What Everyone Is Saying About Quicken WillMaker Plus...

"By far the most comprehensive program we reviewed, offering guidance on everything...."
—**USA Today**

"The most complete of the five products we tried."
—**The Wall Street Journal**

"From a group of tough critics, Nolo's WillMaker got the most praise... superior on every front."
—**Kiplinger's Personal Finance Magazine**

"WillMaker is such an easy-to-use program that users may never need to look at the manual—refreshingly painless."
—**Fortune**

"The most... comprehensive and widely praised of the will writing programs."
—**Chicago Tribune**

"You can complete the documents fairly quickly, or you can spend a great deal of time exploring all the clearly written definitions and explanations...."
—**PC World**

"Even if you know you should see a lawyer... Quicken's question-and-answer technique can help you sort through the options."
—**BusinessWeek**

"The most sophisticated legal software on the market."
—**Worth**

"The level of detail and complexity anticipated by the program makes WillMaker one of the leading legal-advice programs on the market."
—**Inc.**

Keep Up With the Latest in the Law and in This Product

Use Quicken WillMaker Plus's easy Web Update feature to download the latest legal and software updates (requires Internet access). For plain-English legal information on a broad array of estate planning and personal matters, check out www.nolo.com.

Product support (including Web Update) for Quicken WillMaker Plus 2009 ends on **January 1, 2010**. Be sure to register your product to qualify for special upgrade pricing.

Please note that legal documents created and signed before January 1, 2010 will remain legally valid and enforceable if you have used Web Update regularly. You will need to upgrade your software only if you want to create new documents or update existing documents.

An Important Message to Our Readers

This product is not a substitute for legal advice from an attorney. We've done our best to give you useful, accurate legal information, but that's not the same as personalized legal advice. If you want help understanding how the law applies to your particular circumstances, or deciding which estate planning documents are best for you and your family, you should consider seeing a qualified attorney. Estate planning documents are not valid in Louisiana.

Quicken®

WillMaker

ESTATE PLANNING ESSENTIALS

Plus
2009

NOLO

FIFTH EDITION   OCTOBER 2008

Editor   SHAE IRVING

Proofreading   ROBERT WELLS

Index   BAYSIDE INDEXING

Printing   DELTA PRINTING SOLUTIONS, INC.

Willmaker.
    Quicken WillMaker Plus : estate planning essentials. -- 5th ed., 2009 ed.
        p. cm.
    Includes index.
    ISBN-13: 978-1-4133-0902-7 (pbk.)
    ISBN-10: 1-4133-0902-X (pbk.)
    1. Willmaker. 2. Estate planning--United States--Popular works. 3. Wills--United
States--Popular works. 4. Wills--United States--Forms. 5. Estate planning--United
States--Forms. I. Title.
    KF750.W55 2008
    346.7305'2--dc22

                                    2008018180

All product and company names mentioned in Quicken WillMaker Plus are the property of their
respective owners.

Quantity sales: For information on bulk purchases or corporate premium sales, please contact
the Special Sales Department. For academic sales or textbook adoptions, ask for Academic Sales.
800-955-4775, Nolo, 950 Parker Street, Berkeley, CA 94710.

Quicken is a registered trademark of Intuit, Inc., used under license. WillMaker, Nolo and the Nolo
logo are registered trademarks of Nolo. All features, services, terms and conditions subject to change
without notice. Use of the product requires acceptance of the enclosed License Agreement. If you do
not agree to its terms, please return the software for a refund of the purchase price.

Estate planning documents are not valid in Louisiana. This program is not a substitute for legal advice
from an attorney. We've done our best to give you useful, accurate legal information, but that's not
the same as personalized legal advice. If you want help understanding how the law applies to your
particular circumstances, or deciding which estate planning documents are best for you and your
family, you should see a qualified attorney.

Easy upgrade from all versions of Quicken WillMaker and Quicken Lawyer Personal.
Not compatible with Quicken-branded legal software published prior to 2002.

Contributors

Steve Elias received his law degree from Hastings College of the Law in 1969. He worked in California, New York and Vermont as a legal aid lawyer, and in Vermont as a public defender. Steve has written and edited Nolo books on a wide range of topics, including wills, special-needs trusts, criminal law, legal research, patents, trademarks, bankruptcy and, most recently, foreclosures. From 1983 to 1985, Steve worked with Ralph Warner and a couple of NASA scientists—who previously had designed a basic will software program for California—to launch the first version of WillMaker, now Quicken WillMaker Plus. For the next decade, Steve helped to develop and refine WillMaker's legal content. Steve now lives in Lakeport, California, where he provides legal advice to people doing their own bankruptcies and cohosts several radio programs with his wife on community radio station KPFZ 88.1 FM.

Shae Irving has been a Nolo author and editor since 1994, specializing in estate planning and family law issues. She has written or cowritten books and software, including *Prenuptial Agreements: How to Write a Fair and Lasting Contract, Living Wills and Powers of Attorney for California* and *Get It Together: Organize Your Records So Your Family Won't Have To*. Shae is the managing editor of Quicken WillMaker Plus and the primary author of the program's durable power of attorney for finances. Shae graduated from Boalt Hall School of Law at the University of California, Berkeley, and briefly practiced law at a large San Francisco firm before joining Nolo's editorial staff.

Janet Portman is Nolo's Managing Editor. She specializes in residential and commercial landlord/tenant law and legal issues related to courts. She is the author or coauthor of several Nolo books, including *Every Landlord's Legal Guide, Every Tenant's Legal Guide* and *Negotiate the Best Lease for Your Business*. A nationally syndicated columnist with Inman News, Portman's column, "Rent It Right," appears regularly in the *Chicago Tribune, Los Angeles Times* and other prominent newspapers and websites. Janet developed many of the Quicken WillMaker Plus forms for executors.

Mary Randolph earned her law degree from the Boalt Hall School of Law at the University of California, Berkeley. In addition to writing the living trust materials in Quicken WillMaker Plus, she has written several books for Nolo, including *The Executor's Guide: Settling Your Loved One's Estate or Trust, 8 Ways to Avoid Probate, Every Dog's Legal Guide: A Must-Have Book for Your Owner* and *Deeds for California Real Estate*. She lives in the San Francisco Bay Area with her family.

Albin Renauer earned his law degree from the University of Michigan Law School in 1985. He worked as a public interest lawyer in San Francisco and as a staff attorney for Chief Justice Rose Bird of the California Supreme Court, joining Nolo in 1987. Albin's knowledge of law and computer programming made him an integral part of the technical and legal development of many Nolo software programs, including WillMaker, now Quicken WillMaker Plus. He continues to contribute to the software, playing a significant role in developing and maintaining WillMaker's health care directives. Albin is also a coauthor of Nolo's book, *How to File for Chapter 7 Bankruptcy*, and he operates his own Web business, LegalConsumer.com, which provides bankruptcy information and resources for consumers. Albin lives in the San Francisco Bay Area with his family.

Barbara Kate Repa, a longtime lawyer and journalist, has devoted her career to editing and writing about legal issues for consumers. A Nolo author and editor since 1987, she has covered topics ranging from legal humor to workplace issues to estate planning. Former president of both the Bay Area Funeral Society and the California Board of Funeral Directors and Embalmers, Barbara Kate was the primary author of WillMaker's first health care directives and final arrangements document—all of which were added to the software program in the early 1990s. She is currently a senior contributing editor at Caring.com—a website devoted to helping adult children care for their aging parents—where she specializes in legal and end-of-life issues.

Betsy Simmons received her law degree from Golden Gate University School of Law and is now a legal editor at Nolo specializing in estate planning. She edits the Quicken WillMaker Plus will and keeps many of the program's smaller forms up to date. Betsy also edits many popular Nolo titles, including *Plan Your Estate, Make Your Own Living Trust* and *How to Probate an Estate in California*. When Betsy's not at work she enjoys playing soccer and spending time with her family.

Marcia Stewart has been a Nolo editor and author since 1989, writing and editing books on landlord-tenant law, real estate, and other consumer issues. She is the coauthor of *Nolo's Essential Guide to Buying Your First Home, Every Landlord's Legal Guide, Every Tenant's Legal Guide, Leases and Rental Agreements* and *Renters' Rights*—and she has edited dozens of additional Nolo titles. Marcia created many of the Quicken WillMaker Plus forms for home and family.

Ralph "Jake" Warner founded Nolo with Ed Sherman in 1972. When personal computers came along, he became a pioneer of self-help legal software, cocreating the first version of WillMaker (now Quicken WillMaker Plus) in the early 1980s. In addition to running Nolo for much of the past three decades, Warner has been an active editor and author. He wrote many books, including *Get a Life: You Don't Need a Million to Retire Well* and *How to Run a Thriving Business*. Today, he serves as chief executive officer as well as chairman of Nolo's board of directors. During a three-year break earlier this decade, Warner embarked on a new business venture: TallTales Audio, an audio book production company devoted to children's storytelling, online and on CD. Warner holds a law degree from Boalt Hall School of Law at the University of California at Berkeley and an undergraduate degree from Princeton.

Table of Contents

16 Creating a Shared Basic Trust 201

Users' Manual

Appendixes

Index

Your Legal Companion for Estate Planning

If you're like a lot of people, you have a nagging feeling that you need to make a will—but you haven't gotten around to it because it sounds hard or expensive or just unpleasant. (Or maybe you picked up this software because you are the rare individual who loves to plan and get organized. We encourage those tendencies.) We're here to help. With Quicken WillMaker Plus, making a legal will doesn't have to be difficult. In fact, you can probably get it done in under an hour.

You're smart to pay attention to that nagging feeling: Almost everyone needs a will. It lets you leave your property, name a guardian for young children and eliminate uncertainty about your wishes—all of which will spare your family headaches later.

And a will isn't the only thing to think about. In addition, you may want to make a living trust to help your family avoid probate court proceedings after your death. And everyone should consider preparing a living will and durable powers of attorney— important documents that can help you stay in control of your own health care and financial choices while saving your family lots of hassles and heartaches, too. You can use Quicken WillMaker Plus to prepare these legal tools, and more.

Our carefully designed question-and-answer format makes the process as easy as it can be. Our goal is to help you over any hurdles by providing clear guidance and encouragement at every step. We'll get you started by helping you figure out exactly which estate planning documents you need. Just select the options that best describe your life situation—for example, whether you have young children, are financially comfortable or are elderly or ill—and we'll tell you whether it's most important to consider a simple will, a living trust, powers of attorney or something more complex. (Or, if you know which document you want to make first, you can skip this part and get right to it.)

When you select the document you want to start with, we'll tell you a little more about it and then ask you a series of straightforward questions. The software uses your answers to make a legal document that's valid in your state.

If you're not sure how to answer a particular question, you'll find lots of practical and legal information within easy reach. Our onscreen help is there to guide you through questions large and small. (You'll probably be able to use Quicken WillMaker Plus to handle your own basic estate planning, without hiring a lawyer. But we'll always alert you to situations where you might benefit from help from a lawyer or other expert.) When you're done making a document, we'll tell you everything you need to know about how to finalize it and make it legal.

Keep in mind that you can plan your estate a little bit at a time. Start by making just one document, such as your will. When you're ready, come back to the program to make more, perhaps your health care documents or a living trust. You can think of Quicken WillMaker Plus as your estate planning companion, providing trustworthy legal and practical advice along the path that's best for you.

Congratulations on starting your estate planning—it's a wonderful thing to do for your loved ones. We know from long experience that putting a sound estate plan into place can bring peace and satisfaction to those who take the time to do it.

Planning Your Estate With Quicken WillMaker Plus

state planning is the process of arranging for what will happen to your property when you die. (Whatever you own at your death is called your estate.) It can also include:

- making arrangements for the care of your young children in the event of your death
- planning for your own care in case someday you can't make decisions on your own
- taking steps so that your inheritors can avoid probate court proceedings after your death, and
- if you own a large amount of property, planning to avoid federal or state estate tax.

We can help you with all of these issues, and a few others as well. What follows is a discussion of the legal documents you can create with Quicken WillMaker Plus, so you can see what they accomplish and decide whether or not they fit your situation.

> ### Property That Doesn't Pass Through a Will or Trust
>
> Usually, you cannot use a will or trust to leave certain kinds of assets, including:
>
> - bank accounts for which you have named a pay-on-death beneficiary
> - life insurance proceeds (they go to the beneficiary you named in the policy)
> - stocks and bonds for which you have named a transfer-on-death beneficiary
> - property owned as "community property with right of survivorship," which automatically goes to the survivor when one co-owner dies
> - property owned in joint tenancy or tenancy by the entirety (it automatically goes to the surviving owners at your death), and
> - individual retirement accounts (IRAs and 401(k) plans) and certain pension funds (they go to the beneficiary you named in forms provided by the account custodian).

Wills and Basic Living Trusts

Perhaps the most essential reason to make an estate plan is to have a say about who gets your property when you die. To do this, you need a will or a trust. You can make either one with Quicken WillMaker Plus.

If you don't use a will, trust or other legal method to transfer your property when you die, state law determines what happens to your possessions. (See "Dying Without a Will" in Chapter 2.)

What Wills and Basic Living Trusts Can Do

When you make a will or basic living trust with Quicken WillMaker Plus, you can specify who will inherit your property. You can also:

- name alternates, in case your first choices die before you do

- choose someone you trust to oversee the distribution of your property after your death, and
- name a trusted adult to manage the property that a child or young adult inherits from you. (We give you several ways to handle this; they're explained in Chapter 7.)

Comparing Wills and Basic Living Trusts

Both wills and basic living trusts let you leave your property to the people you want to inherit it. You can revoke or change a will or living trust at any time, for any reason, before you die.

The big difference is that assets left in a living trust don't have to go through probate court proceedings at your death. This is because when you create a living trust, you must transfer ownership of the designated property to yourself as "trustee" of the trust. During your lifetime, you still have control over all the property transferred to your living trust and you can do what you want with it—sell it, spend it or give it away. Then, after your death, the person you named to take over as trustee distributes the property to the family and friends you named.

Why avoid probate? For most families, it's a waste of time and money. It typically takes from nine to 18 months to file a deceased person's will with the court, gather the assets, pay debts and taxes and eventually distribute what is left as the will directs. Fees for attorneys, appraisers, accountants and probate court can reduce by about 5% the amount left for survivors to inherit. Unless relatives are fighting over who gets what, or there are big claims against the estate, a court-supervised process is seldom necessary.

Making a living trust involves more paperwork than making a will, because you must transfer ownership of the property to yourself as trustee and conduct future personal business in the name of the trust. But there is no need to file a separate tax return for the trust. All transactions, such as the sale of trust property at a profit, are reported on your personal income tax return.

A trust also offers a way that the trust property can be taken care of if someday you can't handle it yourself. If you become incapacitated, the person you appointed in your trust to take over after your death can step in and manage trust property. If you don't have a trust, close family members may have to go to court to get that kind of authority. (You can also arrange for property management in a durable power of attorney for finances, discussed in Chapter 22.)

A will can do one important thing that a living trust can't: It lets you name someone (called a personal guardian) to raise your young children in the unlikely event that neither you nor the other parent is available.

For a more detailed discussion of wills and trusts, see Chapters 2 and 13.

What Wills and Trusts Can Do

	Will	Basic Living Trust	AB Living Trust
Avoid probate		✓	✓
Reduce estate tax			✓
Keep your estate plan confidential		✓	✓
Set up management of property for minors	✓	✓	✓
Arrange for management of some or all of your property if you become incapacitated		✓	✓
Appoint a guardian to raise young children if you can't	✓		

Quicken WillMaker Plus's basic trust avoids probate but has no effect on estate taxes. If you think your estate may be large enough to owe federal estate taxes, check out the AB Trust, discussed below.

Choosing Between a Will and a Basic Living Trust

Many people create both a will and a living trust. It's common to use a living trust to leave only some assets and leave the rest by will or by another probate-avoidance method. (See "Other Ways to Avoid Probate" in Chapter 13.) In fact, even if you make a living trust, you'll still want to make a simple back-up will to handle property you don't get around to transferring to the trust.

Here are some factors to think about when deciding whether the centerpiece of your estate plan should be a will or a living trust:

Your age. If you're under 60 and healthy, it often makes sense to prepare a will, use simple probate-avoidance devices such as joint tenancy or pay-on-death bank accounts for some property and leave the more complicated estate planning until later.

The size of your estate. The bigger your estate, the bigger the potential probate cost and the less likely that your estate will qualify for simplified probate proceedings (discussed in Chapter 13). Often it makes good sense to concentrate effort on making sure that major assets, such as real estate or business assets, are owned in a way that will avoid probate.

The type of property you own. You don't need a trust to avoid probate for assets like your bank and retirement accounts; it's a matter of filling out simple beneficiary forms that your bank or retirement plan administrator can give you. But transferring real estate outside of probate usually means making a living trust. This process may well be worth the work, but there is more effort required: The living trust will have no effect unless you transfer title of your property to yourself as trustee of your living trust.

The Estate Tax–Reducing AB Trust

The second kind of trust you can make with Quicken WillMaker Plus is an "AB" or bypass trust, which lets married couples avoid both probate and federal estate tax. (Unmarried or same-sex partners cannot use this type of trust because only married heterosexual couples are eligible for federal tax benefits; see "Same-Sex Partners and the Law" in Chapter 4.)

Estate tax is not a concern for most people. The tax is levied on the property you own at your death—but a large amount of property is exempt from taxation. In 2009, that amount is $3.5 million, which means that most people don't need to worry about estate tax. In 2010, the estate tax will vanish completely. But there's another wrinkle: Unless Congress reauthorizes these changes, the estate tax will automatically reappear in 2011, with an exempt amount of $1 million.

If you're married, estate tax is most likely to be an issue when the second spouse dies. (When the first spouse dies, everything left to the survivor passes tax-free.) If the second spouse owns all the couple's property and it's worth more than the estate tax exemption, estate tax will be due. If that's the case, it's worth doing some tax planning, because the tax is steep—45%.

With an AB trust, you leave property first to your spouse (in trust, with certain restrictions) and then, usually, to your children. Because the second spouse never legally owns the deceased spouse's property, her estate won't owe tax on it at her death.

There is also a special kind of AB trust called a "disclaimer trust." With this type of trust, the surviving spouse decides, after the first spouse dies, whether or not to create the tax-saving trust. A disclaimer trust can be useful for couples who aren't sure whether or not estate tax will be a concern for the surviving spouse.

For more about whether an AB trust is right for you, see Chapter 14.

Durable Power of Attorney for Finances

It's a good idea for almost everyone with property or an income to make a durable power of attorney for finances. It's particularly important, however, if you fear that health problems may make it impossible for you to handle your financial matters.

Making a durable power of attorney ensures that someone you trust will be on hand to manage the many practical, financial tasks that will arise if you become incapacitated. For example, bills must be paid, bank deposits must be made and someone must handle insurance and benefits paperwork. Many other matters may need attention as well, from property repairs to managing investments or a small business. In most cases, a durable power of attorney for finances is the best way to take care of tasks like these. See Chapter 22 for more information.

Health Care Directives (Living Will and Power of Attorney)

It's vitally important that those close to you understand the kind of medical treatment you would—or would not—want if you were unable to speak for yourself. You can use Quicken WillMaker Plus's health care directives to describe your health care wishes and name a trusted person to oversee them. The person you name can also make other necessary health care decisions for you if you are too ill or injured to direct your own care.

The program helps you prepare documents that are legal in your state. Depending on where you live, you may get a single document (often called an advance health care directive) or two separate documents (typically called a living will and a durable power of attorney for health care).

For more information about health care directives, see Chapter 23.

Final Arrangements Document

As you go through the process of creating a will, living trust or other estate planning document, your thoughts may turn to how you want your body to be handled after your death.

With our final arrangements document, you can let your loved ones know whether you wish to be buried or cremated, what kind of memorial ceremonies you have in mind and other details related to the final disposition of your body. During a difficult time, this document can provide much needed guidance for your survivors.

To learn more about the final arrangements document, see Chapter 24.

Documents for Executors

Quicken WillMaker Plus offers a number of documents that you can use if you are named as someone's executor—and you can help your own executor by letting him or her know that these forms are available on your computer when they're needed.

An executor, called a personal representative in some states, is the person you name in your will to safeguard and handle your property

after you die. Your executor makes sure that debts and taxes are paid and distributes what's left to your beneficiaries, as your will directs. If someone dies without naming an executor, a court will appoint someone to take the job. This person is most often called an administrator.

Here is a brief description of each of the documents for executors that you can make with Quicken WillMaker Plus.

Information for Caregivers and Survivors

With our Information for Caregivers and Survivors form, you can create a comprehensive guide to the details of your life, from information about your bank accounts to people you'd like contacted in the event of your illness or death.

To prepare this form, the program will walk you through the particulars of your life, asking you to provide details on many topics, including things your loved ones may not know—such as the names of your doctors or whether you have life insurance. The result of this interview will be a document that will greatly aid those who need to care for you or manage your estate.

Executor's Checklist

If you have been named the executor of an estate, you'll want to know what kind of tasks you are expected to perform. The Executor's Checklist is a good introduction.

Of course, every estate (and state) is different. An executor's tasks depend on the size of the estate, the kinds of property the deceased person owned and other factors, such as the needs and expectations of the family. State laws governing the administration of estates also vary.

> **RESOURCE**
> **Help with the executor's job.** For a more thorough guide to an executor's duties, see *The Executor's Guide: Settling a Loved One's Estate or Trust*, by Mary Randolph (Nolo).

Executor's Letter to Financial Institution

If you are the executor or administrator of someone's estate, your tasks include locating and making an inventory of all of the deceased person's property. One category of property you must investigate is bank and other financial accounts held by the deceased. You can use this form to write to financial institutions to find out what accounts or loans the deceased had with that institution, as well as to learn what those accounts were worth at the time of death.

Affidavit of Domicile

An Affidavit of Domicile (sometimes called an Affidavit of Residence) is one of the documents used by an executor to transfer ownership of stock or other securities from the name of the deceased person to the new owner. The purpose of the Affidavit of Domicile is to establish the state of residence of the stockholder (in this case, the deceased person)

Employee Death Benefits Letter

An executor must contact each of the deceased person's former employers to find out whether the estate or survivors are entitled to any death benefits. You can use Quicken WillMaker Plus's Employee Death Benefits Letter to request the information you need.

Life Insurance Claim Form Request

Before a life insurance company will pay the proceeds on a policy, it will ask the beneficiary to fill out a claim form that provides information about the beneficiary. The claim form verifies that the person making the claim is the proper beneficiary under the policy.

Use the Request for Life Insurance Claim Form to provide the life insurance company with the information it needs before it will send out an insurance claim form.

Life Insurance Request for Proceeds Letter

A life insurance company will pay the proceeds of a policy only after it receives confirmation that the insured person has died. The company also needs to verify that the person requesting the proceeds is the beneficiary who is entitled to receive the benefits under the terms of the policy. That's why you must complete and submit its claim form with a cover letter like this one.

Notice to Vehicle Insurance Company of Death

As the executor for someone who owned (or co-owned) an insured vehicle, you will want to be added as a "named insured" to the vehicle insurance policy as soon as possible. This status will give you all the protections and rights that the deceased person had under the policy. It will also give you peace of mind as you manage and care for the vehicle in your role as the executor, and it will ensure that any payments from the insurance company go jointly to you and any other people insured by the policy.

Notice to Homeowners Insurance Company of Death

As with vehicles, you will want to be added as a "named insured" to the deceased person's homeowners insurance policy. This will give you all the rights that the deceased person had under the policy, and it will ensure that any payments from the insurance company go jointly to you as the executor and any other individuals insured under the policy.

Notice to Creditor of Death

Use this form to notify each of the deceased person's creditors of the death and to close the deceased person's credit accounts.

General Notice of Death

An executor may want to notify businesses and organizations of the death. For example, you might want to notify charities to which the deceased person made regular donations. You can use this letter to inform anyone who might need to know of the death.

Requesting Birth or Death Certificates

As you fulfill your duties as executor, you may need to obtain copies of a death or birth certificate. The most convenient way to get copies of a death certificate is to request them from the funeral home or mortuary at the time of the death. Otherwise, you can find forms and instructions online. Many county websites offer birth and death certificate request forms that you can print out and send; others allow you to submit your request electronically and pay by credit card.

To find out your options, go to the official website of the county where the birth or death occurred. You can usually find it by using this formula, substituting the state postal abbreviation for "XX": www. co.[COUNTY_NAME]. [XX].us. For example, you can find the website for King County, Washington, at www.co.king.wa.us.

Forms for Home and Family

We provide a range of forms you can use to take care of your loved ones, pets and property. For example, there are authorizations you can use to give someone else permission to take care of your child, and agreements you can complete to arrange for pet care. Here's some information about each of the forms for your home and family.

Child Care Agreement

If you want to hire someone to care for your children in your home, you should prepare a child care agreement.

Quicken WillMaker Plus's child care agreement allows you to spell out the exact responsibilities of the position and to specify the child care provider's hours, amount and schedule of payment, benefits and other important aspects of the job.

Child Care Instructions

Use this form to provide important information for babysitters and child care providers, such as names and phone numbers of doctors and emergency contacts, and instructions about meals, naps and other details of your child's care.

Authorization for Minor's Medical Treatment

Creating a medical care authorization allows another adult to authorize necessary medical or dental treatment for your child if he or she is injured or becomes ill while under the care of another adult—for example, while playing on a sports team or staying with a babysitter.

Authorization for Foreign Travel With Minor

If your young child will be traveling outside the United States with another adult, you should prepare an authorization for foreign travel. The form provides necessary proof that you have consented to the travel.

Temporary Guardianship Authorization for Care of Minor

If you leave your child in the care of another adult for a few days, weeks or months, you should authorize the caretaker to make any necessary decisions about your child's medical, educational and other care. You can do this by preparing a temporary guardianship authorization.

Elder Care Agreement

Quicken WillMaker Plus's elder care agreement is for people who wish to sign an agreement with an elder care provider who will take care of an older parent or other elderly relative at home. The agreement allows you to spell out the exact responsibilities of the position and to specify the worker's hours, amount and schedule of payment, benefits and other important aspects of the job.

Pet Care Agreement

If you're going on a trip or will otherwise be unable to care for your pet for a period of time, you might leave your animal in the care of a friend, relative or neighbor. If you do so, it's prudent to prepare this written agreement setting out clear instructions for your pet's care and clarifying each party's responsibilities and expectations.

Housekeeping Services Agreement

If you hire someone to clean or take care of your house on a regular basis, you can use our housekeeping services agreement. It allows you to spell out the exact responsibilities of the position and to specify the housekeeper's hours, benefits and other details.

Housesitting Instructions

Use this form to provide detailed housesitting instructions for a person who will care for your home while you are away. You can specify your wishes about your plants and garden, newspapers and mail, telephone calls, appliances and equipment, lights and security, tools and supplies, vehicles and other matters. You can also include important information such as how you can be reached while you are away and whom the housesitter can contact for help in your absence.

Authorization to Drive a Motor Vehicle

Lending your vehicle to someone isn't always as simple as handing over the keys. If the person who borrows your car is pulled over by the police or is involved in an accident, he or she will want to quickly prove that you agreed to the use. Otherwise, the driver may be detained while police investigate whether the car is stolen.

This simple authorization takes just a few minutes to complete, and it provides important legal proof that you've given someone else permission to drive your vehicle. The form is designed for a car, but it will work fine for a motorcycle, truck or other motor vehicle such as a motorboat.

Notice to Put Name on "Do Not Call" List

The best way to stop telemarketers from calling you is to enter your telephone number in the National Do Not Call Registry, available at www.ftc.gov/donotcall. Telemarketers are prohibited from calling numbers listed in the registry. Those who violate the law are subject to stiff fines—up to $11,000 for each offending phone call. A number of states have do not call lists as well. You may want to add your number to your state's registry, if it offers one.

Some companies are exempt from the federal registry's rules. These include long-distance telephone companies, airlines, banks and credit unions. Organizations soliciting money for political organizations or charities are also exempt. But even these businesses and organizations are required to keep their own lists of consumers who say that they do not want to be called again. If you ask a company not to call you, but you get another call within 12 months, you can sue for up to $500.

If you wish to contact a business or organization to request that they cease calling you, you can use our form: Notice to Put Name on "Do Not Call" List. If necessary, you can use this form to prove that the company violated the law by calling you after you asked them not to. End every unwanted call by stating, "Put me on your 'do not call' list." Then follow up by mailing the telemarketer this form that states the same thing, thereby generating irrefutable evidence of your request that they cease calling.

Cancel Membership or Subscription

Use this form to cancel a magazine subscription or your membership in an organization. The form allows you to state the reason for the cancellation—perhaps you have moved or are no longer interested in the subject—although you do not have to provide a reason. You can also use this form to request a refund of your membership or subscription fee, if you believe it is warranted.

Personal Finance Forms

Finally, we offer some forms to help you with basic financial matters. There are forms to use if you need to borrow or lend money, plus a few other useful documents—such as a power of attorney you can use to have someone take care of a specific financial transaction if you're unavailable. Here's a little more information about each form.

General Bill of Sale

Use this form to record the terms of the sale of an item of personal property, such as a car, computer or guitar. When you sell an item with a written bill of sale, you reduce the chance of a dispute arising after the sale.

Special (Limited) Power of Attorney for Finances

A limited power of attorney for finances lets you appoint someone (called your "attorney-in fact") to help you with one or more clearly defined tasks involving your finances or property. For example, you may want to name someone to monitor certain investments for you while you are on vacation—and sell them if necessary. Or you may need someone to sign business or legal papers for you while you are unavailable. This form lets you temporarily delegate authority to someone you trust.

Revocation of Power of Attorney

If you've made a power of attorney, you can change your mind and cancel it at any time. Use this notice of revocation to put an end to any power of attorney, including a durable power—that is, one that is designed to remain in effect even after you become incapacitated.

Promissory Notes

If you are borrowing or lending money, you should create a promissory note. Like an IOU, a promissory note records the terms of the loan, including the period of repayment and the interest rate (if interest will be charged), as well as the borrower's promise to pay back the loan. We provide four different kinds of promissory notes.

Installment payments. This type of promissory note requires the borrower to make the same monthly payment for a specified number of months. You can choose whether or not the borrower will pay interest on the loan.

Balloon payment. This promissory note requires the borrower to pay the same amount of money each month for a specified number of months, followed by a large balloon payment at the end of the repayment period. The borrower must pay interest on the loan.

Payments of interest only. With this type of note, the borrower pays only the interest on the loan each month for a specified number of months, with a balloon payment of the principal and any remaining interest at the end of the loan term.

One lump-sum payment. As the name indicates, this note requires the borrower to make a just one payment on a specified date. You can choose whether the borrower will pay interest on the loan.

Security Agreement for Borrowing Money

Use this form if you are borrowing or lending money and the borrower agrees to provide the lender with a security interest as collateral for the loan. This security agreement allows the borrower to offer tangible personal property as collateral—that is, physical items of property other than real estate, such as a car, jewelry or furniture.

About Wills

Making a will is an excellent way to ensure that your plans for leaving property to family, friends and organizations of your choice are carried out after you die. You can efficiently and safely write your own legal will using the Quicken WillMaker Plus program. But before you start, it is a good idea to read this chapter and Chapter 3, which explain generally what a will can accomplish and how you can use Quicken WillMaker Plus to meet your needs.

Legal Requirements

For a will to be legally valid, both you—the person making the will—and the will itself must meet some technical requirements.

Who Can Make a Will

Before you start your computer and get the Quicken WillMaker Plus program going, make sure you qualify to make a will in the eyes of the law.

Age

To make a will, you must either be:
- at least 18 years old, or
- living in a state that permits people under 18 to make a will if they are married, in the military or otherwise considered legally emancipated.

Mental Competence

You must be of sound mind to prepare a valid will. While this sounds like a subjective standard, the laws generally require that you must:

- know what a will is, what it does and that you are making one
- understand the relationship between you and the people who would normally be provided for in your will, such as a spouse or children
- understand the kind and quantity of property you own, and
- be able to decide how to distribute your belongings.

This threshold of mental competence is not hard to meet. Very few wills are successfully challenged based on the charge that the person making the will was mentally incompetent. It is not enough to show that the person was forgetful or absentminded.

To have a probate court declare a will invalid usually requires proving that the testator was totally overtaken by the fraud or undue influence of another person—and that person then benefited from the wrongdoing by becoming entitled to a large amount of money or property under the will.

Interestingly, the great majority of undue influence contests are filed against attorneys who draw up wills in which they are named to take clients' property. If the person making the will was very old, ill or suffering from dementia when he or she made the will, it is obviously easier to convince a judge that undue influence occurred.

> **SEE AN EXPERT**
>
> **If a contest seems possible.** If you have any serious doubts about your ability to meet the legal requirements for making a will, or you believe your will is likely to be contested by another

person for any reason, consult an experienced lawyer. (See Chapter 25.)

Will Requirements

State law determines whether a will made by a resident of the state is valid. And a will that is valid in the state where it is made is valid in all other states.

Contrary to what many people believe, a will need not be notarized to be legally valid. But adding a notarized document to the will verifying that the will was signed and witnessed can be helpful when it comes time to file the will in probate court. This option is available in all but a handful of states. (See "The Self-Proving Option" in Chapter 10.)

There are surprisingly few legal restrictions and requirements in the will-making process. In most states, a will must:

- include at least one substantive provision—either giving away some property or naming a guardian to care for minor children who are left without parents
- be signed and dated by the person making it
- be witnessed by at least two other people who are not named to take property under the will, and
- be clear enough so that others can under-stand what the testator intended. Nonsensical, legalistic language such as: "I hereby give, bequeath and devise" is both unwise and unnecessary.

Handwritten and Oral Wills

In about half the states, unwitnessed, hand-written wills—called holographic wills—are legally valid. And a few states accept oral wills under very limited circumstances, such as when a mortally wounded soldier utters last wishes.

But handwritten wills are fraught with possible legal problems. Most obviously, after your death, it may be difficult to prove that your unwitnessed, handwritten document was actually written by you and that you intended it to be your will. And it may be almost impossible to prove the authenticity of an oral will.

A properly signed, witnessed will is much less vulnerable to challenge by anyone claiming it was forged or fabricated. If need be, witnesses can later testify in court that the person whose name is on the will is the same person who signed it, and that making the will was a voluntary and knowing act.

Dying Without a Will

If you die without a valid will, money and other property you own at death will be divided and distributed to others according to your state's intestate succession laws. These laws divide all property among the relatives who are considered closest to you according to a set formula—and completely exclude friends and charities.

These legal formulas often do not mirror people's wishes. For example, dividing property according to intestate succession laws is often unsatisfactory if you are married and have no children, because most state laws require your spouse to share your property with your parents. The situation is even worse for unmarried couples. Except in a few states, unmarried partners receive nothing. And even in the states that offer exceptions, benefits aren't automatic—eligible couples must register their partnerships with the state.

Also, if you have minor children, another important reason to make a will is to name a personal guardian to care for them. This is an important concern of most parents, who worry that their children will be left without a caretaker if both parents die. Intestate succession laws do not deal with the issue of who will take care of your children. When you don't name a guardian in your will, it is left up to the courts and social service agencies to find and appoint a personal guardian.

Making Basic Decisions About Your Will

Making a will is not difficult, but it is undeniably a serious and sobering process. Before you begin, get organized and focus on these important questions:

- What do you own? (See Chapter 5.)
- Who should get your property? (See Chapter 6.)
- If you have minor children, who is the best person to care for them, and who is best suited to manage property you leave them? (See Chapter 4 and Chapter 7.)

- Who will see that your property is distributed according to your wishes after your death? (See Chapter 8.)

This manual offers guidance on how to use Quicken WillMaker Plus to give legal effect to your decisions in all of these areas. The ultimate choices, however, are up to you.

Other Ways to Leave Property

A will is not the only way—and in some cases, not the best way—to transfer ownership of your property to another person upon your death. For a discussion of the different ways to pass property after your death, see "Wills and Basic Living Trusts" in Chapter 1.

Making Your Own Will

As a way to decide who gets your property, the will has been around in substantially the same form for about 500 years. For the first 450 years, self-help was the rule and lawyer assistance the exception. When this country was founded, and even during the Civil War, it was highly unusual for a person to hire a lawyer to formally set out what should be done with his or her property. However, in the past 50 years, the legal profession has scored a public relations coup by convincing many people that writing a will without a lawyer is like doing your own brain surgery.

In truth, the hardest part of making a will is figuring out what property you own and who will get it when you die—questions you can answer best. Our will-making program, which has been in wide and successful use for two decades, prompts you to answer the right questions—and produces a will that fits your circumstances and is legal in your state.

But you may have a question about your particular situation that Quicken WillMaker Plus does not answer. Or perhaps you have a very large estate—worth over $2 million—and want to engage in some sophisticated tax planning. Or you may simply be comforted by having a lawyer give your Quicken WillMaker Plus will a once-over. Whenever you have concerns such as these or simply feel that you are in over your head, it may be wise to consult an attorney with knowledge and experience in wills and estate planning. (See Chapter 25.)

Helping Someone Else Make a Will

You can use Quicken WillMaker Plus to help a loved one or friend make a will. But you must be sure that your role is only to type in the will maker's wishes. In other words, the will maker, not you, must decide on the terms of the will.

If your role exceeds these limits, a court could declare the will invalid—and you may even face legal charges.

If you decide to help someone else prepare a will, you may want to take an extra step to document your role: Make an audio or video recording of the process or ask someone else to be present as a witness while you follow the will maker's directions.

> **EXAMPLE:** Betty asks her neighbor, James, to help her make her will because her hands shake too badly to type her responses into the program. She dictates her answers to James and he types them in at her direction. She also tells James to print out the document for her to sign. For extra security, Betty's friend Wendy watches as a witness so she can later testify to James's role, if necessary.

If the person you want to help cannot clearly direct the will-making process, or if you have any concern that the person may not fully understand what it means to make a will, see an experienced estate planning attorney for help.

About Quicken WillMaker Plus Wills

ecause wills reflect how people want to leave their property, they can be as complex and intricate as life. While state laws broadly regulate the procedures for valid will making, you are generally free to write a will to meet your needs. This freedom may seem overwhelming if you are not used to wading through legal documents.

Quicken WillMaker Plus offers considerable help. The program works by asking you to systematically answer questions. As you will soon see, you either already have enough information to answer them easily, or you can quickly get it.

> **TIP**
>
> **Keeping track of important information.** As you prepare to make your will, you may wish to make a list of financial and estate planning advisers you have consulted in the past. It may also be a good time to organize other estate planning documents—such as your living trust documents or life insurance policy—and to record their locations so that others will know where to find them.
>
> With Quicken WillMaker Plus you can make an Information for Caregivers and Survivors form to help with this task. With this document, you can provide a comprehensive guide to the details of your life—ranging from information about your property and your financial accounts to the names and addresses of people you want contacted in the event of your death—for people who will care for you if you ever become incapacitated and those who will wind up your affairs after death. To find out more, click on the Document List button and select Information for Caregivers and Survivors from the list.

What You Can Do With a Quicken WillMaker Plus Will

This chapter gives you a quick survey of what you can and cannot do with the Quicken WillMaker Plus program. Each topic is discussed in greater detail, both in the help screens that run with the program and in other chapters in the manual.

Tailor Your Will to Your Needs

Quicken WillMaker Plus provides you with unique guidance and options based on the state in which you live, your marital status, whether you have children and whether your children are minors. Recognizing that some people have very simple wishes for leaving their property while others' plans are more complex, Quicken WillMaker Plus lets you choose from among several approaches designed to meet your needs. For instance, if you are married, you may choose to:

- leave all property to your spouse
- leave most property to your spouse, with several specific property items going to people you name, or
- divide property among many different people and organizations. (See Chapter 6.)

Name Beneficiaries to Get Specific Property

Quicken WillMaker Plus lets you make an unlimited number of separate gifts—called specific bequests—of cash, personal property or real estate. You may choose to leave these bequests to your spouse, children, grandchildren or anyone else—including friends, business associates, charities or other organizations. You can also use your will to leave property to a living trust, if you've established one. (See Chapter 6.)

> **EXAMPLE:** Using Quicken WillMaker Plus, Marcia leaves her interest in the family home to her spouse Duane, her valuable coin collection to one of her children, her boat to another child, her computer to a charity and $5,000 to her two aunts, in equal shares.

> **EXAMPLE:** Raymond, a lifelong bachelor, follows Quicken WillMaker Plus's directions and leaves his house to his favorite charity. He divides his personal possessions among 15 different relatives and friends.

> **EXAMPLE:** Darryl and Floyd have lived together for several years. Darryl wants to leave Floyd all of his property, which includes his car, time-share ownership in a condominium, a savings account and miscellaneous personal belongings. He can use Quicken WillMaker Plus to accomplish this.

Name Someone to Take All Remaining Property

If you have chosen an approach that lets you divide your property by making specific bequests, Quicken WillMaker Plus also allows you to name people or organizations to take whatever property is left over after you have made the specific bequests. This property is called your residuary estate. (See "Naming Residuary Beneficiaries" in Chapter 6.)

> **EXAMPLE:** Annie wants to make a number of small bequests to friends and charities but to leave the bulk of her property to her friend Maureen. She accomplishes this by using the specific bequest screens to make the small gifts, and then names Maureen as residuary beneficiary. There is no need for her to list the property that goes to Maureen. The very nature of the residuary estate is that the residuary beneficiary—in this case, Maureen—gets everything that is left over after the specific bequests are distributed.

Name Alternate Beneficiaries

Using Quicken WillMaker Plus, all beneficiaries you name take the property you leave them under your will only if they survive you by 45 days. The reason that Quicken WillMaker Plus imposes this 45-day rule is that you do not want to leave your property to a beneficiary who dies very shortly after you do, because that property will then be passed along to that person's inheritors. These beneficiaries are not likely to be the ones you would choose to receive your property.

To account for the possibility that your first choices of beneficiaries will not meet the survivorship requirement, Quicken WillMaker Plus allows you to name alternate beneficiaries for each of your bequests. (See Chapter 6.)

Name a Guardian to Care for Your Children

You may use Quicken WillMaker Plus to name a personal guardian—either an individual or a couple—to care for your minor children until they reach age 18, in case there is no other legal parent to handle these duties. You may name the same guardian for all your children, or different guardians for different children. (It is important, however, that both parents name the same person or couple as guardian for any particular child; see example below.) You will also have the opportunity to explain your choices in your will.

If your children need a guardian after your death, a court will formally review your choice. Your choice will normally be approved unless the person or couple you name refuses to assume the responsibility or the court becomes convinced that the best interests of your children would be better served if they were left in the care of someone else. (See "Your Children" in Chapter 4.)

EXAMPLE: Millicent names her friend Vera to serve as personal guardian in the event that her husband, Frank, dies at the same time she does or is otherwise unavailable to care for their three children. Millicent and Frank die together in an accident. The court appoints Vera as personal guardian for all three children, since her ability to care for them has not been questioned.

If Frank had written a will naming another person to serve as guardian, however, the court would have to choose between those nominated. For this reason, parents should choose the same people as personal guardians if that is possible.

Avoiding Legalese: Per Stirpes and Per Capita

"Per stirpes" and "per capita" are legal jargon for the way children inherit property in place of a deceased parent—for example, one of these terms might govern how a granddaughter would inherit property left to her mother under a will, if her mother died before the will maker. It's not necessary for your will to include these terms. In fact, it's better to avoid them, because they can be interpreted in different ways. Instead, your Quicken WillMaker Plus will lets you set out exactly whom you want to inherit your property, who will take the property if your first choice beneficiary doesn't survive you and the shares that they will inherit.

Name a Manager for Children's Property

You may leave property to your own or other people's children. Or your young children may receive property from some other source. But at your death, property left to minors—especially cash or other liquid assets—will usually have to be managed by an adult until the minors turn 18. In many cases, it may be most prudent to have property left to minors managed for them until they are even older.

Property management involves safeguarding and spending the property for the young person's education, health care and basic living needs; keeping good records of these expenditures; and seeing that income taxes are paid. Management ends at the age you specify in the will. What is left of the property is then distributed to the child.

Quicken WillMaker Plus allows you to name a trusted person—or, if no one is available, you can name an institution such as a bank or trust company—to manage property left to young beneficiaries. The management methods available are different from state to state.

Quicken WillMaker Plus also allows you to name a property guardian who will handle property that other people leave to your children or property that you leave to them outside of your will.

Setting up property management for children is discussed in detail in Chapter 7.

SEE AN EXPERT

Providing for beneficiaries with special needs. It is common to set up management for property that will pass to a beneficiary who has a mental or physical disability, or who manages money poorly. The management provided under Quicken WillMaker Plus is not sufficiently detailed to provide for people with disabilities or those with special problems such as spendthrift tendencies or substance abuse. If you need this type of management, you can turn to Nolo's book, *Special Needs Trusts*, by Stephen Elias, or consult an attorney who specializes in dealing with the needs of people with disabilities. (See Chapter 25.)

Name a Caretaker for Your Pet

Many of us consider our pets to be members of the family. It's not natural to think of them as belongings that we can pass through a will. However, in the eyes of the law, pets are property. That means you can't leave money or other items directly to your pet—but you can use your will to leave your pet to a trusted caretaker. Doing so is a good way to ensure that your pet has a loving home when you die.

With Quicken WillMaker Plus, you can name a caretaker for your pet and leave money to that person for your pet's care. If you choose to leave money to the caretaker, your document will state that you leave it "with the hope that the money will be used for the care and maintenance" of your pet. It will be up to the honor of the caretaker to use the gift as you intend. This shouldn't be a problem if you choose someone you trust to care for your pet.

You can also name an alternate in case your first-choice caretaker is not available when you die. (See "Pets" in Chapter 4.)

Cancel Debts Others Owe You

You can use Quicken WillMaker Plus to relieve any debtors who owe you money at your death from the responsibility of paying your survivors. All you need to do is specify the debts and the people who owe them. Quicken WillMaker Plus will then include a statement in your will canceling the debts. If a debt is canceled in this way, Quicken WillMaker Plus also automatically wipes out any interest that has accrued on it as of your death. (See "Forgiving Debts Others Owe You" in Chapter 9.)

EXAMPLE: Cynthia lent $25,000 at 10% annual interest to her son George as a down payment on a house. She uses Quicken WillMaker Plus to cancel this debt. At Cynthia's death, George need not pay her estate the remaining balance of the loan, or the interest accrued on it.

Designate How Debts, Expenses and Taxes Are Paid

Quicken WillMaker Plus allows you to designate a particular source of money or other specific assets from which your executor should pay your debts, final expenses such as funeral and probate costs and any estate and inheritance taxes. (See Chapter 9.)

EXAMPLE: Brent owns a savings account, a portfolio of stocks and bonds, an R.V. and two cars. He uses Quicken WillMaker Plus to make a will—leaving his R.V. and stocks and bonds to his nephew, his cars to his niece and his savings account to his favorite charity, River Friends. He also designates the savings account as the source of payment of his debts and expenses of probate. Under this arrangement, River Friends will receive whatever is left in the savings account after debts and expenses of probate have been paid.

EXAMPLE: Calvin's estate is valued at over $2 million. It is likely that his estate will owe some federal estate taxes when he dies. He uses Quicken WillMaker Plus to specify that any estate tax he owes should be paid proportionately from all the property subject to the tax. If there is estate tax liability, his executor will require that each of Calvin's beneficiaries pay part of the tax in the same proportion their bequest bears to the value of Calvin's estate as a whole.

Name an Executor

With Quicken WillMaker Plus, you can name an executor for your estate. This person or institution, called a personal representative in some states, will be responsible for making sure the provisions in your will are carried out and your property distributed as your will directs. Quicken WillMaker Plus also produces a letter to your executor that generally explains what the job requires.

Executor or Personal Representative?

The following states use the term "personal representative" instead of "executor," but it means the same thing. If you live in one of these states, you will see the term personal representative in your will.

Alabama	Idaho	New Mexico
Alaska	Maine	North Dakota
Arizona	Michigan	South Carolina
Colorado	Minnesota	South Dakota
Florida	Montana	Utah
Hawaii	Nebraska	Wisconsin

The executor can be any competent adult. Commonly, people name a spouse or other close relative or friend or—for large estates or where no trusted person is able to serve—a financial institution such as a bank or savings and loan. You are free to name two people or institutions to share the job, but doing so is often unwise. (See Chapter 8.)

It is also a good idea to use Quicken WillMaker Plus to name an alternate executor in case your first choice becomes unable or unwilling to serve.

> EXAMPLE: Rick and Phyllis both use Quicken WillMaker Plus to complete wills naming each other as executor in case the other dies first. They both name Rick's father as an alternate executor to distribute their property in the event they die at the same time.

> EXAMPLE: Pat and Babs do not wish to burden their relatives with having to take care of their fairly considerable estate. Each names the Third National Bank as executor after checking that their estate is large enough so that this bank will be willing to take the job.

What You Cannot Do With a Quicken WillMaker Plus Will

Quicken WillMaker Plus allows you to produce a valid and effective will designed to meet most needs. But there are some restrictions built into the program. Some of the restrictions are designed to prevent you from writing in conditions that may not be legally valid. Others are intended to keep the program simple and easy to use.

Make Bequests With Conditions

You cannot make a bequest that will take effect only if a certain condition occurs—an "if, and or but," such as "$5,000 to John if he stops smoking." Such conditional bequests are confusing and usually require someone to oversee and supervise the beneficiaries to be sure they satisfy the conditions in the will. If you doubt this, consider that someone would have to constantly check up on John to make sure he never took a puff—and someone would have to wrench away his property if he ever got caught in the act.

So, to use Quicken WillMaker Plus, you must be willing to leave property to people outright; you cannot make them jump through hoops or change their behavior to get it.

CAUTION
Takers must survive by 45 days. To ensure that property goes to people you want to have it, Quicken WillMaker Plus automatically imposes the condition that each of your beneficiaries must survive you by 45 days. If they do not survive you by that amount of time, the property you had slated for them will pass instead to the person or institution you have named as an alternate beneficiary, or it will go to the one you have named to take your residuary estate.

Write Joint Wills

In the past, it was common for a married couple who had an agreed scheme for how to distribute all their property to write one document together: a joint will. But time has shown that setup to be crawling with problems.

Quicken WillMaker Plus requires that each spouse make his or her own will, even if both agree about how their property is to be distributed. This limitation is not imposed to annoy people or defeat their intentions; there is solid legal reasoning behind it.

Joint wills are intended to prevent the surviving spouse from changing his or her mind about what to do with the property after the first spouse dies. The practical effect is to tie up the property for years in title and probate determinations—often until long after the second spouse dies. Also, many court battles are fought over whether the surviving spouse is legally entitled to revoke any part of the joint will.

There are still some lawyers who will agree to write joint wills for clients, but they take the risk that such wills may become cumbersome or may even be found invalid in later court challenges. For these reasons, it is best for both spouses to write separate wills—a bit more time-consuming, perhaps, but a lot safer from a legal standpoint.

Creating Identical Wills

While you can't create a joint will using Quicken WillMaker Plus, you can create identical wills—that is, two separate wills in which all the provisions (such as beneficiaries and children's guardians) are the same. If you want to do this, the program provides an easy shortcut. See "Creating an Identical Will for a Spouse or Partner," in the Users' Manual.

Explain the Reasons for Leaving Your Property

Most of the time, the act of leaving property to people—or choosing not to leave them anything—speaks for itself. Occasionally, however, people making wills want to explain to survivors the reasons they left property as they did. This might be the case, for example, if you opt to leave one of your two children more property than the other to compensate for the loan you made during your lifetime to help one of them buy a house. Although the desire to make such explanations is understandable, Quicken WillMaker Plus does not allow you to do it in your will, because of the risk that you might add legally confusing language to the document.

However, there is an easy and legally safe way to provide your heirs with explanations for your bequests. You can draft a letter that you can attach to your will, explaining your reasons for leaving property to some people—or not leaving it to others. (See Chapter 12.)

Name Coguardians for Children's Property

You may name only one guardian to care for the property left to your young children. While you may choose different property guardians for different children, you may not name two people to share the responsibility. (See Chapter 7.)

At first glance, it may seem to be a good idea to divide up the job—after all, sometimes two heads are better than one. But naming more than one property guardian often presents more problems than it solves because those two people will have to make every decision together. A difference of opinion could require court intervention, which will cost both time and money. It is better to name just one trustworthy person to make decisions about your children's property, and then name a second equally trustworthy person to take over the job if the first one becomes unavailable.

In contrast, note that you may name a couple to serve as your children's *personal* guardians. A personal guardian makes decisions about the wellbeing of the children, rather than the children's property. When those types of decisions will be made in a family setting with two adults, the ability to name a couple is important—so that either adult may take the child to the doctor or to school, for example.

> **CAUTION**
>
> **Review wills to avoid conflicts.** People who jointly own property or have children together should review their wills together to be sure they do

not provide conflicting information—such as each naming two different guardians for any one child.

Control Property After Death

Property given to others in a Quicken WillMaker Plus will must go to them as soon as you die. You cannot make a bequest by will with the property to be used for a person's life and then be given to a second person when the first person dies. Such an arrangement involves too many variables for both will makers and beneficiaries to handle. You will need to use more complex estate planning strategies to carry out this type of plan. (See Chapter 25.)

> **EXAMPLE:** Emory wants his grand-children to get his house when he dies but wants his wife to have the right to live in the house until her death. Emory cannot use Quicken WillMaker Plus to accomplish this. Emory would have to leave his house in trust to his spouse for her life and then to his grandchildren upon his spouse's death.

Require a Bond for Executors or Property Managers

A bond is like an insurance policy that protects the beneficiaries in the unlikely event that the executor wrongfully spends or distributes estate property. Because the premium or fee that must be paid for a bond comes out of the estate—leaving less money for the beneficiaries—most wills for small or moderate estates do not require one.

Following this general practice, the will produced by the Quicken WillMaker Plus program does not require a bond. Instead, take care to appoint someone you know to be trustworthy.

Leave Property to Your Pet

Animals aren't legally permitted to own property, so you can't use your will to make gifts to your pet. If you name your pet to receive property through your will, that gift will be void and the intended gift and the pet will become part of your residuary estate.

That said, you can use your will to name a caretaker for your pet and to leave money to that person requesting that they use it for the care of your pet. (See "Pets" in Chapter 4.)

Customize a No-Contest Clause

The Quicken WillMaker Plus will contains a standard no-contest clause. This clause states that a beneficiary who challenges your will after your death forfeits any gifts you have made to that beneficiary under your will. The property you left to the beneficiary would be distributed as if they died before you.

> **EXAMPLE:** Marah's will leaves $15,000 to her sister, Karen. Marah's nephew, Nathaniel, is the alternate beneficiary for the gift. Marah leaves the rest of her property to her partner of five years, Luke. After Marah's death, Karen challenges the will, believing that Marah intended to leave her more property and that Luke unfairly influenced Marah. Under the terms of the no-contest clause, the $15,000

gift to Karen is immediately revoked and the money passes to Nathaniel.

In reality, most states will not uphold a no-contest clause if the challenger has a good reason to object to the will—for example, if the challenger shows that the will is not valid because the signer's name was forged. Other states go further and do not uphold no-contest clauses for any reason.

Although states vary in their willingness to uphold no-contest clauses, all Quicken WillMaker Plus wills include a standard no-contest clause for an important purpose: to discourage challenges to your will by those who do not like what you leave them. If a beneficiary challenges your will anyway, and a court decides not to enforce the no-contest clause, the rest of your will is effective as written.

If you do not want to include a no-contest clause, or if you do not like the way the clause would affect the distribution of your estate following a challenge, see an experienced estate planning lawyer for advice.

A Look at a Quicken WillMaker Plus Will

You may find it helpful to take a look at a Quicken WillMaker Plus will, but do not be alarmed if the sample will does not match the one you produce. Your Quicken WillMaker Plus will is tailored to your property, circumstances and state laws. Nearly every paragraph, or clause, of the sample will is followed by an explanation.

Will of Natalie DeJarlais

Part 1. Personal Information

I, Natalie DeJarlais, a resident of the State of California, Alameda County, declare that this is my will.

Part 2. Revocation of Previous Wills

I revoke all wills and codicils that I have previously made.

This provision makes clear that this is the will to be used—not any other wills or amendments to those wills, called codicils, that were made earlier. To prevent possible confusion, all earlier wills and codicils should also be physically destroyed.

Part 3. Marital Status

I am married to Michael Sexton.

Here you identify your spouse if you are married—or your partner, if you are in a registered domestic partnership, civil union or other marriage-like relationship recognized by your state. If you are not married or in a registered partnership, this provision will not appear in your will.

Part 4. Children

I have the following children now living: Sammie DeJarlais and Chester DeJarlais.

This part of your will should list all of your natural-born and adopted children; your stepchildren should not be included here. By naming all your children, you will prevent a child from claiming that he or she was accidentally overlooked in your will. It will also ward off later claims that any child is entitled to take a share of your property against your wishes.

Part 5. Pets

I leave my Boston terrier, Clementine, and $1,500, to Ann Heron, with the hope that the money will be used for Clementine's care and maintenance. If Ann Heron does not survive me, I leave Clementine and $2,000 to Michael Sexton, with the hope that the money will be used for Clementine's care and maintenance.

Here you can leave your pet to a trusted caretaker. You can also leave money to the caretaker with a request that the caretaker use the money for your pet's care.

Part 6. Disposition of Property

A beneficiary must survive me for 45 days to receive property under this will. As used in this will, the phrase "survive me" means to be alive or in existence as an organization on the 45th day after my death.

This language means that to receive property under your will, a person must be alive for at least 45 days after your death. Otherwise, the property will go to whomever you named as an alternate. This language permits you to choose another way to leave your property if your first choice dies within a short time after you do.

This will clause also prevents the confusion associated with the simultaneous death of two spouses, when it is hard to tell who gets the property they have left to each other. Property left to a spouse who dies within 45 days of the first spouse, including a spouse who dies simultaneously, will go to the person or organization named as alternate.

If I leave property to be shared by two or more beneficiaries, and any of them does not survive me, I leave his or her share to the others equally unless this will provides otherwise.

This clause states that if you leave a gift to two or more beneficiaries without stating the percentage each should receive, the beneficiaries will share the gift equally. This clause is included as a catch-all; you can determine the shares for almost every shared gift.

My residuary estate is all property I own at my death that is subject to this will that does not pass under a general or specific bequest, including all failed or lapsed bequests.

This definition is included so that you and your survivors are clear on the meaning of "residuary estate."

I leave $10,000 to Justin Disney. If Justin Disney does not survive me, I leave this property to Bhamita Ranchod.

This language leaves a specific item of property—$10,000—to a named beneficiary, Justin Disney. If Justin Disney does not survive the testator, then Bhamita Ranchod will get the money.

I leave my rare stamp collection to Ann Heron, Eric K. Workman and André Zivkovich in the following shares: Ann Heron shall receive a 1/4 share. Eric K. Workman shall receive a 1/4 share. André Zivkovich shall receive a 1/2 share.

This language leaves a specific item of property—a stamp collection—to three people in unequal shares.

I leave my collection of Nash cars to The Big Sky Auto Museum and Richard Jenkins in equal shares. If Richard Jenkins does not survive me, I leave his or her share of this property to Patricia Jenkins.

This will leaves specific property to an organization and a person equally. Since the testator here was concerned about providing for the possibility that the person would not survive to take the property, she named an alternate for him.

I leave my residuary estate to my spouse, Michael Sexton.

This clause gives the residuary estate—all property that does not pass under this will in specific bequests—to the testator's spouse. Your residuary estate may be defined differently depending on your plans for leaving your property.

If Michael Sexton does not survive me, I leave my residuary estate to Sammie DeJarlais and Chester DeJarlais in a children's pot trust to be administered under the children's pot trust provisions.

If the person named here to take the residuary estate does not survive the testator, the residuary estate will pass to the two people named: the testator's children. The property will be put in one pot for both of the children to use as they mature. Specifics of how this pot trust operates are explained later in the will. Keep in mind that, in this example, the pot trust will come into being only if the testator's spouse does not survive the testator by at least 45 days.

If both of these children are age 18 or older at my death, my residuary estate shall be distributed to them directly in equal shares.

This clause makes clear what should happen if the children are older than the age the testator specified the pot trust should end. In this case, no pot trust will be created; the children will get the property directly and divide it evenly.

If either of these children do not survive me, I leave his or her share to the other child.

This clause explains that if either child here does not survive, the other will get the property directly.

If Michael Sexton, Sammie DeJarlais and Chester DeJarlais all do not survive me, I leave my residuary estate to Delia Holt.

All personal and real property that I leave in this will shall pass subject to any encumbrances or liens placed on the property as security for the repayment of a loan or debt.

This language explains that whoever gets any property under this will also gets the mortgage and other legal claims against the property, such as liens. And anyone who takes property that is subject to a loan, such as a car loan, gets the debt as well as the property.

Part 7. Custodianship Under the Uniform Transfers to Minors Act

All property left in this will to Delia Holt shall be given to James Leung as custodian under the California Uniform Transfers to Minors Act, to be held until Delia Holt reaches age 21. If James Leung is unwilling or unable to serve as custodian of property left to Delia Holt under this will, Michael Eisenberg shall serve instead.

This clause provides that all property left to the child named in the clause will be managed by the person named as the custodian until the child turns the age indicated. An alternate custodian is also named in case the first-choice custodian is unable or unwilling to serve when the time comes.

Part 8. Children's Pot Trust

A. Beneficiaries of Children's Pot Trust

Sammie DeJarlais and Chester DeJarlais shall be the beneficiaries of the children's pot trust provided for in this will. If a beneficiary survives me but dies before the children's pot trust terminates, that beneficiary's interest in the trust shall pass to the surviving beneficiaries of the children's pot trust.

B. Trustee of Children's Pot Trust

Dave Jenkins shall serve as the trustee of the children's pot trust. If Dave Jenkins is unable or unwilling to serve, Keely Jenkins shall serve instead.

C. Administration of the Children's Pot Trust

The trustee shall manage and distribute the assets in the children's pot trust in the following manner.

The trustee may distribute trust assets as he or she deems necessary for a beneficiary's health, support, maintenance and education. Education includes, but is not limited to, college, graduate, postgraduate and vocational studies and reasonably related living expenses.

In deciding whether or not to make distributions, the trustee shall consider the value of the trust assets, the relative current and future needs of each beneficiary and each beneficiary's other income, resources and sources of support. In doing so, the trustee has the discretion to make distributions that benefit some beneficiaries more than others or that completely exclude others.

Any trust income that is not distributed by the trustee shall be accumulated and added to the principal.

D. Termination of the Children's Pot Trust

When the youngest surviving beneficiary of this children's pot trust reaches 18, the trustee shall distribute the remaining trust assets to the surviving beneficiaries in equal shares.

If none of the trust beneficiaries survives to the age of 18, the trustee shall, at the death of the last surviving beneficiary, distribute the remaining trust assets to that beneficiary's estate.

Part 9. Individual Child's Trust

A. Beneficiaries and Trustees

All property left in this will to Bhamita Ranchod shall be held in a separate trust for Bhamita Ranchod until she reaches age 25. The trustee of the Bhamita Ranchod trust shall be Connor Jenkins.

This clause provides that all property given to the child named in the clause shall be held in trust—that is, managed strictly for the benefit of the child—by the person named as the trustee until the child turns the age indicated. An alternate trustee may also be named in case the first-choice trustee is unable or unwilling to serve when the time comes.

B. Administration of an Individual Child's Trust

The trustee of an individual child's trust shall manage and distribute the assets in the trust in the following manner.

Until the trust beneficiary reaches the age specified for final distribution of the principal, the trustee may distribute some or all of the principal or net income of the trust as the trustee deems necessary for the child's health, support, maintenance and education. Education includes, but is not limited to, college, graduate, postgraduate and vocational studies and reasonable living expenses.

This clause lets the trustee spend the trust principal and income for the child's general living, health and educational needs. The clause gives the trustee great latitude in how this is done and what amount is spent.

In deciding whether or not to make a distribution to a beneficiary, the trustee may take into account the beneficiary's other income, resources and sources of support.

This clause lets the trustee withhold the trust principal or income from the trust beneficiary if, in the trustee's opinion, the beneficiary has sufficient income from other sources.

Any trust income that is not distributed by the trustee shall be accumulated and added to the principal.

Every trust involves two types of property: the property in the trust—called the trust principal—and the income that is earned by investing the principal. This clause assures that the trustee must add to the trust principal any income that is earned on the principal, unless the income is distributed to the trust beneficiary.

C. Termination of an Individual Child's Trust

An individual child's trust shall terminate as soon as one of the following events occurs:

- the beneficiary reaches the age stated above, in which case the trustee shall distribute the remaining principal and accumulated net income of the trust to the beneficiary
- the beneficiary dies, in which case the principal and accumulated net income of the trust shall pass under the beneficiary's will, or if there is no will, to his or her heirs, or
- the trust principal is exhausted through distributions allowed under these provisions.

This clause sets out three events that may cause the trust to end. The first is when the minor or young adult reaches the age specified for the trust to end. If the trust ends for this reason, the minor or young adult gets whatever trust principal and accumulated income is left. The trust will also end if the minor or young adult dies before the age set for the trust to end. If the trust ends for this reason, the principal and income accumulated in the trust goes to whomever the young adult named in his or her will to get it or, if there is no will, to the minor or young adult's legal heirs—such as parents, brothers and sisters. A third occurrence that will cause the trust to end is when there is no trust principal left—or so little left that it's no longer financially feasible to maintain it.

Part 10. General Trust Administration Provisions

All trusts established in this will shall be managed subject to the following provisions.

A. Transferability of Interests

The interests of any beneficiary of all trusts established by this will shall not be transferable by voluntary or involuntary assignment or by operation of law and shall be free from the claims of creditors and from attachment, execution, bankruptcy or other legal process to the fullest extent permitted by law.

This important clause removes the trust principal and accumulated income from the reach of the minor or young adult's creditors—while it is being held in the trust. Also, this clause prevents the minor or young adult from transferring ownership of the principal or accumulated interest to others—again, while it is in the trust. Once property is distributed to the minor or young adult, however, there are no restrictions on what he or she can do with it.

B. Powers of the Trustee

In addition to other powers granted a trustee in this will, a trustee shall have the powers to:

1. Invest and reinvest trust funds in every kind of property and every kind of investment, provided that the trustee acts with the care, skill, prudence and diligence under the prevailing circumstances that a prudent person acting in a similar capacity and familiar with such matters would use.

2. Receive additional property from any source and acquire or hold properties jointly or in undivided interests or in partnership or joint venture with other people or entities.

3. Enter, continue or participate in the operation of any business, and incorporate, liquidate, reorganize or otherwise change the form or terminate the operation of the business and contribute capital or loan money to the business.

4. Exercise all the rights, powers and privileges of an owner of any securities held in the trust.

5. Borrow funds, guarantee or indemnify in the name of the trust and secure any obligation, mortgage, pledge or other security interest, and renew, extend or modify any such obligations.

6. Lease trust property for terms within or beyond the term of the trust.

7. Prosecute, defend, contest or otherwise litigate legal actions or other proceedings for the protection or benefit of the trust; pay, compromise, release, adjust or submit to arbitration any debt, claim or controversy; and insure the trust against any risk and the trustee against liability with respect to other people.

8. Pay himself or herself reasonable compensation out of trust assets for ordinary and extraordinary services, and for all services in connection with the complete or partial termination of this trust.

9. Employ and discharge professionals to aid or assist in managing the trust and compensate them from the trust assets.

10. Make distributions to the beneficiaries directly or to other people or organizations on behalf of the beneficiaries.

> *This list of powers should cover the gamut of activities that trustees might be called upon to exercise in administering any trust set up in this will.*

C. Severability

The invalidity of any trust provision of this will shall not affect the validity of the remaining trust provisions.

> *This language ensures that in the unlikely event that a court finds any individual part of this trust to be invalid, the rest of the document will remain in effect.*

Part 11. Personal Guardian

If at my death a guardian is needed to care for my children, I name Ann Heron as personal guardian. If this person is unable or unwilling to serve as personal guardian, I name Michael Eisenberg to serve instead.

Reasons for my choice for guardian for all my children: Ann Heron has established a close relationship with all of the children. She frequently takes care of them when my husband and I must work on weekends—and her training as a doctor makes her especially knowledgeable about handling their health care needs. Best of all, she is a loving and trustworthy friend who has unerring judgment and common sense—an excellent choice to raise the children if Michael and I cannot.

No personal guardian shall be required to post bond.

> *This clause names someone to provide parental-type care for a minor child if there is no legal (biological or adoptive) parent able to provide it. The clause also provides for an alternate to step in if the first choice is not able or willing to act when the moment comes. When making your own will, be aware that if there is another legal parent on the scene, that parent will usually be awarded custody of the children, unless a court concludes that the children would be at risk of harm. The explanation provided for the choice helps ensure that a court will help follow your reasoning—and often helps ensure court approval of your choice of guardian. The clause also provides that the personal guardian need not provide a bond to guarantee faithful performance of his or her duties.*

Part 12. Property Guardian

If at my death, a guardian is needed to care for any property belonging to Sammie DeJarlais or Chester DeJarlais, I name Eric K. Workman as property guardian. If Eric K. Workman is unwilling or unable to serve as property guardian, I name Justin Disney to serve instead.

No property guardian shall be required to post bond.

> *This clause appoints someone to manage property that passes to your children outside of your will. For example, if your children receive inheritance from another relative, proceeds from a life insurance policy or income from a trust, and those instruments do not provide a property guardian, you can name an adult to manage those funds until the children become adults. You may also appoint an alternate property guardian in case your first choice is not able or willing to serve when the time comes. The clause also provides that the personal guardian need not provide a bond—a kind of insurance of good performance—to guarantee that he or she will act faithfully.*

Part 13. Forgiveness of Debts

I wish to forgive all debts specified below, plus accrued interest as of the date of my death: Sheila Jenkins, April 6, 2007, $10,000.

> *Forgiving a debt is equivalent to making a bequest of money. It is a common way to equalize what you leave to all your children when you have loaned one of them some money—that is, the amount that you would otherwise leave that child can be reduced by the amount of the debt being forgiven.*

Part 14. Executor

I name Michael Sexton to serve as my executor. If Michael Sexton is unwilling or unable to serve as executor, I name Ann Heron to serve as my executor.

No executor shall be required to post bond.

> *This clause identifies the choices for executor and an alternate executor who will take over if the first choice is unable or unwilling to serve when the time comes.*

Part 15. Executor's Powers

I direct my executor to take all actions legally permissible to have the probate of my will done as simply and as free of court supervision as possible under the laws of the state having jurisdiction over this will, including filing a petition in the appropriate court for the independent administration of my estate.

This clause sets out the specific authority that the executor will need to competently manage the estate until it has been distributed under the terms of the will. The will language expresses your desire that your executor work as free from court supervision as possible. This will cut down on delays and expense.

When you print out your will, a second paragraph will list a number of specific powers that your executor will have, if necessary. It also makes clear that the listing of these specific powers does not deprive your executor of any other powers that he or she has under the law of your state. The general idea is to give your executor as much power as possible, so that he or she will not have to go to court and get permission to take a particular action.

Part 16. Payment of Debts

Except for liens and encumbrances placed on property as security for the repayment of a loan or debt, I direct all debts and expenses owed by my estate to be paid using the following assets: Account #666777 at Cudahy Savings Bank.

This clause states how debts will be paid. Depending on the choice you make when using Quicken WillMaker Plus, your debts may be paid either from specific assets you designate or from your residuary estate—all the property covered by your will that does not pass through a specific bequest.

Part 17. Payment of Taxes

I direct that all estate and inheritance taxes assessed against property in my estate or against my beneficiaries to be paid using the following assets: Account #939494050 at the Independence Bank, Central Branch.

This clause states how any estate or death taxes owed by the estate or beneficiaries should be paid. This will usually apply only to people whose estate has a net value of $2 million or more. Depending on the choice you make when operating Quicken WillMaker Plus, your taxes may be paid from all of your property, from specific assets you designate or by your executor according to the law of your state.

Part 18. No-Contest Provision

If any beneficiary under this will contests this will or any of its provisions, any share or interest in my estate given to the contesting beneficiary under this will is revoked and shall be disposed of as if that contesting beneficiary had not survived me.

This harsh-sounding clause is intended to discourage anyone who receives anything under the will from challenging its legality for the purpose of receiving a larger share. Many states will not enforce a no-contest clause if the challenger has a good reason for the contest. Other states have passed laws specifically stating that a no-contest clause will not be enforced. If a court decides not to carry out the no-contest clause in your will, the rest of the document will be enforced as written.

/////
/////
/////
/////
/////
/////
/////
/////

These hashmarks will automatically appear to fill up the rest of the page so that your signature appears with some text of the will—one way to help guard against an unethical survivor tampering with the document.

Part 19. Severability

If any provision of this will is held invalid, that shall not affect other provisions that can be given effect without the invalid provision.

This is standard language that ensures that in the unlikely event that a court finds any individual part of your will to be invalid, the rest of the document will remain in effect.

SIGNATURE

I, Natalie DeJarlais, the testator, sign my name to this instrument, this _____ day of _____, _____, at _____. I declare that I sign and execute this instrument as my last will, that I sign it willingly, and that I execute it as my free and voluntary act. I declare that I am of the age of majority or otherwise legally empowered to make a will, and under no constraint or undue influence.

Signature: _____

WITNESSES

We, the witnesses, sign our names to this document, and declare that the testator willingly signed and executed this document as the testator's last will.

In the presence of the testator, and in the presence of each other, we sign this will as witnesses to the testator's signing.

To the best of our knowledge, the testator is of the age of majority or otherwise legally empowered to make a will, is mentally competent and under no constraint or undue influence. We declare under penalty of perjury that the foregoing is true and correct, this _____ day of _____, _____ at _____ _____.

First Witness

Sign your name: _____

Print your name: _____

Address: _____

City, State: _____

Second Witness

Sign your name: _____

Print your name: _____

Address: _____

City, State: _____

About You and Yours

As you go through Quicken WillMaker Plus, you will first be asked to answer a number of questions about yourself and your family. This chapter discusses those questions in the order in which they appear in the program.

Your Name

Enter your name—first, middle if you choose, then last—in the same form that you use on other formal documents, such as your driver's license or bank accounts. This may or may not be the name that appears on your birth certificate.

If you customarily use more than one name for business purposes, list all of them in your Quicken WillMaker Plus answer, separated by aka, which stands for "also known as."

There is room for you to list several names. But use your common sense. Your name is needed here to identify you and all the property you own. Be sure to include all names in which you have held bank accounts, stocks, bonds, real estate or other property. But you need not list every nickname, or names you use for nonbusiness purposes.

Your Gender

Quicken WillMaker Plus also asks you to state whether you are male or female. This is not to be nosy, but so that the screens you see while proceeding through the program and the language in your final document will be easier to read, avoiding the awkward "he or she."

Your Social Security Number

At the end of the interview, Quicken WillMaker Plus will give you the option to enter your nine-digit Social Security number. If you choose to enter it, the number will *not* be included in your will, where it could become part of the public record. Instead, the program will print your Social Security number in a letter for your executor that prints with your will.

Your State

You are asked to specify the state of your legal residence, sometimes called a domicile. This is the state where you make your home now and for the indefinite future. This information is vital for a number of will-making reasons, so it is important to check your answer for accuracy.

Your state's laws affect:

- marital property ownership
- property management options for young beneficiaries
- how your will can be admitted into probate, and
- whether your property will be subject to state inheritance tax.

If you live in two or more states during the year and have business relationships in both, you may not be sure which state is your legal residence.

Choose the state where you are the most rooted—that is, the state in which you:

- are registered to vote
- register your motor vehicles

- own valuable property—especially property with a title document, such as a house or car
- have checking, savings and other investment accounts, and
- maintain a business.

To avoid confusion, it is best to keep all or at least most of your roots in one state, if possible. For people with larger estates, ideally this should be in a state that does not levy an inheritance tax. (See "Estate and Inheritance Taxes" in Chapter 9.)

CAUTION

Wills valid in the United States only. Quicken WillMaker Plus produces valid wills in all of the continental United States except for Louisiana—and the program guides you by showing you screens geared specifically to the state of residence you indicate when using it.

Because the property and probate laws in Puerto Rico and Guam, for example, may differ from a state you have selected to use in making your will, we do not guarantee that a Quicken WillMaker Plus will is valid there. However, some users who reside outside the United States do use Quicken WillMaker Plus to help draft their wills and then have them looked over by an experienced local professional.

CAUTION

If your choice is not clear. If you do not maintain continuous ties with a particular state, or if you have homes in both the United States and another country, consult a lawyer to find out which state to list as your legal domicile when using Quicken WillMaker Plus.

Living Overseas

If you live overseas temporarily because you are in the armed services, your residence will be the home of record you declared to the military authorities.

Normally, your home of record is the state you lived in before you received your assignment, where your parents or spouse live or where you now have a permanent home. If there is a close call between two states, consider the factors listed above for determining a legal residence, or get advice from the military legal authorities.

If you live overseas for business or education, you probably still have ties with a particular state that would make it your legal residence. For example, if you were born in Wisconsin, lived there for many years, registered to vote there and receive mail there in care of your parents who still live in Milwaukee, then Wisconsin is your legal residence for purposes of making a will.

Your County

Including your county in your will is optional but recommended. Including it will help others identify you and track down your property after your death.

Also, a county name may provide those handling your estate with important direction, because wills go through probate in the court system of the county where you last resided, no matter where you died. The one exception is real estate: That property is probated in the court of the county in which it is located.

If you live in Alaska, which is divided into boroughs and judicial districts instead of counties, you may enter the name of your borough. The correct term will appear in your will.

Marital or Domestic Partnership Status

Quicken Willmaker Plus asks you to indicate your marital or domestic partnership status. (When we say "domestic partnership," we mean any marriage-like partnership registered with a state government, including civil unions and reciprocal beneficiary relationships.) The law treats married people and registered domestic partners differently than other will makers, so your answer to this question is important. Rest assured, however, that you will be able to leave your property in almost any way you please, regardless of your relationship status.

It will probably be easy to select your relationship status. However, if you are separated, have filed for divorce or have a same-sex partner, the answer may not be clear. Read the following sections to help you make the best choice.

If you are married or in a registered domestic partnership, you should also review the property ownership laws affecting married and partnered people. (See "Property Ownership Rules for Married People" in Chapter 5.)

The Importance of Your Marital Status

You should make a new will whenever you marry or divorce. (See Chapter 11.)

If your marital status changes but your will does not, your new spouse or ex-spouse may get more or less of your property than you intend. For example, if you marry after making a will and do not provide for the new spouse—either in the will or through transfers outside the will—your spouse, in many states, may be entitled to claim a big share of your property at your death.

Also, if you name a spouse in a will, then divorce or have the marriage annulled and die before making a new will, state laws will produce different, often unexpected, results. In most states, the former spouse will automatically get nothing. In other states, the former spouse is entitled to take the property as set out in the will.

In a few states, registered domestic partnerships provide the same rights and responsibilities as marriage. In those states, changes in your partnership status may affect the distribution of your property. Therefore, like married folks, you should make a new will whenever your domestic partnership status changes.

Divorce

If you're not sure whether or not you are legally divorced, make sure you see a copy of the final order signed by a judge. To track down a divorce order, contact the court clerk in the county where you believe the divorce occurred. You will need to give the first and last names of you and your former spouse and make a good guess at what year the divorce became final. If you cannot locate a final decree of divorce, it is safest to assume you are still legally married.

If the divorce was supposed to have taken place outside the United States, it may be difficult to verify. If you have any reason to think that someone you consider to be a former spouse might claim to be married to you at your death because an out-of-country divorce was not legal, consult a lawyer. (See Chapter 25.)

Separation

Many married couples, contemplating divorce or reconciliation, live apart from one another, sometimes for several years. While this often feels like a murky limbo while you are living it, for will-making purposes, your status is straightforward: You are legally married until a court issues a formal decree of divorce, signed by a judge. This is true even if you and your spouse are legally separated as declared in a legal document. Note that many separation agreements, however, set out rights and restrictions that may affect your ownership of property.

Common Law Marriage

It is uncommon to have a common law marriage. In most states, common law marriage does not exist.

But in the states listed below, couples can become legally married if they live together and either hold themselves out to the public as being married or actually intend to be married to one another. Once these conditions are met, the couple is legally married. And the marriage will still be valid even if they later move to a state that does not allow couples to form common law marriages there.

No matter what state you live in, if either you or the person you live with is still legally married to some other person, you cannot have a common law marriage.

The following states recognize some form of common law marriage:

- Alabama
- Colorado
- District of Columbia
- Georgia (if created before 1/1/97)
- Idaho (if created before 1/1/96)
- Iowa
- Kansas
- Montana
- New Hampshire (for inheritance purposes only)
- Ohio (if created before 10/10/91)
- Oklahoma
- Pennsylvania (if created before 1/1/05)
- Rhode Island
- South Carolina
- Texas, and
- Utah.

In addition, a handful of states—including Florida, Indiana, Mississippi, Nebraska, Nevada, New Jersey and South Dakota—recognize common law marriages if they were created long ago. If you live in one of these states and you entered into what you believe to be a common law marriage before 1970, you may want to consult a lawyer to determine the legal status of your relationship.

There is no such thing as a common law divorce; no matter how your marriage begins, you must go through formal divorce proceedings to end it.

Same-Sex Couples

The laws affecting same-sex couples are in flux. Legally, some states do not recognize same-sex relationships at all, while other states offer a variety of rights to lesbian and gay couples who register their relationships. Currently, California and Massachusetts are the only states that permit same-sex couples to marry. Other states offer benefits similar to marriage for couples who register for them. (For more information, see "Same-Sex Partners and the Law," below.)

When making your will, how you include your partner depends on where you live and the kind of legal commitment you and your partner have made.

If you married your partner in California or Massachusetts. If you married your partner in California or Massachusetts and you still live in one of those states, you may make your will as a married person. Simply indicate that you are married when you make your will. Your document will treat your relationship like any other marriage and will refer to your partner as your spouse.

If you are a California or Massachusetts resident and you did not get married in the state, but are married in another country that offers legalized same-sex marriage, you also may indicate that you are married when you make your will.

If you registered your partnership in the state where you live. If you and your partner registered as partners in a state that offers benefits to same-sex couples and you still live in that state, choose "I have a registered domestic partner," when asked for your relationship status. Although some states use different terms (such as "civil union partners" or "reciprocal beneficiaries") we generally use "domestic partners" to refer to a registered same-sex couple. If, however, you live in a state that uses another term, your finished document will contain the correct term for your state. (If you live in New Jersey, where you may have a domestic partnership or a civil union, you will be asked to select the appropriate term for your relationship.)

If you have not registered your partnership in the state where you live. If you and your partner have not registered with your state or if you no longer live in the state where you registered, you should make your will as a single person by choosing "I'm not married, nor do I have a registered domestic partner." Unless you are a resident of California or Massachusetts, this applies to partners who got married in another country that offers legalized same-sex marriage. At this time, it is safest to assume that U.S. states—other than California or Massachusetts—and the federal

Same-Sex Partners and the Law

State Rules

- California allows same sex-couples to marry. The state also offers registered domestic partnerships that provide the same rights married couples enjoy, including community property rights (see "Property Ownership Rules for Married People" in Chapter 5) and the right to inherit from a deceased partner who didn't make a will. Although it is technically possible that you and your partner can be both married and registered domestic partners under California law, to avoid confusion we ask you to choose one status or the other when you make your will. Doing so will not affect the way your property is distributed after your death.

- Connecticut allows same-sex couples to form civil unions that give partners all the rights of married couples under state law, including inheritance rights.

- The District of Columbia's domestic partnership law gives registered partners many of the same rights as spouses, including inheritance rights.

- Hawaii allows unmarried couples to enter into reciprocal beneficiary relationships, giving each partner most of the inheritance rights of married couples.

- Maine gives registered domestic partners many of the same rights as married couples, including inheritance rights.

- Massachusetts allows same-sex couples to marry.

- New Hampshire allows same-sex couples to form civil unions, giving partners all the rights of married couples under state law, including inheritance rights.

- New Jersey law provides for both domestic partnerships and civil unions, though you can't have both at the same time. (If you are registered as domestic partners and you enter a civil union, your domestic partnership is automatically terminated. In addition, since 2/19/2007, new domestic partnerships are not allowed for people under 62.) Either form of partnership gives the surviving partner the right to inherit from the deceased partner and treats survivors like spouses for inheritance tax purposes.

- Oregon gives registered domestic partners most of the rights that married couples have, including inheritance rights.

- Vermont allows same-sex couples to form civil unions that give partners all the rights of married couples under state law, including inheritance rights.

- Washington gives registered domestic partners many of the same rights as married couples, including inheritance rights. Washington's community property laws do not apply to domestic partners.

Federal Rules

The federal government does not currently recognize any same-sex relationships, no matter what state law says. (This is because of a federal law called the Defense of Marriage Act.) So same-sex couples who marry or register their partnerships are not entitled to the federal estate and gift tax benefits married couples enjoy—or to Social Security benefits, or any of the more than 1,000 other benefits extended to heterosexual married couples.

government will not recognize legal same-sex marriages from other countries, so you cannot depend on your foreign marriage to give you married status in the United States. In this case, to minimize the possibility of a challenge to your will, it's best to make your will as a single person and then name your partner as your primary beneficiary.

Indicating that you are single does not limit your ability to leave property to your partner or to name your partner as executor of your will or guardian of your young children. You can do all of those things in your will.

> **RESOURCE**
> **More information for same-sex couples.** For complete information about the legal issues that same-sex couples face, see *A Legal Guide for Lesbian & Gay Couples*, by Denis Clifford, Frederick Hertz and Emily Doskow (Nolo).

Your Spouse or Domestic Partner

Quicken WillMaker Plus prompts you to provide the full name of your spouse or domestic partner. As with your own name, list all names used for business purposes, following the tips suggested for entering your own name, above.

Also indicate whether your spouse or domestic partner is male or female. This way, the program can refer to him or her with the correct pronoun.

Your Children

Becoming a parent is what may have motivated you to buckle down to the task of writing your will in the first place.

If you are the parent of young children, your will is the perfect place to address some driving concerns you are likely to have if you die before they are grown. These concerns include:

- who will care for your children, and
- who will manage their property.

Quicken WillMaker Plus lets you make these decisions separately. This gives you the option of placing the responsibilities in the hands of the same person or, if need be, naming different people. First, you are asked to name someone to care for your children. Later in the program, you'll deal with the issue of providing property management for your own or other people's young children. (See Chapter 7.)

Identifying Your Children

Quicken WillMaker Plus asks you whether or not you have any children and, if you do, it asks you to name each of them. You are not required to leave property to your children, but it is important that you at least state each child's name. If you don't, it may not be clear whether you intentionally left a child out of your will, or whether the child was accidentally overlooked (called "pretermitted," under the law). A child who is unintentionally omitted from your will—usually because you made your will before he or she was born—has a right to take a share of your estate.

SEE AN EXPERT

Children born after a parent dies.
If a child is conceived before your death but is born after you die, he or she will most likely be entitled to part of your estate even if your will doesn't mention the child. But the law is now rushing to answer a new question posed by advancing medical technology: What happens if a child is conceived *after* the death of a parent? If sperm, eggs or embryos are preserved before the parent's death, a child could be born years later. Individual states are taking different approaches to this matter. Some are giving posthumously conceived children the rights to inherit property and receive other benefits from their deceased parents. Others are refusing such rights. If you are curious about this issue or planning for a posthumously conceived child, you should consult a knowledgeable estate planning lawyer.

When naming your children, you should include all children born to you or legally adopted by you.

If you are the parent of a child who has been legally adopted by a person other than your spouse or partner—or you have otherwise given up your legal parental rights—then you need not name that child in your will.

You should not name stepchildren you have not adopted, since they are not entitled by law to a share of your property when you die. The pretermitted heir rule does not apply to them. Also, Quicken WillMaker Plus offers a number of options that include your children

as a group, and if you include stepchildren in the list and use one of these options, your will might contain provisions you did not intend.

However, you are free to leave your stepchildren as much property in your will as you wish. If you want to treat your children and stepchildren equally and not differentiate between them, when Quicken WillMaker Plus asks how you wish to leave your property, choose the option labeled "Leave it some other way." (See Chapter 6.)

To list your children, enter their full names in the sequence and format you want the names to appear in your will.

CAUTION

Don't use "all my children." Some people are tempted to skimp on naming their children individually and want to fill in "all my children," "my surviving children," "my lawful heirs" or "my issue." Don't do it. That shorthand language is much more confusing than listing each child by name.

Your Children's Birthdates

Quicken WillMaker Plus also asks you to enter your children's dates of birth—month, day, year. The program will automatically compute their ages in years—an important consideration when you are asked to name a personal guardian and provide management for property you or others leave them.

Personal Guardians for Your Minor Children

Among the most pressing concerns of parents with minor children is who will care for the children if one or both of them die before the children reach adulthood.

Although contemplating the possibility of your early death can be wrenching, it is important to face up to it and adopt the best contingency plan for the care of your young children. If the other parent is available, then he or she can usually handle the task.

However, you and the other parent might die close together in time. Or you may currently be a single parent and need to decide what will happen if you do not survive until your children become adults.

This section discusses using Quicken WillMaker Plus to choose a personal guardian to care for the children's basic health, education and other daily needs. Choosing a person to manage your children's property is discussed in Chapter 7.

Reasons for Naming a Personal Guardian

The general legal rule is that if there are two parents willing and able to care for the children, and one dies, the other will take over physical custody and responsibility for caring for the child. In many states, the surviving parent may also be given authority by a court to manage any property the deceased parent left to the children—unless the deceased

parent has specified a different property management arrangement in a will.

But there is no ready fallback plan if both parents of a minor child die or, in the case of a single parent, there is not another parent able or willing to do the job. Using Quicken WillMaker Plus, you can deal with these concerns by naming a personal guardian as well as an alternate. The person you name will normally be appointed by the court to act as a surrogate parent for your minor children if both of the following are true:

- There is no surviving biological or adoptive parent able to properly care for the children.
- The court agrees that your choice is in the best interests of the children.

If both parents are making wills, each should name the same person as guardian for each child. This will help avoid the possibility of a dispute and perhaps even a court battle should the parents die simultaneously. But remember, if one parent dies, the other will usually assume custody and will then be free to make a new will naming a different personal guardian if he or she wishes. In short, if both parents are active caretakers, the personal guardian named in a will cares for the children only if both parents die close together in time.

However, if you feel strongly that the other parent is not the best person to care for the children, be sure to explain your reasoning when the Quicken WillMaker Plus program prompts you to do so. (See "Explaining Your Choice," below.)

Naming Different Guardians for Different Children

One obvious concern when choosing a personal guardian for your children is to keep them together if they get along well with one another. This suggests that it is best to name the same personal guardian for all the children.

There are families, however, where the children are not particularly close to one another but have strong attachments with one or more adults outside the immediate family. For instance, one child may spend a lot of time with a grandparent while another child may be close to an aunt and uncle. Also, in a second or third marriage, a child from an earlier marriage may be closer to a different adult than a child from the current marriage.

In these situations and others, logic dictates other advice: Choose the personal guardian you believe would best be able to care for the child. This may mean that you will choose different personal guardians for different children.

Choosing a Personal Guardian

To qualify as a personal guardian, your choice must be an adult—18 in most states—and competent to do the job. For obvious reasons, you should first consider an adult with whom the child already has a close relationship—a stepparent, grandparent, aunt or uncle, older sibling, babysitter, close friend of the family or even neighbor. Whomever you choose, be sure that person is mature, good-hearted and willing and able to assume the responsibility.

Naming More Than One Person as Guardian

In many cases, it's a poor idea to name more than one person to serve as guardian for your children. Naming multiple guardians raises the possibility that they may disagree about the best way to raise a child, resulting in conflict and perhaps even requiring court intervention. However, there is one situation in which naming two guardians makes good sense: when you want to name a couple to care for your children together.

If you know a couple—for example, your sister and her husband—who are willing and able to take good care of your children, it's fine to name them both as coguardians. The couple will act as your children's surrogate parents. Both of them will be allowed to do things for your children that require legal authority, such as picking up your children from school, authorizing field trips or taking them to the doctor.

Keep in mind, however, that if you name a couple as coguardians, they must be able to agree on what's best for your children. Any severe difference of opinion between them could require court intervention—and this would be difficult for the couple and upsetting to your kids. Also, if you name a couple that parts ways while you are still alive, you should revise your will to name one or the other to care for your children, or choose a different couple to act as coguardians.

The main point is that you must choose carefully when naming a couple as personal coguardians for your children. Select a couple that can make joint decisions without conflict, has a unified parenting style and is likely to stay together a long time. If you have any reservations about the longevity of the couple's relationship or any concerns about either person's parenting style, you may be better off just naming one of them—for example, name just your sister. If you like, you can explain the reasons for your choice in your will. See "Explaining Your Choice," below.

Choosing an Alternate Personal Guardian

Quicken WillMaker Plus lets you name a back-up or alternate personal guardian to serve in case your first choice for each child either changes his or her mind or is unable to do the job at your death. The considerations involved in naming an alternate personal guardian are the same as those you pondered when making your first choice: maturity, a good heart, familiarity with the children and willingness to serve.

If you name a couple as coguardians, the alternate will become the personal guardian only if both coguardians are unable or unwilling to serve.

Explaining Your Choice

Leaving a written explanation of why you made a particular choice for a personal guardian may be especially important if you think a judge may have reason to question your decision.

If you don't want the other parent to have custody. If you are separated or divorced, you may have strong ideas about why the child's other parent, or perhaps a grandparent, should not have custody of your minor children. In an age when many parents live separately, the following predicaments are sadly common:

- "I have custody of my three children. I don't want my ex-husband, who I believe is emotionally destructive, to get custody of our children if I die. Can I choose a guardian to serve instead of him?"
- "I have legal custody of my daughter and I've remarried. My present wife is a much better mother to my daughter than my ex-wife, who never cared for her properly. What can I do to make sure my present wife gets custody if I die?"
- "I live with a man who's been a good parent to my children for six years. My father doesn't like the fact that we aren't married and may well try to get custody of the kids if I die. What can I do to see that my partner gets custody?"

There is no definitive answer to these questions. If you die while the child is still a minor and the other parent disputes your choice in court, the judge will likely grant custody to the other parent, unless that parent:

- has legally abandoned the child by not providing for or visiting the child for an extended period, or
- is clearly unfit as a parent.

It is usually difficult to prove that a parent is unfit, absent serious and obvious problems such as chronic drug or alcohol abuse, mental illness or a history of child abuse. The fact that you do not like or respect the other parent is never enough, by itself, for a court to deny custody to him or her.

EXAMPLE: Susan and Fred, an unmarried couple, have two minor children. Although

Susan loves Fred, she does not think he is capable of raising the children on his own. She uses Quicken WillMaker Plus to name her mother, Elinor, as guardian. If Susan dies, Fred, as the children's other parent, will be given first priority as personal guardian over Elinor, despite Susan's will, assuming the court finds he is willing and able to care for the children. However, if the court finds that Fred should not be personal guardian, Elinor would get the nod, assuming she is fit.

If you honestly believe the other natural parent is incapable of caring for your children properly—or simply will not assume the responsibility—you should reinforce that belief by explaining why you elected to name other people as guardians and alternates.

EXAMPLE: Justine and Paul live together with Justine's minor children from an earlier marriage. The natural father is out of the picture, but Justine fears that her mother, Tamira, who does not approve of unmarried couples living together, will try to get custody of the kids if something happens to her. Justine wants Paul to have custody because he knows the children well and loves them. She can use Quicken WillMaker Plus to name Paul as personal guardian and add a statement making the reasons for this choice clear.

If Justine dies and Tamira goes to court to get custody, the fact that Justine named Paul will give him an advantage. If he is a good parent, he is likely to get custody in most states.

Tips on What to Include

When deciding who should become a child's personal guardian, the courts of all states are required to act in the child's best interests. In making this determination, the courts commonly consider a number of facts, which you might want to include when explaining your choice for personal guardian. They include:

- whom the parents nominated to become the personal guardian
- whether the proposed personal guardian will provide the greatest stability and continuity of care for the child
- which person will best be able to meet the child's needs, whatever these happen to be
- the quality of the relationship between the child and the adults being considered for guardian
- the child's preferences to the extent these can be gleaned, and
- the moral fitness and conduct of the proposed guardians.

If you name your same-sex partner as guardian. If you coparent your children with a same-sex partner, you probably want to nominate your partner as the personal guardian of your children. Whether or not the court will respect your nomination depends on where you live and on two legal relationships: the relationship between you and your partner and the relationship between your partner and your kids.

If your children have another legal parent, perhaps from a prior relationship, the court will choose that parent over your partner unless you provide a good reason not to.

If you live in any of the states that recognize same-sex marriage or marriage-like relationships (such as registered domestic partnerships or civil unions) and your children were born after you and your partner entered into a legal relationship under the laws of that state, then you and your partner are both legal parents under state law and the court should respect your partner's legal right to continue parenting your children after your death. This is true whether or not you nominate your partner in your will, but you should go ahead and make the nomination and explain your reasons for it, as discussed below.

If you live in a state that doesn't offer any legal relationship for same-sex couples, the court will make the final decision about who will care for your children. The court will consider your choice for personal guardian, but it may not understand or fully respect your relationship with your partner.

For these reasons, take advantage of the opportunity to fully explain to the court why you named your partner to care for your children. You might say, for example, "I name my life-partner Ruth Williams as the personal guardian for our son Matthew Price because we conceived and raised him together and she is his only other parent." Or, "I name my domestic partner Richard Bennett as personal guardian for our daughter Jane Bennett-Hines because he is her other legal parent, as recognized by the state of California."

RESOURCE

Learn more about same-sex families. For a detailed discussion of parenting issues for same-sex couples, see *A Legal Guide for Lesbian & Gay Couples*, by Denis Clifford, Frederick Hertz and Emily Doskow (Nolo).

Grandchildren

Quicken WillMaker Plus asks you to name your grandchildren. Name all of them—including those to whom you leave no property. Include children adopted by your child and those born while your child was not married.

It is important that you name all grandchildren, because the rule that allows unintentionally omitted children to take a share of your estate also applies to grandchildren you may have overlooked in your will if their parent—that is, your child—dies before you do. (See "Your Children," above.)

As it does for your own children, Quicken WillMaker Plus automatically provides the statement that if you have not left any property to a grandchild, that is intentional—and therefore eliminates the problem. Again, you are free to leave the grandchild property if you choose. Also, if you have additional grandchildren after making your will, it is wise to make a new will that includes them.

SEE AN EXPERT

If you don't know your family. If family estrangement or other circumstances leave you thinking that you might not know the names of all of your grandchildren—or even

CHAPTER 4 | ABOUT YOU AND YOURS | 59

Chapter 4

your children—seek the advice of a good estate planning lawyer. You'll want to be certain that your will is not subject to unexpected claims.

Keep Your Will Current

Here are two situations in which you should make a new will:

If a child is born to or legally adopted by you after you make your will. You should draft a new will to list the new child. If you do not, that child may challenge your will and receive a share of what you leave.

If one of your children dies before you do and leaves children of his or her own. The laws of many states require that you name and provide for the children of deceased children. If you do not, they may be considered accidentally overlooked, and entitled to part of your property. To protect against this, make a new will, naming these grandchildren so that you can signal that you are aware that these grandchildren exist. You are still free to leave them as little or as much property as you wish in your will.

(See Chapter 11 for information on updating your will.)

Pets

You can use the Quicken WillMaker Plus will to leave your pet to a caretaker you choose. You can also leave money to that person to help with the costs of caring for your pet, although your will cannot force the caretaker to use the money that way. If you want the caretaker to be legally bound to use the money for the care of your pet, you will need a pet trust. See "Setting up a trust for your pet," below.

Using a will to provide for your pet is a simple and inexpensive way to make sure your pet has a caring home after your death. It is not the only way to provide for your pet, but most folks find that it makes the most sense.

Leaving Details About Your Pet's Care

In addition to naming a caretaker for your pet, you may want to leave information and suggestions about your pet's habits and needs. You can use Quicken WillMaker Plus's Information for Survivors and Caregivers form for this purpose. It allows you to leave specifics about each animal, including health needs, food and exercise requirements and sleeping habits. You can also use the document to describe memorial plans or final arrangements for your pet.

SEE AN EXPERT

Setting up a trust for your pet. In a majority of states, you can leave your pet money in a trust, managed by a trustee you name. You'll need to hire an attorney to be sure the document is properly drafted and valid in your state.

Finding a Loving Home for Your Pet

If you're not able to find someone both willing and able to take care of your pet after you die, you're not without options. More and more programs are springing up across the country to help assure people that their pets will have a loving home when they can no longer care for them.

SPCA programs. After the San Francisco SPCA fought, successfully, to save a dog that was to be put to death after its owner died, the organization began a special service to find good homes for the pets of deceased San Francisco SPCA members. The new owners are entitled to free lifetime veterinary care for the pets at the SPCA's hospital. Other SPCAs have created similar programs. Contact local SPCAs and similar organizations in your area for more information.

Veterinary school programs. A number of veterinary schools take in pets whose owners leave substantial endowments to the school. These programs typically provide a homelike atmosphere and lifetime veterinary care for the animals. Here is a list of some schools that currently offer this option:

Indiana
Peace of Mind Program
School of Veterinary Medicine, Purdue University
800-830-0104
www.vet.purdue.edu/development

Kansas
Perpetual Pet Care Program
Kansas State University School of Veterinary
    Medicine
785-532-4013
www.vet.k-state.edu/depts/development/
    perpet/program.htm

Minnesota
PerPETual Pet Care Program
University of Minnesota College of Veterinary
    Medicine
612-626-2343
www.cvm.umn.edu/devalumni/perpetualcare/
    home.html

Oklahoma
Cohn Family Shelter for Small Animals
Oklahoma State University, Center for
    Veterinary Health Sciences
405-744-6728
www.cvhs.okstate.edu

Texas
Stevenson Companion Animal Life-Care
    Center
College of Veterinary Medicine, Texas A&M
    University
979-845-1188
www.cvm.tamu.edu/petcare

Washington
Perpetual Pet Care Program
Washington State University, College of Veterinary
    Medicine
509-335-5021
www.vetmed.wsu.edu

About Your Property

This chapter discusses the grist of will making: what you own, how you own it and what legal rules affect how you can leave it. Once you have considered the information about property in this chapter, you will be ready to use Quicken WillMaker Plus to leave it to others—a task discussed in detail in Chapter 6. If you have children, see Chapter 7 for a discussion of their right to inherit property and your right to disinherit them.

Many readers will not need the information in this chapter. If you plan to leave your property in a lump—that is, without giving specific items of property to specific people—it makes little difference what you own and how you own it. That will be sorted out when you die, and the people you have named to take "all" your property will get whatever you own.

This chapter is important for you to read if either of the following is true:

- You are married or in a registered domestic partnership and you plan to name someone other than your spouse or partner to receive all or most of your property. This includes everyone who has not received a final decree of divorce or dissolution.
- You plan to leave specific items of property to specific people or organizations.

TIP

Keeping track of your property. There are many things your survivors will need to know about your property—and it will help them to have some relevant information about it, including:

- the location of some items
- the location of ownership, warranty and appraisal papers
- the value of some items—especially if they have special significance
- directions for maintaining the property, and
- details about caring for your pets.

You can use Quicken WillMaker Plus's Information for Caregivers and Survivors form for this task.

Inventory Your Valuable Property

The first step is to take inventory—write down the valuable items of property you own. The categories listed below should jog your memory.

Even if you plan to leave everything to your spouse or children, you should make a list. It will help you to avoid overlooking things. And if you make a trust, every item (or group of items) must be specifically described and listed in the trust document.

To help you with this task, Quicken WillMaker Plus provides a property worksheet that you can print out and keep with you as a reference while you make your estate planning documents. You can access the property worksheet from the screen called "Leaving Your Property," which introduces you to the topic of leaving your property to others. Click on the "Property Worksheet" link to start making your list.

Valuable Property	
Animals	Precious metals
Antiques	Real estate
Appliances	Agricultural land
Art	Boat/marina dock
Books	space
Business interests	Co-ops
Sole proprietorship	Condos
Partnership	Duplexes
Corporation	Houses
LLC	Mobile homes
Business property*	Rental property
Cameras and photo	Time-shares
equipment	Undeveloped land
Cash accounts	Vacation houses
Certificates of	Retirement accounts
deposit	Royalties
Checking	Securities
Money market	Bonds
funds	Commodities
Savings	Mutual funds
China, crystal and	Stocks
silver	U.S. bills, notes and
Coins and stamps	bonds
Collectibles	Tools
Computers	Vehicles
Copyrights, patents	Bicycles
and trademarks	Cars
Electronic equipment	Motorcycles
Furniture	Motor homes/RVs
Furs	Planes
Jewelry	Boats
Limited partnership	

* If you own a sole proprietorship

Property You Should Not Include in Your Will

In almost all cases, your will does not affect property that you have arranged to leave by another method. (There's an exception in the state of Washington; see below.)

Property with a right of survivorship. If you hold property in joint tenancy, tenancy by the entirety or community property with right of survivorship, your share of that property automatically belongs to the surviving co-owner after you die. A will provision leaving your share would have no effect unless all co-owners die simultaneously.

Property you place in a trust. Property you place in a trust passes automatically to the beneficiary named in the trust document—you cannot pass this property in your will. This includes property placed in a revocable living trust.

Property for which you've already named a beneficiary. There are many ways to pass property without a will or trust. If you hold a type of property on this list, you should not include the property in your will.

- Money in a pay-on-death bank account. If you want to change the beneficiary, contact the financial institution.
- Property held in beneficiary (transfer-on-death or TOD) form. This may include stocks, bonds and—in a handful of states—real estate or vehicles. To change the beneficiary, you'll need to make a new beneficiary form, deed or title document.
- Proceeds of a life insurance or annuity policy for which you've named a

beneficiary. To make changes, contact the insurance company.

- Money in a pension plan, individual retirement account (IRA), 401(k) plan or other retirement plan. You name the beneficiary on forms provided by the account administrator.

To learn more about these property ownership methods, most of which are designed to avoid probate court proceedings, read the beginning of Chapter 13.

Note for Washington Readers

The state of Washington has changed some of the rules discussed above. If you like, you can leave the following types of property in your will:

- your share of joint tenancy bank accounts
- pay-on-death bank accounts
- transfer-on-death securities or security accounts, and
- property in a living trust.

If you set up one of these devices for leaving your property and then later use your will to change the beneficiary, the property goes to the person you name in your will. However, if you designate a new beneficiary after you make your will—for example, by updating the paperwork for a pay-on-death account or changing your living trust—the gift in the will has no effect. (Wash. Rev. Code § 11.11.020.)

Property You Own With Others

If you are not married or in a registered domestic partnership, and you own property with someone else, you probably own it in tenancy in common. This is the most common way for unmarried people to own property together. Each co-owner is free to sell or give away his or her interest during life or leave it to another at death in a will. To tell whether or not you own property as tenancy in common, check the deed or other title document; it should specifically note that the property is held as a tenancy in common.

> **CAUTION**
> **More rules for married or legally partnered people making wills.** If you are married or in a registered domestic partnership, a whole host of legal rules may affect what property you own jointly and separately. (See "Property Ownership Rules for Married People," below.)

Property on Which You Owe Money

Using Quicken WillMaker Plus, if you leave property on which you owe money, the beneficiary who takes it at your death will also take over the debt owed on that property. This means the beneficiary of the property is responsible for paying off the debt. (But your survivors will not inherit your debt, per se. For example, if you die with nothing to your name except credit card debt, your survivors will not be responsible for paying those bills.)

Property Ownership Rules for Married People

Most people who are married or are in registered domestic partnerships leave all or the greatest share of their property to their surviving spouses or partners. For them, the nuances of marital property law are not important, since the survivor gets the property anyway.

But if you plan to leave your property to several people instead of or in addition to your spouse or partner, the picture becomes more complicated. Under your state's laws, your spouse or partner may own some property you believe is yours. And if you do not own it, you cannot give it away—either now or at your death. Questions of which spouse or partner owns what property are important if your spouse or partner does not agree to your plan for property disposition.

There are two issues to consider:

- What do you own?
- Will your spouse or partner have the right to claim a share of your property after your death? (See "Your Spouse's Right to Inherit from You," below.)

This section will help you determine what you own and so can leave to others in your will. To figure it out, you need to know a little about the laws in your state. When it comes to property ownership, states are broadly divided into two types: community property states and common law property states.

Community Property States		
Alaska[1]	Louisiana	Texas
Arizona	Nevada	Washington
California[2]	New Mexico	Wisconsin
Idaho		

[1] If the couple makes a written agreement stating that they wish their property to be treated as community property

[2] Registered domestic partners are also covered by community property laws.

Common Law States
All other states

Community Property States

If you live in a community property state, there are a few key rules to keep in mind while making your will:

- You can leave your separate property to anyone you wish.
- You can leave half of the community property (property you and your spouse or partner own together) to anyone you wish.
- After your death, your spouse or partner automatically keeps his or her half of the community property.
- If you are in a registered domestic partnership in California, all of the community property rules that apply to married couples also apply to you and your partner.

**Another Option:
Community Property With
Right of Survivorship**

Alaska, Arizona, California, Nevada, Texas and Wisconsin allow a form of community property that works just like joint tenancy—in other words, the surviving spouse or domestic partner automatically inherits the property when the other spouse or partner dies. To take advantage of this type of ownership, the property's title document must state that the property is owned "as community property with right of survivorship," or something similar.

Your Separate Property

The following property qualifies as separate property in all community property states:

- property that you own before marriage
- property that you receive after marriage by gift or inheritance
- property that you purchase entirely with your separate property, and
- property that you earn or accumulate after permanent separation.

In some states, additional types of property—such as personal injury awards received by one spouse during marriage—may also qualify as separate property. (See "Property That Is Difficult to Categorize," below.)

Community property states differ in how they treat income earned from separate property. Most hold that such income is separate. But a number of states take the opposite approach, treating income from separate property as community property.

Normally, separate property stays separate as long as it is not:

- so mixed with marital property that it is impossible to tell what is separate and what is not, or
- transferred in writing by the separate property owner into a form of shared ownership.

Just as separate property can be transformed into shared property, community property can be turned into separate property by a gift from one spouse to the other. The rules differ somewhat from state to state, but, generally speaking, gifts made to transform one type of property into another must be made with a signed document.

Community Property

The basic rule of community property is simple: During a marriage, all property earned or acquired by either spouse or domestic partner is owned 50-50 by each spouse or partner, except for property received by only one of them through gift or inheritance.

More specifically, community property usually includes:

- All income received by either spouse or partner from employment or any other source (except gifts to or inheritance by just one spouse or partner)—for example, wages, stock options, pensions and other employment compensation and business profits. This rule generally applies only to the period when the couple lives together as husband and wife or domestic partners. Most community property states consider income and property acquired after the spouses or partners permanently separate to be the separate property of the spouse or partner who receives it.

- All property acquired with community property income during the marriage.
- All separate property that is transformed into community property under state law. This transformation can occur in several ways, including when one spouse or domestic partner makes a gift of separate property to both of them

or when property is so mixed together that it's no longer possible to tell what property is separate (lawyers call this "commingling").

- As mentioned above, in a few community property states, income earned during marriage from separate property—for example, rent, interest or dividends—is community property. Most community property states consider such income to be separate property, however.

Classifying Property in Community Property States: Some Examples

Property	Community or Separate	Why
A painting you inherited while married	Separate; you can leave it in your will.	Inherited property belongs only to the person who inherited it.
A car you bought before you got married	Separate; you can leave it in your will.	Property owned before marriage is not community property.
A boat you bought with your income while married and registered in your name	Community; you can leave only your half-interest in your will.	It was purchased with community property income (income earned during the marriage).
The family home you and your spouse own together	Community; you can leave only your half-interest in your will.	It was purchased with community property income (income earned during the marriage).
A loan that your brother owes you	Community; you can leave only your half-interest in your will.	The loan was made from community property funds and belongs half to you and half to your spouse.
A fishing cabin you inherited from your father	Separate; you can leave it in your will.	Inherited property belongs only to the person who inherited it.
Stock you and your spouse bought with savings from your spouse's earnings	Community; you can leave only your half-interest in your will.	It was purchased with one spouse's earnings, which are community property during marriage.

EXAMPLE: Beth and Daniel live in Idaho, one of the few community property states where income earned from separate property belongs to the community. Beth inherits 22 head of Angus cattle from her father. Those cattle go on to breed a herd of more than 100 cattle. All the descendants of the original 22 animals are considered income from Beth's separate property and are included in the couple's community property estate.

Property That Is Difficult to Categorize

Normally, classifying property as community or separate property is easy. But in some situations, it can be a close call. There are several potential problem areas.

Businesses. Family businesses can create complications, especially if they were owned before marriage by one spouse or domestic partner and expanded during the marriage or partnership. The key is to figure out whether the increased value of the business is community or separate property. If you and your spouse or partner do not have the same view of how to pass on the business, it may be worthwhile to get help from a lawyer or accountant.

Money from a personal injury lawsuit. Usually, but not always, awards won in a personal injury lawsuit are the separate property of the spouse or partner receiving them. There is no easy way to characterize this type of property. If a significant amount of your property came from a personal injury settlement, research the specifics of your state's law or ask an estate planning expert.

Pensions. Generally, for married people, the part of a pension gained from earnings made during the marriage is considered to be community property. This is also true of military pensions. However, some federal pensions—such as Railroad Retirement benefits and Social Security retirement benefits—are not considered community property, because federal law deems them to be the separate property of the employee earning them. Also, because the federal government does not recognize domestic partnerships, community property rules will not apply to federal benefits acquired by registered domestic partners.

Common Law Property States

Common law property states are all states other than the community property states listed above.

In these states, you own:

- all property you purchased using your property or income, and
- property you own solely in your name if it has a title slip, deed or other legal ownership document.

In common law states, the key to ownership for many types of valuable property is whose name is on the title. If you and your spouse or registered domestic partner take title to a house together—that is, both of your names are on the deed—you both own it. That is true even if you earned or inherited the money you used to buy it. If your spouse or domestic partner earns the money, but you take title in your name alone, you own it.

If the property is valuable but has no title document, such as a computer, then the person whose income or property is used to pay for it owns it. If joint income is used, then you own it together. You can each leave your half in your will, unless you signed an agreement providing for a joint tenancy or a tenancy by the entirety.

EXAMPLE: Will and Jane are married and live in Kentucky, a common law property state. They have five children. Shortly after their marriage, Jane wrote an extremely popular computer program that helps doctors diagnose illness. She has received royalties averaging about $200,000 a year over a ten-year period. Jane has used the royalties to buy a car, boat and mountain cabin—all registered in her name alone. The couple also owns a house as joint tenants. In addition, Jane owns a number of family heirlooms which she inherited from her parents. Throughout their marriage, Jane and Will have maintained separate savings accounts. Will works as a computer engineer and has deposited all of his income into his account. Jane put her unspent royalties in her account, which now contains $75,000.

Jane owns:
- the savings account listed in her name alone
- one-half interest in the house (which, because it is held in joint tenancy, will go to Will at Jane's death)
- the car, boat and cabin, since there are title documents listing them in her name (if there were no such documents, she would still own them because they were bought with her income), and
- her family heirlooms.

Will owns:
- the savings account listed in his name alone, and
- one-half interest in the house (which, because it is held in joint tenancy, will go to Jane at Will's death).

EXAMPLE: Martha and Scott, who are married, have both worked for 30 years as schoolteachers in Michigan, a common law state. Generally, Scott and Martha pooled their income and jointly purchased a house, worth $200,000 (in both their names as joint tenants); cars (one in Martha's name and one in Scott's); a share in a vacation condominium (in both names as joint tenants); and house-hold furniture. Each maintains a separate savings account, and they also have a joint tenancy checking account containing $2,000. In addition, Scott and his sister own a piece of land as tenants in common.

Martha owns:
- her savings account
- half-interest in the house, the joint checking account and the condo (which, because they are held in joint tenancy, will go to Scott at her death)
- her car, and
- half the furniture.

Scott owns:
- his savings account
- half-interest in the house, the joint checking account and the condo (which, because they are held in joint tenancy, will go to Martha at his death)
- his car

- half the furniture, and
- a half-interest in the land he owns with his sister.

Moving From State to State

Complications may set in when a husband and wife acquire property in a common law property state and then move to a community property state. California, Idaho, Washington and Wisconsin treat the earlier-acquired property as if it had been acquired in the community property state. The legal term for this type of property is "quasi-community property." Wisconsin calls it "deferred marital property."

The other community property states do not recognize the quasi-community property concept for will-making purposes. Instead, they go by the rules of the state where the property was acquired. If you and your spouse move from a non-community property state into one of the states that recognizes quasi-community property, all of your property is treated according to community property rules. However, if you move to any of the other community property states from a common law state, you must assess your property according to the rules of the state where the property was acquired.

Couples who move from a community property state to a common law state face the opposite problem. Generally, each spouse retains one-half interest in the community property the couple accumulated while living in the community property state. However, if there is a conflict after your death, it can get messy; courts dealing with the issue have not been consistent.

SEE AN EXPERT

If you move. If you move from a community property state to a common law one, and you and your spouse have any disagreement as to who owns what, it may be wise to check with a lawyer. (See Chapter 25.)

SEE AN EXPERT

Same-sex couples. If you are moving from the state in which you registered your domestic partnership, there is a good chance that the state you are moving to will not recognize the property rights you received through your partnership status. You may want to consult a knowledgeable attorney in your new state to be sure you both fully understand your property rights and have an appropriate plan in place.

Your Spouse's Right to Inherit From You

If you intend to leave your spouse or registered domestic partner very little or no property, you may run into some legal roadblocks. All common law property states (see above) protect a surviving spouse or partner from being completely disinherited—and most assure that a spouse has the right to receive a substantial share of a deceased spouse's property. Community property states offer a different kind of protection.

Spousal Protection in Common Law States

In a common law state, a shortchanged surviving spouse or domestic partner usually has the option of either taking what the will provides, called "taking under the will," or rejecting the gift and instead taking the minimum share allowed by state law, called "taking against the will." In some states, your spouse or partner may have the right to inherit the family residence, or at least use it for his or her life. The Florida constitution, for example, gives a surviving spouse the deceased spouse's residence.

Laws protecting spouses and domestic partners vary among the states. In many common law property states, a spouse is entitled to one-third of the property left in the will. In a few, it is one-half. The exact amount of the spouse's minimum share may also depend on whether there are also minor children and whether the spouse has been provided for outside the will by trusts or other means.

> EXAMPLE: Leonard's will leaves $50,000 to his second wife, June, and the rest of his property, totaling $400,000, to May and April, his daughters from his first marriage. June can choose instead to receive her statutory share of Leonard's estate, which will be far more than $50,000. To the probable dismay of May and April, their shares will be substantially reduced; they will share what is left of Leonard's property after June gets her statutory share.

Of course, these are just options; a spouse who is not unhappy with the share he or she receives by will is free to let it stand. And in almost all states, one spouse or partner can give up all rights to inherit any property by completing and signing a waiver. If you want to make that type of arrangement, consult a lawyer. (See Chapter 25.)

SEE AN EXPERT

Leaving little to a spouse. If you do not plan to leave at least half of your property to your spouse or domestic partner in your will and have not provided for him or her generously outside your will, consult a lawyer.

Family Allowances

Some states provide additional, relatively minor protections for immediate family members. These vary from state to state in too much detail to discuss here. Generally, however, these devices attempt to assure that your spouse and children are not left out in the cold after your death, by allowing them temporary protection (such as the right to remain in the family home for a short period) or funds (typically, living expenses while an estate is being probated).

In many common law states, how much the surviving spouse is entitled to receive depends on what that spouse receives both under the will and outside of the will—for example, through joint tenancy or a living trust—as well as what the surviving spouse owns. The total of all of these is called the augmented estate.

While the augmented estate concept is rather complicated, its purpose is easy to grasp. Basically, almost all property of both spouses is taken into account, and the surviving spouse gets a piece of the whole pie.

Spousal Protection in Community Property States

Most community property states do not give surviving spouses or registered domestic partners the right to take a share of the deceased spouse's or partner's estate. Instead, they try to protect spouses and domestic partners while both are still alive, by granting each spouse or partner half ownership of property and earnings either spouse or partner acquires during the marriage. (See "Community Property States," above.)

However, in a few states—under very limited circumstances—a surviving spouse or domestic partner may elect to take a portion of the deceased spouse's community or separate property. These laws are designed to prevent spouses and domestic partners from being either accidentally overlooked—for example, if one spouse or partner makes a will before marriage or partnership and forgets to change it afterward to include the new spouse or partner—or deliberately deprived of their fair share of property. These protections are available in Alaska (Alaska Stat. §§ 13.12.201 and following), California (California Prob. Code §§ 21610 and following), Idaho (Idaho Code §§ 15-2-202 and following), Washington (Wash. Rev. Code §§ 26.16.240 and following) and Wisconsin (Wis. Stat. §§ 861.02 and following). If you want to learn more about them, consult a lawyer. (See Chapter 25.)

How to Leave Your Property

The heart of will making is deciding who gets your property when you die. For many, this is an easy task: You want it all to go to your spouse or partner, your kids or your favorite charity. For others, it's a little more complicated—for example, you want most of your property to go to your spouse, partner, child or charity, but you also want certain items to go to other people. You may even have a fairly complicated scheme in mind that involves dividing your property among a number of people and organizations.

Chapter 5 introduced some basic concepts about your property and whether you can leave it to others in your will. This chapter explains how to put your plan into effect using the Quicken WillMaker Plus program. If you want to leave all or most of your property to a loved one or favorite charity, the program offers you some shortcuts. Quicken WillMaker Plus also accommodates more complex wishes.

After you name those who will get your property, Quicken WillMaker Plus lets you name alternates—that is, who should get property if your first choices do not survive you.

You do not need to read all of this chapter to figure out how to write the will you want. Start with the discussion that is tailored to your situation:

- married or in a registered domestic partnership, with children
- married or in a registered domestic partnership, with no children
- not married or in a registered domestic partnership, but you have children, or
- not married or in a registered domestic partnership, and you have no children.

If You Are Married or in a Registered Domestic Partnership and You Have Children

Many married or partnered people have simple will-making needs. They want to leave all or most of their property to their spouses or partners. As alternates, they may want to choose their children, or name another person or organization. Quicken WillMaker Plus lets you choose any of those paths easily. And if you do not want to make your spouse or partner the main beneficiary of your will, that option is available, too.

Choosing Beneficiaries

Quicken WillMaker Plus prompts you to choose one of three approaches to leaving your property. You can:

- leave everything to your spouse or domestic partner
- leave most of your property, with some specific exceptions, to your spouse or domestic partner, or
- make a plan that may or may not include your spouse or domestic partner.

The third option offers flexibility. You should choose it if you want to divide up your property more evenly among a number of beneficiaries, or if you want to give all or most of your property to someone other than your spouse or domestic partner. But if you do choose this approach to making your will, be sure that you understand the rules governing what you own and the rights of your spouse or partner. (See "Property Ownership Rules for Married People" and "Your Spouse's Right to Inherit From You" in Chapter 5.)

EXAMPLE: Anne and Robert are a married couple with one young child. Anne wants a simple will, in which she leaves all of her property to Robert. She chooses the first option—everything to your spouse—to get a will that reflects her wishes.

EXAMPLE: Arnie wants his wife to receive most of his property when he dies, but he has a valuable violin that he wants to go to his best friend, Eddie, and a coin collection that he wants his nephew to receive. Arnie chooses the second option— most to your spouse. Then, later in the program, he can name Eddie to receive his violin and his nephew to receive his coin collection.

EXAMPLE: Sylvia is married to Fred. She wants to leave him her share of their investment portfolio and family business but also wants to leave a number of specific property items to different friends, relatives and charities. She chooses the third option when using Quicken WillMaker Plus. The program then prompts her to list specific property items and the person or organization she wants to receive each one. Before she does, Sylvia reviews Chapter 5 to make sure she understands what property is appropriate to leave in her will.

 SKIP AHEAD

When you can skip ahead. If you do not want to name your spouse or registered domestic partner to receive all or most of your property, skip the rest of this section and go to "Making Specific Bequests," below, for a discussion of what comes next.

Choosing Alternates for Your Spouse or Partner

If you want your spouse or registered domestic partner to receive all or most of your property, your next task will be to choose an alternate for your spouse or partner.

The will you create with Quicken WillMaker Plus provides that all beneficiaries—including your spouse—must survive you by 45 days to receive the property you leave them. This is a standard will provision, called a survivorship requirement. It is based on the assumption that if a beneficiary survives you by only a few days or weeks, you would prefer the property to go to another beneficiary that you choose and name in your will.

The alternates you choose will receive the property only if your spouse or domestic partner dies fewer than 45 days after you do.

Depending on your previous choices, Quicken WillMaker Plus offers two or three options for alternates. You can name:

- your child or children, or
- other alternate beneficiaries.

These two approaches to naming alternates are shortcuts. You need not specify which items go to which beneficiaries.

If you named your spouse or domestic partner to receive all your property, you also have a third option: You can make a completely new plan for leaving your property which will take effect only if your spouse does not survive you by at least 45 days. If you make this choice, you can divide your property among a number of alternate beneficiaries.

Each of these approaches to naming alternates is discussed below.

Naming Your Children as Alternates

It is common for married or partnered people who have children to simply leave all or most of their property to the surviving spouse or partner and name the children to take the property as alternates. This means if your spouse or partner does not survive you by 45 days, the property your spouse or partner would have received will pass to your child or children.

If you have more than one child, you must decide how the children should share the property.

> **EXAMPLE:** Meg and Charlie have three grown children. When Charlie makes his will, he leaves everything to Meg and names the children as alternates for her. He directs that all three children should receive equal shares of his property if Meg doesn't survive him and they take it, instead.

If any of your children are minors or young adults, you may:
- specify the share each child will receive; later, you may designate how each child's share will be managed and doled out if a child is under 35 when you die, or

- direct that the property be held in one undivided fund, called a pot trust; under this option, the person you select to serve as trustee will use the assets in the trust for all your children as needed, until your youngest child turns an age you choose—up to age 25.

(See Chapter 7 for a discussion of these methods for managing property left to children.)

> **EXAMPLE:** Julia and Emanuel have three young children. When Julia makes her will, she names Emanuel to inherit most of her property and leaves a few small items to her sister. As alternates for her husband, she picks her children. But because they are too young to manage money or property, later in the program she names her sister to manage any property the children may take under her will while they are still young.

> **EXAMPLE:** Barry and his wife Marta have two young daughters close in age. In his will, Barry leaves Marta all his property and chooses the children as alternate beneficiaries. He also picks the pot trust option and names his mother as trustee. If Marta does not survive him by at least 45 days, all of Barry's property will go into a trust for the two girls, administered by Barry's mother.

Quicken WillMaker Plus also lets you name a second level of alternates—that is, alternates who will take the property a child would have received, if that child does not survive you. You can name an alternate for each child or simply designate that the survivors receive any property that would have gone to a deceased child.

Naming Alternates Who Are Not Your Children

If you decide to specify alternates to receive the property left to your spouse or domestic partner, you may name whomever you want. You are not constrained, as with the first option, to naming only your children as alternates. For instance, you may name a charity, a friend or just one of your children. If your spouse or partner does not survive you by 45 days, the alternates you name will receive the property your spouse or partner would have received. If you name more than one person or organization, you may specify what share each is to receive.

> **EXAMPLE:** Celeste is married with two grown children. The children have both been provided for nicely with money from trusts and are financially secure. In her will, Celeste leaves her husband most of her property, with a few exceptions of some heirlooms for her children. As an alternate for her husband, she names the university where she taught for many years.

You can also name a second level of alternates—that is, alternates to take the property should both your spouse or partner and a first level of alternates you name all die before you do. You can name a back-up alternate for each alternate. If you named more than one first-level alternate, you may also designate that the survivors receive any property that would have gone to a deceased alternate.

Making a Different Plan

This option—Plan B—is available only if you choose to leave all your property to your spouse or registered domestic partner.

It lets you create a whole new plan to take effect if, and only if, your spouse or partner doesn't survive you by 45 days. This option is for people who think like this: I want to leave all my property to my spouse, period. But in case my spouse does not survive me, I want to make a whole new plan from the ground up— my Plan B—that does not include my spouse. So, if my spouse survives me, he or she gets all my property. But if not, I'll have been able to divide my property just as if I weren't married.

Your Plan B can include as many specific bequests as you wish. (See "Making Specific Bequests," below.) After you have made all your specific bequests, you can also name someone to take the rest of your property. This is called your residuary beneficiary. (See "Naming Residuary Beneficiaries," below.) Again, all of these Plan B bequests will take effect only if your spouse or domestic partner does not survive you by 45 days.

> **EXAMPLE:** Sean wants to leave all his property to Eva, his wife, if she's alive when he dies. But thinking about what he would want to happen if Eva were not around to take everything, he decides that he would want to divide his property among several friends, relatives and charities.

When he sits down with Quicken Will-Maker Plus to make his will, Sean names Eva to get all his property. Then, when it's time to name alternates, he chooses the Plan B option and leaves $10,000 to a local food bank, his piano to his niece and the rest of his property to his brother.

If You Do Not Name Alternates

If you leave your entire estate to one person or a group of people, you do not name alternate beneficiaries, and your primary beneficiaries do not survive you, then your estate will be distributed according to the laws of your state. (See "Dying Without a Will" in Chapter 2.)

If You Are Married or in a Registered Domestic Partnership and You Do Not Have Children

Many married or partnered people have simple will-making needs. They want to leave all or most of their property to their spouses or domestic partners. Then, as alternates, they may name one or more other people or organizations. Quicken WillMaker Plus lets you choose this path easily. And if you do not want to make your spouse or partner the main beneficiary of your will, that option is available, too.

Choosing Beneficiaries

Quicken WillMaker Plus prompts you to choose one of three approaches to leaving your property. You can:

- leave everything to your spouse or domestic partner
- leave most of your property, with some specific exceptions, to your spouse or domestic partner
- make a plan that may or may not include your spouse or domestic partner.

The third option offers flexibility. You should choose it if you want to divide up your property more evenly among a number of beneficiaries or if you want to give all or most of your property to someone other than your spouse or partner. If you choose it, be sure that you understand the rules governing what you own and the rights of your spouse or registered domestic partner. (See "Property Ownership Rule for Married People" and "Your Spouse's Right to Inherit From You" in Chapter 5.)

EXAMPLE: Mark and Abby are a young married couple with no children. Mark wants simply to leave everything to Abby in his will. He chooses the first option—everything to your spouse—so that his will reflects his intentions.

EXAMPLE: Paul wants his wife to receive most of his property when he dies, but he wants his golf clubs to go to his best friend, Eric, and wants his niece to take his photography equipment. Paul chooses the second option—most to your spouse. Then, later in the program, he can name Eric to receive his golf clubs and his niece to receive the photography equipment.

EXAMPLE: Eleanor is married to William. She wants to leave William her share of their investment portfolio and family business, but also wants to leave a number of specific items to different friends, relatives and charities. She chooses the third option when using Quicken WillMaker Plus—make a different plan. The program then prompts her to list specific property items and the person or organization she wants to receive each of them. Before she does, Eleanor reviews Chapter 5 to make sure she understands what property is appropriate to leave in her will.

SKIP AHEAD

When you can skip ahead. If you do not want to name your spouse or domestic partner to receive all or most of your property, skip the rest of this section and go to "Making Specific Bequests," below, for a discussion of what comes next.

Choosing Alternates for Your Spouse or Partner

If you want your spouse or domestic partner to receive all or most of your property, your next task will be to choose an alternate for your spouse or partner.

The will you create with Quicken WillMaker Plus provides that all beneficiaries—including your spouse or domestic partner—must survive you by 45 days to receive the property you leave them. This is a standard will provision, called a survivorship requirement. It is based on the assumption that if a beneficiary survives you by only a few days or weeks, you would prefer the property to go to another beneficiary that you name in your will.

The alternates you choose will receive the property only if your spouse or partner does not live at least 45 days longer than you do.

The simplest ways to provide for an alternate are to name:

- one person or organization to receive everything your spouse or partner would have received, or
- more than one person or organization to share the property. If you go that route, the alternates will receive all the property that would have gone to your spouse or partner. You need not specify which items go to which beneficiaries.

Or you can make a new plan for leaving your property—Plan B—which will take effect only if your spouse or partner does not survive you by 45 days. If you choose to make a new plan, you can divide your property among several alternate beneficiaries.

These approaches to naming alternates are discussed below.

Naming Alternates for Your Spouse or Partner

You may name whomever you want as the alternate for your spouse or domestic partner. For instance, you may name a charity, friend or relative. If your spouse or partner does not survive you by 45 days, the alternates you name will receive the property your spouse or partner would have received. If you name more than one person or organization, you may specify what share each is to receive.

EXAMPLE: In her will, Sharon leaves most of her property to her husband, Alex, with a few exceptions of some small items for friends. As an alternate for Alex, she names the charity at which she volunteered for many years.

You can also name a second level of alternates—that is, alternates to take the property should both your spouse and alternate not survive you. You can name a back-up alternate for each alternate. If you named more than one first-level alternate, you may designate that the survivors receive any property that would have gone to a deceased alternate.

Making a Different Plan

If you choose to leave all your property to your spouse or domestic partner, you can create a whole new plan to take effect if, and only if, your spouse or partner doesn't survive you by 45 days. This option is for people who think like this: I want to leave all my property to my spouse, period. But in case my spouse does not survive me, I want to make a whole new plan from the ground up—my Plan B—that does not include my spouse. So, if my spouse survives me, he or she gets all my property. But if not, I'll divide my property just as if I weren't married.

Your alternate plan—Plan B—can include as many specific bequests as you wish. (See "Making Specific Bequests," below.) After you have made all your specific bequests, you can also name someone to take the rest of your property. This is called your residuary beneficiary. (See "Naming Residuary Beneficiaries," below.) Again, all of these Plan B bequests will take effect only if your spouse or domestic partner does not survive you by 45 days.

EXAMPLE: Sean wants to leave all his property to Eva, his wife, if she's alive when he dies. But thinking about what he would want to happen if Eva were not around to take everything, he decides that he would want to divide his property among several friends, relatives and charities.

When he sits down with Quicken WillMaker Plus to make his will, Sean names Eva to take everything. Then, when it's time to name alternates, he chooses the Plan B option and leaves $10,000 to a local food bank, his piano to his niece and everything else to his brother.

If You Do Not Name Alternates

If you leave your entire estate to one person or a group of people, you do not name alternate beneficiaries, and your primary beneficiaries do not survive you, then your estate will be distributed according to the laws of your state. (See "Dying Without a Will" in Chapter 2.)

If You Are Not Married or in a Domestic Partnership and You Have Children

If you are a single parent, your children probably figure prominently in your plans for distributing your property after your death. With that in mind, Quicken WillMaker Plus offers some shortcuts when making your will.

Choosing Beneficiaries

Quicken WillMaker Plus prompts you to choose one of three approaches to leaving your property. You can:

- leave everything to your child or children
- leave most of your property, with some specific exceptions, to your child or children, or
- make a plan that may or may not include your children.

The third option offers flexibility. You should choose it if you want to divide your property more evenly among a number of beneficiaries, or if you want to give all or most of your property to someone other than your children. If you choose it, be sure that you understand the rules governing what you own. (See Chapter 5.)

> **EXAMPLE:** Raquel is a divorced mother of two young children. She wants to leave all her property to the children, in equal shares. She chooses the first option.

> **EXAMPLE:** Carlo, a widower, has one son, who is now 40 years old. Carlo wants to leave most of his property to his son but also make a few small bequests to charities. He chooses the second option. Then, later in the program, he can name the charities and the amounts he wants to leave to each.

> **EXAMPLE:** Brenda has three children, all of whom are grown and financially healthy. She wants to leave a number of specific property items to her children but also to many different friends, relatives and charities. She chooses the third

option when using Quicken WillMaker Plus. The program then asks her to list specific property items and the person or organization she wants to receive each one. Before doing this, Brenda reviews Chapter 5 to make sure she understands what property she can leave in her will.

 SKIP AHEAD

When you can skip ahead. If you do not want to name your child or children to receive all or most of your property, skip the rest of this section and go to "Making Specific Bequests," below, for a discussion of what comes next.

Designating Children's Shares

If you have a number of children, you must decide how you want them to share the property they receive through your will.

> **EXAMPLE:** Charlie has three grown children. When Charlie makes his will, he names the children to receive everything. He directs that all three children should receive equal shares of his property.

If any of your children are minors or young adults, you may:

- specify the share each child will receive; later, you may designate how each child's share will be managed and doled out if a child is under 35 when you die, or
- direct that the property be held in one undivided fund, called a pot trust; under this option, the person you select to serve as trustee will use the assets in the trust for all your children as needed, until

your youngest child turns an age you choose up to age 25.

(See Chapter 7 for an explanation of all of these methods for managing property left to children.)

EXAMPLE: Tess has three children, two teenagers and one 26-year-old son. When she makes her will, she leaves the children most of her property and leaves a few small items to her sister. Because her oldest child is self-supporting, she leaves him just a 1/5 share and leaves the two younger children 2/5 each. Later in the program, Tess names her sister to manage any property the two younger children come to own while they are still young.

EXAMPLE: Frank has two young sons close in age. In his will, he leaves them all his property. He then picks the pot trust option and names his sister as trustee. That means that if the boys inherit Frank's property while they are still young, all of it will go into a trust for them, administered by Frank's sister.

Choosing Alternates for Your Children

If you choose your child or children to receive all or most of your property, your next task will be to choose an alternate for your child.

The will you create with Quicken Will-Maker Plus provides that a beneficiary must survive you by 45 days to receive property through the will. This is a standard will provision, called a survivorship requirement. It is based on the assumption that if a beneficiary survives you by only a few weeks, you would prefer the property to go to another beneficiary that you name in your will.

The alternates you choose for a child will receive the property only if the child does not survive you by at least 45 days.

CAUTION

No alternates necessary for pot trusts. If you chose a pot trust, you don't need to name alternates. If one child does not survive you, the other surviving children will still share the property.

If you have one child, you can either:
- name one or more alternates for that child, or
- make a plan that may or may not include your child and other people or organizations.

If you have more than one child and have designated a share for each child, you can either:
- name one or more alternates for each child, or
- specify that if one child doesn't survive you, the survivors should take the deceased child's share.

If you chose a pot trust, you need not name alternates. If any child does not survive you, the others will share the property.

Naming Alternates for Your Children

You may name whomever you want—for instance, a charity, friend or relative—as the alternate for a child. If the child does not survive you by 45 days, the alternates will receive the property the child would have received. If you name more than one alternate, you may specify the share each is to receive.

EXAMPLE: In her will, Sharon leaves her daughter most of her property and gives the rest to friends. As an alternate for her daughter, she names her daughter's two young children.

Surviving Children

Rather than name alternates for each of your children, you may want to provide that whatever property you leave them will go to all the children who survive you.

EXAMPLE: In his will, Patrick leaves his daughter and two sons all of his property. He specifies that each should receive an equal share. When Quicken WillMaker Plus asks him to name alternates for the children, he specifies that the survivors should take the share.

If You Do Not Name Alternates

If you leave your entire estate to one person or a group of people, you do not name alternate beneficiaries, and your primary beneficiaries do not survive you, then your estate will be distributed according to the laws of your state. (See "Dying Without a Will" in Chapter 2.)

If You Are Not Married or in a Domestic Partnership and You Do Not Have Children

As a single person, you are free to leave your property in any way you choose. Your beneficiaries may be your loved ones or organizations you value highly. You can divide your property as you see fit, whether that means leaving it all to one beneficiary or giving specific items to specific people. Or, you may prefer to combine these approaches, leaving most of your assets to one or more beneficiaries and a few unique items to others. In any case, you'll have the opportunity to choose alternate beneficiaries as well.

Choosing Beneficiaries

Quicken WillMaker Plus prompts you to choose one of three approaches to leaving your property. You can:

- Leave everything to one or more beneficiaries. For example, you might leave everything you own to your girlfriend or to your sisters.
- Leave almost everything to one or more beneficiaries, but also leave some specific items to particular people. For example, you might want to leave all of your property to your sisters, but you want to leave your antique dining table to your neighbor.
- Leave your property some other way. You can leave specific items of property to certain beneficiaries, then choose one or more beneficiaries who will receive everything that's left. For example, you could leave your antique furniture to your sister, your ABC stock to your nephew, your comic book collection to your neighbor and everything else to the American Cancer Society.

If you want to leave specific items of property, be sure that you understand what kinds of property should be left in a will, and what might be passed to your survivors in other ways. (See "Property You Should Not Include in Your Will" in Chapter 5.)

EXAMPLE: Fernando and Robert have been together for many years, but they do not live in a state that offers registered domestic partnerships. When Fernando makes his will, he wants all his property to go to Robert. He chooses the first option—leave everything to one person—to make a will that reflects his wishes.

EXAMPLE: Theresa, whose husband died several years ago, wants to divide her money and possessions among different friends, relatives and charities. She chooses the third option. Quicken WillMaker Plus then asks her to list specific property items and the person or organization she wants to receive each one. Then she names one person who will receive any other property that she owns at her death.

SKIP AHEAD

When you can skip ahead. If you do not want to name one or more beneficiaries to receive all or most of your property, skip the rest of this section and go to "Making Specific Bequests," below, for a discussion of what comes next.

Choosing Alternates

If you specify that one or more beneficiaries should receive all or most of your property, your next task will be to choose alternates.

The will you create with Quicken Will-Maker Plus provides that all beneficiaries must survive you by 45 days to receive the property you leave them. This is a standard will provision, called a survivorship requirement. It is based on the assumption that if a beneficiary survives you by only a few days or weeks, you would prefer the property to go to another beneficiary that you name in your will.

The alternates you choose will receive the property only if your main beneficiaries do not survive for at least 45 days after you die.

Quicken WillMaker Plus offers two options for alternates. You can:

- name alternate beneficiaries, or
- make a completely new plan which will take effect only if your main beneficiaries do not survive you by 45 days. This way, you can divide your property among several alternate beneficiaries.

Naming Alternates

You may name whomever you want as alternates for each of your main beneficiaries. For instance, for each of your main beneficiaries, you may name a charity or a group of friends. If you name more than one person or organization, you may specify the share each is to receive.

If a main beneficiary does not survive you by 45 days, the alternates you name will receive the property he or she would have received.

EXAMPLE: Christine is not married and has no children. She is very close to her sister Karen, and wants to leave all her property to her.

In her will, Christine names Karen as her main beneficiary. As alternates, she names Karen's two children.

EXAMPLE: Ari leaves all of his property to his two brothers Seth and David. Because Seth is more financially stable, he indicates that Seth should get one-quarter of his estate and David should get three-quarters. He names his cousin Rachel as an alternate beneficiary for David's share. She will get three-quarters of Ari's estate if David does not survive Ari. Ari names his favorite charity as an alternate for Seth's share. If Seth does not survive Ari, the charity will get one-quarter of the estate.

If you like, you may also name a second level of alternates—that is, alternates to take the property should both your main and alternate beneficiaries not survive you by 45 days or more.

If you name more than one alternate beneficiary and one or more of them does not survive you, the surviving alternates will receive any property that would have gone to a deceased alternate.

If you name more than one alternate beneficiary but don't name any second alternates for those beneficiaries, the surviving alternate beneficiaries will share the property that any deceased beneficiary would have received.

EXAMPLE: In her will, JoEllen leaves all her property to her partner Katrine. She names her nephews, Jacob and Joseph, as alternates and does not name second alternates. When JoEllen dies, Katrine and Jacob have already passed away. Joseph inherits all of JoEllen's property.

Making a Different Plan

This option lets you create a whole new plan that takes effect only if your main beneficiary or beneficiaries do not survive you by 45 days. Your alternate plan—Plan B—can include as many specific bequests as you wish. (See "Making Specific Bequests," below.)

After you have made all your specific bequests, you can also name someone to take the rest of your property. This is called your residuary beneficiary. (See "Naming Residuary Beneficiaries," below.)

EXAMPLE: Sven wants to leave all his property to Jeannette, his companion, if she's alive when he dies. But thinking about what he would want to happen if Jeannette were not around to get everything, he decides that he would want to divide his property among relatives and charities.

When he sits down with Quicken WillMaker Plus to make his will, Sven names Jeannette to take all of his property. Then, when it's time to name alternates, he chooses the Plan B option and leaves $10,000 to a local food bank, his piano to his niece and everything else to his brother.

If You Do Not Name Alternates

If you leave your entire estate to one person or a group of people, you do not name alternate beneficiaries, and your primary beneficiaries do not survive you, then your estate will be distributed according to the laws of your state. (See "Dying Without a Will" in Chapter 2.)

Making Specific Bequests

This section discusses how to make specific bequests—that is, leave specific property items to specific people or groups. You should read this section if you:

- left most of your property to one or more main beneficiaries but want to leave some items to others
- want to divide your property among several beneficiaries, without leaving most or all of it to one or more main beneficiaries, or
- left everything to one or more beneficiaries, but instead of naming alternates for those beneficiaries, you want to make a Plan B to take effect if your main beneficiaries don't survive you.

Quicken WillMaker Plus lets you make an unlimited number of separate specific bequests. For each one, you must provide this information:

- a description of the item—for example, a house, cash, an heirloom or a car
- the names of the people or organizations you want to get the items, and
- if you wish, the name of an alternate beneficiary, who will receive specific property if your first beneficiary does not survive you by 45 days. You can name more than one alternate beneficiary; if you do, they will share the property.

Describing the Property

The first part of making a specific bequest is to describe the property you want to pass to a certain beneficiary or beneficiaries you have in mind. For example, if you want to leave your guitar to your best friend, you would begin by entering a brief description of the guitar, such as "my 1959 Martin guitar."

When describing an item, be as concise as you can, but use enough detail so that people will be able to identify and find the property. Most often, this will not be difficult: "my baby grand piano," "my collection of blue apothecary jars" or "my llama throw rug" are all the description you will need for tangible items that are easy to locate. If an item is very valuable or could be easily confused with other property, make sure you include identifying characteristics such as location, serial number, color or some other unique feature.

> ! **CAUTION**
> **Do not include property that will pass by other means.** Before describing the property you wish to leave in a specific bequest, take a moment to reflect on what property you are legally able to pass in your will. If you have already arranged to leave property outside your will by using legal devices such as life insurance, pay-on-death bank accounts or living trusts, you usually should not include that property in a specific bequest. (See "Property You Should Not Include in Your Will" in Chapter 5.)

Tips on Describing Property in Your Will

Here is how to identify different types of property with enough detail to prevent confusion:

- **Household furnishings.** You normally need not get very specific, unless an object is particularly valuable. It is enough to list the location of the property: "all household furnishings and possessions in the apartment at 55 Drury Lane."
- **Real estate.** You can simply provide the street address or, for unimproved property, the name by which it is commonly known: "my condominium at 123 45th Avenue," "my summer home at 84 Memory Lane in Oakville," "the vacant lot next to the McHenry Place on Old Farm Road." You do not need to provide the legal description from the deed.

- **Bank, stock and money market accounts.** List financial accounts by their account numbers. Also, include the name and location of the organization holding the property: "$20,000 from savings account #22222 at Independence Bank, Big Mountain, Idaho"; "my money market account #23456 at Beryl Pynch & Company, Chicago, Illinois"; "100 shares of General Foods common stock."
- **Personal items.** As with household goods, it is usually adequate to briefly describe personal items and group them, unless they have significant monetary or sentimental value. For example, items of extremely valuable jewelry should normally be listed and identified separately, while a drawer full of costume jewelry and baubles could be grouped.

Naming Beneficiaries

The second step in making a specific bequest is to name one or more beneficiaries. If you have already entered the name of a beneficiary in the Contact List, select the name from the list and paste it in the beneficiary field. (See the Users' Manual for help.)

Beneficiaries' names need not be the names that appear on their birth certificates; as long as the names you use clearly identify the beneficiaries, all is well.

Minors or Young Adults

If any of the beneficiaries you name is a minor (under 18) or young adult (under 35), you will have a chance, in a later part of Quicken WillMaker Plus, to choose someone to manage the property for them until they are older. (See Chapter 7.)

Multiple Beneficiaries

If you name two or more beneficiaries to share a specific bequest, you will later be asked to specify each person's share. To avoid possible tiffs among your beneficiaries, the property you plan to leave them either should be property that is easily divided—a sum of money or an investment portfolio—or property that you intend to be sold so that the proceeds can be split, such as undeveloped real estate or a valuable collection. For property that requires discretion to divide—family antiques, for example—it may be wiser to leave items separately.

CAUTION

Gifts to caretakers. Some states do not allow caretakers to inherit large amounts of property from the people they care for. These rules are intended to protect those who may be improperly influenced by the people who care for them.

State laws generally provide many sensible exceptions—for example, caretakers who are also close family members can receive gifts without restriction. Unfortunately, these exceptions won't help you if you want to reward an honest and faithful caretaker-friend by making a gift in your will.

If you want to leave a substantial gift (more than a thousand dollars) to someone who cares for you and is not a relative, see an experienced estate planning attorney for advice.

Organizations

You may want to leave property to a charity or a public or private organization—for example, the American Red Cross, the Greenview Battered Women's Shelter or the University of Illinois at Champaign-Urbana.

The organization you name need not be set up as a nonprofit, unless you wish your estate to qualify for a charitable estate tax deduction. (See Chapter 13.) It can be any organization you consider worthy of your bequest. The only limitation is that the organization must not be set up for some illicit or illegal purpose.

The organization you name will receive your gift with no strings attached. You cannot use your will to describe how the property should be used. If you want to do that—for example, if you want a gift to your alma mater to be used as a scholarship for a student who gets above a 3.5 grade point average—see an experienced estate planning attorney for advice.

When naming an organization, be sure to enter its complete name, which may be different from the truncated version by which it is commonly known. Several different organizations may use similar names—and you want to be sure your bequest goes to the one you have in mind. Someone at the organization will be more than happy to help you get it straight.

Your Living Trust

If you've made a living trust, you may have heard of something called a "pour-over" will. This type of will simply takes property you haven't yet transferred to your living trust and leaves it to the trust when you die.

You may want to make a pour-over will so that you need not worry about transferring every minor asset into your living trust. The pour-over will can also cover items of property that you acquire after making the trust, if you don't have a chance to transfer those items to the trust during your life.

Keep in mind, however, that any property you leave through a will—including your pour-over will—may have to go through probate. These are the court proceedings that living trusts are designed to avoid. Take care not to leave property through a pour-over will that is large enough to require probate proceedings. (For more information about probate and how to avoid it, see "About Basic Living Trusts" in Chapter 13.)

If you want to make a pour-over will or add a pour-over bequest to your will, you can do so. You must simply indicate that the living trust is the beneficiary of the property you want to leave through the will. For example, you can leave property to "John Doe as trustee of the John Doe Living Trust, dated January 1, 20xx."

Specifying Shares

If you name a group of beneficiaries to receive specific property, Quicken WillMaker Plus will ask you whether you want them to receive equal or unequal shares of the property. If you want it shared unequally, the shares must add up to one. Quicken WillMaker Plus will warn you if your computations are off.

Do Not Place Conditions on Bequests

Don't place conditions on any of your bequests; it risks making a confusing and even unenforceable will.

Here are some examples of what not to do:

- "I leave my gold Rolex to Andres, but only if he divorces his current wife, Samantha." Such a bequest would not be considered legally valid, because it encourages the breakup of a family.
- "I leave my dental office equipment to Claude, as long as he sets up a dental practice in San Francisco." The reason this bequest is unwieldy becomes obvious once you think ahead to the need for constant supervision. Who would be responsible for tracking Claude's dentistry career and making sure he ends up in San Francisco? What if Claude initially practices in San Francisco, using the equipment he was willed, then moves to grow grapes in the Napa Valley? Must he give up the equipment? To whom?
- "I leave my vintage Barbie doll collection to Collette, if the dolls are still in good condition." Who is to judge whether the dolls are in good condition? What happens if they aren't?

SEE AN EXPERT

When to see a lawyer. If you are determined to place conditions on beneficiaries or property, consult a lawyer who is experienced in drafting bequests that will adequately address these potentially complex arrangements.

EXAMPLE: Fred Wagner wants to leave an undeveloped real estate parcel to his three children, Mary, Sue and Peter. Because he has already paid for Mary's graduate school education, he wants to give Sue and Peter greater percentages of the property in case they want to go back to school, too. He lists his children and the share of his property to which they are entitled this way: Mary Wagner (1/5), Susan Wagner (2/5) and Peter Wagner (2/5).

Naming Alternates

To receive property under your will, a beneficiary must survive you by 45 days. Quicken WillMaker Plus assumes that if a beneficiary survives you by only a few days or weeks, you would prefer the property to pass to an alternate or residuary beneficiary named in your will, rather than have the property pass along with the beneficiary's other property.

With Quicken WillMaker Plus, you can name one or more alternate beneficiaries to take the bequest if your first choices do not survive you by the required period.

EXAMPLE: Joan leaves her horse to her brother Pierre. In case Pierre does not survive her by 45 days and so become eligible to receive this bequest, Joan names her sister Carmen as Pierre's alternate beneficiary.

If you name multiple beneficiaries to receive property, you can name an alternate for each beneficiary.

EXAMPLE: Gideon leaves his house to his three nephews—Aaron, Thomas and Zeke—in equal shares. In case Aaron does not survive him by 45 days, Gideon specifies that the house should then go to the survivors, Thomas and Zeke. In case Thomas does not survive him by 45 days, Gideon names his brother Horace to take Thomas's share. In case Zeke does not survive him by 45 days, Gideon specifies that Aaron and Horace should take Zeke's share.

If you do not name alternates for specific bequests, and the primary beneficiary dies before you do, the property will become part of your residuary estate.

Reviewing Specific Bequests

When you complete a specific bequest—that is, you have identified the property, named the beneficiary and named an alternate beneficiary—Quicken WillMaker Plus will display the beneficiary's name on the screen. You can also view this list by property. You can then add a new bequest or review, change or delete any of the bequests you have made.

Naming Residuary Beneficiaries

Quicken WillMaker Plus will ask you to name a beneficiary for your residuary estate only if either of the following is true:

- You chose not to name one main beneficiary to receive most or all of your property.

- After leaving all your property to one beneficiary, you chose to create an alternate plan, or Plan B, in case your first choice does not survive you. In this case, you name a residuary beneficiary as part of your alternate plan.

If you left all or most of your property to one or more beneficiaries, they will receive property that does not pass in a specific bequest or by means other than your will. In effect, they will automatically become your residuary beneficiaries.

EXAMPLE: When Mikki makes her will, she leaves all her property to her husband, Tyler. By the time she dies, 15 years later, she has acquired a new car, stocks and other items. Everything goes to her husband.

What a Residuary Beneficiary Receives

Your residuary beneficiary receives anything that does not go, for one reason or another, to the beneficiaries you named to receive specific bequests.

Specifically, the residuary beneficiary receives property that:

- you overlook when making your will
- you acquire after you make your will, and
- does not go to the person you named to get it in a specific bequest—for example, because that person died before you did and you did not name an alternate beneficiary, or the alternate also failed to survive you.

EXAMPLE: In her will, Sara, a widow, leaves many different items to many different beneficiaries: books to her daughter, jewelry to a friend, a car to her nephew and so on. She doesn't name alternate beneficiaries for these specific bequests, but she names her daughter as residuary beneficiary.

When Sara dies, some years after making the will, the friend to whom she left the jewelry has already died. The jewelry goes to Sara's daughter, as does the other property that Sara acquired since making her will.

There is no need to describe, in your will, the property the residuary beneficiary will receive. By definition, your residuary estate is the rest of your property that does not pass outside of your will or in a specific bequest, so it is impossible to know exactly what it will include. When your executor inventories your entire estate after your death, he or she will identify your residuary estate.

How to Name Residuary Beneficiaries

You can name one or more individuals or organizations, or a combination of both, as residuary beneficiaries. Use the Contact List to select and paste the name if it is already on the list. (See the Users' Manual for help.)

If you name more than one residuary beneficiary, Quicken WillMaker Plus will ask you what shares you want each to receive.

EXAMPLE: After making a large number of specific bequests in his Quicken WillMaker Plus will, Maurice leaves his residuary estate to his four children, Clara, Heinrich, Lise and Wiebke. He wants Lise and Wiebke each to receive 30% (3/10) of the property and the other two children to each receive 20% (2/10) each. So he indicates that he wants to leave the residuary estate in unequal shares and enters the desired shares on the screen provided for this purpose.

If any of the beneficiaries you name is a minor (under 18) or young adult (under 35), you will have a chance, in a later part of Quicken WillMaker Plus, to choose someone to manage the property for them until they are older. (See Chapter 7.)

Naming Alternates

Quicken WillMaker Plus also asks you to choose an alternate residuary beneficiary, in case your first choice does not survive you by 45 days.

If you do not name alternates for specific bequests, and the primary beneficiary dies before you do, the property will become part of your residuary estate.

> **CAUTION**
>
> **When you need not bother naming alternates.** You do not have to name an alternate residuary beneficiary, and not everyone is

concerned about this issue. Younger people in reasonably good health are usually confident that they can address a beneficiary's premature death by updating their wills. However, many married people are concerned about what will happen if they die close together in time. And older people in poor health may fear that they won't have an opportunity to update their wills if their first choice beneficiaries die before they do.

EXAMPLE: After making many specific bequests, Alfredo leaves his residuary estate to his daughter, Vanessa. He then specifies that if Vanessa does not survive him, her share should go to her two children—Alfredo's grandchildren. If Vanessa does not survive Alfredo, and Alfredo does not write a new will, Vanessa's children would each take one-half of Alfredo's residuary estate.

EXAMPLE: Jack makes a large number of specific bequests to friends and relatives and then leaves his residuary estate to his friend, Joe. He names another friend, Josette, as alternate residuary beneficiary. Josette will be entitled to take property under Jack's will only if Joe does not survive Jack by 45 days and there is property left over after the specific bequests are distributed.

Providing Management for Children's Property

Except for items of little value, minors are not permitted by law to receive property directly. This legal rule is most important if the property is:

- cash or other liquid assets—for example, a savings account that can easily be spent, or
- property that comes with a title document—for example, real estate.

Instead, that property will have to be distributed to and managed by a responsible adult. It is of vital importance to both your own children and any other young beneficiaries that you arrange for this management yourself, in your will. If you don't, a court may need to appoint and supervise someone—an expensive and time-consuming alternative. It's better to make your own choice and state it in your will, instead of leaving the decision to someone else.

TIP

Keeping track of children's property. The person you name to take care of your child's property will need access to financial records related to property that the child will own. For help collecting this information, use Quicken WillMaker Plus's Information for Caregivers and Survivors form.

Property management consists of naming a trusted adult to care for and accurately account for a young person's property until the minor turns a specific age. The property being managed must be held, invested or spent in the best interest of the minor. In other words, someone other than the young person will decide if their inheritances will be spent on college tuition or a new sports car.

Explaining Your Bequests to Your Children

Using Quicken WillMaker Plus, you are free to divide your property among your children as you see fit. If your children are already responsible adults, your prime concern will likely be fairness—given the circumstances and the children's needs. Often, this will mean dividing your property equally among your children. Sometimes, however, the special health or educational needs of one child, the relative affluence and stability of another or the fact that you are estranged from a child will be the impetus for you to divide the property unevenly.

Doing this can sometimes raise serious angst; a child who receives less property may conclude that you cared for him or her less. To clear up confusion, you may wish to explain your choices. Because of the risk of adding illegal or confusing language, Quicken WillMaker Plus does not allow you to make this explanation in your will. Fortunately, there is a sound and sensible way to express your reasons and feelings. Simply prepare a separate letter to accompany your will. (See Chapter 12.)

Quicken WillMaker Plus enables you to establish management for two types of property:

- property that passes to minors under your will (they do not have to be your own children), and
- property that passes to your minor children outside of your will.

For property received under your will, this management may last until the minor turns an age you choose. For property that your minor children receive outside of your will, the management provided by Quicken WillMaker Plus lasts until the children become adults—18 years old in most states.

What Happens If the Minor Does Not Get Property

If you arrange for property management for a minor, but the minor never actually becomes entitled to the property, no harm is done. The management provisions for that minor are ignored. For instance, suppose you identify a favorite niece to take property as an alternate beneficiary and provide management for that property until the niece turns 25. If the niece never gets to take the property because your first-choice beneficiary survives you, no property management will be established for her, since none will be needed.

Property Management for Gifts That Pass Under Your Will

Quicken WillMaker Plus offers three approaches to property management for property that passes to minors under your will:

- the Uniform Transfers to Minors Act— for property left in your will—in all states except South Carolina and Vermont
- the Quicken WillMaker Plus child's trust—for property left in your will—as an alternative to the UTMA and as an option for will makers who live in one of the two states that have not adopted the UTMA, and
- the Quicken WillMaker Plus pot trust— for property left to your children in your will—if at least one of your children is younger than 25 years old.

The Uniform Transfers to Minors Act

The Uniform Transfers to Minors Act (UTMA) allows you to name a custodian to manage property you leave to a minor. The management ends when the minor reaches age 18 to 25, depending on state law.

States are free to adopt or reject the UTMA, which is a model law proposed by a group of legal scholars. All but two states have adopted the UTMA, many making minor changes to it. It is likely that the UTMA will be universally adopted in a few more years.

Age Limits for Property Management in UTMA States

State	Age at Which Minor Gets Property	State	Age at Which Minor Gets Property
Alabama	21	Missouri	21
Alaska	18 to 25	Montana	21
Arizona	21	Nebraska	21
Arkansas	18 to 21	Nevada	18 to 25
California	18 to 25	New Hampshire	21
Colorado	21	New Jersey	18 to 21
Connecticut	21	New Mexico	21
Delaware	21	New York	21
District of Columbia	18 to 21	North Carolina	18 to 21
Florida	21	North Dakota	21
Georgia	21	Ohio	18 to 21
Hawaii	21	Oklahoma	18 to 21
Idaho	21	Oregon	21 to 25
Illinois	21	Pennsylvania	21 to 25
Indiana	21	Rhode Island	21
Iowa	21	South Dakota	18
Kansas	21	Tennessee	21 to 25
Kentucky	18	Texas	21
Maine	18 to 21	Utah	21
Maryland	21	Virginia	18 to 21
Massachusetts	21	Washington	21
Michigan	18 to 21	West Virginia	21
Minnesota	21	Wisconsin	21
Mississippi	21	Wyoming	21

If the UTMA has been adopted in your state, you may use it to specify a custodian to manage property you leave to a minor in your will until the age at which the laws of your state require that it be turned over to the minor. Depending on your state, this varies from 18 to 25. Quicken WillMaker Plus keeps track of the state you indicate as your residence and tells you whether the UTMA is available and, if so, the age at which property management under it must end.

States That Have Not Adopted the UTMA

The UTMA has not been adopted in South Carolina or Vermont.

If you are a resident of one of these states, you can set up property management for any minor or young adult beneficiary using the Quicken WillMaker Plus child's trust, discussed below. If at least one of your children is under 25 years old, you may also use the Quicken WillMaker Plus pot trust, discussed below.

Among the powers the UTMA gives the custodian are the rights to collect, hold, manage, invest and reinvest the property, and to spend it "for the use and benefit of the minor." All of these actions can be taken without getting approval from a court. The custodian must also keep records so that tax returns can be filed on behalf of the minor and must otherwise act prudently in controlling the property.

Special Rule for Life Insurance

Often the major source of property left to children comes from a life insurance policy naming the children as beneficiaries. If you want the insurance proceeds for a particular child to be managed, and you live in a state that has adopted the UTMA, instruct your insurance agent to provide you with the form necessary to name a custodian to manage the property for the beneficiary under the terms of this Act.

The Quicken WillMaker Plus Child's Trust

The Quicken WillMaker Plus child's trust, which can be used in all states, is a legal structure you establish in your will. If you create a trust, any property a minor beneficiary gets will be managed by a person or institution you choose to serve as trustee until the beneficiary turns an age you choose—through age 35. The trustee's powers are listed in your will. The trustee may use trust assets for the education, medical needs and living expenses of the beneficiary. All property you leave to a beneficiary for whom a trust is established will be managed under the terms of the trust.

Because management under the Quicken WillMaker Plus child's trust can be extended through age 35, it is also suitable to use for property left to young adults. (The pros and cons of management options are discussed in "Choosing Among Management Options," below.)

The Quicken WillMaker Plus Pot Trust

The Quicken WillMaker Plus pot trust is a legal structure you can establish in your will. However, instead of creating a separate child's trust for the property you leave to each child, you create one trust for all the property you leave to your children. You name a single trustee to manage the property for the benefit of the children as a group, without regard to how much is spent on an individual child.

For example, if there are three children and one of them needs an expensive medical procedure, all of the property could be spent on that child, even though the other children would receive nothing. While this potential result may seem unfair, it in fact mirrors the reality faced by many families: Some children need more money than others.

The pot trust will last until the youngest child turns an age you specify up to age 25. If there is a significant age gap between your children, the oldest children may have to wait many years past the time they become adults before they receive their shares of the property. For instance, if one of your children is five and another child is 17—and you specify that the pot trust should end when the youngest turns 18—the 17-year-old will have to wait at least until age 30 to receive a share of the property left in the trust.

CAUTION

All or none must go in pot. The Quicken WillMaker Plus pot trust option is available only for property you leave to all of your children as a group. If you want to use the pot trust for some but not all of your children, you will need to see a lawyer. (See Chapter 25.)

When Will Property Management End?

The age at which property management ends depends on the type of management you select.

- **UTMA.** State law determines when property management ends. In some states, you may choose from a limited age range. See "The Uniform Transfers to Minors Act," above.
- **Quicken WillMaker child's trust.** The trust ends when the child turns an age you choose, up to age 35.
- **Quicken WillMaker pot trust.** The trust ends when your youngest child turns an age you choose, up to age 25.
- **Other property management.** Property management for property your child receives outside of your will ends when the child becomes a legal adult—age 18 in most states.

Choosing Among Management Options

For each minor or young adult to whom you leave property in your will, you must decide which management approach to use: the UTMA, a child's trust or the pot trust. This section helps you decide which is best.

SEE AN EXPERT

Needs not covered by Quicken WillMaker Plus. The property management features offered by Quicken WillMaker Plus—the UTMA, child's trust and pot trust—provide the property manager with broad management authority adequate for most minors and young adults. However, they are not designed to:

- provide skilled long-term management of a business
- provide for management of funds beyond age 35 for a person with spendthrift tendencies or other personal habits that may impede sound financial management beyond young adulthood, or
- meet a disabled beneficiary's special needs. A physical, mental or developmental disability will likely require management customized to the beneficiary's circumstances, both to perpetuate the beneficiary's way of life and to preserve the property, while assuring that the beneficiary continues to qualify for government benefits.

To learn more about preparing trusts for people with disabilities, read *Special Needs Trusts* (Nolo), by Stephen Elias. For other situations described here, consult an experienced estate planning attorney. (See Chapter 25.)

Using the UTMA

As a general rule, the less valuable the property involved and the more mature the child, the more appropriate the UTMA is, because it is simpler to use than a child's trust or pot trust. There are a couple of reasons for this.

Because the UTMA is built into state law, banks, insurance companies, brokerage firms and other financial institutions know about it, so it should be easy for the custodian to carry out property management duties. To set up a child's trust or pot trust, the financial institution would have to be given a copy of the trust document and may tie up the proceeding in red tape to be sure the trustee is acting under its terms.

Also, a custodian acting under the UTMA need not file a separate income tax return for the property being managed; it can be included in the young beneficiary's return. However, in a child's trust or a pot trust, both the beneficiary and the trust must file returns.

Because the UTMA requires that management end at a relatively young age, if the property you are leaving is worth $100,000 or less—or if the child is likely to be able to handle more than that by age 21 (25 in Alaska, California, Nevada, Oregon, Pennsylvania or Tennessee)—use the UTMA. After all, $100,000 is likely to be used up before management under the UTMA ends.

Using the Quicken WillMaker Plus Child's Trust

Generally, the more property is worth, and the less mature the young beneficiary, the better it is to use the child's trust, even though doing so creates more work for the property manager than does the UTMA. For example, in a child's trust, the property manager must keep the beneficiary informed, manage trust assets prudently (meeting the requirements of state law) and file a separate tax return for the trust each year.

However, if a minor or young adult stands to get a fairly large amount of property—such as $200,000 or more—you might not want it all distributed by your state's UTMA cutoff age, which is usually 18 or 21. In such circumstances, you may be better off using the Quicken WillMaker Plus child's trust. Under the child's trust, management can last until an age you choose, to age 35.

Choosing an age for a particular beneficiary to get whatever trust property has not been spent on the beneficiary's needs will depend on:

- the amount of money or other property involved
- how much control you would like to impose over it
- the beneficiary's likely level of maturity as a young adult (for small children, this may be difficult to predict, but by the time youngsters reach their teens, you should have a pretty good indication), and
- whether the property you leave, such as rental property or a small business, needs sophisticated management that a young beneficiary is unlikely to master.

Using the Quicken WillMaker Plus Pot Trust

As a general rule, the pot trust makes sense only when you have two or more children and they are young and fairly close in age. For instance, if one of your children were 20 and another child of a later marriage were two, and you specify that the pot trust should end

when the younger child turns 18, the 20-year-old would have to wait until age 36 to receive the property. However, the pot trust option is available to you as long as any of your children is under age 25.

Like the trustee of a child's trust, a pot trust trustee must invest trust assets following the rules set out in state law, communicate regularly with the trust beneficiaries to keep them informed and file annual tax returns. The trustee of the pot trust also has the significant added responsibility of weighing competing claims from the children when deciding how to spend trust assets.

Property Management for Property That Does Not Pass Under Your Will

The UTMA, Quicken WillMaker Plus child's trust and pot trust are good management options for property that minor or young adult beneficiaries receive under your will. However, if you have minor children and they receive property of significant value outside of your will, a court will usually have to step in and appoint a guardian to manage the property under court supervision until the children turn 18.

The two most common ways that children receive property outside of a will are from life insurance or through a living trust. (See Chapter 13.) While it is possible to provide for management of this type of property through your life insurance agent under the UTMA or within the living trust itself, often no such management is established and a property guardianship is required.

In addition, property that your children receive from other sources—the lottery, a gift from an aunt or uncle, earnings from playing in a rock band—may also need to be managed by a property guardian.

It is always better to specify who will be managing any such property that your minor children come to own. Otherwise, the court will appoint someone who may or may not have your children's best interests in mind. If you are using the Quicken WillMaker Plus child's trust, a pot trust or the UTMA to provide management for property you are leaving to your children in your will, the person you have named as trustee or custodian would also be a good choice for property guardian. Another possible choice is the person you chose to be personal guardian, if you think he or she will handle the property wisely for the benefit of the minor. You also may wish to choose someone else entirely. Next, we offer some tips to help you pick the right person.

Naming a Property Manager

You may name one person to manage the property of a minor. You can also name one alternate (sometimes called "successor"), who will take over if your first choice is unable to serve.

Choosing a property manager is an important decision. Name someone you trust, who is familiar with property management and who shares your attitudes and values about how the money should be spent.

CAUTION
Parents do not get the job automatically. You may be surprised to learn that the child's other parent probably will not be able to automatically step in and handle property you leave your children in your will. Rather, unless you provide for management in your will, that other parent usually will have to petition the court to be appointed as the property manager and then handle the property under court supervision until the children turn 18. So, if you want your children's other parent to manage the property you are leaving your children, name that person to manage your children's property.

Keep in mind that you can only name the other parent as custodian or trustee if there is a chance that the other parent will be alive when the child receives the gift. For example, if you leave a gift to the other parent and you name the child as alternate for that gift, you cannot name the other parent to be trustee or custodian of that gift because the child would only receive the property if the other parent is not alive.

Whomever you choose as custodian or trustee, it is essential to get his or her consent first. This will also give you a chance to discuss, in general terms, how you would like the property to be managed to be sure the manager you select agrees with your vision and fully understands the beneficiary's needs.

The next sections offer tips on choosing the right property manager. In most situations, a trusted adult will be the best choice, but in some rare cases, you may want to name an institution, such as a bank.

Choosing a Property Manager

As a general rule, name a trusted adult who lives in or near to the state where the property will be managed—or at least be willing to travel there if needed.

You need not worry about finding a financial wizard to be your property manager because that person will have the power to hire professionals to prepare accountings and tax returns and to give investment advice. Anyone hired for such help may be paid out of the property being managed. The main job is to manage the property honestly, make basic decisions about how to take care of the assets wisely and sensibly mete out the money to the trust beneficiary.

It is usually preferable to combine the personal care and property management functions for a particular minor child in the hands of one person. Think first who is likely to be caring for the children if you die, and then consider whether that person is also a good choice for property manager. If you must name two different people, try to choose people who get along well; they will have to work together.

If you believe that the person who will be caring for the minor is not the best person to handle the minor's finances, consider another adult who is capable and is willing to serve.

For property you leave to young adults who are too old to have a person guardian, select an honest person with business savvy to manage the property.

EXAMPLE: Orenthal and Ariadne agree that Ariadne's sister, Penny, should be guardian of their kids should they both die, but that the $200,000 worth of stock the three kids will inherit might better be handled by someone with more business experience and who will be better able to resist the children's urgings to spend the money frivolously. In each of their wills, they name Penny as personal guardian of the children, but also create trusts for the property they are leaving to their children. They name each other as trustees, and Orenthal's mother, Phyllis, who has investment and business knowledge and lots of experience in handling headstrong adolescents, as the alternate trustee, after obtaining her consent. Orenthal and Ariadne also decide that one of their children, who is somewhat immature, should receive his share of the estate—at least the portion not already disbursed for his benefit by the trustee—upon turning 25, and the other two children should get their shares when they turn 21.

Selecting an Institution as Trustee

If you are using the UTMA, you must name a person as custodian; you cannot name an institution. If you're creating a trust, you can name an institution to serve as trustee, but it is rarely a good idea. Most banks will not accept a trust with less than several hundred thousand dollars' worth of liquid assets.

When banks do agree to take a trust, they charge large management and administrative fees. All trustees are entitled to reasonable compensation for their services—paid from trust assets. But family members or close friends who act as trustees often waive payments or accept far less than banks. If you cannot find an individual you think is suitable for handling your assets and do not have enough property to be managed by a financial institution, you may be better off not creating a trust.

Also, it is common for banks to manage the assets of all trusts worth less than $1 million as part of one large fund, while charging fees as if they were individually managed. Any noninstitutional trustee who invests trust money in a conservatively run mutual fund can normally do at least as well at a fraction of the cost.

Examples of Property Management

Here are some examples of how the Quicken WillMaker Plus property management options might be selected. The following scenarios are only intended as suggestions. Remember, if you live in South Carolina or Vermont, you cannot create an UTMA custodianship.

> EXAMPLE: **Married, adult children age 25 and older.** You want to leave all your property, worth $250,000, to your spouse and name surviving children as alternate beneficiaries. As long as you think the children are all sufficiently mature to handle their shares of the property if your spouse does not survive you, answer no

when Quicken WillMaker Plus asks if you wish to set up property management.

> EXAMPLE: **Married, children aged 2, 5 and 9.** You want to leave all your property, which is worth $250,000, to your spouse and name your children as alternate beneficiaries. You use the property management feature and select the UTMA option to manage the property if it passes to your children. You name your wife's mother— the same person you have named as personal guardian—as custodian, and name your brother as alternate personal guardian and alternate custodian. The property will be managed by the custodian until the age set by your state's law.
>
> You also name your wife's mother as property guardian if management is needed for property your minor children receive outside of your will.
>
> Later, when your children are older and you have accumulated more property, you may wish to make a new will and switch from the UTMA management approach to a pot trust so that the property can be used to meet the children's needs as required.

> EXAMPLE: **Single or married; two minor children from a previous marriage and one minor child with your present partner.** You want to leave all your property, which is worth $250,000, directly to your children. You can use the UTMA, set up the trust for each child or create a pot trust. You should also name a property guardian to

manage any property your minor child might get outside of your will.

CAUTION

Beware of spouse's and domestic partner's property rights. If you are married or in a registered domestic partnership, your spouse or partner may have a right to claim a portion of your property, so it is usually unwise to leave it all to your children unless your spouse or partner agrees with that plan. (See "Property Ownership Rules for Married People" in Chapter 5.)

EXAMPLE: **Single or married; two adult children from a previous marriage—ages 23 and 27—and one minor child with your present partner.** You decide to divide $300,000 equally among the children. To accomplish this, you establish a trust

for each child from the previous marriage and put the termination age at 30. You name your current spouse, who gets along well with the children, as trustee and a local trust company as alternate trustee. Because your third child is an unusually mature teenager, you choose the UTMA for this child and select 21 as the age at which this child takes any remaining property outright. You appoint your wife as custodian and your sister as successor custodian.

EXAMPLE: **Married or single; one daughter, age 32, and three minor grandchildren.** You want to leave $50,000 directly to each of the grandchildren. You establish a custodianship under the UTMA for each grandchild and name your daughter as custodian and her husband as successor custodian.

Choosing an Executor

You should name an executor to wrap up your will. After your death, that person will have legal responsibility for safeguarding and handling your property, seeing that debts and taxes are paid and distributing what is left to your beneficiaries as your will directs.

Executor or Personal Representative?

The following states use the term "personal representative" instead of "executor," but it means the same thing. If you live in one of these states, you will see the term "personal representative" in your will.

Alabama	Idaho	New Mexico
Alaska	Maine	North Dakota
Arizona	Michigan	South Carolina
Colorado	Minnesota	South Dakota
Florida	Montana	Utah
Hawaii	Nebraska	Wisconsin

TIP

Make your will and records accessible. You can help with the executor's first task: locating your will. Keep the original in a fairly obvious place—such as a desk or file cabinet. And make sure your executor has access to it.

Duties of an Executor

Serving as an executor can be fairly easy, or it can require a good deal of time and patience—depending on the amount of property involved and the complexity of the plans for it.

The Executor's Job

Your executor will have a number of duties, most of which do not require special expertise and can usually be accomplished without outside help. An executor typically must:

- obtain certified copies of the death certificate
- locate will beneficiaries
- examine and inventory the deceased person's safe deposit boxes
- collect the deceased person's mail
- cancel credit cards and subscriptions
- notify Social Security and other benefit plan administrators of the death
- learn about the deceased person's property—which may involve examining bankbooks, deeds, insurance policies, tax returns and many other records
- get bank accounts released or, in the case of pay-on-death accounts, get them transferred to their new owner, and
- collect any death benefits from life insurance policies, Social Security, veterans benefits and other benefits due from the deceased's union, fraternal society or employer.

In addition to these mundane tasks, the executor will typically have to:

- file papers in court to start the probate process and obtain the necessary authority to act as executor
- handle the probate court process—which involves transferring property and making sure the deceased's final debts and taxes are paid, and
- prepare final income tax forms for the deceased and, if necessary, file estate tax returns for the estate.

Note for Texas Residents: Independent Administration

Like many states, Texas offers a simplified probate process. In the Lone Star State, it's called "independent administration" and it gives an executor broad powers to act without supervision of the probate court. For example, an independent executor can pay final bills and distribute property without the court's oversight.

Unlike other states, Texas requires a will to contain a bit of special language to request this simplified process. That's why your Quicken Willmaker Plus will refers to your executor as your "independent executor" and includes required language permitting the independent administration of your estate.

SEE AN EXPERT

When to see a lawyer. We've designed your will to request independent administration because it saves money and speeds up probate. If you want your executor to work under the close supervision of a court, see an experienced estate planning attorney for advice.

For these tasks, it may be necessary to hire an outside professional who will be paid out of the estate's assets—a lawyer to initiate and handle the probate process and an accountant to prepare the necessary tax forms. But in some states, because of simplified court procedures and adequate self-help law materials, even these tasks can be accomplished without outside assistance.

For help with the task of educating your executor, you can print out a document titled Letter to Executor, which you can give to the person you name to serve. The document offers guidance on the executor's duties.

RESOURCE

More help for executors. For a complete guide to an executor's duties and details about how to wrap up an estate, see *The Executor's Guide: Settling a Loved One's Estate or Trust*, by Mary Randolph (Nolo).

Posting a Bond

Sometimes, a probate court asks an executor to post a bond—an insurance policy that protects beneficiaries if the executor is dishonest or incompetent—unless your will expressly waives this requirement. As long as you choose an executor you trust, there's no reason your executor should have to go to the trouble of putting up a bond. Furthermore, the cost of the bond—usually about 10% of its face amount—comes out of your estate. If a bond is purchased, your beneficiaries will receive less than they otherwise would.

The will you make with Quicken WillMaker Plus expressly states that no bond is necessary. However, a few states may require the executor to put up a bond if they live in another state—no matter what your will says. (See "Restrictions on Out-of-State Executors," below.)

Getting Paid

The laws of every state provide that an executor may be paid out of the estate. Depending on your state law, this payment may be:

- based on what the court considers reasonable
- a small percentage of the gross or net value of the estate, or
- set according to factors specified in your state's statutes.

An executor who either stands to get a large portion of the estate or is a close family relative, commonly does the work without being paid. Some will makers opt to leave their executors a specific bequest of money in appreciation for serving.

However, outside experts will almost always be paid out of the estate. The amount experts—including lawyers—are paid is totally under the control of the executor. However, a few states set out fees that may be charged by lawyers and other professionals—usually a percentage of the value of the estate.

CAUTION

Beware of lawyers' fees. Lawyers commonly imply that the fee allowed by statute is the fee that they are required to charge for their services. In fact, lawyers are perfectly free to charge by the hour or to set a flat fee that is unrelated to the size of the estate. One of the most important tasks that your executor can perform is to negotiate a reasonable fee with any lawyer he or she may pick to help probate your estate. Be sure you explain this to your choice for executor.

Naming an Executor

Glancing through the list of the executor's duties mentioned above should tip you off about who might be the best person for the job. The prime characteristics are honesty, skill at organizing and finesse in keeping track of details. For many tasks, such as collecting mail and finding important records and papers, it may be most helpful to name someone who lives nearby or who is familiar with your business matters.

Choosing Your Executor

The most important guideline in naming an executor is to choose someone you trust enough to have access to your personal records and finances after your death. Many people choose someone who is also named to get a substantial amount of property under the will. This is sensible, because a person with an interest in how your property is distributed—a spouse, partner, child or close family member—is also likely to do a conscientious job as executor. And he or she will probably also come equipped with knowledge of where your records are kept and an understanding of why you want your property split up as you have directed.

Following are a few more things you may want to consider when making your choice. Whomever you choose, make sure the person you select is willing to do the job. Discuss the possible duties involved with your choice for executor before naming him or her in your will.

Naming Someone Who Lives Out of State

As a practical matter, it's wise to name an executor who lives close to you. It will be more difficult for the executor to handle day-to-day matters from a distance. But if the best person for the job lives far away, there's no law against naming that person in your will. Every state allows out-of-state executors to serve, though most states impose special rules on them. The table below sets out the details.

Naming More Than One Person

While you may name two executors to serve together, doing so is often not wise. Joint executors may act without each other's consent—and if they ever disagree, your estate may be the loser because of lengthy probate delays and court costs.

Naming an Institution

While it is almost always best to choose a trusted person for the job, you may not know anyone who is up to the task of winding up your estate—especially if your estate is large and complicated and your beneficiaries are either very old, very young or just inexperienced in financial matters. If so, you can select a professional management firm to act as your executor. (Banks often provide this service.)

If you are considering naming an institution as executor, be sure the one you choose is willing to act. Most will not accept the job unless your estate is fairly large. Also, institutions charge a hefty fee for acting as executor. They may charge both a percentage of the value of property to be managed and a number of smaller fees for routine services such as buying and selling property.

If You Do Not Name an Executor

If you do not name an executor in your will, the document will still be valid. But your decision will not have been a wise one. It will most often mean that a court will have to scurry to come up with a willing relative to serve. If that fails, the court will probably appoint someone to do the job who is likely to be unfamiliar with you, your property and your beneficiaries. People appointed by the court to serve are usually called administrators.

The laws in many states provide that anyone who is entitled under the will to take over half a person's property has first priority to serve as executor. If no such person is apparent, courts will generally look for someone to serve among the following groups of people, in the following order:

- surviving spouse or registered domestic partner
- children
- grandchildren
- great-grandchildren
- parents
- brothers and sisters
- grandparents
- uncles, aunts, first cousins
- children of deceased spouse or partner
- other next of kin
- relatives of a deceased spouse or partner
- conservator or guardian
- public administrator
- creditors, and
- any other person.

Restrictions on Out-of-State Executors	
Alabama	Nonresident can be appointed executor only if already serving as executor of same estate in another state. (Ala. Code § 43-2-22)
Arkansas	Nonresident executor must appoint an in-state agent to accept legal papers. (Ark. Code Ann. § 28-48-101(b)(6))
Connecticut	Nonresident executor must appoint in-state probate court judge as agent to accept legal papers. (Conn. Gen. Stat. Ann. § 52-60)
Delaware	Nonresident executor must appoint county Register of Wills as the agent to accept legal papers. (Del. Code Ann. Tit. 12, § 1506)
Dist. of Col.	Nonresident executor must publish notices in a newspaper and appoint the probate register as agent to accept legal papers. (D.C. Code Ann. §§ 20-303, 20-343)
Florida	Nonresident can be appointed executor only if he or she is related by blood, marriage or adoption to person making will. (Fla. Stat. Ann. § 733.304)
Illinois	Nonresident executor may be required to post bond, even if will expressly states bond not required. (755 Ill. Comp. Stat. § 5/6-13)
Indiana	Nonresident can serve as executor if resident appointed coexecutor and nonresident posts a bond. Nonresident can serve alone if he or she posts a bond, files a written notice of acceptance and appoints an in-state agent to accept legal papers. (Ind. Code Ann. § 29-1-10-1)
Iowa	Nonresident can serve as executor only if resident appointed coexecutor, unless court allows nonresident to serve alone. (Iowa Code § 633.64)
Kansas	Nonresident executor must appoint an in-state agent to accept legal papers. (Kan. Stat. Ann. § 59-1706)
Kentucky	Nonresident can be appointed executor only if he or she is related by blood, marriage or adoption to person making will. (Ky. Rev. Stat. Ann. § 395.005)
Maryland	Nonresident executor must publish notices in a newspaper and appoint an in-state agent to accept legal papers. (Md. Code Ann. [Est. & Trusts]. §§ 5-105, 5-503)
Massachusetts	Nonresident executor must appoint an in-state agent to accept legal papers. (Mass. Gen. Laws ch. 195, § 8)
Missouri	Nonresident executor must appoint an in-state agent to accept legal papers. (Mo. Rev. Stat. § 473.117)
Nevada	Nonresident can serve as executor only if resident appointed coexecutor. (Nev. Rev. Stat. Ann. § 139.010)
New Hampshire	Nonresident executor must be approved by probate judge and must appoint an in-state agent to accept legal papers. (N.H. Stat. §§ 553:5, 553:25)
New Jersey	Nonresident must post bond unless will waives the requirement. (N.J. Stat. Ann. § 3B:15-1)

Restrictions on Out-of-State Executors (cont'd)	
North Carolina	Nonresident executor must appoint an in-state agent to accept legal papers. (N.C. Gen. Stat. § 28A-4-2)
Ohio	Nonresident can be appointed executor only if he or she is related by blood, marriage or adoption to person making will—or if he or she lives in a state that permits nonresidents to serve. (Ohio Rev. Code Ann. § 2109.21)
Oklahoma	Nonresident executor must appoint an in-state agent to accept legal papers. (Okla. Stat. Ann. tit. 58, § 162)
Pennsylvania	Nonresident can serve as executor only with permission of register of wills. Nonresident executor must file an affidavit stating that estate has no known debts in Pennsylvania, and that he or she will not perform any duties prohibited in home state. (20 Pa. Cons. Stat. Ann. §§ 3157, 4101)
Rhode Island	Nonresident executor must be approved by a judge and must appoint an in-state agent to accept legal papers. (R.I. Gen. Laws §§ 33-8-7, 33-18-9)
Tennessee	Nonresident executor must appoint secretary of state as agent to accept legal papers and may be required to post bond. Nonresident can also serve if resident appointed coexecutor. (Tenn. Code Ann. § 35-50-107)
Texas	Nonresident executor must appoint an in-state agent to accept legal papers. (Tex. Prob. Code Ann. § 78)
Vermont	Nonresident executor must appoint an in-state agent to accept legal papers. Nonresident executor can be appointed only with court approval; court must approve nonresident executor upon request of surviving spouse or civil union partner, adult children or parents or guardians of minor children. (Vt. Stat. Ann. tit. 14, § 904)
Virginia	Nonresident executor must post a bond and appoint an in-state agent to accept legal papers. Bond without a guarantee is permitted. (Va. Code Ann. § 26-59)
Washington	Nonresident executor must post a bond and appoint an in-state agent to accept legal papers. If nonresident is surviving spouse and sole beneficiary of will, or if will expressly states so, bond is not required. (Wash. Rev. Code Ann. §§ 11.28.185, 11.36.010)
West Virginia	Nonresident executor may serve if clerk of the county commission of the county where the probate is conducted serves as nonresident's agent. Nonresident must post bond unless will says otherwise. (W.Va. Code Ann. § 44-5-3)
Wisconsin	Nonresident executor must appoint an in-state agent to accept legal papers. At court's discretion, nonresident executor can be removed or refused appointment solely on grounds of residency. (Wis. Stat. Ann. § 856.23)
Wyoming	Nonresident executor must appoint an in-state agent to accept legal papers. (Wyo. Stat. § 2-11-301)

Naming an Alternate

In case you name someone to serve as executor who dies before you do or for any other reason cannot take on the responsibilities, you should name an alternate to serve instead.

- If you name coexecutors, your alternate executor will serve only if both co-executors are unavailable.
- You may name up to two alternate executors. However, only one of them may serve at a time. Your second alternate will serve only if your executor(s) and your first alternate become unavailable.

EXAMPLE: Marsha names Bill and Jane as her coexecutors. She then names Susan as first alternate and Keith as second alternate. When Marsha dies, if either Bill or Jane is unavailable to be the executor of her estate, the other will serve alone. If both Bill and Jane are unavailable, Susan will serve. In the unlikely event that Bill, Jane and Susan are all unavailable, it will be up to Keith to wrap up Marsha's estate.

In choosing an alternate executor, consider the same factors you did in naming your first choice. (See "Choosing Your Executor," above.)

Debts, Expenses and Taxes

M oney matters have a way of living on—even after your death. But you can easily guide your survivors through the vexing process of dealing with your debts and expenses by including clear instructions in your will.

In your will, you can:

- forgive debts that others owed you during your lifetime
- designate what property should be used to pay debts you owe at death, and
- designate what property should be used to pay state and federal death taxes owed by your estate or due on the property in it.

> **TIP**
> **Keeping track of your debts, expenses and taxes.** At your death, your executor and other survivors may need to learn about the debts you owed and that others owed to you during your life. For help collecting and recording this information, use Quicken WillMaker Plus's Information for Caregivers and Survivors form.

Forgiving Debts Others Owe You

You can release anyone who owes you a debt from the responsibility of paying it back to your estate after you die. You can cancel any such debt—oral or written. If you do, your forgiveness functions much the same as giving a gift; those who were indebted to you will no longer be legally required to pay the money they owed.

Keep in mind that releasing people or institutions from the debts they owe you may diminish the property that your beneficiaries receive under your will.

Quicken WillMaker Plus prompts you to describe any debt you wish to cancel—including the name of the person who owes it, the approximate date the debt was incurred and the amount you wish to forgive. This information is important so that the debt can be properly identified.

Explaining Your Intention

If you forgive a debt, it is likely to come as a pleasant surprise to those living with the expectations that they must repay it. And you will probably give the gesture considerable thought before including such a direction in your will. While the final document will contain a brief clause stating your intention, you may wish to explain your reasoning beyond this bald statement. If you wish to do so, it is best to write your explanation in a brief letter that you attach to your will. (See Chapter 12.)

> **CAUTION**
> **Caution for married or legally partnered people.** If you want to use your will to forgive a debt and the debt was incurred while you were married or legally partnered, you may only have the right to forgive half the debt. There is a special need to be cautious about this possibility in community property states. If your debt is a

community property debt, you cannot cancel the whole amount due unless your spouse or partner agrees to allow you to cancel his or her share of the debt—and puts that agreement in writing.

Liabilities at Your Death

If you live owing money, chances are you will die owing money. If you do, your executor will be responsible for rounding up your property and making sure all your outstanding debts are satisfied before any of the property is put in the hands of those you have named to get it. The property you own at your death—or your estate—may be liable for several types of debts, expenses and taxes.

Debts You Owe

When you leave this credit-happy world, you will likely go out with debts you have not fully paid—personal loans, credit card bills, mortgage loans, income taxes. Whether such debts pass to the beneficiary along with the property, or must be paid out of the estate, depends upon how the debt is characterized. (See "Types of Debts," below.)

Expenses Incurred After Your Death

There are several expenses incurred after you die—including the costs of a funeral, burial or cremation and probate—which may take your survivors by surprise if you do not plan ahead for paying them.

Funeral and burial expenses, for example, typically cost several thousand dollars. And for those who do not plan ahead, the costs may soar even higher. (See Chapter 24.) In addition, probate and estate administration fees typically run about 5% to 7% of the value of the property you leave to others in your will.

Estate and Inheritance Taxes

Estate tax is a concern for few people. The tax is levied on the property you own at death—but a large amount of property is exempt from taxation. (See "Estate and Inheritance Taxes," below.)

Unless you specify otherwise in your will, in most states, these taxes will normally be paid proportionately out of the estate's liquid assets. This means that a beneficiary's property will be reduced by the percentage that the property bears to the total liquid assets. Liquid assets include bank accounts, money market accounts and marketable securities. Real estate and tangible personal property such as cars, furniture and antiques are not included. This could cause a problem if, for example, you left your bank account with $50,000 in it to a favorite nephew and your tax liability—most of which resulted from valuable real property left to another beneficiary—gobbled up all or most of it.

Types of Debts

There are two basic kinds of debts to think about when making a will—secured and unsecured.

When You Need Not Worry—And When You Should

Typically, you do not need to leave instructions about debts if any of the following are true:

- Your debts and expenses are likely to be negligible—or to represent only a tiny fraction of a relatively large estate.
- You are leaving all your property to your spouse or partner or specify that it should be shared among a very few beneficiaries, without dividing it into specific bequests.
- You understand and approve of how your state law deals with debts and expenses.

On the other hand, you may need to be concerned about covering your debts and death taxes when your will-making plan involves dividing up your property among a number of beneficiaries.

And you need to plan more carefully if debts payable by your estate are likely to be large enough to cut significantly into bequests left to individuals and charitable institutions. The danger, of course, is that unless you plan carefully, the people whose bequests are used to pay debts and expenses may be the very people whom you would have preferred to take your property free and clear.

EXAMPLE: Ruth has $40,000 in a money market account and several valuable musical instruments, also worth $40,000. She makes a will leaving the money market account to her daughter and the instruments to her musician son but does not specify how her debts and expenses should be paid. Due to medical bills and an unpaid personal loan from a friend, Ruth dies owing $35,000. After Ruth's death, her executor must follow state law, which first requires that debts be paid out of the residuary estate. But because there is no residuary—all property is used up by specific bequests—a second rule applies that requires that debts be paid out of liquid assets. As a result, the executor pays the $35,000 out of the money market account, leaving the daughter with only $5,000. The son receives the $40,000 worth of musical instruments.

Secured Debts

Secured debts are any debts owed on specific property that must be paid before title to that property fully belongs to its owner.

One common type of secured debt occurs when a major asset such as a car, appliance or business is paid for over a period of time. Usually, the lender of credit will retain some measure of legal ownership in the asset—termed a security interest—until it is paid off.

Another common type of secured debt occurs when a lender, as a condition of the loan, takes a security interest in property already owned by the person applying for the money. For instance, most finance companies require their borrowers to agree to pledge "all their personal property" as security for the loan. The legal jargon for this type of security interest is a non-purchase-money secured debt—that is, the debt is incurred for a purpose other than purchasing the property that secures repayment.

Other common types of secured debts are mortgages and deeds of trust owed on real estate in exchange for a purchase or equity loan, tax liens and assessments that are owed on real estate and, in some instances, liens or legal claims on personal and real property created as a result of litigation or home repair.

If you are leaving property in your will that is subject to a secured debt, you may be concerned about whether the debt will pass to the beneficiary along with the property, or whether it must be paid by your estate.

Debts on Real Estate

Quicken WillMaker Plus passes all secured debts owed on real estate along with the real estate.

EXAMPLE: Paul owes $50,000 under a deed of trust on his home, signed as a condition of obtaining an equity loan. He leaves the home to his children. The deed of trust is a secured debt on real property and passes to the children along with the property.

EXAMPLE: Sonny and Cati, a married couple, borrow $100,000 from the bank to purchase their home and take out a deed of trust in the bank's favor as security for the loan. They still owe $78,000 and are two years behind in property tax payments. In separate wills, Sonny and Cati leave their ownership share to each other and name their children as alternates to take the home in equal shares. The deed of trust is a purchase money secured debt and, if the children get the property, they will also get the mortgage—and responsibility for paying the past due amount in taxes.

Debts on Personal Property

All debts owed on personal property pass to the beneficiaries of the property.

EXAMPLE: Phil owns a 1999 Ferrari. Although the car is registered in Phil's name, the bank holds legal title pending

Phil's payment of the outstanding $75,000 car note. Phil uses Quicken WillMaker Plus to leave the car to his companion Paula. The car note is a secured debt and will pass to Paula with the car.

When the Debt Exceeds the Property Value

Because the property is usually worth more than any debt secured by it, a person who takes the property at your death but does not want to owe money can sell the property, pay off the debt and pocket the difference. However, at times, relying on this approach is not satisfactory—especially when it comes to houses.

For example, if you leave your daughter your house with the hope that it will be her home, you will probably not want her to have to sell the house because she cannot meet the mortgage payments. If you think a particular beneficiary will need assistance with paying a debt owed on property, try to leave the necessary money or valuable assets to him or her as well.

Unsecured Debts

Unsecured debts are all debts not tied to specific property. Common examples are medical bills, most credit card bills, utility bills and probate fees. Your executor must pay these debts and expenses out of property from your estate. A student loan is another common example of an unsecured debt. However, most student loans can be canceled if the borrower dies before the loan is paid off, so the borrower's estate will owe nothing.

Paying Debts and Expenses

Quicken WillMaker Plus offers two options for paying debts, including the expenses of probate. You can:

- designate a particular asset or assets to be used or sold to pay debts and expenses, or
- choose not to designate specific assets, which will mean that your executor will pay the debts and expenses as required by the laws of your state.

Designating Specific Assets

One helpful approach to taking care of debts and expenses is to designate one or more specific assets that your executor must use to pay them. For example, if you designate a savings or money market account to be used for paying off your debts and expenses, and the amount in the account is sufficient to meet these obligations, the other bequests you make in your will won't be affected by your estate's indebtedness.

If you select specific assets to pay your debts and expenses, you'll probably want to select liquid assets over nonliquid assets. Liquid assets are those easily converted into cash at full value: bank and deposit accounts, money market accounts, stocks and bonds. On the other hand, tangible assets such as motor vehicles, planes, jewelry, stamp and coin collections, electronic items and musical instruments must be sold to raise the necessary cash. Hurried sales seldom bring in anywhere near the full value, which means the net worth of your estate will also be reduced.

EXAMPLE: Harry writes mystery books for a living. He has never produced a blockbuster but owns 15 copyrights, which produce royalties of about $70,000 a year. During his life, Harry has traveled widely and collected artifacts from around the world. They have a value of $300,000 if sold carefully to knowledgeable collectors. Harry makes a will leaving his copyrights to his spouse and the artifacts to his children. He also designates that the artifacts should be used to pay his debts and expenses—which total $150,000 at death. Harry's executor, who is not a collector and has little time or inclination to sell the artifacts one by one, sells them in bulk for $140,000—less than half of their true value. To raise the extra $10,000, two of the copyrights are sold, again at less than their true value. As a result, Harry's children receive nothing and his spouse gets less than Harry intended.

Avoid designating property you have left to specific beneficiaries. It is important to review your specific bequests before designating assets to pay debts and expenses. If possible, designate liquid assets that have not been left to specific beneficiaries. Only as a last resort should you earmark a tangible item also left in a specific bequest for first use to pay debts and expenses.

One exception to this general recommendation occurs if you believe you are unlikely to owe much when you die and that the expenses of probate will be low. Then, it makes sense for you to designate a substantial liquid asset left as a specific bequest to also pay debts and expenses.

Covering Your Debts With Insurance

One way to deal with the problem of large debts and small assets is to purchase a life insurance policy in an amount large enough to pay your anticipated debts and expenses and have the proceeds made payable to your estate. You can then specify in your will that these proceeds should be used to pay your debts and expenses—with the rest going to your residuary beneficiary or a beneficiary named in a specific bequest.

But be careful. If large sums are involved, talk with an estate planner or accountant before adopting this sort of plan. Having insurance money paid to your estate subjects that amount to probate. A better alternative may be to provide that estate assets be sold, with the proceeds used to pay the debts. Then have the insurance proceeds made payable directly to your survivors free of probate.

Of course, if the source you specify is insufficient to pay all the bills, your executor will still face the problem of which property to use to make up the difference. For this reason, it is often wise to list several resources and specify the order in which they should be used. Also, make sure that they are worth more than what is likely to be required.

EXAMPLE: Ella, a widow, makes a will that contains the following bequests:

- My house at 1111 Soto Street in Albany, New York, to Hillary Bernette. (The house has an outstanding mortgage of $50,000, for which Hillary will become responsible.)
- My coin collection (appraised at $30,000) to Stanley, Mark and Belinda Bernette.
- My three antique chandeliers to Herbert Perkins.
- The rest of my property to Denise Everread. Although not spelled out in the will, this property consists of a savings account ($26,000), a car ($5,000), a camera ($1,000) and stock ($7,000).

Using Quicken WillMaker Plus, Ella specifies that her savings account and stock be used in the order listed to pay debts and expenses. When Ella dies, she owes $8,000; the expenses of probating her estate total $4,000. Following Ella's instructions, her executor would close the savings account, use $12,000 of it to pay debts and expenses and turn the rest over to Denise along with the stock and camera.

EXAMPLE: Now suppose Ella has only $6,000 in the savings account. When she dies, her executor, following the same instructions, would close the account ($6,000) and sell enough stock to make up the difference ($6,000). The remaining $1,000 worth of stock, the camera and the car would pass to Denise.

> **CAUTION**
>
> **Describe property consistently.** If you designate property both as a specific bequest and as a source for paying your debts, be sure to describe it exactly the same in both instances to avoid confusion.

If You Don't Specify Assets

If you do not specify how you want your debts and expenses to be paid, your executor will need to follow your state's laws, and your Quicken WillMaker Plus will instructs him or her to do so.

Some states require that debts and expenses be paid first out of property in your estate that does not pass under your will. In other states, your debts and expenses must first be paid out of liquid assets such as bank accounts and securities, then from tangible personal property and, as a last resort, from real estate.

Estate and Inheritance Taxes

Before you concentrate on how you want your estate or inheritance taxes to be paid, consider whether you need to be concerned about these types of taxes at all. Most people do not.

These taxes are imposed on the transfer of property after someone dies. Some people confuse probate-avoidance devices, such as living trusts and joint tenancy, with schemes to save on taxes. But avoiding probate does not reduce these taxes.

Whether or not your estate will be required to pay taxes depends on two factors:

- the value of your taxable estate—that is, your net estate minus any gifts or expenses that are tax-exempt, and
- the laws of the state in which you live.

Federal Estate Taxes

Only a fraction of estates end up owing federal estate tax. Primarily, that's because a large amount of property is exempt from the tax, and the exemption is growing steadily bigger. For deaths that occur in 2008, estates smaller than $2 million do not owe estate tax. For deaths that occur in 2009, that amount is $3.5 million.

Planning for estate taxes can be quite complicated. If you think your estate might be large enough to owe estate tax, see Chapter 13, which explains the system.

State Inheritance and Estate Taxes

State taxes normally do not take a deep enough bite to cause serious concern unless your estate is very large. However, because of recent changes to federal and state tax laws, an increasing number of estates owe some state tax. (Some estates may have to pay state tax even if they aren't large enough to owe federal estate tax.) If you own a lot of property—say, more than $500,000 worth—and you're concerned about it, you may want to check with an estate planning or tax lawyer who can bring you up to date on the laws in your state.

If it turns out that your estate owes state taxes, your executor has an obligation to pay them and will therefore deduct them from each bequest unless you state differently in your will, as you can do when using Quicken WillMaker Plus.

SEE AN EXPERT

Getting help with large estates. As you might imagine, financial planning experts have devised many creative ways to plan for paying estate and inheritance taxes. If your estate is large enough to warrant concern about possible federal or state taxes, it is large enough for you to afford a consultation with an accountant, estate planning specialist or lawyer specializing in estates and trusts. (See Chapter 13.)

Choosing How to Pay Taxes

Quicken WillMaker Plus offers the following options for paying estate and inheritance taxes. You can:

- pay them from all property you own at death
- designate specific assets, or
- choose not to specify how your taxes will be paid, leaving that matter up to state law.

If the value of your estate is well below the federal and state tax range, and you have no reasonable expectation that your estate will grow much larger before your death, you may want to skip this discussion of your options for paying taxes and choose the option "Don't specify."

If you are a relatively young, healthy person and your estate is only slightly larger than $2 million, you may want to adopt one of the Quicken WillMaker Plus tax payment options now and worry about more sophisticated tax planning later. After all, by the time you die, federal and state tax rules may have changed many times.

Paying Taxes From All Property You Own

For the purpose of computing estate and inheritance tax liability, your estate consists of all property you legally own at your death, whether it passes under the terms of your will or outside of your will—such as a joint tenancy, living trust, savings bank trust or life insurance policy. Because your estate's tax liability will be computed on the basis of all this property, you may wish to have the beneficiaries of the property share proportionately in the responsibility for paying the taxes.

> EXAMPLE: Julie Johanssen, a widow, owns a house (worth $1 million), stocks ($400,000), jewelry ($150,000) and investments as a limited partner in a number of rental properties ($900,000). To avoid probate, Julie puts the house in a living trust for her eldest son, Warren; puts the stocks in a living trust for another son, Alain; and uses her will to leave the jewelry to a daughter, Penelope, and the investments to her two surviving brothers, Sean and Ivan. She specifies that all beneficiaries of property in her taxable estate share in paying any estate and inheritance taxes.

When Julie dies, the net worth of her estate, which consists of all the property mentioned, is over the amount of the estate tax exemption in the year of her death, so there is federal estate tax liability.

Each of Julie's beneficiaries will be responsible for paying a portion of this liability. Each portion will be measured by the proportion that beneficiary's inheritance has to the estate as a whole.

Designating Specific Assets

As with payment of debts and expenses, it may be a good approach to designate one or more specific property items to satisfy the amount you owe in taxes. Again, if you designate a bank, brokerage or money market account to be used for paying taxes, and the amount in the account is adequate to meet these obligations, the other bequests you make in your will should not be affected.

Of course, if the resource you specify for payment of your estate and inheritance taxes is not sufficient to cover the amount due, your executor will still face the problem of which property will be used to make up the difference. So, again, it is a good idea to list several resources that should be used to pay estate and inheritance taxes.

> CAUTION
> **Guidance for selecting specific assets.**
> If you do choose to select specific assets to be used to pay your taxes, follow the general rules set out in "Paying Debts and Expenses," above.

If You Don't Specify a Method of Payment

If you choose this option, your will directs your executor to pay your estate and inheritance taxes as required by the laws of your state. As with your debts and expenses, your state law controls how your executor is to approach this issue if you do not establish your own plan. Some states leave the method of payment up to your executor, while others provide that all beneficiaries must share the tax burden. Depending on your financial and tax situation and the law of your state, more variables set in than can reasonably be covered here. If you are concerned about the possible legal repercussions of choosing this option, consider researching your state's law. (See Chapter 25.)

Make It Legal: Final Steps

Once you have proceeded through all the Quicken WillMaker Plus screens and responded to all the questions the program poses, your will is nearly finished. There are just a few more steps you must take to make it legally effective so that the directions you expressed in it can be carried out after your death.

No Accents or Umlauts

If your name contains accent marks, umlauts or other special characters, you can type them into WillMaker. *However, those characters will not show up correctly in your printed document unless you change the default font* (Times New Roman). Common Windows fonts that will correctly print special characters include:

- Georgia (serif), and
- Verdana (sans serif).

For details on how to change the fonts of printed documents, see "Changing How Your Documents Look" in Part 7 of the Users' Manual.

Checking Your Will

Before you sign your will, take some time to scrutinize it and make sure it accurately expresses your wishes. You can do this either by previewing it in the program or by printing out a draft copy. (Consult the Users' Manual if you need additional guidance.)

Having an Expert Check Your Will

You may want to have your will checked by an attorney or tax expert. This makes good sense if you are left with nagging questions about the legal implications of your choices, or if you own a great deal of property or have a complicated idea of how you want to leave it. But keep in mind that you are your own best expert on most issues and decisions involved in making a will—what property you own, your relation to family members and friends and your own favorite charities. Also, some attorneys don't support the self-help approach to making a will, so you may have to find one who is cooperative. (See Chapter 25.)

Signing and Witnessing Requirements

To be valid, a will must be legally executed. This means that you must sign your will in front of two witnesses. These witnesses must sign the will not only in your presence, but also in the presence of all the other witnesses.

Requirements for Witnesses

There are a few legal requirements for witnesses. The witnesses need to be of sound mind. In most states, the witnesses need to be 18 or older. Many states also require that the witnesses not be people who will take property under the will. Thus we require that you not use someone to whom you leave property in your will, even as an alternate or residuary beneficiary, as a witness.

As a matter of common sense, the people you choose to be witnesses should be easily available when you die. While this bit of future history is impossible to foretell with certainty, it is usually best to choose witnesses who are in good health, are younger than you are and likely to remain in your geographic area. However, the witnesses do not have to be residents of your state.

The Self-Proving Option

For a will to be accepted by a probate court, the executor must show that the document really is the will of the person it purports to be—a process called proving the will. In the past, all wills were proved either by having one or two witnesses come into court to testify or swear in written, notarized statements called affidavits that they saw you sign your will.

Today, most states allow people to make their wills self-proving—that is, they can be admitted in probate court without the hassle of herding up witnesses to appear in court or sign affidavits. This is accomplished when the person making the will and the witnesses all appear before a notary public and sign an affidavit under oath, verifying that all necessary formalities for execution have been satisfied.

If you live in a state that offers the self-proving option, Quicken WillMaker Plus automatically produces the correct affidavit for your state, with accompanying instructions. With the exception of New Hampshire, the self-proving affidavit is not part of your will, but a separate document. To use it, you and your witnesses must first sign the will as discussed above. Then, you and your witnesses must sign the self-proving affidavit in front of a notary public. This may be done any time after the will is signed but, obviously, it is easiest to do it while all your witnesses are gathered together to watch you sign your will. Most notaries will charge at least a minimal amount for their services—and will require you and your witnesses to present some identification verifying that you are who you claim to be.

Many younger people—who are likely to make a number of wills before they die—decide not to make their wills self-proving, due to the initial trouble of getting a notary at the signing. If you are one of these people, file the uncompleted affidavit and instructions in a safe place in case you change your mind later.

Note for California and Indiana Readers

In California or Indiana, the self-proving feature does not require a separate affidavit. Instead, the fact that the witnesses sign the will under the oath printed above their signatures is sufficient to have the will admitted into probate, unless a challenge is mounted. There is no need to take further steps to make a California or Indiana will self-proving.

States Without Self-Proving Laws

The self-proving option is not available in the District of Columbia, Maryland, Ohio or Vermont. In these states, your executor will be required to prove your will.

Signing Procedure

You need not utter any magic words when signing your will and having it witnessed, but a few legal requirements suggest the best way to proceed:

- Gather all witnesses together in one place.
- Inform your witnesses that the papers you hold in your hand are your last will and testament. This is important, because the laws in many states specifically require that you acknowledge the document as your will before the witnesses sign it. The witnesses need not read your will, however, and there is no need for them to know its contents. If you want to ensure that the contents of the will stay confidential, you may cover all but the signature portion of your will with a separate sheet of paper while the witnesses sign.
- Initial each page of the will at the bottom on the lines provided. The purpose of initialing is to prevent anyone from challenging the will as invalid on the grounds that changes were made to it by someone else.

- Sign the last page on the signature line while the witnesses watch. Use the same form of your name that you stated in your will.
- Ask each of the witnesses to initial the bottom of each page on a line there, then watch as they sign and fill in their addresses on the last page where indicated. Their initials act as evidence if anyone later claims you changed your will without going through the proper legal formalities.

Changing Your Quicken WillMaker Plus Will

Once you have signed your will and had it witnessed, it is extremely important that you do not alter it by inserting handwritten or typed additions or changes. Do not even correct misspellings. The laws of most states require that after a will is signed, any additions or changes to it, even clerical ones, must be made by following the same signing and witnessing requirements as for an original will.

Although it is legally possible to make handwritten corrections on your will before you sign it, that is a bad idea since, after your death, it will not be clear to the probate court that you made the corrections before the will was signed. The possibility that the changes were made later may throw the legality of the whole will into question.

If you want to make changes after your will has been signed and witnessed, there are two ways to accomplish it: You can either make a new will or make a formal addition, called a codicil, to the existing one. Either approach requires a new round of signing and witnessing.

One of the great advantages of Quicken WillMaker Plus is that you can conveniently keep current by simply making a new will. This does away with the need to tack on changes to the will in the form of a codicil and involves no need for additional gyrations. Codicils are not a good idea when using Quicken WillMaker Plus because of the possibility of creating a conflict between the codicil and the original will. It is simpler and safer to make a new Quicken WillMaker Plus will, sign it and have it witnessed.

Storing Your Will

Once your will is properly signed and witnessed, be sure that your executor can easily locate it at your death. Here are some suggestions:

- Store your printed and witnessed will in an envelope on which you have typed your name and the word "Will."
- Place the envelope in a fireproof metal box, file cabinet or home safe. An alternative is to place the original will in a safe deposit box. But before doing that, learn the bank's policy about access to the box after your death. If, for instance, the safe deposit box is in your name alone, the box can probably be opened only by a person authorized by a court, and then only in the presence

of a bank employee. An inventory may even be required if any person enters the box or for state tax purposes. All of this takes time, and in the meantime, your document will be locked away from those who need it.

Helping Others Find Your Will

Your will should be easy to locate at your death. You want to spare your survivors the anxiety of having to search for your will when they are already dealing with the grief of losing you. Make sure your executor, and at least one other person you trust, knows where to find your will.

Making Copies of Your Will

Some people are tempted to prepare more than one signed and witnessed original of their wills in case one is lost. While it is legal in most states to prepare and sign duplicate originals, it is never a good idea. Common sense tells you why: If you later want to change your will, it can be difficult to locate all the old copies to destroy them.

That said, it is sometimes a good idea to make several unsigned copies of your current will. You may want to give one to your executor or other loved ones, so they know your plans.

To share your will, print multiple copies when you finalize your document. Print these copies with a "duplicate" watermark; see Part 4 of the Users' Manual for instructions. Sign your original will and distribute the unsigned copies. We also recommend that you store one unsigned copy with your original will.

If you need more copies later, you can photocopy the unsigned will or print copies from your computer by returning to the program.

Of course, you aren't required to disclose the contents of your will to anyone. If you prefer to keep your will confidential until your death, do not make any copies.

Giving Your Portfolio File a Good Home

Once you have printed out your will, you should make a copy of it in electronic form. Find a safe place to store the copy so that you can use it to restore or update your will if that becomes necessary. Other people should not have access to the computer file without your permission.

As with other unsigned and unwitnessed copies, the copy of your will stored in your computer, or in another electronic format such as on a CD-ROM, does not constitute a valid will. To be valid, a will must be printed out and formally signed and witnessed as discussed above.

Updating Your Will

Your will is an extremely personal document. Information such as your marital status, where you live, the property you own and whether you have children—all are examples of life choices that affect what you include in your will and what laws will be applied to enforce it.

Life wreaks havoc on even the best-laid plans. You may sell one house and buy another. You may divorce. You may have or adopt children. Eventually you will face the grief of losing a loved one. Not all life changes require you to change your will. However, significant ones often do. This chapter tells you when it's necessary to make a new will.

When to Make a New Will

The following occurrences signal that it is time for you to make a new will.

Marrying or Divorcing

Suppose that after you use Quicken WillMaker Plus to leave all or part of your property to your spouse, you get divorced. Under the law in many states, the divorce automatically cancels the bequest to the former spouse. The alternate beneficiary named for that bequest, or, if there is none, your residuary beneficiary, gets the property. In some states, however, your former spouse would still be entitled to take your property as directed in the will. If you remarry, state legal rules become even more murky. (In a few states, these rules also apply to registered domestic partners.)

Rather than deal with all these complexities, follow this simple rule: Make a new will if you marry, divorce, are separated and seriously considering divorce or if you register or dissolve a domestic partnership.

> **SEE AN EXPERT**
>
> **Beware of state laws on spouses' shares.** If you leave your spouse or registered domestic partner out of your will because you are separated, and you die before you become divorced, it is possible that the spouse or partner could claim a statutory share of your estate. (See "Your Spouse's Right to Inherit From You" in Chapter 5.) Consult a lawyer to find out how the laws of your state apply to this situation. (See Chapter 25.)

Getting or Losing Property

If you leave all your property in a lump to one or more people or organizations, there is no need to change your will if you acquire new items of property or get rid of existing ones—those individuals or organizations take all of your property at your death, without regard to what it is.

But if you have made specific bequests of property that you no longer own, it is wise to make a new will. If you leave a specific item—a particular Tiffany lamp, for example—to someone, but you no longer own the item when you die, the person named in your will to receive it may be out of luck. In most states, that person is not entitled to receive another item or money instead. In some states, however, the law presumes that you wanted the beneficiary to have something—and so gives him or her the right to a sum of money equal to the value of the gift. While this may be what you want, it could still disrupt your plan for how you want your property distributed. The legal word for a bequest that fails to make it in this way is ademption. People who do not get to take the property in question are often heard to use an earthier term.

However, in some circumstances, if a specific item has merely changed form, the original beneficiary may still have a claim to it. Examples of this are:

- a promissory note that has been paid and for which the cash is still available, and
- a house that is sold in exchange for a promissory note and deed of trust.

A problem similar to ademption occurs when there is not enough money to go around. For example, if you leave $50,000 each to your spouse and two children, but there is only $90,000 in your estate at your death, the gifts in the will must all be reduced. In legal lingo, this is called an abatement. How property is abated under state law is often problematic.

You can avoid these problems if you adjust the type and amount of your bequests to reflect reality—a task that may require both diligence and the commitment to make a new will periodically.

Adding or Losing Children

Each time a child is born or legally adopted into your family, the new child should be named in the will—where you are asked to name your children—and provided for according to your wishes. If you do not do this, the child might later challenge your will in court, claiming that he or she was overlooked as an heir and is entitled to a substantial share of your property. (See "Your Children" in Chapter 4.)

If any of your children die before you and leave children, you should name those grandchildren in your will. If they are not mentioned in your will, they might later be legally entitled to claim a share of your estate. (See "Grandchildren" in Chapter 4.)

Moving to a Different State

Quicken WillMaker Plus applies several state-specific laws when it helps you create your will. These laws are especially important in two situations.

- If you have set up one form of management for young beneficiaries and then move to a different state, you may find when making a new will that Quicken WillMaker Plus presents you with different management options. This is because some states have adopted the Uniform Transfers to Minors Act and others have not. If you want to see whether your new state offers different management options, see "The Uniform Transfers to Minors Act" in Chapter 7.
- If you are married and do not intend to leave all or most of your property to your spouse, review "Property Rules for Married People" in Chapter 5, which discusses the rules if you move from a community property state to a common law state or vice versa.

Losing Beneficiaries

If a beneficiary you have named to receive a significant amount of property dies before you,

you should make a new will. It is especially important to do this if you named only one beneficiary for a bequest and did not name an alternate—or if the alternate you named is no longer your first choice to get the property.

Losing Guardians or Property Managers

The first choice or alternate named to serve as a personal guardian for your minor children or those you have named to manage their property may move away, become disabled or simply turn out to be someone you consider unsuitable for the job. If so, you will probably want to make a new will naming a different person.

Losing an Executor

The executor of your estate is responsible for making sure your will provisions are carried out. If you decide that the executor you originally named is no longer suitable—or if he or she dies before you do—you should make a new will in which you name another person for the job.

Losing Witnesses

The witnesses who sign your will are responsible for testifying that the signature on your will is valid and that you appeared capable of making a will when you did so. If two or more of your witnesses become unable to fulfill this function, you may want to make a new will with new witnesses—especially if you have some inkling that anyone is likely to contest your will after you die. But a new will is probably not necessary if you have made

your will self-proving. (See "The Self-Proving Option" in Chapter 10.)

How to Make a New Will

It is easy to make a new will using Quicken WillMaker Plus. In fact, a subsequent swoop through the program will proceed even more quickly than the first time through, since you will know what to expect and will likely be familiar with many of the legal concepts you had to learn at first.

If you review your will and wish to change some of your answers, the program will automatically alert you to specific changes that may signal different laws applying to your situation. These include changes in:

- your marital or domestic partner status
- your state of residence
- the number of children you have, and
- your general approach to will making— from simple to complex, or vice versa.

If you make a new will, even if it only involves a few changes, you must follow the legal requirements for having it signed and witnessed just as if you were starting from scratch. If you choose to make your will self-proving, you must also complete a new affidavit.

> **CAUTION**
>
> **In with the new, out with the old.** As soon as you print, sign and have your new will witnessed, it will legally replace all wills you have made before it. But to avoid possible confusion, you should physically destroy all other original wills and any copies of them.

Explanatory Letters

In addition to the tasks that you can accomplish in a Quicken WillMaker Plus will, you may also wish to:

- explain why you are giving property to certain beneficiaries and not to others
- explain disparities in bequests
- express positive or negative sentiments about a beneficiary
- express wishes about how to care for a pet
- explain how shared gifts should be divided, or
- leave your loved ones a statement about your personal experiences, values or beliefs.

Quicken WillMaker Plus does not allow you to do these things in your will for one important reason: The program has been written, tested and tested again with painstaking attention to helping you make your own legal and unambiguous will. If you add general information, personal statements or reasons for making or not making a bequest, you risk the possibility of producing a document with conflicting, confusing or possibly even illegal provisions.

Fortunately, there is a way you can have a final say about personal matters without seriously risking your will's legal integrity. You can write a letter to accompany your will expressing your thoughts to those who survive you.

Since what you put in the letter will not have legal effect as part of your will, there is little danger that your expressions will tread upon the time-tested legal language of the will or cause other problems later. In fact, if

your will is ambiguous and your statement in the letter sheds some light on your intentions, judges may use the letter to help clarify your will. However, if your statements in the letter fully contradict provisions in your will, you may create interpretation problems after your death. For example, if you cut your daughter out of your will and also state in a letter attached to the will that she is your favorite child and that is why you are leaving her the family home, you are setting the stage for future confusion.

Keeping these cautions in mind, writing a letter to those who survive you to explain why you wrote your will as you did—and knowing they will read your reasoning at your death—can give you a great deal of peace of mind during life. It may also help explain potential slights and hurt feelings of surviving friends and family members. This chapter offers some guidance on how you can write a clear letter that expresses your wishes without jeopardizing the legality of your will.

An Introduction for Your Letter

A formal introduction to the letter you leave can help make it clear that what you write is an expression of your sentiments and not intended as a will—or an addition to or interpretation of your will.

After the introduction, you are free to express your sentiments, keeping in mind that your estate may be held liable for any false, derogatory statements you make about an individual or organization.

One suggested introduction follows.

To My Executor:

This letter expresses my feelings and reasons for certain decisions made in my will. It is not my will, nor do I intend it to be an interpretation of my will. My will, which I signed, dated and had witnessed on _____ , is the sole expression of my intentions concerning all my property and other matters covered in it.

Should anything I say in this letter conflict with, or seem to conflict with, any provision of my will, the will shall be followed.

I request that you give a copy of this letter to each person named in my will to take property, or act as a guardian or custodian, and to anyone else you determine should receive a copy.

Expressing Sentiments and Explaining Choices

There is little that a manual such as this can say to guide you in personal expressions of the heart. What follows are some suggestions about topics you might wish to cover.

Explaining Why Gifts Were Made

The Quicken WillMaker Plus requirement that you must keep descriptions of property and beneficiaries short and succinct may leave you unsatisfied. You may have thought hard and long about why you want a particular person to get particular property—and feel frustrated

that you are constrained in your will to listing your wishes in a few simple words. You can remedy that by explaining your feelings in a letter.

EXAMPLE:

[Introduction]

The gift of my fishing boat to my friend Hank is in remembrance of the many companionable days we enjoyed fishing together on the lake. Hank, I hope you're out there for many more years.

EXAMPLE:

[Introduction]

Julie, the reason I have given you the farm is that you love it as much as I do and I know you'll do your best to make sure it stays in the family. But please, if the time comes when personal or family concerns mean that it makes sense to sell it, do so with a light heart—and knowing that it's just what I would have done.

Explaining Disparities in Gifts

You may also wish to explain your reasons for leaving more property to one person than another. While it is certainly your prerogative to make or not make bequests as you wish, you can also guess that in a number of family situations, unbalanced shares may cause hurt feelings or hostility after your death.

Ideally, you could call those involved together during your life, explaining to them why you plan to leave your property as you do. However, if you wish to keep your property plans private until after you die—or would find such a meeting too painful or otherwise impossible—you can attach a letter of explanation to your will.

EXAMPLE:

[Introduction]

I love all my children equally. The reason I gave a smaller ownership share in the house to Tim than to my other children is that Tim received family funds to purchase his own home, so it is fair that my other two children receive more of my property now.

EXAMPLE:

[Introduction]

I am giving the bulk of my property to my son Jason for one reason: Because of his health problems, he needs it more.

Ted and Ellen, I love you just as much, and I am extremely proud of the life choices you have made. But the truth is that you two can manage fine without a boost from me, and Jason cannot.

Offering Suggestions for Shared Gifts

If you are leaving a shared gift that contains a number of specific items—such as "my household furnishings" or "my art collection"—you may have some thoughts on how you'd like your beneficiaries to divide up the property. Of course, you can use your will to control the size of the share that each beneficiary gets, but that that still leaves your survivors to figure out who gets which specific assets. For example, if you leave your entire estate to be shared equally by your three children, how should your executor decide who gets the house, who gets the bank accounts and who gets the cars?

You can use a letter to make suggestions to your executor about how you want your property divided. Your suggestions will not have any legal weight; your executor is required to follow the terms of your will, not the terms of your letter. However, your letter can give your executor valuable guidance about how to distribute property, within the terms of your will.

Even if you don't particularly care who gets which things, you may want to suggest a fair way of figuring it out, such as a lottery for the highly coveted items.

Whatever suggestions you give, be very careful not to contradict any of the gifts you make in your will.

EXAMPLE:

[Introduction]

I have left my library equally to my grand-children. I know each of them has enjoyed many of the books over the years and I want to make sure that each receives a few favorites. I suggest that you hold a drawing to determine the order in which each grandchild will choose a book, with each then taking a volume in turn until their favorites are spoken for. The rest of the library can be distributed—taken or given away—in whatever manner they choose.

Expressing Positive or Negative Sentiments

Whatever your plans for leaving your property, you may wish to attach a letter to your will in which you clear your mind of some sentiments you formed during life. These may be positive —thanking a loved one for kind acts. Or they may be negative—explaining why you are leaving a person out of your will.

EXAMPLE:

[Introduction]

The reason I left $10,000 to my physician Dr. Buski is not only that she treated me competently over the years but that she was unfailingly gentle and attentive. I always appreciated that she made herself available— day or night—and took the time to explain my ailments and treatments to me.

EXAMPLE:

[Introduction]

I am leaving nothing to my brother Malcolm. I wish him no ill will. But over the years, he has decided to isolate himself from me and the rest of the family and I don't feel I owe him anything.

Explaining Choices About Your Pet

As discussed in Chapter 4, the best way to provide a home for your pet is to use your will to name a caretaker for your pet and leave some money to that person to cover the costs of your pet's care. If you like, you can use your explanatory letter to say why you chose a particular person to watch over your animals after your death.

EXAMPLE:

[Introduction]

I have left my dog Cessna to my neighbor Belinda Mason because she has been a loving friend to him, taking care of him when I was on vacation or unwell. I know that Belinda and her three children will provide a caring and happy home for Cessna when I no longer can.

Leaving Details About Your Pet's Care

You may want to provide your pet's caretaker with information and suggestions about your pet's habits and needs. We recommend that you use Quicken WillMaker Plus's Information for Survivors and Caregivers form for this purpose. It allows you to leave specifics about each animal, including health needs, food and exercise requirements and sleeping habits. You can also use the document to describe memorial plans or final arrangements for your pet.

Describing Personal Experiences and Values

Many people are interested in leaving behind more than just property. If you wish, you can also leave a statement about the experiences, values and beliefs that have shaped your life. This kind of letter or document is often known as an "ethical will," and it can be of great worth to those who survive you.

While you could legally include an ethical will statement in your regular will—that is, the one you make to leave your property to others—we recommend that you include these sentiments in your explanatory letter or in a separate document. The reasons are the same

as those mentioned earlier: It's better to avoid including anything potentially confusing or ambiguous in your legal will.

As long as you don't contradict the provisions of your legal will, your options for expressing yourself are limited only by the time and energy you have for the project. You could do something as simple as use your explanatory letter to set out a concise description of your basic values. Or, if you feel inspired, you may leave something much more detailed for your loved ones. Many survivors are touched to learn about important life stories, memories and events. You might also consider including photographs or other mementos with your letter. If writing things down seems like too much effort, you could use an audio or videotape to talk to those who are closest to you. A little thought will surely yield many creative ways to express yourself to those you care for.

RESOURCE

More information about ethical wills. If you want to go beyond writing down some of your experiences and values in your explanatory letter, there is a growing body of websites and literature that can help you explore different ways of making an ethical will. You might begin by visiting www.ethicalwill.com. The site offers some basic free information and sells ethical will-writing kits.

About Living Trusts

A trust is an arrangement under which one person, called the trustee, owns property on behalf of someone else, called the beneficiary. You can create a trust simply by preparing and signing a document called a Declaration of Trust.

The trusts you can make with Quicken WillMaker Plus are called "revocable living trusts." Revocable means you can revoke them at any time. They're called "living" trusts because they're created when you're alive, not at your death like some other kinds of trusts. Sometimes, living trusts are known by their Latin name: *inter vivos* (among the living) trusts.

Quicken WillMaker Plus makes two kinds of revocable living trusts: a basic living trust, which lets you avoid probate, and an AB or bypass trust, which both avoids probate and may also eliminate estate taxes after your death.

About Basic Living Trusts

This basic trust is simple to set up and makes transferring property after your death quick and easy. It does not affect taxes at all.

How a Basic Trust Helps Your Family

If you make a basic living trust, you can save your family a great deal of time and money. The big advantage is that property left through a trust avoids probate. There are other pluses as well.

Avoiding Probate

Unless you make a trust or use some other probate-avoidance method (such as owning real estate in joint tenancy or designating a payable-on-death beneficiary for a bank account), your property will probably have to go through probate before the beneficiaries receive it. Generally, property left through a will must go through probate.

In the probate process, the will (if there is one) is proved valid in court, and debts are paid. Then, the remaining property is distributed to the beneficiaries named in the will, or, if there isn't a will, the closest relatives. The cost of probate varies widely from state to state, but attorney, court and other fees can eat up about 5% of your estate (the property you leave at death), leaving that much less to go to the people you want to get it. If the estate is complicated, the fees can be even larger.

The Cost of Probate	
If you leave property worth:	**Probate may cost about:**
$200,000	$10,000
$500,000	$25,000

At least as bad as the expense of probate is the delay it causes. In many states, probate can take a year or two, during which time the beneficiaries generally get nothing unless the judge allows the immediate family a small "family allowance."

If you own real estate in more than one state, it's usually necessary to have a whole separate probate proceeding in each state. That means the surviving relatives must probably find and hire a lawyer in each state and pay for multiple probate proceedings.

A Miniglossary of Living Trust Terms

Unfortunately, you can't escape legal lingo entirely when you deal with living trusts. A complete onscreen glossary is always available when you're using Quicken WillMaker Plus. (See the Users' Manual.) But keeping it to a minimum, here's what you need to know:

- The person who sets up the living trust (that's you) is called a **grantor**, **trustor** or **settlor**.
- The person who has power over the trust property is called the **trustee**. You are the original trustee of your living trust, so you keep total control over property in the trust. If you and your spouse or partner make a trust together, both of you are trustees.
- The property you transfer to the trustee is called, collectively, the trust property or trust **principal**. (And, of course, there's a Latin version: the trust **corpus**.)

- The person you name to take over as trustee after your death (or, with a shared trust, after the death of both grantors) is called the **successor trustee**. The successor trustee's job is to transfer the trust property to the beneficiaries, following the instructions in the Declaration of Trust. The successor trustee may also manage trust property inherited by young beneficiaries.
- The trust **beneficiaries** inherit the trust property when the grantor dies. With a basic trust, there is just one kind of beneficiary. If you make an AB trust, there are two kinds: the **life beneficiary**, who is always the surviving spouse, and the **final beneficiaries**, who inherit trust property after both spouses have died.

From the family's point of view, probate's headaches are rarely justified. If the estate contains common kinds of property—a house, stocks, bank accounts, a small business, cars—and no relatives are fighting about it, the property merely needs to be handed over to the new owners. In the vast majority of cases, the probate process entails nothing more than tedious paperwork, and the attorney is nothing more than a very highly paid clerk.

Avoiding the Need for a Conservatorship or Guardianship

A living trust can be useful if you become incapable, because of physical or mental illness, of taking care of your financial affairs. That's because the person you named to serve as trustee at your death (or, if you made a shared trust, the other grantor) can take over management of the trust assets. The person who takes over has authority to manage all property in the trust and to use it for your benefit.

> EXAMPLE: Margaret creates a living trust, appointing herself as trustee. The trust states that if she someday can no longer manage her own affairs, her daughter Elizabeth will replace her as trustee.

If there is no living trust and you haven't made other arrangements for someone to take over your finances if you become incapacitated, a court must appoint someone. Typically, the spouse or adult child of the person seeks this authority and is called a conservator or guardian. (See Chapter 22.)

Keeping Your Estate Plan Confidential

When your will is filed with the probate court after you die, it becomes a matter of public record. A living trust, on the other hand, is a private document in most states. Because the living trust document is never filed with a court or other government entity, what you leave to whom remains private. (There is one exception: Records of real estate transfers are always public.)

Some states require that you register your living trust with the local court. But there are no legal consequences or penalties if you don't. (Registration is explained in Chapter 18.)

The only way the terms of a living trust might become public is if—and this is very unlikely—someone files a lawsuit to challenge the trust or collect a court judgment you owe. (See below.)

CAUTION

Special state rules. In a few states, after a grantor dies, the successor trustee must disclose certain facts about the living trust. For details, see Chapter 21.

How a Basic Trust Works

A basic revocable living trust does, essentially, what a will does: leaves your property to the people you want to inherit it. But because a trustee owns your property, your assets don't have to go through probate at your death.

When you create a revocable living trust, you appoint yourself trustee, with full power to manage trust property. Then you transfer ownership of some or all of your property to yourself as trustee. You keep absolute control over the property held in trust. You can:

- sell, mortgage or give away property held in trust
- put ownership of trust property back in your own name
- add property to the trust
- change the beneficiaries
- name a different successor trustee, or
- revoke the trust completely.

> EXAMPLE: Ashley creates a revocable living trust and names herself as trustee. She transfers her valuable property—a house and some stocks—to herself as trustee. As trustee, she can sell, mortgage or give away the trust property, or take it out of the trust and put it back into her name.

If you and your spouse or partner create a trust together, both of you must consent to changes, although either of you can revoke the trust entirely.

After you die, the person you named in your trust document to be "successor trustee" takes over. This person transfers the trust property to the relatives, friends or charities you named as the trust beneficiaries. No probate is necessary for property that was held in trust. In most cases, the whole thing can be handled within a few weeks. When the property has all been transferred to the beneficiaries, the living trust ceases to exist.

If any of your beneficiaries inherit trust property while still young (not yet 35), the successor trustee (or the surviving grantor, if you made a trust with someone) has more responsibility. The successor trustee will follow the instructions you left in the trust document, and either:

- transfer the property inherited by the child to the "custodian" you chose, to manage the property until the child reaches an age specified by your state's law (21 in most states, but up to 25 in a few states), or
- keep the property in a "child's subtrust," using it for the child's benefit, until the child reaches an age you designate.

Both methods are explained in Chapters 15, 16 and 17.

Other Ways to Avoid Probate

A living trust isn't the only probate-avoidance method around. Here are some methods you might want to investigate, to use with or instead of a living trust.

Payable-on-Death Bank Accounts

Payable-on-death bank accounts offer one of the easiest ways to keep money—even large sums of it—out of probate. All you need to do is fill out a simple form, provided by the bank, naming the person you want to inherit the money in the account at your death.

As long as you are alive, the person you named to inherit the money in a payable-on-death (P.O.D.) account has no rights to it. You can spend the money, name a different beneficiary or close the account. At your death, the beneficiary just goes to the bank, shows proof of the death and of his or her identity and collects whatever funds are in the account. The probate court is never involved.

Transfer-on-Death Registration of Securities

Every state but Texas has adopted a law (the Uniform Transfer-on-Death Securities Registration Act) that lets you name someone to inherit your stocks, bonds or brokerage accounts without probate. It works very much like a payable-on-death bank account. When you register your ownership, either with the stockbroker or the company itself, you make a request to take ownership in what's called "beneficiary form." When the papers that show your ownership are issued, they will also show the name of your beneficiary.

After you register ownership this way, the beneficiary has no rights to the stock as long as you are alive. You are free to sell it, give it away or name a different beneficiary. But on your death, the beneficiary can claim the securities without probate, simply by providing proof of death and some identification to the broker or transfer agent. (A transfer agent is a business that is authorized by a corporation to handle stock transfers.)

Transfer-on-Death Deeds for Real Estate

In Arizona, Arkansas, Colorado, Kansas, Missouri, Montana, New Mexico, Nevada, Ohio and Wisconsin, you can prepare a deed now but have it take effect only at your death. These transfer-on-death deeds must be prepared, signed, notarized and recorded (filed in the county land records office) just like a regular deed. But unlike a regular deed, you can revoke a transfer-on-death deed. The deed must expressly state that it does not take effect until death.

Check your state's statute for the rules in your state. Several of the statutes provide deed forms.

Transfer-on-Death Registration for Vehicles

So far, only California, Connecticut, Kansas, Missouri and Ohio offer car owners the sensible option of naming a beneficiary, right on the certificate of title or title application, to inherit a vehicle. If you do this, the beneficiary you name has no rights as long as you are alive. You are free to sell or give away the car, or name someone else as the beneficiary.

To name a transfer-on-death beneficiary, all you do is apply for registration in "beneficiary form." The new certificate lists the name of the beneficiary, who will automatically own the vehicle after your death. You can find more information on the website of your state's motor vehicles department.

Retirement Plans

Retirement plans such as IRAs, 401(k)s and Keoghs don't have to go through probate. All you need to do is name a beneficiary to receive the funds at your death, and no probate will be necessary.

Life Insurance

Life insurance proceeds are subject to probate only if the beneficiary named in the policy is your estate. That's done occasionally if the estate will need immediate cash to pay debts and taxes, but it's usually counterproductive.

Joint Tenancy

Joint tenancy is an efficient and practical way to transfer some kinds of property without probate.

Joint tenancy is a way two or more people can hold title to property they own together. All joint owners (called joint tenants) must own equal shares of the property. (Vermont and Connecticut are exceptions; joint owners there may own unequal shares.) When one joint owner dies, the surviving owners automatically get complete ownership of the property. This is called the "right of survivorship." The property doesn't go through probate court—there is only some simple paperwork to fill out to transfer the property into the name of the surviving owner.

A will doesn't affect who inherits joint tenancy property. So even if your will leaves your half-interest in joint tenancy property to someone else, the surviving owners will still inherit it.

This rule isn't as ironclad as it may sound. You can, while still alive, break the joint tenancy by transferring your interest in the property to someone else (or, in some states, to yourself, but not as a joint tenant).

Joint tenancy often works well when couples acquire real estate or other valuable property together. If they take title in joint tenancy, probate is avoided when the first owner dies—though not (unlike a living trust) when the second owner dies.

Joint tenancy is usually a poor estate planning device when an older person, seeking only to avoid probate, puts solely owned property into joint tenancy with someone else. If you make someone else a co-owner, in joint tenancy, of property that you now own yourself, you give up half ownership of the property. The new owner has rights that you can't take back. For example, the new owner can sell or mortgage his or her share. And federal gift tax may be assessed on the transfer.

There can also be serious problems if one joint tenant becomes incapacitated and cannot make decisions. The other owners must get legal authority to sell or mortgage the property. That may mean going to court to get someone (called a conservator or guardian, in most states) appointed to manage the incapacitated person's affairs. (This problem can be partially dealt with if the joint tenant has signed a document called a "durable power of attorney," giving someone authority to manage her affairs if she cannot. See Chapter 22.) With a living trust, if you (the grantor) become incapacitated, the successor trustee (or the other spouse, if you made a trust together) takes over and has

full authority to manage the property. No court proceedings are necessary.

Several states have abolished or restricted joint tenancy; see below.

State Restrictions on Joint Tenancy

Alaska. No joint tenancies for real estate, except for husband and wife, who may own property as tenants by the entirety. (See below.)

Oregon. A transfer of real estate to husband and wife creates a tenancy by the entirety, not joint tenancy. All other transfers in joint tenancy create a tenancy in common. (See "Property You Own With Others," in Chapter 5.)

Tennessee. A transfer of real estate to husband and wife creates a tenancy by the entirety, not joint tenancy. All other transfers in joint tenancy create a tenancy in common. (See "Property You Own With Others," in Chapter 5.)

Texas. A joint tenancy can be created only if you sign a separate written agreement.

Wisconsin. No joint tenancies between spouses after January 1, 1986. If spouses attempt to create a joint tenancy, it will be treated as community property with right of survivorship. (See below.)

Tenancy by the Entirety

"Tenancy by the entirety" is a form of property ownership that is similar to joint tenancy. About half the states offer it, and it is limited to married couples or same-sex couples who have registered with the state (in states that allow this).

States That Allow Tenancy by the Entirety

Alaska[1]	Maryland	Oklahoma
Arkansas	Massachusetts	Oregon[1]
Delaware[1]	Michigan	Pennsylvania
Dist. of Col.	Mississippi	Rhode Island
Florida	Missouri	Tennessee
Hawaii	New Jersey	Utah[1]
Illinois[1]	New York[1]	Vermont
Indiana[1]	North Carolina	Virginia
Kentucky[1]	Ohio[2]	Wyoming

[1] Allowed for real estate only
[2] Only if created before April 4, 1985

Tenancy by the entirety has many of the same advantages and disadvantages of joint tenancy and is most useful in the same kind of situation: when a couple acquires property together. When one owner dies, the surviving co-owner inherits the property. The property doesn't go through probate.

If property is held in tenancy by the entirety, neither spouse or partner can transfer his or her half of the property alone, either while alive or by will or trust. It must go to the survivor. (This is different from joint tenancy; a joint tenant is free to transfer his or her share to someone else during his or her life.)

EXAMPLE: Fred and Ethel hold title to their house in tenancy by the entirety. If Fred wanted to sell or give away his half-interest in the house, he could not do so without Ethel's signature on the deed.

Community Property With Right of Survivorship

In a few states, married couples (and in California, registered domestic partners) can own property together "as community property with right of survivorship." When one spouse dies, the other automatically inherits the property, without probate. The states that offer this option are Alaska, Arizona, California, Nevada and Wisconsin.

Simplified Probate Proceedings

Many states have begun, slowly, to dismantle some of the more onerous parts of probate. They have created categories of property and beneficiaries that don't have to go through a full-blown probate court proceeding. If your family can take advantage of these procedures after your death, you may not need to worry too much about avoiding probate.

Almost every state has some kind of simplified (summary) probate or out-of-court transfer process for one or more of these categories:

Small estates. Most states offer streamlined probate court procedures for small estates; what qualifies as a small estate varies widely from state to state. In many states, even if your total estate is too large to qualify as a small estate, your heirs can still make use of the simplified procedures if the amount that actually goes through probate is under the limit.

Personal property. If the estate is small, many states also let people collect personal property (that's anything but real estate) they've inherited by filling out a sworn statement (affidavit) and giving it to the person who has the property. Typically, the beneficiary must also provide some kind of proof of his or her right to inherit, such as a death certificate and copy of the will.

Property left to the surviving spouse. In some states, if a surviving spouse inherits less than a certain amount of property, no probate is necessary.

RESOURCE

For more about probate avoidance, see *8 Ways to Avoid Probate*, by Mary Randolph (Nolo).

The Tax-Saving AB (Bypass) Trust

The federal estate tax is imposed after your death, on property you left at your death. Because everyone is entitled to a large estate tax exemption, the tax affects only large estates, and only about 1% of Americans end up owing it.

The Future of the Estate and Gift Tax

In 2001, Congress passed legislation repealing the estate tax—but not until 2010. Meanwhile, the exemption amount is going up, and the tax rates have gone down, meaning that fewer people than ever need to worry about estate

tax. The exact dates and amounts are shown below.

It appears likely that Congress will revive the tax in some form, probably with a high exemption amount, before 2010. In 2011, the estate tax repeal will expire unless Congress votes to renew it.

Congress did not repeal the federal gift tax, although it raised the exemption and lowered the maximum rate. The lifetime gift tax exemption is $1 million, and (unlike the estate tax exemption) will stay there. That means you can make a total of $1 million of taxable gifts before owing any federal gift tax.

How the Estate Tax Will Fade Away			
Year of Death	Unified Estate/ Gift Tax Exemption	Gift Tax Exemption	Highest Estate and Gift Tax Rate
2008	$2 million	$1 million	45%
2009	$3.5 million	$1 million	45%
2010	Estate tax repealed	$1 million	top individual income tax rate (gift tax only)
2011	$1 million unless Congress extends repeal	$1 million	50% unless Congress extends repeal

How an AB Trust May Help Your Family

If you're married, estate tax is most likely to be an issue when the second spouse dies. When the first spouse dies, everything left to the survivor, if he or she is a U.S. citizen, passes tax-free. This rule is called the unlimited marital deduction.

Sounds good. But older couples who have a large combined estate and leave everything to each other may be in for a big estate tax bill on the death of the second spouse. The marital deduction really just postpones estate tax until the second spouse dies.

Say, for example, a husband leaves all his property to his wife. At the husband's death, no estate tax is due. But when the widow dies, the marital deduction won't apply—and now her estate may exceed the amount of the federal estate tax exemption. Her estate will have to pay a much larger tax than if the husband had left his property directly to children or other beneficiaries.

An AB trust can eliminate estate tax for couples who together own up to twice as much as the estate tax exemption. It works by making the first spouse's estate subject to tax at his or her death—but not at the second spouse's. That way, each spouse's estate stays under the estate tax threshold; they're never combined for estate tax purposes. Just how the trust does this is explained in the next section.

Same-sex couples. Married same-sex couples have special concerns when it comes to estate tax planning. Under current laws, same-sex marriage is legal in California and Massachusetts. But the federal government does not now recognize these marriages, which means a surviving same-sex spouse does not inherit property from the deceased spouse free of federal estate tax.

How an AB Trust Works

In a nutshell, an AB trust generally works like this example: The first spouse to die leaves his property to his children, not his spouse. But the children don't get it outright—it's in trust. And the trust gives the surviving spouse the right to any income from the property, and the right to spend the property itself for certain purposes, for the rest of her life. Only at the second spouse's death does the property go outright to the kids.

The tax break comes because the surviving spouse never legally owns the trust property, and so the property isn't part of her estate. If the survivor had inherited the property outright, it would have been subject to estate tax at her death.

> **EXAMPLE:** Thomas and Maria, husband and wife, are in their mid-70s, and each has assets worth $1.9 million. Thomas dies in 2007, and Maria two years later. Here's the tax situation, with and without an AB trust:
>
> - **Without an AB trust.** Thomas leaves everything outright to Maria. No estate tax is assessed because of the marital deduction. But the size of Maria's estate rises to $3.8 million. At her death, all property in excess of the exempt amount in 2009, $3.5 million, is taxed.
> - **With an AB trust.** Thomas and Maria establish an AB trust, with the income to go to the survivor for life and the principal to the children at the survivor's death. When Thomas dies, his $1.9 million is not taxed because

it's below the exempt amount. The value of Maria's estate remains at $1.9 million.

When Maria dies, $3.5 million can be left to anyone free of estate tax, so there is no estate tax liability on her $1.9 million, which goes to the children. The $1.9 million that Thomas left in trust also goes to the children; it isn't taxed, because it was below the exemption amount at Thomas's death. It isn't part of Maria's estate, because she is not considered the owner.

Unlike a basic revocable living trust, an AB trust controls what happens to property for years after the first spouse's death. If you make one, you must be sure that the surviving spouse will be financially and emotionally comfortable receiving only the income from the money or property placed in trust, with the children (or other persons) as the actual owner of the property.

The surviving spouse is entitled to any income that property in the irrevocable trust produces. More important, the trust document gives the survivor the right to use any amount of the principal necessary for his or her "health, education, support and maintenance in accord with his or her accustomed manner of living." This is the broadest standard the IRS allows for an AB trust. (26 CFR 20.2041-1(c)(2).) If the surviving spouse were given broader powers, the IRS would consider her the owner of the property—which would destroy the estate tax advantage of holding the property in trust.

This means that the surviving spouse can, for example, live in a house owned by the irrevocable trust. And if faced with a need to spend trust principal for medical needs or another kind of emergency, she can go ahead.

You can, if you wish, give the surviving spouse the power to decide whether or not to set up a tax-saving bypass trust. This option, and how to decide whether or not an AB trust is right for you, are discussed in Chapter 14.

State Estate and Inheritance Taxes

Even if your estate isn't big enough to owe federal estate tax, the state may still take a bite.

Estate tax. Until 2005, most states didn't impose their own estate tax; instead, they took a share of the federal estate tax paid by large estates. (This is called a "pick-up" or "sop" tax.) But the federal legislation that started the phase-out of the federal estate tax also took away the share of estate tax that states got to keep. To get back some of what they lost, some states are collecting tax from estates that aren't big enough to owe any federal tax. So far, almost half the states have changed their laws so they can keep collecting estate tax.

Inheritance tax. Some states impose a separate tax on a deceased person's property, called an inheritance tax. The tax rate depends on who inherits the property; usually, spouses and other close relatives pay nothing or a low rate.

For each state's rules, see *Plan Your Estate*, by Denis Clifford, or *The Executor's Guide: Settling a Loved One's Estate or Trust*, by Mary Randolph (both published by Nolo).

Other Ways to Save on Estate Taxes

Here are other tax-saving strategies you may want to use in addition to—or instead of—an AB trust.

Annual tax-exempt gifts. If you don't need all your income and property to live on, making sizable gifts while you're alive can be a good way to reduce eventual federal estate taxes before that tax is repealed. Currently, only gifts larger than $12,000 made to one person or organization in one calendar year count toward the personal estate tax exemption. You can give smaller gifts tax-free.

> EXAMPLE: Allen and Julia give each of their two daughters $24,000 every year for four years. They have transferred $176,000 without becoming liable for gift tax.

Other tax-exempt gifts. Other gifts are exempt regardless of amount, including:

- gifts between spouses who are U.S. citizens (gifts to spouses who are not United States citizens are exempt only up to $128,000 per year)
- gifts paid directly for medical bills or school tuition, and
- gifts to tax-exempt charitable organizations.

Charitable trusts. If you want to make a big contribution to a charitable cause you care about—and at the same time cut your income taxes now and guarantee some income for life—then a charitable trust may be for you. They're not just for the very rich; you can contribute to a "pooled" charitable trust with as little as $5,000.

QTIPs and QDOTs. These trusts, known by their catchy acronyms (easier to say than Qualified Terminable Interest Property trust, you have to admit), are mainly used by married couples concerned about estate tax. A QTIP lets couples postpone paying estate tax until the second spouse's death, and also lock in, while both are still alive, who inherits the property at the second spouse's death. A QDOT is useful when a spouse who is not a U.S. citizen stands to inherit a large amount of property.

Life insurance trusts. Although the proceeds of a life insurance policy don't go through probate, they are included in your estate for federal estate tax purposes. You can reduce the tax bill by giving ownership of the policy to a life insurance trust (or to the beneficiary directly) at least three years before your death. But like other estate tax-saving strategies, this one will have to be reassessed in light of the planned estate tax repeal.

What Living Trusts Cannot Do

As wonderful as living trusts can be, they aren't a complete estate plan by themselves. Here are some things that trusts can't do.

Shelter Assets for Purposes of Medicaid Eligibility

You cannot affect your eligibility for Medicaid by holding property in a revocable living trust. Assets held in a living trust are "countable resources" for purposes of Medicaid qualification. Because you have complete control over trust assets, those assets are treated just as if you owned them in your own name.

RESOURCE

Long-Term Care: How to Plan & Pay for It, by Joseph Matthews (Nolo), explains Medicaid eligibility and asset protection in detail.

Convey Your Wishes About Medical Intervention

A living trust has absolutely nothing to do with conveying your wishes about life support systems and other medical intervention at the end of life. You'll need other documents—an advance directive ("living will") and durable power of attorney—to make your wishes clear and legally binding. (See Chapter 23.)

Protect Assets From Creditors

A living trust does not provide any protection from creditors. Because you keep the power to transfer the property back to yourself or revoke the trust entirely, if a creditor sues you and wins, and a court issues a judgment against you, the creditor can seize trust property to pay off the judgment.

Change Your Obligations to Your Family

Most married people leave much, if not all, of their property to their spouses. But if you don't leave your spouse at least half of your property, your spouse may have the right to go to court and claim some of your property after your death. Some or all of the property you had earmarked for other beneficiaries would go to your spouse.

CAUTION

Be cautious if you're getting divorced. You could also run into trouble from a former spouse if you try to transfer assets in or out of trust while your divorce proceeding is pending. Some states have very specific rules about what you may and may not do during this period.

The rights of spouses vary from state to state. The most important differences are between community property states and non-community property states. The details are discussed in "Your Spouse's Right to Inherit From You" in Chapter 5.

SEE AN EXPERT

Don't try to cut out your spouse. If you don't plan to leave at least half of the property in your estate to your spouse, you should consult a lawyer experienced in estate planning.

State law may also give your spouse the right to inherit the family residence, or at least use it for his or her life. The Florida constitution, for example, gives a surviving spouse the deceased spouse's residence. (Fla. Const. Art. 10, § 4.) And Minnesota law requires that a homestead (a dwelling owned and occupied by a deceased person at death) pass to the surviving spouse, regardless of a will provision to the contrary, if the deceased has no descendents. If there are descendents, the homestead goes to the surviving spouse for life and then to the descendents. (Minn. Stat. § 524.2-402.)

Lawsuits by a Child

Children usually have no right to inherit anything from their parents. There are two exceptions: laws that give minor children certain rights and laws that protect children who are unintentionally overlooked in a will.

Minor Children

State law may give your minor children (less than 18 years old) the right to inherit the family residence. The Florida constitution, for example, prohibits the head of a family from leaving his residence in his will (except to his spouse) if he is survived by a spouse or minor child. (Fla. Const. Art. 10, § 4.)

Overlooked Children

State laws protect offspring who appear to have been unintentionally overlooked in a parent's will. As the use of living trusts becomes more widespread, states have begun to expand protection to children who go unmentioned in living trusts.

Typically, these laws protect a child born after the parent's will is signed. The law presumes that the parent didn't mean to cut that child out, but simply didn't get around to writing a new will. The child can claim a share (the size depends on state law) of the deceased parent's property, which may include property in a living trust.

If you don't want to leave any property to one or more of your children, the easy way to avoid any later misunderstandings or legal claims is to make a will and mention each child in it. You don't have to leave a child any property. (See Chapter 4.)

Overlooked grandchildren. Children have no right to inherit from their grandparents unless their parent has died. In that case, the grandchildren can claim whatever the deceased child would have been legally entitled to.

Using a Back-Up Will

Even though you create a living trust, you will almost certainly need a simple back-up will, too. Like a living trust, a will is a document in which you specify what is to be done with your property when you die. You can make your will with Quicken WillMaker Plus. See Chapter 3.

Why Make a Will?

Having a will is important for several reasons.

First, a will is an essential back-up device for property that you don't get around to transferring to your living trust. For example, if you acquire property shortly before you die, you may not think to transfer ownership of it to your trust—which means that it won't pass under the terms of the trust document. But in your back-up will, you can include a clause that says who should get any property that you haven't specifically left to someone.

If you don't have a will, any property that isn't transferred by your living trust or other probate-avoidance device (such as joint tenancy) will go to your closest relatives, in an order determined by state law. These laws may not distribute property in the way you would have chosen. For example, if you die leaving a spouse and children, all the property that isn't subject to a living trust or will may be divided among your spouse and children. If your children are minors, that means there must be a court proceeding to get a guardian appointed to manage the property for them.

Second, in a will you can name someone to be the personal guardian of your minor child, in case you and the child's other parent die while the child is still under 18. You can't do that in a living trust.

Finally, if you want to leave nothing to your spouse or a child, you must make your wishes clear in a will. (State law may give your spouse or minor child the right to claim some of your estate; see Chapter 15, 16 or 17.)

Avoiding Conflicts Between Your Will and Living Trust

When you make both a living trust and a back-up will, pay attention to how the two work together. If your will and your trust document contain conflicting provisions, at the least you will create confusion among your inheritors, and at the worst, bitter disputes—maybe even a lawsuit—among friends and family.

Here are some no-no's:

- Don't leave the same property in your living trust and will, even if it's to the same beneficiary. If you transfer the property to your living trust and name a beneficiary in the trust document, that's all you need to do. Mentioning the property in the will raises the possibility of probate.

- Don't leave the same property to different beneficiaries in your will and your living trust.
- Don't name different people to be executor of your will and successor trustee of your living trust, especially if you think they might quarrel about how your affairs should be handled. There's one important exception: If you make a trust with your spouse, you may want to name your spouse as executor of your will, but not as successor trustee—the successor trustee takes over only after both spouses have died. (See Chapter 15, 16 or 17.)

Pour-Over Wills

Some lawyers advise people who make living trusts to make "pour-over wills" instead of a plain back-up will. A pour-over will takes all the property you haven't gotten around to transferring to your living trust and, at your death, leaves it to the trust.

Pour-over wills (named because everything is "poured over" from the will to your living trust) do not avoid probate. If the value of the property left through a pour-over will is small, however, some states exempt it from probate or offer streamlined probate procedures. This is true whether or not the will is a pour-over one.

If probate is required, a pour-over will actually has a disadvantage that standard wills don't: It forces the living trust to go on for months after your death, because the property left through the will must go through probate before it can be transferred to the trust. Usually, the property left in a living trust can be distributed to the beneficiaries, and the trust ended, within a few weeks after the person's death.

EXAMPLE: Joy transfers her valuable property to her living trust. She also makes a pour-over will, which states that any property she owns at death not specifically left to someone in the will goes to the living trust. When Joy dies, the property left through her will goes to the trust and is distributed to the residuary beneficiary of her living trust, her son Louis. The living trust must be kept going until probate of the will is finished, when property left by the will is poured over into the living trust.

If Joy had simply named Louis as the residuary beneficiary of a plain back-up will, the result would have been the same, but the process would have been simpler. The living trust would have been ended a few weeks after Joy's death. And after probate was finished, Louis would have received whatever property passed through Joy's will.

A pour-over will can be useful if you set up a child's subtrust for a young beneficiary in your living trust. You may want any property that child inherits through your will to go into the subtrust. Otherwise, you would create two trusts for the beneficiary: one in the will and one in your living trust.

EXAMPLE: Jessica makes a living trust and leaves the bulk of her property to her 12-year-old son. She arranges, in the trust document, for any trust property her son inherits before the age of 30 to be kept in a subtrust. Jessica also makes a back-up will, in which she again arranges for a subtrust to be set up if she should die before her son is 30. So if Jessica dies before her son reaches 30, two subtrusts will be set up for him.

If Jessica used a pour-over will, any property her son inherited through the will would go into the subtrust created by her living trust. Only half the paperwork would be necessary.

If you want to add a pour-over bequest to your will, see "Making Specific Bequests" in Chapter 6.

Drawbacks of a Living Trust

A living trust—especially an AB trust—does have unique problems and complications. Most people think the benefits outweigh the drawbacks, but you should be aware of them.

Paperwork

Setting up a living trust isn't difficult or expensive, but it requires some paperwork. The first step is to use Quicken WillMaker Plus to create and print out a trust document, which you should sign in front of a notary public. That's no harder than making a will.

There is, however, one more essential step to making a living trust effective: You must make sure that ownership of all the property you listed in the trust document is legally transferred to you as trustee of the trust.

If an item of property doesn't have a title (ownership) document, you can simply list it on a document called an Assignment of Property. (Quicken WillMaker Plus generates this document automatically.) Most books, furniture, electronics, jewelry, appliances, musical instruments and many other kinds of property can be handled this way.

But if an item has a title document—real estate, stocks, mutual funds, bonds, money market accounts or vehicles, for example—you must change the title document to show that the property is held in trust. For example, if you want to put your house into your living trust, you must prepare and sign a new deed, transferring ownership to you as trustee of the trust (or, in Colorado, to the trust itself). (Chapter 19 explains how.)

Record Keeping

After a revocable living trust is created, little day-to-day record keeping is required. No separate income tax records or returns are necessary as long as you are both the grantor and the trustee. (IRS Reg. § 1.671-4.) Income from property held in the living trust is reported on your personal income tax return.

You must keep written records whenever you transfer property to or from the trust, which isn't difficult unless you transfer a lot of property in and out of the trust. (Chapter 20 discusses transferring property in and out of your living trust.)

EXAMPLE: Monica and David Fielding put their house in a living trust to avoid probate, but later decide to sell it. In the real estate contract and deed transferring ownership to the new owners, Monica and David sign their names "as trustees of the Monica and David Fielding Revocable Living Trust."

An AB trust requires additional record keeping and paperwork after the first spouse dies. It also usually entails legal fees when, at the first spouse's death, the trust may be split into Trust A and Trust B. (One trust contains the deceased spouse's assets and is irrevocable; the other contains the surviving spouse's assets and is revocable.) Splitting the couple's assets in a way that yields the greatest tax benefits can be a tricky job, requiring the services of a good tax lawyer.

The surviving spouse must then obtain a taxpayer ID number for the irrevocable trust and file an annual trust income tax return, IRS Form 1041. This usually isn't a big deal but, like any tax return, it requires some work. The surviving spouse must also keep two sets of records, one of income and transactions involving his or her own property, including property in Trust B, and one for Trust A property.

Transfer Taxes

In most states, transfers of real estate to revocable living trusts are exempt from transfer taxes that are usually imposed on real estate transfers. But in a few states, transferring real estate to your living trust could trigger a tax. (See Chapter 19.)

Difficulty Refinancing Trust Property

Because legal title to trust real estate is held in the name of the trustee, a few banks and title companies may balk if you want to refinance it. They should be sufficiently reassured if you show them a copy of your trust document, which specifically gives you, as trustee, the power to borrow against trust property.

In the unlikely event you can't convince an uncooperative lender to deal with you in your capacity as trustee, you'll have to find another lender (which shouldn't be hard) or transfer the property out of the trust and back into your name. Later, after you refinance, you can transfer it back into the living trust.

No Cutoff of Creditors' Claims

Most people don't worry that after their death, creditors will try to collect large debts from property in the estate. In most situations, the surviving relatives simply pay the valid debts, such as outstanding bills, taxes and last illness and funeral expenses. But if you are concerned about the possibility of large claims, you may want to let your property go through probate instead of a living trust.

If your property goes through probate, creditors have only a certain amount of time to file claims against your estate. A creditor who was properly notified of the probate court proceeding cannot file a claim after the period—about six months, in most states—expires.

> **EXAMPLE:** Elaine is a real estate investor with a good-sized portfolio of property. She has many creditors and is sometimes named in lawsuits. It might be to her advantage to have assets go through a probate, which cuts off the claims of creditors who are properly notified of the probate proceeding.

On the other hand, when property isn't probated, creditors still have the right to be paid (if the debt is valid) from the property. There is no formal claim procedure, however. The creditor may not know who inherited the deceased debtor's property, and once the property is found, the creditor may have to file a lawsuit, which may not be worth the time and expense.

If you want to take advantage of probate's creditor cutoff, you must let all your property pass through probate. If not, there's a good chance the creditor could still sue (even after the probate claim cutoff) and try to collect from the property that didn't go through probate and passed instead through your living trust.

What Kind of Living Trust Do You Need?

Quicken WillMaker Plus makes two kinds of revocable living trusts: a basic trust, which avoids probate, and an AB trust, which avoids both probate and federal estate tax.

When to Use a Basic Probate-Avoidance Trust

Like a will, a basic revocable living trust lets you leave your property to the people you want to inherit it. The main advantage of a living trust is that your assets don't have to go through probate at your death. Consider a living trust if any of the following applies to you:

You're middle-aged or older, or in poor health. As you get older, you'll want to think more about sparing your family the expense and delay of probate.

Simpler probate-avoidance methods aren't available. A living trust is an excellent way to avoid probate for real estate that you own alone and many other miscellaneous assets. But if your money is in bank, brokerage or retirement accounts, it's simpler and equally effective just to name payable-on-death beneficiaries for each account. These methods don't offer all the features of a living trust— most important, you might not be able to name an alternate beneficiary. But especially for younger people, that drawback may be outweighed by convenience.

Your estate probably won't qualify for simplified probate. Most states allow certain amounts or types of property to be transferred without probate or by a streamlined court procedure, even if it's left by will. If your estate is eligible for a simple transfer procedure, you

may not need to create a trust. Simplified probate is available to estates of just a few thousand dollars in some states, all the way up to $200,000 in Nevada. In some states, if a surviving spouse inherits less than a certain amount of property, no probate is necessary.

 RESOURCE
Every state's approach to handling small estates is listed in *The Executor's Guide: Settling a Loved One's Estate or Trust*, by Mary Randolph; *Plan Your Estate*, by Denis Clifford; and *8 Ways to Avoid Probate*, by Mary Randolph, all published by Nolo.

You own out-of-state real estate. Using a living trust can let you avoid probate proceedings in that state, saving your family a big headache.

You aren't worried about big creditors' claims. If you own a business that has many creditors, you may want your assets to go through probate, so that creditors' claims are cut off after a certain period. If creditors don't make their claims by the deadline, your inheritors can take your property free of concern that creditors will surface later and attempt to claim a share.

You're concerned about privacy. A will is filed with the probate court after you die and becomes a matter of public record. A living trust, on the other hand, is not, so what you leave to whom remains private. (There is one exception: Records of real estate transfers are always public.)

You don't mind some extra paperwork. Creating a trust document is no harder than making a will. There is, however, one more essential step to making a living trust effective: You must make sure that ownership of all the property you listed in the trust document is legally transferred to you as trustee of the trust.

You're concerned about incapacity. A living trust can be useful if you become incapable, because of injury or illness, of taking care of your financial affairs. With a trust, the person named to serve as trustee after your death can take over management of the trust assets.

Without a living trust or other arrangements, a court must appoint someone to take over.

When to Use a Regular Tax-Saving AB Trust

A basic living trust does nothing to reduce federal estate tax—for that, you need an AB trust. But should you even be concerned about estate tax? Most people don't need to worry

---

You May Not Need a Living Trust at All

You may already be convinced that you want to avoid probate or save on estate taxes. But before you plunge ahead with a trust, read on. You may *not* need a living trust if:

- **You're young and healthy.** Your estate planning goals are probably simple. You want to make sure that in the unlikely event of your early death, your property will go to the people or institutions you want to get it and, if you have young children, that they are well cared for. You can accomplish those goals by writing a will (in which you name a guardian to raise the children) and buying some life insurance. If you do want to take some probate-avoidance steps now, check out simpler methods, such as payable-on-death bank accounts.
- **You own your big assets jointly with someone else.** If you're married or in a long-term relationship, you probably own many, if not all, of your valuable assets together with your mate. If you

hold title in joint tenancy, tenancy by the entirety or (in some states) community property, the property will go to the survivor, without probate, when the first owner dies. You may decide to wait to create a trust, which will avoid probate at the second death, until later.
- **You can name beneficiaries outside of your will for most of your assets.** You don't need a trust to avoid probate for bank or retirement accounts; all you have to do is fill out a form provided by the bank or account custodian, naming the beneficiary. You can do the same thing for stocks and bonds in almost every state.
- **You don't own much.** Small estates (defined differently by each state) don't have to go through regular probate; streamlined procedures are available. And if you're considering an AB trust, keep in mind that currently only large estates owe estate tax.

about it; only a tiny fraction—fewer than 2%—of estates owe estate tax. But as explained in Chapter 13, legislative changes have made it difficult for some people to know whether or not they should even try to plan for avoiding estate tax.

Currently, the amount that you can leave that is exempt from estate tax is scheduled to rise until 2010, at which time the estate tax will no longer be imposed at all. But unless Congress extends the estate tax repeal, the tax will pop up again in 2011 (with a $1 million exemption). Most observers, however, predict that the estate tax will never go away completely, but that it will survive for very large estates—possibly those worth more than $3.5 million. It all depends on Congress.

Consider an AB trust only if the following apply to you:

You expect to owe estate tax when the second spouse dies. If you and your spouse have combined assets worth more than the amount that is exempt from estate tax, your family may be in for a hefty estate tax bill when the second spouse dies.

But as the exemption amount increases, that scenario becomes more and more remote for most people. Unless you expect to leave a very large amount of property at your death, you don't need an AB trust or other estate tax-saving plan.

An AB trust could actually cost your family money if, when you die, there is no estate tax. That's because the new tax law changes the rules for determining the tax basis of inherited property. Under the current law, the basis of inherited property is the value at the date of death. In most cases, that arrangement is a boon for the person who inherits the property,

because the new basis usually is higher, and a higher ("stepped-up") tax basis means less taxable profit when the property is eventually sold.

But if the estate tax is repealed as scheduled (in 2010), not all inherited property will automatically get a stepped-up basis. Instead, the executor of the estate will be able to choose up to $1.3 million of property in the estate to get a stepped-up basis. If the property is in an AB trust instead of the estate, it won't be eligible to get a date-of-death basis. (Property in a basic revocable trust will qualify for a stepped-up basis.)

If you think your wealth may exceed the amount that is exempt from estate tax, it's a tough call. Whether or not you want to make an AB trust to try to avoid possible eventual tax may depend on two unknowable things: how long you will live and what Congress will do in the next few years.

First, you could simply postpone making an AB trust until the future of the estate tax is decided by Congress. If the tax comes back in 2011, you may need an AB trust after all.

Second, you could use Quicken WillMaker Plus to make a "disclaimer" trust. That's an AB trust that gives the surviving spouse the power to decide, after the first spouse dies, whether or not to put the tax-saving features of the AB trust into effect. (More on this below.)

Third, you can always make an AB trust and revoke it, if the estate tax exemption reaches a level at which you no longer need to worry about estate taxes. But you can't revoke the whole trust after one spouse dies; part of it becomes irrevocable then. The deceased spouse's share of the trust property will be tied up for the rest of the surviving spouse's life, and there's nothing you can do about it.

Estate Tax Exemptions: On the Rise

Year of Death	Estate Tax Exemption
2008	$2 million
2009	$3.5 million
2010	Estate tax repealed
2011	$1 million unless Congress extends repeal

You're married. The AB trust made by Quicken WillMaker Plus is for married couples only. If, however, you're married to someone of the same sex (currently an option only in California and Massachusetts), don't use the Quicken WillMaker Plus AB trust. The AB trust is based on the tax law that lets a surviving spouse inherit from the deceased spouse without owing any estate tax. But the federal government does not now recognize same-sex marriages, which means that a surviving same-sex spouse does not get that tax break.

You and your spouse are in your 50s, 60s or older. If one or both of you expects to live many more years, you can leave everything directly to your spouse, who can inherit an unlimited amount without paying tax (as long as the surviving spouse is a U.S. citizen). The survivor would have a long time to use the money and to plan for reducing eventual estate taxes.

You don't mind restricting the surviving spouse's use of trust property. With an AB trust, the surviving spouse does not have unlimited access to the property inherited from the deceased spouse. Although Quicken WillMaker Plus's AB trust gives the survivor as much control as the IRS will allow (and still get the tax break), there are restrictions. The survivor gets only the income from the deceased spouse's half of the property and can spend principal only for health, education, support and maintenance, in accord with his or her accustomed manner of living.

Family members get along well. You should be confident that the surviving spouse and the children (or other final beneficiaries) won't quarrel over management of the trust property. Until the surviving spouse dies, he or she and the children will essentially share ownership of the trust assets. Children hoping to inherit big sums have been known to resent the parent's use of trust property—forgetting that the parents didn't have to set up the trust and took the trouble to do so solely to benefit the children.

You don't mind some hassles and legal fees after the first spouse dies. After one spouse dies, the survivor will need to consult an attorney (or possibly a certified public accountant) to split the trust into Trusts A and B, or to decide whether or not to create the bypass trust (if you chose the disclaimer trust option). And each year, a trust income tax return will have to be filed for the irrevocable bypass trust.

CAUTION

Keep an eye on the estate tax laws. The uncertainty in the current estate tax law has made it almost inevitable that Congress will soon take up the matter of estate taxes. Otherwise, people simply cannot plan ahead. So, keep up to date as these changes work their way through the political process. If the estate tax really is eliminated, you will almost certainly not want an AB trust.

Avoiding Estate Tax If You're Single

The AB trust produced with Quicken WillMaker Plus works only for married couples. If you're single, or in an unmarried relationship (including a same-sex domestic partnership or marriage, neither of which is treated like traditional marriage for federal tax law purposes), you can use other tax-saving strategies, such as making tax-free gifts and using other kinds of trusts. Check out *Plan Your Estate*, by Denis Clifford (Nolo), which discusses ways that unmarried persons can avoid estate tax at their death, and many other estate planning issues.

The Wills and Estate Planning section of Nolo's website, at www.nolo.com, provides good background information about estate tax avoidance and other estate planning concerns.

When to Use a Disclaimer AB Trust

Consider adding the disclaimer clause to your AB trust if you're not sure whether or not the estate of the second spouse to die will owe estate tax, and you don't want to lock in your choice of an AB trust.

A disclaimer trust works just like a regular AB trust in most ways. The difference is that when the first spouse dies, the surviving spouse isn't forced to split the trust into Trusts A and B. If it looks like creating the irrevocable bypass trust isn't necessary to save on estate taxes (perhaps because the estate tax exemption has gone up and you no longer own enough to be taxed), he or she doesn't have to do it. The surviving spouse can make the decision based on current information—the tax laws and the surviving spouse's resources at the time. Those things are impossible to predict now.

It's good to have this flexibility, especially given the uncertainty in the federal estate tax laws, because splitting an AB trust and maintaining the bypass trust for years takes a fair amount of time and money. A surviving spouse must keep separate records for the assets in the bypass trust and file an annual income tax return for it. If the trust isn't going to save on estate taxes, you don't want to have to go to all that trouble.

If the surviving spouse decides not to split the AB trust, he or she inherits all the trust property (except for items left specifically to other beneficiaries). It stays in the surviving spouse's revocable trust, which requires no special record keeping or tax returns.

If, however, it makes financial sense, the surviving spouse can go ahead and split the AB trust. The spouse decides how much property should go into the irrevocable bypass trust and "disclaims"—turns down—that amount of property. A disclaimer must be made within nine months after the death and is subject to strict legal rules. One important rule is that the spouse cannot benefit from an asset—for example, use the interest generated by a bank account—and then disclaim it.

The bottom line is that whether you make a regular or a disclaimer trust, the surviving spouse will need professional tax advice after the first spouse's death.

EXAMPLE: Steve and his wife Vanita have assets worth almost $3 million—an amount that's subject to estate tax in 2008, when they're doing their planning, but that will no longer be taxed as of 2009, when the estate tax exemption rises to $3.5 million. Because they're not sure if estate tax will be an issue for them, they make an AB trust with a disclaimer clause.

When Steve dies in 2009, it's up to Vanita to decide how much, if anything, to put in the bypass trust. Because of investment downturns, Vanita and Steve's combined assets are worth only about $2 million at Steve's death. Meanwhile the estate tax exemption has jumped to $3.5 million. Vanita talks to a tax lawyer and realizes that she can inherit all the trust property outright, save herself the hassle of creating the irrevocable bypass trust and not owe any estate tax at her death (unless her net worth rises dramatically and unexpectedly).

So she doesn't disclaim any trust property, and as a result it all goes into her revocable survivor's trust. She has complete control over the trust and doesn't need to keep separate records or file tax returns for it.

Don't use a disclaimer trust unless you're both comfortable with giving the surviving spouse complete control over the couple's assets when the first spouse dies—just as if he or she inherited everything outright. This is fine with many couples, who set up AB trusts only for tax savings and will be relieved if the trouble and expense of an AB trust are not necessary. But if you don't want the surviving spouse to control who inherits the trust property at his or her death, you may want to use a regular AB trust. For example, if you want to be sure that your children from a previous marriage will inherit your share of the trust property, then you would not want a disclaimer trust.

One Trust or Two?

If you and your spouse or partner own big assets together, you may want to make a basic probate-avoidance trust together. (If you make an AB trust, you must make one shared trust.)

Many couples prefer to make one shared trust, because that way they don't have to divide co-owned property. For example, to hold a co-owned house in two separate trusts would require the spouses to sign and record a deed transferring a half-interest in the house to each spouse as trustee. And to transfer household furnishings to separate trusts, spouses would have to allocate each item to a trust—or end up transferring a half-interest in a couch to separate trusts.

There is another advantage to making a shared trust if you and your spouse want to leave significant trust property to each other. With a shared trust, property left by one grantor to the survivor stays in the living trust when the first grantor dies; no transfer is necessary. With separate trusts, property left to the survivor must usually be transferred first from the trust to the survivor, and then (to avoid probate) to the survivor's living trust.

If you and your spouse or partner own most of your property together but each of you has some separate property, a shared trust is fine. You can transfer all of it to the trust, and each spouse can name beneficiaries (including each other) to receive his or her separate property.

If, however, you and your spouse own most of your property separately, you may want to make individual trusts. Most couples in this situation fit one of these profiles:

- You and your spouse signed an agreement stating that each spouse's earnings and other income are separate, and you have kept your property separate.
- You are recently married and own little or no property together.
- You each own mostly separate property acquired before your marriage (or by gift or inheritance), which you conscientiously keep from being mixed. Couples who marry later in life and no longer work often fit into this category.

Another reason to make separate trusts is if each of you wants to keep sole control over your own trust property. With a shared trust, each of you has authority over all trust property while both are alive. (See Chapter 16.)

Your decision may be affected by the marital property laws of your state. This section briefly explains the two systems of marital property laws: community property and non-community property. It will help you understand what you own.

Are You Married?

You may not be sure in certain situations:

Same-sex couples. Only California and Massachusetts allow marriage between two people of the same sex.

You're separated but not yet divorced. See a lawyer before you create a trust or transfer property in or out of one. To protect the rights of each spouse, your state may have very specific rules about what you can and cannot do after separation but before your divorce is final.

Common law marriages. In some states, a couple can become legally married by living together, intending to be married and presenting themselves to the world as a married couple. See Chapter 4 for more information.

Community Property States

Alaska*	Nevada
Arizona	New Mexico
California**	Washington
Idaho	Wisconsin
Louisiana	Texas

* If spouses sign a community property agreement

** Registered domestic partners are also covered by California's community property laws.

In these states, the general rule is that spouses share everything 50-50, so it usually makes sense to make one shared marital trust, especially if you have been married for a number of years.

All property earned by either spouse during the marriage, regardless of whose name is on the title slip, is community property. Each spouse owns a one-half interest in it. Property acquired by one spouse by gift or inheritance, however, or before marriage, is not community property; it is the separate property of that spouse. Federal Social Security benefits and certain retirement plan benefits are also separate, not community, property.

EXAMPLE: Rob and Cecile live in Nevada, a community property state. They have been married for 20 years. Except for some bonds that Cecile inherited from her parents, virtually all their valuable property—house, stocks, car—is owned together. The money they brought to the marriage in separate bank accounts has long since been mixed with community property, making it community property, too. Rob and Cecile decide to make a shared living trust.

SEE AN EXPERT
California registered domestic partners should get expert advice. In California, if you and your partner have registered with the state, you are subject to state community property laws just as married couples are. Creating a joint trust could turn property into community property—a result you might not intend, and one

that could have tax and legal consequences down the road.

Non-Community Property States

Alabama	Missouri
Alaska*	Montana
Arkansas	Nebraska
Colorado	New Hampshire
Connecticut	New Jersey
Delaware	New York
District of Columbia	North Carolina
Florida	North Dakota
Georgia	Ohio
Hawaii	Oklahoma
Illinois	Oregon
Indiana	Pennsylvania
Iowa	Rhode Island
Kansas	South Carolina
Kentucky	South Dakota
Maine	Tennessee
Maryland	Utah
Massachusetts	Vermont
Michigan	Virginia
Minnesota	West Virginia
Mississippi	Wyoming

* Spouses can, however, create community property by signing a community property agreement.

In a non-community property state, it's usually fairly easy for spouses to keep track of who owns what. The spouse whose name is on the title document (deed, brokerage account paper or title slip, for example) owns it. If you own most of your property together, you'll probably want to make a shared trust; if you own things separately, consider individual trusts.

EXAMPLE: Howard and Louisa live in Indiana. Both have grown children from prior marriages. When they married, they moved into Howard's house. They both have their own bank accounts and investments, and one joint checking account which they own as joint tenants with right of survivorship.

Each makes an individual living trust. Howard, who dies first, leaves his house to Louisa, but most of his other property is left to his children. The funds in the checking account are not included in his living trust but pass to Louisa, also without probate, because the account was held in joint tenancy. Howard's other accounts go to his children, under the pay-on-death arrangement he has with the bank. (Joint tenancy, pay-on-death accounts and other probate-avoidance methods are discussed in Chapter 13.)

Creating an Individual Trust

When you create your living trust document with Quicken Will-Maker Plus, you have only a few choices to make. Basically, you must decide:

- what property you want to put in your living trust
- whom you want to receive the trust property at your death (these people or organizations are the beneficiaries of your living trust)
- who is to be the successor trustee—the person you want to distribute trust property at your death, and
- how you should arrange for someone to manage trust property if it's inherited by beneficiaries who are too young to handle it without supervision.

You may already have a good idea of how you want to decide these issues. This chapter discusses the factors you should think about as you make each decision. It is organized the same way as the program is (Parts 1 through 6), so that you can easily refer to it while you're actually making your trust document. It's a good idea, though, to read through this chapter before you sit down at the computer—it will make the whole process clearer and easier.

Creating a Valid Living Trust

- ☐ Prepare the trust document with Quicken WillMaker Plus.
- ☐ Print out the trust document and sign it in front of a notary public.
- ☐ Transfer ownership of the property listed in the trust document into your name, as trustee.
- ☐ Update your trust document when needed.

How an Individual Trust Works: An Overview

Here, in brief, are the important points about how an individual trust works:

Control of trust property. You will be the trustee of your living trust, so you'll have control over the property in the trust.

Amendments or revocation. At any time, you can revoke the trust, add property to it, remove property from it or modify any term of the trust document.

After your death. After you die, the person named in the trust document as successor trustee takes over. He or she is responsible for distributing trust property to the beneficiaries and managing any trust property left to a young beneficiary in a child's subtrust (explained later).

EXAMPLE: Lenora sets up a basic revocable living trust to avoid probate. In the trust document, she makes herself the trustee and appoints her son Ben as successor trustee, to take over as trustee after her death. She transfers her valuable property—her house, savings accounts and stocks—to the living trust.

The trust document states that Lenora's grandson, Max, is to receive the stocks when she dies. She provides that if Max is not yet 27 when she dies, the stocks will stay in a "child's subtrust," managed by the successor trustee Ben. Everything else goes to her son Ben.

When Lenora dies, Ben becomes trustee. He follows the terms of the trust document and, in his capacity as trustee, distributes all the trust property except the stocks to himself, without probate.

Ben also manages the stocks inherited by Max, who is 16 at Lenora's death, until his 27th birthday. When all the property in the subtrust is given to Max or spent on his behalf, the subtrust ends.

Part 1: Your Name

Entering this information is easy: Just type in your name. The name you enter will form part of the name of your trust. For example, if you enter "William S. Jorgensen," your trust will be named "The William S. Jorgensen Revocable Living Trust." Your name will also automatically appear as the original trustee of your living trust. (See Part 2, below.)

Enter your name the way it appears on other formal business documents, such as your driver's license or bank accounts. This may or may not be the name on your birth certificate.

> **EXAMPLE:** Your birth certificate lists your name as Rose Mary Green. But you've always gone by Mary and always sign documents as Mary McNee, your married name. You would use Mary McNee on your living trust.
>
> Use only one name; don't enter various versions of your name joined by "aka" (also known as).
>
> If you go by more than one name, be sure that the name you use for your living trust is the one that appears on the ownership documents for property you plan to hold in trust. If it isn't, it could cause confusion later, and you should change the name on your ownership documents before you transfer the property to the trust.

> **EXAMPLE:** You use the name William Dix for your trust but own real estate in your former name of William Geicherwitz. You should prepare and sign a new deed, changing the name of the owner to William Dix, before you prepare another deed to transfer the property to yourself as trustee.

Part 2: Trustees

To be legally valid, every trust must have a trustee—a person or institution to manage the property held in trust. When you create a living trust with this program, you are the trustee now. You will name someone else to be the successor trustee, who will take over after you have died.

The Original Trustee

You will be the original trustee of your living trust. As trustee, you will have complete control over the property that will be held in the trust.

As a day-to-day, practical matter, it makes little difference that your property is now held in trust. You won't have any special duties as trustee of your trust. You do not even need to file a separate income tax return for the living trust. If the property generates income, just report it on your personal income tax return, as if the trust did not exist.

You have the same freedom to sell, give away or mortgage trust property as you did before you put the property into the living trust. The only difference is that you must now sign documents in your capacity as trustee.

EXAMPLE: Celeste wants to sell a piece of land that is owned in her name as trustee of her living trust. She prepares a deed transferring ownership of the land to the new owner, and signs the deed as "Celeste Tornetti, trustee of the Celeste Tornetti Revocable Living Trust dated February 4, 2004."

! CAUTION

You can't name someone else as trustee. In the unlikely event you don't want to be the original trustee of your living trust, you cannot use Quicken WillMaker Plus; you need to see an estate planning lawyer to draw up a more specialized living trust. Naming someone else as trustee has important tax consequences and means you give up control over trust property.

The Successor Trustee

You must choose a successor trustee—someone to act as trustee after your death or incapacity. The successor trustee has no power or responsibility while you are alive and capable of managing your affairs.

The Successor Trustee's Duties If You Are Incapacitated

If you become physically or mentally incapacitated and unable to manage your affairs, the successor trustee takes over management of the property in your living trust. But who should decide that it's time for the successor trustee to take over, if the issue ever comes up?

In the trust document, you'll name someone (and two alternates) to make this determination. These people do not have to be doctors; ideally, you will choose people who know you well and can give an unbiased opinion about whether or not you need help taking care of financial matters.

If there's ever a question of your ability to manage the trust, the successor trustee will ask your first choice for an opinion of your capacity. If that person isn't available, the successor trustee will go to your second, and if necessary, third choice. If one of them states, in writing, that because of your condition, the successor trustee needs to take over as trustee, then the successor can do so.

If the successor trustee takes over management of the trust, he or she has authority to use trust property for your health care, support and welfare. The law requires the trustee to act honestly and prudently in managing the property. And because you are no longer the trustee, the new trustee must file an income tax return for the trust. At your death, any remaining trust property is distributed to your beneficiaries.

The successor trustee has no power over property not in your living trust and no authority to make medical decisions for you. For this reason, it's also wise to create documents called durable powers of attorney, giving the successor trustee authority to manage property not held in trust and to make health care decisions. (See Chapters 22 and 23.)

The Successor Trustee's Duties After Your Death

After your death, the successor trustee takes over as trustee. His or her primary responsibility is to distribute trust property to the beneficiaries named in your Declaration of Trust. That is usually a straightforward process. An outline of the steps the successor trustee needs to take to transfer certain common kinds of property is in Chapter 21.

The successor trustee may have long-term duties if the trust document creates a child's subtrust for trust property inherited by a young beneficiary (this is explained in Part 6, below).

Choosing a Successor Trustee

The person or institution you choose as successor trustee will have a crucial role: to manage your trust property (if you become incapacitated) or distribute it to your beneficiaries (after your death).

Obviously, when you are giving someone this much power and discretion, you should choose someone with good common sense whom you trust completely. If you don't know anyone who fits this description, think twice about establishing a living trust. Most people pick an adult son or daughter, other relative or close friend.

In most situations, the successor trustee will not need extensive experience in financial management; common sense, dependability and complete honesty are usually enough. A successor trustee who may have long-term responsibility over a young beneficiary's trust property needs more management and financial skills than a successor trustee whose only job is to distribute trust property. The successor trustee does have authority, however, under the terms of the trust document, to get any reasonably necessary professional help—from an accountant, lawyer or tax preparer, perhaps—and pay for it out of trust assets.

Institutions as Successor Trustees

Normally, your first choice as successor trustee should be a flesh-and-blood person, not the trust department of a bank or other institution. Institutional trustees charge hefty fees, which come out of the trust property and leave less for your family and friends. And most aren't even interested in "small" living trusts—ones that contain less than several hundred thousand dollars worth of property.

But if there's no close relative or friend you think is capable of serving as your successor trustee, probably your best bet is to consider naming a private trust services company as successor trustee. Typically, their fees are pricey, but less than a bank's, and your affairs will probably receive more personal attention.

For a very large living trust, another possibility is to name a person and an institution as cosuccessor trustees. The bank or trust services company can do most of the paperwork, and the person can keep an eye on things and approve all transactions.

Usually, it makes sense to name just one person as successor trustee, to avoid any possibility of conflicts. But it's legal and may be desirable to name more than one person. For example, you might name two or more of your children, if you don't expect any disagreements between them and you think one of them might feel hurt and left out if not named.

Having more than one successor trustee is especially likely to cause serious problems if the successor trustees are in charge of the property you have left to a young beneficiary in a child's subtrust. The trustees may have to manage a young beneficiary's property for many years and will have many decisions to make about how to spend the money—greatly increasing the potential for conflict. (Children's subtrusts are discussed in Part 6, below.)

If you appoint cotrustees, you'll have to decide how they'll have authority to act—that is, whether each one can act independently or if they must all agree before they can act. Obviously, it's easy to let each act without waiting for formal, written consent from the others. You may, however, prefer to have them all formally agree before taking action on behalf of the trust.

If you name more than one successor trustee, and one of them can't serve, the others will serve. If none of them can serve, the alternate you name (later in this section of the program) will take over.

It's perfectly legal to name a beneficiary of the trust (someone who will receive trust property after your death) as successor trustee. In fact, it's common.

EXAMPLE: Mildred names her only child, Allison, as both sole beneficiary of her living trust and successor trustee of the living trust. When Mildred dies, Allison uses her authority as trustee to transfer the trust property to herself.

The successor trustee does not have to live in the same state as you do. But if you are choosing between someone local and someone far away, think about how convenient it will be for the person you choose to distribute the living trust property after your death. Someone close by will probably have an easier job, especially with real estate transfers. But for transfers of property such as securities and bank accounts, it usually won't make much difference where the successor trustee lives.

Obviously, before you finalize your living trust, you must check with the person or institution you've chosen to be your successor trustee. You want to be sure your choice is willing to serve.

If you don't, you may well create problems down the line. The person you've chosen may not want to serve, for a variety of reasons. And even if the person would be willing, if he or she doesn't know of his or her responsibilities, transfer of trust property after your death could be delayed.

If you choose an institution, you must check out the minimum size of trust it will accept and the fees it charges for management, and make arrangements for how the institution will take over as trustee at your death.

Avoiding Conflicts With Your Will and Other Documents

Your living trust gives your successor trustee the authority to manage trust property if you become incapacitated. To avoid conflicts, it's a good idea to name your successor to two other posts:

- In your will, appoint your successor trustee to be executor, to be responsible for distributing property that doesn't pass through your living trust.
- In your durable power of attorney for finances, appoint your successor trustee to be your attorney-in-fact, to have authority to make financial and property management decisions for property (except trust property) if you become incapacitated.

Payment of the Successor Trustee

Typically, the successor trustee of a simple probate-avoidance living trust isn't paid. This is because, in most cases, the successor trustee's only job is to distribute the trust property to beneficiaries soon after the grantor's death. Often, the successor trustee inherits most of the trust property.

An exception is a successor trustee who manages the property in a child's subtrust. In that case, the successor trustee is entitled, under the terms of the trust document, to "reasonable compensation." The successor trustee decides what is reasonable and takes it from the trust property left to the young beneficiary.

Allowing the successor trustee to set the amount of the payment can work well, as long as your successor trustee is completely trustworthy. A young beneficiary who feels the trustee's fees are much too high will have to go to court to challenge them.

Naming an Alternate Successor Trustee

Quicken WillMaker Plus asks you to name an alternate, in case your first choice as successor trustee is unable to serve.

If you named more than one successor trustee, the alternate won't become trustee unless none of your original choices can serve.

> **EXAMPLE:** Caroline names her two children, Eugene and Vanessa, as successor trustees. She names a close friend, Nicole, as alternate successor trustee. When Caroline dies, Vanessa is ill and can't serve as trustee, so Eugene acts as sole successor trustee. If he becomes unable to serve, Nicole would take over.

If no one you named in the trust document can serve, the last trustee to serve has the power to appoint, in writing, another successor trustee. (See Chapter 21.)

> **EXAMPLE:** To continue the previous example, if Nicole were ill and didn't have the energy to serve as successor trustee, she could appoint someone else to serve as trustee.

Part 3: Property to Be Put in Trust

Now you're getting to the heart of the program. In this part, you must list each item of property you want to transfer to your living trust. It will take some thought to decide what property to include and how to list it in the trust document. (Later in the program, you will name beneficiaries to receive each item of trust property at your death.)

This is a crucial step: Any property you don't list will not go into your living trust and will not pass under the terms of the trust. It may instead have to go through probate.

Adding property to the trust later. If you mistakenly leave something out or acquire more valuable property after you create your trust, you can add it to your living trust later. Chapter 20 explains how.

> ⓘ **CAUTION**
>
> **Listing property in the trust document is not enough.** If an item has a title (ownership) document, such as a deed or title slip, you must change the title document to show that you, as trustee, are the legal owner of the property. If you don't, the trust won't work. *You should transfer ownership as soon as possible after you print out and sign your Declaration of Trust.* Instructions are in Chapter 19.

Decide What Property to Hold in Trust

What items should you hold in trust to avoid probate fees? Think about including:

- houses and other real estate
- jewelry, antiques, furs and valuable furniture
- stock in a closely held corporation
- stock, bond and other security accounts held by brokerages
- small business interests
- patents and copyrights
- precious metals
- valuable works of art
- valuable collections of stamps, coins or other objects.

You don't need to put everything you own into a living trust to save money on probate. For some assets, you may decide to use other probate-avoidance devices instead of a living trust. (See Chapter 13.)

When you list your property in the program, you can group items, if you're leaving them all to one beneficiary. For example, if you want to leave all your books to your best friend, there's no need to describe each one individually—unless your collection includes some particularly valuable or important books that you want to make extra sure get to the beneficiary.

> ⓘ **CAUTION**
>
> **If you're married or in a domestic partnership.** If you are married but are making an individual trust, remember that you can leave only the property you own. To be sure you understand what you own and what your spouse owns, see Chapter 16, Part 3. Similarly, if you and your same-sex partner have registered your relationship with the state, be sure you know how state law affects your rights. In California, for example, registered domestic partners are covered by state community property laws.

Real Estate

The most valuable thing most people own is real estate: their house, condominium or land. Many people create a living trust just to make sure a house doesn't go through probate. You can probably save your family substantial probate costs by transferring your real estate through a living trust.

If you own the property with someone else, however, you may not want to transfer your real estate to an individual living trust. (See "Co-Owned Property," below.)

Co-op apartments. If you own shares in a co-op corporation that owns your apartment, you'll have to hold your shares in trust. Some corporations are reluctant to let a trustee own shares; check the co-op corporation's rules to see if the transfer is allowed.

Small Business Interests

The delay, expense and court intrusion of probate can be especially detrimental to an ongoing small business. Using your living trust to transfer business interests to beneficiaries quickly after your death is almost essential if you want the beneficiaries to be able to keep the business running.

If you want to control the long-term management of your business, however, a revocable living trust is not the right vehicle. See an estate planning lawyer to draft a different kind of trust, with provisions tailored to your situation.

Different kinds of business organizations present different issues when you want to hold your interest in trust:

Sole proprietorships. If you operate your business as a sole proprietorship, with all business assets held in your own name, you can simply transfer your business property to yourself as trustee. You should also transfer the business's name itself; that transfers the customer goodwill associated with the name.

Partnership interests. If you operate your business as a partnership with other people, you can probably transfer your partnership share to yourself as trustee. If there is a partnership certificate, it must be changed.

Some partnership agreements require the people who inherit a deceased partner's share of the business to offer that share to the other partners before taking it. But that happens after death, so it shouldn't affect your ability to transfer the property through a living trust.

It's not common, but a partnership agreement may limit or forbid holding your interest in trust. If yours does, you and your partners may want to see a lawyer before you make any changes.

Solely owned corporations. If you own all the stock of a corporation, you should have no difficulty transferring it to yourself as trustee.

Closely held corporations. A closely held corporation is a corporation that doesn't sell shares to the public. All its shares are owned by a few people who are usually actively involved in running the business. Normally, you can use a living trust to transfer shares in a closely held corporation by listing the stock in the trust document and then having the stock certificates reissued in your name as trustee.

You'll want to check the corporation's bylaws and articles of incorporation to be sure that you will still have voting rights in your capacity as trustee of the living trust; usually, this is not a problem. If it is, you and the other shareholders should be able to amend the corporation's bylaws to allow it.

There may, however, be restrictions that affect the transfer of shares. Check the corporation's bylaws and articles of incorporation, as well as any separate shareholders' agreements. One fairly common rule is that surviving shareholders (or the corporation) have the right to buy the shares of a deceased shareholder. In that case, you can still use a living trust to transfer the shares, but the people who inherit them may have to sell them.

Limited liability companies. If your small business is an LLC, you'll need the consent of a majority or all of the other owners (check your operating agreement) before you can transfer your interest to yourself as trustee. That shouldn't be a problem; they'll just want to know that you, as trustee of your own trust, will have authority to vote on LLC decisions. Another way to address this concern would be to transfer your economic interest in the LLC, but not your right to vote.

Bank Accounts

It's not difficult to transfer bank accounts to your living trust. But you may well decide that you don't need to. That's because you can directly designate a beneficiary for the funds in a bank account. If you do, you don't need to transfer those accounts to a living trust just to avoid probate. Their contents won't go through probate in the first place.

This option can be especially useful for personal checking accounts, which you may not want to transfer to your living trust—it can be difficult to cash checks that say the account is owned by a revocable living trust.

A living trust, however, offers one advantage that most pay-on-death arrangements do not: You can name an alternate beneficiary to receive the account if your first choice isn't alive at the time of your death. Pay-on-death accounts are discussed in Chapter 13.

Vehicles and Property That Is Often Sold

Some kinds of property are cumbersome to keep in a living trust. It's not a legal problem, just a practical one. Two common examples are:

- **Cars or other vehicles you use.** Having registration and insurance in your name as trustee could be confusing, and some insurance companies might balk. If you have valuable antique autos or a mobile home that is permanently attached to land and considered real estate under your state's law, however, you may want to go ahead and hold them in trust. You should be able to find an insurance company that will cooperate.

- **Property you buy or sell frequently.** If you don't expect to own the property at your death, there's no compelling reason to hold it in trust. (Remember, the probate process you want to avoid doesn't happen until after your death.) On the other hand, if you're buying property, it's no more trouble to acquire it in your name as trustee.

Life Insurance

If you own a life insurance policy at your death, the insurance company will give the proceeds to the named beneficiary, without probate. (The proceeds are, however, considered part of your estate for federal estate tax purposes.)

If you have named a minor or young adult as the beneficiary, you may want to name your living trust instead. Then, in the trust document, you name the child as beneficiary of any insurance proceeds paid to the trust and arrange for an adult to manage the policy proceeds if the beneficiary is still young when you die. If you don't arrange for management of the money, and the beneficiary is still a minor (under 18) when you die, a court will have to appoint a financial guardian after your death. (Young beneficiaries are discussed in Part 6, below.)

Passing the proceeds of a life insurance policy through your living trust is a bit more complicated than leaving other property this way. You must take two steps:

1. Name the living trust as the beneficiary of your life insurance policy. (Your insurance agent will have a form that lets you change the beneficiary of the policy.)
2. When you list property items in the living trust document, list the proceeds of the policy, not the policy itself. (See "How to Describe Trust Property," below.)

Securities

If you buy and sell stocks regularly, you may not want to go to the trouble of acquiring and selling them using your authority as trustee of the trust.

Fortunately, there's an easier way to do it: Hold your stocks in a brokerage account that is owned in your name as trustee. All securities in the account are then held in trust, which means that you can use your living trust to leave all the contents of the account to a specific beneficiary. If you want to leave stock to different beneficiaries, you can either establish more than one brokerage account or leave one account to more than one beneficiary to own together.

Stock in closely held corporations. See "Small Business Interests," above.

An Alternative: Transfer-on-Death Registration

All states but Louisiana and Texas now allow ownership of securities to be registered in a "transfer-on-death" form. You can designate someone to receive the securities, including mutual funds and brokerage accounts, after your death. No probate will be necessary. Ask your broker about the forms you need to fill out to name a beneficiary for your securities.

Cash

It's common for people to want to leave cash gifts to beneficiaries—for example, to leave $5,000 to a relative, friend or charity. Don't, however, just type in "$5,000 cash" when you list the property you want to transfer to the living trust. There's no way to hold cash in trust unless its source is identified.

You can, however, easily accomplish your goal by transferring ownership of a cash account—a savings or money market account, for example—to yourself as trustee of your trust. You can then name a beneficiary to receive the contents of the account. So if you want to leave $5,000 to cousin Fred, all you have to do is put the money in a bank or money market account, transfer it to your living trust and name Fred, in the trust document, as the beneficiary of the account.

If you don't want to set up a separate account to leave a modest amount of cash to a beneficiary, think about buying a savings bond and leaving it to the beneficiary or leaving one larger account to several beneficiaries.

> EXAMPLE: Michael would like to leave some modest cash gifts to his two grown nephews, Warren and Brian, whom he's always been fond of. He puts $5,000 into a money market account and then transfers the account into his living trust. In his trust document, he names Warren and Brian as beneficiaries of the account. After Michael's death, the two nephews will inherit the account together, and each will be entitled to half of the funds.

Co-Owned Property

If you co-own property with someone, you can hold your share of the property in trust. But whether or not you will want to depends on how you hold title to the property.

If you do decide to transfer just your interest in co-owned property to your living trust, you don't need to specify that your share is one half or some other fraction. For example, if you and your sister own a house together, you need only list "the house at 7989 Lafayette Court,

Boston, MA." Your trust document will simply state that you have transferred all your interest in that property to the trust.

If you are married and want to transfer only your share of property you own together with your spouse, see Chapter 16, Part 3.

If You're Not Sure How You Hold Title

If you own real estate with someone else but aren't sure how you hold title, look at the deed. It should say how title is held: in joint tenancy, tenancy in common, tenancy by the entirety, or community property or community property with right of survivorship (in community property states). In a community property state, if the deed says the property is owned "as husband and wife," that means community property.

Property Held in Joint Tenancy

Property owned in joint tenancy does not go through probate until the last surviving owner dies. When one co-owner (joint tenant) dies, his or her share goes directly to the surviving co-owners, without probate. So if avoiding probate is your only concern, you don't need to transfer joint tenancy property to your living trust. A living trust does, however, offer more flexibility than joint tenancy.

Beneficiaries. If you transfer your share of joint tenancy property to a living trust, the joint tenancy is destroyed. You can leave your share of the property to anyone you choose—it won't automatically go to the surviving co-owners.

Simultaneous death. Joint tenancy doesn't avoid probate if the joint owners die simultaneously. If that happens, each co-owner's interest in the property is passed to the beneficiaries named in the residuary clauses of their wills. If there's no will, the property passes to the closest relatives, under state law.

If you hold the property in your living trust, you can name an alternate beneficiary to receive your share of the property. You're assured that probate will be avoided even in the (statistically very unlikely) event of simultaneous death.

Property Held in Tenancy by the Entirety

Tenancy by the entirety is, basically, a kind of joint tenancy that's only for married couples (and for registered same-sex couples, in states where that's available). It is allowed in the states listed in Chapter 13.

You cannot hold your half-interest in tenancy by the entirety property in an individual living trust. Neither owner can transfer his or her half of the property alone, either while alive or by will or trust. (This is different from joint tenancy; a joint tenant is free to transfer his or her share to someone else during his life.)

Community Property

Community property is another form of ownership that's only for married couples in the states listed below (or for registered domestic partners, in California). If you and your spouse together own community property, you should probably create a shared living trust. See Chapter 14.

Community Property States		
Alaska*	Louisiana	Washington
Arizona	Nevada	Wisconsin
California	New Mexico	Texas
Idaho		

* If spouses sign a community property agreement.

Retirement Plans

Individual retirement accounts cannot be held in trust. Instead, avoid probate by naming a beneficiary to inherit whatever's left in your retirement account at your death. The plan administrator or account holder can provide forms on which to designate your beneficiary.

You can name a living trust as a beneficiary, but there's rarely a reason to. Under current IRS rules, money left to a trust must be distributed based on the life expectancy of the trust beneficiary.

RESOURCE

IRAs, 401(k)s & Other Retirement Plans: Taking Your Money Out, by Twila Slesnick and John C. Suttle (Nolo), explains the options of those who inherit money in a retirement account.

Other Valuable Property

Other valuable items—everything from jewelry and antiques to boats and airplanes—can also be placed in trust.

How to Describe Trust Property

When Quicken WillMaker Plus asks you to list the property you want to hold in your trust, describe each item clearly enough so that the successor trustee can identify the property and transfer it to the right person. No magic legal words are required.

Think about whom the property will ultimately go to. If you're leaving everything to one person, or just a few, there's less need to go into great detail. But if there will be a number of trust beneficiaries and objects could be confused, be more specific about each one. When in doubt, err on the side of including more information.

Rules for Entering Descriptions of Trust Property

- Don't use "my" in a description. Don't, for example, enter "my books" or "my stereo system." That's because once the property is in the living trust it doesn't belong to you anymore—it belongs to the trust.
- Don't begin a description with a capital letter (unless it must begin with a proper name, like "Steinway"). That's because the descriptions will be inserted into a sentence in the trust document, and it would look odd to see a capital letter in the middle of a sentence.
- Don't end a description with a period. Again, this is because the descriptions will be inserted into a sentence in the trust document.

If the property you're describing is valuable—expensive jewelry or artworks, for example—describe it in detail, much as you would if you were listing it on an insurance policy.

Here are some sample descriptions:

Real estate
- "the house at 321 Glen St., Omaha, NE"
- "the house at 4444 Casey Road, Fandon, Illinois, and the 20-acre parcel on which it is located"

Usually, the street address is enough. It's not necessary to use the "legal description" found on the deed, which gives a subdivision plat number or a metes-and-bounds description. But if the property has no street address—for example, if it is undeveloped land out in the country—you will need to carefully copy the full legal description, word for word, from the deed.

If you own a house and several adjacent lots, it's a good idea to indicate that you are transferring the entire parcel to your living trust by describing the land as well as the house.

If you own the property with someone else and are transferring only your share, you don't need to specify the share you own. Just describe the property. The trust document will show that you are transferring all your interest in the property, whatever share that is, to the living trust.

Bank accounts
- "Savings Account No. 9384-387, Arlington Bank, Arlington, MN"
- "Money Market Account 47-223 at Charles Schwab & Co., Inc., San Francisco, CA"

Household items

- "all the furniture normally kept in the house at 44123 Derby Ave., Ross, KY"
- "the antique brass bed in the master bedroom in the house at 33 Walker Ave., Fort Lee, New Jersey"
- "all furniture and household items normally kept in the house at 869 Hopkins St., Great Falls, Montana"

Sole proprietorship business property

- "Mulligan's Fish Market"
- "Fourth Street Records and CDs"
- "all accounts receivable of the business known as Garcia's Restaurant, 988 17th St., Atlanta, GA"
- "all food preparation and storage equipment, including refrigerator, freezer, hand mixers and slicer used at Garcia's Restaurant, 988 17th St., Atlanta, GA"

As explained in "Decide What Property to Hold in Trust," above, you should both list the name of the business and separately list items of business property.

Partnership interest

- "Don and Dan's Bait Shop Partnership owned by the grantor before being held in this living trust"

Because a partnership is a legal entity that can own property, you don't need to list items of property owned by the partnership.

Shares in a closely held corporation

- "The stock of ABC Hardware, Inc."

Shares in a solely owned corporation

- "all shares in the XYZ Corporation"
- "all stock in Fern's Olde Antique Shoppe, Inc., 23 Turnbridge Court, Danbury, Connecticut"

Securities

- "all securities in account No. 3999-34-33 at Smith Brokerage, 33 Lowell Place, New York, NY"
- "200 shares of General Industries, Inc., stock"
- "Good Investment Co. mutual fund account No. 888-09-09"

Life insurance proceeds

- "the proceeds of Acme Co. Life Insurance Policy #9992A"

Miscellaneous items

- "Macintosh laptop computer (serial number 129311)"
- "the medical textbooks in the office at 1702 Parker Towers, San Francisco, CA"
- "the stamp collection usually kept at 321 Glen St., Omaha, NE"
- "the collection of European stamps, including [describe particularly valuable stamps], usually kept at 440 Loma Prieta Blvd., #450, San Jose, CA"
- "the Martin D-35 acoustic guitar, serial number 477597"
- "the signed 1960 Ernie Banks baseball card kept in safe deposit box 234, First National Bank of Augusta, Augusta, IL"
- "the Baldwin upright piano kept at 985 Dawson Court, South Brenly, Massachusetts"

Part 4: Beneficiaries of Trust Property

Once you've entered a list of the property you're going to hold in trust, the next step is to say whom you want to inherit that property. Quicken WillMaker Plus lets you name a beneficiary for each item of trust property separately or name one beneficiary to receive everything.

The beneficiaries you name in your trust document are not entitled to anything while you are alive. You can amend your trust document and change the beneficiaries any time you wish.

SEE AN EXPERT

Rights of a spouse or child. If you are married and don't plan to leave at least half of what you own to your spouse, consult a lawyer experienced in estate planning. State law may entitle your spouse to claim some of the property in your living trust.

In most circumstances, you don't have to leave anything to your children. But if you want to disinherit a child, you should make a will and specifically mention the child in it. (See Chapter 4.)

How Do You Want Your Property Distributed?

Quicken WillMaker Plus asks you first whether you want to leave all your trust property to one beneficiary (or more than one, to share it all) or leave different items to different beneficiaries.

The simplest approach is to leave all your trust property to one person or to one or more persons to share. If you choose that option, all you have to do is name each beneficiary and then name an alternate beneficiary for each, who will inherit the trust property if a primary beneficiary does not survive you by five days. (Alternates are discussed below.)

If you choose to leave different items to different beneficiaries, you will be shown a list of all the property items you listed earlier. You can then name beneficiaries for them.

Minors or Young Adults

You can name minors (children under 18) to inherit trust property. If a beneficiary you name is a minor or a young adult who can't yet manage property without adult help, you can arrange for an adult to manage the trust property for the beneficiary. Quicken WillMaker Plus lets you do this after you have named all your beneficiaries. (See Part 6, below.)

Your Successor Trustee

It's very common, and perfectly legal, to make the person you named to be successor trustee (the person who will distribute trust property after your death) a beneficiary as well.

> **EXAMPLE:** Nora names her son Liam as successor trustee of her living trust. She also names him as sole beneficiary of her trust property. When Nora dies, Liam, acting as trustee, will transfer ownership of the trust property to himself.

Naming More Than One Beneficiary to Share Property

You can name more than one beneficiary to share any item of trust property. Simply list their names in the box on the screen. Type the names one per line; don't join the names with an "and." (See the Users' Manual for examples.)

Always use the beneficiaries' actual names; don't use collective terms such as "my children." It's not always clear who is included in such descriptions. And there can be serious confusion if one of the people originally included as a group member dies before you do.

Obviously, if you name cobeneficiaries for a piece of property that can't be physically divided—a cabin, for example—give some thought to whether or not the beneficiaries are likely to get along. If they are incompatible, disagreements could arise over taking care of property or deciding whether or not to sell it. If they can't settle their differences, any co-owner could go to court and demand a partition—a court-ordered division and sale—of the property.

Cobeneficiaries will share the property equally unless you state otherwise. We'll ask you, after you enter the names, whether or not you want an item of trust property to be shared equally by the beneficiaries.

> EXAMPLE: Georgia wants to leave her house to her two children, Ross and Ryan, but wants Ross to have a 75% share of it. She enters their names and then, on a later screen, enters their interests, in fractions: ¾ for Ross and ¼ for Ryan.

When the children inherit the property, they own it together. But Ross will be liable for 75% of the taxes and upkeep cost and entitled to 75% of any income the house produces. If they sell it, Ross will be entitled to 75% of the proceeds.

Beneficiaries for Your Share of Co-Owned Trust Property

If you own property together with someone else, you will name beneficiaries for your share of the property. At your death, only your interest in the property will go to the beneficiary you name.

Pay attention to who will end up as co-owners of the property after your death. If, for example, you and your brother own a house together, and you leave your share to your daughter—who detests her uncle—problems are likely.

Entering Beneficiaries' Names

When you enter a beneficiary's name, use the name by which the beneficiary is known for purposes such as a bank account or driver's license. Generally, if the name you use clearly and unambiguously identifies the person, it is sufficient.

If you name an institution (charitable or not) to inherit trust property, enter its complete name. It may be commonly known by a shortened version, which could cause confusion if there are similarly named organizations. Call to ask if you're unsure. (An institution that stands to inherit some of your money will be more than happy to help you.) Also be sure to specify if you want a branch or part of a national organization to receive your gift—for example, a local chapter of the Sierra Club.

Alternate Beneficiaries

Quicken WillMaker Plus allows you to name an alternate for every person you name as a primary beneficiary. The alternate will get the property left to the primary beneficiary if your first choice does not live for more than 120 hours (five days) after your death. This "survivorship" period ensures that if you and a primary beneficiary die simultaneously or almost so, the property will go to the alternate beneficiary you chose, not to the primary beneficiary's heirs.

> EXAMPLE: Laura leaves all her trust property to her sister Jean, and names her daughter as alternate beneficiary. Laura and Jean are seriously injured in a car accident; Jean dies a day after Laura does. Because Jean did not survive Laura by at least five days, the trust property she would have inherited from Laura goes to Laura's daughter instead.
>
> If there had been no survivorship requirement, at Laura's death the trust property would have gone to Jean; when she died a day later, it would have gone to her heirs.

You don't have to name an alternate for a charitable (or other) institution you name as a beneficiary. If the institution is well established, it is probably safe to assume that it will still exist at your death.

With other beneficiaries, however, there is always the chance that the primary beneficiary may not survive you, so it's a good idea to name an alternate. If you don't name an alternate, the property that beneficiary would have received will be distributed to the person or institution you name, in the next part of the program, as your "residuary beneficiary." (See Part 5, below.)

You can name more than one person or institution as alternate beneficiaries. If you do, they will share the property equally unless you state otherwise.

Part 5: Residuary Beneficiaries

If you leave all your trust property to one person (or a group of people to share), you will not name a residuary beneficiary. But if you made any specific gifts you will name a residuary beneficiary for your living trust. The person or organization you name will receive:

- any trust property for which both the primary and alternate beneficiaries you named die before you do
- any trust property that you didn't leave to a named beneficiary (this could include property you transfer to the trust later and don't name a beneficiary for)
- any property you leave to your living trust through your will (such a will is called a pour-over will), and
- any property that you actually transferred to yourself as trustee but didn't list in the trust document.

Often, the residuary beneficiary of a living trust doesn't inherit anything from the trust. Usually, naming a residuary beneficiary is just a back-up measure, to guard against the extremely small chance that both a primary and alternate trust beneficiary do not survive you.

Part 6: Property Management for Young Beneficiaries

If any of your beneficiaries (including alternate and residuary beneficiaries) might inherit trust property before they are ready to manage it without an adult's help, you should arrange for someone else to manage it for them for a while. There are several ways to go about it:

- **Leave the property to an adult to use for the child.** Many people don't leave property directly to a child. Instead, they leave it to the child's parent or to the person they expect to have care and custody of the child if neither parent is available. There's no formal legal arrangement, but they trust the adult to use the property for the child's benefit.
- **Name a custodian under a law called the Uniform Transfers to Minors Act (UTMA).** In almost every state, you can name a "custodian" to manage property you leave a child until the child reaches 18 or 21, depending on state law (up to 25 in some states). If you don't need management to last beyond that age, a custodianship is preferable.
- **Create a child's subtrust.** You can use Quicken WillMaker Plus to establish a "child's subtrust" in your living trust. If you do, your successor trustee will manage the property you left the child and dole it out for education, health and other needs. The subtrust ends at

whatever age you designate (up to 35), and any remaining property is turned over to the child outright.

Subtrusts and custodianships are explained below.

CAUTION

Children with special needs. These property management options are not designed to provide long-term property management for a child with serious disabilities. For information on providing for a child with special needs, see *Special Needs Trusts*, by Stephen Elias (Nolo).

Should You Arrange for Management?

It's up to you whether or not to make arrangements, in the trust document, to have someone manage trust property if it is inherited by young beneficiaries.

The consequences of forgoing management for trust property inherited by a young beneficiary depend on whether the beneficiary is over or under age 18 at your death.

Children Under 18 Years Old

Minors—children under 18—cannot, legally, own or manage significant amounts of property. An adult must be in charge if the minor acquires more than a few thousand dollars' worth of property. (The exact amount depends on state law.)

If your minor beneficiaries won't inherit anything of great value—if you're leaving them objects that have more sentimental than monetary value—you don't need to arrange for an adult to manage the property.

But if a beneficiary inherits valuable trust property while still a minor, and you have not arranged for the property to be managed by an adult, a court-appointed guardian may have to manage the property.

Contrary to what you might expect, a child's parent does not automatically have legal authority to manage any property the child inherits. So even if one or both of the beneficiary's parents are alive, they may have to ask the court to grant them that authority, and will be subject to the court's supervision. If neither parent is alive, there may be no obvious person for the court to appoint as property guardian. In that case, it may be even more important for you to name someone in your living trust.

There is one other option: In most states, the successor trustee can appoint a custodian for property inherited by a minor. If the value of property exceeds a certain amount—$10,000 in most states—a court must approve the appointment. And the custodianship must end at 18 in most states, earlier than many parents would choose. So it's still better to name a custodian yourself.

Young Adults 18 to 35 Years Old

If someone who is 18 or older inherits trust property, you do not need, legally, to have anyone manage the property on the beneficiary's behalf. And if you don't make any arrangements, the beneficiary will get the property with no strings attached. But you can arrange for property management to last until a beneficiary turns any age up to 35.

There is no legal requirement that management for a trust beneficiary's property must end at 35, but we think 35 is a reasonable cutoff. If you don't want to give a beneficiary free rein over trust property by the time he or she reaches 35, you probably need to see a lawyer and tailor a plan to the beneficiary's needs.

Which Is Better: Subtrust or Custodianship?

Using Quicken WillMaker Plus, you can create either a child's subtrust or a custodianship under the Uniform Transfer to Minors Act (if it's available in your state). Both are safe, efficient ways of managing trust property that a young person inherits. Under either system, the person in charge of the young beneficiary's property has the same responsibility to use the property for the beneficiary's support, education and health.

The most significant difference is that a child's subtrust can last longer than a custodianship, which must end at age 18 to 21 in most states (up to 25 in a few). For that reason, a child's subtrust is a good choice when a child could inherit a large amount of property.

Because an UTMA custodianship is much easier to administer, it is usually preferable if the beneficiary will inherit no more than about $50,000 worth of trust property ($100,000 or more if the child is quite young). That amount is likely to be used up for living and education expenses by the time the beneficiary is 21, so there's no need to create a subtrust that can continue beyond that age.

A custodianship has other advantages as well:

- Handling a beneficiary's property is easier with a custodianship than with a trust. A custodian's powers are written into state law, and most institutions, such as banks and insurance companies, are familiar with the rules. Trusts, on the other hand, vary in their terms. So before a bank lets a trustee act on behalf of a beneficiary, it may demand to see and analyze a copy of the Declaration of Trust.

- You can name whomever you wish to be a custodian, and you can name different custodians for different beneficiaries. So if you want to arrange custodianships for grandchildren, for example, you could name each child's parent as custodian. A child's subtrust is not quite so flexible: The successor trustee will be the trustee of all children's subtrusts created for your young beneficiaries.

- If the property in a subtrust earns income, and that income isn't distributed quickly to the beneficiary, the trust will have to pay tax on it. The federal tax rate on such retained income may be higher than it would be if the young beneficiary were taxed on it. The trustee may well need to hire experts to help with trust accounting and tax returns.

Custodianships

Think a custodianship is right for your family? Here's how it works.

How a Custodianship Works

In the trust document, you name someone to serve as custodian for a particular beneficiary. That person manages any trust property the young beneficiary inherits until the beneficiary reaches the age at which state law says the custodianship must end. Each state's age is listed in Chapter 7.

> **EXAMPLE:** In her living trust, Sandra leaves 100 shares of General Motors stock to her niece, Jennifer. She names Hazel, Jennifer's mother, as custodian under the Illinois Uniform Transfers to Minors Act.
>
> After Sandra's death, her successor trustee gives the stock to the custodian, Hazel. She will manage it for Jennifer until Jennifer turns 21, the age Illinois law says she must be given the property outright.

In some states, you can specify—within limits—at what age the custodianship will end. If your state allows this, we'll ask you to enter the age at which you want the custodianship to end.

> **EXAMPLE:** If Sandra, in the previous example, lived in New Jersey, the state's law would allow her to choose any age from 18 to 21 for the custodianship to end.

The Custodian's Responsibilities

A custodian has roughly the same responsibility as the trustee of a child's subtrust: to manage the beneficiary's property wisely and honestly. The custodian's authority and duties are set out by state law (the Uniform Transfers to Minors Act, as enacted by your state). No court directly supervises the custodian.

The custodian must:

- manage the property until the beneficiary reaches the age at which, by law, he or she gets the property outright
- use the property or income to pay for expenses such as the young beneficiary's support, education and health care
- keep the property separate from his or her own property, and
- keep separate records of transactions. The custodian does not have to file a separate income tax return; income from the property can be reported on the young beneficiary's return. (By comparison, the trustee of a child's subtrust must file a separate tax return for the subtrust.)

A custodian who needs to hire an accountant, tax lawyer or other expert can use the property to pay a reasonable amount for the help.

If state law allows it, the custodian is entitled to reasonable compensation and reimbursement for reasonable expenses. The payment, if any is taken, comes from the custodial property.

Choosing a Custodian

You can name a different custodian for each young beneficiary, if you wish.

In most cases, you should name the person who will have physical custody of the minor child. That's almost always one of the child's parents. If the beneficiary is your child, name the child's other parent unless you have serious reservations about that person's ability to handle the property for the child.

Only one person can be named as custodian for one beneficiary. You can, however, name an alternate custodian to take over if your first choice is unable to serve.

Children's Subtrusts

Quicken WillMaker Plus allows you to set up a separate child's subtrust for each young beneficiary.

How a Child's Subtrust Works

In your trust document, you state the age at which the beneficiary should receive trust property outright. If at your death the beneficiary is younger than the age you specified, a subtrust will be created for that beneficiary. (If the beneficiary is older, he or she gets the trust property with no strings attached, and no subtrust is created.) Each beneficiary gets a separate child's subtrust.

Quicken WillMaker Plus is set up so that the successor trustee will serve as trustee of any children's subtrusts. If you want different people to manage property inherited by different beneficiaries, you may want to use a custodianship instead of a child's subtrust. (To appoint someone else to be trustee of a child's subtrust, the trust document would have to be changed significantly; see a lawyer.)

Whatever trust property the beneficiary is entitled to receive upon your death will go into the child's subtrust, if the child is still under the age set for termination of the subtrust. The trustee will manage the subtrust property and use it as necessary for the beneficiary's health, education and support. After your death, the subtrust cannot be revoked or amended. Until then, you are free to change your mind about having a subtrust set up for a particular beneficiary.

The child's subtrust will end when the beneficiary reaches the age you designated in your Declaration of Trust. This can be any age up to and including 35. The trustee will then give the beneficiary what remains of the subtrust property.

EXAMPLE: In his trust document, Stanley names his 14-year-old son Michael as beneficiary of $100,000 worth of stock. He specifies that any stock Michael becomes entitled to when Stanley dies should be kept in a subtrust until Michael is 25, subject to the trustee's right to spend it on Michael's behalf.

Stanley dies when Michael is 19. The stock goes into a subtrust for him, managed by the successor trustee of Stanley's living trust. The trustee uses the stock (or the income it produces) to pay for Michael's education and support. Michael receives what's left of the stock when he turns 25.

EXAMPLE: Victoria creates a living trust and leaves her trust property to her daughters, who are 22 and 25. She specifies that any trust property they inherit should stay in children's subtrusts until each daughter reaches 30. Victoria names her sister, Antoinette, as successor trustee.

Victoria dies in a car accident when one daughter is 28 and the other is 31. The 28-year-old's half of the trust property stays in a subtrust, managed by Antoinette, until she turns 30. The 31-year-old gets her half outright; no subtrust is created for her.

The Trustee's Duties

The subtrust trustee must:

- manage and invest subtrust property until the beneficiary reaches the age set out in the trust document
- keep the beneficiary (or the beneficiary's guardian, if the beneficiary is a minor) reasonably well informed about how the assets are being invested
- use subtrust property or income to pay for expenses such as the beneficiary's support, education and health care, and
- keep separate records of subtrust transactions and file income tax returns for the subtrust.

The trustee's powers and responsibilities are spelled out in the trust document. A trustee who needs to hire an accountant, tax lawyer or other expert can use subtrust assets to pay a reasonable amount for the help.

The trust document also provides that the trustee of a subtrust is entitled to reasonable compensation for acting as trustee. The trustee decides what is a reasonable amount; the compensation is paid from the subtrust assets.

For more on the trustee's responsibilities, see Chapter 21.

Declaration of Trust

Part 1. Trust Name

This revocable living trust shall be known as the Sheila Jenkins Revocable Living Trust.

Part 2. Declaration of Trust

Sheila Jenkins, called the grantor, declares that she has transferred and delivered to the trustee all her interest in the property described in Schedule A attached to this Declaration of Trust. All of that property is called the "trust property." The trustee hereby acknowledges receipt of the trust property and agrees to hold the trust property in trust, according to this Declaration of Trust.

The grantor may add property to the trust.

Part 3. Terminology

The term "this Declaration of Trust" includes any provisions added by valid amendment.

Part 4. Amendment and Revocation

A. Amendment or Revocation by Grantor

The grantor may amend or revoke this trust at any time, without notifying any beneficiary. An amendment must be made in writing and signed by the grantor. Revocation may be in writing or any manner allowed by law.

B. Amendment or Revocation by Other Person

The power to revoke or amend this trust is personal to the grantor. A conservator, guardian or other person shall not exercise it on behalf of the grantor, unless the grantor specifically grants a power to revoke or amend this trust in a Durable Power of Attorney.

Part 5. Payments From Trust During Grantor's Lifetime

The trustee shall pay to or use for the benefit of the grantor as much of the net income and principal of the trust property as the grantor requests. Income shall be paid to the grantor at least annually. Income accruing in or paid to trust accounts shall be deemed to have been paid to the grantor.

Part 6. Trustees

A. Trustee

Sheila Jenkins shall be the trustee of this trust.

B. Trustee's Responsibilities

The trustee in office shall serve as trustee of all trusts created under this Declaration of Trust, including children's subtrusts.

C. Terminology

In this Declaration of Trust, the term "trustee" includes successor trustees or alternate successor trustees serving as trustee of this trust. The singular "trustee" also includes the plural.

D. Successor Trustee

Upon the death or incapacity of Sheila Jenkins, the trustee of this trust and of any children's subtrusts created by it shall be Richard Jenkins. If Richard Jenkins is unable or unwilling to serve as successor trustee, Ann Heron shall serve as trustee.

E. Resignation of Trustee

Any trustee in office may resign at any time by signing a notice of resignation. The resignation shall be delivered to the person or institution who is either named in this Declaration of Trust, or appointed by the trustee under Section F of this Part, to next serve as the trustee.

F. Power to Appoint Successor Trustee

If no one named in this Declaration of Trust as a successor trustee or alternate successor trustee is willing or able to serve as trustee, the last acting trustee may appoint a successor trustee and may require the posting of a reasonable bond, to be paid for from the trust property. The appointment must be made in writing, signed by the trustee and notarized.

G. Bond

No bond shall be required for any trustee named in this Declaration of Trust.

H. Compensation

No trustee shall receive any compensation for serving as trustee, unless the trustee serves as a trustee of a child's subtrust created by this Declaration of Trust.

I. Liability of Trustee

With respect to the exercise or non-exercise of discretionary powers granted by this Declaration of Trust, the trustee shall not be liable for actions taken in good faith. Such actions shall be binding on all persons interested in the trust property.

Part 7. Trustee's Management Powers and Duties

A. Powers Under State Law

The trustee shall have all authority and powers allowed or conferred on a trustee under Arizona law, subject to the trustee's fiduciary duty to the grantors and the beneficiaries.

B. Specified Powers

The trustee's powers include, but are not limited to:

1. The power to sell trust property, and to borrow money and to encumber trust property, including trust real estate, by mortgage, deed of trust or other method.

2. The power to manage trust real estate as if the trustee were the absolute owner of it, including the power to lease (even if the lease term may extend beyond the period of any trust) or grant options to lease the property, to make repairs or alterations and to insure against loss.

3. The power to sell or grant options for the sale or exchange of any trust property, including stocks, bonds, debentures and any other form of security or security account, at public or private sale for cash or on credit.

4. The power to invest trust property in every kind of property and every kind of investment, including but not limited to bonds, debentures, notes, mortgages, stock options, futures and stocks, and including buying on margin.

5. The power to receive additional property from any source and add it to any trust created by this Declaration of Trust.

6. The power to employ and pay reasonable fees to accountants, lawyers or investment experts for information or advice relating to the trust.

7. The power to deposit and hold trust funds in both interest-bearing and non-interest-bearing accounts.

8. The power to deposit funds in bank or other accounts, whether or not they are insured by the FDIC.

9. The power to enter into electronic fund transfers or safe deposit arrangements with financial institutions.

10. The power to continue any business of the grantor.

11. The power to institute or defend legal actions concerning this trust or the grantor's affairs.

12. The power to execute any documents necessary to administer any trust created by this Declaration of Trust.

13. The power to diversify investments, including authority to decide that some or all of the trust property need not produce income.

Part 8. Incapacity of Grantor

If the grantor becomes physically or mentally incapacitated, whether or not a court has declared the grantor incompetent or in need of a conservator or guardian, the successor trustee named in Part 6 shall be trustee.

The determination of the grantor's capacity to manage this trust shall be made by Patricia Jenkins. The successor trustee shall, if necessary, ask Patricia Jenkins to state, in writing, an opinion as to whether or not the grantor is able to continue serving as trustee. The successor trustee may rely on that written opinion when determining whether or not to begin serving as trustee.

If the successor trustee is unable, after making reasonable efforts, to obtain a written opinion from Patricia Jenkins, the successor trustee may request an opinion from Eric Workman and may rely on that opinion.

If the successor trustee is also unable, after making reasonable efforts, to obtain a written opinion from Eric Workman, the successor trustee may request an opinion from Delia Holt and may rely on that opinion.

If the successor trustee is unable, after making reasonable efforts, to obtain a written opinion from Patricia Jenkins, Eric Workman or Delia Holt, the successor trustee may request an opinion from a physician who examines the grantor, and may rely on that opinion.

The trustee shall use any amount of trust income or trust property necessary for the grantor's proper health care, support, maintenance, comfort and welfare, in accordance with the grantor's accustomed manner of living. Any income not spent for the benefit of the grantor shall be accumulated and added to the trust property. Income shall be paid to the grantor at least annually. Income accruing in or paid to trust accounts shall be deemed to have been paid to the grantor.

The successor trustee shall manage the trust until the grantor is again able to manage her affairs. The determination of the grantor's capacity to again manage this trust shall be made in the manner specified just above.

Part 9. Death of a Grantor

When the grantor dies, this trust shall become irrevocable. It may not be amended or altered except as provided for by this Declaration of Trust. It may be terminated only by the distributions authorized by this Declaration of Trust.

The trustee may pay out of trust property such amounts as necessary for payment of the grantor's debts, estate taxes and expenses of the grantor's last illness and funeral.

Part 10. Beneficiaries

At the death of the grantor, the trustee shall distribute the trust property as follows:

Richard Jenkins shall be given Sheila Jenkins's interest in 100 shares of Applied Dynamics stock. If Richard Jenkins does not survive Sheila Jenkins, that property shall be given to Patricia Jenkins.

David Jenkins shall be given Sheila Jenkins's interest in the trust property not otherwise specifically and validly disposed of by this Part. If David Jenkins does not survive Sheila Jenkins, that property shall be given to Richard Jenkins.

Part 11. Terms of Property Distribution

All distributions are subject to any provision in this Declaration of Trust that creates a child's subtrust or a custodianship under the Uniform Transfers to Minors Act.

A beneficiary must survive the grantor for 120 hours to receive property under this Declaration of Trust. As used in this Declaration of Trust, to survive means to be alive or in existence as an organization.

All personal and real property left through this trust shall pass subject to any encumbrances or liens placed on the property as security for the repayment of a loan or debt.

If property is left to two or more beneficiaries to share, they shall share it equally unless this Declaration of Trust provides otherwise. If any of them does not survive the grantor, the others shall take that beneficiary's share, to share equally, unless this Declaration of Trust provides otherwise.

Part 12. Custodianships Under the Uniform Transfers to Minors Act

Any property to which David Jenkins becomes entitled under Part 10 of this Declaration of Trust shall be given to Richard Jenkins, as custodian for David Jenkins under the Arizona Uniform Transfers to Minors Act, until David Jenkins reaches the age of 21. If Richard Jenkins is unable or ceases to serve as custodian, Ann Heron shall serve as custodian.

Part 13. Grantor's Right to Homestead Tax Exemption

If the grantor's principal residence is held in trust, the grantor has the right to possess and occupy it for life, rent-free and without charge except for taxes, insurance, maintenance and related costs and expenses. This right is intended to give the grantor a beneficial interest in the property and to ensure that the grantor does not lose eligibility for a state homestead tax exemption for which she otherwise qualifies.

Part 14. Severability of Clauses

If any provision of this Declaration of Trust is ruled unenforceable, the remaining provisions shall stay in effect.

Certification of Grantor

I certify that I have read this Declaration of Trust and that it correctly states the terms and conditions under which the trust property is to be held, managed and disposed of by the trustee, and I approve the Declaration of Trust.

_____   _____
Sheila Jenkins, Grantor and Trustee   Date

Certification of Acknowledgment of Notary Public

State of _____

County of _____

On _____, before me, _____ ,
a notary public for said state, personally appeared _____ ,
personally known to me (or proved to me on the basis of satisfactory evidence) to be the person whose name is subscribed to the within instrument, and acknowledged to me that she/he executed the same in her/his authorized capacity and that by her/his signature on the instrument the person, or the entity upon behalf of which the person acted, executed the instrument.

Witness my hand and official seal.

_____

NOTARY PUBLIC for the State of _____

My commission expires _____ .

Schedule A
Property Placed in Trust

1. 100 shares of Applied Dynamics stock.
2. House at 2100 Fortuna Street, Phoenix, Arizona.
3. Condominium at 57-A Alpine Way, Tahoe City, California.

Creating a Shared Basic Trust

When you create your living trust document with Quicken Will-Maker Plus, you have only a few choices to make. Basically, you must decide:

- what property you want to put in your living trust
- whom you want to receive the trust property at your death (these people or organizations are the beneficiaries of your living trust)
- who is to be the successor trustee—the person you want to distribute trust property at your death, and
- how you should arrange for someone to manage trust property if it's inherited by beneficiaries who are too young to handle it without supervision.

You may already have a good idea of how you want to decide these issues. This chapter discusses the factors you should think about as you make each decision. It is organized the same way as the program is (Parts 1 through 6), so that you can easily refer to it while you're actually making your trust document. It's a good idea, though, to read through this chapter before you sit down at the computer—it will make the whole process clearer and easier.

Creating a Valid Living Trust

- ☐ Prepare the trust document with Quicken WillMaker Plus.
- ☐ Print out the trust document and sign it in front of a notary public.
- ☐ Transfer ownership of the property listed in the trust document into your name, as trustee.
- ☐ Update your trust document when needed.

How a Shared Basic Trust Works: An Overview

Here, in brief, are the important points about how a shared trust works:

Control of trust property. Both grantors will be trustees of your living trust, so you'll both have control over the property in the trust. Either of you can act on behalf of the trust—sell or give away trust property, for example. (As a practical matter, the consent of both may be necessary—see Part 3, below.)

Amendments or revocation. Either grantor can revoke the trust or add separately owned property to it at any time. Both, however, must consent to change any terms of the trust document—who gets what property, or who is named as successor trustee, for example.

This way either grantor can, by revoking the trust, return the situation to exactly what it was before the trust was formed. (Co-owned property is returned to both grantors, and separately owned property to its owner.) But while both grantors are living, neither can alone change what they've decided on in the trust—who should get what property when each one dies.

Death of the first grantor. When the first grantor dies, the shared living trust is automatically split into two trusts:

- Trust #1 contains the deceased grantor's share of trust property, except any trust property left to the survivor.
- Trust #2 contains the survivor's share, including any trust property left by the deceased grantor to the survivor.

The survivor is sole trustee of both trusts. The survivor must distribute the deceased grantor's property (what's in Trust #1) exactly as he or she instructed in the trust document, with no modifications. The survivor is also responsible for managing any Trust #1 property left to a young beneficiary in a child's subtrust (explained later in the chapter). When all the property in Trust #1 is distributed to the beneficiaries, Trust #1 ceases to exist.

Continuation of the living trust. Trust #2 (the survivor's) goes on as before, with the addition of any trust property the survivor inherited from the deceased grantor.

Death of the second grantor. At this point, the person named in the trust document as successor trustee takes over. He or she is responsible for distributing trust property to the beneficiaries and managing any trust property left to a young beneficiary in a child's subtrust (explained later).

EXAMPLE: Harry and Maude, a married couple, set up a shared revocable living trust to avoid probate. In the trust document, they appoint their niece Emily as successor trustee, to take over as trustee after they have both died. They transfer much of their co-owned property—their house, savings accounts and stocks—to themselves as trustees. Maude also puts some of her family heirlooms, which are her separate property, in the trust.

The trust document states that Maude's brother is to receive the heirlooms when she dies; everything else goes to Harry. Harry leaves all his trust property to Maude.

Maude dies first. The trust splits into Trust #1, which contains Maude's heirlooms, and Trust #2, which contains everything else: Harry's trust property and the trust property he inherits from Maude. Harry becomes the sole trustee of both trusts.

Following the terms of the trust document, Harry distributes Maude's heirlooms (Trust #1) to her brother, without probate. When the property is distributed, Trust #1 ceases to exist. Harry doesn't have to do anything with the trust property Maude left him; it's already in Trust #2.

When Harry dies, Emily becomes trustee and distributes the trust property following Harry's instructions in the trust document.

Part 1: Your Names

This part is easy: Just enter your names. The names you enter will form part of the name of your trust. For example, if you enter "William S. Jorgensen" and "Helga M. Jorgensen," your trust will be named "The William S. Jorgensen and Helga M. Jorgensen Revocable Living Trust." Your names will also appear as the original trustees of your living trust. (See Part 2, below.)

Enter your name the way it appears on other formal business documents, such as your driver's license or bank accounts. This may or may not be the name on your birth certificate.

If you go by more than one name, use only one; don't enter various versions of your name joined by "aka" (also known as). Be sure that the name you use is the one that appears on the ownership documents for property you plan to hold in trust. If it isn't, it could cause confusion later, and you should change the name on your ownership documents before you transfer the property to yourself as trustee.

EXAMPLE: You use the name William Dix for your trust, but own real estate in your former name of William Geicherwitz. You should prepare and sign a new deed, changing the name of the owner to William Dix, before you prepare another deed to transfer the property to your living trust.

Part 2: Trustees

To be legally valid, every living trust must have a trustee—someone to manage the property held in trust. When you create a revocable living trust with this program, both grantors are the trustees while you are alive. You'll name someone else to be the successor trustee, to take over after both of you have died.

The Original Trustees

Both grantors will be the original trustees of your living trust. That way, both of you have control over trust property, and taxation doesn't get complicated.

SEE AN EXPERT

You can't name someone else as trustee. In the unlikely event you don't want to be the trustees or want only one of you to be trustee, you cannot use Quicken WillMaker Plus. See an estate planning lawyer.

As a day-to-day, practical matter, it makes little difference that your property is now held in trust. You won't have any special duties as trustees of your trust. You do not even need to file a separate income tax return for the living trust. If the property generates income, just report it on your personal income tax return, as if the trust did not exist.

You have the same freedom to sell, give away or mortgage trust property as you did before you put the property into the living trust. The only difference is that you must now sign documents in your capacities as trustees.

EXAMPLE: Celeste and Robert want to sell a piece of land that is owned in the name of their living trust. They prepare a deed transferring ownership of the land from the trust to the new owner, and sign the deed as "Celeste Tornetti and Robert Tornetti, trustees of the Celeste Tornetti and Robert Tornetti Revocable Living Trust dated February 4, 20xx."

It's important to realize that once the property is held in trust, either trustee has authority over it. That means that either one can sell or give away any of the trust property—including any property that was co-owned or was the separate property of the other grantor before it was transferred to the trust. In practice, however, both of you will probably have to consent to transfer real estate out of the living trust. Especially in community property states, buyers and title insurance companies usually insist on both owners' signatures on transfer documents.

If you don't want to give your spouse or partner legal authority over your separately owned property, it's best to make separate living trusts. (See Chapter 14.)

The Trustee After One Grantor's Death or Incapacity

When one grantor dies or becomes incapacitated and unable to manage his or her affairs, the other becomes sole trustee.

But who should decide that it's time for an original trustee to step aside, if the issue ever comes up?

In the trust document, you'll name someone (and two alternates) to make this determination. These people do not have to be doctors; ideally, you will choose people who know you well and can give an unbiased opinion about whether or not you need help taking care of financial matters.

If there's ever a question of your ability to manage the trust, the successor trustee will ask your first choice for an opinion of your capacity. If that person isn't available, the successor trustee will go to your second, and if necessary, third choice. If one of them states, in writing, that because of your condition, the successor trustee needs to take over as trustee, then the successor can do so.

If one trustee takes over management of trust property, he or she has no power over property not held in trust, and no authority to make health care decisions for the incapacitated trustee. For this reason, it's also wise for each of you to create documents called durable powers of attorney, giving the other spouse or partner authority to manage property not owned in the name of the trust

and to make health care decisions. (See Chapters 22 and 23.)

After one grantor's death, the survivor, as trustee, is responsible for distributing trust property of the deceased grantor that is not left to the surviving grantor. The survivor must follow the deceased grantor's wishes as they are set out in the trust document. The survivor has no legal power to modify the deceased grantor's intentions in any way. (See Chapter 21.)

The survivor may have long-term duties if the trust document creates a child's subtrust for trust property inherited by a young beneficiary. It falls to the surviving trustee to manage trust property left to a young beneficiary in this way, possibly for many years (this is explained in Part 6, below).

The Successor Trustee

You must also choose a successor trustee—someone to act as trustee after both of you have died or become incapacitated. The successor trustee has no power or responsibility if at least one original trustee is alive and capable of managing the trust.

The Successor Trustee's Duties After Both Grantors' Deaths

After both original trustees have died, the successor trustee named in the trust document takes over as trustee. The successor trustee's primary responsibility is to distribute trust property to the beneficiaries named in the trust document. That is usually a straightforward process that can be completed in a few weeks. (More about this in Chapter 21.)

The successor trustee may, however, have long-term duties if the trust document creates a child's subtrust for trust property inherited by a young beneficiary (this is explained in Part 6 below).

The Successor Trustee's Duties If Either Grantor Is Incapacitated

The successor trustee will take over as trustee before both trustees have died if both trustees are unable to manage their affairs. Incapacity is determined by the person named in the trust document for this purpose. (See "The Trustee After One Grantor's Death or Incapacity," above.) In this situation, the successor trustee has broad authority to manage the property in the living trust and use it for both grantors' health care, support and welfare. The law requires him or her to act honestly and prudently. And because the grantors are no longer the trustees, the new trustee must file an annual income tax return for the trust.

Choosing a Successor Trustee

The person or institution you choose as successor trustee will have a crucial role: to distribute trust property to your beneficiaries after you have died. And if you and the other grantor become incapacitated, the successor will manage trust property on your behalf; if you leave property to a young beneficiary in trust, the successor will manage that property until the beneficiary is old enough to handle it alone.

Obviously, when you are giving someone this much power and discretion, you should choose someone with good common sense whom you trust completely. If you don't know anyone who fits this description, think twice about establishing a living trust. Most people pick an adult son or daughter, other relative or close friend.

Keep in mind that the successor trustee does not take over until both grantors have died (or become incapacitated). That means that after one grantor's death, the survivor will probably have plenty of time to amend the trust document and name a different successor trustee if he or she wishes.

In most situations, the successor trustee will not need extensive experience in financial management; common sense, dependability and complete honesty are usually enough. A successor trustee who may have long-term responsibility over a young beneficiary's trust property needs more management and financial skills than a successor trustee whose only job is to distribute trust property. The successor trustee does have authority, however, under the terms of the trust document, to get any reasonably necessary professional help— from an accountant, lawyer or tax preparer, perhaps—and pay for it out of trust assets.

Usually, it makes sense to name just one person as successor trustee, to avoid any possibility of conflicts. But it's legal and may be desirable to name more than one person. For example, you might name two or more of your children, if you don't expect any disagreements between them and you think one of them might feel hurt and left out if not named.

Having more than one successor trustee is especially likely to cause serious problems if the successor trustees are in charge of the property you have left to a young beneficiary in a child's subtrust. The trustees may have to manage a young beneficiary's property for many years and will have many decisions to make about how to spend the money—greatly increasing the potential for conflict. (Children's subtrusts are discussed in Part 6, below.)

If you appoint cotrustees, you'll have to decide how they'll have authority to act—that is, whether each one can act independently or if they must all agree before they can act. Obviously, it's easy to let each act without waiting for formal, written consent from the others. You may, however, prefer to have them all formally agree before taking action on behalf of the trust.

If you name more than one successor trustee, and one of them can't serve, the others will serve. If none of them can serve, the alternate you name (in the next section of the program) will take over.

It's perfectly legal to name a beneficiary of the trust (someone who will inherit trust property) as successor trustee. In fact, it's common.

> **EXAMPLE:** Mildred and James name their only child, Allison, to be successor trustee of their living trust. They name each other as trust beneficiaries, and Allison as alternate beneficiary. When James dies, his share of the trust property goes to Mildred. When Mildred dies, Allison uses her authority as trustee to transfer the remaining trust property to herself, the beneficiary.

Institutions as Successor Trustees

Normally, your first choice as successor trustee should be a flesh-and-blood person, not the trust department of a bank or other institution. Institutional trustees charge hefty fees, which come out of the trust property and leave less for your family and friends. And most aren't interested in "small" living trusts—ones that contain less than several hundred thousand dollars' worth of property.

But if there's no close relative or friend you think is capable of serving as your successor trustee, probably your best bet is to consider naming a private trust services company as successor trustee. Typically, their fees are pricey, but less than a bank's, and your affairs will probably receive more personal attention.

For a very large living trust, another possibility is to name a person and an institution as cosuccessor trustees. The bank or trust services company can do most of the paperwork, and the person can keep an eye on things and approve all transactions.

The successor trustee does not have to live in the same state as you do. But if you are choosing between someone local and someone far away, think about how convenient it will be for the person you choose to distribute the living trust property after your death. Someone close by will probably have an easier job, especially with real estate transfers. But for transfers of property such as securities and bank accounts, it usually won't make much difference where the successor trustee lives.

Obviously, before you finalize your living trust, you should check with the person you've chosen to be your successor trustee. You want to be sure your choice is willing to serve. If you don't, you may well create problems down the line. The person you've chosen may not want to serve, for a variety of reasons. And even if the person would be willing, if he or she doesn't know of his or her responsibilities, transfer of trust property after your death could be delayed.

If you choose an institution, you must check out the minimum size of trust it will accept and the fees it charges for management and make arrangements for how the institution will take over as trustee.

Avoiding Conflicts With Your Will and Other Documents

When you make a living trust with your spouse or partner, the document gives him or her authority to manage trust property if you ever become incapacitated. It's usually a good idea to also appoint your spouse or partner to be your:

- executor, to distribute property left through your will after your death, and
- attorney-in-fact in your Durable Power of Attorney for Finances, to manage property not held in trust if you become incapacitated.

Payment of the Successor Trustee

Typically, the successor trustee of a simple probate-avoidance living trust isn't paid. This

is because, in most cases, the successor trustee's only job is to distribute the trust property to beneficiaries soon after the grantor's death—and often, the successor trustee inherits most of the trust property anyway.

An exception is a successor trustee who manages the property in a child's subtrust. In that case, the successor trustee is entitled, under the terms of the trust document, to "reasonable compensation." The successor trustee decides what is reasonable and takes it from the trust property left to the young beneficiary.

Allowing the successor trustee to set the amount of the payment can work well, as long as your successor trustee is completely trustworthy. If the young beneficiary feels the trustee's fees are much too high, he or she will have to go to court to challenge them.

Naming an Alternate Successor Trustee

We'll ask you to name an alternate successor trustee, in case your first choice is unable to serve.

If you name two or more successor trustees, the alternate won't become trustee unless none of your original choices can serve.

> EXAMPLE: Caroline and Oscar name their two grown children, Eugene and Vanessa, as successor trustees. They name a close friend, Nicole, as alternate successor trustee. After Caroline and Oscar have died, Vanessa is ill and can't serve as trustee. Eugene acts as sole successor trustee. If he is unable to serve or dies, Nicole will take over.

If no one you named in the trust document can serve, the last trustee to serve has the power to appoint, in writing, another successor trustee. (See Chapter 21.)

EXAMPLE: To continue the previous example, if Nicole were ill and didn't have the energy to serve as successor trustee, she could appoint someone else to serve as trustee.

Part 3: Property to Be Put in Trust

In this part of the program, you must list each item of property—both jointly owned and separately owned—you want to transfer to your living trust. It will take some thought to decide what property to include and how to list it in the trust document. (Later in the program, you will name beneficiaries to receive each item of trust property at your death.)

This is a crucial step. Any property you don't list will not go into your living trust and will not pass under the terms of the trust. It may instead have to go through probate.

Adding property to the trust later. If you mistakenly leave something out or acquire more valuable property after you create your trust, you will be able to add it to your living trust. Chapter 20 explains how.

CAUTION

Listing property in the trust document is not enough. If an item has a title (ownership) document, such as a deed or title slip, you must change the title document to show

that you, as trustee, are the legal owner of the property. If you don't, the trust won't work. *You should transfer ownership as soon as possible after you print out and sign your Declaration of Trust.* Instructions are in Chapter 19.

Inventory Your Valuable Property

Before you begin to list your property in the program, sort out what you have and who owns it: you, your spouse or partner, or both of you. You need to label each item this way because each grantor names beneficiaries for his or her share of the trust property separately. Chapter 5 has tips on taking inventory of what you own.

After you've made an inventory, the next section will help you decide which items you want to hold in trust so they don't have to go through probate after your death.

Grouping Items

When you list your property in the program, you can group items if you're leaving them all to one beneficiary. For example, if you want to leave all your books to your daughter, there's no need to describe each one individually—unless your collection includes some particularly valuable or important books that you want to make extra sure get to the beneficiary.

Who Owns It?

You'll need to say who owns each item when you enter it in the program. This is because only your share of the trust property is distributed at your death.

For many couples, especially if they've been together a long time, nearly everything is owned together. But one or both of you may own a sizable amount of property separately. If you're married, your state's laws may give both spouses ownership rights in property that you may think is owned by only one spouse. If you're unsure about who owns what, read this section, which explains the ownership rules for your state.

Community Property States

Alaska*	Nevada
Arizona	New Mexico
California**	Texas
Idaho	Washington
Louisiana	Wisconsin

* If spouses sign a community property agreement

** Registered domestic partners are also covered by California's community property laws.

If you live in a community property state and you aren't sure who owns what, don't rely on whose name is on the title document. For example, if while you were married you bought a house with money you earned, your spouse legally owns a share of that property—even if only your name is on the deed.

Generally, any property that either spouse earns or acquires during the marriage (before permanent separation) is community property. Both spouses (the "community") own it together, and each spouse can leave his or her half-interest through a will or living trust. The main exception to this shared ownership rule

is that property one spouse acquires by gift or inheritance belongs to that spouse alone. Property acquired before marriage also belongs to each spouse separately.

Even separate property may, however, turn into community property if it is mixed ("commingled") with community property. For example, if you deposit separate property funds into a joint bank account and then make more deposits and withdrawals, making it impossible to tell what part of the account is separate money, it's all considered community property.

Survivorship Community Property

In Alaska, Arizona, California, Nevada and Wisconsin, couples can hold title to community property in a way that entails a right of survivorship. When property is held this way, after the first spouse dies, the survivor automatically owns all the property, without probate. So if you have survivorship community property, you don't need to put it into a living trust to avoid probate.

Non-Community Property States

Alabama	Missouri
Alaska*	Montana
Arkansas	Nebraska
Colorado	New Hampshire
Connecticut	New Jersey
Delaware	New York
District of Columbia	North Carolina
Florida	North Dakota
Georgia	Ohio

Hawaii

Illinois

Indiana

Iowa

Kansas

Kentucky

Maine

Maryland

Massachusetts

Michigan

Minnesota

Mississippi

Oklahoma

Oregon

Pennsylvania

Rhode Island

South Carolina

South Dakota

Tennessee

Utah

Vermont

Virginia

West Virginia

Wyoming

* Spouses can, however, create community property by signing a community property agreement.

In these states, it is usually fairly simple to figure out who owns what. If the property has a title document—for example, a deed to real estate or a car title slip—then the spouse whose name is on the title is the owner. If the property doesn't have a title document, it belongs to the spouse who paid for it or received it as a gift. (It's possible, though, that if there were a dispute, a judge could determine, based on the circumstances, that a spouse whose name is not on the title document might own an interest in the property.)

If the trust is revoked, the property will be returned to each spouse based on the same ownership rights they had before the property was held in trust.

Decide What Property to Hold in Trust

Now that you've got a list of what you own, you're ready to decide what items you want

to hold in trust to avoid probate fees. Think about including:

- houses and other real estate
- jewelry, antiques, furs and valuable furniture
- stock in a closely held corporation
- stock, bond and other security accounts held by brokerages
- small business interests
- money market and bank accounts
- patents and copyrights
- precious metals
- valuable works of art, and
- valuable collections of stamps, coins or other objects.

You don't need to put everything you own into a living trust to save money on probate. For some assets, you may decide to use other probate-avoidance devices instead of a living trust. And at least some of the property left to a surviving spouse can probably be transferred without a full-blown probate court proceeding. (See Chapter 13.)

Real Estate

The most valuable thing most people own is real estate: their house, condominium or land. You can probably save your family substantial probate costs by transferring your real estate through a living trust.

In some situations, however, you may not want to hold your real estate in living trust. See the discussions below on:

- Property Held in Joint Tenancy
- Property Held in Tenancy by the Entirety, and
- Community Property States.

<table>
<tr><td>

If You're Not Sure How You Hold Title

If you own real estate with someone else but aren't sure how you hold title, look at the deed. It should say how title is held: in joint tenancy, tenancy in common, tenancy by the entirety, or community property or community property with right of survivorship (in community property states). In a community property state, if the deed says the property is owned "as husband and wife," that means community property.

</td></tr>
</table>

If either of you own real estate with someone else, you can transfer just your interest in it to your living trust. You won't need to specify that your share is one-half or some other fraction. For example, if you and your sister own a house together, you need only list "the house at 7989 Lafayette Court, Boston, MA." Your trust document will state that you have transferred all your interest in that property to the trust. The share of the property owned by your sister, obviously, is not included.

Co-op apartments. If you own shares in a co-op corporation that owns your apartment, you'll have to hold your shares in trust. Some corporations are reluctant to let a trustee own shares; check the co-op corporation's rules to see whether the transfer is allowed.

Small Business Interests

The delay, expense and court intrusion of probate can be especially detrimental to an ongoing small business. Using your living trust to transfer business interests to beneficiaries quickly after your death is almost essential if you want the beneficiaries to be able to keep the business running.

If you want to control the long-term management of your business, however, a revocable living trust is not the right vehicle. See an estate planning lawyer to draft a different kind of trust, with provisions tailored to your situation.

Different kinds of business organizations present different issues when you want to hold your interest in trust:

Sole proprietorships. If you operate your business as a sole proprietorship, with all business assets held in your own name, you can simply transfer your business property to yourself as trustee. You should also transfer the business's name itself; that transfers the customer goodwill associated with the name.

Partnership interests. If you operate your business as a partnership with other people, you can probably transfer your partnership share to yourself as trustee. If there is a partnership certificate, it must be changed.

Some partnership agreements require the people who inherit a deceased partner's share of the business to offer that share to the other partners before taking it. But that happens after death, so it shouldn't affect your ability to transfer the property through a living trust.

It's not common, but a partnership agreement may limit or forbid holding your interest in trust. If yours does, you and your partners may want to see a lawyer before you make any changes.

Solely owned corporations. If you own all the stock of a corporation, you should have no difficulty transferring it to yourself as trustee.

Closely held corporations. A closely held corporation is a corporation that doesn't sell shares to the public. All its shares are owned by a few people who are usually actively involved in running the business. Normally, you can use a living trust to transfer shares in a closely held corporation by listing the stock in the trust document and then having the stock certificates reissued in your name as trustee.

You'll want to check the corporation's bylaws and articles of incorporation to be sure that you will still have voting rights in your capacity as trustee of the living trust; usually, this is not a problem. If it is, you and the other shareholders should be able to amend the corporation's bylaws to allow it.

There may, however, be restrictions that affect the transfer of shares. Check the corporation's bylaws and articles of incorporation, as well as any separate shareholders' agreements. One fairly common rule is that surviving shareholders (or the corporation) have the right to buy the shares of a deceased shareholder. In that case, you can still use a living trust to transfer the shares, but the people who inherit them may have to sell them.

Limited liability companies. If your small business is an LLC, you'll need the consent of a majority or all of the other owners (check your operating agreement) before you can transfer your interest to yourself as trustee. This shouldn't be a problem; they'll just want to know that you, as trustee of your own trust, will have authority to vote on LLC decisions. Another way to address this concern would be to transfer your economic interest in the LLC, but not your right to vote.

Bank Accounts

It's not difficult to transfer bank accounts to your living trust. But you may well decide that you don't need to. That's because you can directly designate a beneficiary for the funds in a bank account. If you do, you don't need to transfer those accounts to a living trust just to avoid probate. Their contents won't go through probate in the first place.

This option can be especially useful for personal checking accounts, which you may not want to transfer to your living trust—it can be difficult to cash checks on accounts owned in a trustee's name.

A living trust, however, offers one advantage that most pay-on-death arrangements do not: You can name an alternate beneficiary to receive the account if your first choice isn't alive at your death. Pay-on-death accounts are discussed in Chapter 13.

Jointly owned accounts. If you want to hold a joint account in your living trust, things are more complicated, and you may just want to name a payable-on-death beneficiary for the account instead. The reason is that almost all joint accounts have what's called the "right of survivorship," which means that when one owner dies, the survivor automatically owns all the money in the account. A provision in a will or living trust can't override that. So no matter what your living trust says, the share of the first grantor to die will go to the survivor; the money in the account will go to a trust beneficiary only when the second grantor dies.

> EXAMPLE: Joan and Alex have a joint savings account. They go to the bank and change the registration card on

the account to read "Joan and Alex Crookshank, trustees of the Joan and Alex Crookshank Revocable Living Trust dated August 23, 20xx." In the trust document, Alex leaves his half of the account to his friend Max. Joan leaves hers to her daughter Linda. Alex dies first. The account is now owned by Joan, and when she dies, all the funds will go to Linda. Max won't inherit anything.

Vehicles and Property That Is Often Sold

Some kinds of property are cumbersome to keep in a living trust. It's not a legal problem, just a practical one. Two common examples are:

- **Cars or other vehicles you use.** Having registration and insurance in your name as trustee could be confusing, and some insurance companies might balk. If you have valuable antique autos, or a mobile home that is permanently attached to land and considered real estate under your state's law, however, you may want to go ahead and hold them in trust. You should be able to find an insurance company that will cooperate.
- **Property you buy or sell frequently.** If you don't expect to own the property at your death, there's no compelling reason to hold it in trust. (Remember, the probate process you want to avoid doesn't happen until after your death.) On the other hand, if you're buying property, it's no more trouble to acquire it in your name as trustee.

Life Insurance

If you own a life insurance policy at your death, the insurance company will give the proceeds to the named beneficiary, without probate. (The proceeds are, however, considered part of your estate for federal estate tax purposes.)

If you have named a minor or young adult as the beneficiary, you may want to name your living trust instead. Then, in the trust document, you name the child as beneficiary of any insurance proceeds paid to the trust and arrange for an adult to manage the policy proceeds if the beneficiary is still young when you die. If you don't arrange for management of the money, and the beneficiary is still a minor (under 18) when you die, a court will have to appoint a financial guardian after your death. (Young beneficiaries are discussed in Part 6, below.)

Passing the proceeds of a life insurance policy through your living trust is a bit more complicated than leaving other property this way. You must take two steps:

1. Name the living trust as the beneficiary of your life insurance policy. (Your insurance agent will have a form that lets you change the beneficiary of the policy.)
2. When you list property items in the living trust document, list the proceeds of the policy, not the policy itself. (See "How to Describe Trust Property," below.)

Securities

If you buy and sell stocks regularly, you may not want to go to the trouble of acquiring and selling them using your authority as trustee of the trust.

Fortunately, there's an easier way to do it: Hold your stocks in a brokerage account that is owned in your name as trustee. All securities in the account are then held in trust, which means that you can use your living trust to leave all the contents of the account to a specific beneficiary. If you want to leave stock to different beneficiaries, you can either establish more than one brokerage account or leave one account to more than one beneficiary to own together.

An Alternative: Transfer-on-Death Registration

All states but Louisiana and Texas now allow ownership of securities to be registered in a "transfer-on-death" form. You can designate someone to receive the securities, including mutual funds and brokerage accounts, after your death. No probate will be necessary. Ask your broker about the forms you need to fill out to name a beneficiary for your securities.

Stock in closely held corporations. See "Small Business Interests," above.

Cash

It's common for people to want to leave cash gifts to beneficiaries—for example, to leave $5,000 to a relative, friend or charity. Don't, however, just type in "$5,000 cash" when you list the property you want to hold in trust. There's no way to own cash as a trustee, unless that cash is specifically identified.

The way to identify the cash is to transfer ownership of a cash account—a savings or money market account, for example—to yourself as trustee. You can then name a beneficiary to receive the contents of the account. So if you want to leave $5,000 to cousin Fred, all you have to do is put the money in a bank or money market account, transfer it to yourself as trustee and name Fred, in the trust document, as the beneficiary of the account.

If you don't want to set up a separate account to leave a modest amount of cash to a beneficiary, think about buying a savings bond and leaving it to the beneficiary or leaving one larger account to several beneficiaries.

> **EXAMPLE:** Michael would like to leave some modest cash gifts to his two grown nephews, Warren and Brian, whom he's always been fond of. He puts $5,000 into a money market account and then transfers the account to himself as trustee. In his trust document, he names Warren and Brian as beneficiaries of the account. After Michael's death, the two nephews will inherit the account together, and each will be entitled to half of the funds.

Property Held in Joint Tenancy

Property owned in joint tenancy does not go through probate until the last surviving owner dies. When one co-owner (joint tenant) dies, his or her share goes directly to the surviving co-owners, without probate. So if avoiding probate is your only concern, you and the other grantor don't need to transfer your joint tenancy property to your living trust.

Joint tenancy doesn't avoid probate, however, if the joint owners die simultaneously—there is no survivor to inherit the other's share. If you die at the same time, each owner's half-interest in the joint tenancy property is passed to the beneficiaries named in the residuary clauses of their wills. If you didn't make a will, the property passes to your closest relatives under state "intestate succession" law.

If you're concerned about what would happen to the property in the (statistically very unlikely) event that you and your spouse or partner died simultaneously, you have two choices.

- You can name a beneficiary, who would inherit the property in the event of simultaneous death, in your back-up will. If the property passes under your will, however, it will probably go through probate.
- You can hold the property in your living trust, and each owner can name the other as primary beneficiary and name an alternate beneficiary to receive his or her share of the property in case of simultaneous death. It's a bit more paperwork, but you're assured that probate will be avoided even in the event of simultaneous death.

There's another reason to use a living trust for joint tenancy property: if you want to leave your share of the property to someone besides the other joint tenant(s). Joint tenancy property automatically goes to the surviving co-owners when one co-owner dies. But if you transfer joint tenancy property to a living trust, the joint tenancy is destroyed, and you can leave your share to anyone you please.

Property Held in Tenancy by the Entirety

You and your spouse or registered domestic partner may hold title to property in "tenancy by the entirety"—basically, a kind of joint tenancy that's only for married couples (and same-sex couples that have registered with the state). Not all states have this form of ownership; see Chapter 13 for a list.

Like joint tenancy, tenancy by the entirety property does not go through probate when one owner dies; it automatically goes to the survivor. So if avoiding probate is your only concern, you and your spouse or partner don't need to transfer your tenancy by the entirety property to your living trust. Also like joint tenancy property, tenancy by the entirety property doesn't avoid probate if you both die simultaneously. If you're concerned about that possibility, you have two choices: Name a beneficiary in your back-up will, or hold the property in trust. These options are discussed just above.

Community Property States

Alaska*	Nevada
Arizona	New Mexico
California	Texas
Idaho	Washington
Louisiana	Wisconsin

* If spouses sign a community property agreement

If you and your spouse or registered domestic partner own significant community property, and you want to leave it to each other, you may not want to transfer it to your living trust. Your options depend on what state you live in.

Alaska, Arizona, California, Nevada or Wisconsin. In these states, you may want to take advantage of an option that lets you avoid probate completely for community property. You can add the right of survivorship to your community property so that when one spouse dies, the other automatically owns it.

California also allows community property that isn't held with an express right of survivorship to pass outside of probate, via two different procedures. For real estate, the surviving spouse or partner simply files a one-page affidavit (sworn statement) with the county recorder's office. The affidavit states that he or she is entitled to full ownership of the property. For other property, the survivor requests a Spousal Property Order from the probate court, which then authorizes the transfer into the survivor's name.

Idaho offers a simple probate procedure when the surviving spouse is the only beneficiary. The survivor files a petition with the probate court, and the court issues an order stating that he or she now owns everything.

Washington offers no probate shortcuts for community property. It goes through probate just like everything else.

New Mexico allows a surviving spouse to take title to a home held in community property without probate. But there are several limitations: It's allowed only after a six-month waiting period, only if probate isn't necessary for any other assets and only if all debts and taxes have been paid.

In any state, community property does not avoid probate when the second spouse dies. To avoid probate then, the property must be left via a living trust or other probate-avoidance device.

Community property also doesn't avoid probate if both spouses die simultaneously. If you're concerned about that possibility, you can hold the property in trust, and each spouse can name the other as primary beneficiary and name an alternate beneficiary to receive his or her share of the property in case of simultaneous death. It's a bit more paperwork, but you're assured that probate will be avoided even in the event of simultaneous death.

Retirement Plans

Individual retirement accounts cannot be held in trust. Instead, avoid probate by naming a beneficiary to inherit whatever's left in your retirement account at your death. The plan administrator or account holder can provide forms on which to designate your beneficiary.

Because retirement account funds don't go through probate (as long as you name a beneficiary other than your estate), there is usually no reason to name your trust as the beneficiary. If you do name a revocable living trust as the beneficiary of your retirement account, then (under current IRS rules) after your death required minimum distributions will be based on the life expectancy of the trust beneficiary.

RESOURCE

IRAs, 401(k)s & Other Retirement Plans: Taking Your Money Out, by Twila Slesnick and John C. Suttle (Nolo), explains the options of those who inherit money in a retirement account.

Other Valuable Property

Other valuable items   everything from jewelry and antiques to boats and airplanes—can also be placed in trust.

How to Describe Trust Property

When we ask you to list the property you want to hold in trust, describe each item clearly enough so that the surviving trustee or successor trustee can identify the property and transfer it to the right person. No magic legal words are required.

Think about whom the property will ultimately go to. If you're leaving everything to one person, or just a few, there's less need to go into great detail. But if there will be a number of trust beneficiaries, and objects could be confused, be more specific about each one. When in doubt, err on the side of including more information; describe particularly valuable items in detail, much as you would if you were listing them on an insurance policy.

Here are some sample descriptions:

Real estate

- "the house at 321 Glen St., Omaha, NE"
- "the house at 4444 Casey Road, Fandon, Illinois, and the 20-acre parcel on which it is located"

Usually, the street address is enough. It's not necessary to use the "legal description" found on the deed, which gives a subdivision plat number or a metes-and-bounds description. But if the property has no street address—for example, if it is undeveloped land out in the country—you will need to carefully copy the full legal description, word for word, from the deed.

If you own a house and several adjacent lots, it's a good idea to indicate that you are transferring the entire parcel to your living trust by describing the land as well as the house.

If you own the property with someone else and are transferring only your share, you don't need to specify the share you own. Just describe the property. The trust document will show that you are transferring all your interest in the property, whatever share that is, to the living trust.

Bank accounts

- "Savings Account No. 9384-387, Arlington Bank, Arlington, MN"
- "Money Market Account 47-223 at Charles Schwab & Co., Inc., San Francisco, CA"

Household items

- "all the furniture normally kept in the house at 44123 Derby Ave., Ross, KY"
- "the antique brass bed in the master bedroom in the house at 33 Walker Ave., Fort Lee, New Jersey"
- "all furniture and household items normally kept in the house at 869 Hopkins St., Great Falls, Montana"

Sole proprietorship business property

- "Mulligan's Fish Market"
- "Fourth Street Records and CDs"
- "all accounts receivable of the business known as Garcia's Restaurant, 988 17th St., Atlanta, GA"
- "all food preparation and storage equip-ment, including refrigerator, freezer,

hand mixers and slicer, used at Garcia's Restaurant, 988 17th St., Atlanta, GA"

As explained in "Decide What Property to Hold in Trust," above, you should both list the name of the business and separately list items of business property.

Partnership interest

- "Don and Dan's Bait Shop Partnership owned by the grantor before being held in this living trust"

Because a partnership is a legal entity that can own property, you don't need to list items of property owned by the partnership.

Shares in a closely held corporation

- "The stock of ABC Hardware, Inc."

Shares in a solely owned corporation

- "all shares in the XYZ Corporation"
- "all stock in Fern's Olde Antique Shoppe, Inc., 23 Turnbridge Ave., Danbury, CT"

Securities

- "all securities in account No. 3999-34-33 at Smith Brokerage, 33 Lowell Place, New York, NY"
- "200 shares of General Industries, Inc. stock"
- "Good Investment Co. mutual fund account No. 888-09-09"

Life insurance proceeds

- "the proceeds of Acme Co. Life Insurance Policy #9992A"

Miscellaneous items

- "Macintosh laptop computer (serial number 129311)"
- "the medical textbooks in the office at 1702 Parker Towers, San Francisco, CA"
- "the stamp collection usually kept at 321 Glen St., Omaha, NE"
- "the collection of European stamps, including [describe particularly valuable stamps], usually kept at 440 Loma Prieta Blvd., #450, San Jose, CA"
- "the Martin D-35 acoustic guitar, serial number 477597"
- "the signed 1960 Ernie Banks baseball card kept in safe deposit box 234, First National Bank of Augusta, Augusta, IL"
- "the Baldwin upright piano kept at 985 Dawson Court, South Brenly, Massachusetts"

Rules for Entering Descriptions of Trust Property

- Don't use "my" or "our" in a description. Don't, for example, enter "my books" or "my stereo system." That's because once the property is in the living trust, it doesn't belong to you anymore—it belongs to the trust.
- Don't begin a description with a capital letter (unless it must begin with a proper name, like "Steinway"). That's because the descriptions will be inserted into a sentence in the trust document, and it would look odd to see a capital letter in the middle of a sentence.
- Don't end a description with a period. Again, this is because the descriptions will be inserted into a sentence in the trust document.

Part 4: Beneficiaries of Trust Property

Once you've entered a list of the property you're going to hold in trust, the next step is to say whom you want to inherit that property. In the trust document, you and your spouse or partner must each name beneficiaries—the family, friends or organizations who will receive your share of the trust property.

Each spouse or partner names beneficiaries separately, because each one's trust property is distributed when that spouse or partner dies. When the first spouse or partner dies, his or her trust property will be distributed to the beneficiaries he or she named. If it is left to the other spouse or partner, it stays in the trust. When the second spouse or partner dies, the rest of the property in the trust is distributed to his or her beneficiaries.

> EXAMPLE: Roger and Marilyn Foster create a shared living trust. Each puts co-owned and separately owned property in the trust. When Roger dies, Marilyn takes over as sole trustee and distributes Roger's trust property to the beneficiaries he named in the trust document. Her property, including the trust property she inherits from Roger, stays in the living trust.

The beneficiaries you name in your trust document are not entitled to any trust property while both spouses or partners are alive. You can amend your trust document and change the beneficiaries any time you wish.

SEE AN EXPERT

Rights of a spouse, partner or child. If you are married and don't plan to leave at least half of what you own to your spouse or registered domestic partner, consult a lawyer experienced in estate planning. State law may entitle your spouse or partner to claim some of the property in your living trust. In most circumstances, you don't have to leave anything to your children. But if you want to disinherit a child, you should make a will and specifically mention the child in it. (See Chapter 4.)

How Do You Want Your Property Distributed?

We'll ask you first whether you want to leave all your trust property to one beneficiary (or more than one, to share it all) or leave different items to different beneficiaries.

Many couples want to leave all trust property to the survivor. If you choose that option, we'll insert your spouse's or partner's name (entered earlier) as beneficiary of all your trust property. All you have to do is name an alternate beneficiary, who will inherit your trust property if your spouse or partner does not survive you by five days. (Alternates are discussed below.)

If you choose to leave different items to different beneficiaries, you will be shown a list of all the property items you listed earlier. You can then name beneficiaries for them.

Your Spouse or Partner

It's common for spouses and partners to leave each other all or a substantial portion of the property in their shared trust. In a shared trust, if one grantor leaves the other trust property, it stays in the living trust when the first grantor dies.

> **EXAMPLE:** Max and Joan make a shared basic living trust. Each leaves all his or her trust property to the other. Max dies first. All his interest in trust property stays in what is now Joan's living trust. Joan has the right to amend the trust document to name beneficiaries for the trust property that is now hers. (See Chapter 21.)

Children From Prior Marriages

If you have children from a prior marriage, you may well want to leave them property in your living trust. A common way to do this is to leave the children specific items—real estate, life insurance policy proceeds, bank accounts or whatever—and leave everything else to your spouse or partner.

A more complicated way of ensuring that both your current spouse and children from an earlier marriage are taken care of is to create an AB trust. It gives the surviving spouse the right to use income from (or live in) certain property for his or her life; then the property goes to the children. (See Chapter 14.)

Minors or Young Adults

You can name minors (children under 18) to inherit trust property. If a beneficiary you name is a minor or a young adult who can't yet manage property without help, you can arrange for an adult to manage the trust property for the beneficiary. (See Part 6, below.)

Your Successor Trustee

It's very common and perfectly legal to make the person you named to be successor trustee (the person who will distribute trust property after the second grantor dies) a beneficiary as well.

> **EXAMPLE:** Nora and Sean name their son Liam as successor trustee of their living trust. Each spouse names the other as sole beneficiary of his or her trust property, and both name Liam as alternate beneficiary. When Nora dies, her trust property goes to Sean and stays in the trust. After Sean's death, Liam, acting as trustee, will transfer ownership of the trust property to himself.

Naming More Than One Beneficiary to Share Property

You can name more than one beneficiary to share any item of trust property. Simply list their names in the box on the screen. Type the names one per line; don't join the names with an "and." (See the Users' Manual for examples.)

Always use the beneficiaries' actual names; don't use collective terms such as "my children." It's not always clear who is included in such descriptions. And there can be serious confusion if one of the people originally included as a group member dies before you do.

Obviously, if you name cobeneficiaries for a piece of property that can't be physically divided—a cabin, for example—give some thought to whether or not the beneficiaries are likely to get along. If they are incompatible, disagreements could arise over taking care of property or deciding whether or not to sell it. If they can't settle their differences, any co-owner could go to court and demand a partition—a court-ordered division and sale—of the property.

Cobeneficiaries will share the property equally unless you state otherwise. We'll ask you, after you enter the names, whether or not you want an item of trust property to be shared equally among the beneficiaries.

> **EXAMPLE:** Georgia wants to leave her house to her two children, Ross and Ryan, but wants Ross to have a 75% share of it. She enters their names and then, on a later screen, enters their interests, in fractions: 3/4 for Ross and 1/4 for Ryan.
>
> When the children inherit the property, they own it together. But Ross will be liable for 75% of the taxes and upkeep cost, and entitled to 75% of any income the house produces. If they sell it, Ross will be entitled to 75% of the proceeds.

Entering Beneficiaries' Names

When you enter a beneficiary's name, use the name by which the beneficiary is known for purposes such as a bank account or driver's license. Generally, if the name you use clearly and unambiguously identifies the person, it is sufficient.

If you name an institution (charitable or not) to inherit trust property, enter its complete name. It may be commonly known by a shortened version, which could cause confusion if there are similarly named organizations. Call to ask if you're unsure. (An

institution that stands to inherit some of your money will be more than happy to help you.) Also be sure to specify if you want a branch of a national organization to receive your gift—for example, a local chapter of the Sierra Club.

Beneficiaries for Co-Owned Trust Property

As you name your beneficiaries, remember that when it comes to property you and your spouse or partner co-own, you're naming people to receive only your share. When one of you dies, only his or her interest in the co-owned property will go to the named beneficiary.

> **EXAMPLE:** Marcia and Perry transfer all the property they own together into their living trust. Marcia names Perry as the beneficiary of all her interest in the trust property. Perry names Marcia to inherit all of his half except his half-interest in their vacation cabin, which he leaves to his son from a previous marriage, Eric. If Perry dies first, Perry's half-interest in the cabin will go to Eric, who will co-own it with Marcia.

Alternate Beneficiaries

You can name an alternate beneficiary for every person you name as a primary beneficiary. The alternate will get the property left to the primary beneficiary if your first choice does not live for more than 120 hours (five days) after your death. This "survivorship" period ensures that if you and a primary beneficiary die simultaneously or almost so, the property will go to the alternate beneficiary you chose, not to the primary beneficiary's heirs.

> **EXAMPLE:** Laura and her husband Juan Carlos make a shared living trust. Laura leaves all her trust property to Juan Carlos and names her daughter from a previous marriage as alternate beneficiary. Laura and Juan Carlos are seriously injured in a car accident; Juan Carlos dies a day after Laura does. Because Juan Carlos did not survive Laura by at least five days, the trust property he would have inherited from Laura goes to Laura's daughter instead.
>
> If there had been no survivorship requirement, the trust property would have gone to Juan Carlos; when he died a day later, it would have gone to the beneficiaries he had named.

You don't have to name an alternate for a charitable (or other) institution you name as a beneficiary. If the institution is well established, it is probably safe to assume that it will still exist at your death.

With other beneficiaries, however, there is always the chance that the primary beneficiary may not survive you, so it's a goood idea to name an alternate.

You can name more than one person or institution as alternate beneficiaries. If you do, they will share the property equally (unless you state otherwise).

Part 5: Residuary Beneficiaries

If you leave all your trust property to one beneficiary (or a group of beneficiaries to share) you will not name a residuary beneficiary. But if you made any specific gifts, each grantor must name a residuary beneficiary. The person or organization you name will receive:

- any trust property for which both the primary and alternate beneficiaries you named die before you do
- any trust property that you didn't leave to a named beneficiary (this could include property you transfer to the trust later and don't name a beneficiary for, and trust property that was owned by the other grantor, which he or she left you)
- any property you leave to your living trust through your will (such a will is called a pour-over will), and
- any property that you actually transferred to yourself as trustee but didn't list in the trust document.

Often, the residuary beneficiary of a living trust doesn't inherit anything from the trust. Usually, naming a residuary beneficiary is just a back-up measure, to guard against the extremely small chance that both a primary and alternate trust beneficiary do not survive you.

Part 6: Property Management for Young Beneficiaries

If any of the beneficiaries (including alternate and residuary beneficiaries) named by either grantor might inherit trust property before they are ready to manage it without an adult's help, that grantor should arrange for someone to manage it for them for a while. There are several ways to go about it:

- **Leave the property to an adult to use for the child.** Many people don't leave property directly to a child. Instead, they leave it to the child's parent or to the person they expect to have care and custody of the child if neither parent is available. There's no formal legal arrangement, but they trust the adult to use the property for the child's benefit.
- **Name a custodian under a law called the Uniform Transfers to Minors Act (UTMA).** In almost every state, you can name a custodian to manage property you leave a child until the child reaches 18 or 21, depending on state law (up to 25 in some states). If you don't need management to last beyond that age, a custodianship is preferable.
- **Create a child's subtrust.** You can use Quicken WillMaker Plus to establish a "child's subtrust" in your living trust. If you do, the surviving trustee (or the successor trustee, after both grantors' death) will manage the property you left the child and dole it out for education, health and other needs. The subtrust ends at whatever age you designate (up to 35), and any remaining property is turned over to the child outright.

Subtrusts and custodianships are explained below.

> **CAUTION**
>
> **Children with special needs.** These property management options are not designed to provide long-term property management for a child with serious disabilities. For information on this kind of planning, see *Special Needs Trusts*, by Stephen Elias (Nolo).

Should You Arrange for Management?

Each grantor chooses whether or not to arrange to have someone manage trust property if it is inherited by young beneficiaries.

The consequences of forgoing management for trust property inherited by a young beneficiary depend on whether the beneficiary is over or under age 18 at your death.

Children Under 18 Years Old

Minors—children under 18—cannot, legally, own or manage significant amounts of property. An adult must be in charge if the minor acquires more than a few thousand dollars' worth of property. (The exact amount depends on state law.)

If your minor beneficiaries won't inherit anything of great value—if you're leaving them objects that have more sentimental than monetary value—you don't need to arrange for an adult to manage the property.

But if a beneficiary inherits valuable trust property while still a minor, and you have not arranged for the property to be managed by an adult, a court-appointed guardian may have to manage the property. Contrary to what you might expect, a child's parent does not automatically have legal authority to manage any property the child inherits. So even if one or both of the beneficiary's parents are alive, they will have to ask the court to grant them that authority and will be subject to the court's supervision. If neither parent is alive, there may be no obvious person for the court to appoint as property guardian. In that case, it may be even more important for you to name someone in your living trust.

There is one other option: In most states, the successor trustee can name a custodian to manage property inherited by a minor. If the value of the property exceeds a certain amount—$10,000 in most states—a court must approve the appointment. And the custodianship must end at 18 in most states, earlier than many parents would choose. So it's still better to name a custodian yourself.

Young Adults 18 to 35 Years Old

If someone who is 18 or older inherits trust property, you do not need, legally, to have anyone manage the property on the beneficiary's behalf. And if you don't make any arrangements, the beneficiary will get the property with no strings attached. But you can arrange for property management to last until a beneficiary turns any age up to 35.

There is no legal requirement that management for a trust beneficiary's property must end at 35, but we think 35 is a reasonable cutoff. If you don't want to let a beneficiary get his or her hands on trust property by the time he or she reaches 35, you probably need to see a lawyer and tailor a plan to the beneficiary's needs.

Which Is Better: Subtrust or Custodianship?

Using Quicken WillMaker Plus, you can create either a child's subtrust or a custodianship under the Uniform Transfer to Minors Act (if it's available in your state). Both are safe, efficient ways of managing trust property that a young person inherits. Under either system, the person in charge of the young beneficiary's property has the same responsibility to use the property for the beneficiary's support, education and health.

The most significant difference is that a child's subtrust can last longer than a custodianship, which must end at age 18 to 21 in most states (25 in a few states). (Each state's rule is set out in Chapter 7.) For that reason, a child's subtrust is a good choice when a child could inherit a large amount of property.

Because an UTMA custodianship is much easier to administer, it is usually preferable if the beneficiary will inherit no more than about $50,000 worth of trust property ($100,000 or more if the child is quite young). That amount is likely to be used up for living and education expenses by the time the beneficiary is 21, so there's no need to create a subtrust that can continue beyond that age.

A custodianship has other advantages as well:

- Handling a beneficiary's property is much easier with a custodianship than with a trust. A custodian's powers are written into state law, and most institutions, such as banks and insurance companies, are familiar with the rules. Trusts, on the other hand, vary in their terms. So before a bank lets a trustee act on behalf of a beneficiary, it may demand to see and analyze a copy of the Declaration of Trust.

- You can name whomever you wish to be a custodian, and you can name different custodians for different beneficiaries. So if you want to arrange custodianships for grandchildren, for example, you could name each child's parent as custodian. A child's subtrust is not quite so flexible: The surviving grantor, or the successor trustee if you are the second grantor to die, will be the trustee of all children's subtrusts created for your young beneficiaries.

- If the property in a subtrust earns income, and that income isn't distributed quickly to the beneficiary, the trust will have to pay tax on it. The federal tax rate on such retained income may be higher than it would be if the young beneficiary were taxed on it. The trustee may well need to hire experts to help with trust accounting and tax returns.

Custodianships

Think a custodianship is right for your family? Here's how it works.

How a Custodianship Works

In the trust document, you name someone to serve as custodian for a particular beneficiary. That person manages any trust property the young beneficiary inherits from you until the beneficiary reaches the age at which state law says the custodianship must end. (See the list in Chapter 7.)

EXAMPLE: Sandra and Don make a living trust. Sandra leaves 100 shares of General Motors stock to her niece, Jennifer Frankel. She names Hazel Frankel, Jennifer's mother, as custodian under the Illinois Uniform Transfers to Minors Act.

After Sandra's death, Don, as trustee, turns the stock over to the custodian, Hazel. She will manage it for Jennifer until Jennifer turns 21, the age Illinois law says she must be given the property outright.

In some states, you can specify—within limits—at what age the custodianship will end. If your state allows this, the program will ask you to enter the age at which you want the custodianship to end.

EXAMPLE: If Sandra, in the previous example, lived in New Jersey, the state's law would allow her to choose any age from 18 to 21 for the custodianship to end.

The Custodian's Responsibilities

A custodian has roughly the same responsibility as the trustee of a child's subtrust: to manage the beneficiary's property wisely and honestly. The custodian's authority and duties are set out by a law called the Uniform Transfers to Minors Act, as enacted by your state. No court directly supervises the custodian.

The custodian must:

- manage the property until the beneficiary reaches the age at which, by law, he or she gets the property outright.
- use the property or income to pay for expenses such as the young beneficiary's support, education and health care
- keep the property separate from his or her own property, and
- keep separate records of transactions. The custodian does not have to file a separate income tax return; income from the property can be reported on the young beneficiary's return. (By comparison, the trustee of a child's subtrust must file a separate tax return for the subtrust.)

A custodian who needs to hire an accountant, tax lawyer or other expert can use the property to pay a reasonable amount for the help.

If state law allows it, the custodian is entitled to reasonable compensation and reimbursement for reasonable expenses. The payment, if any is taken, comes from the custodial property.

Choosing a Custodian

You can name a different custodian for each young beneficiary, if you wish.

In most cases, you should name the person who will have physical custody of the minor child. That's almost always one of the child's parents. If the beneficiary is your child, name the child's other parent unless you have serious reservations about that person's ability to handle the property for the child.

Only one person can be named as custodian for one beneficiary. You can, however, name an alternate custodian to take over if your first choice is unable to serve.

Children's Subtrusts

Quicken WillMaker Plus allows you to set up a separate child's subtrust for each young beneficiary.

How a Child's Subtrust Works

In your trust document, you state the age at which the beneficiary should receive trust property outright. If at your death the beneficiary hasn't reached that age, a subtrust will be created for that beneficiary. (If the beneficiary is older, he or she gets the trust property with no strings attached, and no subtrust is created.) Each beneficiary gets a separate child's subtrust.

Quicken WillMaker Plus is set up so that the surviving trustee, or the successor trustee after both original trustees die, will serve as trustee of all children's subtrusts. If you want different people to manage property inherited by different beneficiaries, you may want to use a custodianship instead of a child's subtrust. (To appoint someone else to be trustee of a child's subtrust, the trust document would have to be changed significantly; see a lawyer.)

Whatever trust property the beneficiary is entitled to inherit will go into the child's subtrust, if the child is still under the age set for termination of the subtrust. The trustee will manage the subtrust property and use it as necessary for the beneficiary's health, education and support. Once in operation, the subtrust cannot be revoked or amended. Until then, you are free to change your mind about having a subtrust set up for a particular beneficiary.

The child's subtrust will end when the beneficiary reaches the age designated in the Declaration of Trust. This can be any age up to and including 35. The trustee will then give the beneficiary what remains of the subtrust property.

> **EXAMPLE:** In the trust document that Stanley makes with his wife Natalie, he names his 14-year-old son Michael as beneficiary of $100,000 worth of stock. He specifies that any stock Michael becomes entitled to when Stanley dies should be kept in a subtrust until Michael is 25, subject to the trustee's right to spend it on Michael's behalf.
>
> Stanley dies when Michael is 19. The stock goes into a subtrust for him, managed by Natalie. She uses the stock (and the income it produces) to pay for Michael's education and support. Michael receives what's left of the stock when he turns 25.

> **EXAMPLE:** Roger and Victoria create a living trust and leave their trust property to the other. They name their daughters, who are 22 and 25, as alternate beneficiaries, and arrange for any trust property they inherit to stay in children's subtrusts until each daughter reaches 30.

They name Victoria's sister, Antoinette, as successor trustee.

Roger and Victoria die in a car accident when one daughter is 28 and the other is 31. The 28-year-old's half of the trust property stays in a subtrust, managed by Antoinette, until she turns 30. The 31-year-old gets her half outright; no subtrust is created for her.

The Subtrust Trustee's Duties

The subtrust trustee must:

- manage and invest subtrust property until the beneficiary reaches the age set out in the trust document
- keep the beneficiary (or the beneficiary's guardian, if the beneficiary is a minor) reasonably well informed about how trust assets are being invested
- use subtrust property or income to pay for expenses such as the beneficiary's support, education and health care
- keep separate records of subtrust transactions, and
- file income tax returns for the subtrust.

The trustee's powers and responsibilities are spelled out in the trust document. A trustee who needs to hire an accountant, tax lawyer or other expert can use subtrust assets to pay a reasonable amount for the help.

The trust document also provides that the trustee of a subtrust is entitled to reasonable compensation for acting as trustee. The trustee decides what is a reasonable amount; the compensation is paid from the subtrust assets.

For more on the trustee's responsibilities, see Chapter 21.

Declaration of Trust

Part 1. Trust Name

This revocable living trust shall be known as the Richard Jenkins and Patricia Jenkins Revocable Living Trust.

Part 2. Declaration of Trust

Richard Jenkins and Patricia Jenkins, called the grantors, declare that they have transferred and delivered to the trustees all their interest in the property described in Schedules A, B and C attached to this Declaration of Trust. All of that property is called the "trust property." The trustees hereby acknowledge receipt of the trust property and agree to hold the trust property in trust, according to this Declaration of Trust.

Either grantor may add property to the trust.

Part 3. Terminology

The term "this Declaration of Trust" includes any provisions added by valid amendment.

Part 4. Character of Trust Property

While both grantors are alive, property held in this trust shall retain its original character as community or separate property, as the case may be.

If the trust is revoked, the trustee shall distribute the trust property listed on Schedule A to the grantors as their community property. The trust property listed in Schedule B shall be distributed to Patricia Jenkins as her separate property, and the trust property listed in Schedule C shall be distributed to Richard Jenkins as his separate property.

Part 5. Amendment and Revocation

A. Revocation by Grantor

Either grantor may revoke this trust at any time, without notifying any beneficiary. Revocation may be made in writing or any manner allowed by law.

B. Amendment by Grantors

While both grantors are alive, this Declaration of Trust may be amended only by both of them acting together. All amendments must be in writing and signed by both grantors.

C. Amendment or Revocation by Other Person

The power to revoke or amend this trust is personal to the grantors. A conservator, guardian or other person shall not exercise it on behalf of either grantor, unless a grantor specifically grants a power to revoke or amend this trust in a Durable Power of Attorney.

Part 6. Payment From Trust During Grantors' Lifetimes

The trustees shall pay to or use for the benefit of the grantors as much of the net income and principal of the trust property as the grantors request. Income shall be paid to the grantors at least annually. Income accruing in or paid to trust accounts shall be deemed to have been paid to the grantor.

Part 7. Trustees

A. Original Trustees

Richard Jenkins and Patricia Jenkins are the trustees of this trust. Either alone may act for or represent the trust in any transaction.

B. Trustee at Death of Original Trustee

Upon the death of Richard Jenkins or Patricia Jenkins, the surviving trustee shall serve as sole trustee.

C. Trustee's Responsibilities

The trustee in office shall serve as trustee of all trusts created under this Declaration of Trust, including children's subtrusts.

D. Terminology

In this Declaration of Trust, the term "trustee" includes successor trustees or alternate successor trustees serving as trustee of this trust. The singular "trustee" also includes the plural.

E. Successor Trustee

Upon the death or incapacity of the surviving trustee, or the incapacity of both trustees, Delia Holt shall serve as trustee. If Delia Holt is unable or unwilling to serve as successor trustee, Natalie DeJarlais shall serve as trustee.

F. Resignation of Trustee

Any trustee in office may resign at any time by signing a notice of resignation. The resignation must be delivered to the person or institution who is either named in this

Declaration of Trust, or appointed by the trustee under Section G of this Part, to next serve as the trustee.

G. Power to Appoint Successor Trustee

If no one named in this Declaration of Trust as a successor trustee or alternate successor trustee is willing or able to serve as trustee, the last acting trustee may appoint a successor trustee and may require the posting of a reasonable bond, to be paid for from the trust property. The appointment must be made in writing, signed by the trustee and notarized.

H. Bond

No bond shall be required for any trustee named in this Declaration of Trust.

I. Compensation

No trustee shall receive any compensation for serving as trustee, unless the trustee serves as a trustee of a child's subtrust created by this Declaration of Trust.

J. Liability of Trustee

With respect to the exercise or nonexercise of discretionary powers granted by this Declaration of Trust, the trustee shall not be liable for actions taken in good faith. Such actions shall be binding on all persons interested in the trust property.

Part 8. Trustee's Management Powers and Duties

A. Powers Under State Law

The trustee shall have all authority and powers allowed or conferred on a trustee under California law, subject to the trustee's fiduciary duty to the grantors and the beneficiaries.

B. Specified Powers

The trustee's powers include, but are not limited to:

1. The power to sell trust property, and to borrow money and to encumber trust property, including trust real estate, by mortgage, deed of trust or other method.

2. The power to manage trust real estate as if the trustee were the absolute owner of it, including the power to lease (even if the lease term may extend beyond the period of any trust) or grant options to lease the property, to make repairs or alterations and to insure against loss.

3. The power to sell or grant options for the sale or exchange of any trust property, including stocks, bonds, debentures and any other form of security or security account, at public or private sale for cash or on credit.

4. The power to invest trust property in every kind of property and every kind of investment, including but not limited to bonds, debentures, notes, mortgages, stock options, futures and stocks, and including buying on margin.

5. The power to receive additional property from any source and add it to any trust created by this Declaration of Trust.

6. The power to employ and pay reasonable fees to accountants, lawyers or investment experts for information or advice relating to the trust.

7. The power to deposit and hold trust funds in both interest-bearing and non-interest-bearing accounts.

8. The power to deposit funds in bank or other accounts uninsured by FDIC coverage.

9. The power to enter into electronic fund transfer or safe deposit arrangements with financial institutions.

10. The power to continue any business of either grantor.

11. The power to institute or defend legal actions concerning this trust or the grantors' affairs.

12. The power to execute any documents necessary to administer any trust created by this Declaration of Trust.

13. The power to diversify investments, including authority to decide that some or all of the trust property need not produce income.

Part 9. Incapacity of Grantors

If Richard Jenkins or Patricia Jenkins becomes physically or mentally incapacitated, whether or not a court has declared the grantor incompetent or in need of a conservator or guardian, the other grantor shall be sole trustee until the incapacitated grantor is again able to manage his or her affairs.

If both grantors become incapacitated, the successor trustee named in Part 7 of this Declaration of Trust shall serve as trustee.

The determination of a grantor's capacity to manage this trust shall be made by Michael Sexton. The successor trustee shall, if necessary, ask Michael Sexton to state, in writing, an opinion as to whether or not the grantor is able to continue serving as trustee. The successor trustee may rely on that written opinion when determining whether or not to begin serving as trustee.

If the successor trustee is unable, after making reasonable efforts, to obtain a written opinion from Michael Sexton, the successor trustee may request an opinion from David

Jenkins and may rely on that opinion.

If the successor trustee is unable, after making reasonable efforts, to obtain a written opinion from Michael Sexton or David Jenkins, the successor trustee may request an opinion from a physician who examines the grantor, and may rely on that opinion.

The trustee shall manage the trust property and use any amount of trust income or trust principal necessary for the proper health care, support, maintenance, comfort and welfare of both grantors, in accordance with their accustomed manner of living. Income shall be paid to the grantors at least annually. Income accruing in or paid to trust accounts shall be deemed to have been paid to the grantor.

Part 10. Death of a Grantor

The first grantor to die shall be called the "deceased grantor." The other grantor shall be called the "surviving grantor."

Upon the deceased grantor's death, the trustee shall divide the property of the Richard Jenkins and Patricia Jenkins Revocable Living Trust listed on Schedules A, B and C into two separate trusts, Trust #1 and Trust #2. The trustee shall serve as trustee of Trust #1 and Trust #2.

Trust #1 shall contain all the property of the Richard Jenkins and Patricia Jenkins Revocable Living Trust owned by the deceased grantor before it was held in trust, plus accumulated income, except trust property left by the terms of this trust to the surviving grantor. Trust #1 shall become irrevocable at the death of the deceased grantor. The trustee shall distribute the property in Trust #1 to the beneficiaries named in Part 11 of this Declaration of Trust.

Trust #2 shall contain all the property of the Richard Jenkins and Patricia Jenkins Revocable Living Trust owned by the surviving grantor before it was held in trust, plus accumulated income, and any trust property left by the deceased grantor to the surviving grantor. It shall remain revocable until the death of the surviving grantor.

The trustee may pay out of trust property such amounts as necessary for payment of debts, estate taxes and expenses of the last illness and funeral of the deceased or surviving grantor.

Part 11. Beneficiaries

A. Richard Jenkins's Beneficiaries

At the death of Richard Jenkins, the trustee shall distribute the trust property listed on Schedule C, plus accumulated interest; the share of the property on Schedule A owned by

Richard Jenkins before it was transferred to the trustee, plus accumulated interest; and if Richard Jenkins is the second grantor to die, any property listed on Schedule B left to him by Patricia Jenkins, plus accumulated interest; as follows:

1. Patricia Jenkins shall be given all Richard Jenkins's interest in all the furniture in the house at 3320 Windmill Road, Auburn, California, the condominium at 19903 Forest Way, #43, Wawona, California, and the house at 3320 Windmill Road, Auburn, California. If Patricia Jenkins does not survive Richard Jenkins, that property shall be given to Ann Heron.

2. James Leung shall be given all Richard Jenkins's interest in account no. 3301-A94 at International Brokers, San Francisco, California. If James Leung does not survive Richard Jenkins, that property shall be given to Andre Zivkowich.

3. Ann Heron shall be given all Richard Jenkins's interest in the trust property not otherwise specifically and validly disposed of by this Part. If Ann Heron does not survive Richard Jenkins, that property shall be given to the Nature Conservancy and Mills College, in equal shares.

B. Patricia Jenkins's Beneficiaries

At the death of Patricia Jenkins, the trustee shall distribute the trust property listed on Schedule B, plus accumulated interest; the share of the property on Schedule A owned by Patricia Jenkins before it was transferred to the trustee, plus accumulated interest; and if Patricia Jenkins is the second grantor to die, any property listed on Schedule C left to her by Richard Jenkins, plus accumulated interest; as follows:

1. Richard Jenkins shall be given all Patricia Jenkins's interest in the trust property. If Richard Jenkins does not survive Patricia Jenkins, that property shall be given to Ann Heron.

2. Ann Heron shall be given all Patricia Jenkins's interest in the trust property not otherwise specifically and validly disposed of by this Part.

C. Property Left to the Surviving Grantor

Any trust property left by the deceased grantor to the surviving grantor shall remain in the surviving grantor's revocable trust, Trust #2.

D. Terms of Property Distribution

All distributions are subject to any provision in this Declaration of Trust that creates a child's subtrust or a custodianship under the Uniform Transfers to Minors Act.

A beneficiary must survive the grantor for 120 hours to receive property under this Declaration of Trust. As used in this Declaration of Trust, to survive means to be alive or in existence as an organization.

All personal and real property left through this trust shall pass subject to any encumbrances or liens placed on the property as security for the repayment of a loan or debt.

If property is left to two or more beneficiaries to share, they shall share it equally unless this Declaration of Trust provides otherwise. If any of them does not survive the grantor, the others shall take that beneficiary's share, to share equally, unless this Declaration of Trust provides otherwise.

Part 12. Children's Subtrusts

A. Beneficiaries for Whom Subtrusts May Be Created

1. If Ann Heron becomes entitled to any trust property under Part 11.B before reaching the age of 29, that trust property shall be kept in a separate child's subtrust, under the provisions of this Part, until Ann Heron reaches the age of 29. The subtrust shall be known as the "Richard Jenkins and Patricia Jenkins Revocable Living Trust, Ann Heron Subtrust."

2. If Ann Heron becomes entitled to any trust property under Part 11.A before reaching the age of 29, that trust property shall be kept in a separate child's subtrust, under the provisions of this Part, until Ann Heron reaches the age of 29. The subtrust shall be known as the "Richard Jenkins and Patricia Jenkins Revocable Living Trust, Ann Heron Subtrust."

B. Powers of Subtrust Trustee

The trustee may distribute as much of the net income or principal of the child's subtrust as the trustee deems necessary for the beneficiary's health, support, maintenance or education. Education includes, but is not limited to, college, graduate, postgraduate and vocational studies and reasonably related living expenses.

In deciding whether or not to make a distribution, the trustee may take into account the beneficiary's other income, resources and sources of support. Any subtrust income not distributed by the trustee shall be accumulated and added to the principal of the subtrust.

The trustee is not required to make any accounting or report to the subtrust beneficiary.

C. Assignment of Subtrust Assets

The interests of the beneficiary of a child's subtrust shall not be transferable by voluntary or involuntary assignment or by operation of law before receipt by the beneficiary. They shall be free from the claims of creditors and from attachments, execution, bankruptcy or other legal process to the fullest extent permitted by law.

D. Compensation of Trustee

Any trustee of a child's subtrust created under this Declaration of Trust is entitled to reasonable compensation, without court approval, out of the subtrust assets for ordinary and extraordinary services, and for all services in connection with the termination of any subtrust.

E. Termination of Subtrust

A child's subtrust shall end when any of the following events occurs:

1. The beneficiary reaches the age specified in Section A of this Part. If the subtrust ends for this reason, the remaining principal and accumulated income of the subtrust shall be given outright to the beneficiary.

2. The beneficiary dies. If the subtrust ends for this reason, the subtrust property shall pass to the beneficiary's heirs.

3. The trustee distributes all subtrust property under the provisions of this Declaration of Trust.

Part 13. Homestead Rights

If the grantors' principal residence is held in this trust, grantors have the right to possess and occupy it for life, rent-free and without charge, except for taxes, insurance, maintenance and related costs and expenses. This right is intended to give grantors a beneficial interest in the property and to ensure that the grantors, or either of them, do not lose eligibility for a state homestead tax exemption for which either grantor otherwise qualifies.

Part 14. Severability of Clauses

If any provision of this Declaration of Trust is ruled unenforceable, the remaining provisions shall stay in effect.

Certification of Grantors

We certify that we have read this Declaration of Trust and that it correctly states the terms and conditions under which the trust property is to be held, managed and disposed of by the trustees, and we approve the Declaration of Trust.

_____   _____
Richard Jenkins, Grantor and Trustee   Date

_____   _____
Patricia Jenkins, Grantor and Trustee   Date

CERTIFICATION OF ACKNOWLEDGMENT OF NOTARY PUBLIC

State of _____

County of _____

On _____, before me, _____,
a notary public for said state, personally appeared Richard Jenkins and Patricia Jenkins, proved
to me on the basis of satisfactory evidence to be the persons whose names are subscribed
to the within instrument, and acknowledged to me that they executed the same in their
authorized capacity and that by their signatures on the instrument the persons, or the entity
upon behalf of which the persons acted, executed the instrument.

Witness my hand and official seal.

_____

NOTARY PUBLIC

My commission expires _____

Schedule A

SHARED PROPERTY PLACED IN TRUST

1. All the furniture in the house at 3320 Windmill Road, Auburn, California.

2. The condominium at 19903 Forest Way, #43, Wawona, California.

3. The house at 3320 Windmill Road, Auburn, California.

Schedule B

PATRICIA JENKINS'S SEPARATE PROPERTY PLACED IN TRUST

1. Scudder International Fund Account 993-222-1.

2. The four-volume American stamp collection kept at 3320 Windmill Road, Auburn, California.

Schedule C

RICHARD JENKINS'S SEPARATE PROPERTY PLACED IN TRUST

1. Account no. 3301-A94 at International Brokers, San Francisco, California.

Creating an AB Trust

When you create your AB living trust document with Quicken WillMaker Plus, you must decide:

- whether you want to make a "disclaimer" AB trust, which gives the surviving spouse the option of not splitting the AB trust when the first spouse dies (in case by that time the AB trust isn't necessary to save on estate taxes)
- what property you want to hold in trust
- whether or not you would like to leave some items of trust property at your death to someone other than your spouse
- whom you want to be the final beneficiaries (the people who will inherit trust property after both spouses have died)
- who is to be the successor trustee (the person or institution who, after both spouses have died, will distribute the trust property), and
- how you should arrange for someone to manage trust property inherited by beneficiaries who are too young to handle it without supervision.

This chapter discusses the factors you should think about as you make each decision. It is organized the same way as the program is (Parts 1 through 6), so that you can easily refer to it while you're actually making your trust document. It's a good idea, though, to read through this chapter before you sit down at the computer—it will make the whole process clearer and easier.

Creating a Valid Living Trust

☐ Prepare the trust document with Quicken WillMaker Plus.

☐ Print out the trust document and sign it in front of a notary public.

☐ Transfer ownership of the property listed in the trust document into your name, as trustee.

☐ Update your trust document when needed.

How an AB Trust Works: An Overview

Here, in brief, are the important points about an AB trust:

Control of trust property. You and your spouse will both be trustees of your living trust, so you'll both have control over the property held in trust. Either spouse can act on behalf of the trust—sell or give away trust property, for example. (As a practical matter, the consent of both spouses may be necessary—see Part 2, below.)

Amendments or revocation. Both spouses must consent to change any terms of the trust document—for example, who is named as successor trustee or final beneficiary.

Either spouse can, however, revoke the trust. This way either spouse can return the situation to exactly what it was before the trust was formed. (Co-owned property is returned to both spouses, and separately owned property to the owner-spouse.)

Death of the first spouse. What happens after the death of the first spouse depends on what kind of AB trust you made. If you made a regular AB trust, without the disclaimer option, then the AB trust must be split into two trusts. The surviving spouse will want to hire expert help to decide exactly how assets should be divided.

- **Trust A, the bypass trust.** This trust contains the deceased spouse's share of trust assets, except any items of trust property left directly to someone other than the surviving spouse. This trust is now irrevocable; its terms cannot be changed. The surviving spouse has the right to use Trust A property but does not own it outright.
- **Trust B, the survivor's trust.** This trust contains the surviving spouse's share of trust property. The surviving spouse has complete control over and ownership of Trust B property. The survivor can also amend the trust document—for example, to name a new final beneficiary for Trust B property.

The surviving spouse is sole trustee of both trusts, and both will exist until the second spouse dies.

If you chose the disclaimer trust option, the surviving spouse must decide whether or not to create the bypass trust. If no bypass trust is created, the surviving spouse receives all trust property in the survivor's trust.

Death of the second spouse. When the second spouse dies, the person named in the trust document as successor trustee takes over and distributes the trust property to the final beneficiaries. The successor trustee also manages any trust property left to a young beneficiary in a child's subtrust (explained later).

EXAMPLE: William and Kay, a married couple, set up an AB living trust. In the trust document, they name their two grown children, Emily and Brendan, as final beneficiaries. They appoint Emily as successor trustee, to take over as trustee after they have both died. They decide to transfer much of their co-owned property—their house and some valuable furniture and art—to their names as trustees of the trust. Kay also puts some family heirlooms, which are her separate property, in the trust.

Kay provides, in the trust document, that her brother is to receive the heirlooms when she dies; everything else goes to William, in trust, and then to the children. William leaves all his trust property to Kay, in trust, and then to the children.

Kay dies first. William, as sole trustee, gives the heirlooms to Kay's brother, as the trust document instructs. He then splits the trust into Trust A and Trust B, each of which contains half of the couple's co-owned property. To accomplish this split, William enlists the help of an experienced estate planning attorney, who explains the tax consequences of dividing the property in different ways.

After Kay's death, William decides to make a change in his living trust document. In an amendment to the trust document, he names his 12-year-old granddaughter, Cecile, to inherit some of his trust property. He states that if Cecile is not yet 25 when he dies, the trust property she inherits will stay in a child's subtrust, managed by the successor trustee.

When William dies, Emily becomes trustee and distributes the trust property following the instructions in the trust document. She also manages the property inherited by Cecile, who is 21 at William's death, until her 25th birthday. When all the property is given to the beneficiaries, the trust ends.

Part 1: Your Names

This part is easy; just enter your names. The names you enter will determine the name of your trust. For example, if you enter "William S. Jorgensen" and "Helga M. Jorgensen," your trust will be named "The William S. Jorgensen and Helga M. Jorgensen AB Revocable Living Trust." Your names will also appear as the original trustees of your living trust. (See Part 2, below.)

Enter your name the way it appears on other formal business documents, such as your driver's license or bank accounts. This may or may not be the name on your birth certificate.

If you go by more than one name, use only one; don't enter various versions of your name joined by "aka" (also known as). Be sure that the name you use is the one that appears on the ownership documents for property you plan to hold in trust. If it isn't, it could cause confusion later, and you should change the name on your ownership documents before you transfer the property to yourselves as trustees.

EXAMPLE: You use the name William Dix for your trust but own real estate in your former name of William Geicherwitz. You should prepare and sign a new deed, changing the name of the owner to William Dix, before you prepare another deed to transfer the property to yourself as trustee.

Part 2: Trustees

To be legally valid, every living trust must have a trustee—someone to manage the property held in trust. When you create a revocable living trust with this program, you and your spouse are the trustees while you are alive. You'll name someone else to be the successor trustee, to distribute trust property to the final beneficiaries after both you and your spouse have died.

Your Duties as Trustees

You and your spouse will be the original trustees of your living trust. That way, both of you have control over trust property, and taxation doesn't get complicated.

SEE AN EXPERT
You can't name someone else as trustee. In the unlikely event you and your spouse don't want to be the trustees or want only one of you to be trustee, you cannot use Quicken WillMaker Plus. See an estate planning lawyer.

While Both Spouses Are Alive and Well

As trustees, both of you will have complete control over the property that is held in trust.

As a day-to-day, practical matter, it makes little difference that your property is held in trust. You won't have any special duties as trustees of your trust. You do not even need to file a separate income tax return for the living trust. If trust property generates income, just report it on your personal income tax return, as if the trust did not exist.

You have the same freedom to sell, give away or mortgage trust property as you did before you put the property in trust. The only difference is that if you and your spouse must sign documents relating to the property, you do so in your capacity as trustees.

> **EXAMPLE:** Celeste and Robert want to sell a piece of land that they hold in their AB trust. They prepare a deed transferring ownership of the land to the new owner and sign the deed as "Celeste Tornetti and Robert Tornetti, trustees of the Celeste Tornetti and Robert Tornetti AB Living Trust dated February 4, 20xx."

It's important to realize that once the property is held in trust, either trustee (spouse) has authority over it. That means that either spouse can sell or give away any of the trust property—including any property that was co-owned or was the separate property of the other spouse before it was transferred to the trust. In practice, however, both spouses will probably have to consent to transfer real estate out of the living trust. Especially in community property states, buyers and title insurance companies usually insist on both spouses' signatures on transfer documents.

If One Spouse Becomes Incapacitated

If one spouse becomes incapacitated and unable to manage his or her affairs, the other becomes sole trustee. (If the other spouse has already died, the successor trustee takes over.) But who should decide that it's time for one spouse to step aside, if the issue ever comes up?

In the trust document, you'll name someone (and two alternates) to make this determination. These people do not have to be doctors; ideally, you will choose people who know you well and can give an unbiased opinion about whether or not you need help taking care of financial matters.

If there's ever a question of your ability to manage the trust, your spouse will ask your first choice for an opinion of your capacity. If that person isn't available, your spouse will go to your second, and if necessary, third choice. If one of them states, in writing, that because of your condition, your spouse needs to take over as sole trustee or that the successor trustee needs to take over as trustee, then the spouse or the successor can do so.

A spouse who takes over as sole trustee under these circumstances has no power over property not held in the living trust, and no authority to make health care decisions for the incapacitated spouse. For this reason, it's also wise for each spouse to create documents called durable powers of attorney, giving the other spouse authority over more than trust property. (See Chapters 22 and 23.)

After One Spouse's Death

After one spouse dies, the surviving spouse is sole trustee. The survivor's first task is to oversee the division of the trust into two trusts, Trust A (the deceased spouse's trust) and Trust B (the survivor's). If the trust document contains the "disclaimer" clause, the surviving spouse has the option of not splitting the trust, and to instead inherit all trust property. Either way, the surviving spouse will need expert tax advice before acting. (See Chapter 21.)

Once the trust is split, it's up to the survivor to manage the deceased spouse's trust property, which is now in Trust A. The trust made by Quicken WillMaker Plus gives the surviving spouse the broadest possible authority allowed by IRS rules. (See Chapter 21.)

The survivor has two other possible duties:

- Distributing trust property to other beneficiaries. If the deceased spouse left items of trust property directly to any beneficiaries, the surviving spouse must distribute them, following the terms of the trust document. The surviving spouse has no legal power to modify the deceased spouse's intentions in any way. (See Chapter 21.) Usually, the process takes only a few weeks.
- Managing property left to a young person. If the deceased spouse left trust property to a young beneficiary and directed that it should stay in trust, the surviving spouse will be in charge of the property. This job will last until the beneficiary is old enough, under the terms of the trust, to receive the trust property outright. (See Part 6, below.)

The Successor Trustee

You and your spouse must choose a successor trustee—someone to act as trustee after both of you have died or can no longer manage your affairs. The successor trustee has no power or responsibility if at least one spouse is alive and capable of managing the trust.

The Successor Trustee's Duties After Both Spouses' Deaths

After both spouses have died, the successor trustee takes over as trustee of Trust A and Trust B. The successor trustee's job is to distribute trust property to the final beneficiaries. That is usually a straightforward process that can be completed in a few weeks. (How to transfer certain common kinds of property is explained in Chapter 21.)

The successor trustee may also have long-term duties, if the trust document creates a child's subtrust for trust property inherited by a young beneficiary (this is explained in Part 6, below).

The Successor Trustee's Duties If Both Spouses Are Incapacitated

The successor trustee will take over as trustee before both spouses have died only if neither spouse is able to manage the trust. A successor trustee who thinks that neither spouse can still manage the trust will ask the person you named, in the trust document, for an opinion of your capacity. If your first choice isn't available, the trustee will go to the people you named as your second, and if necessary, third choice. If one of them states, in writing, that because of your condition, the successor trustee needs to take over as trustee, then the successor trustee can do so. (See "If One Spouse Becomes Incapacitated," above.)

In this situation, the successor trustee has broad authority to manage the property in the living trust and use it for both spouses' health care, support and welfare. The law requires him or her to act honestly and prudently. And because the grantors are no longer the trustees, the new trustee must file an annual income tax return for the trust.

Choosing a Successor Trustee

The person or institution you choose as successor trustee will have a crucial role: to distribute trust property to your beneficiaries after you and your spouse have died. And if you and your spouse become incapacitated, the successor will manage trust property on your behalf; if you leave property to a young beneficiary in trust, the successor will manage that property until the beneficiary is old enough to handle it alone.

Obviously, when you are giving someone this much power and discretion, you should choose someone with good common sense whom you trust completely. If you don't know anyone who fits this description, think twice about establishing a living trust. Most people pick an adult son or daughter, other relative or close friend.

In most situations, the successor trustee will not need extensive experience in financial management; common sense, dependability and complete honesty are usually enough.

A successor trustee who may have long-term responsibility over a young beneficiary's trust property needs more management and financial skills than a successor trustee whose only job is to distribute trust property. The successor trustee does have authority, however, under the terms of the trust document, to get any reasonably necessary professional help— from an accountant, lawyer or tax preparer, perhaps—and pay for it out of trust assets.

Usually, it makes sense to name just one person as successor trustee, to avoid any possibility of conflicts. But it's legal and may be desirable to name more than one person. For example, you might name two or more of your children, if you don't expect any disagreements between them and you think one of them might feel hurt and left out if not named.

Having more than one successor trustee is especially likely to cause serious problems if you leave property to a young beneficiary in a child's subtrust. The trustees may have to manage a young beneficiary's property for many years and will have many decisions to make about how to spend the money— greatly increasing the potential for conflict. (Children's subtrusts are discussed in Part 6, below.)

If you name more than one successor trustee, and one of them can't serve, the others will serve. If none of them can serve, the alternate you name (in the next section of the program) will take over.

It's perfectly legal to name a beneficiary of the trust (someone who will inherit trust property) as successor trustee. In fact, it's common.

EXAMPLE: Mildred and James name their only child, Allison, to be both final beneficiary and successor trustee of their AB living trust. When James dies, Mildred manages both Trust A and Trust B. When Mildred dies, Allison uses her authority as trustee to transfer the property in both Trust A and Trust B to herself, the final beneficiary.

Institutions as Successor Trustees

Normally, your first choice as successor trustee should be a flesh-and-blood person, not the trust department of a bank or other institution. Institutional trustees charge hefty fees, which come out of the trust property and leave less for your beneficiaries. And most aren't even interested in small living trusts—ones that contain less than several hundred thousand dollars' worth of property.

But if there's no close relative or friend you think is capable of serving as your successor trustee, probably your best bet is to consider naming a private trust services company. Typically, their fees are pricey but less than a bank's, and your affairs will probably receive more personal attention.

For a very large living trust, another possibility is to name a person and an institution as cosuccessor trustees. The bank or trust services company can do most of the paperwork, and the person can keep an eye on things and approve all transactions.

Avoiding Conflicts With Your Will and Other Documents

Your AB living trust gives your spouse the authority to manage trust property if you become incapacitated. To avoid conflicts, you should also give your spouse authority to make other decisions if you can't:

- In your will, appoint your spouse to be executor, to be responsible for distributing property left through your will.
- In your durable power of attorney for finances, appoint your spouse to be your "attorney-in-fact," to have authority to make decisions about property not held in trust if you become incapacitated.

If you do choose different people to be your attorney-in-fact and successor trustee, each will have a role if you become incapacitated. The successor trustee will be in charge of all trust property, and the attorney-in-fact will have authority over property not held in trust.

The successor trustee does not have to live in the same state as you do. But if you are choosing between someone local and someone far away, think about how convenient it will be for the person you choose to distribute the living trust property after your death. Someone close by will probably have an easier job, especially with real estate transfers. But for transfers of property such as securities and bank accounts, it usually won't make much difference where the successor trustee lives.

Obviously, before you and your spouse finalize your trust, you must check with the person you've chosen to be your successor trustee. You want to be sure your choice is willing to serve. If you don't, you may well create problems down the line. The person you've chosen may not want to serve, for a variety of reasons. And even if the person would be willing, if he or she doesn't know of his or her responsibilities, transfer of trust property after your death could be delayed.

If you choose an institution, you must check out the minimum size of trust it will accept and the fees it charges for management and make arrangements for how the institution will take over as trustee at the second spouse's death.

Payment of the Successor Trustee

Typically, the successor trustee of an AB trust isn't paid. This is because, in most cases, the successor trustee's only job is to distribute the trust property to the final beneficiaries—and often, the successor trustee inherits the property anyway.

An exception is a successor trustee who manages the property in a child's subtrust. In that case, the successor trustee is entitled, under the terms of the trust document, to "reasonable compensation." The successor trustee decides what is reasonable and takes it from the trust property left to the young beneficiary.

Allowing the successor trustee to set the amount of the payment can work well, as long as your successor trustee is completely trustworthy. A young beneficiary who feels the trustee's fees are much too high will have to go to court to challenge them.

Naming an Alternate Successor Trustee

We'll ask you to name an alternate successor trustee, in case your first choice is unable to serve.

If you name two or more successor trustees, the alternate won't become trustee unless none of your original choices can serve.

> **EXAMPLE:** Caroline and Oscar name their two grown children, Eugene and Vanessa, as successor trustees. They name a close friend, Nicole, as alternate successor trustee. After Caroline and Oscar have died, Vanessa is ill and can't serve as trustee. Eugene acts as sole successor trustee. If he were also unable to serve, Nicole would take over.

If no one you named in the trust document can serve, the last trustee to serve has the power to appoint, in writing, another successor trustee. (See Chapter 21.)

> **EXAMPLE:** To continue the previous example, if Nicole were ill and didn't have the energy to serve as successor trustee, she could appoint someone else to serve as trustee.

Part 3: Property to Be Put in Trust

In this part of the program, you and your spouse must list each item of property—both jointly owned and separately owned—you want to hold in trust. It will take some thought to decide what property to include and how to list it in the trust document.

This is a crucial step. Any property you don't list will not go into your living trust and will not pass under the terms of the trust. It may instead have to go through probate.

Adding property to the trust later. If you mistakenly leave something out or acquire more valuable property after you create your trust, you will be able to add it to your living trust. Chapter 20 explains how.

> **CAUTION**
> **Listing property in the trust document is not enough.** If an item has a title (ownership) document, such as a deed or title slip, you must change that document to show that you, as trustee, are the legal owner of the property. If you don't, the trust won't work. *You should transfer ownership as soon as possible after you print out and sign your Declaration of Trust.* Instructions are in Chapter 19.

Inventory Your Valuable Property

Before you begin to list your property in the program, sort out what you have. First, get out a pencil or your word processor and list all the valuable items of property you own. The categories listed in Chapter 5 should jog your memory.

Making a list helps for two reasons. First, when you make your trust document, you'll have to list and describe every item (or group of items, in some circumstances) anyway. You

can group items together if it will be clear what you mean and you don't feel a need to specifically describe any item in the group. For example, if you want to leave all your books through your trust, there's no need to describe each one individually—unless your collection includes some particularly valuable or important books that you want to make extra sure get to the beneficiary.

Second, listing your assets this way will help you get an idea of their total monetary value. If either of you owns assets worth more than the federal estate tax exempt amount, an AB trust won't completely shelter your estate from federal estate tax. You may want to explore other ways of lessening the tax burden.

For purposes of estimating your net worth, you don't need precise figures—so don't run out and get appraisals. After all, your assets and their value will undoubtedly change before your death. You just need a ballpark estimate.

Who Owns What?

You'll need to label each item as "his, hers or ours" when you enter it in the program. This is because when the first spouse dies, you need to know what property should be divided between Trust A and Trust B. And you might want to leave some of your separate property items to someone other than your spouse.

For many couples, especially if they've been married a long time, nearly everything is owned together. But if you haven't been married long, or have been married before, you may own a sizable amount of property separately. If you're unsure about who owns what, read this section, which explains the ownership rules of your state.

Community Property States

Alaska*	Nevada
Arizona	New Mexico
California	Texas
Idaho	Washington
Louisiana	Wisconsin

* If spouses sign a community property agreement.

If you live in a community property state and you aren't sure who owns what, don't rely on whose name is on the title document. For example, if while you were married you bought a house with money you earned, your spouse legally owns a share of that property—even if only your name is on the deed.

Generally, any property that either spouse earns or acquires during the marriage (before permanent separation) is community property. Both spouses (the "community") own it together. The main exception to this rule is that property one spouse acquires by gift or inheritance, or acquired before the marriage, belongs to that spouse alone.

Even separate property may, however, turn into community property if it is mixed ("commingled") with community property. For example, if you deposit separate property funds into a joint bank account and then make more deposits and withdrawals, making it impossible to tell what part of the account is separate money, it's all considered community property.

Non-Community Property States

Alabama	Kansas
Alaska*	Kentucky
Arkansas	Maine
Colorado	Maryland
Connecticut	Massachusetts
Delaware	Michigan
District of Columbia	Minnesota
Florida	Mississippi
Georgia	Missouri
Hawaii	Montana
Illinois	Nebraska
Indiana	New Hampshire
Iowa	New Jersey
New York	South Carolina
North Carolina	South Dakota
North Dakota	Tennessee
Ohio	Utah
Oklahoma	Vermont
Oregon	Virginia
Pennsylvania	West Virginia
Rhode Island	Wyoming

* Spouses can, however, create community property by signing a community property agreement.

In these states, it is usually fairly simple to figure out who owns what. If the property has a title document—for example, a deed to real estate or a car title slip—then the spouse whose name is on the title is the owner. If the property doesn't have a title document, it belongs to the spouse who paid for it or received it as a gift. (It's possible, though, that if there were a dispute, a judge could determine, based on the circumstances, that a spouse whose name is not on the title document might own an interest in the property.)

If the trust is revoked, the property will be returned to each spouse based on the same ownership rights they had before the property was held in trust.

How Much Property to Put in Your AB Trust

Now that you've got a list of what you and your spouse own, you're ready to decide what items you want to hold in trust. You need to think about two issues: the total value of property you want to hold in trust, and what kinds of property are best suited to an AB trust. This section discusses "how much"; the next one discusses "which assets."

How Much the AB Trust Can Shelter

If you make an AB trust with Quicken WillMaker Plus, you and your spouse can shelter from estate tax twice the amount of the federal estate tax exemption. That amount depends on the year of the first spouse's death, as shown below.

The Estate Tax Exemption	
Year of Death	**Estate Tax Exemption**
2008	$2 million
2009	$3.5 million
2010	Estate tax repealed
2011	$1 million unless Congress extends repeal

EXAMPLE: Maureen and Lester have a net worth of $3 million, shared equally. They create an AB trust together. Lester dies in 2008, when he can leave up to $2 million free of estate tax. His $1.5 million worth of trust property passes to the bypass trust (Trust A). His estate doesn't owe any tax because the amount he leaves is below the federal estate tax exemption for that year.

When Maureen dies in 2009, her property (let's say its value has remained at $1.5 million, though of course it could have gone up or down) is now subject to tax. But because it is also under the estate tax exemption for that year, no tax is due.

The Regular AB Trust

If you don't expect your half of your combined estate to exceed the estate tax exemption, you can safely put everything in your AB trust. No estate tax will be due.

If, however, either spouse has an estate that exceeds the federal estate tax exemption in the year of death, and you create a regular AB trust (without a disclaimer clause, as discussed below), the estate will owe federal estate tax. This is true even if the total combined value of the couple's estates is less than the amount that could be sheltered by an AB trust.

EXAMPLE: Lidia and Mark create an AB trust, and Lidia dies in 2008. At her death, her share of the trust property is worth $2.8 million—more than the $2 million that can pass tax-free in 2008. Her estate owes federal estate tax. When Mark dies in 2009, his estate is valued at $2.0 million, too. But in 2009, an estate of that size doesn't owe any tax.

Obviously, none of us knows when we're going to die. So for purposes of estate planning (only!), you may want to take the most pessimistic route possible and assume that the bypass trust will become operational—that is, a spouse will die—in the year you create the trust.

The Disclaimer AB Trust

Another way to deal with the uncertainty is to make a disclaimer trust, as discussed in Chapter 14. Including the disclaimer clause in your Quicken WillMaker Plus trust allows the surviving spouse to decide, after the first spouse dies, how much trust property (if any) should go into the bypass trust. The spouse can "disclaim" property he or she would otherwise inherit, sending that property (under the terms of the trust document) into the bypass trust.

The only limit is that the spouse cannot transfer more than the amount of the current estate tax exemption—which means that the bypass trust won't ever be large enough to be subject to estate tax.

> **EXAMPLE:** Charlotte and her husband Winston make a disclaimer trust. They leave everything to each other and name their children as the final beneficiaries.
>
> When Winston dies in 2008, the couple's trust property is worth $2.5 million. The federal estate tax exemption for that year is $2 million.
>
> After talking with a tax expert, Charlotte decides to split the AB trust into Trust A, the bypass trust, and Trust B, her

survivor's trust. She further decides she wants $1 million to go into the bypass trust. That will leave $1.5 million under her complete control. She figures that even if she invests wisely and increases the value of her holdings, estate tax still won't be due at her death.

To put this plan into effect, Charlotte's lawyer draws up a disclaimer—a document in which Charlotte gives up (disclaims) $1 million of the trust property. Under the terms of the trust document, the property goes into Trust A, the bypass trust. Charlotte will have the right to use the income it produces and to spend the principal itself for certain purposes allowed by law. At her death it will go to the couple's children.

> **CAUTION**
> **Watch out for state estate taxes.** Because of recent changes in federal and state tax laws, estate taxes imposed by states are becoming of greater concern to many people.
> Before 2005, if an estate was big enough to pay federal estate tax, the state could claim a share of the money. This tax was called a pick-up or sponge tax. It didn't actually increase the tax paid; the state was merely entitled, by federal law, to take a certain percentage of the federal tax due. But states no longer get a share of federal estate taxes. To make up for this loss of revenue, some states have enacted their own estate taxes, which are no longer connected to the federal system. Estates may have to pay state tax even if they aren't large enough to pay federal estate tax. State tax rates, however, are generally much lower than federal estate tax rates.

This is true even if you use an AB trust. If you leave an amount of property that might exceed your state's threshold for state estate tax, you may owe state tax even though your estate doesn't exceed the threshold for federal estate tax.

> **EXAMPLE:** Roy and his wife Ann, who are Rhode Island residents, make an AB trust. At Roy's death, his share of the couple's property is $800,000. That amount goes in Trust B, the deceased spouse's trust. Because Roy's estate is under the federal estate tax threshold, it does not owe federal estate tax. It will, however, owe Rhode Island estate tax, because that state no longer just imposes a pick-up estate tax; it currently taxes estates of $675,000 or more.

In most cases, the state tax amount will not be huge. But if you're concerned about it, see a tax lawyer in your state (and, if you own real estate elsewhere, in that state, too) who can bring you up to date on this rapidly changing area of the law.

What to Do If One Spouse Owns More Than the Estate Tax Exemption

If your individual estate may exceed the estate tax exemption, you need to think about how much of your property you want to leave to your AB trust. For example, if you and your spouse have shared property worth $5 million, and your share is worth $4 million, if you leave it all to your Trust A, part of it will be subject to estate tax.

There are several strategies to deal with this issue:

- Use a disclaimer trust, as discussed above.

- Use an AB trust with a "formula" clause. This clause directs that only property worth up to the amount of the estate tax exemption in the year of death be put into Trust A, the bypass trust. It's especially desirable if it seems likely that one spouse will long outlive the other; the survivor will have many years to use the money and take measures to reduce eventual estate taxes. (Quicken WillMaker Plus does not make a formula trust.)

- Leave some of your property (whatever exceeds the exempt amount) directly to your spouse, who won't pay tax on it because of the marital deduction.

- Leave some of your property (whatever exceeds the exempt amount) in a QTIP or QDOT trust; this lets you defer tax until the death of the second spouse and control who inherits it after the surviving spouse dies. (Quicken WillMaker Plus does not make QTIP or QDOT trusts.)

- If one spouse's estate is much larger than the other's, equalize the size of the estates by transferring some property to the spouse with less property. This may bring the other spouse's estate below the estate tax exemption, or at least reduce the amount of tax owed.

- Leave all your property to the bypass trust, fully expecting that some estate tax may be due at your death. If you don't expect the second spouse to live much longer than the first spouse, this may actually save money on taxes, by making each spouse's estate closer in value.

- Reduce the size of your estate by making tax-free gifts of some of your property while you're alive.

SEE AN EXPERT

If you need more. As you can see, there's no one solution that's right for everyone, especially in light of the estate tax law uncertainty. If you own more property than an AB trust can currently shelter, see a lawyer to discuss which strategy is right for you.

What Kinds of Property to Hold in Trust

Think about including:
- houses and other real estate
- jewelry, antiques, furs and valuable furniture
- stock in a closely held corporation
- stock, bond and other security accounts held by brokerages
- small business interests
- money market and bank accounts
- patents and copyrights
- precious metals
- valuable works of art, and
- valuable collections of stamps, coins or other objects.

Real Estate

The most valuable thing most people own is their real estate: their house, condominium or land. You'll probably want to hold your real estate in your AB trust.

If you or your spouse owns real estate with someone else, you can transfer just your interest in it to your living trust. You won't need to specify that your share is one-half or some other fraction. For example, if you and your sister own a house together, you need only list "the house at 7989 Lafayette Court, Boston, MA." Your trust document will state that you have transferred all your interest in that property to the trust. The share of the property owned by your sister, obviously, is not included.

Co-op apartments. If you own shares in a co-op corporation that owns your apartment, you'll have to hold your shares in trust. Some corporations are reluctant to let a trustee own shares; check the co-op corporation's rules to see whether the transfer is allowed.

Small Business Interests

The delay, expense and court intrusion of probate can be especially detrimental to an ongoing small business. And if a business is a major asset, you'll want to include it in your trust to avoid estate tax.

SEE AN EXPERT

If you want to control the long-term management of your business. A revocable living trust is not the right vehicle for arranging business management. See an estate planning lawyer to draft a different kind of trust, with provisions tailored to your situation.

Different kinds of business organizations present different issues when you want to hold your interest in your living trust:

Sole proprietorships. If you (or you and your spouse) operate your business as a sole proprietorship, with all business assets held in your own name, you can simply transfer your business property to yourselves as trustees. You should also transfer the business's name itself; that transfers the customer goodwill associated with the name.

Partnership interests. If you operate your business as a partnership with other people, you can probably transfer your partnership share to your living trust. If there is a partnership certificate, it must be changed.

Some partnership agreements require the people who inherit a deceased partner's share of the business to offer that share to the other partners before taking it. But that happens after death, so it shouldn't affect your ability to transfer the property through a living trust.

It's not common, but a partnership agreement may limit or forbid holding your interest in a living trust. If yours does, you and your partners may want to see a lawyer before you make any changes.

Solely owned corporations. If you own all the stock of a corporation, you should have no difficulty transferring it to you and your spouse as trustees.

Closely held corporations. A closely held corporation is a corporation that doesn't sell shares to the public. All its shares are owned by a few people who are usually actively involved in running the business. Normally, you can use a living trust to transfer shares in a closely held corporation by listing the stock in the trust document and then having the stock certificates reissued in the trustees' names.

You'll want to check the corporation's bylaws and articles of incorporation to be sure you will still have voting rights in your capacity as trustee of the living trust; usually, this is not a problem. If it is, you and the other shareholders should be able to amend the corporation's bylaws to allow it.

There may, however, be restrictions that affect the transfer of shares. Check the corporation's bylaws and articles of incorporation, as well as any separate shareholders' agreements. One fairly common rule is that surviving shareholders (or the corporation) have the right to buy the shares of a deceased shareholder. In that case, you can still use a living trust to transfer the shares, but the people who inherit them may have to sell them.

Limited liability companies. If your small business is an LLC, you'll need the consent of a majority or all of the other owners (check your operating agreement) before you can transfer your interest to yourself as trustee. Getting the other owners to agree shouldn't be a problem; they'll just want to know that you, as trustee of your own trust, will have authority to vote on LLC decisions. Another way to address this concern would be to transfer your economic interest in the LLC, but not your right to vote.

Bank Accounts

It's not difficult to transfer bank accounts to your living trust.

You may not, however, want to hold your personal checking accounts in a living trust—it can be difficult to cash checks on accounts owned in a trustee's name.

Jointly owned accounts. If you want to hold a joint account in your living trust, things are more complicated, and you may just want to name a payable-on-death beneficiary for the account instead. The reason is that almost all joint accounts have what's called the "right of survivorship," which means that when one owner dies, the survivor automatically owns all the money in the account. A provision in a will or living trust can't override that. So no matter what your living trust says, the share of the first spouse to die will go to the survivor; the money in the account will go to a trust beneficiary only when the second spouse dies.

EXAMPLE: Joan and Alex have a joint savings account. They go to the bank and change the registration card on the account to read "Joan and Alex Crookshank, trustees of the Joan and Alex Crookshank AB Revocable Living Trust dated August 23, 20xx." In the trust document, Alex leaves his half of the account to his friend Max. Alex dies first. The account is now owned by Joan; Max won't inherit anything.

Vehicles and Property That Is Often Sold

Some kinds of property are cumbersome to keep in a living trust. It's not a legal problem, just a practical one. Two common examples are:

- **Cars or other vehicles you use.** Having registration and insurance in your name as trustee could be confusing, and some insurance companies might balk. If you have valuable antique autos, or a mobile home that is permanently attached to land and considered real estate under your state's law, however, you may want

to go ahead and hold them in trust. You should be able to find an insurance company that will cooperate.
- **Property you buy or sell frequently.** If you don't expect to own the property at your death, there's no compelling reason to hold it in trust. (Remember, probate and taxes aren't issues until after your death.) On the other hand, if you're buying property, it's no more trouble to acquire it in your name as trustee.

Life Insurance

If you own a life insurance policy at your death, the insurance company will give the proceeds to the named beneficiary without probate. The proceeds are, however, considered part of your estate for federal estate tax purposes.

If you have named a minor or young adult as the beneficiary of an insurance policy, you may want to name your living trust instead. Then, in the trust document, you name the child as beneficiary of any insurance proceeds paid to the trust and arrange for an adult to manage the policy proceeds if the beneficiary is still young when you die. If you don't arrange for management of the money, and the beneficiary is still a minor (under 18) when you die, a court will have to appoint a financial guardian after your death. (Young beneficiaries are discussed in Part 6, below.)

Passing the proceeds of a life insurance policy through your living trust is a bit more complicated than leaving other property this way. You must take two steps:

1. Name the living trust as the beneficiary of your life insurance policy. (Your

insurance agent will have a form that lets you change the beneficiary of the policy.)

2. When you list property items in the living trust document, list the proceeds of the policy, not the policy itself. ("How to Describe Trust Property," below, contains sample descriptions.)

Securities

If you buy and sell stocks regularly, you may not want to go to the trouble of acquiring and selling them using your authority as trustees of the trust. Fortunately, there's an easier way to do it: Hold your stocks in a brokerage account that you own as trustees. All securities in the account are then held in your trust. In most states, you can also register securities in "beneficiary" form so that they avoid probate, without holding them in trust.

Stock in closely held corporations. See "Small Business Interests," above. In most states, you can also register securities in "beneficiary" form so they avoid probate without holding them in trust.

Cash

If you want to leave a few cash gifts to beneficiaries—for example, $5,000 to a relative, friend or charity—in addition to leaving the bulk of your property to your spouse, you can do so. You can't, however, just list "$5,000 cash" in your trust document— you must identify exactly where that cash is coming from. The way to do it is to hold a cash account (a savings or money market account, for example) in your trust and name a beneficiary to receive the contents of the

account. So to leave $5,000 to cousin Fred, all you have to do is put the money in a bank or money market account, transfer it to yourself as trustee and name Fred, in the trust document, as the beneficiary of the account.

Especially if the amounts involved are small, it may be simpler, however, to just name a payable-on-death beneficiary for a bank account. (See Chapter 13.)

Community Property

Alaska*	Nevada
Arizona	New Mexico
California	Texas
Idaho	Washington
Louisiana	Wisconsin

* If spouses sign a community property agreement.

Community property (owned by both spouses equally) held in your living trust will stay community property. Separately owned property (property of only one spouse) will remain the separate property of the spouse. That means that community property held in trust is still eligible for the favorable tax treatment given community property at one spouse's death. (Both halves of community property left to the surviving spouse get a date-of-death tax basis for income tax purposes, if the value of the property has gone up.)

If either spouse revokes the living trust, ownership of the property will go back to the spouses as it was before the property was held in the living trust. Community property goes back to both spouses equally, and separate property goes to the spouse who owned it.

Retirement Plans

Individual retirement accounts cannot be held in trust.

You can name a living trust as a beneficiary, but it's usually not a good idea. Under current IRS rules, money left to a trust is distributed based on the life expectancy of the trust beneficiary.

 RESOURCE
IRAs, 401(k)s & Other Retirement Plans: Taking Your Money Out, by Twila Slesnick and John C. Suttle (Nolo), explains the options of those who inherit money in a retirement account.

Other Valuable Property

Other valuable items—everything from jewelry and antiques to boats and airplanes—can also be placed in trust.

How to Describe Trust Property

When we ask you to list the property you want to hold in your trust, describe each item clearly enough so that it will get to the right person after your death. Most or all of your trust property will go for the use of your spouse, in Trust A. If, however, you're going to leave an item as a specific gift, just make sure your surviving spouse (or successor trustee, if you're the second spouse to die) can identify the property and transfer it to the beneficiary. No magic legal words are required.

Rules for Entering Descriptions of Trust Property

- Don't use "my" in a description. Don't, for example, enter "my books" or "my stereo system." That's because once the property is in the living trust, it doesn't belong to you anymore—it belongs to the trust.
- Don't begin a description with a capital letter (unless it must begin with a proper name, like "Steinway"). That's because the descriptions will be inserted into a sentence in the trust document, and it would look odd to see a capital letter in the middle of a sentence.
- Don't end a description with a period. Again, this is because the descriptions will be inserted into a sentence in the trust document.

Think about whom the property will ultimately go to. If you're leaving everything to one person, or just a few, there's less need to go into great detail. But if there will be a number of trust beneficiaries and objects could be confused, be more specific about each one. When in doubt, err on the side of including more information; describe particularly valuable items much as you would if you were listing them on an insurance policy.

Here are some sample descriptions:

Real estate
- "the house at 321 Glen St., Omaha, NE"
- "the house at 4444 Casey Road, Fandon, Illinois, and the 20-acre parcel on which it is located"

Usually, the street address is enough. It's not necessary to use the "legal description" found on the deed, which gives a subdivision plat number or a metes-and-bounds description. But if the property has no street address—for example, if it is undeveloped land out in the country—you will need to carefully copy the full legal description, word for word, from the deed.

If you own a house and several adjacent lots, it's a good idea to indicate that you are transferring the entire parcel to your living trust by describing the land as well as the house.

If you own the property with someone else and are transferring only your share, you don't need to specify the share you own. Just describe the property. The trust document will show that you are transferring all your interest in the property, whatever share that is, to the living trust.

Bank accounts
- "Savings Account No. 9384-387, Arlington Bank, Arlington, MN"
- "Money Market Account 47-223 at Charles Schwab & Co., Inc., San Francisco, CA"

Household items
- "all the furniture normally kept in the house at 44123 Derby Ave., Ross, KY"
- "the antique brass bed in the master bedroom in the house at 33 Walker Ave., Fort Lee, New Jersey"
- "all furniture and household items normally kept in the house at 869 Hopkins St., Great Falls, Montana"

Sole proprietorship business property
- "Mulligan's Fish Market"
- "Fourth Street Records and CDs"
- "all accounts receivable of the business known as Garcia's Restaurant, 988 17th St., Atlanta, GA"
- "all food preparation and storage equipment, including refrigerator, freezer, hand mixers and slicer used at Garcia's Restaurant, 988 17th St., Atlanta, GA"

As explained in "What Kinds of Property to Hold in Trust," above, you should both list the name of the business and separately list items of business property.

Partnership interest
- "the Don and Dan's Bait Shop Partnership owned by the grantor before being held in this living trust"

Because a partnership is a legal entity that can own property, you don't need to list items of property owned by the partnership.

Shares in a closely held corporation
- "The stock of ABC Hardware, Inc."

Shares in a solely owned corporation
- "all shares in the XYZ Corporation"
- "all stock in Fern's Olde Antique Shoppe, Inc., 23 Turnbridge Court, Danbury, Connecticut"

Securities
- "all securities in account No. 3999-34-33 at Smith Brokerage, 33 Lowell Place, New York, NY"
- "200 shares of General Industries, Inc., stock"

- "Good Investment Co. mutual fund account No. 888-09-09"

Life insurance proceeds

- "the proceeds of Acme Co. Life Insurance Policy #9992A"

Miscellaneous items

- "Macintosh laptop computer (serial number 129311)"
- "the medical textbooks in the office at 1702 Parker Towers, San Francisco, CA"
- "the stamp collection usually kept at 321 Glen St., Omaha, NE"
- "the collection of European stamps, including [describe particularly valuable stamps], usually kept at 440 Loma Prieta Blvd., #450, San Jose, CA"
- "the Martin D-35 acoustic guitar, serial number 477597"
- "the signed 1960 Ernie Banks baseball card kept in safe deposit box 234, First National Bank of Augusta, Augusta, IL"
- "the Baldwin upright piano kept at 985 Dawson Court, South Brenly, Massachusetts"

Part 4: Specific Beneficiaries

Once you've entered a list of the property you're going to hold in trust, the next step is to say whom you want to inherit it. With an AB trust, this is pretty simple, because each spouse leaves all or the bulk of his or her trust property to the other, in Trust A. (This is true whether or not you use the disclaimer trust option.) So all each spouse has to do is name:

- beneficiaries for any specific gifts—items you don't want to leave to the surviving spouse in Trust A, and
- the final beneficiaries, who inherit all the trust property after both spouses have died. (See Part 5, below.)

EXAMPLE: Roger and Marilyn create an AB trust. Each puts co-owned and separately owned property in the trust. They name their three children as final beneficiaries. When Roger dies, Marilyn takes over as sole trustee and splits the AB trust into Trust A (the irrevocable bypass trust) and Trust B (her ongoing revocable trust). When Marilyn dies, the successor trustee distributes the property to the children.

The beneficiaries you name in your trust document are not entitled to any trust property while both spouses are alive. You can amend your trust document and change the beneficiaries until your death.

> **CAUTION**
> **Children's rights to inherit.** In most circumstances, you don't have to leave anything to your children. But if you want to disinherit a child, it's a good idea to make a will and specifically mention the child in it. (See Chapter 4.)

Choosing Specific Beneficiaries

We'll ask you first whether you want to make any specific gifts or just leave all trust property in Trust A for your spouse (and, eventually, the final beneficiaries). Just skip this part if you want to leave everything to your spouse in the bypass trust. If you choose to make some specific gifts, we'll show you a list of all the items you listed earlier. You can choose any number of them and name beneficiaries (including your spouse, if you wish) for them.

If you leave your spouse a specific gift, it will stay in his or her revocable living trust—not in Trust A, the irrevocable bypass trust—if you are the first to die.

> EXAMPLE: Max and Joan make an AB trust. Max wants Joan to have some property outright, with no restrictions, so he leaves some items to her directly as specific gifts. Max dies first. The specific gifts go into Trust B, Joan's revocable living trust. (See Chapter 21.)

As you name your specific beneficiaries, remember that when it comes to property you and your spouse co-own, you're naming people to receive only your share. Only your interest in the co-owned property will go to the beneficiary.

> EXAMPLE: Marcia and Perry transfer all the property they own together into their living trust. Perry leaves his half-interest in the couple's vacation cabin to his son from a previous marriage, Eric. When Perry dies, his half-interest in the cabin will go to Eric, who will co-own it with Marcia.

Alternate Beneficiaries

You can name an alternate beneficiary for every person you name as a specific beneficiary.

The alternate will get the property left to the primary beneficiary if your first choice does not live for more than 120 hours (five days) after your death. This survivorship period ensures that if you and a primary beneficiary die simultaneously or almost so, the property will go to the alternate beneficiary you chose, not to the primary beneficiary's heirs.

You don't have to name an alternate for a charitable (or other) institution you name as a beneficiary. If the institution is well established, it is probably safe to assume that it will still exist at your death.

You can name more than one person or institution as alternate beneficiaries. If you do, they will share the property equally unless you state otherwise.

Common Concerns

Here are some issues that may come up when you name beneficiaries.

Naming Minors or Young Adults

You can name minors (children under 18) to inherit trust property. If a beneficiary you name is a minor or a young adult who can't yet manage property without help, you can arrange for an adult to manage the trust property for the beneficiary. (See Part 6, below.)

Naming Your Successor Trustee as a Beneficiary

It's very common, and perfectly legal, to make the person you named to be successor trustee (the person who will distribute trust property after the second spouse dies) a beneficiary as well.

> **EXAMPLE:** Nora and Sean name their son Liam as successor trustee of their AB trust. They name Liam and his sister Meg as final beneficiaries. After Nora and Sean have both died, Liam, acting as trustee, will transfer ownership of the trust property to himself and Meg.

Naming More Than One Beneficiary to Share Property

You can name more than one beneficiary to share any item of trust property. Obviously, give some thought to whether or not the beneficiaries are likely to get along. If they are incompatible, disagreements could arise over taking care of property or deciding whether or not to sell it.

Cobeneficiaries will share property equally unless you state otherwise. We'll ask you, after you enter their names, whether or not you want them to get equal shares.

> **EXAMPLE:** Georgia wants to leave her house to her two children, Ross and Ryan, but wants Ross to have a 75% share of it. She enters their names and then, on a later screen, enters their interests, in fractions: 3/4 for Ross and 1/4 for Ryan.
>
> When the children inherit the property, they own it together. But Ross will be liable for 75% of the taxes and upkeep cost and entitled to 75% of any income the house produces. If they sell it, Ross will be entitled to 75% of the proceeds.

Entering Beneficiaries' Names

When you enter a beneficiary's name, use the name by which the beneficiary is known for purposes such as a bank account or driver's license. Generally, if the name you use clearly and unambiguously identifies the person, it is sufficient.

If you name an institution (charitable or not) to inherit trust property, enter its complete name. It may be commonly known by a shortened version, which could cause confusion if there are similarly named organizations. Call to ask if you're unsure. (An institution that stands to inherit some of your money will be more than happy to help you.) Also be sure to specify if you want a specific branch of a national organization to receive your gift—for example, a local chapter of the Sierra Club.

Cobeneficiaries. Simply enter their names in the box on the screen. Type the names one per line.

Always use the beneficiaries' actual names; don't use collective terms such as "my children." It's not always clear who is included in such descriptions. And there can be serious confusion if one of the group dies before you do.

Part 5: Final Beneficiaries

Final beneficiaries are the people or organizations that inherit trust property after both spouses have died.

How It Works

Each spouse names final beneficiaries separately, although in most cases they name the same people. If they do name the same people, then the final beneficiaries inherit trust property after the second spouse dies.

> **EXAMPLE:** Peggy and Michael make their AB trust, naming their two children as final beneficiaries. The children won't inherit anything until after Peggy and Michael have both died; then they will inherit the property in Trusts A and B.

You and your spouse, however, can name different final beneficiaries. That's because each of you chooses final beneficiaries for your share of the trust property. For example, if you have children from a previous marriage, you may want to name them as your final beneficiaries, while your spouse names someone else.

> **EXAMPLE:** Peggy and Basil both have children from previous marriages. When they make their AB trust, each names his own children as final beneficiaries. Basil dies first; his share of the trust property goes into Trust A, the bypass trust, for Peggy to use until her death. Peggy's share goes into Trust B, which she owns outright. When Peggy dies five years later, her children get the Trust B property, and Basil's children inherit the Trust A property.

Things may work a little differently if you choose to include the disclaimer option in your trust document, essentially making the bypass trust optional.

If the spouses name the same final beneficiaries, nothing changes. After both spouses have died, those final beneficiaries will inherit all the trust property, whether or not the surviving spouse decided to create the bypass trust.

If the spouses name different final beneficiaries, however, they can't be sure what trust property the final beneficiaries of the first spouse to die will inherit. Those beneficiaries might not inherit anything from the trust. That's because the surviving spouse decides how much trust property, if any, goes into the bypass trust. If the surviving spouse decides that a bypass trust isn't necessary to save on estate taxes, it won't be created, and there will be nothing for the final beneficiaries of that trust to inherit when the second spouse dies.

> **EXAMPLE:** Clarisse and Harold make a disclaimer trust. Clarisse names her daughter from a previous marriage as her final beneficiary, and Harold names his son from his previous marriage.
>
> When Harold dies, the estate tax exemption has risen so high that his widow Clarisse decides there's no tax reason to split the AB trust and create the irrevocable bypass trust. So, under the terms of the trust, she does nothing and inherits all the trust property. When she dies, the property goes to her final beneficiary, her daughter. Harold's son inherits no trust property.

This isn't a problem unless the spouses name different final beneficiaries and both want to be sure that their own final beneficiaries will inherit. In that situation, a disclaimer trust isn't a good idea.

Choosing Final Beneficiaries

Most couples name their children as their final beneficiaries, but you can name anyone you wish. (If for some reason you don't want to leave anything to a child, you should make a will and specifically mention the child in it. See Chapter 13.)

Here are some other common choices.

The Successor Trustee

It's fine to name someone as both your successor trustee and a final beneficiary.

Charities

You can name a charity as a final beneficiary, but doing so raises some issues you should think about.

Problems may arise only if your estate owes federal estate tax at your death—that is, your estate exceeds the amount of the estate tax threshold in the year in which you die. Because gifts made to charities are not subject to estate tax, any tax due will be taken out of the amounts left to other, noncharitable final beneficiaries. They may end up getting less than you intended.

 SEE AN EXPERT

If you think your estate may run into this problem, see an estate planning lawyer. You may want to customize your trust document to

include a provision stating that taxes are to be paid from the charity's share. This way, the other beneficiaries will get their entire shares, and the charity will get what's left.

More Than One Final Beneficiary

You can name more than one final beneficiary. If you do, you can specify what share of your trust property you want each one to inherit. You cannot, however, specify who gets what particular items; they will share all the property.

Always use the beneficiaries' actual names, not terms such as "my children." It's not always clear who is included in such groups. And there can be serious confusion if one of the group dies before you do.

Minors or Young Adults

If a final beneficiary is a minor or a young adult, you can arrange for someone to manage the trust property for the beneficiary. (See Part 6, below.)

Final Beneficiaries' Rights

Choose your final beneficiaries carefully. After one spouse has died, final beneficiaries have certain legal rights even before they inherit trust property. If they believe the surviving spouse is spending bypass trust assets wastefully or in violation of the terms of the trust document, they could go to court. They could ask a judge to order the surviving spouse to manage the trust assets differently, or even to appoint a different person as trustee. Such conflicts are rare—but you should be confident that your final beneficiaries understand that you are going to the trouble of setting up an AB trust to benefit them, that doing so is a generous act on your part and that they should defer to the surviving spouse's decisions about the use of bypass trust property.

You may require the surviving spouse to give final beneficiaries copies of the annual trust income tax return, however. We'll ask you whether or not you want to require this.

If You Change Your Mind

After the first spouse dies, his or her final beneficiaries can't be changed. But if you are the surviving spouse, you can change the beneficiaries of your own revocable trust. (See Chapter 21.)

Part 6: Property Management for Young Beneficiaries

If any of the beneficiaries (including alternates) named by either spouse might inherit trust property before they are ready to manage it without an adult's help, you should arrange for someone to manage it for them for a while.

Your Options

There are several ways to arrange for an adult to manage property inherited by a young person:

- **Leave the property to an adult to use for the child.** Many people don't leave property directly to a child. Instead, they leave it to the child's parent or to the person they expect to have care and custody of the child if neither parent is available. There's no formal legal arrangement, but they feel confident that the adult will use the property for the child's benefit.
- **Name a custodian under the Uniform Transfers to Minors Act (UTMA).** In almost all states, you can name a custodian to manage property you leave a child until the child reaches 18 or 21, depending on state law (up to 25 in several states). If you don't need management to last beyond that age, a custodianship is probably the way to go.
- **Create a child's subtrust.** You can use Quicken WillMaker Plus to establish a child's subtrust in your living trust. If you do, your surviving spouse (or the successor trustee, after both spouses' death) will manage the property left to the child and dole it out for education, health and other needs. The subtrust ends at whatever age you designate, up to 35, and then any remaining property is turned over to the child outright.

Subtrusts and custodianships are explained below.

RESOURCE

Children with special needs. These property management options are not designed to provide long-term property management for a child with serious disabilities. For information on this kind of planning, see *Special Needs Trusts*, by Stephen Elias (Nolo).

Should You Arrange for Management?

Each spouse chooses whether or not to arrange to have someone manage trust property that's inherited by young beneficiaries.

The consequences of forgoing management for trust property inherited by a young beneficiary depend on whether the beneficiary is over or under age 18 at your death.

Children Under 18 Years Old

Minors—children under 18—cannot, legally, own or manage significant amounts of property. An adult must be in charge if the minor acquires more than a few thousand dollars' worth of property. (The exact amount depends on state law.)

If your minor beneficiaries will inherit objects that have more sentimental than monetary value, you don't need to arrange for an adult to manage the property.

But if a beneficiary inherits valuable trust property while still a minor, and you have not arranged for the property to be managed by an adult, a court-appointed guardian may have to manage the property. Contrary to what you might expect, a child's parent does not automatically have legal authority to manage any property the child inherits. So even if one or both of the beneficiary's parents are alive, they will have to ask the court to grant them that authority and will be subject to the court's supervision. If neither parent is alive, there may be no obvious person for the court to appoint as property guardian. In that case, it may be even more important for you to name someone in your living trust.

There is one other option: In most states, the successor trustee can name a custodian to manage property inherited by a minor. If the value of property exceeds a certain amount—$10,000 in most states—a court must approve the appointment. And the custodianship must end at 18 in most states—earlier than many parents may choose. So it's still better to name a custodian yourself.

Young Adults 18 to 35 Years Old

If a living trust beneficiary is 18 or older when he or she inherits trust property, you do not need, legally, to have anyone manage the property on the beneficiary's behalf. And if you don't make any arrangements, the beneficiary will get the property with no strings attached. But you can arrange for property management to last until a beneficiary turns any age up to 35.

There is no legal requirement that management for a trust beneficiary's property must end at 35, but we think 35 is a reasonable cutoff. If you don't want to give a beneficiary free rein over trust property by the time he or she reaches 35, you probably need to see a lawyer and tailor a plan to the beneficiary's needs.

Which Is Better: Subtrust or Custodianship?

Using Quicken WillMaker Plus, you can create either a child's subtrust or a custodianship under the Uniform Transfer to Minors Act (if it's available in your state). Both are safe, efficient ways of managing trust property that a young person inherits. Under either system, the person in charge of the young beneficiary's property has the responsibility to use the property for the beneficiary's support, education and health.

The most significant difference is that a child's subtrust can last longer than a custodianship, which must end at age 21 in most states (25 in several states). For that reason, a child's subtrust is a good choice when a child could inherit a large amount of property.

Because an UTMA custodianship is much easier to administer, it is usually preferable if the beneficiary will inherit no more than about $50,000 worth of trust property ($100,000 or more if the child is quite young). That amount is likely to be used up for living and education expenses by the time the beneficiary is 21, so there's no need to create a subtrust that can continue beyond that age.

A custodianship has other advantages as well:

- Handling a beneficiary's property can be easier with a custodianship than with a trust. A custodian's powers are written into state law, and most institutions, such as banks and insurance companies, are familiar with the rules. Trusts, on the other hand, vary in their terms. So

before a bank lets a trustee act on behalf of a beneficiary, it may demand to see and analyze a copy of the Declaration of Trust.

- You can name whomever you wish to be a custodian, and you can name different custodians for different beneficiaries. So if you want to arrange custodianships for grandchildren, for example, you could name each child's parent as custodian. A child's subtrust is not quite so flexible: The surviving spouse, or the successor trustee if you are the second spouse to die, will be the trustee of all children's subtrusts created for your young beneficiaries.

- If the property in a subtrust earns income, and that income isn't distributed quickly to the beneficiary, the trust will have to pay tax on it. The federal tax rate on such retained income may be higher than it would be if the young beneficiary were taxed on it. The trustee may well need to hire experts to help with trust accounting and tax returns.

Custodianships

Think a custodianship is right for your family? Here's how it works.

How a Custodianship Works

In the trust document, you name someone to serve as custodian for a particular beneficiary. That person manages any trust property the young beneficiary inherits from that spouse until the beneficiary reaches the age at which state law says the custodianship must end. (See the list in Chapter 7.)

> **EXAMPLE:** Sandra and Don make an AB trust. Sandra leaves, as a specific gift, 100 shares of General Motors stock to her niece, Jennifer Frankel. She names Hazel Frankel, Jennifer's mother, as custodian under the Illinois Uniform Transfers to Minors Act.
>
> After Sandra's death, Don, as trustee, turns the stock over to the custodian, Hazel. She will manage it for Jennifer until Jennifer turns 21, the age Illinois law says she must be given the property outright.

In some states, you can specify—within limits—at what age the custodianship will end. If your state allows this, we'll ask you to enter an age at which you want the custodianship to end.

> **EXAMPLE:** If Sandra, in the previous example, lived in Nevada, state law would allow her to choose any age from 18 to 25 for the custodianship to end.

The Custodian's Responsibilities

A custodian has roughly the same responsibility as the trustee of a child's subtrust: to manage the beneficiary's property wisely and honestly. The custodian's authority and duties are set out by a law called the Uniform Transfers to Minors Act, as enacted by your state. No court directly supervises the custodian.

The custodian must:

- manage the property until the beneficiary reaches the age at which, by law, he or she gets the property outright
- use the property or income to pay for expenses such as the young beneficiary's support, education and health care
- keep the property separate from his or her own property, and
- keep separate records of transactions. The custodian does not have to file a separate income tax return; income from the property can be reported on the young beneficiary's return. (By comparison, the trustee of a child's subtrust must file a separate tax return for the subtrust.)

A custodian who needs to hire an accountant, tax lawyer or other expert can use the property to pay a reasonable amount for the help.

If state law allows it, the custodian is entitled to reasonable compensation and reimbursement for reasonable expenses. The payment, if any is taken, comes from custodial property.

Choosing a Custodian

You can name a different custodian for each young beneficiary, if you wish.

In most cases, you should name the person who will have physical custody of the minor child. That's almost always one of the child's parents. If the beneficiary is your child, name the child's other parent unless you have serious reservations about that person's ability to handle the property for the child.

Only one person can be named as custodian for one beneficiary. You can, however, name an alternate custodian to take over if your first choice is unable to serve.

Children's Subtrusts

Quicken WillMaker Plus allows you to set up a separate child's subtrust for each young beneficiary.

How a Child's Subtrust Works

In your trust document, you state the age at which the beneficiary should receive trust property outright. If at your death the beneficiary hasn't reached that age, a subtrust will be created for that beneficiary. (If the beneficiary is older, he or she gets the trust property with no strings attached, and no subtrust is created.) Each beneficiary gets a separate child's subtrust.

Quicken WillMaker Plus is set up so that the surviving spouse, or the successor trustee after both spouses die, will serve as trustee of all children's subtrusts. If you want different people to manage property inherited by different beneficiaries, you may want to use a custodianship instead of a child's subtrust. (To appoint someone else to be trustee of a child's subtrust, the trust document would have to be changed significantly; see a lawyer.)

Whatever trust property the beneficiary is entitled to receive will go into the child's subtrust, if the child is still under the age set for termination of the subtrust. The trustee will manage the subtrust property and use it as necessary for the beneficiary's health,

education and support. After the spouse's death, the subtrust cannot be revoked or amended. Until then, that spouse is free to change his or her mind about having a subtrust set up for a particular beneficiary.

The child's subtrust will end when the beneficiary reaches the age designated by the spouse in the Declaration of Trust. This can be any age up to and including 35. The trustee will then give the beneficiary what remains of the subtrust property.

EXAMPLE: In the AB trust that Oliver makes with his wife Natalie, Oliver leaves a specific gift, $100,000 worth of stock, to his 14-year-old grandson Michael. He specifies that the stock should be kept in a subtrust until Michael is 25, subject to the right of the trustee (Natalie) to spend it on his behalf.

Oliver dies when Michael is 19. The stock goes into a subtrust for him, managed by Natalie. She uses the stock (and the income it produces) to pay for Michael's education and support. Michael receives what's left of the stock when he turns 25.

EXAMPLE: Herb and Laura create an AB trust and leave all their trust property to the other. They name their daughters, who are 22 and 25, as final beneficiaries and arrange for any trust property they inherit to stay in subtrusts until each daughter reaches 30. They name Laura's sister, Antoinette, as successor trustee.

Herb and Laura die in a car accident when one daughter is 28 and the other is 31. The 28-year-old's half of the trust property stays in a subtrust, managed by Antoinette, until she turns 30. The 31-year-old gets her half outright; no subtrust is created for her.

The Subtrust Trustee's Duties

The subtrust trustee must:

- manage and invest subtrust property until the beneficiary reaches the age set out in the trust document—which can take years
- keep the beneficiary (or the beneficiary's guardian if the beneficiary is a minor) reasonably well informed about how trust assets are being invested
- use subtrust property or income to pay for expenses such as the beneficiary's support, education and health care, and
- keep separate records of subtrust transactions and file annual income tax returns for the subtrust.

The trustee's powers and responsibilities are spelled out in the trust document. If the subtrust trustee needs to hire an accountant, tax lawyer or other expert, he or she can use subtrust assets to pay a reasonable amount for the help.

The trust document also provides that the trustee of a subtrust is entitled to reasonable compensation for his or her work as trustee. The trustee decides what is a reasonable amount; the compensation is paid from the subtrust assets.

For more on the trustee's responsibilities, see Chapter 21.

Declaration of Trust

Part 1. Trust Name

This trust shall be known as the Richard Jenkins and Patricia Jenkins AB Living Trust.

Part 2. Declaration of Trust

Richard Jenkins and Patricia Jenkins, called the grantors, declare that they have set aside and hold in this trust all their interest in the property described in the attached Schedules A, B and C. All of that property is called the "trust property."

The trustees acknowledge receipt of the trust property and agree to hold it in trust, according to this Declaration of Trust.

The trust property shall be used for the benefit of the trust beneficiaries and shall be administered and distributed by the trustees in accordance with this Declaration of Trust.

The term "this Declaration of Trust" includes any provisions added by valid amendment.

Part 3. Character of Trust Property

While both grantors are alive, property transferred to this trust shall retain its original character as community or separate property, as the case may be. If the trust is revoked, the trustee shall distribute the trust property to the grantors based on the same ownership rights they had before the property was held in trust.

Part 4. Adding Property to the Trust

Either grantor, or both, may add property to this trust at any time.

Part 5. Grantors' Rights

A. Payments From Trust During Grantors' Lifetimes

The trustees shall pay to or use for the benefit of the grantors as much of the net income and principal of the trust property as the grantors request. Income shall be paid to the grantors at least annually. Income accruing in or paid to trust accounts shall be deemed to have been paid to the grantors.

B. Rights Retained by Grantors

As long as both grantors are alive, both retain all rights to income, profits and control of the trust property listed on Schedule A.

As long as Richard Jenkins is alive, he retains all rights to income, profits and control of any property listed on Schedule C.

As long as Patricia Jenkins is alive, she retains all rights to income, profits and control of any property listed on Schedule B.

Part 6. Amendment and Revocation

A. Revocation by Grantor

As long as both grantors are alive, either one may revoke this trust at any time, without notifying any beneficiary. Revocation may be in writing or any manner allowed by law.

B. Amendment by Grantor

While both grantors are alive, this Declaration of Trust may be amended only by both of them acting together. All amendments must be in writing and signed by both grantors.

After the death of one grantor, the surviving spouse can amend his or her revocable living trust, Trust B, the Surviving Spouse's Trust, as defined in Part 14.

C. Amendment or Revocation by Other Person

The power to revoke or amend this trust is personal to the grantors. A conservator, guardian or other person may not exercise it on behalf of either grantor unless the grantor specifically grants the power to revoke or amend this trust in a Durable Power of Attorney.

Part 7. Homestead Rights

If the grantors' principal residence is held in this trust, the grantors have the right to possess and occupy it for life, rent-free and without charge, except for taxes, insurance, maintenance and related costs and expenses. This right is intended to give the grantors a beneficial interest in the property and to ensure that the grantors, or either of them, do not lose eligibility for a state homestead tax exemption for which either grantor otherwise qualifies.

Part 8. Trustees

A. Original Trustees

Richard Jenkins and Patricia Jenkins are the trustees of this trust and any other trust or child's subtrust created under this Declaration of Trust. Either original trustee alone may act for and represent the trust in any transaction.

B. Trustee at Death of Original Trustee

When one original trustee dies, the other shall serve as sole trustee.

C. Successor Trustee at Death of Both Original Trustees

When both original trustees have died, Sheila Jenkins shall serve as trustee. If Sheila Jenkins is unable or unwilling to serve as successor trustee, Michael Sexton shall serve as trustee.

D. Trustee's Responsibility

The trustee in office shall serve as trustee of all trusts, including any child's subtrust, created under this Declaration of Trust.

E. Terminology

The term "trustee" includes successor trustees or alternate successor trustees serving as trustee of this trust. The singular "trustee" also includes the plural.

F. Resignation of Trustee

Any trustee in office may resign at any time by signing a notice of resignation. The resignation shall be delivered to the person or institution who is either named in this Declaration of Trust, or appointed by the trustee under Section G of this Part, to next serve as the trustee.

G. Power to Appoint Successor Trustee

If no one named in this Declaration of Trust to serve as trustee is willing and able to serve as trustee, the last acting trustee may appoint a successor trustee and may require the posting of a reasonable bond, to be paid for with the trust property. The appointment must be made in writing, signed by the trustee and notarized.

H. Bond

No bond shall be required of any trustee named in this Declaration of Trust.

I. Compensation

No trustee shall receive compensation for serving as trustee, unless the trustee serves as a trustee of Trust A, the Bypass Trust, or of a child's subtrust created by this Declaration of Trust.

J. Liability of Trustee

With respect to the exercise or non-exercise of discretionary powers granted by this Declaration of Trust, the trustee shall not be liable for actions taken in good faith. Such actions shall be binding on all persons interested in the trust property.

Part 9. Trustee's Powers and Duties

A. Power Under State Law

To carry out the provisions of this Declaration of Trust, the trustee shall have all authority and powers allowed or conferred under California law, subject to the trustee's fiduciary duty to the grantors and the beneficiaries.

B. Specified Powers

The trustee's powers include, but are not limited to:

1. The power to sell trust property, and to borrow money and to encumber trust property, including trust real estate, by mortgage, deed of trust or other method.

2. The power to manage trust real estate as if the trustee were the absolute owner of it, including the power to sell, lease (even if the lease term may extend beyond the period of any trust) or grant options to lease the property, to make repairs or alterations and to insure against loss.

3. The power to sell or grant options for the sale or exchange of any trust property, including stocks, bonds, debentures and any other form of security or security account, at public or private sale for cash or on credit.

4. The power to invest trust property in every kind of property and every kind of investment, including but not limited to bonds, debentures, notes, mortgages, stock options, futures and stocks, and including buying on margin.

5. The power to receive additional property from any source and add to any trust created by this Declaration of Trust.

6. The power to employ and pay reasonable fees to accountants, lawyers, investment experts or other professionals for information or advice relating to the trust.

7. The power to deposit and hold trust funds in both interest-bearing and non-interest-bearing accounts.

8. The power to deposit funds in bank or other accounts, whether or not they are insured by the FDIC.

9. The power to enter into electronic fund transfers or safe deposit arrangements with financial institutions.

10. The power to continue any business of either grantor.

11. The power to institute or defend legal actions concerning this trust or the grantors' affairs.

12. The power to execute any documents necessary to administer any trust created by this Declaration of Trust.

13. The power to diversify investments, including authority to decide that some or all of the trust property need not produce income.

Part 10. Incapacity of Grantors

A. Incapacity of One Grantor

While both grantors are alive, if one of them becomes physically or mentally incapacitated, whether or not a court has declared the grantor incompetent or in need of a conservator or guardian, the other grantor shall serve as sole trustee, until the incapacitated grantor is no longer incapacitated.

B. Incapacity of Both Grantors

If both grantors become physically or mentally incapacitated, the successor trustee named in Part 8 shall serve as trustee until at least one of the grantors is no longer incapacitated.

The successor trustee shall pay trust income at least annually to, or for the benefit of, the grantors. Income accruing in or paid to trust accounts shall be deemed to have been paid to the grantors. The trustee may also spend any amount of trust principal necessary, in the trustee's discretion, for the health, education, support, comfort, welfare and maintenance of the grantors, in accordance with their accustomed standard of living, until at least one grantor is no longer incapacitated, or until the grantors' deaths.

C. Incapacity of Surviving Spouse

If, after the death of one spouse, the surviving spouse becomes physically or mentally incapacitated, the successor trustee shall serve as trustee of Trust A and Trust B and of any other trusts created by this Declaration of Trust. The successor trustee shall serve as trustee until the surviving spouse is no longer incapacitated.

The trustee shall pay income from Trust B at least annually to, or for the benefit of, the surviving spouse. The trustee may also spend any amount of Trust B principal necessary, in the successor trustee's discretion, for the health, education, support, comfort, welfare and maintenance of the surviving spouse, in accordance with his or her accustomed standard of living.

Any income not spent for the benefit of the surviving spouse shall be accumulated and added to Trust B.

D. Determination of Incapacity

The determination of a grantor's capacity to manage this trust shall be made by Natalie DeJarlais. The successor trustee shall, if necessary, ask Natalie DeJarlais to state, in writing, an opinion as to whether or not the grantor is able to continue serving as trustee. The successor trustee may rely on that written opinion when determining whether or not to begin serving as trustee.

If the successor trustee is unable, after making reasonable efforts, to obtain a written opinion from Natalie DeJarlais, the successor trustee may request an opinion from James Leung and may rely on that opinion.

If the successor trustee is also unable, after making reasonable efforts, to obtain a written opinion from James Leung, the successor trustee may request an opinion from Andre Zivkovich and may rely on that opinion.

If the successor trustee is unable, after making reasonable efforts, to obtain a written opinion from Natalie DeJarlais, James Leung or Andre Zivkovich, the successor trustee may request an opinion from a physician who examines the grantor, and may rely on that opinion.

Part 11. Beneficiaries

A. Wife's Beneficiaries

At the death of Patricia Jenkins, the trustee shall distribute her share of the trust property listed on Schedule A and any separate property listed on Schedule B as specified in this section.

If Patricia Jenkins is the first grantor to die, her trust property shall be transferred to and administered as part of Trust A, the Bypass Trust, as defined in Part 13. If she is the second grantor to die, her trust property shall be given to her final beneficiaries, named in Part 13.

B. Husband's Beneficiaries

At the death of Richard Jenkins, the trustee shall distribute his share of the trust property listed on Schedule A and any separate property listed on Schedule C as specified in this section.

Michael Sexton shall be given Richard Jenkins's interest in the +collection of antique coins, in safety deposit box #145 at First National Bank in Oakland, California.

If Richard Jenkins is the first grantor to die, his remaining trust property shall be transferred to and administered as part of Trust A, the Bypass Trust, as defined in Part 13. If he is the second grantor to die, his remaining trust property shall be given to his final beneficiaries, named in Part 13.

Part 12. Division of Trust Property Into Trust A and Trust B

At the death of the first grantor to die, the trustee shall divide the property held in the Richard Jenkins and Patricia Jenkins AB Living Trust between two separate trusts, known as Trust A, the Bypass Trust, and Trust B, the Surviving Spouse's Trust. The trustee does not need to physically segregate the trust assets to divide them between Trust A and Trust B. The trustee shall exclusively determine what records, documents and actions are required to establish and maintain Trust A and Trust B.

A. Trust A Property

After the trustee makes any specific gifts of the deceased spouse provided for in Part 11, the trustee shall place all remaining trust property of the deceased spouse in a trust known as Trust A, the Bypass Trust. The "trust property of the deceased spouse" is, for purposes of this provision, all trust property owned individually by the deceased spouse at the time it was transferred to the trustees, plus shared ownership trust property with a total value equal to one-half the total value, at the time of the deceased spouse's death, of the shared ownership trust property listed on Schedule A of this trust document.

B. Trust B Property

The trustee shall place all trust property of the surviving spouse in a trust known as Trust B, The Surviving Spouse's Trust. The "trust property of the surviving spouse" is, for purposes of this provision, all trust property owned individually by the surviving spouse at the time it was transferred to the trustees, plus shared ownership trust property with a total value equal to one-half the total value, at the time of the deceased spouse's death, of the shared ownership trust property listed on Schedule A of this trust document.

Part 13. Terms of Trust A, the Bypass Trust

All property held in Trust A shall be administered as follows:

A. Revocation

Trust A is irrevocable.

B. Life Beneficiary

The surviving spouse is the life beneficiary of Trust A.

C. Payments From Trust A

The trustee shall pay to or spend for the benefit of the surviving spouse the net income of Trust A at least quarterly. Income accruing in or paid to trust accounts shall be deemed to have been distributed to the surviving spouse. The trustee shall also pay to or spend for the benefit of the surviving spouse any sums from the principal of Trust A necessary for the surviving spouse's health, education, support and maintenance, in accordance with his or her accustomed manner of living.

D. Trustee's Responsibilities and Compensation

The trustee has the rights and responsibilities set out in Part 8.

The trustee is entitled, without court approval, to reasonable compensation from the assets of Trust A for services rendered managing Trust A. The trustee is not required to make any accounting or report to trust beneficiaries.

E. Final Beneficiaries

At the death of the life beneficiary, the trustee shall distribute the property of Trust A, the Bypass Trust, to the final beneficiaries of the deceased spouse.

Patricia Jenkins's final beneficiaries are Keely Jenkins and Connor Jenkins.

Richard Jenkins's final beneficiary is David Jenkins. If David Jenkins does not survive the life beneficiary, his interest shall be given to Michael Sexton.

Part 14. Terms of Trust B, the Surviving Spouse's Trust

A. Surviving Spouse's Rights

During his or her life, the surviving spouse retains all rights to all income, profits and control of the property in Trust B.

B. Amendment and Revocation

The surviving spouse may amend or revoke Trust B at any time during his or her lifetime, without notifying any beneficiary. Trust B becomes irrevocable at the death of the surviving spouse.

C. Beneficiaries

At the death of the surviving spouse, the trustee shall make any specific gifts of the surviving spouse provided for in Part 11, and then distribute all remaining property of Trust B to the surviving spouse's final beneficiaries, named in Part 13.

Part 15. Terms of Property Distribution

All distributions are subject to any provision in this Declaration of Trust that creates a child's subtrust or a custodianship under the Uniform Transfers to Minors Act.

A beneficiary must survive the grantor for 120 hours to receive property under this Declaration of Trust. As used in this Declaration of Trust, to survive means to be alive or in existence as an organization.

All personal and real property left through this trust shall pass subject to any encumbrances or liens placed on the property as security for the repayment of a loan or debt.

If property is left to two or more beneficiaries to share, they shall share it equally unless this Declaration of Trust provides otherwise. If any of them does not survive the grantor, the others shall take that beneficiary's share, to share equally, unless this Declaration of Trust provides otherwise.

Part 16. Simultaneous Death

If both grantors die simultaneously, or under such circumstances as to render it difficult or impossible to determine who predeceased the other, for purposes of this living trust it shall be conclusively presumed that both died at the same moment, and neither survived the other. The trustee shall make any specific gifts provided for in Part 11, and then distribute all remaining property to each spouse's final beneficiaries, named in Part 13.

Part 17. Payment of Grantors' Debts and Taxes

The trustee may pay out of trust property such amounts as necessary for payment of debts, estate taxes and expenses of the last illness and funeral of either spouse.

Part 18. General Administrative Provisions

A. Controlling Law

The validity of this trust and construction of its provisions shall be governed by the laws of California.

B. Severability of Clauses

If any provision of this Declaration of Trust is ruled unenforceable, the remaining provisions shall nevertheless remain in effect.

Part 19. Custodianships Under the Uniform Transfers to Minors Act

If Keely Jenkins becomes entitled to trust property under Part 11.A or Part 13.E.1 of this Declaration of Trust, the property shall be given to Sheila Jenkins as custodian for Keely Jenkins under the California Uniform Transfers to Minors Act. The custodianship shall end when Keely Jenkins reaches age 21. If Sheila Jenkins is unable or ceases to serve as custodian, Michael Sexton shall serve as custodian.

If Connor Jenkins becomes entitled to trust property under Part 11.A or Part 13.E.1 of this Declaration of Trust, the property shall be given to Sheila Jenkins as custodian for Connor Jenkins under the California Uniform Transfers to Minors Act. The custodianship shall end when Connor Jenkins reaches age 21. If Sheila Jenkins is unable or ceases to serve as custodian, Michael Sexton shall serve as custodian.

If David Jenkins becomes entitled to trust property under Part 11.B or Part 13.E.2 of this Declaration of Trust, the property shall be given to Sheila Jenkins as custodian for David Jenkins under the California Uniform Transfers to Minors Act. The custodianship shall end when David Jenkins reaches age 18. If Sheila Jenkins is unable or ceases to serve as custodian, Ann Heron shall serve as custodian.

/////

/////

/////

/////

/////

/////

/////

Certification of Grantors

We certify that we have read this Declaration of Trust and that it correctly states the terms and conditions under which the trust property is to be held, managed and disposed of by the trustees, and we approve the Declaration of Trust.

_____   _____
Richard Jenkins, Grantor and Trustee   Date

_____   _____
Patricia Jenkins, Grantor and Trustee   Date

Certification of Acknowledgment of Notary Public

State of _____

County of _____

On _____, before me, _____ ,
a notary public for said state, personally appeared _____ ,
who proved to me on the basis of satisfactory evidence to be the person(s) whose name(s) is/
are subscribed to the within instrument, and acknowledged to me that he/she/they executed
the same in his/her/their authorized capacity(ies) and that by his/her/their signature(s) on the
instrument the person, or the entity upon behalf of which the person(s) acted, executed the
instrument.

I certify under PENALTY OF PERJURY under the laws of the State of California that the
foregoing is true and correct.

Witness my hand and official seal.

_____
Signature of Notary Public

_____
Printed Name

Notary Public for the State of California

Residing at: _____

[NOTARIAL SEAL]   My commission expires: _____

SCHEDULE A

SHARED PROPERTY PLACED IN TRUST

1. House at 14731 Henderson Street, Berkeley, California.

2. 150 shares in Capital Equipment Corporation.

SCHEDULE B

WIFE'S SEPARATE PROPERTY PLACED IN TRUST

All Patricia Jenkins's interest in the following property:

1. House at 1545 Meadow Way, Malibu, California.

SCHEDULE C

HUSBAND'S SEPARATE PROPERTY PLACED IN TRUST

All Richard Jenkins's interest in the following property:

1. Collection of antique coins, in safety deposit box #145 at First National Bank in Oakland, California.

Signing, Storing and Registering Your Trust

You're getting close, but you're not quite done. You'll have a valid living trust when you've completed the program, printed out your living trust document and signed it. Here's what to do next.

Before You Sign

When you've printed out the trust document, take plenty of time to read it. Carefully. Make sure it says what you want it to say. Check to be sure you have:

- included all property you want to leave through the trust
- clearly and accurately identified all property (double check any account or serial numbers, for example)
- included all beneficiaries to whom you want to leave property
- spelled beneficiaries' names correctly and consistently, and
- made adequate arrangements for management of trust property that young beneficiaries might inherit.

If you want to make changes, go back to the part of the program you need to change, enter the new data and print out another trust document. (If you need help, see the Users' Manual.)

Consulting a Lawyer

Although in most instances it isn't necessary, you may also want to have an experienced estate planning lawyer look over the trust document before you sign it. We recommend that you see a lawyer if:

- You're unsure about the legal effect of anything in the trust document.
- You want to make changes, even if they seem insignificant, to the trust document.

The cost of paying an estate planning attorney to review the trust document should be reasonable, especially compared to the cost of having an attorney do the whole thing from scratch. (Chapter 25 discusses how to find a lawyer and get the most help for your legal fees.)

A word of caution: Be aware that a lawyer who has a set way of doing things may disparage your efforts. Find a lawyer who respects what you've learned and done.

Signing Your Trust Document in Front of a Notary

To create a valid living trust, you must sign the trust document. A living trust document, unlike a will, does not need to be signed in front of witnesses. (In Florida, two witnesses are required; a witness statement automatically prints out with a Florida trust document.) But you do need to sign your living trust document in front of a notary public for your state. If you create a shared living trust, both of you need to sign the trust document in front of the notary. If anyone challenges the authenticity of your signature after your death, the notarization will serve as evidence that it is genuine. And some institutions (stock brokerage houses, for example) may require that the signature be notarized before they will transfer assets into your name as trustee.

You can usually find a notary at a bank, title or escrow company, real estate brokerage or library. Or check the yellow pages under "Notaries Public."

Getting a signature notarized is quite simple. You show some evidence of your identity, and then the notary watches you sign the trust document and signs and dates it, too. The notary also stamps a notarial seal on the document.

Your living trust document includes, at the end of the document, lines for your signature and a place for the notarization. The notarization form should be valid in most places, but if the notary public for your state wants to modify it, that's fine; some states require slightly different wording.

You must also sign the Assignment of Property that prints out with your trust document. This is the form that shows that you are transferring certain kinds of personal property to the trust. (See Chapter 19.) It doesn't have to be notarized.

Making Copies

You will probably need copies of the trust document to transfer certain kinds of property (stocks, for example) to yourself in your capacity as trustee. (The details are in Chapter 19.) If a broker, bank or other institution wants to see your trust document, use a photocopy of the original trust document—the one you signed and had notarized. Do not just print out and sign another copy. Each copy you actually sign becomes, legally, an original trust document. Later, if you amend or revoke your living trust, you don't want lots of duplicate original trust documents floating around.

You should give a copy of the trust document to anyone you named to be a custodian of trust property inherited by a young beneficiary. The custodian may need it to show his or her authority to manage the property on behalf of the beneficiary.

It's not usually advisable to give copies of the trust document to beneficiaries. The problem is that if you later revoke or amend the trust but don't collect all the old copies, outdated copies of your trust document will still exist.

States That Provide for Registration of Living Trusts		
Alaska	Idaho	Missouri
Colorado[2]	Maine[1]	Nebraska[1]
Florida[1]	Michigan	North Dakota
Hawaii		

[1] Not mandatory

[2] Registration of a revocable living trust not required until the grantor's death; no registration required if all trust property is distributed to the beneficiaries then.

Registering the Trust

Some states require that the trustee of a trust register the trust with the local court. But there are no legal consequences or penalties if you don't.

Registration of a living trust doesn't give the court any power over the administration of the trust, unless there's a dispute. Registration serves to give the court jurisdiction over any disputes involving the trust—for example, if after your death, a beneficiary wants to object to the way your successor trustee distributed the trust property. But if you don't register your trust, the result is the same: The court still has jurisdiction if a disgruntled relative or creditor files suit. (The only exception is that if a court demands that a trustee register a trust, and the trustee refuses, the trustee can be removed.)

To register a revocable living trust, the trustee must file a statement with the court where the trustee resides or keeps trust records. The statement must include:

- the name and address of the trustee
- an acknowledgment of the trusteeship
- the name(s) of the grantor(s)
- the name(s) of the original trustee(s), and
- the date of the trust document.

A trust can be registered in only one state at a time.

Storing the Trust Document

Store your living trust document, the software CD and the manual where you keep important papers such as your will or durable power of attorney. A fireproof box in your home or office is fine. If you want to be extra careful, a safe deposit box is a good choice.

Make sure your successor trustee (or your spouse or partner, if you made a trust together) knows where the original trust document is and can get hold of it soon after your death. The new trustee will need it to carry out your instructions on how to manage and distribute trust property. The new trustee will also need the information in Chapter 21 to carry out his or her duties.

Copies of your trust document stored on your computer are not valid living trusts. The trust document must be printed out and signed to create a trust.

Transferring Property to the Trust

After you sign your living trust document, you have a valid living trust. But the trust is of absolutely no use to you until the property you listed in the trust document is actually transferred into your name as trustee (or, in Colorado, to the name of the trust itself). Lawyers call this "funding" the trust.

Funding your living trust is crucial. It takes some time and paperwork, but it's not difficult. You should be able to do it yourself, without a lawyer. This chapter shows you how.

> **CAUTION**
>
> **Don't put this off!** Failing to transfer property to the trustee's name is the most common and serious mistake people make when creating a living trust. If you don't get around to preparing and signing the transfer documents, the trust document will have no effect on what happens to your property after your death. Instead, the property will pass through your will, if you have one (you should—see Chapter 13). If you don't have a will, the property will go to certain close relatives, according to state law. Either way, your probate- and tax-avoidance goals will not be met.

Making a Certification or Abstract of Trust

When you go to transfer property in or out of your living trust, a bank or other institution may ask to see the trust document. The institution wants to know that the trust exists and that you really have the authority you say you do.

If you don't want to show your trust document, in most cases you can use a shorter version of it, called a certification, certificate, abstract or memorandum of trust (different states use different names). This document gives institutions the information they need but lets you keep some key provisions private. Notably, you don't have to disclose the names of the beneficiaries to whom you're leaving trust property. A certification is almost universally accepted in place of an entire trust document.

Many states have laws stating that if a certification of trust includes certain information, institutions must accept it in lieu of the entire trust document. California law, for example, states that someone who refuses to accept a valid certification and demands to see the whole trust document may be liable for any monetary loss suffered by the trust grantor.

With Quicken WillMaker Plus, you can make a certification that meets the requirements of many states (for example, California). Even if it doesn't contain everything your state's form does, it will still be acceptable in a great many cases. However, an institution may insist that you use the form that has been approved by your state legislature. The states that have their own requirements are listed below. You can look up your state's law if you need to; see Chapter 25 for tips. In addition, institutions such as banks and title companies may have their own forms, which they would prefer you to use.

Whenever you want to create a certification, you can use Quicken WillMaker Plus to print out a new one. The only additional information you need to give is the date the trust document was signed, along with your current address.

You should sign the certification in front of a notary public. If you and your spouse or

States With Their Own Certification Rules

Most states have enacted statutes setting out the contents for a certification of trust. If your certification meets the state requirements, institutions must accept it or be liable to you for your losses.

If you want to look up your state's statute, start at www.nolo.com/statute/state.cfm. You can also find it in a law library.

State	Statute Sections on Certification of Trust	State	Statute Sections on Certification of Trust
Alabama	Ala. Code § 19-38-1013	Nevada	Nev. Rev. Stat. § 164.410
Arkansas	Ark. Rev. Stat. § 28-73-1013	New Hampshire	N.H. Rev. Stat. Ann. § 564-B:10-1013
California	Cal. Prob. Code § 18100.5	New Mexico	N.M. Stat. Ann. § 46A-10-1012
Delaware	Del. Code Ann. § 3591		
Dist. of Columbia	D.C. Code Ann. § 19-1310.13	North Carolina	N.C. Gen. Stat. § 36C-10-1013
Florida	Fla. Stat. Ann. § 736.1017	Ohio	Ohio Rev. Code § 5810.13
Idaho	Idaho Code § 68-115	Oregon	Or. Rev. Stat. § 130.860
Indiana	Ind. Code § 30-4-4-5	Pennsylvania	20 Pa. Cons. Stat. Ann. § 7790.3
Iowa	Iowa Code § 633A.4604		
Kansas	Kan. Stat. Ann. § 58a-1013	Rhode Island	R.I. Gen. Laws § 34-4-27
Maine	Me. Rev. Stat. tit. 18-B, § 1013	South Carolina	S.C. Code Ann. § 62-7-1013
Michigan	Mich. Comp. Laws Ann. § 565.432	South Dakota	S.D. Cod. Laws Ann. § 55-4-42
		Tennessee	Tenn. Code Ann. § 35-15-1013
Minnesota	Minn. Stat. § 501B.56	Utah	Utah Code Ann. § 75-7-1013
Mississippi	Miss. Code Ann. § 91-9-7	Virginia	Va. Code § 55-550.13
Missouri	Mo. Rev. Stat. § 456.10-1013	West Virginia	W.Va. Code § 36-1-4a
Nebraska	Neb. Rev. Stat. § 30-39,102 and following	Wyoming	Wyo. Stat. § 4-10-814

partner made the trust together, you both need to sign the certification. If one has died, the survivor can make a certification.

A sample is shown below.

Property Without Title Documents

If an item doesn't have an official title document, you can hold it in trust very easily, with a document called an Assignment of Property. Quicken WillMaker Plus automatically assembles this document; you can print it out when you print the trust document itself.

The Assignment of Property lists every item of trust property that you've indicated doesn't have a title document, plus ones you weren't sure about. It simply says that you're transferring all those items to you as the trustee of your trust. All you need to do is sign it and keep it with your trust document.

Examples of Items Without Title Documents		
Appliances	Computers	Stereos
Artwork	Dishes	Tools
Books	Furniture	
Clothing	Jewelry	

Remember that the Assignment of Property works only for items that do not have their own specific title documents. If an item has a title document—for example, the deed to a house or the title slip to a car—you'll need to create a new one. The rest of this chapter explains how.

Real Estate

To transfer real estate (also called real property) into your trust, you must prepare and sign a new deed, transferring ownership. You can fill out a new deed yourself; it's not difficult.

Co-op apartments. If you own a co-op apartment, you can't use a deed to transfer your shares in the co-op. You will have to check the co-op corporation's rules to see if the transfer is allowed. Some co-ops resist such transfers because they are afraid a trustee isn't a proper shareholder in the corporation. You can probably overcome any resistance you encounter by reminding the powers that be that for all practical purposes, you and the trust are the same—you have the same tax identification number, for example.

Preparing the Deed

First, get a deed form. In many places, you can find blank deed forms in stationery or office supply stores. If you can't find what you need there, try a local law library; look for books on "real property" that have deed forms you can photocopy. You can use a "quitclaim" or "grant" deed form. (If you use a grant deed, you are promising the new owner (the trustee) that you have good title to the property. If you use a quitclaim deed, you are promising only to transfer whatever interest you own in the property. The distinction isn't important when you control the trust.)

Certification of Trust

The trustee of the Sheila Jenkins Revocable Living Trust declares as follows:

Part 1. Existence and Name of Trust/Grantor

Sheila Jenkins, called the grantor, created a revocable living trust, known as the Sheila Jenkins Revocable Living Trust, by Declaration of Trust dated August 15, 2007. This trust has not been revoked, modified or amended in such a way that would contradict what is stated in this Certification of Trust and remains in full force and effect.

Grantor's address is:
900 Lincoln Street
Tucson, Arizona 85745

Part 2. Amendment and Revocation

The grantor may amend or revoke the Sheila Jenkins Revocable Living Trust at any time, without notifying any beneficiary. The power to revoke or amend the trust is personal to the grantor. A conservator, guardian or other person shall not exercise it on behalf of the grantor, unless the grantor specifically grants a power to revoke or amend the trust in a Durable Power of Attorney.

Part 3. Trustee

Sheila Jenkins is the currently acting trustee of the trust.

The trustee in office shall serve as trustee of all trusts created under the Declaration of Trust, including children's subtrusts.

Part 4. Title to Trust Assets

Title to trust assets should be taken in the name of Sheila Jenkins, trustee of the Sheila Jenkins Revocable Living Trust, dated August 15, 2007.

Part 5. Trustee's Management Powers and Duties

Powers Under State Law

The trustee shall have all authority and powers allowed or conferred on a trustee under Arizona law, subject to the trustee's fiduciary duty to the grantors and the beneficiaries.

Specified Powers

The trustee's powers include, but are not limited to:

1. The power to sell trust property, and to borrow money and to encumber trust property, including trust real estate, by mortgage, deed of trust or other method.

2. The power to manage trust real estate as if the trustee were the absolute owner of it, including the power to lease (even if the lease term may extend beyond the period of any trust) or grant options to lease the property, to make repairs or alterations and to insure against loss.

3. The power to sell or grant options for the sale or exchange of any trust property, including stocks, bonds, debentures and any other form of security or security account, at public or private sale for cash or on credit.

4. The power to invest trust property in every kind of property and every kind of investment, including but not limited to bonds, debentures, notes, mortgages, stock options, futures and stocks, and including buying on margin.

5. The power to receive additional property from any source and add it to any trust created by this Declaration of Trust.

6. The power to employ and pay reasonable fees to accountants, lawyers or investment experts for information or advice relating to the trust.

7. The power to deposit and hold trust funds in both interest-bearing and non-interest-bearing accounts.

8. The power to deposit funds in bank or other accounts, whether or not they are insured by the FDIC.

9. The power to enter into electronic fund transfers or safe deposit arrangements with financial institutions.

10. The power to continue any business of the grantor.

11. The power to institute or defend legal actions concerning this trust or the grantor's affairs.

12. The power to execute any documents necessary to administer any trust created by this Declaration of Trust.

13. The power to diversify investments, including authority to decide that some or all of the trust property need not produce income.

This Certification of Trust is being signed by the currently acting trustee.

_____   _____
Sheila Jenkins, Grantor and Trustee   Date

Certification of Acknowledgment of Notary Public

State of _____

County of _____

On _____, before me, _____,

a notary public in and for said state, personally appeared _____,

who proved to me on the basis of satisfactory evidence to be the person whose name is
subscribed to the within instrument, and acknowledged to me that she/he executed the same
in her/his authorized capacity, and that by her/his signature on the instrument the person, or
the entity upon behalf of which the person acted, executed the instrument.

Witness my hand and official seal.

_____
Notary Public

_____

[NOTARIAL SEAL]   My commission expires: _____

RESOURCE

If you're in California, you can find deed forms and instructions for filling them out in *Deeds for California Real Estate,* by Mary Randolph (Nolo).

Deed forms vary somewhat, but they all require the same basic information. Type in:

- The current owners' names. If you are the sole owner, or if you and someone else co-own the property and you are transferring just your share, only your name goes here. If you and your spouse own the property together and are transferring it to a shared trust, type in both of your names. Use exactly the same form of your name as is used on the deed that transferred the property to you and you used in your living trust document.
- The new owner's name. Fill in your name(s) as trustee(s) exactly as it (they) appears in the first paragraph of your trust document, and the date you signed the trust document in front of a notary public.

TIP

Transferring Colorado real estate. Colorado law makes it advantageous to hold real estate under the name of the trust itself, not the trustee. So if you hold Colorado real estate in trust, the new owner's name should be, for example, "The Jonathan L. Geery Living Trust, dated November 15, 20xx." (Colo. Rev. Stat. § 38-30-108.5.)

- The "legal description" of the property. Copy the description exactly as it appears on the previous deed.

If you co-own the property with someone and are transferring only your share, you must also state, with the legal description, that you are transferring only that share (a one-half interest, for example) or that you are transferring "all your interest in" the property.

EXAMPLE: Amanda, who owns a house with her sister, wants to transfer her half of the property to her living trust. When she fills out a new deed, she can insert either "a one-half interest in" or "all my interest in" before the legal description of the real estate.

After everything is filled in, sign and date the deed in front of a notary public for the state in which the property is located. Everyone you listed as a current owner, who is transferring his or her interest in the property to the trustee, must sign the deed.

Recording the Deed

After the deed is signed, you need to "record" it—that is, put a copy of the notarized deed on file in the county office that keeps local property records. In most places, the land records office is called the county recorder's office, land registry office or county clerk's office.

Just take the original, signed deed to the land records office. For a small fee, a clerk will make a copy and put it in the public records. You'll get your original back, stamped with a reference number to show where the copy can be found in the public records.

Transfer Taxes

In most places, you will not have to pay a state or local transfer tax when you transfer real estate to yourself as trustee. Most real estate transfer taxes are based on the sale price of the property and do not apply when no money changes hands. Others specifically exempt transfers where the real owners don't change—as is the case when you transfer property to yourself as trustee of a revocable living trust.

Before you record your deed, you can get information on transfer tax from the county tax assessor, county recorder or state tax officials. Many counties now make this information available online; check your county's website.

California Property Taxes

In California, increases in real estate taxes are limited by constitutional amendment (Proposition 13). The assessed value of the property can't go up more than 2% annually until a piece of property is sold. When the property is sold, however, the house is taxed on its market value. Transferring real property to yourself as trustee of your own revocable living trust—or back to yourself—does not trigger a reassessment for property tax purposes. (Cal. Rev. & Tax Code § 62(d).)

You may, however, have to file a form called a Preliminary Change of Title Report with the county tax assessor. Call the assessor to find out.

Insurance

After you have transferred ownership of real estate, call your insurance agent to report the change. The company will change its records on the policy, but the change shouldn't affect your coverage or the cost of the policy.

Due-on-Sale Mortgage Clauses

Many mortgages contain a clause that allows the bank to call ("accelerate") the loan—that is, demand that you pay the whole thing off immediately—if you transfer the mortgaged property. Fortunately, in most instances lenders are forbidden by federal law to invoke a due-on-sale clause when property is transferred into a living trust. The lender can't call the loan if the borrower is a trust beneficiary and the transfer is "unrelated to occupancy" of the premises. (Garn-St. Germain Depository Institutions Act of 1982 (96 Stat. 1505).)

Bank Accounts and Safe Deposit Boxes

It should be simple to reregister ownership of a bank account as trustee of your living trust or open a new account in the trustee's name. Just ask the bank what paperwork you need to submit.

The bank will be concerned with the authority granted to the trustees to act on behalf of the trust. Depending on the kind of account, the bank may want to know if the trustees have the power to borrow money, put funds in a non-interest-bearing account or engage in electronic transfers. (The trust document created by Quicken WillMaker Plus includes all these powers.)

To verify your authority, the bank may want to see a copy of your trust document or have you fill out its own form, often called a Trust Certification.

If you want to transfer title to a safe deposit box, you'll have to reregister its ownership, too. The bank will have a form for you to fill out.

Credit Unions

If you want to transfer a credit union account to your living trust, you cannot simply change the name on the account. Because credit unions are membership organizations, the trust must qualify as a member of the credit union. Most credit unions accept living trusts as members. Ask your credit union for instructions.

Vehicles

Most people don't hold vehicles in trust, for reasons discussed in Part 3 of Chapters 15, 16 and 17. But if you want to hold a vehicle in trust, you must fill out a change of ownership document and have title to the vehicle reissued in the trustee's name. The title certificate to your vehicle may contain instructions. If you have questions, call your state's motor vehicles agency or check its website.

You need special forms to transfer some vehicles to your name as trustee, including:

- **Airplanes.** The Federal Aviation Administration, which registers all aircraft, has forms for you to use. For information about its Civil Aviation Registry, check out the FAA's website at www.faa.gov.
- **Large boats.** The Coast Guard has its own forms. (See www.uscg.mil.)

Securities

How you transfer stocks, bonds and other securities to your living trust depends on whether you hold your stocks in a brokerage account or separately.

Brokerage Accounts

If you hold your stocks, bonds or other securities in a brokerage account, either change the account to your name as trustee or open a new account in that name. Simply contact your broker and ask for instructions. The brokerage company will probably have a straightforward form that you can fill out, giving information about the trustees and their authority.

If not, you will probably need to send the broker:

- a copy of the trust document or a certification of trust (see "Making a Certification or Abstract of Trust," above), and
- a letter instructing the holder to transfer the brokerage account to (or open a new account in) your name as trustee.

After you've submitted your request, get written confirmation that the account's ownership has in fact been changed.

With some brokerage houses, you may run into a slight glitch. Here's what happens: When you go to transfer your account into your name as trustee, the brokerage house assigns it a new account number. Suddenly your property schedule, where you listed the account, has the wrong account number on it.

What to do? Just amend your property schedule to show the new account number. (See Chapter 21.) Then replace the old schedule with the new one, and you're all set.

Stock Certificates

If you have the stock certificates or bonds in your possession—most people don't—you must get new certificates issued, showing that you hold the shares in trust. Ask your broker for help. If the broker is unwilling or unable to help, write to the "transfer agent" of the corporation that issued the stock. You can get the address from your broker or the investor relations office of the corporation. The transfer agent will give you simple instructions.

You will probably have to send in:

- your certificates or bonds
- a form called a "stock or bond power," which you must fill out and sign, and
- a copy of the trust document or a certification of trust.

The stock or bond power may be printed on the back of the certificates; if not, you can probably find a copy at an office supply store. Send these documents to the transfer agent with a letter requesting that the certificates be reissued in your name as trustee of the living trust.

Stock in closely held corporations. See "Business Interests," below.

Government Securities

To transfer government securities—for example, Treasury bills or U.S. bonds—have your broker contact the issuing government agency, or do it yourself.

Mutual Fund Accounts

Ask the company that issues the mutual fund what it requires for you to reregister ownership of your mutual fund account in your living trust's name. Most will send you an easy-to-use form to fill out. In addition, it will usually want a copy of your trust document or a certification of trust. (See "Making a Certification or Abstract of Trust," above.)

Business Interests

How you transfer small business interests to your living trust depends on the way the business is owned.

Sole Proprietorships

First, list the business, by name, as an item of property in the trust document. That transfers the name and whatever customer goodwill goes with it.

Because you own the business assets in your own name (a sole proprietorship, unlike a corporation, is not an entity that can own property), you transfer them as you would any other valuable property. (See "Inventory Your Valuable Property" in Chapter 5.)

If you have a registered trademark or service mark, you must reregister ownership in the living trust's name.

RESOURCE

Trademark: Legal Care for Your Business & Product Name, by Stephen Elias (Nolo), contains sample forms for reregistering trademarks.

Solely Owned Corporations

If you own all the stock of a corporation, you shouldn't have any problem transferring it to yourself as trustee of your living trust. Follow these four steps:

Step 1: Fill out the stock transfer section on the back of the certificate.

Step 2: Mark the certificate "cancelled" and place it in your corporate records book.

Step 3: Reissue a new certificate in your name as trustee.

Step 4: Show the cancellation of the old certificate and the issuance of the new certificate on the stock ledger pages in your corporate records book.

Closely Held Corporations

Normally, you can transfer your shares in a closely held corporation to your living trust by following corporate bylaws and having the stock certificates reissued in the living trust's name. But first, check the corporation's bylaws and articles of incorporation, as well as any separate shareholders' agreements, to see if there are any restrictions on such transfers. If an agreement limits or forbids transfers, it will

have to be changed before you can hold your shares in trust.

CAUTION

Special rules for S corps. If you own shares in an S corporation, you cannot hold them in trust unless the trust is "qualified" under IRS rules. Consult a tax adviser.

Partnership Interests

To transfer a partnership interest, you must notify your business partners and modify the partnership agreement to show that your partnership interest is now held in trust. If there is a partnership certificate, it must also be changed.

Occasionally a partnership agreement limits or forbids transfers to a trustee. If so, you and your partners may want to see a lawyer before you make any changes.

Limited Liability Companies

You should get the consent of all of the other owners before you can transfer your interest to yourself as trustee. (Even if your operating agreement requires the consent of only a majority of the other owners, it's a good idea to have everyone's consent, just to head off any difficulties.) Getting the other owners to agree shouldn't be a problem; they'll just want to know that you, as trustee of your own trust, will have authority to vote on LLC decisions.

To make the transfer, you'll need a document transferring your interest. You can use the Approval of Transfer of Membership form in *Your Limited Liability Company: An Operating Manual*, by Anthony Mancuso (Nolo).

Limited Partnerships

Limited partnerships are a form of investment governed by securities laws. Contact the partnership's general partner to find out what paperwork is necessary to hold your interest in trust.

Copyrights

If you want to hold your interest in a copyright in trust, you should list the copyright in the trust document and then sign and file, with the U.S. Copyright Office, a document transferring all your rights in the copyright to yourself as trustee. Sample transfer forms are in *The Copyright Handbook*, by Stephen Fishman (Nolo).

Patents

If you own a patent and want to hold it in trust, you should prepare a document called an "assignment" and record it with the Patent and Trademark Office in Washington, DC. There is a small fee for recording. Sample assignment forms and instructions are in *Patent It Yourself,* by David Pressman, and *What Every Inventor Needs to Know About Business & Taxes*, by Stephen Fishman (both published by Nolo).

Property That Names the Trust as Beneficiary

You can name your living trust as beneficiary of a life insurance policy, individual retirement account (IRA) or Keogh account. You don't (can't, in the case of retirement accounts) transfer the policy or account itself to the trust. You are the owner. The living trust is the beneficiary, which will receive the proceeds at your death.

Living With Your Living Trust

As a day-to-day, practical matter, it makes little difference that your property is now held in your revocable living trust. You have no special paperwork to prepare, forms to file or other duties to perform as the trustee of your own trust. But you may need to change your trust to reflect changed circumstances in your life. This chapter explains how.

What to Do If...

This section tells you how to proceed if you run into any of these common situations.

Trust Property Earns Income

No separate income tax records or returns are necessary as long as you are the trustee of your own living trust. (IRS Reg. § 1.671-4.) Income from property in the trust must be reported on your personal income tax return.

However, if a trust is ongoing after a grantor dies—for example, a child's subtrust or a bypass trust created after an AB trust grantor dies—you may need to file a trust tax return. See Chapter 21.

You Sell or Give Away Trust Property

You have complete control over the property you hold in the living trust. If you want to sell or give away any of it, simply go ahead, using your authority as trustee. You (or you and your spouse or partner, if you made a trust together) just sign ownership or transfer documents (the deed, bill of sale or other document) in your capacity as trustee of the living trust.

EXAMPLE: Mel holds his house in his living trust. When he sells it, he signs the new deed as "Melvin Owens, trustee of the Melvin Owens Revocable Living Trust dated June 8, 20xx."

If you and your spouse or partner made a trust together, either of you has authority over trust property. That means that either of you can sell or give away any of the trust property—including the property that was co-owned or was the other's separate property before it was transferred to the trust. In practice, however, both of you will probably have to consent to transfer real estate out of the living trust. Especially in community property states, buyers and title insurance companies usually insist on both spouses' signatures on transfer documents.

If for any reason you want to take property out of the trust but keep ownership of it, you can transfer it to yourself. The process is, essentially, the reverse of the process you followed to transfer the property to the trust. (See Chapter 19.)

EXAMPLE: Janice wants to take her house out of her living trust but keep ownership in her own name. She makes the deed out from "Janice Yamaguchi, trustee of the Janice Yamaguchi Revocable Living Trust dated November 6, 20xx" to "Janice Yamaguchi."

If you take property out of the trust, you will also need to make some changes to your trust document:

- Modify the property schedule of your trust document to reflect the change. If you don't, the schedule will still show that the property is owned by the trust, and the discrepancy could be confusing to the people who carry out your wishes after your death.

- If the property doesn't have a title document, create and print out an Assignment of Property form, showing that you've transferred the item back to you as an individual.
- If you named a specific beneficiary to receive the item, delete that trust provision, using a trust amendment.

"Amending Your Trust Document," below, shows how to make these changes using Quicken WillMaker Plus.

EXAMPLE: Wendy and Brian made a basic living trust several years ago. Wendy transferred a valuable antique dresser, which she inherited from her father before she was married, to the living trust. It's listed on Schedule B of the trust document as her separate property. The trust document provides that the dresser will go to her son at her death. But she's changed her mind and wants her daughter to have the dresser right now.

After Wendy gives the dresser to her daughter, she uses Quicken WillMaker Plus to prepare and print out three documents. First, she prepares a new Schedule B, deleting the dresser from the list of property, and replaces the old Schedule B attached to the trust document. Second, she prepares an Assignment of Property, showing that she's transferred the dresser from herself as trustee to herself. Third, she prepares

an amended trust document, omitting the paragraph that left the dresser to her son. After she signs the amendment in front of a notary public, her trust document reflects her wishes.

You Add Valuable Property to the Trust

If you add property to your living trust, you may need to amend the trust document (as well as the property schedule) to name a beneficiary to inherit the property. (See "Amending Your Trust Document," below.)

You Change Your Mind About a Beneficiary or Trustee

You may simply change your mind about whom you want to inherit trust property, or whom you want to serve as your successor trustee. To change these or other terms of your living trust, you'll need to make a trust amendment.

You Marry or Have a Child

If you get married or have a child, you'll almost certainly want to amend your trust document to provide for your new spouse or offspring. (Your spouse or child may be entitled, under state law, to some of your property; see Chapter 13.)

You Get Divorced

If you divorce, you should revoke your living trust. In several states, provisions of a living trust that affect a spouse are automatically revoked by divorce, but you shouldn't rely on these laws. Better to have it in writing.

You Move to Another State

Your living trust is still valid if you prepare it in one state and then move to another. You may, however, need to take some actions after your move:

- Your new state may require you to register your living trust document with the local court. (See Chapter 18.)
- You may want to amend the trust document if the new state's laws differ on matters such as marital property rights or property management for young trust beneficiaries.

Your New State Has Different Marital Property Laws

If you and your spouse move to another state, in most cases, the move does not change who owns what. But everything you and your spouse acquire in the new state is subject to that state's laws regarding ownership.

EXAMPLE: Leah and Ben move from Texas, a community property state, to Illinois, a non-community property state. In Texas, money either spouse earned from working belongs to both spouses equally, which means that the car Leah bought with her salary is jointly owned by Leah and Ben. That doesn't change when they move to Illinois. After they move, however, each spouse's salary is his or her separate property.

If, however, you move from a non-community property state to a community property state, the move may change which spouse owns what. California, Idaho, Washington and Wisconsin have rules that treat certain property you bring with you as if you had acquired it in the community property state. Here's the general rule: If the property would have been community property had you acquired it in the new state, it is treated like community property at death or divorce. (The legal term for such property is "quasi-community property" or, in Wisconsin, "deferred marital property.") This means that each spouse owns half of this property and can leave only that share at death. One important exception: These rules usually don't apply to real estate.

EXAMPLE: Carlo and Sylvia, a married couple, move from New York to California. Their car, bought in New York with Carlo's earnings and registered in his name, is quasi-community property— which means that once Carlo and Sylvia settle in California, the car would be considered to belong to both of them if they divorce or one of them dies.

Obviously, this can be a very complicated subject. The good news is that you need be concerned about this issue only if all of these three things are true:

- You move to California, Idaho, Washington or Wisconsin from a non-community property state.
- You are concerned that because of the move, trust property that was formerly

owned by only one spouse might now be considered to be owned by both.

- In the trust document, you did not leave at least a half-interest in that property to your spouse.

In this situation, you have two options:

- Make a trust amendment, changing ownership of the property from separate property to community property. If you made a basic trust, have both spouses name beneficiaries for the property. If you made an AB trust, it will probably be going to the surviving spouse anyway.
- See a lawyer who's knowledgeable about your new state's law. If the property you're concerned about is valuable, the cost of an expert will be well worth the peace of mind you get.

The New State Has Different Rules About Property Management for Young Beneficiaries

Your state's law determines the choices you have when it comes to arranging for someone to manage property left to young beneficiaries. In all states, you can use Quicken WillMaker Plus to create a child's subtrust for any beneficiary who might inherit trust property before he or she is 35. But state law determines whether or not you have another option: appointing someone to be the custodian of trust property inherited by a young beneficiary. (See Chapter 15, 16 or 17, Part 6.)

Only South Carolina and Vermont do not allow custodianships. If you move from either of those states, you may want to create a trust amendment, changing your trust document to let you create a custodianship.

If you move after you have already created a custodianship, the custodianship will still be valid. You can, however, create a trust amendment that deletes the old custodianship clause and adds a new one that conforms to your new state's law.

Your New State Gives Spouses or Children Different Rights

Different states entitle surviving spouses (and in some unusual circumstances, children) to claim different shares of a deceased spouse's estate. (See Chapter 13.) If you haven't left much property to your spouse or child and are concerned that either might challenge your estate plan after your death, you'll want to know what your new state's laws say. You may want to amend your trust document or other parts of your estate plan.

> **SEE AN EXPERT**
> **See an estate planning lawyer.** If you haven't left at least half of your property to your spouse, we recommend that you see an estate planning lawyer.

Your Spouse or Partner Dies

If you and your spouse or partner made a shared living trust, when one dies the other will probably inherit some, if not all, of the deceased grantor's trust property outright.

Basic Living Trust

The survivor may need to amend his or her trust to name beneficiaries for property inherited from the deceased spouse. (See Chapter 21.) The survivor may also want to amend the trust document if he or she left property to the now-deceased spouse or partner.

AB Trust

With an AB trust, the deceased spouse's property goes into Trust A, the bypass trust. The surviving spouse has certain rights over bypass trust property but doesn't own it outright. The final beneficiaries of that property are already set (they were named by the deceased spouse) and can't be changed.

There is, however, work for the survivor, who must see to it that the trust assets are split into Trust A (the bypass trust, the irrevocable trust that contains the deceased spouse's trust property) and Trust B (the revocable trust that contains the survivor's trust property). If the trust contains the disclaimer clause, then the surviving spouse must decide whether to split the property into Trust A and Trust B and, if so, how much property should go into Trust A. That process is explained in Chapter 21.

A Major Beneficiary Dies

You may need to amend your trust document if a major beneficiary dies.

Basic Trust

If you made a basic trust and left much or all of your trust property to one person, and that person dies before you do, you may well want to amend your trust document. If you named an alternate beneficiary for the deceased beneficiary, there's not an urgent need to

amend the trust document; the alternate will inherit the property. But amending it makes sense, so that you can name another alternate beneficiary.

AB Trust

If you made an AB trust with your spouse, then your spouse is your main beneficiary. If, however, you left a few items of trust property to others, and one of those beneficiaries dies before you do, you may want to amend your trust document to name a new beneficiary for the property. Also, if the final beneficiary (or one of them) dies, you and your spouse may want to amend the trust to name a new beneficiary.

Your Estate Tax Situation Changes

If you've made an AB trust, keep an eye on the law and on your net worth. Because the estate tax exemption is rising rapidly (see Chapter 13), you may find that you don't need a tax-saving AB trust after all. If both spouses are still alive, you can revoke your AB trust and create a basic probate-avoidance trust instead. That will save you paperwork, money (because you would need to hire an expert to help you with the AB trust when the first spouse died) and hassle (because an AB trust ties up the property of the first spouse to die).

If, however, you made a disclaimer trust, you don't need to revoke it even if you are no longer concerned about estate taxes. That's because when the first spouse dies, the surviving spouse has the power to decide not to split the AB trust to create the irrevocable bypass trust.

You might find, though, that your wealth increases much more rapidly than you expected—perhaps because of a surprise inheritance or business success. If your newfound wealth might mean an estate tax bill after your death, you might want to look into creating an AB trust. (Chapter 14 explains when an AB trust makes sense.)

> ⓘ **CAUTION**
> **Keep an eye on the estate tax laws.** The uncertainty in the estate tax legislation passed in 2001 has made it almost inevitable that Congress will soon take up the matter of estate taxes. So keep up to date as these changes work their way through the political process. If the estate tax really is permanently eliminated, or the exemption amount is fixed so high that you don't need to worry about estate tax (more likely), you will almost certainly not want an AB trust.

Amending Your Trust Document

Quicken WillMaker Plus makes it easy for you to amend your trust document even after you've signed it. By using the program to create and print out an amended trust document or a new property schedule, you can change, for example:

- beneficiaries
- successor trustees
- custodians (people who will manage trust property inherited by young beneficiaries), or
- property in the trust.

If you create and print out an amended trust, you should sign it in front of a notary public and attach it to the signed original trust document. Then give a copy to anyone who already has a copy of the original trust document.

> ⓘ **CAUTION**
> **Do not change the trust document except with the amendment module of Quicken WillMaker Plus.** Any other changes could create serious problems for your beneficiaries or even invalidate your trust.

Who Can Amend Your Trust Document

Who can amend the terms of a living trust document depends on whether you created an individual living trust or a shared one.

Someone Acting on Your Behalf

The trust document you create with Quicken WillMaker Plus cannot be amended or revoked by someone acting on your behalf, unless you give that authority in another document.

That means someone who is appointed by a court to handle your affairs (a conservator or guardian) or someone you have given authority to act for you in a document called a power of attorney (your "attorney-in-fact") cannot amend the trust document absent specific authorization. If you want to give your attorney-in-fact authority to amend your living trust, you must specifically grant this authority in your power of attorney. (See Chapter 22.)

Individual Living Trust

If you created an individual living trust, you can amend the trust document at any time.

Shared Basic Living Trust

If you made a trust with your spouse or partner, then while both of you are alive you both must agree to amend any provision of the trust document—for example, to change a beneficiary, a successor trustee or the property management set up for a young beneficiary.

After one grantor dies, the shared living trust is split into two trusts, one of which can no longer be amended. (This is explained in Chapter 21.)

AB Trust

While both spouses are alive, both must agree to amend any provision of the living trust document—for example, to change a final beneficiary, a successor trustee or the property management set up for a young beneficiary.

After one spouse dies, the AB trust is split into two trusts, and the couple's jointly owned property is divided between them. (This is explained in Chapter 21.) Trust A, the bypass trust, cannot be amended.

If the couple made a disclaimer trust, however, the surviving spouse may decide not to create the bypass trust at the first spouse's death. In that case, the trust is treated just like a basic shared trust. (See Chapter 14.)

Adding or Deleting Property

If you acquire valuable items of property after you create your living trust, you should promptly add them to the trust. You might also want to remove some items.

Basic Trust, or AB Trust If Both Spouses Are Still Alive

For a basic trust, or an AB trust when both spouses are still alive, there are four steps to take:

Step 1: Use the amendment module of Quicken WillMaker Plus to create a revised Property Schedule A, B or C of your trust document, adding new items or deleting old ones. (See the Users' Manual.) If you made an individual trust, you have only one schedule, Schedule A. If you made a shared trust, Schedule A lists your co-owned property, and Schedules B and C list separate property.

Step 2: Print out the new schedule and replace the old one on your signed original trust document. That's all you have to do; schedules don't have to be signed.

Step 3: If you added property, transfer ownership of the property to yourself as trustee. You'll need to change the property's title document or, if the item doesn't have a title document, use the Assignment of Property form, showing that you are holding the item in trust. (See Chapter 19.) If you removed an item, transfer it out of the trust, either by changing its title document (a deed, for example) or using an Assignment of Property that transfers it from you as trustee to you as individual.

Step 4: If you need to name a beneficiary for property you've added, create an amended trust document, as discussed below. You won't need to amend your trust document if you left all your trust property to one person, if you want the new property to go to the residuary beneficiary of a basic trust or if you made an AB trust and want the property to go to your spouse.

EXAMPLE: Rose and her husband Michael created a trust several years ago. Now they're buying a house and take title as "Rose Morris and Michael Morris, Trustees of the Rose Morris and Michael Morris Revocable Living Trust dated January 13, 1997." They then prepare a revised Schedule A (which lists co-owned property) of their trust document, print it out and replace the old Schedule A.

Because their trust document leaves all their property to each other, they do not need to amend their trust document.

AB Trust If One Spouse Has Died

After one spouse has died, and the trust has been split into Trusts A and B, you cannot use Quicken WillMaker Plus to add or remove property from either Trust A (the bypass trust) or Trust B (the survivor's trust). Trust A cannot be changed in any way after one spouse dies.

Trust B cannot be changed with this program because the original property schedules, prepared when you created the trust, are no longer accurate or meaningful. They show only what was in the combined AB trust, and which spouse owned it originally.

When one spouse dies, you should have new property schedules prepared, showing

which property is now held in the new Trust A and new Trust B. If you want to add or delete any property from your Trust B, you'll need to modify this new Trust B property schedule. You may also want to amend the provision in the trust document that stated whom you were leaving the property to.

If you want to add or delete property, see the lawyer who helped you divide the trust property into Trust A and Trust B and draw up your new property schedules.

Changing Provisions of the Trust Document

If you want to change your signed trust document, you will create what's called an "amended and restated" version of it. When you return to the program after signing your original trust document, you'll go through the trust interview again, make your changes and then print out the entire trust document. The new trust document will be labeled as an amended and restated version of the original. It will also state that whatever property you already hold in the trust doesn't have to be transferred again; it stays in trust. (If you created an entirely new trust, signed on a different date, you would have to transfer all trust property from the old trust to the new one.)

Shared Trust If One Grantor Has Died

After one grantor has died, you cannot use the program to make changes to the trust document. If you're the surviving grantor and want to make changes to your ongoing survivor's trust, you have two options: Have a lawyer draw up an amendment, or make a new, individual trust.

Amendments. There are limits to what you can change after one grantor dies. Of course, you cannot change any of the deceased grantor's directions about who inherits his or her trust property. But if you see a lawyer for customized amendments, you can:

- name a different successor trustee
- name or change beneficiaries to inherit your trust property
- name a different person to make incapacity decisions, or
- change property management for young beneficiaries.

Revocation. Some survivors prefer to revoke the original trust and make a new one, in their name only, so that at their death it's clear who owned everything. To do this, however, you must be sure to transfer property from the old trust to the new—a bit of paperwork that you may find worth the effort.

Changing Trust Language

Probably the most common kind of change is to modify one or more provisions. For example, if you want to change successor trustees, you'll need to change the original provision that named your old choice so that it names your new choice. You can make this change with the amendment part of Quicken WillMaker Plus. The program will then prepare an amended trust document for you to print out and sign. An example is shown below.

Sample Amended and Restated Trust Document (first page)

The Richard Jenkins and Patricia Jenkins Revocable Living Trust

Amended and Restated Declaration of Trust

Richard Jenkins and Patricia Jenkins are the grantors of the Richard Jenkins and Patricia Jenkins Revocable Living Trust created under the Declaration of Trust dated May 20, 20xx (the "Declaration of Trust"). Richard Jenkins and Patricia Jenkins are also the trustees appointed and acting under the terms of that Declaration of Trust. Under the power reserved to the grantors by Part 5 of the Declaration of Trust, the grantors hereby amend and restate the Declaration of Trust as set out in this document.

The trustees hereby consent to the terms of this amended and restated Declaration of Trust. The parties agree that, upon execution of this instrument, the Declaration of Trust shall be replaced in whole, and the terms of this amended and restated Declaration of Trust shall supersede the terms of that Declaration of Trust for all purposes.

The grantors and the trustees confirm that all assets currently titled in the name of the trustees of the Richard Jenkins and Patricia Jenkins Revocable Living Trust shall continue to be held by the trustees as assets of the amended and restated trust.

Part 1. Trust Name

This revocable living trust shall be known as the Richard Jenkins and Patricia Jenkins Revocable Living Trust.

Part 2. Declaration of Trust

Richard Jenkins and Patricia Jenkins, called the grantors, declare that they have transferred and delivered to the trustees all their interest in the property described in Schedules A, B and C attached to this Declaration of Trust. All of that property is called the "trust property." The trustees hereby acknowledge receipt of the trust property and agree to hold the trust property in trust, according to this Declaration of Trust.

Either grantor may add property to the trust.

Revoking Your Living Trust

If you're like most people, amending your living trust will take care of your changing circumstances over the years, and you will never need to revoke your trust. But there are, of course, a few exceptions to that rule.

You can revoke your living trust at any time. Revoking a living trust (unlike revoking a will) requires some work: You must transfer ownership of all the trust property out of your name as trustee.

Who Can Revoke Your Trust

If you created an individual living trust, you can revoke it at any time.

Either grantor can revoke a shared basic trust or AB trust, wiping out all terms of the trust. The trust property is returned to each person according to how they owned it before transferring it to the trust.

> EXAMPLE: Yvonne and Andre make a basic probate-avoidance living trust together. Each transfers separately owned property to the trust. They also transfer ownership of their house, which they own together, to the trust. Later Yvonne revokes the living trust. She transfers the property she owned back to herself, and the property her husband owned back to him. The co-owned property goes back to both of them.

The trust document cannot be revoked by someone acting on your behalf unless you have specifically granted that authority. If you made a shared trust, and you are the survivor, you can revoke only your revocable trust. So if you made a basic trust, you can revoke Trust #2; if you made an AB trust, you can revoke Trust B.

How to Revoke Your Trust

To revoke your living trust, follow these steps:

Step 1: Transfer ownership of trust property from yourself as trustee back to yourself. Basically, you must reverse the process you followed when you transferred ownership of the property to yourself as trustee. (See Chapter 19.) You can make the transfer because of your authority as trustee of the trust.

Step 2: Use Quicken WillMaker Plus to prepare a document called a Revocation of Trust. After you've printed your trust document, when you start the program again, it will ask you whether or not you've signed the trust document, creating a legally valid trust. If you have, the program will take you to a screen that lets you choose "Revoke Trust."

Step 3: Print out the Revocation of Trust and sign it in front of a notary public.

Step 4: If you registered your trust with the local court (a procedure authorized in certain states; see Chapter 18), notify the court that the trust has been terminated.

A sample is shown below.

Revocation of the Richard Jenkins and Patricia Jenkins AB Living Trust

We, Richard Jenkins and Patricia Jenkins, hereby revoke the Richard Jenkins and Patricia Jenkins AB Living Trust, created by Declaration of Trust signed May 20, 20xx, according to the power reserved to the grantors by Part 6 of the Declaration of Trust.

All property held in the trust shall be returned to the grantors.

CERTIFICATION OF ACKNOWLEDGMENT OF NOTARY PUBLIC

State of _____

County of _____

On _____, before me, _____,
a notary public for said state, personally appeared Richard Jenkins and Patricia Jenkins, personally known to me (or proved to me on the basis of satisfactory evidence) to be the persons whose names are subscribed to the within instrument, and acknowledged to me that they executed the same in their authorized capacities and that by their signatures on the instrument the persons, or the entity upon behalf of which the persons acted, executed the instrument.

Witness my hand and official seal.

_____

NOTARY PUBLIC

My commission expires _____.

After a Grantor Dies

The benefit of a revocable living trust doesn't come until after the grantor's death, when trust property is transferred to beneficiaries without probate or shifted into an irrevocable, tax-saving trust. The all-important responsibility of handling that transfer falls to the surviving grantor if you made a trust together, or your successor trustee if you made an individual living trust.

This chapter outlines the responsibilities of the person who is in charge of a trust after a grantor dies, so you can understand what the successor trustee will have to do.

When your successor takes over, possibly many years from now, he or she will need to check current state law.

RESOURCE

More information for trustees. Your successor trustee can find extensive information, when it's necessary, in these two Nolo books: *How to Probate an Estate in California*, by Julia Nissley, and *The Executor's Guide: Settling a Loved One's Estate or Trust*, by Mary Randolph.

What Happens When a Grantor Dies: An Overview

The process works differently depending on whether you made an individual living trust or a shared trust with your spouse or partner.

Individual Trust

When the grantor, who is also the trustee, dies, the successor trustee named in the Declaration of Trust takes over as trustee. The new trustee is responsible for distributing the trust property to the beneficiaries named in the trust document.

The Successor Trustee's Duties: Individual Trust

- Notify beneficiaries that the trust exists, if necessary.
- Get an appraisal of valuable trust property.
- Prepare an Affidavit of Assumption of Duties.
- Distribute trust property to beneficiaries named in the trust document.
- Manage trust property left in a child's subtrust, if any.
- File the deceased grantor's final income tax returns, if necessary. (This is the responsibility of the executor of the estate, if there was a will.)

The trust continues to exist only as long as it takes the successor trustee to distribute trust property to the beneficiaries.

The successor trustee is also in charge of managing any property left to a young beneficiary in a child's subtrust. A subtrust will exist until the beneficiary is old enough to get the property outright (at the age specified in the trust document), so if there's a subtrust the successor trustee may have years of work ahead. (See "Administering a Child's Subtrust," below.)

If trust property inherited by a young beneficiary is to be managed by a custodian under the Uniform Transfers to Minors Act, the person named as custodian will be responsible for that property. That person may or may not be the successor trustee. (See "Administering a Custodianship" below.)

Basic Shared Trust

When a couple creates a basic probate-avoidance living trust with Quicken WillMaker Plus, both grantors are trustees. When the first one dies, the surviving grantor becomes sole trustee.

The trust itself is automatically split into two trusts:

- Trust #1 contains the deceased grantor's share of trust property, excluding any trust property left to the survivor. Its terms cannot be changed, and it cannot be revoked.
- Trust #2 contains the survivor's share, including any of the deceased grantor's share of the trust property that is left to the survivor. (The Declaration of Trust provides that trust property left to the survivor stays in the living trust. If it did not contain such a provision, the property would have to be transferred from the living trust to the survivor and then, if the survivor wanted it to avoid probate, back to the living trust again.) The survivor is still free to revoke Trust #2 or amend its terms.

The survivor is sole trustee of Trust #1, Trust #2 and any children's subtrusts set up for the deceased grantor's young beneficiaries. (See "Administering a Child's Subtrust," below.)

It's the survivor's job to distribute the property in Trust #1 to the beneficiaries the deceased grantor named in the trust document. If, as is common, much of the trust property is left to the survivor, that person will have little to do—the trust property he or she inherits is already in the living trust and does not need to be transferred. (More about this later in the chapter.)

Trust #2 goes on as before, as a revocable living trust. It contains only the survivor's property, and the survivor is free to change any terms of the trust.

For example, the survivor may want to amend the trust document to name beneficiaries for the property inherited from the deceased grantor.

> **EXAMPLE:** Edith and Jacques create a basic shared living trust. They transfer their house, which they own together, into the trust and name each other as beneficiaries. Edith names her son as alternate beneficiary.
>
> When Jacques dies, Edith inherits his half-interest in the house. Because of the way the trust document is worded, she doesn't have to change the trust document to name a beneficiary for this half-interest in the house. Both halves will go to her son at her death. She may, however, want to amend the trust to make her son the primary beneficiary and name someone else to be alternate beneficiary.

When the second grantor dies, the successor trustee named in the trust document takes over as trustee. The process of winding up the living trust is the same as that for an individual trust.

The Surviving Grantor's Duties

- Get an appraisal of valuable trust property.
- Prepare an Affidavit of Assumption of Duties.
- Distribute the deceased grantor's share of the trust property to beneficiaries named in the trust document.
- Manage property left in a child's subtrust, if any.
- File tax returns, if necessary. (This is the executor's responsibility, if a will named someone else as executor of the estate.)

EXAMPLE: Harry and Maude, a married couple, set up a basic revocable living trust. They appoint Maude's cousin Emily as successor trustee, to take over as trustee after they have both died. They transfer ownership of much of their co-owned property to the trust. Maude also puts some family heirlooms, which are her separate property, in the living trust.

In the trust document, Maude leaves her heirlooms to her younger sister. She leaves her half of the trust property she and Harry own together to Harry.

When Maude dies, Harry becomes the sole trustee. Following the terms of the trust document, he distributes Maude's heirlooms (Trust #1) to her sister, without probate. Maude's half of the property they had owned together stays in the trust (Trust #2); no transfer is necessary.

Harry later decides to amend the trust document to name his nephew, Burt, as successor trustee instead of Maude's cousin Emily. When Harry dies, Burt becomes trustee and distributes the trust property following Harry's instructions in the trust document. When he has given all the property to Harry's beneficiaries, the trust ends.

AB Trust

When a married couple creates an AB living trust with Quicken WillMaker Plus, both spouses are trustees. When the first spouse dies, the surviving spouse becomes sole trustee.

What happens next depends on how the trust was structured.

If the trust document contains the disclaimer trust option, then the surviving spouse must decide whether or not to create Trust A, the bypass trust. If the survivor concludes that it's worthwhile to create the trust, she must disclaim (turn down) trust assets she would otherwise inherit. The disclaimed property goes into the bypass trust.

If there is no disclaimer clause in the trust document, then the survivor must see that the AB trust is split into two trusts. (See "Special Considerations for AB Trusts," below.)

- Trust A, the Bypass Trust, contains half (by value) of the couple's shared trust property, and the deceased spouse's separately owned property. This trust's terms cannot be changed, and it cannot be revoked.
- Trust B is the surviving spouse's trust. It includes the rest of the couple's shared trust property, any trust property the deceased spouse left directly to the surviving spouse and the survivor's separately owned property, if any. The

surviving spouse is free to revoke it or amend its terms.

The survivor is sole trustee of Trust A, Trust B and any children's subtrusts set up for the deceased spouse's young beneficiaries.

When the second spouse dies, the successor trustee named in the trust document takes over as trustee of Trusts A and B. The process of winding up the trusts is the same as that for an individual trust (discussed above).

EXAMPLE: Gary and his wife Beth set up an AB living trust, naming their daughter Emily as successor trustee and final beneficiary. They transfer ownership of much of their co-owned property—their house, bank accounts and stocks—to the trust. Beth also puts some family heirlooms, which are her separate property, in the trust.

In the trust document, Beth leaves her heirlooms to her younger sister. She leaves her half of the trust property she and Gary own together to Gary, in trust.

When Beth dies, Gary becomes the sole trustee. Following the terms of the trust document, he distributes Beth's heirlooms to her sister, without probate. He also sees to it that half of the trust property they had owned together goes into Trust A, and the other half into Trust B.

When Gary dies, Emily becomes trustee and distributes the property in Trusts A and B to herself. When it has all been transferred to her, Trusts A and B cease to exist.

Who Serves as Trustee

With a basic shared trust or an AB trust, when one grantor dies, the survivor serves as trustee. With an individual trust, or when the surviving grantor dies, the successor trustee is in charge.

The Surviving Spouse's Duties: AB Trust

- Notify beneficiaries that the trust exists, if necessary.
- Get an appraisal of valuable trust property.
- Prepare an Affidavit of Assumption of Duties.
- Distribute any specific gifts of trust property made by the deceased spouse to beneficiaries named in the trust document.
- Manage property left in a child's subtrust, if any.
- Get expert help to divide trust property into Trust A (bypass trust) and Trust B (survivor's trust) or, if it's a disclaimer trust, to decide whether or not to create Trust A and how much property to put into it.
- Get federal tax ID number for Trust A and file annual income tax returns.
- File tax returns, if necessary. (This is the executor's responsibility, if a will named someone else as executor of the estate.)

More Than One Successor Trustee

If more than one person is named in the trust document as successor trustee, they all serve together. The trust document may require them all to agree before taking any action with regard to the living trust property, or it may allow them to act independently.

If one of the trustees cannot serve, the others remain as trustees. The person named as alternate successor trustee does not take over unless all the people named as successor trustees cannot serve.

If a Trustee Resigns

A trustee can resign at any time by preparing and signing a letter of resignation. The ex-trustee should deliver the notice to the person who is next in line to serve as trustee (see table below).

If no one named in the trust document can serve, the last acting trustee can appoint someone else to take over. The appointment must be in writing, signed and notarized.

Removing a Trustee

Very rarely, a beneficiary becomes seriously unhappy with the way a trustee handles trust property. For example, the beneficiary of a child's subtrust might complain that the trustee isn't spending enough of the trust property on the beneficiary's education. If the dispute can't be worked out, the beneficiary can file a lawsuit to try to force the removal of the trustee.

Getting an Appraisal

Whoever serves as trustee when a grantor dies should promptly get written appraisals of the market value of all significant trust assets. It's important for at least two reasons:

- Whoever inherits property gets a new tax basis in that property: the market value at the date of death. The new owner needs to know what that market value is to correctly figure tax liability later, when the property is eventually sold.
- If the executor or trustee needs to file a federal estate tax return (see Chapter 17), there is a choice of valuing the assets either as of the date of death or six months later. Getting a reliable estimate soon after the death means there will be something to compare it to later.

Who Serves as Trustee			
	Individual Trust	**Basic Shared Trust**	**AB Trust**
When first grantor dies	Successor trustee(s)	Surviving grantor	Surviving spouse
When second grantor dies	N/A	Successor trustee(s)	Successor trustee(s)
If successor trustee can't serve	Alternate successor trustee(s)	Alternate successor trustee(s)	Alternate successor trustee(s)

Preparing an Affidavit of Assumption of Duties

The successor trustee may be asked to show proof that he or she actually has authority to act on behalf of the trust. This is especially likely for transactions involving real estate.

It may be enough for the trustee to show both the trust document and the grantor's death certificate. Another way is to prepare a sworn statement (affidavit) setting out the facts that give the trustee authority, and to record (file in the public records) this document in the county land records office.

In most states, there isn't any set form for this kind of statement, but it should include:

- the name of the trust
- the date the trust was signed, and
- the name of the successor trustee.

The trustee should sign the statement in front of a notary public and attach a certified copy of the death certificate. Certified copies of the death certificate are available from the county or state vital records office; in many places, you can order them online.

Notifying Beneficiaries

Trustees must always keep trust beneficiaries informed about administration of the trust. This rule is intended to make sure that the beneficiaries have enough information to enforce their legal rights—for example, to make sure that trust assets aren't being mismanaged.

With a simple probate-avoidance trust, there is usually not much need for communication with beneficiaries. (The successor trustee may

be, in fact, the only beneficiary.) The trust exists only long enough for the trustee to gather and distribute the assets.

With an AB trust, there is a greater need to keep final beneficiaries informed about trust administration. What these beneficiaries will inherit from the trust is directly affected by the trustee's actions.

General Rules

A successor trustee who thinks beneficiaries of the trust don't know about it should promptly notify them when the grantor dies. A simple letter, telling the beneficiary that the trust has become irrevocable because of the grantor's death, and that the successor trustee is now in charge of trust assets and will distribute them as soon as is practical, will do in most states.

Special State Requirements

Some states have very specific rules about how and when the successor trustee must notify beneficiaries about the existence of the trust. The notice must include certain information and be formatted in a certain way. By the time your trust becomes irrevocable, it's likely that more states will have adopted this kind of notice requirement. A successor trustee should always check current state law and may want to consult a lawyer.

RESOURCE

Help for California trustees. *How to Probate an Estate in California*, by Julia Nissley (Nolo), contains a form successor trustees can use to give the required notice.

Transferring Property to Beneficiaries

After a grantor dies, the trustee must transfer property to beneficiaries in these situations:

- **Individual trust.** All trust property must be transferred.
- **Basic shared trust, when one grantor dies.** The survivor must transfer the deceased grantor's trust property.
- **Basic shared trust, when both grantors have died.** The successor trustee must transfer the trust property of the second grantor to die.
- **AB trust, when one spouse dies.** The surviving spouse must transfer any property specifically left to beneficiaries and not left in Trust A, the irrevocable trust.
- **AB trust, when both spouses have died.** The successor trustee must transfer the property in Trusts A and B to the final beneficiaries.

The procedure for transferring trust property to the beneficiaries who inherit it depends on the kind of property the trustee is dealing with. Generally, a copy of the grantor's death certificate (both grantors', if the trust property was originally co-owned) and a copy of the trust document are necessary. In some cases, the trustee will need to prepare some other paperwork.

Specific requirements for transferring property vary slightly from place to place, and the trustee may have to make inquiries to banks, stock brokerages and other institutions about current procedures, but here are the general rules. A trustee who runs into difficulties has the authority to get help—from a lawyer, accountant or other expert—and pay for it from trust assets.

RESOURCE

How to Probate an Estate in California, by Julia Nissley (Nolo), contains instructions on transferring the trust assets of a deceased California resident.

Property Without Title Documents

For trust property that doesn't have a title document—furniture, for example—the task of the trustee is quite simple. The trustee must promptly distribute the property to the beneficiaries named in the trust. If the trustee thinks it's a good idea, have the recipient sign a receipt.

Property With Title Documents

If an item of trust property has a title document that shows ownership in the name of the original trustee, the trustee must prepare and sign a new title document transferring ownership to the beneficiary. Usually, the trustee will need a copy of the trust document and of the trust grantor's death certificate if the property is in someone else's possession.

Basically, the process of transferring trust property to beneficiaries is the reverse of transferring it into the trust in the first place. (That process is explained in Chapter 19.) For example, you need a deed to transfer real estate to your trust; to transfer it back out again, your successor trustee will also need a deed. If the trustee is dealing with a third party—for example, a brokerage company—it can help with the transaction or at least tell the successor trustee what documents are required.

Preparing and Filing Tax Returns

Final personal tax returns and, if necessary, state or federal estate tax returns must be filed. Doing so is the responsibility of the executor named in the decedent's will. Usually, the same person is both executor and trustee.

A federal estate tax return must be filed if the decedent's gross estate was large enough. (See Chapter 13.) It's a complicated document, due nine months after the decedent's death, and will require expert help. Again, the trustee is entitled to pay for professional help out of the trust assets.

Administering a Child's Subtrust

If a trustee must manage a child's subtrust, the job will last until the beneficiary is old enough to receive the property outright.

EXAMPLE: Carl sets up a living trust and names his two young children as beneficiaries. He specifies that if the children are younger than 30 when he dies, the property they are to receive from the trust should be kept in a separate children's subtrust for each child.

When Carl dies, one child is 30; the other is 25. The 30-year-old will receive her trust property with no strings attached. But a child's subtrust will be created for the 25-year-old. Carl's

successor trustee is responsible for managing the property and turning it over to the child when he turns 30.

The trustee must:

- invest subtrust property prudently
- act honestly and in the best interests of the beneficiary
- keep beneficiaries informed about the administration of the trust
- use the income from subtrust property, or the subtrust property itself, to pay for the beneficiary's health, support, maintenance or education
- file an annual trust income tax return, and
- give the remaining subtrust property to the beneficiary when he or she reaches the age designated in the trust document.

The trustee can use subtrust assets to get professional assistance if necessary. For example, the trustee might want to pay a tax preparer for help with the subtrust's income tax return or consult a financial planner for investment advice.

The trust document also provides that the trustee of a subtrust is entitled to reasonable compensation for his or her work as trustee. The trustee decides what is a reasonable amount; the compensation is paid from the subtrust assets.

Administering a Custodianship

Someone who is appointed, in the trust document, to be the custodian of trust property inherited by a young beneficiary has about the same management responsibilities as the trustee of a child's subtrust. The specifics are set out in the Uniform Transfers to Minors Act, as adopted by the particular state's legislature.

A custodian, however, does not have to file a separate income tax return. Any income from the property is reported on the beneficiary's own return.

Special Considerations for AB Trusts

Dividing the assets of the trust when one spouse dies is the most complicated part of using an AB trust. The uncertainty surrounding the estate tax makes these decisions even thornier. The surviving spouse will need to get expert help from an experienced estate planning attorney to reap the greatest tax benefits.

Deciding Whether or Not to Split the Trust

If you chose to make a disclaimer AB trust, then the threshold question for the surviving spouse is whether or not to split the AB trust and create the tax-saving bypass trust. The trust document, remember, says that if the spouse decides that dividing the trust is too much trouble and not worth the tax savings, then everything can just stay in the survivor's trust.

EXAMPLE: Judith and Colin make an AB trust and include the disclaimer provision. They both live many years longer. When Colin dies, tax laws have

changed, and the estate tax exemption is so high that Judith no longer has to worry about a big estate tax bill at her death. So to save herself the hassle and expense of creating and managing the irrevocable bypass trust, she exercises her authority under the trust document and does not split the AB trust. As a result, all the trust property stays in Judith's revocable survivor's trust.

The surviving spouse does, however, have the option of splitting the AB trust and treating it just like a regular AB trust.

EXAMPLE: Gwen and Michael also make a disclaimer trust. But when Gwen dies, Michael concludes that unless he acts, his estate could be liable for a big estate tax bill at his death. So he decides to go ahead and split the AB trust, creating the irrevocable bypass trust and the revocable survivor's trust. After consulting an estate planning lawyer, he decides to disclaim about a third of the trust property, which under the terms of the trust document means that property goes into the bypass trust. The rest goes into his survivor's trust.

Deciding How to Split the Assets

The goal is to divide the couple's jointly owned trust assets in a way that Trust A and Trust B each contain half of the total value of those assets. The assets can be divided in any way, as long as each trust (Trust A, the bypass trust, and Trust B, the survivor's) holds assets of equal value. Every item does not have to be divided 50-50. For example, if the trust contained stock worth $200,000, all of it could be put into Trust A, if other co-owned trust property of equal value were allocated to Trust B.

There are several factors to consider when deciding what property goes in which trust. One is the likelihood that the asset will increase in value. For example, say a surviving spouse puts the couple's $400,000 house in Trust A, because she thinks it could well be worth $600,000 by the time of her death. If that happens, the increase in value won't be subject to estate tax. (That's because, remember, the house was subject to tax at the first spouse's death.) But if real estate values are expected to sink, she might be better off putting stocks in Trust A—or, since nobody knows what's going to happen, to hedge her bets and split ownership of the house and the stocks between Trust A and Trust B.

Another factor that affects a family residence is the chance that the surviving spouse will want to sell it. An individual owner who sells his or her house gets a big (currently $250,000) exemption from capital gains tax; a trust does not. So if the house is held in the bypass trust, more capital gains tax may be owed if the house is sold.

SEE AN EXPERT
As you can see, this gets complicated fast. It's well worth the cost to consult an expert with good real-world experience.

Preparing the Paperwork

The surviving spouse does not need to create a new trust document to create Trusts A and B. But some other documents are required:

- New property schedules, listing what's in Trust A and Trust B.
- For property with title documents (real estate or stocks, for example), new title documents showing that property is now owned by the trustee of "The John Donaldson and Corrine Donaldson AB Revocable Trust, Trust A." The surviving spouse signs these documents, in her capacity as trustee of both trusts.
- For property without title documents, a new Assignment of Property, showing that these items are held in Trust A or Trust B.

The Surviving Spouse's Duties and Rights

Once the AB trust has been divided into Trust A and Trust B, the surviving spouse has new responsibilities as trustee of Trust A. That trust is now very different from the couple's original living trust: It is irrevocable, and it exists as a separate taxable entity.

As trustee of Trust A, the surviving spouse must:

- Get a federal taxpayer ID number from the IRS for the trust.
- Manage the property prudently.
- Keep separate, clear tax records of all transactions involving Trust A property.
- File federal (Form 1041) and state income tax returns for Trust A every year.

If the spouse needs help from an accountant, tax preparer or lawyer, the trust authorizes her to pay for it from trust assets.

If the grantors required it in the trust document, the trustee must give the final beneficiaries a copy of the trust's federal income tax return each year. The trustee also has a responsibility to keep the final beneficiaries reasonably well informed about management of the trust assets.

The trustee owes a duty of complete honesty and responsibility to the final beneficiaries; this is called a "fiduciary duty." As trustee, the survivor must act in the best interest of those beneficiaries—but the trust document also authorizes the survivor to use trust assets for her own benefit, as discussed in Chapter 13.

The trustee is entitled, without court approval, to reasonable compensation from the assets of Trust A for serving as trustee. Usually the surviving spouse doesn't take compensation. But if the spouse becomes incapacitated, and the successor trustee takes over, the successor may want to take some trust money as compensation for the time and effort spent looking after the trust.

Durable Power of Attorney for Finances

Many people fear that they may someday become seriously ill and unable to handle their own financial affairs—that they might be unable to pay bills, make bank deposits, watch over investments or collect insurance and government benefits. As you grow older or face the possibility of an incapacitating illness, it's wise to plan for such a contingency. Fortunately, there's a simple way to do so: preparing a durable power of attorney for finances.

A durable power of attorney for finances is an inexpensive, reliable legal document. In it, you name someone who will make your financial decisions if you become unable to do so yourself.

This person is called your attorney-in-fact, or in some states, your agent. (Your document will include the correct term for your state.)

If you ever do become incapacitated, the durable power of attorney will likely appear as a minor miracle to those who are close to you.

CAUTION

The perils of forging a signature. If someone becomes incapacitated, panicky family members may consider just faking the signatures necessary to carry on routine financial matters. It may seem perfectly acceptable to sign Aunt Amanda's name to a check if the money is used to pay her phone bill.

But this is forgery—and it's a crime. The law is strict in this area to guard against dishonest family members who might loot a relative's assets.

Forging a signature on checks, bills of sale, tax returns or other financial documents may work for a while, but it will probably be discovered eventually. And then the court proceeding everyone was trying to avoid will be necessary—and a judge will not be eager to put a proven liar in charge of a relative's finances.

Important Terms

- **Principal.** The person who creates and signs the power of attorney document, authorizing someone else to act for him or her. If you make a durable power of attorney for finances, you are the principal.
- **Attorney-in-Fact.** The person who is authorized to act for the principal. In many states, the attorney-in-fact is also referred to as an agent of the principal—and some states use the term "agent" exclusively. Your power of attorney will include the correct term for your state.
- **Alternate Attorney-in-Fact.** The person who takes over as attorney-in-fact if your first choice cannot or will not serve. Also called successor attorney-in-fact or successor agent, depending on the state.
- **Durable Power of Attorney.** A power of attorney that will remain in effect even if the principal becomes incapacitated. This is the kind of power of attorney you make with Quicken WillMaker Plus.
- **Incapacitated.** Unable to handle one's own financial matters or health care decisions. Also called disabled or incompetent in some states. Usually, a physician makes the determination.

TIP

Keeping track of information for your attorney-in-fact. The attorney-in-fact you name may need to know a vast number of details about your property and how you deal with it. With Quicken WillMaker Plus you can make an Information for Caregivers and Survivors form to help with this task. With this document, you can provide a comprehensive guide of the details of your life—ranging from information about your property and your financial accounts, to the names and addresses of people you want contacted in the event of your illness—to the person who will care for you in the event of your incapacity. To find out more, click on the Document List button and select Information for Caregivers and Survivors from the list.

What Quicken WillMaker Plus Can Do

Quicken WillMaker Plus allows you to create your own durable power of attorney for finances. Using Quicken WillMaker Plus, you can:

- name your attorney-in-fact
- appoint someone to replace your attorney-in-fact if he or she cannot serve, and
- state exactly how much authority you want your attorney-in-fact to have over your finances.

In addition to your durable power of attorney for finances, Quicken WillMaker Plus prints out a number of related documents. The first of these is an information sheet for you to give to your attorney-in-fact, explaining what his or her responsibilities will be. There are also several forms designed to make your attorney-in-fact's job easier—including forms for delegating tasks to others and resigning from the job if that becomes necessary. Finally, Quicken WillMaker Plus produces a form that you can use to revoke your durable power of attorney if you change your mind. Each document is explained in this chapter.

What This Document Can Do

Almost everyone with property or an income can benefit from a durable power of attorney for finances. It's particularly important, however, to have a durable power of attorney if you fear that health problems may make it impossible for you to handle your financial matters.

The main reason to make a durable power of attorney for finances is to avoid court proceedings if you become incapacitated. If you don't have a durable power of attorney, your relatives or other loved ones will have to ask a judge to name someone to manage your financial affairs. These proceedings are commonly known as conservatorship proceedings. Depending on where you live, the person appointed to manage your finances is called a conservator, guardian of the estate, committee or curator.

If You Are Married

If you are married, don't assume that your spouse will automatically be able to manage all of your finances if you cannot do so.

Your spouse does have some authority over property you own together—for example, your spouse may pay bills from a joint bank account or sell stock in a joint brokerage account. There are significant limits, however, on your spouse's right to sell property that both of you own. For example, in most states, both spouses must agree to the sale of co-owned real estate or cars. Because an incapacitated spouse can't consent to such a sale, the other spouse's hands are tied.

And when it comes to property that belongs only to you, your spouse has no legal authority. You must use a durable power of attorney to give your spouse authority over your property.

EXAMPLE: New York residents Michael and Carrie have been married for 47 years. Their major assets are a home and stock. They own the home in both their names as joint tenants. The stock was bought only in Michael's name, and the couple has never transferred it into shared ownership. Michael becomes incapacitated and requires expensive medical treatment. Without a durable power of attorney, Carrie cannot sell the stock to pay for medical costs.

EXAMPLE: Janice's husband, Hal, is incapacitated and living in a nearby nursing home. Janice wants to raise money by selling Hal's old car, which he can no longer drive, but she can't because she doesn't have a durable power of attorney and the title is in Hal's name.

If You Have a Living Trust

A central purpose of a revocable living trust is to avoid probate. (See Chapter 13.) But the trust can also be useful if you become incapable of taking care of your financial affairs. That's because the person who will distribute trust property after your death— called the successor trustee—can also, in most cases, take over management of the trust property if you become incapacitated.

But few people transfer all their property to a living trust, and the successor trustee has no authority over property that the trust doesn't own. So although a living trust may be helpful, it is not a complete substitute for a durable power of attorney for finances.

The two documents work well together, however, especially if you name the same trusted person to be your attorney-in-fact and the successor trustee of your living trust. That person will have authority to manage property both in and out of your living trust. You can also give your attorney-in-fact the power to transfer items of your property into your living trust. (See "Specific Financial Powers," below.)

EXAMPLE: Consuela, a widow, owns all the stock of a prosperous clothing manufacturing corporation. To avoid probate, she transfers the stock into a living trust, naming her brother, Rodolfo, as successor trustee. If Consuela becomes incapacitated, Rodolfo will become acting trustee and manage the stock in the trust for Consuela's benefit.

Consuela also prepares a durable power of attorney for finances and names Rodolfo as her attorney-in-fact. That gives him authority over assets she does not transfer to the trust—for example, her bank accounts and car. In her durable power of attorney, she also gives Rodolfo the power to transfer property into her living trust, if he feels that's in her best interest.

Avoiding Conservatorship Proceeding

Conservatorship proceedings can be complicated, expensive and even embarrassing. Your loved ones must ask the court to rule that you cannot take care of your own affairs—a public airing of a very private matter. Court proceedings are matters of public record; in some places, a notice may even be published in a local newspaper. If relatives fight over who is to be the conservator, the proceedings will surely become even more disagreeable, sometimes downright nasty. And all of this causes costs to mount up, especially if lawyers must be hired.

If a judge decides to appoint a conservator, there is no guarantee that the person who gets the job will be the person you would have chosen. A judge may ask you to express a preference for conservator—and will strongly consider what you say—but even this will not ensure that your choice will serve. To increase the chances that your wishes will be followed, you can use the durable power of attorney you make with Quicken WillMaker Plus to name your attorney-in-fact as conservator, if a court must ever appoint one. (See "Nominating a Conservator or Guardian," below.)

If you don't name a conservator in your power of attorney document, state law generally provides a priority list for who should be appointed. For example, a number of states make the person's spouse or registered domestic partner the first choice as conservator, followed by an adult child, parent and brother or sister.

In many states, the law allows the court to appoint whoever it determines will act in your best interests.

The appointment of a conservator is usually just the beginning of court proceedings. Often the conservator must:

- post a bond—a kind of insurance policy that pays if the conservator steals or misuses property
- prepare detailed financial reports—or hire a lawyer or accountant to prepare them and periodically file them with the court, and
- get court approval for certain transactions, such as selling real estate or making slightly risky investments.

All of this, of course, costs money—your money.

A conservatorship isn't necessarily permanent, but it may be ended only by the court.

You can probably avoid the troubles of a conservatorship if you take the time to create a durable power of attorney for finances now. When you make a durable power of attorney, you give your attorney-in-fact full legal authority to handle your financial affairs. A conservatorship proceeding would be necessary only if no one were willing to serve as attorney-in-fact, if the attorney-in-fact wanted guidance from a court or a close relative thought the attorney-in-fact wasn't acting in your best interests.

If You Own Joint Tenancy Property

Joint tenancy is a way that two or more people can own property together. The most notable feature of joint tenancy is that when one owner dies, the other owners automatically get the deceased person's share of the property. But if you become incapacitated, the other owners have very limited authority over your share of the joint tenancy property.

For example, if you and someone else own a bank account in joint tenancy, and one of you becomes incapacitated, the other owner is legally entitled to use the funds. The healthy joint tenant can take care of the financial needs of the incapacitated person simply by paying bills from the joint account. But the other account owner has no legal right to endorse checks made out to the incapacitated person. In practice, it might be possible—if not technically legal—to get an incapacitated person's checks into a joint account by stamping them "For Deposit Only," but that's not the easiest way to handle things.

Matters get more complicated with other kinds of joint tenancy property. Real estate is a good example. If one owner becomes incapacitated, the other has no legal authority to sell or refinance the incapacitated owner's share.

In a durable power of attorney, you can give your attorney-in-fact authority over property you own in joint tenancy—including real estate and bank accounts.

What This Document Cannot Do

The expense and intrusion of a conservatorship are rarely desirable. In a few situations, however, special concerns justify the process. For example, you may not know anyone who could handle the job of managing your finances—or you may expect disgruntled family members to cause trouble for the person you choose as your attorney-in-fact. In these situations, it's probably better not to make a durable power of attorney for finances. In some other situations, a document other than a durable power of attorney for finances will better meet your needs.

Provide Court Supervision of Your Finances

If you can't think of someone you trust enough to appoint as your attorney-in-fact, with broad authority over your property and finances—and who is willing to take on the responsibility—don't create a durable power of attorney. A conservatorship, with the safeguard of court supervision, may be worth the extra cost and trouble for this purpose.

Protect Against Family Fights

A durable power of attorney is a powerful legal document. Once you've finalized yours, anyone who wants to challenge your plans for financial management will face an uphill battle in court. But if you expect that family members will challenge your document or make continual trouble for your attorney-in-fact, a conservatorship may be preferable. Your relatives may still fight, but at least the court will be there to keep an eye on your welfare and your property.

SEE AN EXPERT

Help if your family is feisty. If you expect family fights and feel uncomfortable making a durable power of attorney for finances, you may want to talk with a knowledgeable lawyer. He or she can help you weigh your concerns and options, and decide whether a durable power of attorney is the best option for you. (See Chapter 25.)

Authorize Health Care Decisions

A durable power of attorney for finances does not give your attorney-in-fact legal authority to make health care decisions for you. To make sure that your wishes for health care are known and followed, you should use Quicken WillMaker Plus to create a health care directive. (See Chapter 23.)

Authorize Decisions About Marriage, Adoption, Voting or Wills

You cannot authorize your attorney-in-fact to marry, adopt, vote in public elections or make a will on your behalf. These acts are considered too personal to delegate to someone else.

Give Powers Delegated to Others

If you've already given someone legal authority to manage some or all of your property, you cannot delegate that authority to your attorney-in-fact.

For example, if you become incapacitated, your attorney-in-fact will not be able to:

- control property in a living trust you created giving the successor trustee power over that property, or

- manage your interest in a partnership business if you have a signed agreement giving your partners authority to do so.

Create, Modify or Revoke a Trust

Quicken WillMaker Plus's power of attorney form doesn't allow you to give your attorney-in-fact permission to create, modify or revoke a trust on your behalf—with one exception. If you've already set up a revocable living trust, you may give your attorney-in-fact the power to transfer property to that trust.

About Your Attorney-in-Fact

This section explains more about the responsibilities the person you name as attorney-in-fact will have toward you and your property.

Possible Powers

Commonly, people give an attorney-in-fact broad power over their finances. But it's up to you. Using Quicken WillMaker Plus, you can give your attorney-in-fact authority to do some or all of the following:

- use your assets to pay your everyday expenses and those of your family
- handle transactions with banks and other financial institutions
- buy, sell, maintain, pay taxes on and mortgage real estate and other property
- file and pay your taxes
- manage your retirement accounts
- collect benefits from Social Security, Medicare or other government programs or civil or military service

- invest your money in stocks, bonds and mutual funds
- buy and sell insurance policies and annuities for you
- operate your small business
- claim or disclaim property you get from others
- make gifts of your assets to organizations and individuals that you choose
- transfer property to a living trust you've already set up, and
- hire someone to represent you in court.

(These powers are discussed in detail a little later in this chapter.)

Quicken WillMaker Plus allows you to tailor your durable power of attorney for finances to fit your needs by choosing which powers you grant and placing certain conditions and restrictions upon the attorney-in-fact. For example, you can give your attorney-in-fact authority over your real estate, with the express restriction that your house may not be sold.

Legal Responsibilities

The attorney-in-fact you appoint in your durable power of attorney is a fiduciary—someone who holds a position of trust and must act in your best interests. The law requires your attorney-in-fact to:

- handle your property honestly and prudently
- avoid conflicts of interest
- keep your property completely separate from his or her own, and
- keep adequate records.

These standards do not present problems in most simple situations. For example, if you

just want your attorney-in-fact to sign for your pension check, deposit it in your bank account and pay for your basic needs, there is little possibility of uncertainty or dispute.

Sometimes, however, these rules impose unnecessary hardships on an attorney-in-fact. For example, your property may already be mixed with that of your attorney-in-fact, and it may make good sense for that to continue. Quicken WillMaker Plus allows you to insert clauses in your power of attorney document that permit your attorney-in-fact to deviate from some of the rules above, so that the attorney-in-fact's freedom isn't unnecessarily fettered. (See "Additional Duties and Responsibilities," below.)

Liability for Mistakes

Your attorney-in-fact must be careful with your money and other property. State laws require an attorney-in-fact to act as a prudent person would under the circumstances. That means the primary goal is not to lose your money.

The attorney-in-fact may, however, make careful investment moves on your behalf. For example, if your money is in a low-interest bank account, the attorney-in-fact might invest the money in government bonds, which pay higher interest but are still very safe.

Because most people choose a spouse, close relative or friend to be attorney-in-fact, your Quicken WillMaker Plus power of attorney makes your attorney-in-fact liable only for losses resulting from intentional wrongdoing or extreme carelessness—not for a well-meaning decision that turns out badly.

When Court Supervision May Be Required

An attorney-in-fact is not directly supervised by a court; that's the whole point of naming one. The attorney-in-fact is not required to file reports with any courts or government agencies.

But a court may become involved if someone close to you fears that the attorney-in-fact is acting dishonestly or not in your best interests. It's rare, but close relatives or friends may ask a court to order the attorney-in-fact to take certain actions. Or they may ask the court to terminate the power of attorney and appoint a conservator to look after your affairs. If a conservator is appointed for you, the attorney-in-fact will have to account to the conservator—or the conservator may revoke your durable power of attorney altogether. As mentioned above, you can use your durable power of attorney for finances to name your attorney-in-fact as your first choice for conservator.

Some states have statutes that set out specific procedures for such court actions. For example, a California statute authorizes any interested person, including relatives and friends of the principal, to ask a court to resolve questions relating to the durable power of attorney. Tennessee law provides that the next of kin can petition a court to require an attorney-in-fact to post a bond—something like an insurance policy, generally issued by a surety company.

Even if your state does not have a statute specifically authorizing court actions, someone interested in your welfare and upset with the attorney-in-fact could still go to court and ask for a conservator to be appointed.

Record-Keeping Responsibilities

Your attorney-in-fact is legally required to keep accurate and separate records for all transactions made on your behalf. Good records are particularly important if the attorney-in-fact ever wants to resign and turn the responsibility over to another person.

Record keeping isn't an onerous requirement. The attorney-in-fact must simply be able to show where and how your money has been spent. In most instances, it's enough to have a balanced checkbook and receipts for bills paid and claims made. And because the attorney-in-fact will probably file tax returns on your behalf, income and expense records may be necessary.

EXAMPLE: Keiji appoints Kathryn, his niece, to serve as his attorney-in-fact. Keiji receives income from his savings, two IRAs, Social Security and stock dividends. Kathryn must keep records of the income for bank and tax purposes.

You and your prospective attorney-in-fact should discuss and agree on what record keeping is appropriate. The attorney-in-fact may also want to review your current records now to make sure they're in order. If you don't have clear records, the attorney-in-fact may have to spend a lot of time sorting things out later.

As part of managing your finances, the attorney-in-fact may hire a bookkeeper, accountant or other financial adviser and pay for the services from your property.

> **TIP**
> **Getting help with organizing.** If, like many people, you keep records in haphazardly labeled shoe boxes and file folders, this may be a good time to get organized. For help getting organized, use Quicken WillMaker Plus's Information for Caregivers and Survivors form.

The Basics of Your Durable Power of Attorney

In almost every state, you can create a valid power of attorney if you are at least 18 years old and of sound mind. (In Alabama, you must be at least 19 years old. In Nebraska, you must be at least 19 or married.) This mental competency requirement isn't hard to meet. Generally, you must understand what a durable power of attorney for finances is and does—and you must understand that you are making one.

To make your durable power of attorney with Quicken WillMaker Plus, you must enter some basic identifying information about yourself. This section explains the questions the program poses, in the order they appear.

Your Name

If you have already used Quicken WillMaker Plus to prepare your will, living trust, health care directives or final arrangements, your name will automatically appear on the screen that requests this information.

If it does not, enter your name the way it appears on formal business documents, such as your driver's license, bank accounts or real estate deeds. This may or may not be the name that appears on your birth certificate.

If you have used different names in important documents, you can list all of them on the screen, separated by aka, which stands for "also known as." Be sure to enter all names in which you hold bank accounts, stocks, bonds, real estate and other property. This will make it far easier for your attorney-in-fact to get his or her job done.

If you use more than one name and you're up for some extra work, you may also consider settling on one name for your Quicken WillMaker Plus document, and then changing your other documents to conform. That will clean up your records and save your attorney-in-fact some trouble later on. To change your name on official documents and records—for example, bank accounts, deeds or Social Security records—you'll have to contact the appropriate government office or financial institution to find out what documentation they'll need.

Your Gender

Quicken WillMaker Plus asks whether you are male or female so that your durable power of attorney document will include the correct gender pronoun instead of the awkward "he or she" and "his or her."

Your Address

Enter the complete address of your residence. If during the course of the year you live in more than one state, use the address in the state where you vote, register vehicles, own valuable property, have bank accounts or run a business. If you've already made your will, health care directives or a living trust, be consistent: Use the same address for every document.

Your Social Security Number

Your Social Security number can be very useful for your attorney-in-fact. It may help him or her to obtain your financial information and take care of your affairs. However, we do not ask you to include the number in your document. Growing concerns about identity theft make it important for you to protect this sensitive piece of information. Some states even forbid Social Security numbers on documents that will be placed in the public records. That said, you should be sure that your attorney-in-fact knows your Social Security number. Write it down and ask your attorney-in-fact to keep it safe.

When Your Document Takes Effect

Your durable power of attorney for finances is effective as soon as you sign it. This means that your attorney-in-fact can start acting on your behalf whenever you choose. If you need someone to help you keep an eye on your finances, you may want your attorney-in-fact

to start acting for you right away. On the other hand, you may prefer that your attorney-in-fact use the document only if you are unable to handle matters yourself, either because you are temporarily ill or injured or because of long-term incapacity.

If you want your attorney-in-fact to use the document only if you become incapacitated and unable to take care of your finances, be sure to clearly convey those wishes to the person you name. If you don't trust that your attorney-in-fact will refrain from using the document unless and until you are incapacitated, consider naming someone else to represent you.

 SEE AN EXPERT

Springing powers of attorney. You may have heard of "springing" powers of attorney—that is, documents that become effective only if you are incapacitated. Many people like the idea of these documents, because no one can take action regarding your finances until at least one doctor certifies that you're not well enough to manage them yourself. Unfortunately, there are many inconveniences involved in making a springing document and getting it accepted. Because of the hassles involved, many experts advise that you make an immediately effective power of attorney document. If you feel strongly that you want a springing document instead, consult an attorney.

Choosing Your Attorney-in-Fact

Next, Quicken WillMaker Plus asks you to name your attorney-in-fact. This is the most important decision you must make when you create a durable power of attorney.

Depending on the powers you grant, the attorney-in-fact may have tremendous power over your property. You need to choose someone you trust completely. Fortunately, most of us know at least one such person—usually a spouse, relative or close friend. If there's no one you trust completely with this authority, a durable power of attorney isn't for you.

Remember that you can't count on anyone to keep an eye on the attorney-in-fact once he or she takes over your finances. If your attorney-in-fact handles your affairs carelessly or dishonestly, the only recourse would be a lawsuit—usually not a satisfactory approach. Lawsuits are burdensome and expensive, and would entangle your loved ones in all the legal red tape a power of attorney is designed to avoid. And there's no guarantee that money an incompetent attorney-in-fact lost would ever be recovered. This reality is not intended to frighten you needlessly, but simply to underscore the need to make a careful choice about who will represent you.

Any competent adult can serve as your attorney-in-fact; the person most definitely doesn't have to be a lawyer. But don't appoint someone without first discussing it with that person and making sure he or she accepts this serious responsibility. If you don't, you may well cause problems down the line. The person you've chosen may not want to serve, for a variety of reasons. And even if the person would be willing, if he or she doesn't know of his or her responsibilities, confusion and delay are inevitable if you become incapacitated.

TIP

Getting help. Quicken WillMaker Plus prints out an information sheet you can give to your attorney-in-fact explaining the responsibilities of the job. You can use this document to help you remember the main issues when talking with your attorney-in-fact about his or her duties.

In most situations, the attorney-in-fact does not need extensive experience in financial management; common sense, dependability and complete honesty are enough. Your attorney-in-fact can get any reasonably necessary professional help—from an accountant, lawyer or tax preparer, perhaps—and pay for it out of your assets.

Sometimes it's tough to know whom to choose. Perhaps your mate is ill or wouldn't be a good choice for other reasons. Or you may not know anyone that you feel entirely comfortable asking to take over your financial affairs. Or, if you have an active, complex investment portfolio or own a business, you might decide that your attorney-in-fact needs business skills, knowledge or management abilities beyond those of the people closest to you.

If you're not sure whom your attorney-in-fact should be, read the rest of this section and discuss the issue with those close to you. If you can't come up with a family member or close friend to name, you may want to consider asking your lawyer, business partner or banker to serve as attorney-in-fact. If you really know and trust the person, it may be a good option for you. Keep in mind that it's better not to make a durable power of attorney than to entrust your affairs to someone in whom you don't have complete confidence.

Discussing Your Wishes

Set aside time to talk with your attorney-in-fact about when he or she should start taking care of financial tasks for you. You can agree with your attorney-in-fact that he or she should not exercise any authority under the document unless you become completely unable to take care of yourself and your property—or unless you otherwise direct him or her to do so. With respect to exercising authority under the document, your attorney-in-fact is legally required to follow your wishes.

If you become dissatisfied with your attorney-in-fact's actions, and you are still of sound mind, you can revoke the durable power of attorney and end your attorney-in-fact's power to act for you.

CAUTION

Avoiding family conflict. If there are long-standing feuds among family members, they may object to your choice of attorney-in-fact or the extent of the authority delegated. If you foresee any such conflicts, it's wise to try to defuse them in advance. A discussion with the people who are leery of the power of attorney might help. If you still feel uncomfortable after talking things over, you may want to discuss the troubles with a knowledgeable lawyer. A lawyer can review your estate planning documents and might help you feel reassured that your plans will be carried out as you wish.

Poor Choices for Attorney-in-Fact

Here are some suggestions on whom to avoid when you're choosing an attorney-in-fact:

- To carry out duties and responsibilities properly and promptly, it's usually best that the attorney-in-fact live nearby. Although overnight mail, faxes, email and other technological wonders have made it easier to conduct business long distance, it's still best for your attorney-in-fact to be close at hand—or at least willing to travel and spend time handling your affairs when needed. After all, this is the person who will be responsible for day-to-day details of your finances: opening your mail, paying bills, looking after property and so on. Of course, many families are spread across the country these days. If there's only one person you trust enough to name as attorney-in-fact, and he or she lives far away, you may have to settle for the less than ideal situation.

- Don't name an institution, such as a bank, as attorney-in-fact. It isn't legal in some states, and it's definitely not desirable. Serving as attorney-in-fact is a personal responsibility, and there should be personal connection and trust between you and your attorney-in-fact. If the person you trust most happens to be your banker, appoint that person, not the bank.

If You Are Married

If you're married, you'll probably want to name your spouse as your attorney-in-fact unless there is a compelling reason not to do so. There are powerful legal and practical reasons, in addition to the emotional ones, for appointing your spouse. The main one is that naming anyone else creates the risk of conflicts between the attorney-in-fact and your spouse over how to manage property that belongs to both spouses.

> **EXAMPLE:** Henry and Amelia, a married couple, each create a durable power of attorney for finances. Henry names Amelia as his attorney-in-fact, but Amelia names her sister Anna. Later, Amelia becomes unable to manage her financial affairs, and Anna takes over as her attorney-in-fact. Soon Anna and Henry are arguing bitterly over what should be done with the house and investments that Henry and Amelia own together. If they can't resolve their differences, Henry or Anna may have to go to court and ask a judge to determine what is in Amelia's best interests.

However, if your spouse is ill, quite elderly or simply not equipped to manage your financial affairs, you may have to name someone else as attorney-in-fact. The wisest course is for you and your spouse to agree on whom the attorney-in-fact should be, perhaps one of your grown children.

SEE AN EXPERT

Divorce may not end your spouse's authority. If your spouse is your attorney-in-fact, that designation does not automatically end if you get divorced, except in Alabama, California, Colorado, Illinois, Indiana, Kansas, Minnesota, Missouri, Ohio, Pennsylvania, Texas, Washington and Wisconsin. In any state, after a divorce you should revoke the power of attorney and create a new one, naming someone else as your new attorney-in-fact.

If You Have a Living Trust

If you have created a revocable living trust to avoid probate or minimize estate taxes, the successor trustee you named in the trust document will have power over the trust property if you become incapacitated. If you and your spouse made a living trust together, the trust document almost certainly gives your spouse authority over trust property if you become incapacitated.

Creating a durable power of attorney for finances doesn't change any of this. Your attorney-in-fact will not have authority over property in your living trust. To avoid conflicts, it is usually best to have the same person managing both trust property and nontrust property if you become incapacitated. So, normally, you'll name the same person as successor trustee and as your attorney-in-fact.

> **EXAMPLE:** Carlos, a widower, prepares a revocable living trust to avoid probate and a durable power of attorney for finances in

case he becomes incapacitated. He names his son, Jeffrey, as successor trustee of the living trust and attorney-in-fact under the durable power of attorney.

Several years later, Carlos has a stroke and is temporarily unable to handle his everyday finances. Jeffrey steps in to deposit his father's pension checks and pay monthly bills, using his authority as attorney-in-fact. As successor trustee, he also has legal authority over the property Carlos transferred to his living trust, including Carlos's house.

Appointing More Than One Person

In general, it's a bad idea to name more than one attorney-in-fact, because conflicts between them could disrupt the handling of your finances. Also, some banks and other financial institutions prefer to deal with a single attorney-in-fact.

Still, it is legal to name more than one person—and Quicken WillMaker Plus allows you to name up to three people to serve together. But if you're tempted to name more than one person simply so that no one feels hurt or left out, think again. It may be better to pick one person for the job and explain your reasoning to the others now. If you name more than one person and they don't get along, they may wind up resolving their disputes in court. The result might be more bad feelings than if you had just picked one person to be attorney-in-fact, and explained your choice, in the first place.

Making Decisions

If you name more than one attorney-in-fact, you'll have to grapple with the question of how they should make decisions. You can require co-agents to carry out their duties in one of two ways:

- they must all reach agreement before they take any action on your behalf, or
- they may make decisions independent of one another.

Both methods have strengths and pitfalls, and there's no hard-and-fast rule on which is better. Choose the approach that feels most comfortable to you.

Requiring your attorneys-in-fact to act jointly ensures that decisions are made carefully and with the knowledge of everyone involved, but coordinating multiple decision makers can be burdensome and time-consuming. On the other hand, allowing your attorneys-in-fact to act separately makes it easy to get things done, but allowing two or three people to make independent decisions about your finances can lead to poor record keeping and general confusion. For example, your attorneys-in-fact may independently take money out of your bank accounts or buy and sell stock without full knowledge of what the others are doing to manage your investments.

If There Is a Disagreement

If your attorneys-in-fact get into a dispute that interferes with their ability to represent you properly, they may need help working things out. Getting help could mean submitting the dispute to mediation or arbitration—or going to court to have a judge decide what's best. Your attorneys-in-fact can decide how they want to handle the matter, keeping in mind that their foremost responsibility is to act in your best interest. The downside of all this is not just that there could be confusion and delays in handling your finances, but that you'll probably be the one to pay the costs of settling the dispute. All these are reasons to name just one attorney-in-fact.

If One or More Cannot Serve

If you name more than one attorney-in-fact, and one of them can't serve, the others will continue to serve. If none of them can serve, an alternate can take over.

SEE AN EXPERT

If you want to name more than three people. The best approach is usually to choose just one attorney-in-fact. But Quicken WillMaker Plus allows you to name up to three people to serve together. Asking two or three people to manage your finances may prove unwieldy enough—counting on more than three to coordinate their actions on your behalf would be a logistical nightmare. If you want to name more than three attorneys-in-fact, talk with a lawyer.

Naming Alternates

It's a good idea to name someone to take over as your attorney-in-fact in case your first choice can't serve or needs to resign. Quicken

WillMaker Plus allows you to name up to two alternate attorneys-in-fact, officially called successors. Your first alternate would take over if your initial choice can't serve. The second alternate would take the job only if your first and second choices can't keep it.

When naming alternates, use the same criteria that you used to make your first choice for attorney-in-fact. Your alternates should be every bit as trustworthy and competent. If you don't know anyone you trust well enough to name as a first or second alternate, skip the matter altogether.

Someone who is asked to serve as an alternate attorney-in-fact may be worried about possible liability for the acts of the original attorney-in-fact. To protect against this, the Quicken WillMaker Plus power of attorney form states that a successor attorney-in-fact is not liable for any acts of a prior attorney-in-fact.

You can also authorize your attorney-in-fact to appoint someone to serve if all those you named cannot. You do this by giving your attorney-in-fact permission to delegate tasks to others. (See "Additional Duties and Responsibilities," below.) Allowing your attorney-in-fact to delegate his or her job to someone else eliminates the risk that the position might become vacant because of the original attorney-in-fact's disability or resignation. If this occurs, and you haven't named a successor or none of your successors are available, your durable power of attorney would be useless. There would have to be a conservatorship proceeding to find someone to manage your finances.

If You Name More Than One Attorney-in-Fact

If you name more than one attorney-in-fact, the person you name as a first alternate will take over only if all of your attorneys-in-fact must give up the job. If any number of your first choices can continue to serve, they may do so alone, without the addition of your alternate.

If you name a second alternate, that person will take over only in the extremely unlikely event that all of your named attorneys-in-fact and your first alternate cannot serve.

Specific Financial Powers

Using Quicken WillMaker Plus, you can give your attorney-in-fact up to 14 specific financial powers. The powers may put an enormous amount of control over your finances into the hands of your attorney-in-fact, and it's important that you understand exactly what each power authorizes your attorney-in-fact to do. To that end, we walk you through each power, one at a time, asking whether you want to grant it or not.

If you grant all the powers, your attorney-in-fact will be able to handle your investments, real estate, banking and other financial tasks. The attorney-in-fact can use your assets to pay your debts and expenses—including home maintenance, taxes, insurance premiums, wage claims, medical care, child support, alimony and your personal allowance. The attorney-in-fact can sign deeds, make gifts, pay school expenses and endorse and deposit checks.

As you go through the list of powers, you may find yourself feeling concerned about how much power you're putting in someone else's hands. These feelings are not unusual, as the lists of actions your attorney-in-fact can take are long, exhaustive and perhaps a bit overwhelming. As reassurance, keep in mind your attorney-in-fact's overriding legal duty to act carefully—and always with your best interests at heart. (See "About Your Attorney-in-Fact," above.) If you still find yourself feeling uncomfortable, take some time to reflect on your choice of attorney-in-fact; be sure you've chosen the best person for the job.

Each of the financial powers is explained here. They are numbered as they appear in the Quicken WillMaker Plus program.

Real Estate Transactions

This power puts the attorney-in-fact in charge of any real estate you own. Your attorney-in-fact must, for example, use your assets to pay your mortgage and taxes and arrange for necessary repairs and maintenance to your home. Most important, the attorney-in-fact may sell, mortgage, partition or lease your real estate.

The attorney-in-fact may also take any other action connected to real estate. For example, your attorney-in-fact may:

- buy or lease real estate for you
- refinance your mortgage to get a better interest rate
- pay off legal claims on your property
- buy insurance for your property
- build, remodel or remove structures on your property
- grant easements over your property, and
- bring or defend lawsuits over real estate.

Restricting the Sale of Your Home

Losing your home, especially if you've lived there many years, can be a disturbing prospect. Some people feel strongly that the attorney-in-fact should not sell their home—no matter what happens. If you want to grant the real estate power but forbid your attorney-in-fact from selling or mortgaging your home, Quicken WillMaker Plus allows you to include that restriction.

But think carefully before you tie the hands of your attorney-in-fact in this way. You certainly don't want to lose your home—but a financial emergency may make it necessary. Ideally, you'll trust the person you name as your attorney-in-fact to use discretion to make the decision based on your best interests—particularly if you have named your spouse or other co-owner of your home to serve as your attorney-in-fact.

Personal Property Transactions

Personal property here means physical items of property—for example, cars, furniture, jewelry, computers and stereo equipment. It does not include real estate or intangible kinds of property such as stocks or bank notes.

If you grant this power, your attorney-in-fact can buy, sell, rent or exchange personal property on your behalf. Your attorney-in-fact can also insure, use, move, store, repair or pawn your personal things. Again, all actions must be taken in your best interest.

EXAMPLE: Paul names his wife, Gloria, as his attorney-in-fact for financial matters. When he later goes into a nursing home, his old car, which he can no longer use, becomes an expense Gloria cannot afford. As Paul's attorney-in-fact, she has legal authority to sell the car.

Stock, Bond, Commodity and Option Transactions

This power gives your attorney-in-fact the power to manage your securities—including stocks, bonds, mutual funds, certificates of deposit, commodities and call and put options. Your attorney-in-fact can buy or sell securities on your behalf, accept or transfer certificates or other evidence of ownership and exercise voting rights.

CAUTION

Brokers may use different forms. Many brokerage houses have their own durable power of attorney forms. If yours does, it's a good idea to use it in addition to your Quicken WillMaker Plus power of attorney. Using your broker's form will make things easier for your attorney-in-fact, because your broker will have no need to investigate your power of attorney and quibble over its terms. The broker will already have its form on file and will understand exactly what your attorney-in-fact is authorized to do.

Banking and Other Financial Institution Transactions

One of the most common reasons for making a durable power of attorney is to arrange for someone to handle banking transactions. If you give your attorney-in-fact authority to handle your bank accounts, your bills can be paid, and pension or other checks can be deposited in your accounts even if you can no longer take care of these matters yourself.

EXAMPLE: Virginia, who is in her 70s, is admitted to the hospital for emergency surgery. She's too weak to even think about paying her bills or depositing her Social Security check—and, anyway, she can't get to the bank. Fortunately, she earlier created a durable power of attorney for finances, naming her niece Marianne as her attorney-in-fact. Marianne can deposit Virginia's check and sign checks to pay the bills that come while Virginia is in the hospital.

Your attorney-in-fact may open and close accounts with banks, savings and loans, credit unions or other financial institutions on your behalf. The attorney-in-fact may write checks on these accounts, endorse checks you receive and receive account statements. The attorney-in-fact also has access to your safe deposit box, to withdraw or add to its contents.

In most states, the attorney-in-fact may also borrow money on your behalf and pledge your assets as security for the loan.

CAUTION

Financial institutions may use different forms. Many banks and other financial institutions have their own durable power of attorney forms. Even though granting Quicken WillMaker Plus's banking power will give your attorney-in-fact authority to act on your behalf at any financial institution, it's a good idea to use the financial institution's form in addition to your Quicken WillMaker Plus form. Using the form that your financial institution is most familiar with will make it easier for your attorney-in-fact to get things done.

Signing Checks and Other Documents

Many people wonder how the attorney-in-fact signs checks and other documents on behalf of the principal. Exact procedures vary depending on both local custom and the procedures of a particular financial institution or government agency. In some places, after establishing authority with a particular institution or agency, the attorney-in-fact will sign his or her own name to checks and documents, followed by "POA" or other language such as "under power of attorney dated June 15, 2003." In other locations, the attorney-in-fact will first sign your name and then his or her own name, followed by the "POA" designation.

Business Operating Transactions

This power gives your attorney-in-fact authority to act for you in operating a business that you own yourself or that you run as a partnership, limited liability company or corporation. Subject to the terms of a partnership agreement, operating agreement or corporate rules set out in the bylaws and shareholders' agreements, your attorney-in-fact may:

- sell or liquidate the business
- merge with another company
- prepare, sign and file reports, information and returns with government agencies
- pay business taxes
- enforce the terms of any partnership agreement in court, and
- exercise any power or option you have under a partnership agreement.

If your business is a sole proprietorship, the attorney-in-fact may also:

- hire and fire employees
- move the business
- change the nature of the business or its methods of operation, including selling, marketing, accounting and advertising
- change the name of the business
- change the form of the business's organization—that is, enter into a partnership agreement or incorporate the business
- continue or renegotiate the business's contracts
- enter contracts with lawyers, accountants or others, and
- collect and spend money on behalf of the business.

If you're a sole proprietor, a durable power of attorney is a very useful way to let someone else run the business if you become unable to do so. No court proceedings are required for the attorney-in-fact to take over if you become incapacitated, so there should be no disruption of your business. Be sure to work out a business plan with the person you plan to appoint as your attorney-in-fact; explain what you want for your business and how you expect it to be managed.

> **CAUTION**
>
> **Check your existing agreements.** If you operate your business with other people as a partnership, limited liability company or closely held corporation, your business agreement should cover what happens if a partner or shareholder becomes incapacitated. Typically, the other business owners can operate the business during the incapacitated person's absence or even buy out his or her share. A durable power of attorney will not affect these rules you already have in place.

> **EXAMPLE:** Mike wants his wife, Nancy, to be his attorney-in-fact to manage his finances if he becomes incapacitated. Mike, a house painter, runs the M-J Painting Co. with his equal partner, Jack. Their agreement provides that if one partner becomes incapacitated, the other has exclusive authority to operate the business.
>
> If Jack and Nancy have conflicts over money, however, there could be some problems. Mike, Jack and Nancy should think through the arrangement carefully and may want to consult a lawyer. Whatever they decide on should be spelled out in detail in the partnership agreement. They may also want to create a customized durable power of attorney, with the lawyer's help, that sets out the details of the business arrangements.

Insurance and Annuity Transactions

This power allows your attorney-in-fact to buy, borrow against, cash in or cancel insurance policies or annuity contracts for you and your spouse, children and other dependent family members. The attorney-in-fact's authority extends to all your policies and contracts, whether they name you or someone else as the beneficiary—that is, the person who will receive any proceeds of the policy when you die.

The one exception to this rule covers insurance policies you own with your spouse. Under these policies, your spouse must consent to any transaction that affects the policy. So if your attorney-in-fact is not your spouse, he or she will have to obtain your spouse's permission before taking action. Especially in community property states, even policies that are in one spouse's name may in fact be owned by both spouses. (See "Property Ownership Rules for Married People" in Chapter 5.) If you have questions about who owns your insurance policies, consult a lawyer. (See Chapter 25.)

If you already have an insurance policy or annuity contract, your attorney-in-fact can keep paying the premiums or cancel it—whichever he or she decides is in your best interests.

Your attorney-in-fact is also permitted to change and name the beneficiaries of your insurance policies or annuity contracts. This is a broad power, and it's a good idea to discuss your wishes about it with your attorney-in-fact. If you don't want your attorney-in-fact to change your beneficiary designations, make that clear. If you have strong feelings about whom the designated beneficiary of any new policies should be, you can discuss that as well.

There is one important limitation on your attorney-in-fact's ability to designate beneficiaries. Your attorney-in-fact cannot name himself or herself as beneficiary on a renewal, extension or substitute for an existing policy unless he or she was already the beneficiary before you signed the power of attorney.

Estate, Trust and Other Beneficiary Transactions

This power authorizes your attorney-in-fact to act on your behalf to claim or disclaim property you get from any other source. For example, if you were entitled to money from a trust fund, your attorney-in-fact could go to the trustee—the person in charge of the trust—and press your claim on your behalf. Or, if you didn't really need the money and it would cause your eventual estate tax bill to increase, your attorney-in-fact could turn down the cash.

Disclaiming property—saying that you don't want it—can be a good idea if taking it would increase the size of your estate and generate a big estate tax bill at your death. (For more about estate taxes, see Chapter 13.)

Transferring Property to Your Living Trust

A revocable living trust is a legal structure you create by preparing and signing a document that specifies who will receive certain property at your death. Living trusts are designed to avoid probate, though some may also help you save on estate taxes or set up long-term property management. (See Chapter 13.)

If you've already set up a living trust, this power gives your attorney-in-fact the authority to transfer items of your property to that trust. But your attorney-in-fact can transfer property into your living trust only if you've given him or her authority over that type of property elsewhere in your document. For example, if you want your attorney-in-fact to be able to transfer real estate into the living trust, you must also grant the real estate power. And if you want your attorney-in-fact to transfer bank accounts to your living trust, you must also grant the banking transactions power.

Legal Actions

This provision allows your attorney-in-fact to act for you in all matters that involve courts or government agencies. For example, your attorney-in-fact can bring or settle a lawsuit on your behalf. He or she can also accept court papers intended for you and hire an attorney to represent you in court, if necessary. Unless your attorney-in-fact is a lawyer, he or she may not actually represent you in court but must hire someone to do so. If you lose a lawsuit, the attorney-in-fact can use your assets to pay the winner whatever you owe.

Personal and Family Care

This is an important power. It gives the attorney-in-fact the authority to use your assets to pay your everyday expenses and those of your family. The attorney-in-fact can spend your money for your family's food; shelter; education; cars; medical and dental care; membership dues for churches, clubs or other organizations; pets; vacations; and travel. The attorney-in-fact is allowed to spend as much as it takes to maintain the standard of living to which you, your spouse, children and anyone else you usually support are accustomed.

If you regularly take care of others—for example, you are the primary caretaker for a disabled sibling or parent—your attorney-in-fact can use your assets to continue to help those people.

Government Benefits

This power allows your attorney-in-fact to apply for and collect any benefits you may be entitled to from Social Security, Medicare, Medicaid or other government programs, or civil or military service. To collect most government benefits, your attorney-in-fact must send the government office a copy of the durable power of attorney to prove his or her authority. Social Security is an exception, however. (See below.)

Retirement Plan Transactions

This power gives your attorney-in-fact authority over retirement plans such as IRAs and Keogh plans. The attorney-in-fact may select payment options and designate beneficiaries—the people who will take any money left in the fund at your death. He or she can also change current beneficiary designations, make voluntary contributions to your plan, change the way the funds are invested and roll over plan benefits into other retirement plans. The attorney-in-fact may also perform any other actions authorized by the plan, including borrowing from it.

CAUTION

This power is powerful. The power to change the beneficiaries of your retirement funds is a drastic one. Talk with your attorney-in-fact to be sure he or she understands your wishes with respect to this power.

Tax Matters

This provision gives your attorney-in-fact authority to act for you in all state, local and federal tax matters. The attorney-in-fact can prepare and file tax returns and other documents, pay tax due, contest tax bills and collect refunds. To file a tax return on your behalf, the attorney-in-fact must include a copy of the power of attorney with the return. The attorney-in-fact is also authorized to receive confidential information about you from the IRS.

The IRS Power of Attorney Form

The IRS has its own power of attorney form, but you don't need to use it. It is primarily designed to allow attorneys, accountants and other professionals to receive confidential tax information on behalf of clients. It is not a comprehensive, durable power of attorney for tax matters. The Quicken WillMaker Plus form gives your attorney-in-fact the power to receive confidential information from the IRS, plus the authority to handle any tax matters that arise.

Social Security Checks

To collect your Social Security benefits, your attorney-in-fact will have to take the power of attorney document to a local Social Security office. A representative will interview the attorney-in-fact and establish him or her as your "representative payee"—that is, someone entitled to receive your Social Security checks for you.

If you're creating a power of attorney that's effective immediately, you can save your attorney-in-fact some work by simply contacting the Social Security Administration and naming your attorney-in-fact as your representative payee. However, that means your attorney-in-fact will start receiving your Social Security checks right away, and you may not want that. If it's not yet time for the attorney-in-fact to take control under an immediately effective document, or if you're creating a springing power of attorney, you're better off granting the government benefits power and letting the attorney-in-fact deal with the Social Security Administration when the time comes.

In addition to granting the government benefits power, you might also consider having your Social Security check deposited directly into a bank account where your attorney-in-fact will have access to the funds without the hassles of dealing with the SSA. You can set up a direct deposit arrangement at any time, as long as you are of sound mind.

To appoint a representative payee or arrange for direct deposit of your benefits, contact the SSA at 800-772-1213.

Making Gifts

This last financial power allows your attorney-in-fact to make gifts of your property. You may already know that you want your attorney-in-fact to be able to give away your property under some circumstances. On the other hand, allowing your attorney-in-fact to make gifts might feel like giving up too much control.

Reasons to Allow Gifts

There are many reasons why you might want to permit your attorney-in-fact to make gifts of your property. Here are a few of the most common.

Estate tax savings. If you have substantial assets and are concerned about your eventual estate tax liability, you may be planning to reduce estate taxes by giving away some of your property while you are still alive. If you have set up this sort of gift-giving plan, you'll probably want to authorize your attorney-in-fact to continue it.

Other gift-giving plans. There are lots of reasons to give gifts that have nothing to do with estate planning and avoiding taxes. You may, for example, want to donate regularly to your church or a favorite charity. Or perhaps you've made a commitment to help a family member with college or starting up a business.

Family emergencies. All of us are occasionally caught off guard by unexpected financial troubles. You may want your attorney-in-fact to be able to help out if a loved one faces such an emergency.

Possible Gift Tax Consequences

If your attorney-in-fact gives away more than a certain amount—currently $12,000—to any one person or organization in one calendar year, a federal gift tax return will probably have to be filed.

Several kinds of gifts, however, are not taxable regardless of amount: gifts to your spouse, gifts that directly pay for medical expenses or tuition and gifts to tax-exempt charities. Gift tax may eventually have to be paid, but unless you make hundreds of thousands of dollars' worth of taxable gifts during your life, no tax will actually be due until after your death. Because your attorney-in-fact is required to act in your best interest, making large gifts could put him or her in a bind. On one hand, your attorney-in-fact may feel that you would want to make a sizable gift—even if it's a taxable one—to a particular person or organization. On the other hand, if you have a large estate that is likely to owe estate tax at your death, he or she won't want to increase your eventual tax liability.

For this reason, if you do permit your attorney-in-fact to make gifts, it's particularly important that you explain, ahead of time, what you intend and whether you have any limits.

CROSS-REFERENCE
More information about estate taxes. If you want to learn more about estate and gift taxes, see Chapter 13. For help beyond this book, see *Plan Your Estate*, by Denis Clifford (Nolo). It's

a detailed guide to estate planning, including all major methods of reducing or avoiding estate and gift taxes. If you still have questions, talk with a knowledgeable attorney.

Gifts to the Attorney-in-Fact

First, you must decide whether you want to allow your attorney-in-fact to make gifts to himself or herself. Because this raises some unique issues, you must consider it separately from the question of gifts to other people.

If you want to allow gifts to your attorney-in-fact, you must place an annual limit on them. This is because of a tricky legal rule called a general power of appointment. If your attorney-in-fact has an unlimited power to give your property to himself or herself, and he or she dies before you do, the attorney-in-fact could become the legal owner of all your property. In this case, your attorney-in-fact would be subject to taxes based not only on his or her own assets, but on yours as well.

To avoid this problem, you must limit the amount of money your attorney-in-fact may accept in any given year. To avoid trouble with gift taxes, you may want to let the current gift tax threshold be your guide and set the limit at $12,000 or less. Whatever amount you choose, be sure it's far less than what you're worth. If you set the limit too high, you may inadvertently create a general power of appointment—and increase the chances that your attorney-in-fact will use too much of your property for his or her own purposes.

Gifts to the Alternate Attorney-in-Fact

You may want to allow your primary attorney-in-fact to receive gifts of your property, but not your alternate attorney-in-fact. Quicken WillMaker Plus allows you to include this restriction in your power of attorney document. If you allow gifts to your first choice attorney-in-fact, and you've also named an alternate attorney-in-fact, the program will ask you whether or not your alternate is allowed to receive gifts of your property.

If you wish to allow your alternate to make gifts to himself or herself, that's fine, too. If you do allow gifts to your alternate, the annual gift limit will be the same as the amount you set for your first choice attorney-in-fact.

Gifts to Others

After you've decided whether you want to allow gifts to your attorney-in-fact, Quicken WillMaker Plus asks you about gifts to other people and organizations. If you're comfortable giving your attorney-in-fact broad authority, you can allow gifts to anyone your attorney-in-fact chooses. Or, you can specify the people and organizations to whom your attorney-in-fact may give your property.

If you give your attorney-in-fact broad authority to make gifts, be sure to discuss your intentions. Your attorney-in-fact should have a sound understanding of your plans for giving gifts—including the recipients you have in mind, under what circumstances gifts should be made and in what amounts.

Forgiving Loans

When you give your attorney-in-fact the power to make gifts, you also give the power to forgive or cancel debts others owe you. If anyone owes you money and you've authorized your attorney-in-fact to make gifts to them, be sure you let your attorney-in-fact know which debts you want to be paid and which may be forgiven.

If you've authorized gifts to your attorney-in-fact and he or she owes you money, your attorney-in-fact can forgive those debts, too. But for these debts, your attorney-in-fact can't cancel amounts worth more than his or her maximum gift amount in any calendar year. For example, your son, whom you've named as attorney-in-fact, owes you $20,000. You've placed the annual gift limit at $7,000. He can forgive his debt to you at the rate of $7,000 per year.

Remember that any gifts your attorney-in-fact makes must be in your best interest or according to your explicit instructions. For example, your attorney-in-fact may make annual gifts to each of your three children to reduce your estate tax liability. Or, he or she may make periodic gifts to your niece because you promised to help her with college costs. Your attorney-in-fact should follow the guidelines you have set out in the power of attorney document.

Talk With Your Attorney-in-Fact

It's critically important that you talk with your attorney-in-fact, not just to be sure he or she is willing to take on the job of handling your finances, but to be sure he or she understands what that job entails. Sit down and discuss the list of powers you grant, being especially careful to cover those areas where your attorney-in-fact might exercise a lot of personal discretion.

Now is the time to clarify any special needs or concerns that you have. For example, if there are certain items of personal property you'd never want your attorney-in-fact to sell, note them down and let your attorney-in-fact know how you feel. Or, if you are allowing your attorney-in-fact to make gifts to help out family members or other loved ones who need help, talk frankly about whom you'd feel comfortable helping, as well as when and to what extent.

There is one caveat here: While it is wise to let your attorney-in-fact know what your wishes are, it's generally a bad idea to create a lot of complicated restrictions for him or her. There is no way to know what the future will bring—and, ideally, your attorney-in-fact will have enough flexibility to take whatever actions he or she deems necessary to take care of you. It is important to let your attorney-in-fact know what you want, but also to trust him or her enough to make the right decisions when the time comes.

Additional Duties and Responsibilities

After you've named your attorney-in-fact and decided which financial powers to grant, you have just a few more choices to make about how your attorney-in-fact will carry out his or her duties. These last few questions include:

- whether you want your attorney-in-fact to make periodic reports to anyone about your finances
- whether you want to allow your attorney-in-fact to delegate tasks to others
- whether your attorney-in-fact may benefit financially from actions taken on your behalf
- whether the attorney-in-fact must keep his or her property separate from yours, and
- whether you want to pay your attorney-in-fact.

Periodic Reports

Quicken WillMaker Plus lets you require the attorney-in-fact to issue reports to people you name. Unless you require it, your attorney-in-fact doesn't have to report to anyone about your finances. In most cases, that arrangement is fine.

But in some circumstances, you may want to require reports. For example, if the attorney-in-fact is in charge of your business, investors may need to receive periodic financial statements, audited or reviewed by an accountant. Or perhaps you want to defuse a potentially explosive personal conflict by

reassuring suspicious family members that they'll receive regular reports about your finances. Quicken WillMaker Plus allows you to require quarterly or semi-annual reports to people who you name.

EXAMPLE: Theodore, who is ill, appoints his son, Jason, as his attorney-in-fact for finances. Theodore's two other children, Nancy and Ed, live out of state and aren't on the best of terms with Jason.

To prevent conflict between his children over Jason's handling of Theodore's finances, Theodore decides to require Jason to give Nancy and Ed semi-annual reports of all financial transactions he engages in as attorney-in-fact.

CAUTION

Special requirements for attorneys-in-fact in Utah. If you live in Utah, your attorney-in-fact will have additional reporting responsibilities. These involve what the state calls "interested persons"—that is, anyone who may inherit property under your will or, if you don't make a will, your inheritors according to state law. Here's what your attorney-in-fact must do:

- If you become incapacitated, your attorney-in-fact must notify all interested persons that he or she is your attorney-in-fact and provide them with his or her address. The attorney-in-fact has 30 days from the date of your incapacity to do this. However, since it is usually difficult to pin down the particular date on which someone becomes incapacitated, it is perhaps wiser for the attorney-in-fact to notify people within a month of first taking action under the power of attorney document.

- If any interested person requests it, your attorney-in-fact must provide a copy of the durable power of attorney.
- If any interested person requests it, your attorney-in-fact must provide an annual accounting of the assets to which the durable power of attorney applies, unless you specify that reports are not required, as Quicken WillMaker Plus permits you to do.
- Your attorney-in-fact must notify all interested persons when you die.
- If your attorney-in-fact turns over the job to an alternate, the new attorney-in-fact has ten days to notify inheritors of the change. The new attorney-in-fact must comply with all the reporting requirements listed above.

There are a couple of things you can do to help your attorney-in-fact comply with these requirements. First, give the attorney-in-fact the Information for the Attorney-in-Fact that prints out with your power of attorney document. It explains these reporting rules. Second, if you've made a will, give your attorney-in-fact a list of all the people to whom you are leaving property. It's not necessary to disclose exactly what you're leaving to each person, but without a simple list of names, your attorney-in-fact will have no sure way of knowing who needs to be contacted under the law. (If you make your will using Quicken WillMaker Plus, there's an easy way to provide this list: It prints out at the end of the Letter to Executor that accompanies your will.)

This Utah law is unusual because it places such strict reporting requirements on the attorney-in-fact. Before taking action under the power of

About Reports

The idea of making your attorney-in-fact accountable to people may appeal to you. But before you enter a long list of names of people to whom your attorney-in-fact must make reports, ask yourself whether or not these reports are truly necessary.

One of the most important reasons for making a durable power of attorney is to give control of your finances to someone you trust completely, bypassing the court system. One big advantage of this tactic is that you spare your attorney-in-fact the hassle and expense of preparing reports and accountings for a court.

If you want someone to keep tabs on your attorney-in-fact, think again about whether you truly trust the person you've named.

The Quicken WillMaker Plus power of attorney document requires that all reports include income received by you and expenses incurred. If you want other details included, be certain your attorney-in-fact knows what they are.

Unless the timing of reports is governed by a business agreement or other legally binding document, you are free to require quarterly or semi-annual reports. Weigh the need for the reports against the inconvenience to your attorney-in-fact and the expense of preparing the reports. If you have a very anxious relative, for example, you may want to authorize quarterly reports. Making these reports could be less hassle for your attorney-in-fact than dealing with constant interference from your family members. If the situation is not so tense, semi-annual reports will probably do fine.

attorney document, your attorney-in-fact may want to look at the Utah statutes to find the current requirements. The law is contained in Sections 75-5-501(2) and (3) of the Utah Code, which can easily be found online. (See Nolo's Legal Research Center at www.nolo.com/statute/state.cfm.)

Delegating Powers

If your attorney-in-fact resigns from the job, the alternate you named will take over. But if there is no alternate available, or if your attorney-in-fact is only temporarily unavailable, the attorney-in-fact will need to find another person to do the job.

If you allow it, your attorney-in-fact can turn over all or part of his or her duties to someone else in this situation. This reassignment of duties is called delegation.

If you allow your attorney-in-fact to delegate tasks, he or she is free to turn over any or all of the job to a competent third person. This person may step in temporarily or permanently, depending on the situation.

EXAMPLE: Caroline names her son, Eugene, as her attorney-in-fact for finances, effective immediately. She names a close friend, Nicole, as alternate attorney-in-fact. A year later, Eugene goes on vacation for three weeks, so he delegates his authority over Caroline's bank accounts to Nicole until he returns.

EXAMPLE: Anthony names his wife, Rosa, as his attorney-in-fact; his son Michael is the alternate attorney-in-fact. When Rosa declines to serve because of her own poor health, Michael takes over but soon finds that other responsibilities make it impossible to continue. He delegates all his authority to his sister, Theresa.

Quicken WillMaker Plus prints out a form that your attorney-in-fact can use to delegate authority to someone else. The new representative will use the signed form, along with your power of attorney document, to act on your behalf.

Exceptions to Legal Responsibilities

As discussed, your attorney-in-fact must always act in your best interests, must act honestly and prudently when managing your property and must keep good records. However, you may want to allow your attorney-in-fact to deviate from some standard legal duties, including:

• avoiding conflicts of interest, and
• keeping your property completely separate from his or her own.

Conflicts of Interest

In most states, an attorney-in-fact has no right to engage in activities from which he or she personally stands to benefit. Such activities, which create conflicts of interest between the principal and attorney-in-fact, are called self-dealing. The attorney-in-fact's motive is irrelevant. If the transaction is challenged in court, it is presumed fraudulent until the attorney-in-fact proves otherwise.

EXAMPLE: David is the attorney-in-fact for his elderly mother, Irene. After Irene's failing eyesight makes it impossible for her to drive, David decides to buy her car from her. He looks up the car's fair market value to make sure he is paying a fair amount, writes a check and deposits it in Irene's bank account.

This transaction is forbidden, even though David isn't cheating Irene, unless Irene's power of attorney specifically allows David to benefit from his management of her property and finances.

The ban on self-dealing is intended to protect you; after all, the attorney-in-fact is supposed to be acting on your behalf. It's quite sensible, however, to give the attorney-in-fact permission to self-deal if he or she is your spouse, a close family member, a business partner or another person whose finances are already intertwined with yours. Quicken WillMaker Plus allows you to grant this permission in your power of attorney document.

EXAMPLE: Maurice wants Alice, his best friend, to serve as his attorney-in-fact. They have been involved in many real estate transactions together—including several current projects. Maurice doesn't want to risk disrupting these projects or curtailing Alice's ability to do business, so he specifically states in his durable power of attorney that Alice may benefit from transactions she undertakes on Maurice's behalf as his attorney-in-fact.

Making Gifts

When you grant financial powers to your attorney-in-fact, you may allow him or her to receive gifts of your property. (See "Making Gifts," above.) If you explicitly grant the gift-making power in your document, receiving permitted gifts is not considered a conflict of interest. In other words, it's perfectly fine to forbid your attorney-in-fact from using your power of attorney document for personal benefit while also allowing him or her to receive some of your property as a gift.

Mixing Funds

An attorney-in-fact is never allowed to mix or commingle your funds with his or her own unless the power of attorney specifically authorizes it. You will probably want to grant that authority if you appoint your spouse, mate or immediate family member as attorney-in-fact, and your finances are already thoroughly mixed together in joint bank or security accounts.

EXAMPLE: Jim and Eduardo have been living together for 25 years. They have a joint checking account and share all basic living expenses. Each names the other as his attorney-in-fact. To avoid any possible problems, Jim and Eduardo both include, in their powers of attorney, specific provisions that allow commingling of funds.

If You Named More Than One Attorney-in-Fact

Delegation becomes more complicated if you've named more than one attorney-in-fact.

Attorneys-in-Fact Who Must Act Jointly

If you require your attorneys-in-fact to act together in all that they do, it's a good idea to give them the power to delegate responsibilities. This is to avoid trouble in the event that one or more of your attorneys-in-fact becomes unable to act on your behalf. If this happens, the unavailable attorney-in-fact can use the Quicken WillMaker Plus delegation form to give his or her authority to the remaining attorneys-in-fact, temporarily or permanently. Your remaining attorneys-in-fact can use the delegation form to prove that they are permitted to act alone. If you don't grant the delegation power, an attorney-in-fact who will be unavailable will have to execute an affidavit—a sworn, notarized statement—that he or she cannot act for you. (If one of your attorneys-in-fact permanently resigns, he or she can sign a resignation form; the remaining attorneys-in-fact can use that form to prove their authority.)

In the unlikely event that all of your attorneys-in-fact will be temporarily unavailable, they can get together to choose a person to take over.

Attorneys-in-Fact Who May Act Separately

If you've authorized your attorneys-in-fact to act independently, allowing them to delegate tasks is probably not necessary or wise. The main reason for allowing delegation is to ensure that someone will always be on hand to take care of your finances. In your situation, if just one of your attorneys-in-fact is temporarily unable to act on your behalf, the others may simply act alone, without any special documents or fuss. And you can name up to two alternate attorneys-in-fact to take over if all of your attorneys-in-fact must step down. (See "Naming Alternates," above.)

Allowing delegation in your situation could, in fact, create much unnecessary confusion. Because your attorneys-in-fact may act independently, they could each delegate tasks to individuals that they choose—without consulting each other. When it comes to your finances, it's better not to open the door to that sort of chaos.

Different Powers for Alternate Attorneys-in-Fact

While you might want to give your first-choice attorney-in-fact full power to benefit personally from transactions conducted on your behalf, or to mix your funds with his or hers, you may not feel comfortable giving an alternate attorney-in-fact the same authority. This is often the case for those who name a spouse or partner as attorney-in-fact and then name alternates with whom they are not so close or financially entwined. Quicken WillMaker Plus allows you to specify whether an alternate attorney-in-fact should have the same power as your first choice, or whether you want to restrict the alternate's authority when it comes to personal benefit and mixing funds.

Paying Your Attorney-in-Fact

Quicken WillMaker Plus asks you whether or not you want to pay your attorney-in-fact. If you do, you can specify your payment arrangement.

In family situations, an attorney-in-fact is normally not paid if the duties won't be complicated or burdensome. If your property and finances are extensive, however, and the attorney-in-fact is likely to devote significant time and effort managing them, it seems fair to offer compensation for the work. Discuss and resolve this issue with the proposed attorney-in-fact before you finalize your document.

If you decide to pay your attorney-in-fact something for managing your financial affairs, Quicken WillMaker Plus allows you to set your own rate—for example, $10,000 per year, $10 per hour or some other figure on which you agree. Or, if you don't want to decide on an amount right now, you can allow your attorney-in-fact to determine a reasonable wage when he or she takes over. No single strategy works best for everyone. Choose the approach—and the amount—that feels right to you.

EXAMPLE: Frederick is quite wealthy. He owns and operates a successful chain of convenience stores in a large city. He also owns a house, several pieces of investment property and a wide array of stocks. When he is diagnosed with a life-threatening illness, he creates a durable power of attorney for finances appointing his close friend Barbara as his attorney-in-fact. Because he expects Barbara to watch over his business as well as tend to his other financial affairs, he feels it's appropriate to pay her for her services. Frederick and Barbara settle on a rate of $15,000 per year for her services.

EXAMPLE: Martin creates a durable power of attorney naming his brother, Andrew, as attorney-in-fact. Martin owns a complex investment portfolio, and the brothers agree that Andrew should be paid if he has to manage Martin's finances. They consider an hourly wage but decide not to be that specific now. In his durable power of attorney, Martin states that Andrew may pay himself "reasonable" fees for his services.

If You Named More Than One Attorney-in-Fact

If you named more than one attorney-in-fact and you want to pay them, the amount you enter—for example, $5,000 per year or $12 per hour—applies to each one. If you want to allow your attorneys-in-fact to determine a reasonable amount for their services, each is allowed to set his or her own fee.

Nominating a Conservator or Guardian

It is possible, though highly unlikely, that a court proceeding could be brought to invalidate or overrule your durable power of attorney for finances. (See "Invalidation," below.) If your document is invalidated for any reason, a judge will appoint someone to manage your finances. This person is usually called a "guardian of your estate" or "conservator of your estate."

You can use Quicken WillMaker Plus to nominate your attorney-in-fact to serve as your financial guardian or conservator, if a court must appoint someone to that position. The court will follow your recommendation unless there is a compelling reason not to do so—for example, if someone has proved that your attorney-in-fact is mishandling your money. (Again, this type of outcome is very rare.)

If you do not nominate your attorney-in-fact to serve as the guardian or conservator of your estate, your power of attorney document will not mention the issue at all. In this case, the court would appoint a guardian or conservator by determining what would be in your best interests, but would do so without input from you.

Making It Legal

After you've done the hard work of putting together a durable power of attorney, you must carry out some simple tasks to make sure the document is legally valid and will be accepted by the people with whom your attorney-in-fact may have to deal. This section explains what to do.

Before You Sign

Before you finalize your power of attorney, you may want to show it to the banks, brokers, insurers and other financial institutions you expect your attorney-in-fact to deal with on your behalf.

Discussing your plans with people at these institutions before it is final—and giving them a copy of the durable power of attorney, after you sign it, if you wish—can make your attorney-in-fact's job easier. An institution may require that you include specific language in your durable power of attorney, authorizing the attorney-in-fact to do certain things on your behalf. You may have to go along if you want cooperation later. If you don't want to change your durable power of attorney, find another bank that will accept the document as it is.

Signing and Notarizing

A durable power of attorney is a serious document, and to make it effective you must observe certain formalities when you sign the document.

In all states but California, you must sign your durable power of attorney in the presence of a notary public for your state. (In California, you may choose whether to have your document notarized or witnessed. See "For California Residents: Making the Choice," below.) In many states, notarization is required by law to make the durable power of attorney valid. But even where law doesn't require it, custom usually does. A durable power of attorney that isn't notarized may not be accepted by people with whom your attorney-in-fact tries to deal.

The notary public watches you sign the durable power of attorney and then signs it, too, and stamps it with an official seal. The notary will want proof of your identity, such as a driver's license that bears your photo and signature. The notary's fee is usually inexpensive—$5 to $10 in most places.

Finding a notary public shouldn't be a problem; many advertise in the yellow pages. Or check with your bank, which may provide notarizations as a service to customers. Real estate offices and title companies also have notaries.

If you are gravely ill, you'll need to find a notary who will come to your home or hospital room. To arrange it, call around to notaries listed in the yellow pages. Expect to pay a reasonable extra fee for a house call.

Witnessing

Most states don't require the durable power of attorney to be signed in front of witnesses. (See "States That Require Witnesses," below.) Nevertheless, it doesn't hurt to have a witness or two watch you sign, and sign the document themselves. Witnesses' signatures may make the power of attorney more acceptable to lawyers, banks, insurance companies and other entities the attorney-in-fact may have to deal with. Part of the reason is probably that some other legal documents with which people are more familiar—including wills and health care directives—must be witnessed to be legally valid.

Witnesses can serve another function, too. If you're worried that someone may challenge your capacity to execute a valid durable power of attorney later, it's prudent to have witnesses. If necessary, they can testify that in their judgment you knew what you were doing when you signed the document.

The witnesses must be present when you sign the document in front of the notary. Witnesses must be mentally competent adults, preferably ones who live nearby and will be easily available if necessary. The person who will serve as attorney-in-fact should not be a witness. In most states, the attorney-in-fact does not have to sign the durable power of attorney document. (There are, however, a few exceptions; see below.)

States That Require Witnesses

State	No. of Witnesses	Other Requirements
Arizona	1	Witness may not be your attorney-in-fact, the spouse or child of your attorney-in-fact or the notary public who acknowledges your document.
California	2	Witnesses are required only if your document is not notarized. The attorney-in-fact may not be a witness.
Connecticut	2	The attorney-in-fact may not be a witness.
District of Columbia	2	Witnesses are necessary only if your power of attorney is to be recorded. (See "Recording," below.) The attorney-in-fact may not be a witness.
Florida	2	The attorney-in-fact may not be a witness.
Georgia	2	The attorney-in-fact may not be a witness. In addition, one of your witnesses may not be your spouse or blood relative.
Illinois	1	The attorney-in-fact may not be a witness.
Michigan	2	Witnesses are necessary only if your power of attorney is to be recorded. (See "Recording," below.) The attorney-in-fact may not be a witness.
Oklahoma	2	Witnesses may not be your attorney-in-fact, or anyone who is related by blood or marriage to you or your attorney-in-fact.
Pennsylvania	2	Witnesses are necessary only if the power of attorney is finalized with a mark (rather than a signature) or if it is signed by another person on behalf of and at the direction of the principal. Witnesses may not be your attorney-in-fact or the person who signs the document for you, if you can't sign it yourself.
South Carolina	2	The attorney-in-fact may not be a witness.
Vermont	1	Witness may not be your attorney-in-fact, or the notary public who acknowledges your document.
Wisconsin	2	Witnesses may not be your attorney-in-fact, anyone related to you by blood, marriage or adoption or anyone entitled to a portion of your estate under your will.

For California Residents: Making the Choice

If you live in California, your durable power of attorney is valid if you have it notarized *or* if you sign it in front of two witnesses. Some people feel most comfortable using both methods together, but you are legally required to choose only one. Quicken WillMaker Plus lets you indicate how you want to finalize your document.

When choosing a method, there's one important consideration to keep in mind. If your power of attorney grants your attorney-in-fact authority over your real estate, you should absolutely have your document notarized. This is because you will have to put a copy of your document on file in the county recorder's office (see "Recording," below)—and in order to record your document, it must be notarized.

Obtaining the Attorney-in-Fact's Signature

In the vast majority of states, the attorney-in-fact does not have to agree in writing to accept the job of handling your finances. The exceptions to this rule are California, Georgia, Montana, New Hampshire, Pennsylvania, Vermont and Wisconsin.

California

In California, your attorney-in-fact must date and sign the durable power of attorney before taking action under the document. Ask the attorney-in-fact to read the Notice to Person Accepting the Appointment as Attorney-in-Fact at the beginning of the form. If your attorney-in-fact will begin using the power of attorney right away, he or she should date and sign the designated blanks at the end of the notice. If you've asked your attorney-in-fact not to use the document unless or until you become incapacitated, there's no need to obtain the signature now. Your attorney-in-fact can sign later, if it's ever necessary.

Georgia

In Georgia, your attorney-in-fact must sign the durable power of attorney document and complete an Acceptance of Appointment form. The acceptance form states that the attorney-in-fact understands the legal responsibilities involved in serving as an attorney-in-fact and agrees to carry out the duties to the best of his or her ability.

First, have your attorney-in-fact read and sign the acceptance form that prints out along with your power of attorney document. (After signing, the attorney-in-fact should attach the acceptance form to the original, finalized power of attorney document.) Then, ask the attorney-in-fact to sign the designated blank at the end of the power of attorney document itself, after your own signature.

If you've asked your attorney-in-fact not to use the document unless or until you become incapacitated, you don't have to obtain the attorney-in-fact's signatures right away. Keep the acceptance form together with the original power of attorney document. Your attorney-in-fact can complete it and sign the power of attorney later, if it ever becomes necessary to use the document.

Montana

If you live in Montana, we recommend that you ask your attorney-in-fact to sign the acceptance statement at the end of your durable power of attorney document. (You'll find it after the notary's acknowledgment.) It confirms that the attorney-in-fact willingly takes on the responsibilities of the job. Montana law states that having your attorney-in-fact sign this statement is optional, and that your attorney-in-fact becomes legally responsible simply by acting on your behalf. Nevertheless, the statement is included in Montana's official power of attorney form, and asking your attorney-in-fact to sign it will avoid any confusion about whether he or she understands the seriousness of the job.

New Hampshire and Pennsylvania

In New Hampshire or Pennsylvania, your attorney in fact must complete and sign an acknowledgment form. This simple form ensures that your attorney-in-fact understands the legal responsibilities involved in acting on your behalf. When you print out your durable power of attorney, it will be accompanied by an acknowledgment form for your attorney-in-fact to sign.

If your attorney-in-fact will begin using the power of attorney right away, give the acknowledgment form to him or her along with the finalized, original power of attorney document. Your attorney-in-fact must complete the form and attach it to the power of attorney before taking action under the document.

If you've asked your attorney-in-fact not to use the power of attorney unless or until you become incapacitated, keep the acknowledgment form together with the original power of attorney document. Your attorney-in-fact can complete it later, if it ever becomes necessary to use the power of attorney.

Wisconsin and Vermont

If you live in Wisconsin or Vermont, your attorney-in-fact must sign the power of attorney before taking action under the document. If your attorney-in-fact will begin using the power of attorney right away, ask him or her to print and then sign his or her full name in the designated blanks at the end of the form. If you've asked your attorney-in-fact not to use the document unless or until you become incapacitated, there's no need to obtain the attorney-in-fact's signature now. He or she can sign the document later, if it's ever necessary.

Recording

You may need to put a copy of your durable power of attorney on file in the land records office of the counties where you own real estate, called the county recorder's or land registry office in most states. This is called recording, or registering in some states.

Mandatory Recording

Just two states, North Carolina and South Carolina, require you to record a power of attorney for it to be durable—that is, for it to remain in effect if you become incapacitated.

In other states, you must record the power of attorney if it gives your attorney-in-fact authority over your real estate. Essentially, this means you must record the document if you granted the real estate power. In this case, if you don't record the document, your attorney-in-fact won't be able to sell, mortgage or transfer your real estate.

Recording makes it clear to all interested parties that the attorney-in-fact has power over the property. County land records are checked whenever real estate changes hands or is mortgaged; if your attorney-in-fact attempts to sell or mortgage your real estate, there must be something in the records that proves he or she has authority to do so.

There is no time limit on when you must record a durable power of attorney. So if you've created a document that won't be used unless and until you become incapacitated, you may not want to record it immediately. Your attorney-in-fact can always record the document later, if he or she ever needs to use it.

Even if recording is not legally required, you can do so anyway; officials in some financial institutions may be reassured later on by seeing that you took that step.

Note for North Carolina Readers

In your state, a durable power of attorney must be:

- recorded with the Register of Deeds, and
- filed with the clerk of the Superior Court within 30 days after recording, unless the durable power of attorney waives the requirement that the attorney-in-fact file inventories and accountings with the court. Your Quicken WillMaker Plus power of attorney form waives this filing requirement.

Note for Illinois, Kentucky and Minnesota Readers

If you live in Illinois, Kentucky or Minnesota, when you review your power of attorney document, you'll notice a "preparation statement" at the very end of it. The preparation statement is a simple listing of the name and address of the person who prepared the document. Quicken WillMaker Plus adds this statement because, in these three states, you cannot record your document without it.

In most cases, the name of the principal and the name of the person who prepared the document will be the same: your own. Occasionally, however, someone may use Quicken WillMaker Plus to prepare a form for another person—an ailing relative, for example. In that case, the name and address of the person who stepped in to help should appear in the preparation statement.

Where to Record

In most states, each county has its own office for a recorder or registry of deeds. If you're recording to give the attorney-in-fact authority over real estate, take the durable power of attorney to the office in the county where the real estate is located. If you want your attorney-in-fact to have authority over more than one parcel of real estate, record the power of attorney in each county where you own property. If you're recording for any other reason, take the document to the office in the county where you live.

How to Record

Recording a document shouldn't be complicated, though some counties can be quite fussy about their rules (See below.) You may even be able to record your document by mail, but it's safer to go in person. Typically, the clerk makes a copy for the public records. It will be assigned a reference number, often in terms of books and pages—for example, "Book 14, Page 1932 of the Contra Costa County, California, records." In most places, it costs just a few dollars per page to record a document.

> **CAUTION**
> **Check your county's recording procedures before you finalize your document.** Some counties will ask you to meet very particular requirements before they will put your power of attorney on file. Or, if you don't adhere to their rules, they will charge you an extra fee for filing the document.

For example, in some counties you may be required to file an original document, rather than a photocopy, with the land records office. In this case, you'll need to make a second original, being sure to have it signed, notarized and witnessed (if necessary), just like the first.

And some counties require a margin of a certain number of inches at the top of the first page of a power of attorney. This is where they put the filing stamp when you record the document. Local customs vary widely here; some counties will accept a standard one-inch margin while others ask for a margin of two, three or even four inches. When you make your document, Quicken WillMaker Plus lets you set the correct number of inches for the top margin of the first page.

To avoid hassles and extra expenses, you should call the land record's office before you finalize your power of attorney to make sure you're prepared to meet any special requirements for putting it on file.

What to Do With the Signed Document

Your attorney-in-fact will need the original power of attorney document, signed and notarized, to act on your behalf. So, if you want your attorney-in-fact to start using the document right away, give the original document to the attorney-in-fact.

If you named more than one attorney-in-fact, give the original document to one of them. Between them, they will have to work out the best way to prove their authority. For example, they may decide to visit some financial institutions or government offices together to establish themselves as your attorneys-in-fact. Or they may need to take turns with the document. Some agencies, such as the IRS, will accept a copy of the document, rather than the original: Such flexible policies make things easier on multiple attorneys-in-fact who need to share the original document.

Making and Distributing Copies

If you wish, you can give copies of your durable power to the people your attorney-in-fact will need to deal with—in banks or government offices, for example. If the durable power is in their records, it may eliminate hassles for your attorney-in-fact later because they will be familiar with the document and

What to Do With the Additional Documents

Quicken WillMaker Plus prints out several additional documents along with your durable power of attorney form. These are discussed throughout the chapter, but here is a quick summary of these documents and what you should do with them.

Information for an Attorney-in-Fact

This sheet is intended to help your attorney-in-fact understand the job. It discusses the attorney-in-fact's duties and responsibilities, including the duty to manage your property honestly and prudently and to keep accurate records. You should give a copy to the person you name in your document and take some time to talk together about the responsibilities involved.

Delegation of Authority

If you allow your attorney-in-fact to delegate tasks to others, he or she may want to use Quicken WillMaker Plus's Delegation of Authority form. Give a copy to your attorney-in-fact. Or, if your power of attorney won't be used right away, keep the form with your power of attorney document so your attorney-in-fact will have easy access to it later.

Resignation of Attorney-in-Fact

Your attorney-in-fact can use the Resignation of Attorney-in-Fact form to resign from the job. He or she should fill out the form and send it to the alternate attorney-in-fact. If you name more than one attorney-in-fact, the one who resigns may send the form to the others. Give a copy of this form to your attorney-in-fact along with your power of attorney document. Or, if your power of attorney won't be used right away, keep the forms together in a safe place known by your attorney-in-fact; he or she can obtain them if it becomes necessary.

Notice of Revocation of Durable Power of Attorney

If you ever want to revoke your power of attorney, prepare and sign a Notice of Revocation. Keep a copy of this form on file in case you need it later.

Notice of Revocation of Recorded Power of Attorney

If you record your power of attorney, then change your mind and want to cancel the document, you must also record a Notice of Revocation. To do this, you can use Quicken WillMaker Plus's Notice of Revocation of Recorded Power of Attorney form. Keep a blank copy on file for future use.

expecting your attorney-in-fact to take action under it.

If your power of attorney won't be used unless and until you become incapacitated, however, it may seem premature to contact people and institutions about a document that may never go into effect. It's up to you.

Be sure to keep a list of everyone to whom you give a copy. If you later revoke your durable power of attorney, notify each institution of the revocation. (See "Revoking Your Durable Power of Attorney," below.)

Keeping Your Document Up to Date

If you make a power of attorney that your attorney-in-fact won't use unless and until you become incapacitated, it's a good idea to revoke it and create a new one every five to seven years, especially if your circumstances have changed significantly. A durable power of attorney never expires, but if the document was signed many years before it is used, the attorney-in-fact may have more difficulty getting banks, insurance companies or people in government agencies to accept it.

Revoking Your Durable Power of Attorney

After you make a power of attorney, you can revoke it at any time, as long as you are of sound mind. But to make the revocation legally effective, you must carefully follow all the procedures set out in this section.

If You Move to Another State

If you move to another state, it's best to revoke your old durable power of attorney as described below and create a new one, complying with all regulations of your new state. This is true even though your old power of attorney may be acceptable under your new state's laws.

If you don't make a new document, your attorney-in-fact may run into problems that are more practical than legal. For example, the document may need to be recorded with the local land records office in the new state. If the document does not meet certain requirements, the recorder's office in the new state may not accept it. Making a new document will ensure that things will go smoothly for your attorney-in-fact.

Who Can Revoke

Only you, or someone a court appoints to act for you, can revoke your power of attorney.

When You Can Revoke

You can revoke your durable power of attorney as long as you are of sound mind and physically able to do so. The sound mind requirement is not difficult to satisfy. If someone challenged the revocation, a court would look only at whether or not you understood the consequences of signing the revocation. (The competency requirement is the same as that required to create a valid power of attorney in the first place; see "Possible Challenges to Your Document," below.)

SEE AN EXPERT

If you and your attorney-in-fact can't agree. An attorney-in-fact who refuses to accept a revocation can create serious problems. If you get into such a dispute with your attorney-in-fact, consult a lawyer. (See Chapter 25.)

If a Conservator or Guardian Is Appointed

If your attorney-in-fact is satisfactorily handling your financial affairs while you can't, it's very unlikely that a court will need to appoint a conservator for you. And if it does become necessary, you can use your document to name your attorney-in-fact to the post. (See "Nominating a Conservator or Guardian," above.)

If, however, you or a family member objected to the attorney-in-fact's actions, a court might appoint someone else as conservator. In a few states, appointment of a conservator automatically revokes a durable power of attorney. In that case, the conservator would become solely responsible for your property and financial matters.

In many states, the conservator would have the legal authority to revoke your durable power of attorney. Someone appointed to take physical care of you—usually called a guardian or guardian of the person—not your property, may also, depending on state law, have the power to revoke a financial power of attorney.

When to Revoke

If you've prepared a power of attorney that won't be used unless you're incapacitated, years may elapse between the time you sign the durable power of attorney and when it is put to use. During that interval—or even after your attorney-in-fact starts using the document, as long as you are mentally competent—you may decide you need to revoke the durable power of attorney. Here are the most common situations in which you should revoke a power of attorney and start over.

Changing the Terms

There is no accepted way to amend a power of attorney. If you want to change or amend a durable power of attorney, the safe course is to revoke the existing document and prepare a new one. Don't go back and modify your old document with pen, typewriter or correction fluid—you could throw doubt on the authenticity of the whole thing.

> **EXAMPLE:** Tom signed a durable power of attorney several years ago. Now he is in declining health and wants to add to the authority he gave his attorney-in-fact, Sarah, giving her the power to sell his real estate if necessary. Tom should revoke his old durable power of attorney and create a new one, granting the additional authority.

Similarly, you should revoke your durable power of attorney if you change your mind about your choice of attorney-in-fact. If you create a durable power of attorney that won't be used until later, the person you named to be your attorney-in-fact may become unavailable before he or she is needed. Or you may simply change your mind. If that's the case, you can revoke the durable power of attorney before it is ever used.

Moving to Another State

If you move to a different state, your attorney-in-fact may run into some trouble getting others to accept the validity of a power of attorney signed in your old state. It's best to revoke your power of attorney and prepare a new one.

Losing the Document

If you lose your signed power of attorney document, it's wise to formally revoke it, destroy any copies and create a new one. Very few people are likely to accept your attorney-in-fact's authority if they can't look at the document granting the authority. By officially revoking the lost version, you reduce chances that the old power of attorney might someday resurface and confuse matters.

Marrying or Divorcing

If you get married after signing a durable power of attorney, you'll probably want to designate your new spouse to be your attorney-in-fact, if he or she wasn't the person you named originally.

If you name your spouse as your attorney-in-fact and later divorce, you will probably want to revoke the power of attorney and

create a new one, naming someone else as the attorney-in-fact.

In a number of states, the designation is automatically ended if you divorce the attorney-in-fact. In that case, any alternate you named would serve as attorney-in-fact. You still may want to create a new power of attorney—one that doesn't mention your former spouse and lets you name another alternate attorney-in-fact.

Revoking Your Document

There are two ways to revoke your power of attorney. You can:

- prepare and sign a document called a Notice of Revocation, or
- destroy all existing copies of the document.

The first method is always preferable, because it creates proof that you really revoked the power of attorney.

Some states may allow you to revoke your power of attorney simply by preparing a new one. It's still advisable, however, to prepare a separate Notice of Revocation and notify everyone who needs to know about the revocation.

Preparing a Notice of Revocation

The purpose of a Notice of Revocation is to notify the attorney-in-fact and others that you have revoked the durable power of attorney.

Quicken WillMaker Plus prints out two kinds of Notice of Revocation forms for you to use. If you didn't record your durable power of attorney in the county land records office, choose the Notice of Revocation for an unrecorded document. If you did record the original durable power of attorney, you must also record the revocation; choose the Notice of Revocation for a recorded document.

Signing and Notarizing the Document

You must sign and date the Notice of Revocation. It need not be witnessed, but witnessing may be a prudent idea—especially if you have reason to believe that someone might later raise questions regarding your mental competence to execute the revocation. If you want witnesses' signatures, Quicken WillMaker Plus offers that option. Choose the appropriate revocation document and indicate that you will have it witnessed.

Sign the Notice of Revocation in front of a notary public. (For more on notarization, see "Making It Legal," above.)

Recording the Document

If you recorded the original durable power of attorney at your local recorder of deeds office, you must also record the revocation.

But even if the original durable power of attorney was not recorded, you can record a revocation if you fear that the former attorney-in-fact might try to act without authorization. If the revocation is part of the public records, people who check those records in dealing with the real estate later will know that the former attorney-in-fact is no longer authorized to act on your behalf.

Note for North Carolina Readers

When you register the revocation in the Register of Deeds Office, it must be accompanied by a document showing that a copy of the revocation notice has been delivered to—or served on—the former attorney-in-fact. This document is called a proof of service.

The revocation must be served on the attorney-in-fact by the county sheriff or someone else authorized by law to serve legal papers.

Notifying Others

It's not enough to sign a revocation, or even to record it, for it to take effect; there's one more crucial step. You must notify the former attorney-in-fact and all institutions and people who have dealt or might deal with the former attorney-in-fact. Each of them must receive a copy of the Notice of Revocation.

If you don't give this written notification, people or institutions who don't know the durable power of attorney has been revoked might still enter into transactions with the former attorney-in-fact. If they do this in good faith, they are legally protected. You may well be held legally liable for the acts of your attorney-in-fact, even though you have revoked his or her authority. In other words, once you create a durable power of attorney, the legal burden is on you to be sure everyone knows you have revoked it.

Who Needs to Know?

When you're ready to send out revocation notices, try to think of everyone with whom the attorney-in-fact has had, or may have, dealings. These may include:

- banks
- mortgage companies
- title companies
- stockbrokers
- insurance companies
- Social Security offices
- Medicare or Medicaid offices
- military or civil service offices
- the IRS
- pension fund administrators
- post offices
- hospitals
- doctors
- schools
- relatives
- business partners
- landlords
- lawyers
- accountants
- real estate agents, and
- maintenance and repair people.

EXAMPLE: Before Michael undergoes a serious operation, he makes a durable power of attorney. After his convalescence, Michael revokes the power of attorney in writing. He sends a copy of the revocation to Colette, his attorney-in-fact, but neglects to send a copy to his bank. Colette, fraudulently acting as Michael's attorney-in-fact, removes money from Michael's accounts and spends it. The bank isn't responsible to Michael for his loss.

When the Power of Attorney Ends

A durable power of attorney for finances is valid until you revoke it, you die or there is no one to serve as your attorney-in-fact. A court can also invalidate a power of attorney, but that happens very rarely.

Revocation

As long as you are mentally competent, you can revoke a power of attorney for finances at any time, whether or not it has taken effect. All you need to do is fill out a simple form, sign it in front of a notary public and give copies to the attorney-in-fact and to people or institutions with whom the attorney-in-fact has been dealing. (See "Revoking Your Durable Power of Attorney," above.) You can use Quicken WillMaker Plus to print out a revocation form.

EXAMPLE: Susan prepares a durable power of attorney naming her closest friend, Tina, as her attorney-in-fact. Three years later, they have a bitter fight. Susan prepares a one-page document that revokes the durable power of attorney and gives Tina a copy. She destroys the old document and then prepares a new one, naming her sister Joan as her attorney-in-fact.

Invalidation

Even if you sign a durable power of attorney for finances, if you become incapacitated there is a remote possibility that a disgruntled relative could ask a court to appoint a conservator to manage your financial affairs.

It's rare, but a power of attorney could be ruled invalid if a judge concludes that you were not mentally competent when you signed the durable power of attorney, or that you were the victim of fraud or undue influence. The power of attorney could also be invalidated for a technical error, such as the failure to sign your document in front of witnesses if your state requires it. If that happens, the judge could appoint a conservator to take over management of your property.

In most states, if a court appoints a conservator, the attorney-in-fact becomes accountable to the conservator—not just to you—and the conservator has the power to revoke your durable power of attorney if he or she doesn't approve of the way your attorney-in-fact is handling your affairs. In a few states, however, your durable power of attorney is automatically revoked, and the conservator assumes responsibility for your finances and property.

Divorce

In a handful of states (see "Choosing Your Attorney-in-Fact," above), if your spouse is your attorney-in-fact and you divorce, your ex-spouse's authority is immediately terminated. If you named an alternate attorney-in-fact in your power of attorney, that person takes over as attorney-in-fact. If you didn't name an alternate, your power of attorney ends.

In any state, however, others may question the validity of a document created before a divorce that names the ex-spouse as attorney-in-fact. For this reason, if you get divorced you should revoke your durable power of attorney and make a new one.

No Attorney-in-Fact Is Available

A durable power of attorney must end if there's no one to serve as the attorney-in-fact. To avoid this, Quicken WillMaker Plus lets you name up to two alternate attorneys-in-fact, so someone will be available to serve if your first choice can't do the task.

For a bit of extra insurance, you can also allow the alternate attorney-in-fact to delegate his or her duties to someone else. (See "Delegating Powers," above.)

Death

A durable power of attorney ends when the principal dies. In most states, however, if the attorney-in-fact doesn't know of your death and continues to act on your behalf, his or her actions are still valid.

If you want your attorney-in-fact to have any authority over winding up your affairs after your death, grant that authority in your will—and in your living trust, if you make one. (See Chapter 8 for information about executors; see Chapter 13 for more on living trusts.)

Possible Challenges to Your Document

A common fear is that your durable power of attorney for finances will not be accepted by those around you. While rare, challenges are sometimes raised by people who feel you were not of sound mind when you signed the document or who fear that the document is not legally valid.

Your Mental State

You must be of sound mind when you create your durable power of attorney for finances. When you sign the document, no one makes a determination about your mental state. The issue will come up only if someone goes to court and challenges the durable power of attorney, claiming that you weren't mentally competent when you signed it. That kind of lawsuit is very rare.

Even in the highly unlikely event of a court hearing, the competency requirement is not difficult to satisfy. If you understood what you were doing when you signed your durable power of attorney, that's enough. To make this determination, a judge would probably question any witnesses who watched you sign the document and others who knew you well at the time. There would be no general inquiry into your life. It wouldn't matter, for example, that you were occasionally forgetful or absentminded around the time when you signed your power of attorney document.

The Document's Validity

It's reasonable for someone to want to make sure that your durable power of attorney is still valid and hasn't been changed or revoked. To reassure other people, your attorney-in-fact can show that person the power of attorney document. To lay any fears to rest, it clearly states that any person who receives a copy of the document may accept it without the risk of legal liability—unless he or she knows that the document has been revoked.

Laws in most states also protect people who rely on apparently valid powers of attorney. For example, many states have laws stating that a written, signed power of attorney is presumed valid, and a third party may rely on it.

As a last resort, the attorney-in-fact can sign a sworn statement or affidavit in front of a notary public, stating that as far as he or she knows, the durable power of attorney has not been revoked and that you are still alive. Most states have laws that make such a statement conclusive proof that the durable power of attorney is in fact still valid.

The Powers Granted

Any other person who relies on a durable power of attorney must be sure that the attorney-in-fact has the power he or she claims to have. That means the person must examine the document, to see what power it grants.

The Quicken WillMaker Plus power of attorney document is very specific about the attorney-in-fact's powers. For example, if you

Heading Off Problems

If you think someone is likely to go to court and challenge the legitimacy of your durable power of attorney or claim that you were coerced into signing it, you can take several steps to head off problems:

- **See a lawyer.** An experienced estate planning lawyer can answer questions about your durable power of attorney and about your other estate planning documents as well. For example, you may also be expecting challenges to your will, a trust or health care wishes. You can talk with a lawyer about all of these issues. The point is to have the lawyer put your fears to rest by answering your questions and reviewing or modifying your documents. He or she can help to ensure that your estate plan will hold up under the challenges of your stubborn relatives. Your attorney can also testify about your mental competency, should the need arise.

- **Sign your document in front of witnesses.** You can sign your document in front of witnesses, even if your state does not require it. (See "Making It Legal," above.) After watching you sign, the witnesses themselves sign a statement that you appeared to know what you were signing and that you signed voluntarily. If some one later challenges your competency, these witness statements will be strong evidence that you were of sound mind at the time you signed your document.

- **Get a doctor's statement.** You may also want to get a doctor's statement around the time you sign your durable power of attorney. The doctor should write, date and sign a short statement saying that he or she has seen you recently and believes you to be mentally competent. You can attach this statement to your power of attorney document. Then, if necessary, your attorney-in-fact can produce the statement as evidence that you were of sound mind when you signed your power of attorney.

- **Make a videotape.** You can also videotape a statement of your intent to make and sign the durable power of attorney. Be warned, however, that using a videotape may work against you. The person challenging your power of attorney will want to use any visible quirks of behavior or language as evidence that you were not in fact competent when you made your document. If you do make a videotape, keep it with your power of attorney document.

give your attorney-in-fact authority over your banking transactions, the document expressly states that the attorney-in-fact is empowered to write checks on your behalf. Your attorney-in-fact can point to the paragraph that grants that authority, so a doubting bank official can read it in black and white.

An attorney-in-fact who runs into resistance should seek, politely but insistently, someone higher up in the bureaucracy.

Health Care Directives

Every adult can benefit from making health care directives—that is, documents in which you express your health care wishes and appoint a person to make decisions for you if, someday, you can no longer speak for yourself.

If you're older or in ill health, you surely understand why these documents are important. But if you're younger—perhaps using this program to help prepare health care documents for a loved one—consider making documents for yourself now, even if you don't think it's necessary.

While it's true that the elderly and the seriously ill should make health care directives to smooth the way for decision making at the end of life, we tend to avoid another, disturbing truth: Younger, healthy adults should also have health care directives, because an incapacitating accident or unexpected illness can occur at any time. In fact, if you look at the painful stories that make headlines (see "A Little Bit of History," below), you'll quickly notice that the bitterest family fights over end-of-life health care don't happen when a patient is very old or has a long illness. The worst disputes arise when tragedy strikes a younger adult who never clearly expressed any wishes about medical treatment.

Here, we walk you through the process of making your own customized health care directives. (If you're looking for a living will or durable power of attorney for health care, you're in the right place. They are both types of health care directives.)

It won't take long to make your preferences known: You can most likely prepare your documents in less than an hour. That hour might save your family days, months or even years of confusion and grief.

A Little Bit of History

Your right to direct your own health care is now well established. But that wasn't always the case. Just a few decades ago, heart-wrenching legal battles were fought to win permission to create a document stating that life-prolonging treatments should be terminated—or continued—at the end of life.

Landmark cases involving Karen Ann Quinlan and Nancy Cruzan—two young women who became brain damaged and unable to communicate their wishes—opened the way to laws supporting health care documents. Now, every state has a law that permits you to express your health care wishes and requires medical personnel to follow those wishes—or transfer you to the care of someone else who will do so.

What Happens If You Don't Make Documents

If you do not prepare health care documents, state law tells your doctors what to do. In some states, they may decide what kind of medical care you will receive. Most states, however, require doctors to consult your spouse, registered domestic partner or an immediate relative. The person entitled to make decisions on your behalf is called your "surrogate." A few states allow a "close friend" to act as surrogate.

If there is a dispute about who should be your surrogate, it may have to be resolved in court.

Whether required by law or not, if there is a question about whether surgery or some other serious procedure is authorized, doctors will usually turn for guidance to a close relative—spouse, registered domestic partner, parent, child. Friends and unmarried partners, although they may be most familiar with your wishes for your medical treatment, are rarely consulted, or—worse still—are sometimes purposefully left out of the decision-making process.

Problems arise when loved ones and family members disagree about what treatment is proper and everyone takes sides, claiming they want what is best for the patient. Battles over medical care may even end up in court, especially now that some religious organizations finance lawsuits to block the removal of feeding tubes from permanently unconscious patients. In court, a judge, who usually has little medical knowledge and no familiarity with the patient, must decide the course of treatment. Such battles—which are costly, time-consuming and painful to those involved—are unnecessary if you have the care and foresight to prepare a formal document to express your wishes for your health care.

What You Can Do With This Program

This program allows you to create comprehensive health care documents that are valid for your state. With these documents, you can clearly express your preferences for medical care if you become unable to communicate your wishes. Specifically, you can:

- appoint a trusted person, called your "health care agent" in most states, to oversee your medical care if you become unable to speak for yourself
- name the doctor you'd like to supervise your care
- specify whether or not you want your life prolonged with medical treatments and procedures
- identify specific medical treatments and procedures that you want provided or withheld, and
- provide instructions for donating your organs, tissues or body after death.

You can also state any general wishes you have about your care, such as where you would like to be cared for (for example, in a particular hospice facility or at home, if possible) or any special directions that may affect your comfort or awareness (for instance, whether you would like to receive full doses of pain medication even if it makes you unaware of the presence of family and friends).

TIP

Keep track of other health care information. In addition to your health care directives, caregivers need other medical information as well. You can use Quicken WillMaker Plus to make an Information for Caregivers and Survivors form to help with this task. Among other details, the form includes the names of and contact information for your health care providers and information about your insurance coverage. This important information will be a great help to those who take care of you in the event of your incapacity. To find out more, click "Document List" and select Information for Caregivers and Survivors from the list.

The Basics of Health Care Directives

This section explains what you need to know about health care directives before you start making yours, including:

- the different types of health care directives you may need to make
- what your state's documents are called
- who is legally permitted to make health care directives
- how to help someone else make health care directives
- when the documents take effect, and
- how to make sure your documents cover all the issues that are important to you.

Types of Health Care Directives

A health care directive is any document in which you set out instructions or wishes for your medical care. Most states provide two basic documents for this purpose:

- A durable power of attorney for health care, in which you name someone you trust to oversee your health care and make medical decisions should you become unable to do so.
- A living will, in which you spell out any wishes about the types of care you do or do not wish to receive if you are unable to speak for yourself. Your doctors and the person you name as your agent in your durable power of attorney for health care must do their best to follow any instructions you leave.

The exact names of these documents vary from state to state, and some states combine the two into a single form, usually called an "advance health care directive." The table below shows how your state handles it.

Who Can Make Health Care Directives

To make a health care directive, you must be able to understand what the document means, what it contains and how it works. People with physical disabilities may make valid health care documents; they can direct another to sign for them if they are unable to do so. (See the next section for more information on helping others with documents.)

In most states, you must be 18 years old to make a valid document directing your health care. (In Alabama, you must be 19. In Nebraska, you must be 19 or married.)

Helping Someone Else Make Health Care Directives

If the person you want to help is of sound mind and wants to write down health care wishes, your job should not be difficult. You can use this program to explain the process, answer questions and help prepare and finalize the right documents.

But if you think someone who needs help will resist your efforts, you need to carefully consider the way you approach the subject.

Explaining why the documents are important. If you're concerned about a loved one who is becoming mentally or physically frail, you might begin by simply talking about the benefits of the documents. Some people may be moved by a request to plan ahead because it will relieve anxiety and pressure for you and other caretakers. Others may be more inclined to make health care documents if

What Your Documents Are Called

State	Number of Documents	Living Will	Durable Power of Attorney for Health Care
Alabama	1	Advance Directive for Health Care	
Alaska	1	Advance Health Care Directive	
Arizona	2	Living Will	Health Care Power of Attorney
Arkansas	2	Declaration	Durable Power of Attorney for Health Care
California	1	Advance Health Care Directive	
Colorado	2	Declaration as to Medical or Surgical Treatment	Durable Power of Attorney for Health Care
Connecticut	1 or 2	Document Concerning Health Care and Withholding or Withdrawal of Life Support Systems	Appointment of Health Care Representative
		If you name a health care agent and leave health care instructions, your wishes will be combined into a single form called Health Care Instructions and Appointment of Health Care Representative.	
Delaware	1	Advance Health Care Directive	
Dist. of Col.	2	Declaration	Durable Power of Attorney for Health Care
Florida	2	Living Will	Designation of Health Care Surrogate
Georgia	1	Advance Directive for Health Care	
Hawaii	1	Advance Health Care Directive	
Idaho	1	Living Will and Durable Power of Attorney for Health Care	
Illinois	1 or 2	Declaration	Durable Power of Attorney for Health Care
		If you name a health care agent and leave health care instructions, your wishes will be combined into a single Durable Power of Attorney for Health Care form.	
Indiana	2	Living Will Declaration	Durable Power of Attorney for Health Care and Appointment of Health Care Representative
Iowa	2	Declaration	Durable Power of Attorney for Health Care
Kansas	2	Declaration	Durable Power of Attorney for Health Care Decisions
Kentucky	1	Advance Directive	
Maine	1	Advance Health Care Directive	
Maryland	1	Advance Directive	
Massachusetts	2	Document Directing Health Care	Health Care Proxy
Michigan	2	Document Directing Health Care	Patient Advocate Designation
Minnesota	1	Health Care Directive	

What Your Documents Are Called (cont'd)

State	Number of Documents	Living Will	Durable Power of Attorney for Health Care
Mississippi	1	Advance Health Care Directive	
Missouri	2	Declaration	Durable Power of Attorney for Health Care
Montana	2	Declaration	Durable Power of Attorney for Health Care
Nebraska	2	Declaration	Durable Power of Attorney for Health Care
Nevada	2	Declaration	Durable Power of Attorney for Health Care Decisions
New Hampshire	1	Advance Directive	
New Jersey	1 or 2	Instruction Directive	Proxy Directive
		If you name a health care agent and leave health care instructions, your wishes will be combined into a single form called a Combined Advance Directive for Health Care.	
New Mexico	1	Advance Health Care Directive	
New York	2	Document Directing Health Care	Health Care Proxy
North Carolina	2	Advance Directive	Health Care Power of Attorney
North Dakota	1	Health Care Directive	
Ohio	2	Declaration	Durable Power of Attorney for Health Care
Oklahoma	1	Advance Directive for Health Care	
Oregon	1	Advance Directive	
Pennsylvania	2	Living Will	Health Care Power of Attorney
Rhode Island	2	Declaration	Durable Power of Attorney for Health Care
South Carolina	1 or 2	Declaration	Health Care Power of Attorney
		If you name a health care agent and leave health care instructions, your wishes will be combined into a single Health Care Power of Attorney form.	
South Dakota	2	Living Will Declaration	Durable Power of Attorney for Health Care
Tennessee	1	Advance Health Care Directive	
Texas	2	Directive to Physicians and Family or Surrogates	Medical Power of Attorney
Utah	1	Advance Health Care Directive	
Vermont	1	Advance Directive	
Virginia	1	Advance Medical Directive	
Washington	2	Health Care Directive	Durable Power of Attorney for Health Care
West Virginia	2	Living Will	Medical Power of Attorney
Wisconsin	2	Declaration to Physicians	Power of Attorney for Health Care
Wyoming	1	Advance Health Care Directive	

they understand that doing so is the best way for them to stay in control and get the kind of medical care they want. (You can emphasize that whomever they name to make decisions for them must follow their instructions in every possible way.)

Helping someone who is becoming forgetful or absentminded. Of course, when you talk with someone who's struggling with increasing mental frailty, you will have to be sensitive to feelings about deteriorating mental abilities. Frustration, shame or a sense of loss may well make your loved one more resistant to your help. You may want to underscore that planning is a good thing for anybody— including the young and healthy—just in case it's necessary someday.

Ultimately, however, you should never try to force someone to follow a certain course because you think it's best. If you strong-arm someone whose mental abilities are waning, and the documents you make are later challenged in court, you could find yourself in a lot of legal trouble.

Signing for someone with physical disabilities. You could also get into big trouble if you fake signatures on any legal documents. Even if the person you're helping asks you to sign his or her name, don't do it.

Someone who is physically unable to sign health care documents can direct you to sign them, but you must carefully follow the instructions in "Making It Legal," below.

When Your Documents Take Effect

Your health care documents will take effect only if someday you are so ill or injured that you cannot make and express health care decisions. Generally, this means that:

- You can't understand the nature and consequences of the health care options available to you (including significant benefits, risks and alternatives), and
- You are unable to communicate your own wishes for care, either orally, in writing or through gestures.

If there is some question about your ability to understand your treatment choices or communicate clearly, your doctor (with the input of your health care agent or close relatives) will decide whether it is time for your health care directives to become operative.

Of course, in order for any of this to happen, medical personnel must know about your documents. In most instances, you can ensure that your directives become part of your medical record when you are admitted to a hospital or other care facility. But your need for care could arise unexpectedly or while you are away from home, so it's a good idea to give copies of your documents to several people. (See "Making and Distributing Copies," below.)

What Your Documents Can Cover

Each state may say what makes a health care document legal. Many states list what you can include in your documents and define specific medical terms—and all states set out rules for having your document witnessed or notarized.

If your state law demands a specific form or precise language, the health care documents you produce with this program will contain it. However, in some instances, your documents may go beyond what is addressed by your state law. For example, your state's law may be silent on whether individuals can direct their own health care if they become permanently unconscious, or your state's law may specifically restrict you from removing life support if you are pregnant, or your state's form may not provide a place for you to address your wishes about donating your organs after death. However, if you want to address these issues when using this program, you may do so.

The U.S. Supreme Court has ruled that the U.S. Constitution guarantees your right to direct your own health care. A state law that restricts your rights contradicts this ruling. The Court also ruled that if an individual has left "clear and convincing evidence" of medical wishes, those wishes should be followed. By far the best way to make your wishes known is to leave detailed written instructions.

If your choices are contrary to what your state law allows, your health care directive will state that your instructions should be respected anyway, and followed in keeping with your constitutional right to direct your own health care.

On the off chance that anyone later challenges your health care directive in a court because it goes beyond your state's law, there is an additional legal failsafe. Your document contains a paragraph that allows the rest of your health care directive to be enforced as written even if any one of the directions you leave is found to be legally invalid.

Entering Your Personal Information

To begin making your health care documents, we ask you to provide some basic identifying information about yourself. (We assume here that you are making documents for yourself. If that is not the case, enter the information for the person you are helping.)

Your State

You are asked to specify the state of your legal residence, sometimes called a domicile. This is the state where you make your home now and for the indefinite future. This information is essential, because the program produces health care directives that are geared to the laws of the state you select. (If you travel to another state, your document will be honored in that state as long as it meets the requirements of the state where you live.)

If you divide up the year living in two or more states, you may not be sure which state is your legal residence. To decide, choose the state where you are the most rooted—that is, the state in which you:

- are registered to vote
- register your car
- own valuable property—especially property with a title document, such as a house
- have checking, savings and investment accounts, or
- maintain a business.

> **CAUTION**
>
> **Don't make documents for more than one state.** If you regularly spend time in more than one state, you might be tempted to make health care documents for each—but you shouldn't. The reason is simple: Creating a new health care document almost always revokes an older one. In almost all cases, you cannot have two documents simultaneously in force. Besides, it is not necessary. As mentioned above, all states honor health care directives made in other states as long as they are valid in the state where they were made. You should make and sign your directive in the state in which you legally reside.

Your Name

Enter your name in the same form that you use on other formal documents, such as your driver's license or bank accounts. If you customarily use more than one name for official purposes, list all of them, separated by aka ("also known as").

There is room for you to list several names. But use your common sense. For purposes of your health care directive, your name is needed to identify you and to match you with your medical records. Be sure to include any names you have used on other medical documents such as prior hospital or doctor records.

Your Gender

Many states have restrictions or special considerations that may apply if a woman's health care directive takes effect while she is pregnant. If you are a woman, it may be necessary for you to answer a few more questions to address this possibility. (See "How Pregnancy May Affect Your Wishes," below.)

We also use information about your gender to make your documents and instructions grammatically elegant and accurate, avoiding the cumbersome use of "he or she" and "his or her."

Additional Information

A few states ask you to provide more biographical information, such as your address or birthdate. If your state does, we will ask you for the additional information, and your documents will contain it, too.

Naming Your Primary Physician

Next, you can name a doctor to serve as your primary physician. This is the doctor who will:

- oversee your medical care, and
- make legally significant determinations regarding your mental capacity and the state of your health, if necessary.

You will probably want to name a primary physician if you already have an established relationship with a doctor you trust and with whom you have discussed—or will discuss—your health care wishes. (See "Talking to Your Doctor," below.)

If you don't have an established relationship with a doctor, you can skip to the next part of the program.

What Your Primary Physician Does

Your primary physician may be required to make important decisions about your mental state and your overall health. For example, your health care documents will take effect if you ever lack the capacity to make health care decisions for yourself, and somebody may need to decide whether or not that time has come. The doctor you name will be responsible for making the determination.

In addition, your health care documents may set out instructions for end-of-life care in very specific situations—for instance, you may leave one set of instructions to take effect if you are permanently unconscious and another to govern your care if you are terminally ill. (You'll learn more about this in "Specifying Your Health Care Wishes," below.) Your primary physician will diagnose these conditions, putting your specific instructions into effect.

Choosing Your Primary Physician

If you have more than one doctor and you're not sure which one to pick, think about who would do the best job of supervising your overall care. This may be your family doctor or general practitioner, rather than a specialist.

If you're really on the fence, you can talk to each doctor you're considering. You may find that one of them seems more comfortable taking on the responsibility of managing your care or you might just get a better sense of whom to pick.

Another possibility is to name one doctor as your first choice and another as an alternate.

Choosing an Alternate

The program also asks you to name an alternate physician. Choose your alternate with the same care you use for your first pick. Keep in mind that this doctor may be responsible for making critical decisions about your care. If there isn't a second doctor you know and trust, skip this question.

Talking to Your Doctor

It's wise to talk to your doctor about your treatment preferences before you finalize your health care documents. Talking with your primary physician (and alternate, if any) is especially important because he or she will be in charge of other caregivers. Make sure your doctor understands your health care wishes and is willing to follow them. If you have questions or concerns about specific treatments, your doctor should be able to answer them. If you have other, more subjective concerns about a particular medical condition, such as the effects of certain treatments or how the condition is likely to affect you, discuss those, too.

Let your doctor know that you are completing a health care directive. If you will name an agent, be sure your doctor knows how to contact that person in an emergency. Better still, introduce your agent to your doctor if you have not already done so.

Naming Your Health Care Agent

This is one of the most important parts of the program. It's where you name the person who will work with your doctors to direct your health care and make treatment decisions for you if you are unable to do so. This person is usually called your "health care agent," though some states use a term such as "representative," "proxy" or "surrogate." Your health care documents will use the correct term for your state.

We strongly recommend that you appoint a health care agent—and at least one alternate—if you know someone you trust enough to take the job. The chances that your health care wishes will be enforced increase greatly if you name someone to supervise your care and speak for you if necessary.

And because life is unpredictable, there is no way your health care instructions can cover every possible health-related situation that might arise. Rapidly developing technology and new medical treatments underscore the need for flexible decision making. The best approach is to choose a trusted person who fully understands your feelings, beliefs and wishes.

If you absolutely cannot think of anyone you trust to oversee your medical care, you can skip this part of the program. It is better not to name anyone than to name someone who is not likely to strongly assert your wishes.

It's still a good idea to put your wishes for final health care in writing. Medical personnel are legally bound to follow your written wishes—or to find someone who will. If you do not name a health care agent, make an extra effort to discuss your wishes for medical care with a doctor or patient representative likely to be involved in providing that care.

What a Health Care Agent Does

If you become unable to direct your own health care, your agent will:

- supervise any treatment instructions you set out in your health care documents, and

- make decisions about any health care matters your documents do not cover.

Your health care power of attorney can give your agent very broad authority to direct your medical care. Or you can fine-tune your document by answering some questions about your agent's specific powers, discussed below.

To carry out your wishes and make decisions for you, your agent will always be allowed to:

- review your medical records
- grant releases to medical personnel so that they can perform necessary treatments
- go to court, if necessary to ensure your wishes are followed
- hire and fire medical personnel, and
- visit you in a hospital or other health care facility.

This should allow your agent to do everything needed to make sure your health care wishes are carried out—and if they are not, to get you transferred to another facility or to the care of another doctor who will enforce them.

Your Agent's Responsibility to You

You may be concerned that by naming a health care agent, you are giving up control of your own medical treatment—but you needn't worry. Your agent is legally required to follow your known wishes and to act in your best interest. If you leave written health care instructions, your agent is required to follow them, as are your doctors. On the other hand, if you want to leave certain treatment decisions entirely in the hands of your agent, you may do so.

Mental Health Care Decisions

Most states define health care to include mental health. To leave no confusion on the matter, our health care documents explicitly give your agent the power to make mental health decisions for you. This may include the power to discuss mental health treatments with your health care providers, to request or change medications or even to admit you to a mental health care facility if necessary. However, some states require special documents or authorization before they will allow a health care agent to authorize extreme treatments, such as shock therapy, or to commit someone under their care to a psychiatric facility.

If you have particular concerns about your mental health treatment, you can fill out a special medical health care directive, giving your agent the maximum authority allowed by your state's laws. The Bazelon Center for Mental Health Law, at www.bazelon.org/issues/advancedirectives/index.htm, offers a detailed mental health care directive that allows you to express your preferences on a wide range of treatment issues, such as:

- medication preferences
- electroconvulsive therapy, and
- involuntary commitment to a mental health facility.

The Health Insurance Portability and Accountability Act (HIPAA)

If you've recently visited a doctor, you know there's a law that requires patients to sign forms regarding medical privacy and the release of medical information. This federal law is called HIPAA, the Health Insurance Portability and Accountability Act. Some folks have worried that HIPAA requirements apply to your agent's powers under your health care documents, and that you must prepare special HIPAA release forms to give your agent the authority to take over your health care decisions for you. In fact, this is not the case. An agent is authorized to obtain the medical information necessary to put your document into effect and carry out your wishes.

The health care power of attorney you make with this program contains an explicit statement that your agent is allowed to act as your personal representative under HIPAA, authorized to receive full medical information about you. We took this extra step to avert any hassles for your agent.

The decisions your agent makes for you must always agree with what you direct in your health care documents and any other wishes you make known to him or her. If a situation arises in which your agent does not know your specific wishes, your agent must make the decision that he or she believes you would make if you were capable of doing so. (For a possible exception in New Hampshire, see "Note for New Hampshire Readers: When

Your Agent May Override Your Objections," below.)

To ensure you get the care you want, one of the most important things to do is talk with your agent (and other loved ones) about your wishes. For tips on having this important conversation, see "Talking to Your Agent," below.

You may wonder what happens if your health care agent lets you down. If someone goes to court and proves that your agent is harming you by acting in ways that you would not want, a court could revoke your agent's authority. In this case, the first person to take

over would be an alternate agent you've named in your power of attorney for health care. If you haven't named an alternate or if your alternate is not available, the court will appoint a guardian or conservator to make your health and personal care decisions. (See "Nominating a Guardian," below.)

Choosing Your Agent

The person you name as your health care agent should be someone you trust and someone with whom you feel confident discussing your wishes. Choose someone who respects your

---

Note for New Hampshire Readers: When Your Agent May Override Your Objections

New Hampshire, like most other states, requires your agent and medical providers to make an effort to inform you of any proposed medical treatments, or of any proposal to withdraw or withhold treatment from you. Usually, your caretakers may not provide or withhold treatments if you object, even if you are determined to be incapacitated and incapable of making informed health care choices.

In New Hampshire, however, you can state that your agent should carry out your treatment wishes when your health care providers have determined that you are no longer capable of making informed decisions—even if you verbally object to those treatments when the time comes. When you make your health care

document, we ask you whether or not you want to give your agent this power.

You may want to grant this authority if you are concerned about being diagnosed with Alzheimer's disease or another form of severe dementia. Dementia may cause you to become argumentative and resist the reasoned treatment decisions that you made before you became ill.

This power can make it much easier for your agent to carry out your wishes if you ever become incapable of making rational decisions. But do think carefully before you add it to your document. It places an enormous amount of authority in your agent's hands. Before granting the power, be certain your agent is someone you completely trust to treat you well, and that he or she fully understands your wishes for care.

right to get the kind of medical care you want, even if he or she doesn't completely agree with your wishes.

You can choose your spouse or partner, a relative or a close friend. Keep in mind that your agent may have to assert your wishes in the face of medical personnel and family members who may be driven by their own beliefs and interests, rather than yours. If you foresee the possibility of conflict in enforcing your wishes, be sure to choose someone who is strong-willed and assertive.

> **CAUTION**
> **How marriage or divorce may affect your document.** The document you create with this program revokes the appointment of your spouse or registered domestic partner if you file for divorce or legally separate. If this happens, you should prepare a new document, or know that an alternate agent will step in to serve.
>
> It's also a good idea to prepare a new health care document if you get married, unless your new spouse is already named as your health care agent. You are never required to name your spouse as your health care agent, but if you want to name someone else, be sure you do it in a document created after the date of your marriage. If you have an old document naming someone other than your spouse as your agent, some states will consider it automatically revoked when you marry.

While you need not name someone who lives in the same state as you do, proximity is one factor to consider. If you have a protracted illness, the person you name may be called upon to spend weeks or months near your bedside, making sure health care providers abide by your wishes for treatment.

Finally, if you have made—or are planning to make—a durable power of attorney for finances (see Chapter 22), you should think strongly about naming the same person to oversee both your finances and your health care. If you decide not to name the same person—perhaps because one has a much better head for business and the other is likely to be better at your bedside—keep in mind that your health care agent and your agent for finances may have to work very closely at times. (For example, your agent for finances will be responsible for paying your medical and insurance bills at your health care agent's direction.)

Naming More Than One Agent: A Bad Idea

This program allows you to name just one person at a time to serve as your agent. We believe it's unwise to name two people to serve together, even if you know two people who are willing to take the job. There may be problems, brought on by passing time and human nature, with naming co-agents. In the critical time during which your representatives will be overseeing your wishes, they could disagree or suffer a change of heart, rendering them ineffective as lobbyists on your behalf while they argue with each other.

If you know of two people you would like to name as your agents, choose one to serve first and name the other as your alternate.

State Restrictions on Who Can Serve as Your Agent

A number of states have rules about who can serve as your agent. Attending physicians and other health care providers are commonly prohibited from serving. Some states presume that the motivations of such people may be clouded by self-interest. For example, a doctor may be motivated to provide every medical procedure available—to try every heroic or experimental treatment—even if that goes against a patient's wishes. On the other side, treatments may sometimes be withheld because of concerns about time or cost.

Before you select an agent, consult the list below for the specifics of your state's agent requirements and restrictions before you select an agent.

Choosing Alternate Agents

You may name one or two alternate agents. Your first alternate will serve only if your first choice becomes unavailable. Your second alternate will step in only if your primary agent and first alternate are unable or unwilling to act or cannot quickly be located.

Use the same principles to choose your alternates as you did when making your first pick: trustworthiness, dependability, assertiveness and availability.

Do not choose as an alternate someone who is disqualified by state law from serving in your state. (See the list below.)

Granting Specific Powers to Your Agent

After you name your agent, the program will ask you some questions about granting specific powers to him or her. This section explains each of these powers.

Withdrawing Life-Prolonging Procedures

It is important to specify whether or not your agent may direct health care providers to withhold or withdraw life-prolonging procedures when you are close to death.

A life-prolonging procedure or treatment is one that would only prolong the process of dying or sustain a condition of permanent unconsciousness. In other words, the patient would die soon—or die without regaining meaningful consciousness—whether or not the treatment was administered.

It is generally agreed that cardiopulmonary resuscitation (CPR), dialysis, artificial respiration and complicated invasive surgery are life-prolonging procedures when performed on a terminally ill or permanently comatose patient. (For more information, see below.)

In most states, agents automatically have the power to withdraw life-prolonging procedures. In other states, if you wish to grant the power it must be specifically spelled out in your health care document.

To avoid any confusion, the document you make with this program will clearly state whether or not your agent has the power to withdraw life-prolonging procedures, knowing that to do so may result in your death. You will be instructed to sign or initial this specific clause to underscore that you knowingly granted or denied this power to your agent.

State Law Restrictions on Agents

Alabama

Your health care proxy may not be:

- your treating health care provider
- an employee of your treating health care provider, unless the employee is related to you, or
- under the age of 19.

Alaska

Your health care agent may not be an owner, operator or employee of the health care institution at which you are receiving care, unless related to you by blood, marriage or adoption.

Arizona

Your health care agent must be at least 18 years old.

Arkansas

Your health care agent must be at least 18 years old.

California

Your health care agent may not be:

- your treating health care provider or an employee of your treating health care provider, unless the individual is your registered domestic partner or is related to you, or you and the employee both work for your treating health care provider
- an operator or employee of a community care facility, unless the individual is your registered domestic partner or is related to you, or you and the employee both work at the community care facility
- an operator or employee of a residential care facility for the elderly, unless the individual is your registered domestic partner or is related to you, or you and the employee both work at the residential care facility.

Colorado

Your health care agent must be at least 21 years old.

Connecticut

If, when you appoint your health care agent and attorney-in-fact for health care decisions, you are a patient or a resident of, or have applied for admission to, a hospital, residential care home, rest home with nursing supervision or chronic and convalescent nursing home, your health care agent and attorney-in-fact for health care decisions may not be:

- an operator, unless the operator is related to you by blood, marriage or adoption
- an administrator, unless the administrator is related to you by blood, marriage or adoption, or
- an employee, unless the employee is related to you by blood, marriage or adoption.

In any case, your health care agent and attorney-in-fact for health care decisions may not be:

- under the age of 18
- a witness to the document appointing him or her as your health care representative
- your attending physician, or
- an employee of a government agency which is financially responsible for your medical care—unless that person is related to you by blood, marriage or adoption.

Delaware

Your health care agent may not be an owner, operator or employee of a long-term health care institution where you are receiving care, unless he or she is related to you by blood, marriage or adoption.

State Law Restrictions on Agents (continued)

District of Columbia
Your health care attorney-in-fact may not be your health care provider.

Florida
Your health care surrogate may not be a witness to the document naming your health care representative.

Georgia
Your health care agent may not be a physician or health care provider who is directly involved in your health care.

Hawaii
Your health care agent may not be an owner, operator or employee of your treating health care provider, unless the person is related to you by blood, marriage or adoption.

Idaho
Your health care agent may not be:
- your treating health care provider
- an employee of your health care provider, unless the employee is related to you
- an operator of a community care facility, or
- an employee of an operator of a community care facility, unless the employee is related to you.

Illinois
Your health care agent may not be:
- your health care provider, or
- your attending physician.

Indiana
No restrictions on who may serve as your attorney-in-fact and health care representative.

Iowa
Your health care agent may not be:
- your health care provider, or
- an employee of your health care provider, unless these individuals are related to you by blood, marriage or adoption—limited to parents, children, siblings, grandchildren, grandparents, uncles, aunts, nephews, nieces and great-grandchildren.

Kansas
Your health care agent may not be:
- your treating health care provider
- an employee of your treating health care provider, or
- an employee, owner, director or officer of a health care facility.

These restrictions do not apply, however, if your agent is:
- related to you by blood, marriage or adoption, or
- a member of the same community of people to which you belong who have vowed to lead a religious life and who conduct or assist in conducting religious services and actually and regularly engage in religious, charitable or educational activities or the performance of health care services.

Kentucky
Your health care surrogate may not be an employee, owner, director or officer of a health care facility where you are a resident or patient, unless they are:
- related to you more closely than first cousins, once removed, or
- a member of the same religious order.

State Law Restrictions on Agents (continued)

Maine

Your health care agent may not be an owner, operator or employee of a residential long-term health care institution in which you are receiving care, unless he or she is related to you by blood, marriage or adoption.

Maryland

Your health care agent may not be an owner, operator or employee—or the spouse, parent, child or sibling of an owner, operator or employee—of a health care facility where you are receiving treatment unless he or she would qualify as your surrogate decision maker under Maryland law or is appointed before you receive, or contract to receive, health care from the facility.

Massachusetts

Your health care agent may not be an operator, administrator or employee of a facility where you are a patient or resident or have applied for admission, unless the operator, administrator or employee is related to you by blood, marriage or adoption.

Michigan

Your patient advocate must be at least 18 years old.

Minnesota

Your health care agent may not be your treating health care provider or an employee of your treating health care provider, unless he or she is related to you by blood, marriage, registered domestic partnership or adoption.

Mississippi

Your health care agent may not be an owner, operator or employee of a residential long-term care facility where you are receiving treatment, unless related to you by blood, marriage or adoption.

Missouri

Your health care attorney-in-fact may not be:
- your attending physician
- an employee of your attending physician, or
- an owner, operator or employee of the health care facility where you live, unless:
- you and your attorney-in-fact are related as parents, children, siblings, grandparent or grandchildren, or
- you and your attorney-in-fact are members of the same community of people who have vowed to lead a religious life and who conduct or assist in conducting religious services and actually and regularly engage in religious, charitable or educational activities or the performance of health care services.

Montana

Your health care agent must be at least 18 years old.

Nebraska

Your health care attorney-in-fact may not be:
- under the age of 19, unless he or she is married
- a witness to your durable power of attorney for health care
- your attending physician
- an employee of your attending physician, unless the employee is related to you by blood, marriage or adoption
- a person unrelated to you by blood, marriage or adoption who is an owner, operator or employee of a health care provider of which you are a patient or resident, or

State Law Restrictions on Agents (continued)

- a person unrelated to you by blood, marriage or adoption who is presently serving as a health care attorney-in-fact for ten or more people.

Nevada

Your health care attorney-in-fact may not be:

- your health care provider
- an employee of your health care provider
- an operator of a health care facility, or
- an employee of a health care facility, unless he or she is your spouse, legal guardian or next of kin.

New Hampshire

Your health care agent may not be:

- your health care provider
- an employee of your health care provider, unless the employee is related to you
- your residential care provider, or
- an employee of your residential care provider, unless the employee is related to you.

New Jersey

Your health care representative may not be:

- under the age of 18, or
- an operator, administrator or employee of a health care institution in which you are a patient or resident, unless the operator, administrator or employee is related to you by blood, marriage, domestic partnership or adoption, or, in the case of a physician, is not your attending physician.

New Mexico

Your health care agent may not be an owner, operator or employee of a health care facility at which you are receiving care—unless related to you by blood, marriage or adoption.

New York

Your health care agent may not be:

- under the age of 18, unless he or she is the parent of a child, or married
- your attending physician
- presently appointed agent for ten or more other people, unless he or she is your spouse, child, parent, brother, sister or grandparent
- an operator, administrator or employee of a hospital if, at the time of the appointment, you are a patient or resident of, or have applied for admission to, such hospital. This restriction shall not apply to:
  - an operator, administrator or employee of a hospital who is related to you by blood, marriage or adoption, or
  - a physician, who is not your attending physician, except that no physician affiliated with a mental hygiene facility or a psychiatric unit of a general hospital may serve as agent for you if you are living in or being treated by such facility or unit unless the physician is related to you by blood, marriage or adoption.

North Carolina

Your health care agent must be at least 18 years old.

North Dakota

Your health care agent may not be:

- your treating health care provider
- an employee of your treating health care provider, unless the employee is related to you
- an operator of a long-term care facility, or
- an employee of an operator of a long-term care facility, unless the employee is related to you.

State Law Restrictions on Agents (continued)

Ohio

Your health care attorney-in-fact may not be:

- under the age of 18
- your attending physician
- an administrator of any nursing home in which you are receiving care
- an employee or agent of your attending physician, or
- an employee or agent of any health care facility in which you are being treated.

These restrictions do not apply, however, if your attorney-in-fact is 18 years of age or older and a member of the same religious order as you—or is related to you by blood, marriage or adoption.

Oklahoma

Your health care proxy must be at least 18 years old.

Oregon

Your health care representative may not be:

- under the age of 18
- your attending physician or an employee of your attending physician, unless the physician or employee is related to you by blood, marriage or adoption, or
- an owner, operator or employee of a health care facility in which you are a patient or resident, unless related to you by blood, marriage or adoption—or appointed before you were admitted to the facility.

Pennsylvania

Your health care agent may not be:

- your attending physician or other health care provider, unless related to you by blood, marriage or adoption, or
- an owner, operator or employee of a health care provider from which you are receiving care, unless related to you by blood, marriage or adoption.

Rhode Island

Your health care agent may not be:

- your treating health care provider
- an employee of your treating health care provider, unless the employee is related to you
- an operator of a community care facility, or
- an employee of an operator of a community care facility, unless the employee is related to you.

South Carolina

Your health care agent may not be:

- under the age of 18
- your health care provider at the time you execute your health care power of attorney, unless he or she is related to you
- a spouse or employee of your health care provider, unless he or she is related to you, or
- an employee of the nursing care facility where you live, unless he or she is related to you.

South Dakota

No restrictions on who may serve as your health care agent.

Tennessee

Your health care agent may not be:

- your treating health care provider
- an employee of your treating health care provider, unless he or she is related to you by blood, marriage or adoption
- an operator of a health care institution

State Law Restrictions on Agents (continued)

- an employee of an operator of a health care institution, unless he or she is related to you by blood, marriage or adoption, or
- your conservator, unless you are represented by an attorney who signs a specific statement—required by Tennessee Code § 34-6-203(c).

Texas

Your health care agent may not be:

- your health care provider
- an employee of your health care provider, unless the employee is related to you
- your residential care provider, or
- an employee of your residential care provider, unless the employee is related to you.

Utah

Your health care agent may not be:

- your health care provider, or
- an owner, operator or employee of the health care facility at which you are receiving care, unless related to you by blood, marriage or adoption.

Vermont

Your health care agent may not be:

- your health care provider, or
- an owner, operator, employee, agent or contractor of a residential care facility, health care facility or correctional facility in which you reside, unless related to you by blood, marriage, civil union or adoption.

Virginia

Your health care agent must be at least 18 years old.

Washington

Your health care agent may not be:

- your physician
- your physicians' employee, or
- an owner, administrator or employee of the health care facility where you live or receive care.

These restrictions do not apply, however, if your representative is your spouse, adult child or sibling.

West Virginia

Your health care representative may not be:

- your treating health care provider
- an employee of your treating health care provider, unless he or she is related to you
- an operator of a health care facility serving you, or
- an employee of an operator of a health care facility, unless he or she is related to you.

Wisconsin

Your health care agent may not be:

- your health care provider or the spouse or employee of your health care provider unless he or she is related to you, or
- an employee or spouse of an employee of the health care facility in which you live or are a patient, unless he or she is related to you.

Wyoming

Your health care agent may not be an owner, operator or employee of a residential or community care facility where you are receiving care, unless he or she is related to you by blood, marriage or adoption.

Note for Utah and Wisconsin Readers: Admitting You to a Nursing Home

In most states, a health care agent automatically has the power to decide whether or not to admit you to a nursing home or other long-term care facility—whether for a short stay or a long one. In Utah or Wisconsin, however, you must specifically state whether or not you want your agent to have the power to admit you for anything other than a short-term stay for recuperation or rest. The program will ask you to express your wishes on this matter.

Granting this authority to your health care agent does not mean that you want or prefer to be admitted to a nursing home or residential care facility. As with other matters, your agent must follow your specific wishes. For example, if you would consent to be admitted to a nursing home only as a last resort, you can give your agent the power to admit you, but make sure he or she understands your feelings and preferences.

Keep in mind that if you do not grant this authority and your situation changes or deteriorates to the extent that your health care providers and agent agree that admitting you to a long-term care facility is best for you, your agent may be required to initiate court proceedings in order to get you the care you need.

Ultimately, the choice is deeply personal. The best you can do is make the choice that feels right to you now—and be sure to talk with your agent about your wishes.

Doing this ensures that your wishes will be honored in any state.

Note that giving your agent the power to make this decision is *not* the same as telling your agent what decision to make. Later in the program, you can leave specific instructions about whether or not you want to receive life-prolonging procedures—and when. Your agent is legally bound to follow your wishes. Here, you are just giving your agent power to direct your care on this matter. You should grant your agent this power if you know that you do not want some or all life-prolonging procedures when you are close to death.

Withdrawing Food and Water

If you are close to death and cannot communicate your wishes for health care, it is also likely that you will not be able to eat or drink normally. The medical solution to this is to provide you with food and water—as a mix of nutrients and fluids—through tubes inserted in a vein or into your stomach, depending on your condition. This is typically called "artificially administered nutrition and hydration," though your state may use a slightly different term.

Even though artificially administered food and water is often considered a life-prolonging procedure, it is critical that you state your wishes about this issue separately from other life-prolonging procedures. The withdrawal of food and water from terminally ill or permanently unconscious patients has proven to be a bitterly contested personal and political issue. The document you make with this program explicitly states your wishes on this matter so there is no chance of confusion about what you want. You should grant your agent this power if there are any circumstances under which you would not want to receive artificially administered food and water.

Authorizing Organ, Tissue or Body Donation

Using this program, you can give your agent the authority to carry out your wishes for organ, tissue or body donation after your death—or specify that your agent should not have this power.

In almost all cases, it's wise to give your agent the power to assert your wishes about anatomical gifts. If you want to be a donor, giving your agent clear authority to approve your donation will help to expedite the procedure. (Donations must be carried out quickly in order to succeed.) If you don't want to donate, your agent can ensure your wishes are carried out by speaking firmly on your behalf, even in the face of others who may disagree with your choice. And if you're not sure what you want, you can be assured that someone you trust will have the authority to make a decision based on the circumstances when the time comes.

If you give your agent this authority, a little later in the program you will have the opportunity to provide further instructions about anatomical gifts—or to assert that you do not want to be an organ donor, if that is your wish. (See "Stating Your Wishes for Organ Donation," below.) Your agent must try to follow any wishes you express.

If you don't grant your agent this authority and the question of whether or not to donate

your organs arises after your death, your doctors will ask your next of kin to make the decision.

Authorizing an Autopsy

In some circumstances, such as a sudden or suspicious death, state law may require an autopsy. In these cases, a medical examiner does not need to get permission before proceeding.

In other situations, your loved ones or family members may request an autopsy—for example, if they have questions about the cause of your death or wish to advance society's medical knowledge about a little-understood disease, such as Alzheimer's. You can use the program to give or refuse consent to this type of autopsy, or you can give your agent the power to make the decision for you. Here is a little information about each choice.

Advantages of authorizing an autopsy. Your first option is to state that you authorize an autopsy after your death. This doesn't mean there will be an autopsy; it just allows your loved ones to get more information about your death if they feel they need it.

This type of information can provide comfort to grieving family members, but there is a practical reason for it as well: An autopsy may reveal conditions that could be inherited by other members of your family, giving them opportunities for early diagnosis and treatment.

When you may not want to authorize an autopsy. Your second option is to refuse consent to an autopsy after your death. You may want to avoid an autopsy for personal or practical reasons. For example, some people have religious concerns about the procedure. If that's true for you, you may want to discuss the issue with a clergymember or other spiritual adviser before making your decision.

The most common practical reason for refusing an autopsy is the cost. A complete autopsy can cost several thousand dollars and is usually not covered by insurance. Before you consent to an autopsy, you may want to investigate the costs and be sure your estate has money on hand to cover them.

In rare cases, grants are available to cover the cost of an autopsy. For example, in cases of Alzheimer's or dementia, the National Institutes of Health provides some autopsy services without charge to the family. In order to receive these benefits, however, you must be enrolled in a research program before your death.

Letting your agent decide. When you consider the pros and cons of consenting to an autopsy, you may find that the third option is best. It allows you to leave the matter in your agent's hands.

Whether or not an autopsy is helpful or prudent will depend on the circumstances of your death—many of which are unpredictable ahead of time. If you talk to your agent about your general feelings and wishes, he or she can make a decision when the time comes, taking into account all the circumstances.

Authorizing Disposition of Your Remains

Unless you specify otherwise, your closest family members will decide whether your body will be buried or cremated. This program offers three ways to express your wishes about this decision.

Directing your agent to follow existing wishes. If you want to write down your preferences for final arrangements, including burial or cremation, you can use our "final arrangements" letter for this purpose. It allows you to prepare a detailed document stating your preferences about burial, cremation and a funeral or memorial services. (See Chapter 24.) Once you have done this—or prepared a similar document—you can select the option that states you have already made arrangements that your agent should follow. You will then have the opportunity to describe the document or arrangements you've made, so that your agent and others can locate your papers and carry out your wishes when the time comes.

Letting your agent decide. If you choose this option, your agent will have the power to decide how your body should be handled after you die. You can either leave these matters entirely in the hands of your agent or, better for everyone involved, discuss your wishes with your agent and other loved ones.

Letting family decide. If there is some reason that you do not want to give your agent the authority to make decisions about burial or cremation, you can select the third option, which denies your agent this power. The practical result is that your closest family members will make decisions about your remains, following any wishes that you may have expressed.

If You Give Your Agent This Power: Special Signing Requirements

In some states, if you grant your agent the authority to make decisions about your burial or cremation, you must follow special directions when you finalize your document.

For example, if you live in Nevada, your durable power of attorney for health care decisions may be signed by two witnesses or notarized. Usually, the choice is yours. However, if you grant your agent the power to direct your final arrangements, you must have the document notarized—and witnesses are not necessary.

The program will provide the correct finalization instructions for your state, depending on the choices you make when you prepare your document. To learn whether your state has special requirements, see "State Witnessing and Notarizing Requirements," below.

Talking to Your Agent

It may not be an easy conversation to start, but those who make the effort to discuss the hard topic of what kind of medical care they want at the end of life usually find the effort worth the price. You'll probably want to begin by talking with your agent; then, if you can, discuss your feelings with close family members and friends as well. If the topic seems too difficult to broach, consider using a relevant news item, television show or film as a catalyst for discussion.

There are three basic goals when talking with your agent:

- making sure the person you've picked is willing to take on the responsibility of acting on your behalf
- sharing your written directions and other wishes, and
- allowing your agent to ask questions so you are both clear on what you want.

During your discussion, your agent may ask about issues you haven't considered. This is a great chance for each of you to clarify the understanding between you so that you both can feel confident that your agent will know what to do if he or she must represent you.

If you have a regular doctor, you may want to encourage your doctor and your agent to meet and establish communication. If you are already a patient in a medical facility, your agent will also want to get to know the social worker or patient representative of the facility.

Why are these discussions so important? First, it gives you the opportunity to let people know that you are preparing health care documents, and why you feel strongly about doing so.

Second, it is impossible to foresee all of the circumstances or illnesses that may arise and address them in your documents. Giving people a clear understanding of your personal views and values can avoid future disagreements as to how your written desires should be applied to specific circumstances.

In discussing your values, you may want to cover some or all of the following:

- your overall attitude toward life, including what gives you feelings of purpose and meaning and how you feel about your independence

- fears you may have about no longer being able to speak for yourself or make your own decisions
- any strong feelings you have about medical treatments that you do or do not wish to receive at the end of your life, including life support and feeding tubes
- what a phrase such as "death with dignity," or "no heroic measures" actually means to you
- anything you want others to know about the spiritual or religious part of your life and how it affects your feelings about serious illness and death
- what you might want for comfort and support when you are close to death (for example, to have certain people present, to be read to or to have music playing)
- your feelings about doctors and caregivers, in general, as well as any opinions about specific caregivers, and
- what you want after your death, including feelings about organ donation, an autopsy and final arrangements (for example, burial, cremation or memorial ceremonies).

Obviously, these conversations are not always easy to initiate or carry out, but they present all involved with an opportunity for greater peace of mind. Your loved ones will know your true wishes, and you may find that this is not only a chance to gain clarity and understanding, but also a bridge to closer relationships.

Nominating a Guardian

In most cases, your health care agent will be able to make all necessary health care and personal decisions for you, perhaps working with a financial agent you've named under a durable power of attorney for finances (this document is discussed in Chapter 22). However, although it's unlikely, there may come a time when a court must name someone to make personal decisions for you that go beyond the authority granted in your health care documents. If you need a great deal of help, this person, usually called a "guardian of the person" or "conservator of the person," may be granted the power to decide where you live, what you eat, the clothes you wear or what your daily activities will be.

You can use this program to nominate your agent to serve as guardian if it's ever necessary. Doing so strengthens your statement that you want your agent to speak for you in all matters relating to both your health and personal care.

In almost all cases, a court will appoint the person you nominate to be your conservator or guardian. The only time a court will override your nomination is if someone proves to the court that your choice is unlikely to act in your best interests. These types of disputes are very rare.

If your agent is unavailable. If you nominate your agent as your guardian or conservator and your agent is not willing or able to take the job if called on, your document will automatically nominate any alternate agents you have named, in the order designated.

If you don't nominate your agent. If you don't nominate your agent as guardian or conservator and a court must later appoint one, who gets the job depends on where you live. In some states, your health care agent is automatically nominated for the position. In others, priority is given to your spouse—or registered domestic partner in a few states—followed by close relatives in an order established by state law.

Nominating a guardian or conservator of your estate. While a guardian or conservator of your person is responsible for your personal comfort and care, a guardian or conservator of your estate is responsible for your finances. If you make a durable power of finances, you can nominate your financial agent to serve as the guardian or conservator of your estate if that ever becomes necessary. (Again, see Chapter 22 for more information about durable powers of attorney for finances.)

Specifying Your Health Care Wishes

After you have named (or declined to name) a health care agent, the program offers you the opportunity to express your wishes and feelings about medical treatment in as much detail as you choose. You have four basic options:

- leave all health care decisions in the hands of your agent, if you have named one
- make a general statement that you do not wish to receive life support when death is imminent
- make a general statement that you wish to be kept alive as long as possible, or
- specify different treatment wishes for different situations.

In this section, you will also have a chance to express any additional general wishes about end-of-life health care.

You Control Your Health Care If You Are Able

Most people know it is a good idea to write down their health care wishes. But some run smack into a psychological roadblock. They are worried that they may experience a change of heart or mind later—and that they will receive more or less medical care than they would want in a particular situation.

If this concerns you, it may help to keep the following in mind:

First, the directions set out in your health care documents will be followed only if you someday become unable to communicate your wishes about your treatment. If, for example, you indicate in a health care directive that you do not wish to have water provided, health care providers will not deny you a glass of water as long as you are able to communicate your wishes for one—even through gestures.

Second, you can change or revoke your written health care wishes at any time. If you find that your document no longer accurately expresses your wishes for your medical care, you can easily create a new one to meet your needs. (See "Revoking Your Documents," below.)

Types of Medical Care: What You Should Know

Here, we briefly discuss some medical procedures that you should be familiar with before you provide directions about your care. Dry or off-putting as it may seem, it's a good idea to at least read quickly through the sections below to gain a basic understanding of:

- what the term "life-prolonging" means from a medical perspective
- what "artificially provided food and water" is and when it may be necessary, and
- what constitutes comfort or "palliative" care.

However, you will not need to deal with these definitions if you are already certain of any of the following:

- You want your agent to make all decisions for you.
- You want all procedures to be withheld.
- You want all procedures to be provided.

If any of these apply to you, you can skip directly to "If Your Wishes Are Simple," below.

Life-Prolonging Medical Care

When completing your health care instructions, we ask for your preferences about life-prolonging treatments or procedures. Many people need a little more information before answering these questions.

A life-prolonging procedure or treatment is one that would only prolong the process of dying or sustain a condition of permanent unconsciousness. In other words, the patient would die soon—or die without regaining meaningful consciousness—whether or not the treatment was administered. This section describes the most common life-prolonging treatments—a respirator, cardiopulmonary resuscitation (CPR), surgery and so on—in some detail.

Bear in mind that the types of medical procedures that are available will change over time. Technological advances mean that currently unfathomable procedures and treatments will become available and treatments that are now common will become obsolete. Also, the treatments that are available vary drastically depending on the sophistication of medical facilities.

Blood and blood products. Partial or full blood transfusions may be recommended to combat diseases that impair the blood system, to foster healing after a blood loss or to replenish blood lost through surgery, disease or injury.

Cardiopulmonary resuscitation (CPR). CPR is used when a person's heart or breathing has stopped. CPR includes applying physical pressure and using mouth-to-mouth resuscitation. Electrical shocks are also used if available. CPR is often accompanied by intravenous drugs used to normalize body systems. A final step in CPR is often attaching the patient to a respirator.

Diagnostic tests. Diagnostic tests are commonly used to evaluate urine, blood and other body fluids and to check on all bodily functions. Diagnostic tests can include X-rays and more sophisticated tests of brainwaves or other body systems. Some tests—including surgery—can be expensive, painful and invasive.

It Does Not Get More Personal Than This

For many people, the desire to direct what kind of medical care they want to receive is driven by a very specific event—watching a loved one die, having an unsatisfactory brush with the medical establishment or preparing for serious surgery.

Your ultimate decisions are likely to be influenced by factors such as your medical history, your knowledge of other people's experiences with life-prolonging medical procedures or your religious beliefs. If you are having great difficulty deciding about your preferences for medical care, take a few moments to figure out what's getting in your way. If you are unsure about the meaning or specifics of a particular medical treatment, turn to a doctor you trust for a more complete explanation. If the impediment is fear of sickness or death, talk over your feelings with family members and friends.

Dialysis. A dialysis machine is used to clean and add essential substances to the blood—through tubes placed in blood vessels or into the abdomen—when kidneys do not function properly. The entire cleansing process takes three or more hours and is performed on most dialysis patients two or three times a week. With portable dialysis machines, it is possible for some patients to have the procedure performed at home rather than in a hospital or other advanced care facility.

Drugs. The most common and most controversial drugs given to seriously ill or comatose patients are antibiotics—administered by mouth, through a feeding tube or by injection. Antibiotics are used to arrest and squelch infectious diseases. Patients in very weakened conditions may not respond even to massive doses of antibiotics.

Many health care providers argue that infectious diseases can actually be a benefit to those in advanced stages of an illness, since they may render a patient unconscious, and presumably not in pain, or help to speed up the dying process. Others contend that if an antibiotic can eliminate symptoms of an illness, it is almost always the proper medical treatment.

Drugs may also be used for pain. If, within your health care directive, you state that you do not want drugs to prolong your life, they will still be administered for pain control unless you specifically indicate that you do not want them. (See below.)

Respirator. A mechanical respirator or ventilator assists or takes over breathing for a patient by pumping air in and out of the lungs. Patients are connected to respirators either by a tube that goes through the mouth and throat into the lung or attaches directly to the lung surgically.

Respirators are often used to stabilize patients who are suffering from an acute trauma or breathing crisis, and they are removed as soon as they are no longer needed. If a respirator has been attached to a person who is terminally ill or in a permanent coma, however, most doctors will resist removing the machinery unless there is clear written direction that this is what the patient would want.

Surgery. Surgical procedures such as amputation are often used to stem the spread of life-threatening infections or to keep vital organs functioning. Major surgery such as a heart bypass is also typically performed on patients who are terminally ill or comatose. You might want to consider the cost, time spent recovering from the invasive surgery and inevitability of death when deciding whether to include surgery in your final medical treatment.

Artificially Administered Food and Water

If you are close to death from a serious illness or permanently comatose, you may not be able to survive without the administration of food and water. Unless you indicate that treatment should be withheld, doctors will provide you with a mix of nutrients and fluids through tubes inserted in a vein, into your stomach through your nose or directly into your stomach through a surgical incision, depending on your condition.

Intravenous (IV) feeding, where fluids are introduced through a vein in an arm or a leg, is a short-term procedure. Tube feeding, however, can be carried on indefinitely.

Permanently unconscious patients can sometimes live for years with artificial feeding and hydration without regaining consciousness. If food and water are removed, death will occur in a relatively short time due to dehydration, rather than starvation. Such a course of action generally includes a plan of medication to keep the patient comfortable.

When you make your health care documents, you can choose whether you want artificially administered food and water withheld or provided. This decision is difficult for many people. Keep in mind that as long as you are able to communicate your wishes, by whatever means, you will not be denied food and water if you want it.

RESOURCE

Where to get more help. If you are not sure whether or not you would want to receive artificially administered food and water, you may wish to talk with your doctor or do some more research on your own. The following book is a good resource that may help you sort out your feelings about the issue: *Hard Choices for Loving People: CPR, Artificial Feeding, Comfort Care and the Patient With a Life-Threatening Illness*, by Hank Dunn (A & A Publishers). This well-written resource features a good discussion of the issues surrounding artificial nutrition and hydration, exploring the various medical, religious and philosophical views on the subject. You can download the entire text of the book for free from www.hardchoices.com.

Palliative Care

If you want death to occur naturally—without life-prolonging intervention—it does not mean you must forgo treatment to alleviate pain or keep you comfortable. In fact, the health care directive you make with this program will state that you wish to receive any care that is necessary to keep you pain-free, unless you specifically state otherwise.

This type of care, sometimes known as "comfort care," is now more commonly called "palliative care." Rather than focusing on a cure or prolonging life, palliative care emphasizes quality of life and dignity by

In an Emergency: DNR Orders

In addition to the health care documents produced by this program, you may want to make a Do Not Resuscitate, or DNR, order. A DNR order tells emergency medical personnel that you do not wish to be administered cardiopulmonary resuscitation (CPR). DNR orders are used both in hospitals and in situations where a person might require emergency care outside of the hospital.

You may want to consider a DNR order if you:

- have a terminal illness
- are at significant risk for cardiac or respiratory arrest, or
- have strong feelings against the use of CPR under any circumstances.

In most states, any adult may secure a DNR order. But a few states allow you to create an order only if you have been diagnosed with a terminal illness.

Because emergency response teams must act quickly in a medical crisis, they often do not have the time to determine whether you have a valid health care directive explaining treatments you want provided or withheld. If they do not know your wishes, they must provide you with all possible life-saving measures. But if emergency care providers see that you have a valid DNR order—which is often made apparent by an easily identifiable bracelet, anklet or necklace—they will not administer CPR.

If you ask to have CPR withheld, you will not be given:

- chest compression
- electric shock treatments to the chest
- tubes placed in the airway to assist breathing
- artificial ventilation, or
- cardiac drugs.

If you want a DNR order, or if you would like to find out more about DNR orders, talk with a doctor. In many states, a doctor's signature is required to make the DNR valid—he or she will often need to obtain and complete the necessary paperwork. If the doctor does not have the form or other information you need, call the Health Department for your state and ask to speak with someone in the Division of Emergency Medical Services.

If you obtain a DNR order, discuss your decision with your family or other caretakers and tell them where your form is located. Even if you are wearing identification, such as a bracelet or necklace, keep your form in an obvious place. You might consider keeping it by your bedside, on the front of your refrigerator, in your wallet or in your suitcase if you are traveling. If your DNR order is not apparent and immediately available, or if it has been altered in any way, CPR will most likely be performed.

helping a patient to remain comfortable and free from pain until life ends naturally.

Studies have shown that palliative care services are greatly appreciated by the family and friends of dying patients. Numerous organizations promote public awareness of palliative care options, and information about treatment options is widely available on the Internet. (See below.) However, despite the wide recognition of the benefits of palliative care, a major nationwide study in 2002 revealed that relatively few people get the palliative care they should. Most hospitals do not have integrated palliative care plans among their treatment options. Very few doctors understand it well, and it is still not emphasized in medical training. As a result, many people die in hospital intensive care units, sometimes in severe pain, not knowing their suffering could have been greatly eased. You may wish to spend some time educating yourself about palliative care so that you can discuss your wishes with your health care agent and your treatment providers. When you complete your health care directive, you will have the opportunity to express any particular wishes you have about palliative care.

 RESOURCE

Where to get more help. The following resources can help you understand your options when it comes to palliative care:

Websites

- www.growthhouse.org. A nationwide clearing-house of palliative care information and resources.

- www.pbs.org/wnet/onourownterms. On Our Own Terms is a website created in conjunction with a Bill Moyers/PBS documentary on end-of-life treatment. The site features interviews with professionals, patients and loved ones sharing insights and perspectives on making these difficult choices.

Books

- *Handbook for Mortals: Guidance for People Facing Serious Illness,* by Joanne Lynn, M.D., and Joan Harrold, M.D. (Oxford University Press)
- *Caring for Patients at the End of Life: Facing an Uncertain Future Together,* by Timothy E. Quill (Oxford University Press)
- *The Needs of the Dying: A Guide for Bringing Hope, Comfort, and Love to Life's Final Chapter,* by David Kessler (Harper Paperbacks).

If Your Wishes Are Simple

After you've familiarized yourself with the types of medical treatment that are typically administered at the end of life, it is time to express your own wishes. To begin, the program offers several ways for you to indicate your preferences if you don't want to delve into the specifics of different types of treatments. These are:

- leaving all decisions in the hands of your health care agent, if you've named one
- making a general statement that you do not want your life prolonged when you are close to death, or
- making a general statement that you want your life to be prolonged as long as possible, no matter what your condition.

Letting your agent make all treatment decisions. The first question you will be asked is whether you want to express specific wishes for medical treatment or whether you want your agent to make all decisions for you. If you specify your wishes for treatment, your agent will make decisions for you only on matters you do not specifically address.

Of course, the best way to be sure you'll get the medical care you want if you are someday unable to speak for yourself is to clearly state any preferences that you have. This is especially true if your choices could be considered in any way controversial. For instance, the withholding of artificially administered food and water (feeding tubes) has proved to be a culturally and politically contentious issue in recent years. If you know that you do not want to receive artificially administered food and water (feeding tubes) when you are close to death, it's wise to continue with the program so you can make that wish explicit.

However, if illness or exhaustion have left you feeling that it is too much to formulate and express specific wishes—or if the most important thing to you is simply to name a trusted agent who can act for you—you can leave all decision-making authority in the hands of your agent. If you do, the program won't ask for more information about your treatment wishes, and you can quickly finish up your documents.

On the other hand, if you indicate that you want to specify your wishes for medical treatment, you will first be given the opportunity to make one of two simple statements about your wishes:

Asking that your life not be prolonged when you are close to death. If you choose this option, your document will specify that you do not want to receive life-prolonging treatments when you are close to death from any of the conditions defined by your state's law. Usually, this means that your life will not be artificially prolonged if you are close to death from a terminal condition or are diagnosed as being permanently unconscious. (If you want more information about these specific medical conditions, see the next section.)

You will also be asked to specifically state whether or not you want to receive artificially administered food and water if you are in any of these conditions.

If you make this choice, you will still receive palliative care—that is, treatment to keep you comfortable—unless you specifically state that you do not want it.

Asking for all life-prolonging measures. This option is the opposite of the one just above. If you choose it, your document will state that you want your life to be prolonged for as long as possible within the limits of generally accepted health care standards. This includes receiving artificially administered food and water when you are close to death from a terminal condition or permanently unconscious.

If You Want to Specify Care for Different Situations

Despite rapid technological advances in medicine, much about the end of life remains uncharted. For example, medical experts disagree over whether comatose patients can feel pain and over whether some treatments are universally effective.

People who have strong feelings about what medical care they want to receive are usually guided by personal experience rather than extensive medical knowledge. For example, if you have watched a parent suffer a prolonged death while attached to a respirator, you may opt not to have a respirator as part of your medical care. If a friend who was diagnosed as terminally ill was much improved by a newly developed antibiotic, you may demand that drugs be administered to you, no matter what the medical prognosis.

To accommodate such wishes, while balancing the unknowns of medicine, some flexibility is built into health care documents. You can specify that you should receive different kinds of medical care under certain conditions defined by your state's law. In most states, this means you can leave specific instructions for the care you want when you are permanently unconscious and when you are diagnosed to be close to death from a terminal condition. In a few states, other conditions are covered as well.

For example, medical personnel usually give those diagnosed to be terminally ill a short time to live—less than six months or so. Some people feel that the best medical care under such a prognosis would be to have as much pain and suffering alleviated as possible through drugs and IVs, without any heroic medical maneuvers, such as invasive surgery or painful diagnostic tests.

However, patients often prove doctors wrong. Some people who are expected to die of a terminal illness within a few months stabilize or improve and live on for many years. If you opt to direct that no life-prolonging treatments

be provided, you gamble that your condition will not improve—a gamble you must weigh against the chances you will beat the odds.

Permanently unconscious patients can be kept alive for many years with some mechanical assistance to keep breathing, circulation and other vital bodily functions operating. While chances are statistically miniscule that these patients will ever regain consciousness, in these cases there is a chance that the diagnoses were incorrect in the first place.

There is no general rule to offer on this topic. You must be guided by your own very personal definitions of quality of life. Some people direct that all possible medical treatments be administered to them if they become permanently unconscious, just in case a medical cure becomes available. Others feel strongly that life without consciousness would completely lack meaning—and direct that all medical procedures, including food and water, be discontinued. Still others walk the middle ground, opting to be kept alive by feeding tubes, but not by other life-sustaining measures.

If you are having a difficult time making this choice, you may get good guidance by discussing the matter with a doctor or other experienced health care worker you trust. Internet resources also discuss the medical, spiritual and philosophical aspects of this decision (see below).

If you want to direct that you receive different types of treatment in different situations, the following information will help you understand and evaluate the various conditions for which you can leave directions.

Where to Go for More Help

The growing awareness of health care directives is coupled with a growing number of resources you can turn to if you need help completing your directive or have specific questions about it.

A local senior center may be a good place to go for help. Many of them have trained health care staff on hand who are willing to discuss health care options.

The patient representative or social worker at a local hospital may also be a good person to contact for help. And if you have a regular physician, by all means discuss your concerns with him or her.

Local special groups and clinics may help you fill out your directive—particularly hospice or other organizations set up to meet the needs of the severely ill, such as AIDS or cancer groups. Check your telephone book for a local listing—or call one of the group's hotlines for more information or a possible referral. In addition, www.growthhouse.org has an extensive listing of local resources.

There are also a number of seminars offered. Beware of groups that offer such seminars for a hefty fee, however. Hospitals and senior centers often provide them free of charge.

Close to Death From a Terminal Condition

Generally, a terminal condition is any disease or injury from which doctors believe there is no chance of recovery and from which death is likely to occur within a short time—such as the final stages of cancer.

State laws on health care directives define terminal condition slightly differently, but commonly refer to it as "incurable" or "hopeless." Many state laws explain in addition that a patient who is terminally ill will die unless artificially supported through life-sustaining procedures.

Most states require that one or two physicians verify that the patient has a terminal condition before health care instructions will go into effect. In some states, this verification must be in writing.

Permanently Unconscious

Permanent unconsciousness may be caused by various medical conditions, head traumas or other body injuries.

While permanently unconscious people appear to go through sleep cycles and to respond to some noises and physical stimulation, medical experts disagree about whether a permanently unconscious person is capable of experiencing pain or discomfort. Most permanently unconscious people do not require mechanical assistance with breathing or circulation but must be provided food and water—usually through tubes inserted in the veins or stomach—if the condition persists.

Generally, people who lose consciousness either recover it within a short time (often a matter of hours, days or sometimes weeks) or enter a permanent coma or a persistent vegetative state in which it is extremely unlikely that they will ever regain consciousness. Medical personnel usually declare that a person who remains in a persistent vegetative state for many months without change has passed into a terminal condition.

Once unconsciousness is diagnosed as permanent, the chances of recovery are statistically extremely low. But medical technology (respirators and tube feeding and hydration) can typically keep an unconscious person alive indefinitely—48 years in one case. Consequently, the only way to allow a permanently unconscious person to die naturally may be to discontinue tube feeding and hydration.

To complicate matters, the external symptoms of permanent unconsciousness are somewhat subjective and can be misdiagnosed or the subject of dispute. The highly publicized case of Terri Schiavo involved a Florida woman kept alive by feeding tubes for more than ten years. While most medical experts declared her to be unconscious of her surroundings, at least one doctor offered the opinion that her responses to stimuli were not just reflexive, but were, in fact, evidence that she was conscious of her environment. (After her death, an autopsy showed that she had massive and irreversible brain damage and was indeed in a persistent vegetative state.)

Other factors, such as overmedication, can cause an unresponsive, unconscious condition that may abate once the treatment is halted or changed. To guard against misdiagnosis, many states require two physicians, at least one of whom is an expert on such conditions, to declare a patient permanently unconscious before any stated wishes are carried out.

In cases such as these, the person you appoint as your health care agent can play a crucial role, to make sure that diagnoses are not made in haste or that second opinions can

be sought if there is reason to doubt the initial diagnosis.

Other Medical Conditions

A few states define a condition where death may not be imminent but the medical condition is nonetheless irreversible. If your state's official form addresses a condition like this, we allow you to choose the kind of treatment you want.

Special Conditions: State-by-State

If you live in one of the following states, you will be asked about the additional condition or conditions listed here. As you prepare your document, Quicken WillMaker defines these conditions to help you make your decisions about care.

Florida	End-Stage Condition
Maryland	End-Stage Condition
North Carolina	Advanced Dementia
Oklahoma	End-Stage Condition
Oregon	Advanced Progressive Illness
Pennsylvania	End-Stage Medical Condition
Tennessee	End-Stage Condition
Texas	Irreversible Condition

If the Burdens of Treatments Outweigh the Benefits

In addition to addressing your care in the specific conditions outlined above, you will also have the opportunity to give your agent or other surrogate decision maker the power to withhold or withdraw medical treatments if he or she determines that they are not in your best interest. (This option is not allowed in Oregon, which requires a health care form that covers only certain conditions.)

This broad, catch-all instruction will be offered to you only if you have stated that you do not wish to receive life-prolonging treatment or artificially administered food and water in all other conditions. It lets your decision maker evaluate your situation and direct that treatments be withheld in situations that may go beyond those conditions defined by your state's law. One good example of this is late-stage Alzheimer's disease, which can fall outside the definitions of both "terminal condition" and "permanent unconsciousness."

If you grant this power, a clause like the following will appear in your document:

If I have expressed, in this document or in any other manner, a clear wish regarding a specific treatment or condition, I want that wish to be followed. In all other situations, I direct that my life not be prolonged and that life-prolonging procedures not be provided or continued, in accordance with what my agent determines to be my best interest. In determining my best interest, my agent shall weigh the burdens of treatment against the expected benefits, considering my personal values to the extent known to my agent.

Your known wishes carry much weight in determining what is in your "best interest." In some states, they are conclusive—that is, the law says that a patient's wish is, by definition, the patient's "best interest." In other states, your doctor has some say in determining your best interest when it comes to medical decisions. Regardless of the law in your state, including this provision in your document should shorten the debate by putting clear authority in the hands of your appointed decision maker.

Who Makes the Decision?

If you appoint a health care agent, he or she will be making the determination of whether or not a particular treatment is in your best interest. If you do not appoint a health care agent, you can still include this power in your document. The decision will be placed in the hands of whomever the law appoints as your surrogate decision maker—usually a spouse, registered domestic partner or other close family member.

Do understand that if you grant this power, you are giving your decision maker considerable authority to decide what's best for you. Be sure to talk with your agent, if you have named one, and other loved ones about any specific benefits or burdens that matter to you. For example, would the burden of having to leave your home and spend the rest of your days in a hospital be so significant that you would not wish to receive life-prolonging treatment?

You can also include any strong feelings and preferences for your treatment when you are asked to provide additional instructions or wishes for your health care, in the next part of the program.

Expressing Other Wishes for Your Care

For some people, health care directives—no matter how detailed about things like respirators and surgery—do not reach the heart of their concerns: spiritual matters, money available for care, dying with dignity, quality of life or the well-being of those who care for them.

If you have such concerns, you should discuss them with your health care agent if you have named one—but you can also include them in your written health care instructions. We ask you whether you would like to describe, in your own words, your feelings on any of the following topics:

- the location of your care
- palliative care
- limits or exceptions for pain relief
- personal or religious values, and
- any additional wishes.

This section provides you with a little more information about each option.

> **CAUTION**
>
> **State your wishes carefully to avoid confusion.** You don't want your health care instructions to be confusing to those charged with carrying them out. Be sure that any wishes you specify here do not conflict with other directions you have given.

Location of Care

If where you receive care in the final months, weeks or days of your life is very important to you, you have many ways to set out your wishes. You may state a specific location that you would prefer, such as "at home" or at a particular hospital or hospice facility. Or, you may want to make a more general statement of your preferences, such as any location that lets you be with loved ones at all times.

On the other hand, you may wish to make clear that the location of your care is not as important as getting the treatment you desire. Perhaps you feel that if getting the care you want means being in the intensive care unit of a hospital, you would want to be there. You can state that whatever it takes to prolong your life is more important than where your care is administered.

Location of care may also arise as an issue surrounding diseases such as Alzheimer's or other types of severe dementia. If you have preferences regarding nursing homes or other long-term care options, you may say so.

When specifying wishes for the location of your care, be mindful of creating possible inconsistencies with other health care instructions you have given. For example, if you've expressed a wish for continuation of life-prolonging treatments during a terminal illness, and you've also expressed a preference to receive care at home, make clear which factor is more important. That is, are you willing to forgo some care in order to remain at home, or does the availability of life-sustaining treatment trump your concern about location?

Most important, don't forget to discuss your feelings and wishes with your doctor, your health care agent (if you have named one) and other loved ones.

Palliative Care

Whether or not you want to forgo treatments designed to prolong your life, your health care directive will state that you wish to receive treatment to keep you comfortable and alleviate pain. As discussed above, this type of care is commonly called comfort care or palliative care. Such care attempts not only to provide physical comfort, but also tends to emotional and spiritual needs as well.

If you wish, you can use your document to express any additional or specific wishes you have regarding the way comfort care should be administered. For example, if you prefer a particular course of treatment for pain, including specific medications, you can describe that here.

In addition, you can use this section to describe any wishes or arrangements you have made for hospice or other end-of-life comfort care, and you can set out specific feelings about what would help you remain comfortable at the end of your life. Perhaps you'd like some particular music played, or to have favorite stories, poems or passages read aloud during your final days, when you may be too weak to speak for yourself. This kind of wish is appropriate for this section as well as a discussion with your doctor and loved ones.

Pain Relief Exceptions

Unless you specify otherwise, your health care document authorizes your doctors to provide you with as much medication as they deem necessary to keep you pain-free. If for any reason you do not want this, you may state your wishes in this section.

For example, you may wish to specify that you do not want particular types of pain drugs. Or, you may state that you do not want so much pain medication that it compromises your ability to remain alert and aware of your loved ones.

Personal or Religious Values

At the end of life, health care issues inevitably arise that are not covered by specific directions. When that happens, a statement of your overall philosophy or religious beliefs on matters of medical treatment and dying can help your care providers make decisions on your behalf.

This can be a difficult subject to address, but you may want to consider topics such as:

- your overall goals for your health care
- any fears that you have
- your spiritual or religious beliefs or traditions
- your beliefs about when life would no longer be worth living, and
- your thoughts about how your medical condition may affect your family— personally, practically, financially or otherwise.

Certainly, you should not feel obligated to write a treatise on these matters in your health care directive. If you have any particularly strong feelings, however, they are worth noting. You should also make a particular point to discuss these issues with your health care agent, if you have named one, and other loved ones.

Any Other Wishes or Statements

Finally, we provide a place where you can write out any other feelings or preferences for your health care. You may use this section to write whatever you like, being careful not to create conflicts with any instructions you've already given. In addition, you will want to be sure you've thoroughly discussed your other wishes with your health care agent or other caretakers.

How Pregnancy May Affect Your Wishes

There is one limited situation in which your specific directions about health care might be challenged or ignored: if you are pregnant. Many states' laws say that doctors may not withdraw or withhold life support from a pregnant woman—or that such treatment may not be withheld if the fetus can be brought to term.

These state restrictions have rankled many supporters of women's rights and are legally suspect under U.S. Supreme Court rulings that the Constitution protects women's right to choose whether or not to bear children.

For this reason, if you might become pregnant, this program asks you to say whether you want your health care directions to be:

- given no effect if you are pregnant, or
- carried out as written.

If you specify that your health care directives be given no effect, your health care providers will have the discretion to decide what care is appropriate. They are most likely to administer whatever life-prolonging procedures are available—particularly if the fetus is at least four or five months old and potentially viable and unharmed.

If you choose that your health care directions be carried out as written if you are pregnant, beware that you may meet some resistance from the medical establishment. This is particularly true if you have directed that life-prolonging treatment, food and water or palliative care should be withheld. And you are more apt to run into resistance the more advanced your pregnancy becomes. If you are into the second trimester—fourth through sixth months—doctors are likely to administer all medical care they deem necessary to keep you and the fetus alive.

By the third trimester, it may be practically impossible to overcome a state's proscription against withholding life-prolonging medical care.

If you have strong feelings about overcoming your state's strictures—that is, you live in a state that renders your directive completely ineffective if you are pregnant, but you wish to have it enforced—it is important for you to discuss your wishes and alert your health care agent to lobby on your behalf. It would also be wise to write a brief explanation of your thoughts on this specific issue in the "other wishes" section of your health care directive. (See "Expressing Other Wishes for Your Care," above.)

State Laws on Pregnancy and Health Care Directives

No Effect: The law in your state does not allow your document directing health care to take effect when you are pregnant.

To Term: The law in your state will not allow your document directing health care to take effect if you are pregnant and your doctors believe the fetus could be brought to term while you are receiving life-sustaining treatment.

No Statute: Your state does not have any law about prohibiting withdrawal of life support if you are pregnant.

Alabama	No Effect
Alaska	To Term
Arizona	You may state whether or not you want your health care directions to be carried out if you are pregnant and it is possible for the fetus to develop to the point of live birth.
Arkansas	To Term
California	No Statute
Colorado	To Term
Connecticut	No Effect
Delaware	To Term
Dist. of Col.	No Statute
Florida	Life-prolonging procedures will be provided unless you have expressly stated that your health care surrogate may authorize that life-prolonging procedures may be withheld if you are pregnant, or if your health care surrogate obtains court approval for withholding life-prolonging procedures.
Georgia	Life-sustaining procedures will be provided unless the fetus could not develop to the point of live birth and you expressly state that you want your health care instructions carried out.
Hawaii	No Statute
Idaho	No Effect
Illinois	To Term

State Laws on Pregnancy and Health Care Directives (continued)

Indiana	No Effect
Iowa	To Term
Kansas	No Effect
Kentucky	No Effect
Maine	No Statute
Maryland	You may indicate whether or not you want your health care directions carried out in the event of your pregnancy.
Massachusetts	No Statute
Michigan	If you are pregnant, your health care representative cannot make any medical decision to withhold or withdraw treatment that would result in your death.
Minnesota	You may indicate whether or not you want your health care directives to be carried out in the event of your pregnancy.
Mississippi	No Statute
Missouri	No Effect
Montana	To Term
Nebraska	To Term
Nevada	To Term
New Hampshire	Life-sustaining treatment will be provided unless your doctors conclude that such treatment will not permit the fetus to develop to the point of live birth, or that such treatment will cause you physical harm or prolong severe pain that cannot be alleviated by medication.
New Jersey	You may indicate whether or not you want your health care directions to be carried out in the event of pregnancy.
New Mexico	No Statute
New York	No Statute
North Carolina	No Statute

State Laws on Pregnancy and Health Care Directives (continued)

State	
North Dakota	Life-sustaining procedures will be provided unless those procedures will not permit the fetus to develop to the point of live birth, or your doctor concludes that prolonging your life would cause you physical harm or severe pain, or would prolong severe pain that cannot be alleviated by medication.
Ohio	To Term
Oklahoma	You may indicate whether or not you want your health care directions carried out in the event of pregnancy.
Oregon	No Statute
Pennsylvania	Life-sustaining procedures will be provided unless your doctors conclude that the fetus could not develop to the point of live birth with continued application of those life-sustaining procedures, or prolonging your life would be physically harmful to you or cause you pain that could not be alleviated by medication.
Rhode Island	No Effect
South Carolina	No Effect
South Dakota	Life-sustaining procedures will be provided unless your doctors conclude that the fetus could not develop to the point of live birth with continued application of those life-sustaining procedures, or that prolonging your life would cause you physical harm or prolong severe pain that cannot be alleviated by medication.
Tennessee	No Statute
Texas	No Effect
Utah	No Effect
Vermont	You may indicate whether or not you want your health care directions carried out in the event of pregnancy.
Virginia	No Statute
Washington	No Effect
West Virginia	No Statute
Wisconsin	No Effect
Wyoming	No Statute

Stating Your Wishes for Organ Donation

Before finalizing your health care documents, you can express your wishes on one more matter: donating your organs, tissues or body after death.

If you already know whether or not you want to be an organ donor—or have already made arrangements to donate your organs or body—simply follow the instructions on the screen to indicate your wishes or plans. (Skip to "Making Your Wishes Known," below, for help.) If you are not yet certain whether you want to be a donor, the following information may help you make your decision.

The Need for Donated Organs

Although the number of organ donations has been steadily and slowly rising, the need for organs still far exceeds the number of organs donated. Nearly 100,000 people are currently waiting for lifesaving organ transplant surgery. Based on current rates of donation, one in three of them will die before receiving a transplant.

Religious Views and Concerns

Most major religions support organ donation. Reverence for life is the basis for almost all religious traditions, and organ donation is viewed as a lifesaving act of compassion and generosity. Donated organs must be removed immediately after death, however, and some religions strongly believe that a deceased person's body should remain undisturbed for a number of days. For the practitioner of a religion that holds both of these views—such as many types of Buddhism—a dilemma may arise. On one hand, it is beneficial and compassionate to donate organs, while on the other, it may violate the body. If you are uncertain about the right choice for you, it may be helpful to discuss the issue with your religious or spiritual adviser.

For a brief statement of different religions' views on organ donation, visit www.transweb.org.

Costs of Organ Donation

It will not cost your family anything if you want to donate your organs. The recipient pays the expenses, usually through insurance.

The Organ Donation Procedure

Before an organ is removed from a donor, doctors who are not involved in the procedure must certify that the patient is deceased. The body is then kept on a respirator to keep blood flowing through the organ until it can be removed and given to a waiting recipient. All of this usually takes about 24 hours.

Donation does not disfigure the body and does not interfere with having a funeral, even an open-casket service.

Making Your Wishes Known

Your health care directive is a good place to state your wishes regarding organ donation. Using this program you can choose from the following four options:

Indicate that you have already made arrangements or signed a document expressing your

donation wishes. If you choose this option, you will be asked to briefly describe the arrangements you have made or the document you have signed, including its location.

Other Ways to Make Your Wishes Clear

If you want to be a donor, there are a few more steps you can take to be sure your wishes are carried out. First, if your state offers a donor card—for example, a card or sticker that accompanies your driver's license—it's a good idea to obtain it and fill it out. It can alert others to your wishes in the event of an accident, when your health care documents may not be immediately available.

Second, many states now have donor registries, where you can sign up to donate any usable organs or tissues at your death. These registries, which are run by the state or by a nonprofit organization, provide computerized, confidential lists to authorized medical personnel 24 hours a day. You can check the Internet to see whether a donation registry is available in your state.

Finally, and most important, you should discuss your views about organ donation with your health care agent, close relatives and friends. Even if you've put your wishes in your health care directive and filled out a separate donor card, it's possible that an objection by a close family member could defeat your wishes after death. The best thing you can do is let those close to you know that you feel strongly about donating your organs.

Leave specific instructions about organ, tissue or body donation in your health care document. If you have not made arrangements to donate your organs but you know that you want to be a donor, you can add specific instructions directly to your health care directive. If you choose this option, you may state whether you want to donate any needed organs or body parts, or only specific ones that you name. You will also be able to indicate the purposes for which your donation must be used, including transplant, therapy, research, education or any necessary purpose that is allowed by law.

Indicate that you do not want to donate your organs. If you choose this option, your health care document will clearly state that you don't want to be a donor.

Leave the decision to your agent. If you named a health care agent, you can let him or her make organ donation decisions. If you choose this option, it will be helpful to discuss your feelings with, and offer some guidance to, your agent.

Making It Legal

When you arrive at this part of the program, know that you have finished with the hard parts of making your health care directives. You have overcome the lure of procrastination to assert your right to keep control over your own health care.

However, you still must comply with a few technical requirements before your documents will be legally valid and binding. Very detailed, state-specific instructions will print out with your documents. But here's a brief overview of what you must do.

Signing Your Documents

Every state requires that you sign your documents—or direct another person to sign them for you.

But do not sign them immediately. You must sign your documents in the presence of witnesses or a notary public—sometimes both, depending on state law. That way, there is at least one other person who can attest that you were of sound mind and of legal age when you made the documents.

Signing for Someone Else

If you are helping someone else prepare health care documents and that person is too ill or weak to sign them, you or another person may sign the documents at his or her direction. The document will print with a special place for you to add the signer's name and signature.

The person making the document and the signer should appear together in front of the witnesses and/or notary public (see below), so that someone can observe the signing and confirm, if it is ever necessary, that it is what the document maker wanted and directed.

Having Your Documents Witnessed and Notarized

In most states, witnesses must sign your documents. In some states, you may have your documents notarized instead of witnessed. In others, you will be required to have both witnesses and a notary sign your document. Each state's rule is listed below. Note that a few states have different requirements for the document directing your health care and the document naming your agent.

Witnessing

Many states require that two witnesses see you sign your health care documents and that they verify in writing that you appeared to be of sound mind and signed the documents without anyone else influencing your decision.

Each state also has rules about who may serve as your witnesses. In many states, for example, a spouse, another close relative or any person who would inherit property from you is not allowed to act as a witness for the document directing health care. And many states prohibit your attending physician from being a witness. The goal of these laws is to be sure your witnesses do not have a personal or professional interest in your health care, and, therefore, a conflict of interest.

If your state has restrictions on who may serve as witnesses to your health care documents, those restrictions are listed below and will also be noted on your documents, just before the witness signature lines.

Notarization

A notary public is an individual who is authorized by the state to verify signatures on documents. It shouldn't be difficult to find a notary. Many are listed in the yellow pages. Many hospitals also have a notary on staff.

Depending on your circumstances, you may take your document to the notary, or the notary may come to you. The notary will watch you sign the document and may then sign the notary language on the form or fill in a separate form and attach it to your document.

Be prepared to show the notary some identification and to pay a small fee for the services. If you are a patient in a hospital, the service may be free of charge.

The table below, as well as the instructions accompanying your documents, will tell you whether your state requires that your documents be notarized and whether there are any restrictions on who may serve as the notary.

Glossary of Witnessing Terms

When you read the requirements for witnesses in your state, you may find some unfamiliar words. Here are brief definitions of some terms that commonly occur.

Beneficiary. Any person who is entitled to inherit property from a deceased person.

Beneficiary of a will. Any person or organization named in a will to receive property, either as a first choice or if the first choice as beneficiary does not survive the person making the will.

Claim against the estate. Any right that a person has to receive property from a person's estate. This may arise under a will or living trust, from a contract or because of a legal liability that the deceased owes to the person.

Devisee. Any person who either is entitled to inherit property from a person under state law or who has been named to inherit property in a will or living trust.

Heir at law. Any person who qualifies to inherit property from a person under state law. Usually, heirs at law are spouses, children, parents, brothers and sisters. However, if none of these people exist, an heir at law might be a niece, a nephew or even a distant cousin.

Inherit by operation of law. When a person dies owning property that has not been left by a will or by some other legal device such as a living trust, the property will be distributed according to the laws of the state where the person died—that is, by operation of law. These laws—commonly referred to as the "laws of intestate succession"—usually give property first to a spouse and children and then to parents, brothers and sisters.

Presumptive heir. Someone who would inherit property under state law unless a child was later born to the current owner of the property the presumptive heir expects to receive.

State Witnessing and Notarizing Requirements

Alabama

Advance Directive for Health Care
Two witnesses are required. Neither of your witnesses may be:

- under the age of 19
- your health care proxy
- the person who signed your advance directive for you, if you were unable to sign it yourself
- related to you by blood, marriage or adoption
- entitled to any portion of your estate by operation of law or under your will, or
- directly financially responsible for your medical care.

Alaska

Advance Health Care Directive
Must either be signed by two adult witnesses or notarized.

If you choose to have the document witnessed, neither of your witnesses may be:

- your health care agent
- your health care provider
- an employee of your health care provider, or
- an employee of the health care institution or health care facility where you are receiving health care.

In addition, at least one of your witnesses must not be related to you by blood, marriage or adoption—and must not be entitled to any part of your estate under a will or codicil (amendment to a will).

Arizona

Living Will

Health Care Power of Attorney
Both documents must be signed by at least one witness or notarized.

If you choose to have the document witnessed, you may choose to have one or two witnesses. If you choose to have one witness, your witness may not be:

- any person involved in providing your health care
- related to you by blood, marriage or adoption, or
- entitled to any part of your estate by operation of law or under your will.

If you have two witnesses, your witnesses do not need to meet the last two requirements on the list above.

If you choose to have your document notarized, the notary may not be:

- your health care agent, or
- any person involved in providing your health care.

Arkansas

Declaration

Durable Power of Attorney for Health Care
Both documents must be signed by two witnesses who are at least 18 years old.

California

Single document: Advance Directive for Health Care
Must either be signed by two witnesses or notarized.

If you choose to have the document witnessed, neither of your witnesses may be:

State Witnessing and Notarizing Requirements (continued)

- your health care agent
- your health care provider
- an employee of your health care provider
- the operator of a community care facility
- an employee of a community care facility
- the operator of a residential care facility for the elderly, or
- an employee of a residential care facility for the elderly.

In addition, one of your witnesses must not be related to you by blood, marriage or adoption—and must not be entitled to any part of your estate by operation of law or under your will.

Finally, if you are in a skilled nursing facility, the document must also be witnessed by a patient advocate or ombudsman. (This requirement applies whether the document is witnessed or notarized.)

Colorado

Declaration as to Medical or Surgical Treatment

Durable Power of Attorney for Health Care
Both documents must be signed by two witnesses and may also be notarized.

If you choose to have the document witnessed, neither of your witnesses may be:

- a physician
- an employee of your attending physician
- an employee of a health care facility where you are a patient
- a person with a claim against your estate, or
- a person entitled to any part of your estate by operation of law or under your will.

In addition, if you are a patient or resident of a health care facility, the witnesses cannot be patients of that facility.

Connecticut

Health Care Instructions and Appointment of Health Care Agent and Attorney-in-Fact for Health Care Decisions
Must be signed by two witnesses.

Although the law does not restrict who can serve as a witness, we suggest that your witnesses be at least 18 years old and the person named to serve as your health care agent and your attorney-in-fact for health care decisions not act as a witness. You and your witnesses may also sign in front of a notary public, but you are not required to do so.

Document Concerning Withholding or Withdrawal of Life Support Systems
Must be signed by two witnesses. Although the law does not restrict who can serve as a witness, we suggest that your witnesses be at least 18 years old and the person named to serve as your health care agent and your attorney-in-fact for health care decisions not act as a witness.

Appointment of Health Care Agent and Attorney-in-Fact for Health Care
Must be signed by two witnesses. Although the law does not restrict who can serve as a witness, we suggest that your witnesses be at least 18 years old and the person named to serve as your health care agent and your attorney-in-fact for health care decisions not act as a witness.

Delaware

Advance Health Care Directive
The document must be signed by two witnesses. Neither of your witnesses may be:

- under the age of 18

State Witnessing and Notarizing Requirements (continued)

- related to you by blood, marriage or adoption
- an owner, operator or employee of a residential long-term health care institution in which you are a resident
- a person directly financially responsible for your medical care
- a person with a claim against any portion of your estate, or
- a person entitled to any portion of your estate by operation of law or under your will.

If you are a resident of a sanitarium, rest home, nursing home, boarding home or related institution, one of the witnesses must be, at the time you sign the Advance Health Care Directive, a patient advocate or ombudsman designated by the Division of Services for Aging and Adults with Physical Disabilities or the Public Guardian.

District of Columbia

Declaration
Must be signed by two witnesses. Neither of your witnesses may be:

- under the age of 18
- related to you by blood or marriage
- your attending physician
- an employee of your attending physician
- an employee of a health care facility where you are a patient
- the person who signed your declaration for you, if you were unable to sign it yourself
- a person entitled to any part of your estate by operation of law or under your will, or
- a person directly financially responsible for your medical care.

If you are a patient in a skilled care facility, one witness must be a patient advocate or ombudsman.

Durable Power of Attorney for Health Care
Must be signed by two witnesses. Neither of your witnesses may be:

- under the age of 18
- your health care attorney-in-fact
- your health care provider, or
- an employee of your health care provider.

In addition, one of your witnesses must not be related to you by blood, marriage or adoption and must not be entitled to any part of your estate by operation of law or under your will.

Florida

Living Will
Must be signed by two witnesses, one of whom must not be your spouse or related to you by blood.

Designation of Health Care Surrogate
Must be signed by two witnesses, both of whom must be at least 18 years old. Neither witness may be your health care surrogate. In addition, one of your witnesses must not be your spouse or a blood relative.

Georgia

Advance Directive for Health Care
Must be signed by two witnesses. Neither of your witnesses may be:

- under the age of 18
- your health care agent
- a person who is directly involved in your health care, or

State Witnessing and Notarizing Requirements (continued)

- a person who will knowingly inherit anything from you or knowingly gain a financial benefit from your death.

In addition, only one of your witnesses may be an employee, agent or medical staff member of the hospital, skilled nursing facility, hospice or other health care facility in which you are receiving health care. (This witness is still prohibited from being directly involved in your health care.)

Hawaii

Advance Health Care Directive

Must be signed by two witnesses or notarized. If you choose to have the document witnessed, neither of your witnesses may be:

- your health care agent
- a health care provider, or
- an employee of a health care provider facility.

In addition, at least one of your witnesses must not be related to you by blood, marriage or adoption—and must not be entitled to any part of your estate by operation of law or under your will.

Idaho

Living Will and Durable Power of Attorney for Health Care

Idaho law does not require that your documents be witnessed or notarized. However, witnesses are recommended to avoid concerns that the document was forged, that you were forced to sign it or that it does not represent your wishes. If you choose to have your documents witnessed, we suggest that your witnesses be at least 18 years old and that your health care agent not act as a witness.

Illinois

Declaration

Must be signed by two witnesses. Neither of your witnesses may be:

- under the age of 18
- the person who signed your declaration for you, if you were unable to sign it yourself
- a person entitled to any part of your estate by operation of law or under your will, or
- a person directly financially responsible for your medical care.

Durable Power of Attorney for Health Care

Must be signed by one witness who is at least 18 years old.

Indiana

Living Will Declaration

Must be signed by two witnesses. Neither of your witnesses may be:

- under the age of 18
- your parent, spouse or child
- a person entitled to any part of your estate
- a person directly financially responsible for your medical care, or
- the person who signed your declaration for you, if you were unable to sign it yourself.

Durable Power of Attorney for Health Care and Appointment of Health Care Representative
Must be notarized.

Iowa

Declaration

Durable Power of Attorney for Health Care
Both documents must follow the same requirements:

State Witnessing and Notarizing Requirements (continued)

Must be signed by two witnesses or notarized.

If you choose to have the document witnessed, neither of your witnesses may be:

- under the age of 18
- your health care agent
- your health care provider, or
- an employee of your health care provider.

In addition, one of your witnesses must not be related to you by blood, marriage or adoption within the third degree of consanguinity (parents, children, siblings, grandchildren, grandparents, uncles, aunts, nephews, nieces and great-grandchildren).

Kansas

Declaration

Must be signed by two witnesses or notarized. Neither of your witnesses may be:

- under the age of 18
- the person who signed your declaration for you, if you were unable to sign it yourself
- related to you by blood or marriage
- entitled to any part of your estate by operation of law or under your will, or
- directly financially responsible for your health care.

Durable Power of Attorney for Health Care Decisions

Must be signed by two witnesses or notarized.

If you choose to have the document witnessed, neither of your witnesses may be:

- under the age of 18
- your agent for health care decisions
- related to you by blood, marriage or adoption

- entitled to any part of your estate by operation of law or under your will, or
- directly financially responsible for your health care.

Kentucky

Advance Directive

Must be signed by two witnesses or notarized. Neither of your witnesses nor the notary may be:

- related to you by blood
- your beneficiary by operation of Kentucky law
- your attending physician
- an employee of a health care facility where you are a patient, unless the employee serves as a notary public, or
- directly financially responsible for your health care.

Maine

Advance Health Care Directive

The document must be signed by two witnesses. Although the law does not restrict who can serve as a witness, we suggest that your witnesses be at least 18 years old and that your health care agent not act as a witness.

Maryland

Advance Directive

The document must be signed by two witnesses. The person you name as your health care agent cannot serve as a witness. In addition, at least one of your witnesses must be a person who is not entitled to any portion of your estate, and who is not entitled to any financial benefit by reason of your death.

State Witnessing and Notarizing Requirements (continued)

Massachusetts

Document Directing Health Care

Health Care Proxy

Both documents must be signed by two witnesses. Neither of your witnesses may be:

- under the age of 18, or
- your health care agent.

Michigan

Document Directing Health Care

Must be signed by two witnesses. Although the law does not restrict who can serve as a witness, we suggest that your witnesses be at least 18 years old and that your patient advocate not act as a witness.

Patient Advocate Designation

Must be signed by two witnesses. Neither of your witnesses may be:

- under the age of 18
- your spouse, parent, child, grandchild or sibling
- your patient advocate
- your physician
- an employee of your life or health insurance provider
- an employee of a health care facility where you are a patient
- an employee of a home for the aged where you live, or
- entitled to any portion of your estate by operation of law or under your will.

Minnesota

Health Care Directive

Must be signed by two witnesses or notarized. Neither your witnesses nor the notary may be your health care agent.

If you choose to have the document witnessed, at least one of the witnesses may not be a health care provider or employee of a provider directly attending to you.

If you choose to have the document notarized, the notary may not be your health care agent.

Mississippi

Advance Health Care Directive

Must be signed by two witnesses or notarized.

If you choose to have the document witnessed, neither of your witnesses may be:

- under the age of 18
- your health care agent
- a health care provider, or
- an employee of a health care provider or facility.

In addition, one witness must not be related to you by blood, marriage or adoption, and must not be entitled to any part of your estate by operation of law or under your will.

Missouri

Declaration

Must be signed by two witnesses. Neither of your witnesses may be:

- under the age of 18, or
- the person who signed your declaration for you, if you were unable to sign it yourself.

Durable Power of Attorney for Health Care

If you grant your agent power to direct your burial or cremation, your document must be signed in front of two witnesses and notarized. If you do not grant this power, only the notary is necessary.

State Witnessing and Notarizing Requirements (continued)

Montana

Declaration

Durable Power of Attorney for Health Care

Both documents must be signed by two witnesses. Although the law does not restrict who can serve as a witness, we suggest that your witnesses be at least 18 years old and that your health care agent not act as a witness.

Nebraska

Declaration

Must be signed by two witnesses or notarized. If you choose to have the document witnessed, neither of your witnesses may be:

- under the age of 18, or
- an employee of your life or health insurance provider.

In addition, one witness may not be a director or employee of your treating health care provider.

Durable Power of Attorney for Health Care

If you grant your agent power to direct your burial or cremation, your document must be signed by two witnesses and notarized. Neither of your witnesses may be:

- your attorney-in-fact for health care decisions
- your attending physician
- your spouse, parent, child, grandchild or sibling
- your presumptive heir or known devisee, or
- an employee of your life or health insurance provider.

In addition, one of your witnesses must not be an administrator or employee of your health care provider.

If you do not grant your agent the power to direct your burial or cremation, you may choose to have your document signed by two witnesses (subject to the requirements above) or notarized.

Nevada

Declaration

Must be signed by two witnesses. Although the law does not restrict who can serve as a witness, we suggest that your witnesses be at least 18 years old and that your attorney-in-fact for health care decisions not act as a witness.

Durable Power of Attorney for Health Care Decisions

If you grant your agent power to direct your burial or cremation, your document must be notarized. If you do not grant this power, you may choose to have your document signed by two witnesses or notarized. If you choose to have the document witnessed, neither of your witnesses may be:

- under the age of 18
- your attorney-in-fact for health care decisions
- a health care provider
- an employee of a health care provider
- the operator of a health care facility, or
- an employee of the operator of a health care facility.

In addition, one of your witnesses must not be related to you by blood, marriage or adoption and must not be entitled to any part of your estate by operation of law or under your will.

New Hampshire

Advance Directive

Must be signed by two witnesses or notarized. If you choose to have the document witnessed, neither of your witnesses may be:

- under the age of 18

State Witnessing and Notarizing Requirements (continued)

- your health care agent
- your attending physician or advanced registered nurse practitioner (ARNP) or a person acting under the direction or control of the attending physician or ARNP
- your spouse, or
- entitled to any part of your estate by operation of law or under your will.

In addition, no more than one witness may be a health or residential care provider or such provider's employee.

New Jersey

Combined Advance Directive for Health Care

Instruction Directive

Proxy Directive

Any document must be signed by two witnesses or notarized.

If you choose to have the document witnessed, neither of your witnesses may be:

- under the age of 18, or
- your health care representative.

New Mexico

Advance Health Care Directive

The law does not require that your advance directive be witnessed. However, witnesses are recommended to avoid concerns that the document might be forged, that you were forced to sign it or that it does not genuinely represent your wishes. If you choose to have your document witnessed, we suggest that your witnesses be at least 18 years old.

New York

Document Directing Health Care

Health Care Proxy

Both must be signed by two witnesses. Neither of your witnesses may be:

- under the age of 18
- your health care agent, or
- the person who signed the declaration for you, if you were unable to sign it for yourself.

If you reside in a mental health facility, your witnesses must meet additional requirements. Ask your mental health care provider for more information.

North Carolina

Advance Directive

Must be signed by two witnesses and notarized. Neither of your witnesses may be:

- related to you by blood or marriage
- your attending physician or mental health treatment provider
- a licensed health care provider who is (1) an employee of your attending physician or mental health treatment provider, (2) an employee of the health facility in which you are a patient, or (3) an employee of a nursing home or any adult care home where you reside.
- a person entitled to any part of your estate by operation of law or under your will, or
- a person with a claim against you or your estate.

Health Care Power of Attorney

Must be signed by two witnesses and notarized. Neither of your witnesses may be:

- under the age of 18
- related to you by blood or marriage

State Witnessing and Notarizing Requirements (continued)

- your attending physician or mental health treatment provider
- a licensed health care provider who is (1) an employee of your attending physician or mental health treatment provider, (2) an employee of the health facility in which you are a patient, or (3) an employee of a nursing home or any adult care home where you reside.
- a person entitled to any part of your estate by operation of law or under your will, or
- a person with a claim against you or your estate.

North Dakota

Health Care Directive
Must be signed by two witnesses or notarized. Neither the witnesses or the notary may be:

- under the age of 18
- your spouse or another person related to you by blood, marriage or adoption
- your health care agent
- a person entitled to any part of your estate upon your death, or
- a person with a claim against your estate.

In addition, at least one witness must not be a health care or long-term care provider providing you with direct care or an employee of the health care or long-term care provider providing you with direct care. (This restriction does not apply to the notary.)

Ohio

Declaration
Must be signed by two witnesses or notarized. If you choose to have the document witnessed, neither of your witnesses may be:

- under the age of 18
- related to you by blood, marriage or adoption
- your attending physician
- an administrator of a nursing home where you receive care, or
- the person who signed your declaration, if you were unable to sign it yourself.

Durable Power of Attorney for Health Care
Must be signed by two witnesses or notarized. If you choose to have the document witnessed, neither of your witnesses may be:

- under the age of 18
- related to you by blood, marriage or adoption
- your attorney-in-fact
- your attending physician, or
- an administrator of a nursing home where you receive care.

Oklahoma

Advance Directive for Health Care
If you grant your agent power to direct your burial or cremation, your document must be signed in front of two witnesses and notarized. If you do not grant this power, only the witnesses are necessary. Neither of your witnesses may be:

- under the age of 18
- related to you by blood, marriage or adoption, or
- a person who might inherit from you.

Oregon

Advance Directive
Must be signed by two witnesses.
Neither of your witnesses may be:

- your health care representative, or

State Witnessing and Notarizing Requirements (continued)

- your attending physician.

One witness may not be:

- related to you by blood, marriage or adoption
- an owner, operator or employee of a health care facility where you are a resident, or
- a person entitled to any part of your estate upon your death.

Pennsylvania

Declaration

Durable Power of Attorney for Health Care

Both documents must be signed by two witnesses. Neither of your witnesses may be:

- under the age of 18, or
- the person who signed your declaration for you, if you were unable to sign it yourself.

Rhode Island

Declaration

Must be signed by two witnesses. Your witnesses may not be related to you by blood or marriage.

Durable Power of Attorney for Health Care

If you grant your agent power to direct your burial or cremation, your document must be notarized. If you do not grant this power, you may choose to have your document signed by two witnesses or notarized.

If your document will be notarized, the notary may not be:

- related to you by blood, marriage or adoption, or
- entitled to any part of your estate by operation of law or under your will.

If you choose to have the document witnessed, neither of your witnesses may be:

- under the age of 18
- your health care agent
- a health care provider
- an employee of a health care provider
- the operator of a community care facility, or
- an employee of an operator of a community care facility.

In addition, one of your witnesses must not be related to you by blood, marriage or adoption and must not be entitled to any part of your estate by operation of law or under your will.

South Carolina

Declaration

Must be signed by two witnesses and notarized. Neither of your witnesses may be:

- related to you by blood, marriage or adoption
- your attending physician
- an employee of your attending physician
- a person directly financially responsible for your medical care
- a person entitled to any part of your estate by operation of law or under your will
- a beneficiary of your life insurance policy, or
- a person who has a claim against your estate.

No more than one of your witnesses may be an employee of a health care facility where you are a patient. If you are in a hospital or nursing care facility when you sign your declaration, at least one of your witnesses must be an ombudsman designated by the state.

Health Care Power of Attorney

Must be signed by two witnesses and notarized. Neither of your witnesses may be:

- your health care agent

State Witnessing and Notarizing Requirements (continued)

- your attending physician
- an employee of your attending physician
- related to you by blood, marriage or adoption
- directly financially responsible for your medical care
- the beneficiary of an insurance policy on your life
- a person with a claim against your estate at the time you sign your document, or
- a person entitled to any portion of your estate by operation of law or under your will.

In addition, only one witness may be an employee of a health facility in which you are a patient.

South Dakota

Living Will Declaration

Must be signed by two witnesses, both of whom are at least 18 years old, and may also be notarized, although notarization is optional.

Durable Power of Attorney for Health Care

Must be signed by two witnesses, both of whom are at least 18 years old.

Tennessee

Advance Health Care Directive

Must be signed by two witnesses or a notary. If you choose to have your document witnessed, both witnesses must be competent adults and neither may be your health care agent. In addition, at least one of your witnesses must not be related to you by blood, marriage or adoption—and must not be entitled to any part of your estate by operation of law or under your will.

Texas

Directive to Physicians and Family or Surrogates

Must be signed by two witnesses. Your witnesses must be at least 18 years old. In addition, at least one of your witnesses may not be:

- your health care agent
- related to you by blood or marriage
- your attending physician
- an employee of your attending physician
- an employee of a health care facility in which you are a patient if the employee is providing direct care to you or is an officer, director, partner or business office employee of the health care facility or of any parent organization of the health care facility, or
- a person who is entitled to or has a claim against any part of your estate after your death.

Medical Power of Attorney

Must be signed by two witnesses. Your witnesses must be at least 18 years old. In addition, at least one of your witnesses may not be:

- your health care agent
- related to you by blood or marriage
- your attending physician
- an employee of your attending physician
- an employee of a health care facility in which you are a patient if the employee is providing direct care to you or is an officer, director, partner or business office employee of the health care facility or of any parent organization of the health care facility, or
- a person who is entitled to or has a claim against any part of your estate after your death.

State Witnessing and Notarizing Requirements (continued)

If you grant your agent the power to direct your burial or cremation, you must also have your document notarized.

Utah

Advance Health Care Directive
Must be signed by one witness. Your witness may not be:

- under the age of 18
- your health care agent
- related to you by blood or marriage
- a health care provider who is providing care to you
- an administrator at a health care facility where you are receiving care
- a person directly financially responsible for your medical care
- a person entitled to any part of your estate by operation of law or under your will, or
- the person who signed your document for you, if you were unable to sign it yourself.

If you grant your agent power to direct your burial or cremation, your document must be signed in front of two witnesses.

Vermont

Advance Directive
Must be signed by two witnesses. Neither witness may be:

- under the age of 18
- your health care agent, or
- your spouse, reciprocal beneficiary, parent, adult sibling, adult child or adult grandchild.

In addition, if you are a patient in a hospital, nursing home or residential care facility, a

designated person must sign the document after explaining it to you. Ask a patient representative for help with this requirement.

Virginia

Advance Medical Directive
If you grant your agent power to direct your burial or cremation, your document must be signed in front of two witnesses and notarized—and your health care agent must sign the part of the document that grants the power.

If you do not grant your agent power to direct your burial or cremation, only the witnesses are necessary.

Your witnesses must be over the age of 18. In addition, we suggest that your health care agent not act as a witness.

Washington

Health Care Directive
Must be signed by two witnesses. Neither of your witnesses may be:

- related to you by blood or marriage
- your attending physician
- an employee of your attending physician
- an employee of a health care facility where you are a patient
- a person entitled to any part of your estate by operation of law or under your will, or
- a person with a claim against your estate.

Durable Power of Attorney for Health Care
Must be signed by two witnesses. Although the law does not restrict who can serve as a witness, we suggest that your witnesses be at least 18 years old and that your health care agent not act as a witness.

State Witnessing and Notarizing Requirements (continued)

West Virginia

Living Will

Medical Power of Attorney

Both documents must meet the same requirements:

Must be signed by two witnesses and notarized.

Neither of your witnesses may be:

- under the age of 18
- your health care representative or successor representative
- the person who signed your document, if you were unable to sign it yourself
- related to you by blood or marriage
- your attending physician
- a person directly financially responsible for your medical care, or
- a person entitled to any part of your estate by operation of law or under your will.

Wisconsin

Declaration to Physicians

Must be signed by two witnesses. Neither of your witnesses may be:

- related to you by blood, marriage or adoption
- your health care provider
- an employee of your health care provider, other than a chaplain or a social worker
- an employee of an inpatient health care facility where you are a patient, other than a chaplain or a social worker
- a person directly financially responsible for your medical care
- a person who has a claim against your estate, or

- a person entitled to any part of your estate by operation of law or under your will.

Power of Attorney for Health Care

Must be signed by two witnesses. Neither of your witnesses may be:

- under the age of 18
- your health care agent
- related to you by blood, marriage or adoption
- your health care provider
- an employee of your health care provider, other than a chaplain or a social worker
- an employee of an inpatient health care facility where you are a patient, other than a chaplain or a social worker
- a person directly financially responsible for your medical care, or
- a person with a claim against your estate.

Wyoming

Advance Health Care Directive

Must be signed by two witnesses or notarized. If you choose to have the document witnessed, both witnesses must be competent adults who know you personally. In addition, neither of your witnesses may be:

- your health care agent
- a treating health care provider
- an employee of a treating health care provider
- the operator of a community care facility
- an employee of an operator of a community care facility
- the operator of a residential care facility, or
- an employee of an operator of a residential care facility.

Making and Distributing Copies

Ideally, you should make an effort to make your wishes for your future health care widely known. Keep the originals of your health care documents and, at a minimum, give copies to your agent, if you named one, and to the doctors or medical facility most likely to be treating you. Also consider giving copies to:

- any physician with whom you now consult regularly
- the office of the hospital or other care facility in which you are likely to receive treatment
- the patient representative of your HMO or insurance plan
- immediate family members—spouse, children, siblings, and
- trusted friends.

Some people are hesitant to discuss the particulars of their medical care with other people, feeling that it is an intensely private issue. However, in the case of health care directives, you must weigh your desire for privacy against the need for the documents to be effective. Your carefully reasoned medical directive will simply be wasted words unless you make sure it gets into the hands of the people who need to know about it.

Keeping Your Documents Up to Date

Review your health care documents occasionally—at least every few years—to make sure they still accurately reflect your wishes for your medical care. Advances in technology and changes in health prompt many people to change their minds about the kind of health care they want.

In addition, you should consider making new documents if:

- You move to another state.
- You get married. You should prepare new health care documents if you get married, unless your new spouse is already named as your health care agent. You are never required to name your spouse as your health care agent, but if you want to name someone else, be sure you do it in a document created after the date of your marriage. If you have an old document naming someone other than your spouse as your agent, some states will consider it automatically revoked when you marry.
- You get divorced. If you divorce or separate, revoke your health care documents and make new ones. In most cases, your former spouse's authority as agent terminates automatically if you file for divorce, but you should still create a new document to make your wishes clear.
- You made a health care directive many years ago, because your state's law controlling them has probably changed substantially.
- The agent you named to supervise your wishes becomes unable to do so.

Revoking Your Documents

If you have a change of heart and want to revoke or cancel your health care documents, you can do so at any time.

If you want to revoke the appointment of your health care agent (or an alternate agent), most states require that you either deliver a written notice to your agent and health care providers, or personally inform your primary physician that you no longer want your agent to serve. You may revoke other health care choices simply by informing or demonstrating to your health care providers and others who know about your wishes that you want to revoke them.

But the best practice is to revoke any document in writing—if you are well enough to do so. You should also tear up the original document and ask anyone who has a copy to return it to you to be destroyed. The program will print a revocation form that you can keep for later use, if you need it.

As a practical matter, even if you prepare a written revocation, it is important to tell everyone who knows about your document that you have revoked it.

A New Document Trumps an Old One

If there is more than one health care directive, and there is any discrepancy between the two, the statements in the most recent one win. Technically, there is no need to formally revoke an earlier document. However, confusion may arise if an old document still exists—for example, if it covers issues on which the newer document is silent. For this reason, you should do all you can to make sure your old document is clearly revoked and destroyed. And of course you should make sure that your new document is properly finalized, that you give it to your doctor and your health care agent and that it is placed in your medical records.

Final Arrangements

M ost people avoid the subject of death—and are especially uncomfortable thinking about their own mortality. You, too, may be tempted to leave the details of your final arrangements to those who survive you. But there are two good reasons not to do this: care and cost.

Making Final Arrangements in Advance

Anyone who has lost a loved one knows how agonizing it can be to plan an appropriate commemoration. And most people have attended funerals or memorial services that seem uniquely unsuited to the person who has died.

Letting your survivors know whether you'd like to be buried or cremated, and what kind of ceremonies you envision, saves them the pain of making such decisions at a difficult time. Many family members and friends also find that an open discussion is a great relief—especially if death is likely to occur soon.

Planning some of these details in advance and doing wise comparison shopping can also save money. For many people, after buying a home and car, after-death goods and services are the most expensive thing they ever pay for.

Without some direction, your survivors may choose the most expensive goods and services available, to assuage their own feelings of grief or obligation or perhaps due to pressure from funeral industry providers. The best way to prevent this from happening is to write down your preferences. You can use this program to do just that, creating a final arrangements document to point the way for your loved ones.

A Will Is Not the Way

Despite what many people think, a will is a poor place to express your death and burial preferences. It probably won't be located and read until several weeks after you die—too late to help your family. It's better to write up a separate document such as the one you can prepare with this program.

CAUTION
Get organized for your family. Making a final arrangements document won't do any good unless your loved ones can find it when the time comes. Here are two suggestions for making sure your wishes aren't overlooked:

- Use Quicken WillMaker Plus to make an Information for Caregivers and Survivors form. It provides the location of all your important paperwork, including your final arrangements document. This form also lets you document other essential information, such as financial accounts and medical information. To learn more, click "Document List" and select "Information for Caregivers and Survivors" from the list.
- Turn to *Get It Together*, by Melanie Cullen with Shae Irving (Nolo). This comprehensive workbook walks you step by step through the process of gathering and organizing all your important records and personal information. You can order a customized binder to arrange your work.

The Legal Effect of Your Document

Your final arrangements document provides valuable guidance for your family members. It will tell them what kind of body disposition and services you want and direct them to any sources you've set aside for payment. As long as your wishes are reasonable and financially feasible, they should be carried out as you intend.

If relationships among your loved ones are amicable, this should be all you need. You can talk with those who will be most likely to carry out your wishes and give them a copy of your instructions—or be sure they know where to find them when the time comes.

If a dispute arises among your loved ones —for example, between your partner or spouse and other relatives—funeral industry personnel are usually bound to follow any written instructions you left. The greatest sticking points arise when the deceased person has not provided in advance for payment of the arrangements. (See "Paying for Final Arrangements," at the end of this chapter.) Court battles over preferences for body or funeral ceremonies almost never arise, primarily because of the lack of time and the costs of litigation.

Most disputes arise where more than one person is in charge—say you have three children—and they disagree over a fundamental decision, such as whether your body should be buried or cremated. Such disputes can be avoided if you are willing to put your wishes in writing.

If You're Worried About Family Fights

If you are concerned that your family may not agree with your final wishes—or if you expect them to argue with each other after your death—you can add legal force to your document by combining it with a health care directive.

It may not be possible to make your wishes ironclad. (State laws on the subject vary widely, and many are unclear or full of loopholes.) But a health care directive can help, primarily by allowing you to appoint someone to be sure your postdeath preferences are carried out.

The primary function of a health care directive is to set out wishes for medical treatment in an emergency or at the end of life. And one of the most important parts of making a health care directive is naming your health care agent—that is, the person who will oversee your medical care and make treatment decisions for you if you are unable to do so yourself. You can also give your health care agent the power to carry out your wishes for the disposition of your body and other final arrangements. (Using this program, you can make a health care directive that specifically includes this power.)

To provide guidance for your agent, you can simply attach your final arrangements document to your health care directive. After your death, if family members object to your wishes or squabble with each other about what's best, your health care agent is legally authorized to step in to ensure that you get what you wanted.

See Chapter 23 for more information on health care directives.

Expressing Your Wishes for Organ Donation

There are many ways to express your wishes for organ or body donation. You may have already indicated, on your driver's license or in another document, that you want to be a donor. You can also use your health care directive to state whether or not you wish to be a donor. Taken together, your health care directive and final arrangements document will act as a comprehensive guide to your end-of-life wishes.

If You Have Already Made Some Final Arrangements

If you have already made arrangements for burial or cremation, you may wonder whether it is necessary to make a final arrangements document. It is probably wise to do so. The program gives you the opportunity to describe any existing arrangements, and it may also direct your attention to issues that you have not yet addressed. The result is a comprehensive document that provides essential directions for your survivors.

What Happens If There Is No Document

If you die without leaving written instructions about your preferences, state law determines who has the right to control how your remains will be disposed. In most states, the right—and the responsibility to pay—rests with the following people, in order:

- spouse or registered domestic partner
- child or children
- parent or parents
- next of kin, or
- a court-appointed public administrator.

Getting Started

Before you jump into the details of your final arrangements document, you may want to spend some time thinking about the big picture. It may be easier to answer specific questions once you have a general sense of what you want.

How to approach this is up to you. You may find it helpful to talk with family or friends about end-of-life issues, reflecting on what appeals to you—and what doesn't. Perhaps you have participated in after-death events that you have particularly liked, or where you have felt noticeably uncomfortable. All these things can help to point the way.

If you want to do some additional research, you might browse the Funeral Consumers Alliance website at www.funerals.org. This nonprofit organization's "Frequently Asked Questions" page is a good place to begin exploring your options.

When you're ready, this program invites you to put the details in writing. We'll guide you through a number of topics, one at a time:

- burial or cremation
- mortuary or cremation facility
- embalming

- casket or urn
- pallbearers
- transportation to grave
- headstone, monument or burial marker
- epitaph
- funeral or memorial ceremonies
- obituary, and
- financial plans.

You need answer only the questions you want to. While it helps to be as specific as possible, your final arrangements document can be as brief or as extensive as you wish. If there is an issue you don't care to address, simply skip it. If you like, you can always come back to the program later, either to change your answers or create a more detailed document.

If You Are an Organ Donor

You should state your preference for burial or cremation even if you have arranged to donate some organs or your entire body. (See Chapter 23 for more about organ donation.) Keep in mind that if one or more of your organs is donated, the rest of your body must be disposed of or buried. And even if you have arranged to have your entire body donated, there is the possibility the donation might not be accepted for some reason. And, finally, after the medical institution has finished using the body for teaching or research in one or two years, it must be disposed of or buried.

Burial or Cremation

One of the most important questions we will ask you is whether you want your body to be buried or cremated.

If your body will be buried, you can state your preferences for a burial site. If you choose cremation, you will be asked whether you want your ashes to be scattered, buried or interred, or kept with a loved one.

Body Burial

While more people are choosing cremation than in the past, most bodies in the United States are buried. Depending on your wishes, your body may be buried immediately after death or several days later, after a funeral or other memorial service.

The Burial Process

A body may be buried in the ground, generally in a cemetery plot, or aboveground in the chamber of a mausoleum or family crypt. Typically, burial includes placing the body in a casket. However, if you want your body to be buried immediately, a casket may not be necessary. (Although required by many individual cemeteries, a casket is not a legal requirement for burials in the United States.)

Burial Costs

Burial can be expensive. The national average cost for a traditional funeral, with burial and headstone or monument, is $6,500. Depending upon the costs of products, services and ceremonies, burial can cost several times as much as cremation.

How Much Does Burial Cost?

Product or Service	Cost Estimate
Immediate burial, without embalming or casket	$700 to $4,000
In-ground cemetery plot	$400 or more
Labor charge for interment in a cemetery plot	$500 to $2,500
Casket	$500 to $20,000
Grave liner or in-ground vault, required by many cemeteries (but not by law) to help maintain a level, unshifting landscape	$500 to $10,000
Above-ground crypt	$1,500 or more
Mortuary services, including transfer of remains, embalming, visitation, funeral, funeral booklet or cards, preparing an obituary and ordering the death certificate	$3,000 or more—plus cost of casket, flowers, burial plot, interment, headstone or burial marker

Leaving Instructions

If you have decided where you wish to be buried, record that information. If you have already purchased a gravesite and any other related products or services, describe your arrangements—and attach any related documents (for example, your contract with the cemetery) to your final arrangements document when you print it out.

If you haven't bought a gravesite, but you know where you'd like to be buried, you can state your preference. There is no guarantee

that it will be available when you die, but your survivors will know what you had in mind.

Cremation

The number of people who choose to be cremated is steadily increasing. For some, the relatively low cost makes this choice an easy one. But there are many other reasons why someone might prefer to be cremated—for example, you may want to have your ashes scattered or kept by a loved one at home.

Religious Concerns

Many religions accept cremation. Islam; the Baha'i faith; and the Greek, Jewish and Russian Orthodox faiths oppose cremation outright. The Catholic Church has significantly relaxed its views about cremation in the past decade. If you are thinking of choosing cremation and have religious concerns, speak with your spiritual adviser.

The Cremation Process

Cremation is the burning of a body at extreme heat, resulting in a fine residue of ash and bone. The cremated remains (sometimes called "cremains," though we'll call them "ashes" here) may be buried, scattered or kept in an urn. A temporary casket is required to contain the body during cremation. Cremation caskets are generally made of unfinished wood, cardboard, pressboard or canvas. The cremation facility supplies the temporary casket.

Complete cremation arrangements usually include local transportation of the body to the cremation facility, visitation with the body prior to cremation, a temporary container for remains, cremation, a memorial service, preparation of an obituary, ordering the death certificate and the scattering or other disposition of the ashes.

Cremation Costs

As with burial, cost may play a part in your decision. Here are some cost estimates.

How Much Does Cremation Cost?

Product or Service	Cost Estimate
Cremation	$400 to $1,800
Cremation with scattering at sea	$1,200 to $2,400
Niche in columbarium	$850 to $6,000, averaging about $3,000

What to Do With Cremated Remains

If you choose to have your body cremated, we will ask what you'd like your survivors to do with your ashes. You can state that you'd like your ashes to be:

- scattered over land or water
- buried
- stored aboveground, or
- kept with family or friends.

After you make your initial selection, we'll ask you to provide more details about your wishes. If you want to divide your ashes among two or more of these options, select the one that feels most important to you. When you provide details, you can state exactly what you'd like your survivors to do, including how you want your ashes to be divided.

Scattering or Burying Ashes

If you choose to have your ashes scattered or buried, you should be aware of state or local laws that may affect your wishes.

Check state rules about scattering ashes. Some people wish to have their ashes scattered over some area that has special significance for them—such as a garden, a lookout point or the ocean.

Laws and restrictions on the scattering of ashes vary from state to state. To find out your state's laws, check with a local cremation facility or your state's health department (see "Finding your state's laws," below).

Scattering Services

Most people opt to have family members or friends scatter their ashes in private, in their own time and style. However, there are companies that arrange to transport and scatter cremated remains over land or sea. If you decide to hire one of these services in advance, make sure you understand its pricing structures. Also, attach a copy of any written agreement to your final arrangements document.

Going Green

Burials and cremations can be hard on the environment. Embalming chemicals, metal caskets, concrete burial vaults and cremation facility emissions take a surprising toll. If you want to make plans that minimize environmental effects, here are some options:

Choose a green cemetery. The Green Burial Council can help you find providers that avoid toxins, use biodegradable materials and even help to preserve open space. Visit www.greenburialcouncil.org for more information.

Say no to embalming. Embalming fluid contains toxic chemicals—including up to three gallons of formaldehyde—that can seep into soil and ground water. Embalming rarely serves a legitimate purpose and is almost never required. See "Embalming," below.

Ask for a biodegradable container. You can use a simple wood casket, cardboard box or shroud for burial. There are also biodegradable urns for ashes that will be buried. See "Caskets and Urns," below.

Avoid vaults. Vaults are large containers, usually made from reinforced concrete, that are placed in the ground before a burial. They're not required by law, but many cemeteries demand them because they make it easier to maintain the landscape. The result is that, every year, more than 1.5 million tons of reinforced concrete are buried along with caskets and bodies.

You can look for a cemetery that doesn't require vaults. In a few states, you can even refuse a vault on religious grounds. You may be required to pay an extra fee for grave maintenance.

Cremation conservation. Cremation uses the fewest resources, but it's not entirely clean. It burns fossil fuels and carries the risk of mercury pollution from incinerated fillings. Newer cremation facilities are more efficient, using about half the fuel. If you have amalgam fillings in your teeth, you can ask that they be removed before cremation.

TIP

Cashing in your crowns. If you want your dental work to be extracted prior to burial or cremation, metals can be redeemed for cash. (You can also cash in on replaced dental work during your life.) Garfield Refining Company buys dental metals—gold or semiprecious crowns, bridges and inlays. For more information, visit Garfield online at www.garfieldrefining.com.

Check state and local laws about burying ashes. Ashes can be buried in the ground. Local zoning ordinances may restrict where the burial may take place—such as that they must be buried a specified distance from a residence.

If you wish to have a family member or friend bury your ashes, it is a good idea to first check local zoning ordinances to see whether burial is permitted on the site you have chosen. Ashes can also be buried in a cemetery, either in a special urn garden or in a plot. It is not necessary to place the ashes in an urn before burial, although some places may require a plot liner to prevent the earth from sinking over time.

RESOURCE

Finding your state's laws. You can find information about your state's laws and common practices by contacting the state health department or related agency that governs cemetery and funeral activities. To easily locate this department online, start at the state website: www.[xx].gov, substituting the state's postal abbreviation for "xx." You should then find a listing for the office you need.

Mortuaries and Cremation Facilities

From an economic standpoint, choosing the institution to handle your burial or cremation is one of the most important decisions you can make. If you consider this issue now, you'll have to think about your options,

shop around if necessary—and then make recommendations to your survivors. That said, you may also want to give your loved ones some leeway. Circumstances may change significantly by the time of your death—for example, you may move or an institution may go out of business. Your survivors may need some flexibility when it comes time to carry out your plans.

A good mortuary is equipped to handle many of the details related to disposing of a person's remains. These include:

- collecting the body from the place of death
- storing it until burial or cremation
- making arrangements for burial or cremation
- conducting funeral ceremonies
- preparing the body for burial or cremation, and
- arranging to have the body transported for burial or cremation.

The mortuary can also help with administrative details, such as preparing an obituary and ordering copies of the death certificate.

If you wish to be cremated, the cremation facility may also be able to provide these services for you.

When you make your final arrangements document, you can suggest the mortuary and/ or cremation facility you'd like your survivors to use. If you want your family to handle the disposition of your remains without involving a mortuary or cremation facility (this is rare, but it can be done), you may say so.

Below, you'll find more information on choosing the right facility—or taking a more independent approach.

Choosing a Facility

It is important that you find the mortuary or cremation facility that best meets your needs in terms of style, proximity and cost. Comparison shopping is fairly easy, because mortuaries and cremation facilities must by law give price lists to consumers who visit their facilities—and must disclose prices and other information to those who ask for it over the phone.

You can compare prices and services at local facilities before you make your choice. You may also consider joining a funeral consumer group, or memorial society, to make the task easier. These nonprofit groups can help you locate a mortuary and make other decisions and plans. For a small membership fee, you will receive information about local service providers, including costs. You can also take advantage of the society's discounted rates for funeral products and services.

To locate a group in your area, contact the Funeral Consumers Alliance (FCA) at www.funerals.org or 800-765-0107. For help locating and evaluating cremation facilities, you may want to contact the Cremation Association of North America at www. cremationassociation.org or 312-245-1077.

Making Independent Plans

There is a trend in America for people to care for their own dead, minimizing or even eliminating the involvement of funeral industry personnel. This could mean everything from preparing the body to burying it or transporting it to the cremation facility.

Most states do allow individuals to act completely on their own. But there are rules about how people may proceed. For example, most states have laws that regulate the depth of a site for a body burial. A few states throw up roadblocks to acting independently, requiring that a funeral director handle the disposition of a deceased person.

If you are considering directing that a family member or friend handle your disposition independently, the following resources can help you make your plans:

- The Funeral Consumers Alliance website, www.funerals.org, offers extensive resources to help you make your own plans.
- *Caring for the Dead: Your Final Act of Love*, by Lisa Carlson (Upper Access Press). This book will help you understand how to take care of a body and what laws may apply. It includes a state-by-state guide to funeral and burial practices, as well as directories of cremation facilities and nonprofit funeral consumer groups.
- *Coming to Rest: A Guide to Caring for Our Own Dead*, by Richard Spiegel and Julie Wiskind (Dovetail). This guide covers details from washing the body and arranging ceremonies to complying with legal requirements and completing paperwork.

If you want to research your state's laws and common practices, see "Finding your state's laws," above.

Embalming

When making your final arrangements document, you will be asked whether or not you want your body to be embalmed. Embalming is a process in which the blood is drained and replacement fluids are pumped into the body to temporarily retard its disintegration. While it has now become a common procedure, embalming is rarely necessary; refrigeration serves the same purpose.

Originally considered a barbaric and pagan ritual, embalming first gained popularity during the Civil War, when bodies of the war dead were transported over long distances. When the war ended, embalming was promoted (mostly by those who performed the service) as a hygienic means of briefly preserving a body.

When Embalming Is Required

There is a popular misconception that embalming is always required by law after death. In fact, it is legally required only in some states and only in a few instances, such as:

- when a body will be transported by plane or train from one country or state to another
- where there is a relatively long time—usually a week or more—between the death and burial or cremation, and
- in some cases, where the death occurred because of a communicable disease.

If Your Body Is Not Embalmed

If you choose not to be embalmed, your body will be refrigerated until the time of burial. If you choose, you can still have a funeral or other service with an open casket.

The only effect of not being embalmed will be that if you opt to be buried, your body will begin to decompose within days instead of weeks.

Embalming Costs

The cost of embalming ranges from about $200 to $900, depending on your location and on the individual setting the rate. Refrigeration is usually much less costly, involving a daily charge of about $50. Some facilities provide refrigeration free of charge.

Caskets and Urns

Whether you choose to be buried or cremated, you will have the option to state your wishes for a casket or an urn. You may want both—for example, if you'd like a temporary casket for a funeral before your cremation and an urn for your ashes afterward.

Choosing your own casket or urn may seem like more than you want to think about right now, but there's a very practical reason to consider your preferences and make them known: Doing so may save your survivors thousands of dollars.

First, caskets and urns carry the biggest mark-up of all funeral goods and services. Second, grieving survivors aren't always capable of making sound decisions. This is a setup for overspending. Your loved ones may choose something elaborate and costly, not knowing that you would have been satisfied with simple arrangements.

On the other hand, if you want something ornate and you can afford it, now's your chance to make your wishes known.

Caskets

For immediate burial, a simple container or pine box is all that is necessary. But you may prefer to have a casket—and the cemetery you've chosen may require it. If there will be a service before burial with your body present, the type of container is entirely up to you. You may want something luxurious, something economical, or, if the viewing or service will be at home or in another private place, you may not feel the need for any type of container at all.

If your remains will be cremated but you first want to have a funeral or memorial service with your body present in a casket, your survivors may simply rent one. This is not as odd as it may sound; it is done quite frequently. A rental casket has a disposable liner.

Caskets are usually made from wood, metal, fiberglass or plastic and are available in a wide range of finishes, colors and styles. For example, the fittings or hinges may be finished in gold or silver, with a shine or antique finish. The inside of the casket is usually lined with cloth, which is also available in different fabrics

and colors. The closure may be simple, or it may be fitted with a gasket or protective sealer, promising protection from the elements—at significant additional cost.

A casket may cost anywhere from $500 to $20,000 or more, averaging about $2,330. Casket rentals run about $600, on average. You may want to shop around and compare prices. Under federal law, a funeral home cannot charge you a fee if you provide your own casket, whether homemade or purchased from an outside source.

Urns

If your remains will be cremated and scattered, the cremation facility will provide a temporary container, and you won't need an urn. If you want your survivors to place your ashes in a columbarium or grave or to keep them at home, they will need a container of some sort.

Cremation urns are available in a wide range of materials and styles, from bronze book replicas to colorful porcelain vases. Attractive biodegradable urns are available for burial at sea. If your remains will be divided, smaller "keepsake" containers are available to hold just a portion of them.

If the cremated remains will be interred or buried, the columbarium or cemetery may impose restrictions on the size, shape or type of urn that you may use.

Cremation urns start at about $35 for simple wooden boxes and can run as high as $5,000 to $10,000 for materials such as gilded porcelain.

Shopping for Caskets and Urns

For more information, and to compare prices on caskets and urns, you can turn to the following resources:

- CasketXpress (www.casketxpress.com) and UrnXpress (www.urnxpress.com) allow you to browse a wide range of styles.
- The Funeral Consumers Alliance (www.funerals.org or 800-765-0107) provides information to help you get a fair deal on a casket or urn. The organization can also help you locate independent casketmakers or artisans if you are interested in a low-cost or specialized container.

Pallbearers

In some funeral ceremonies, the casket is carried to and from the place where the ceremony is held—and sometimes again carried from a vehicle to a burial site. The covering traditionally draped over a casket is called a pall, and the people who carry the casket are called pallbearers.

If you envision a ceremony in which your casket will be carried, you can name the people you would wish to serve as pallbearers. Close friends and relatives are common choices. While women were not historically named as pallbearers, there is no logical reason to exclude them.

Your choices need only be physically able to lift and carry. And factor in that some people's psychological makeup may make them better or worse choices for the job.

The number of pallbearers usually ranges from four to eight, but you can name as many or as few as you wish. If you know of no one to nominate—or know just a couple of people you want to name—a mortuary should be able to provide people to help.

Transportation to Grave

You may have a preference about the type of vehicle that will carry your body to the burial site or cremation facility, usually after a funeral ceremony. This might be a horse-drawn carriage, a favorite antique car or a stretch limousine.

If you have selected a mortuary to handle some of your arrangements, it may have only one type of vehicle available. If the vehicle customarily provided is not what you would want for yourself, check to be sure the mortuary will allow you to provide your own—and be sure that it will not add its transportation charge to your costs. If this is important issue to you, check with the mortuary you selected earlier and, if its arrangements about transportation are not satisfactory, shop for another mortuary.

Headstones, Monuments and Burial Markers

Headstones and monuments are upright grave markers (picture the traditional, rounded tombstone), generally used with in-ground burials in a cemetery. In contrast, burial markers are flat and flush to the ground or other surface (picture a plaque), and may be used with an in-ground burial or affixed to a vault above the ground. Burial markers are often used in mausoleums, columbariums and family crypts. Also, because of space constraints and maintenance considerations, many cemeteries now prefer burial markers for graves in the ground.

Headstones, monuments and burial markers come in an almost endless array of shapes and sizes, from the common tombstone to elaborate sculptures and designs. For example, a headstone or burial marker might be embossed with flowers, figures or a photograph. It might bear the logo of a fraternal organization or a military insignia. New "green" cemeteries may use simple stones or just a planting of wildflowers to mark a grave. Designs are limited only by the constraints of cemetery policy, the craft of the builder and your budget. (An Internet search for "burial monument" or "grave marker" will turn up numerous providers to help you compare styles and prices.)

Traditional headstones and monuments are most often made from marble or granite. Both stones come in a variety of colors and shades. With granite, the darkest shades provide the best long-term resistance to erosion. Burial markers are usually made from stone or from various metals—such as steel, bronze or copper.

Headstones and burial markers start at about $400 and run into the thousands. An individual mausoleum or crypt costs about $20,000, and a family mausoleum (containing eight to ten caskets) can run as much as $2 million.

Epitaphs

Perhaps the most entertaining aspect of making final arrangements is choosing the words that you wish to appear on your burial marker. These words are known as your epitaph. Your epitaph can be extremely simple, stating only the years you were born and died—or it can reflect your personality by including a witty saying, favorite phrase or poem.

Famous Epitaphs

I am ready to meet my Maker. Whether my Maker is prepared for the great ordeal of meeting me is another matter.
—Winston Churchill

*Cast a cold eye
On life, on death
Horseman, pass by!*
—W.B. Yeats

3.14159265358979323846264338327950288...
—Ludolph van Ceulen computed π (pi) to 35 digits

Here lies one whose name was writ in water.
—John Keats

She did it the hard way.
—Bette Davis

The best is yet to come.
—Francis Albert Sinatra

That's all folks!
—Mel Blanc

Ceremonies

Death often involves at least one ceremony and sometimes more. To sort out the details for yourself and your survivors, you might find it helpful to consider the types of services that can occur at the following times:

- before burial or cremation
- at the time of burial or when ashes are scattered or interred, or
- after burial or cremation.

You may want a ceremony at each of these times—or at none of them. When you make your final arrangements document, you can leave instructions for each type of ceremony. If you don't want any services, the program allows you to say so. Or, if you have no preferences, you can indicate that and leave these decisions to your loved ones.

Ceremonies Before Burial or Cremation

Most people want at least one ceremony or gathering to be held before their remains are buried or cremated, even if it is a simple one. A wake or funeral is a way for your friends and family members to say goodbye to you, to comfort one another and to grieve.

That said, there may be good reasons why this type of ceremony is not right for you. You may live far from most of your friends and family members, meaning they would have to drop everything and attend the ceremony at great personal cost. In these circumstances, many people opt not to have a large funeral but instead prefer a memorial ceremony— usually held days or weeks after the burial— that more people can attend. (You may of course request a small gathering before your burial or cremation, followed later by a larger memorial ceremony.)

If you do want one or more ceremonies to be held before your body is buried or cremated, it's a good idea to write down your wishes. The more details you arrange while you are alive, the fewer decisions will be left for your survivors at a time when decisions are likely to be hard for them to make.

Here is basic information about common types of services before burial or cremation, to help you make your plans.

Viewing, Visitation or Wake

A viewing, visitation or wake is an opportunity for family and friends to view your body or to sit with you after you've died. For many, it is a quiet, meditative time. For others, it will be a time to gather with family and friends for remembering and honoring your life.

A viewing or visitation is commonly held in the viewing room of a funeral home or mortuary. However, you may wish to have it in another place, such as your home, a community hall or a church. It all depends on your wishes and the options available to you.

Traditionally, a wake is a gathering characterized by both sadness and gaiety—a celebration of the life that has passed and a send-off to whatever comes next. A wake is often held in the home of the deceased person, but many mortuaries now offer their facilities and services for one- or two-day wakes. A wake can be an important part of the grieving process, giving family and friends an opportunity to come together and comfort each other.

If you want a viewing, visitation or wake, you may wish to consider:

- where and when the gathering should be held
- who should be invited
- whether you will have a casket and, if so, whether it should be open or closed, and
- whether you want music, readings, certain types of food or drink, or other details for the gathering. (For wakes, there is of course no limit to the number of details you could specify. Some people have directed their loved ones to wear bright-colored clothing, bring their favorite pets or read a favorite poem.)

Funeral

A traditional funeral is a brief ceremony, most often held in a funeral home chapel or a church. The body is usually present, either in an open or a closed casket. Beyond that, there are no absolutes or requirements about what constitutes a funeral. If the deceased person adhered to a particular religion, funerals often include a brief mass, blessing or prayer service.

In some traditions, only family members attend the funeral, while friends and the general public are invited to attend other scheduled ceremonies. In other locales and traditions, this is reversed, and the funeral is the less private event.

Some concerns you may wish to address when planning a funeral are:

- where the ceremony should be held
- who should be invited
- whether clergy should be invited to lead the ceremony or participate in it and specific names of clergy you would like

- any music you would like played, along with the names of the musicians or singers you would like to perform it
- preferences for a eulogy or other readings, and the name of the person or people you would like to speak
- whether you want your body present at the ceremony or a picture displayed instead, and
- whether you want to suggest that friends donate to a certain organization instead of sending flowers.

If you'd like family and friends to gather at a reception after your funeral, you may specify that as well. Aside from where the reception should be held, you may want to consider the following details:

- who should be invited
- what kind or food and beverages should be served, and
- whether you want to request specific music, activities or entertainment for the gathering.

Burial, Interment or Scattering Ceremonies

In addition to or instead of holding a ceremony before burial, it is common to hold a brief ceremony at the gravesite at which a religious leader, relative or close friend says a few prayers or words of farewell. This type of ceremony may also be appropriate after cremation, at the time your ashes are scattered or interred.

If this is something you want, and you have an idea of who should be there, who should speak and what they should say, describe those details.

Ceremonies After Burial or Cremation

Ceremonies after burial or cremation may range from a reception immediately following a burial or the scattering of ashes to a memorial ceremony held days, weeks or even months after death. Memorial ceremonies may be held anywhere—a mortuary, a religious building, a home, outside or even a restaurant.

Memorial ceremonies are more often the choice of those who wish to have an economic, simple commemoration. While funeral directors, grief counselors or clergy members may be involved in memorial ceremonies, they are not the people to consult for objective advice. Many will advocate that traditional funerals—traditionally more costly and less personalized—are most effective in helping survivors through the mourning process. The truth is that most survivors are likely to take the greatest comfort in attending a ceremony that reflects the wishes and personality of the deceased person.

The details you may want to consider for a reception or memorial ceremony after burial or cremation are largely the same as those for wakes or funerals. For lists to jog your thinking, see "Ceremonies Before Burial or Cremation," above.

Your Obituary

An obituary is a notice printed in a newspaper or other publication after your death. It informs people that you have died and provides some biographical information about you. In addition, the obituary may specify the time and place of your funeral or memorial service and include other details, such as wishes for donations to be made in your name.

Where Will Your Obituary Be Published?

Think about the places where your obituary might be published—newspapers, newsletters, magazines or online. You might want to recommend to your survivors that specific publications run your obituary. For example, you might suggest that your obituary be published in newspapers in the various communities where you have lived and worked. If you work for a company or organization that publishes a newsletter, provide the contact information for the newsletter. If you are well known, you may want to recommend specific magazines or other publications that would be interested in publishing an article about your life.

In the past, newspapers published two types of notices: death notices, which were paid notices supplied by the family, and obituaries, which were statements written by the newspaper's editorial department. Nowadays, the distinction has blurred for many newspapers and both paid and nonpaid statements are often grouped together. We refer to both types of notices as "obituaries."

If you are well known in the community or the field in which you work, a newspaper or other publication will likely publish a detailed obituary or even an article about your life, and there won't be a fee associated with that. Otherwise, the length of your obituary depends on the local newspaper's obituary policy and fees, your budget and how much you wish to say.

Making the Choice

When you make your final arrangements document, you can state that:

- you have already written an obituary that you would like your survivors to publish
- you have not written an obituary, but would like to leave some guidelines for your survivors
- you do not want your survivors to publish an obituary, or
- you have no preferences for the publication of your obituary.

If you anticipate that your family will publish only a brief death notice, you may want to indicate that you have no preference and leave the decisions to them. But if you know that any source—be it a newspaper, website, organizational newsletter or church bulletin—will want to publish information about you after your death, it will help your survivors to know what these sources are and what you do or don't want your obituary to say.

Leaving Instructions

If you prefer to draft your own obituary, we will ask you to state where it is located, so your survivors can easily find it when they need it.

If you don't want to draft a full obituary, you can provide some guidance about what you'd like your survivors to include in your obituary and where they should publish it.

When deciding what to include, you may want to consider the following topics:

- where and when you were born
- family information, including the names of your spouse or partner, children, grandchildren, parents and siblings
- where you went to school
- information about your work
- military service
- community or recreational organizations
- awards or achievements
- special interests or hobbies
- whether or not you want people to send flowers in your name
- whether or not you want people to make donations to a particular charity or organization in your name, and
- anything else you'd like others to know or remember about you.

Guarding Sensitive Information

Unfortunately, obituaries have become popular sources of information for identity thieves. You may want to use caution when supplying details for a death notice. Instead of providing a full birthdate, you might give just the month and year—for example, March 1927. For married women, you may choose to omit the maiden name, a common bit of information used to gain access to financial and other critical accounts.

You may also want to select a photograph to include with your obituary. Your instructions can state which photograph you prefer and where your survivors can find it.

Following are a few sample obituaries to help you draft your own obituary or leave instructions for your survivors. For more examples, look at your newspaper or its website. This should give you many ideas for structuring your obituary.

EXAMPLE: Paul Ralph Dillon, 67, 12 Sunset Lane, Mill Valley, died Thursday, October 5, in San Francisco. Funeral services will be at 10 a.m. Saturday at Grace Cathedral Episcopal Church in San Francisco.

EXAMPLE: Paul Ralph Dillon, 67, 12 Sunset Lane, Mill Valley, died Thursday, October 5, in San Francisco. A native of Springfield, Massachusetts, and a graduate of the Stanford Law School, Mr. Dillon worked as a patent attorney and was a founding partner of Dillon & Winkler, a San Francisco patent law firm. He is survived by his wife, Margaret Evans-Dillon of Mill Valley and two sons, Mark Dillon of Los Angeles and James Dillon of Sacramento. Services will be at 10 a.m. Saturday at Grace Cathedral Episcopal Church in San Francisco.

EXAMPLE: Margaret Evans-Dillon, 71, 12 Sunset Lane, Mill Valley, died Friday, January 11, in Mill Valley. A native of Pleasanton, Ms. Evans-Dillon was an ardent supporter of environmental causes in Marin County and one of the founders of the Marin Environmental Education Program, a series of programs that integrate environmental concerns into local class studies. In 1998, Ms. Evans-

Dillon created Mill Valley Waterkeepers to preserve Mill Valley's watershed and plant and animal life. Ms. Evans-Dillon also served on the Board of the Marin Agricultural Land Trust.

Ms. Evans-Dillon was the daughter of Grace and Woodward Evans of Pleasanton. Her father, Woodward Evans, served as city manager and city attorney for Pleasanton. Ms. Evans-Dillon attended San Francisco State University and received paralegal certification from the University of San Francisco. She worked for twelve years as a paralegal in San Francisco, specializing in patent and copyright law, before marrying Paul Dillon in 1973. Paul Dillon passed away in 1989.

She is survived by two sons, Mark Dillon of Los Angeles and James Dillon of Sacramento. Services are at 12 noon Sunday at St. Anselm Church in Ross. In lieu of flowers, memorial contributions can be sent to the Marin Agricultural Land Trust, P.O. Box 809, Point Reyes Station, CA 94956.

Paying for Final Arrangements

Whatever arrangements you make, you have two main options for covering costs. You can:
- pay everything up front (in a lump sum or installments), or
- decide what you want and leave enough money for your survivors to pay the bills.

If you don't do any of these things, and your estate doesn't have enough money to cover the costs, your survivors will have to pay for any final expenses.

Paying in Advance

If you want to pay in advance, either all at once or under a payment plan, be sure you're dealing with a reputable provider of goods and services, and document your arrangements very clearly.

There are reasons to be cautious about paying up front. Though there are a number of legal controls on how the funeral industry can handle and invest funds earmarked for future services, there have been many reported instances of mismanaged and stolen funds. A great many other abuses go unreported by family members too embarrassed or grief stricken to complain.

In addition, when mortuaries go out of business, customers who have prepaid may be left without a refund and without recourse. Also, many individuals who move during their lifetimes discover that their prepayment funds are nonrefundable—or that there is a substantial financial penalty for withdrawing or transferring them. In addition, money paid now may not cover inflated costs of the future, meaning that survivors will be left to cover what's left.

Setting Aside Funds

A safe, simple and flexible option is to set aside funds that your survivors can use to cover the costs of your final plans.

After making your plans and estimating the cost, you can tuck away that sum (perhaps adding a bit to cover inflation or unexpected expenses) in a money market or other accessible fund. Tell the bank or financial institution that you want to set up a payable-on-death account. You can designate a beneficiary—a good choice might be the executor of your will or successor trustee of your living trust—who can claim the money immediately upon your death. The beneficiary will have no legal obligation to use these funds for your final arrangements, so make sure that person understands what the funds are for and that you trust him or her to do as you ask.

Leaving Instructions

We ask you to write out your financial plans in a few sentences. You'll also want to make sure your survivors have immediate access to any of the documents they'll need to carry out your arrangements, such as a prepayment contract or bank account information.

What to Do With Your Finished Document

After you have printed, dated and signed your final arrangements document, you may need to take a few more steps to ensure it works as you intend.

If you have paperwork to keep with your document, such as receipts or contracts, gather everything together. Attach the papers to your final arrangements document or create a binder or folder where you can store everything in the same place.

If you'll use your final arrangements document in conjunction with a health care directive (as discussed at the beginning of this chapter), you should attach your final arrangements document to the directive.

Store your documents where your loved ones can readily find them. You may want to make photocopies for people who should be aware of your wishes, and tell them where to find the originals, if necessary. It's a good idea to keep a list of folks to whom you've given copies, in case you need to retrieve them later.

Changing or Revoking Your Document

You can change or cancel your document at any time. There is no formal way to do this, so simply tear up the original. If you've given copies to others, be sure to get those copies back so you can destroy them, too. Then make a new document that reflects your current wishes.

If You Need More Help

You probably won't need a lawyer's help to make a will, a living trust or any of the other Quicken WillMaker Plus legal documents. But you may come up with questions about your particular situation that should be answered by an expert. This is especially likely if you have a very large estate, must plan for an incapacitated minor or have to deal with the assets of a good-sized small business. We highlight these and other "red flags" throughout the manual and program.

Learning More

If you've read most of this manual and started making your own will, living trust, health care directive or other document, you may know more about estate planning than a fair number of lawyers do. If you have questions that these materials don't address, you may want to consult some other self-help books or websites before you consult a pricey expert. It's often worth the money to pay a good lawyer for advice about your specific situation; it's rarely worth it to pay by the hour for education. Reading some background information before hiring a lawyer is usually the best approach.

Here are some places to get more in-depth information about estate planning:

- *Plan Your Estate*, by Denis Clifford (Nolo). This book explains how to draw up a complete estate plan making use of a will, living trust and other devices. It introduces more complex estate planning strategies, including various types of tax-saving trusts for the very wealthy.

- *8 Ways to Avoid Probate*, by Mary Randolph (Nolo). If you're interested in learning more about some of the probate-avoidance techniques discussed in this manual, check out this book.

- *Special Needs Trusts: Protect Your Child's Financial Future*, by Stephen Elias (Nolo). This book will help you understand and draft a trust to protect a disabled child. Even if you decide to have a lawyer draw up or finalize the trust, you will be armed with the information you need to get the best possible help.

- *The Executor's Guide: Settling a Loved One's Estate or Trust*, by Mary Randolph (Nolo). This is an invaluable handbook for anyone asked to serve as an executor. It can also help you prepare your estate for your own executor, to make the job as easy as possible.

- *Prenuptial Agreements: How to Write a Fair and Lasting Contract*, by Katherine E. Stoner and Shae Irving. Estate planning is often an important component of writing a prenuptial agreement. If you're planning to be married and considering a written agreement, this book will walk you through the process, including lots of guidance to help you communicate and negotiate a plan that will please both of you.

Nolo Blogs

Nolo's experts are now blogging about day-to-day legal issues that affect your life. For useful, and often entertaining, information about wills, trusts, and other estate planning issues, visit Nolo's Everyday Estate Planning Blog at blogs.nolo.com/estateplanning.

What Kind of Expert Do You Need?

If you have questions, the first thing to decide is what type of expert you should seek. Questions about estate taxes may be better (and less expensively) answered by an experienced accountant than a lawyer. Or if you're wondering what type of life insurance to buy, you may be better off talking to a financial planner.

Consult a lawyer if you have specific questions about a provision of your will, living trust or other estate planning device. Also see a lawyer if you want to get into more sophisticated estate planning—for instance, if you want to establish a charitable trust or a detailed plan to avoid estate taxes.

Different Ways to Get Legal Advice From a Lawyer

Although many consumers (and some lawyers) don't know it yet, the way lawyers and their customers structure their relationships is changing fast. Lawyers used to insist on taking responsibility (and fees) for creating an entire estate plan. But in what has become a very competitive market, many lawyers now offer piecemeal services, tailored to just what a customer wants.

This means you no longer have to walk into a lawyer's office, turn over your legal problems and wait for an answer—and a bill. Instead, you can often buy what you need, whether it's a bit of advice, a single estate planning document, a review of a document

you've prepared with this program or regular coaching as you handle a probate court proceeding on your own.

If you adopt this approach, you and the lawyer should sign an agreement that clearly sets out your roles and states that the lawyer is not acting in a traditional role, but instead giving you limited services or representation. Without this type of agreement, lawyers fear that dissatisfied clients might later hold them responsible for more than they actually agreed to take on. The agreement should make things clear to you too, so you know what to expect from the lawyer. (For more, see "Working With a Lawyer," below.)

Finding a Lawyer

Finding a competent lawyer who charges a reasonable fee and respects your efforts to prepare your own estate planning documents may not be easy. First of all, you'll want to find a lawyer who specializes in estate planning. Most general practice lawyers are simply not sufficiently educated in this field to competently address complicated problems. Here are some other ways to look for help.

Personal Recommendations

The best way to find a lawyer is to get a recommendation from someone you trust. So ask your relatives and friends—especially those you know who have substantial assets and have likely made an estate plan. You may also want to ask those who run their own businesses. They are likely to have a relationship with a lawyer, and if that lawyer doesn't handle estate planning, he or she probably knows someone who does.

Finally, you might check with people you know in any social or other organization in which you are involved. Senior citizens' centers and other groups that advise and assist older people may have a list of local lawyers who specialize in wills and estate planning and are well regarded.

Advice by Phone

If you want advice on a single matter, $40 to $50 will buy you a phone call with a lawyer licensed in your state. You can talk for as long as you want about the subject of your call.

This "Ask an Attorney" service is offered by ARAG, a large provider of prepaid legal insurance. The attorneys who staff the phones are screened (they must be licensed and in good standing with their state bar association) and monitored by ARAG. They are also forbidden from offering to sell you more services—which means they have no incentive to recommend more than you need. There's also a money-back guarantee if you're not satisfied. To use the service, visit www.aragdirect.com.

Group Legal Plans

Some unions, employers and consumer action organizations offer group legal plans to their members or employees, who can obtain legal assistance free or for low rates. If you are a member of such a plan, check with it first. Your problem may be covered free of charge. If it is, and you are satisfied that the lawyer

you are referred to is knowledgeable in estate planning, this route is probably a good choice.

Some plans, however, give you only a slight reduction in a lawyer's fee. In that case, you may be referred to a lawyer whose main virtue is the willingness to reduce fees in exchange for a high volume of referrals. Chances are you can find a better lawyer outside the plan and negotiate a similar fee.

Living Trust Seminars

Newspapers, radio and TV are full of ads for free "seminars" on living trusts. Usually, these events are nothing more than elaborate pitches for paying a lawyer $1,000 to $1,500 to write a living trust. Is it worth it? Probably not.

For a relatively small estate, Quicken WillMaker Plus should be all that you need. For more complicated estate planning, you will almost surely get better, less expensive and more personal service from a local estate planning specialist.

Attorney Directories

A lawyer directory will give you the names of attorneys who practice in your area. You will probably find several who specialize in estate planning and will give you an initial consultation for a low fee.

Following are two directories that may help you. Be sure to take the time to check out the credentials and experience of any lawyer who is listed.

Nolo's Lawyer Directory. Nolo offers a directory that provides a detailed profile for each attorney with information to help you select the right lawyer for you. Attorneys use their profiles to describe their experience, education and fees, and also tell you something about the lawyer's general approach to practicing law. (For example, each lawyer states whether he or she is willing to review documents or coach clients who are doing their own legal work.) Nolo has confirmed that every listed attorney has a valid license and is in good standing with his or her local bar association.

West's Legal Directory. This directory lists most lawyers in the United States—more than 700,000 of them. You can look for a lawyer by location and legal practice category; there's a good chance you'll find more than one estate planning lawyer in your area. You can find the directory at lawyers.findlaw.com or in your local law library.

Attorney Referral Services

Your local county bar may have an attorney referral service, which differs from a directory in that a referral service will gather some information about your legal needs and match you with attorneys who might be a good fit for you. Usually you'll get only a few names of attorneys to consider, chosen for you by the knowledgeable people running the referral service, rather than having an entire directory to choose from on your own.

Working With a Lawyer

Before you talk to a lawyer, decide what kind of help you really need. Do you want someone to advise you on a complete estate plan, or just to review the documents you prepare to make sure they look all right? If you don't clearly tell the lawyer what you want, you may find yourself agreeing to turn over all your estate planning work.

One good strategy is to do some background research and write down your questions as specifically as you can. If the lawyer doesn't give you clear, concise answers, try someone else. If the lawyer acts wise but says little except to ask that the problem be placed in his or her hands—with a substantial fee, of course—watch out. You're either dealing with someone who doesn't know the answer and won't admit it (common) or someone who finds it impossible to let go of the "me expert, you plebeian" philosophy (even more common).

Lawyer fees usually range from $100 to $350 or more per hour. But price is not always related to quality. It depends on the area of the country you live in, but generally, fees of $150 to $200 per hour are reasonable in urban areas. In rural areas and smaller cities, $100 to $150 is more like it. The fee of an experienced specialist may be 10% to 30% higher than that of a general practitioner, but the specialist will probably produce results more efficiently and save you money in the long run.

Be sure you settle your fee arrangement— preferably in writing—at the start of your relationship. In addition to the hourly fee, you should get a clear, written commitment from the lawyer about how many hours your problem should take to handle.

RESOURCE
For more information about working with lawyers and holding down legal fees, see the "Rights and Disputes" area of Nolo's website at www.nolo.com. Click on "Go to Court or Mediate," then select "Working With a Lawyer."

Doing Your Own Legal Research

There is often a viable alternative to hiring a lawyer to resolve legal questions that affect your estate planning documents: You can do your own legal research. Doing your own legal research can provide some real benefits if you are willing to learn how to do it. Not only will you save some money, you will gain a sense of mastery over an area of law, generating confidence that will stand you in good stead should you have other legal problems.

Fortunately, researching wills, living trusts and related estate planning issues is an area generally well suited to doing your own legal research. Most problems do not involve massive or abstruse legal questions. Often you need only check the statutes of your state to find one particular provision.

RESOURCE
Nolo's website, www.nolo.com, offers a section on estate planning that covers a range of topics including living trusts and estate and gift taxes. You can also find links to state and federal statutes from the site.

Legal Research: How to Find & Understand the Law, by Stephen Elias and Susan Levinkind (Nolo), gives instructions and examples explaining how to conduct legal research.

Finding Statutes in a Law Library

You can always find state statutes at a law library or, usually, at the main branch of a public library. Depending on the state, statutes are compiled in books called statutes, revised statutes, annotated statutes, codes or compiled laws. For example, the Vermont statutes are found in a series called *Vermont Statutes Annotated*, while Michigan's laws are found in two separate sets of books: *Michigan Statutes* or an alternate series called *Michigan Compiled Laws*. (The term "annotated" means that the statutes are accompanied by information about their history and court decisions that have interpreted them.) The reference librarian can point you toward the books you need.

After you've found the books, check the index for provisions dealing with the specific subject that concerns you—for example, wills, revocable living trusts or powers of attorney. Generally, you will find what you want in the volume of statutes dealing with your state's basic civil or probate laws. Statutes are numbered sequentially, so once you get the correct number in the index, it will be easy to find the statute you need.

Once you find a law in the statute books, it's important to look at the update pamphlet in the back of the book (called the "pocket part") to make sure your statute hasn't changed or been repealed. Pocket parts are published only once per year, so brand-new laws often have not yet made it to the pocket part. Law libraries subscribe to services and periodicals that update the statute books on a more frequent basis than the pocket parts. You can ask a law librarian to help you find the materials you need.

Finally, you may find summaries of relevant court cases immediately following the statute. (These are the annotations mentioned just above.) If so, you'll want to skim them. If a summary looks like it might help answer your question, read the full court case cited there. (Ask the librarian for help finding the case, or turn to the legal research resource listed above.)

Finding Statutes Online

All states have made their statutes available on the Internet. You can find them by visiting the legal research area of Nolo's website at www. nolo.com/statute/state.cfm. Choose your state to search or browse the statutes.

In addition, almost every state maintains its own website for pending and recently enacted legislation. If you hear about a proposed or new law and you want to look it up, you can use your state's website to find not only the most current version of a bill, but also its history. To find your state's website, open your browser and type in www.state.[your state's postal code].us. Your state's postal code is the two-letter abbreviation you use for mailing addresses. For example, NY is the postal code for New York, so to find New York's state website, type www.state.ny.us. When you open your state's home page, look for links under "government." All states have separate links to their legislatures, and they offer many different ways to look up bills and laws. You can also find any state's legislature through the National Conference of State Legislatures at www.ncsl.org.

Users' Manual Table of Contents

Appendixes

Getting the Most Out of Quicken WillMaker Plus

Welcome to Quicken WillMaker Plus 2009. Quicken WillMaker Plus makes it easy for you and your immediate family to create wills, living trusts and other legal documents for planning your estate and handling personal and financial matters.

You don't need legal training or estate planning experience to create documents with Quicken WillMaker Plus. The onscreen interviews provide easy-to-understand guidance every step of the way. And if you need more help than you see onscreen, the two product manuals are just a click away:

- This Users' Manual explains how to use the program.
- The Legal Manual provides legal and practical answers to help you create specific documents.

You can view electronic versions of both manuals at any time from within Quicken WillMaker Plus. Many screens have links that take you directly to the sections of the manuals that relate to the question you're answering

This part of the Users' Manual gives you a preview of how the program works, along with some tips for using it to your best advantage.

How Quicken WillMaker Plus Works

Two points are key to understanding Quicken WillMaker Plus:

- The program interviews you and uses your answers to create documents.
- Much of the document-creation work happens invisibly, behind the scenes.

Interviews at Your Own Pace

Each document you can create with Quicken WillMaker Plus has its own interview. You click through the questions and answer them at your own pace.

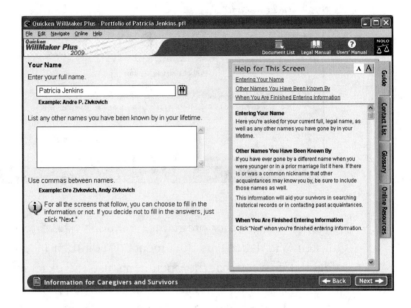

When you finish an interview, the program combines your answers with the appropriate legal language and displays the completed document for you to review.

Unlike some other programs, you don't type directly into Quicken WillMaker Plus documents or edit their language. This safeguard ensures that the documents use the exact language needed to make them legally valid. When you need to make changes to a document, you go back to the appropriate sections of the document interview and change your answers there.

Because Quicken WillMaker Plus customizes later interview questions based on the answers you give to earlier ones, a changed answer may affect the rest of your interview—so after you make a change to a document you may be asked to go back and review some (or all) of the interview questions you've already answered.

You can produce any document in Quicken WillMaker Plus in one sitting, but there's no point in rushing. Relax and take your time—after all, Quicken WillMaker Plus doesn't charge by the hour. Read the "Help for This Screen" section of the onscreen Guide and consider it thoughtfully. You can always stop a document interview and come back later; it's easy to pick up exactly where you left off.

When you're satisfied with your document, print and sign it, following the signing instructions that we provide for every document. These instructions tell you how to finalize your document and make it legal; for instance, signing your will in front of two witnesses or having your living trust notarized.

Looking Behind the Scenes

Part of what makes Quicken WillMaker Plus easy to use is the work the program does invisibly, without your noticing. For example, when you type in a person's name, the program automatically creates an entry for that person in the Contact List section of the program, where contact information is stored for reuse.

While you can get along fine without knowing most of what Quicken WillMaker Plus is doing behind the scenes, learning a little about what's happening in the background can help you use the program more efficiently and effectively. This manual's "Behind the Scenes" features alert you to actions the program is taking and tell you how they may affect you. Look for the "Behind the Scenes" icon shown below:

Read these notes to become a "power user" of Quicken WillMaker Plus.

Not Just Wills: Create Living Trusts, Health Care Directives and More

You can create many types of legal documents with Quicken WillMaker Plus:

- estate planning documents (such as wills, living trusts, health care directives and durable powers of attorney for finances)
- executor documents (such as letters to creditors, financial institutions and others)

- home and family documents (such as housesitting instructions and agreements for taking care of children, pets or elders), and
- personal finance documents (such as bills of sale and promissory notes).

To take full advantage of the program's estate planning offerings, click **Learn More** on the "Which Estate Planning Documents Do You Need?" screen in the program's introduction. You'll then be asked to specify your life circumstances—for instance, whether or not you're married or have children. After only a few clicks, the program recommends a set of estate planning documents that are right for you.

Knowing about the full range of available documents will help you get the most from the program—for example, you can use it to create a quick pet care agreement and some housesitting instructions before you head off on a trip. The complete list of documents you can create with Quicken WillMaker Plus is available in the program's Document List. (See "Exploring the Document List" in Part 3.)

Getting Started

t's easy to start using Quicken WillMaker Plus. Typically, you'll need to:

1. Install Quicken WillMaker Plus.
2. Start the program.
3. Register your copy of the program.
4. Update your version of the program.
5. Get oriented to the screen elements.
6. Figure out which estate planning documents you need.
7. Begin creating documents.

Steps 3 through 6 are optional, but we strongly recommend that you go through them all—especially Step 4, which ensures that you are using the most up-to-date version of the program.

This part of the manual takes you through all of the above steps except creating documents; you'll read about that in Part 3.

Making Sure Your System Meets the Requirements

Before you install Quicken WillMaker Plus, check that your system meets these minimum requirements:

- **Computer.** Pentium 133 (Pentium II 300 recommended)
- **Operating System.** Windows 2000/XP/Vista
- **Memory.** 32 MB RAM (64 MB RAM recommended)
- **Hard Disk Space.** 19 MB (28 MB to install)
- **Monitor.** Super VGA (800 x 600) with 256 colors (16-bit color recommended)
- **CD-ROM Drive.** 2x speed
- **Internet Connection.** 14.4 Kbps modem required to access online features (56 Kbps or higher recommended)
- **Printer.** Any printer supported by Windows 2000/XP/Vista
- **Software.** Microsoft Internet Explorer 6.0 or higher; Adobe Acrobat Reader (optional).

Installing Quicken WillMaker Plus

You install Quicken WillMaker Plus by running the installer. Here's how:

1. Insert the Quicken WillMaker Plus disc into your CD-ROM drive to launch the automatic setup program. If the automatic setup program doesn't launch automatically when you insert the Quicken WillMaker Plus CD, see "Jump-Starting the Setup Program" in Part 7.

2. Follow the instructions that appear onscreen to complete installation. If you're prompted to restart your computer after installation, do so.

 SKIP AHEAD

Skip ahead if your installation is now complete. If you need more information to help you perform the above steps, see the discussions just below. If not, skip ahead to "Starting Quicken WillMaker Plus."

Checking Out the Program Folder

Before using your newly installed version of Quicken WillMaker Plus, we suggest you take a look at the information in the **Quicken WillMaker Plus 2009** program folder on your hard drive.

To open the program folder and check out its contents, follow these steps:

1. From the Windows taskbar, choose **Start > Programs** (or **All Programs**) **> Quicken WillMaker Plus 2009**.

2. Click **Troubleshooting** to open the file and skim its contents. It contains late-breaking and situation-specific information for troubleshooting or preventing problems.

3. If you've used a previous version of the program, click **What's New** to open the file and see what's new compared to your older version.

Starting Quicken WillMaker Plus

You can start the program in either of the following ways:

- by double clicking the Quicken WillMaker Plus icon on your desktop (if you chose this option during installation), or
- by choosing (from the Windows taskbar) **Start > Programs** (or **All Programs**) **> Quicken WillMaker Plus 2009** (folder) **> Quicken WillMaker Plus 2009** (program).

If you used an older version of Quicken WillMaker or Quicken Lawyer to create a file with a .pfl extension on your computer, you're asked if you'd like to open it after installation. Click **Yes** if you want your old documents to show up in the Document List when you get to it, or click **No** to work with a brand-new file.

> CAUTION
>
> **Quicken WillMaker Plus 2009 may not convert all of your documents.** Be aware that some documents from earlier versions of the program can't be opened—and some may require you to review and update your interviews. The program will convert as many of your documents as possible, but sometimes extensive legal updates require us to significantly change the format of a particular document.

The first time you use the program, you won't go straight to the Document List. Instead, you'll encounter a series of introductory screens starting with the "Welcome to Quicken WillMaker" screen.

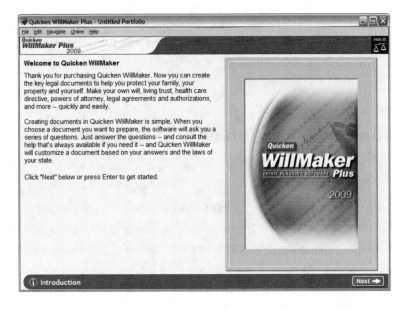

You aren't required to stop and read these screens; you can come back to them later by choosing **Navigate > Go to Introduction**. However, going through the introduction takes only a few minutes—and it's a great way to make sure you take advantage of all the features and services available with the program.

Registering Your Copy of the Program

Registering your copy of Quicken WillMaker Plus gives you access to a variety of services and benefits, including technical support. We recommend that you register as soon as you reach the "Online Registration" screen in the program's introduction.

To register your copy:

1. Do one of the following:
   - From the "Online Registration" screen in the program's introduction, click **Register Now**.
   - From anyplace else in the program, choose **Online > Online Registration**.

2. Follow the directions on the online registration page.

If you don't have an Internet connection, look in the back of your printed manual for a registration card that you can fill out and send in.

Updating Your Version of the Program

Because software boxes sometimes sit on shelves for a while, the version of Quicken WillMaker Plus that you bought may not be the most current. We regularly update the program to accommodate changing laws or fix problems our users report. To make sure you're running the latest version, use Web Update, a feature that downloads and installs any revisions we've made to the program.

Run Web Update the first time you use the program and as often as possible thereafter—either automatically at program start-up (the default preference for the program) or manually at intervals you choose.

Running Web Update Manually

To run Web Update manually:

1. Do one of the following:
   - From the "Keep Quicken WillMaker Up to Date" screen in the program's introduction, click **Web Update**.
   - From anyplace else in the program, choose **Online > Web Update**.
2. Follow the directions that appear on screen.

> **TIP**
>
> **If you have Internet connection problems.** If you're having trouble connecting to the Internet from within Quicken WillMaker Plus, open your Web browser as you normally would from outside the program, then return to the program and try again. If problems persist, see "Handling Web Update Problems" in Part 7.

Enabling and Disabling Automatic Updates

By default, Quicken WillMaker Plus checks for newer versions every time you start up the program (as long as you have an open Internet connection). If it detects a newer version, you're prompted to download and install the newer files (which may take a few minutes). The program will then restart.

If you'd rather not have these checks done automatically, you can turn off this feature by changing the default preference. If you decide to change this preference—we recommend that you don't—be sure to run Web Update manually at regular intervals.

To change the "automatic update" preference:

1. Choose **Edit > Preferences**.
2. Click the check box next to **Automatically check for updates when the program starts** to mark it with a ✔—or to clear the ✔ from the box if it's already checked. If the check box is empty, the program will check for updates only when you run Web Update manually.

Getting Oriented

The introductory screens not only help you take care of initial business, they also orient you to the program's look and feel, pointing out handy resources that can help you with your program tasks.

The program's general screen layout makes everything you need obvious:

- The onscreen Guide is right up front, providing plenty of basic information to help you understand the current task and answer any questions you may have about it.
- The **Next** button at the bottom of the screen clearly points you to your next task.
- If you want to take a detour or a break before going to the next task, you can click the **Back** button or choose from a variety of menu and navigation options at the top of the screen. (If you're not sure what a particular menu command means, see the descriptions in Appendix A.)

When you start creating documents, you'll encounter a wider variety of onscreen options (explained in Part 3), but for now, the options explained here should be pretty much all you need to know.

Figuring Out Which Estate Planning Documents You Need

Before you start creating Quicken WillMaker Plus documents, you can find out which estate planning documents are best for you. At the "Which Estate Planning Documents Do You Need?" screen in the program's introduction, click **Learn More**. (If you aren't currently in the introduction, choose **Navigate > Go to Introduction** and click through the first few screens to reach this screen.)

If you click the **Learn More** button, you'll see a list of several common life situations that may apply to you:

- You're Young and Without Dependents

- You're Paired Up, But Not Married
- You Have Young Children
- You're Middle-Aged and Financially Comfortable
- You're Elderly or Ill.

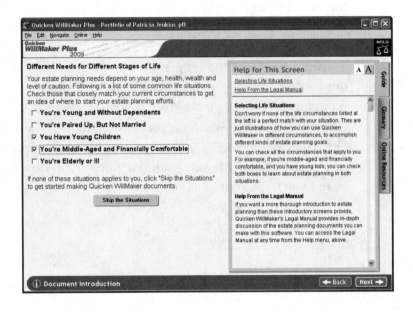

Check the boxes next to the situations that apply to you and click **Next**. This takes you to information screens for each of these situations, which suggest and explain documents that fit your situation. Checking the box on each information screen adds the suggested documents to your Document List. (The Document List is explained in Part 3 of this manual.)

Quitting and Restarting Quicken WillMaker Plus

You can quit Quicken WillMaker Plus by doing any of the following:

- Choose **File > Exit**.
- Click the close box (marked with an "**X**") in the upper right-hand corner of the program.
- Press ALT+F4.

Any changes you've made to your documents since the last time you saved your data are automatically saved when you quit. By default, the **Automatically save changes** feature is turned on. If you've turned **Automatically save changes** off (in **Edit > Preferences**) the program prompts you to save your changes when you quit. For more information on saving your data, see "Saving Your Portfolio" in Part 5.

You can restart the program just as you started it the first time, either from the Windows taskbar or by double clicking the program's icon on your desktop. If you completed the program's introduction before you quit, you'll go directly to the Document List. The Document List is your main jumping-off point for creating documents (or for working with documents you've already created) —and you'll find out all about it in Part 3.

Creating Wills and Other Legal Documents

Creating documents with Quicken WillMaker Plus is simple: You select the type of document you want to create and answer the interview questions for that document. When you've finished the interview, the program generates the document for you, with all the legal niceties in place.

This part of the Users' Manual orients you to the Document List (where you choose a document to work on) and describes how to start, proceed through and complete document interviews.

Exploring the Document List

The Document List in Quicken WillMaker Plus is your home base in the program, similar to the home page for a website. It's the screen you see when you start the program (unless you haven't yet navigated through the series of introductory screens discussed in Part 2). You can easily get to the Document List from most other parts of the program.

Navigating to the Document List

To get to the Document List:

- on the navigation bar, click **Document List**, or
- choose **Navigate > Go to Document List**.

At the Document List, you can view all your document options, choose a document to work on and launch its interview. But first, you should get oriented to the Document List screen and its elements.

Getting Oriented to the Document List

The Document List includes the following elements:

① **Drop-Down List of Categories**

The category you select from this list determines which document names show up in the list below it. The main categories are:

- "Estate Planning"
- "Executors"

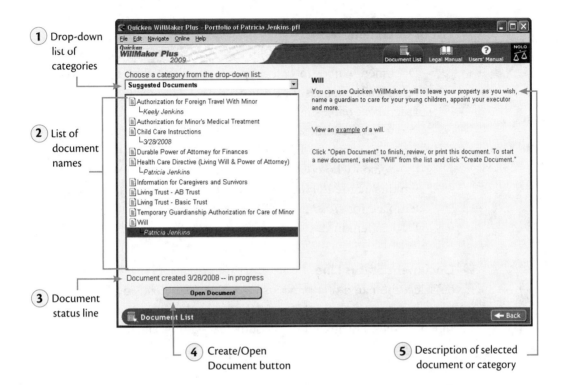

1 Drop-down list of categories

2 List of document names

3 Document status line

4 Create/Open Document button

5 Description of selected document or category

- "Home and Family," and
- "Personal Finance."

You can also choose:

- "All Documents," which displays all available document names, or
- "Suggested Documents," which displays the program's suggestions for estate planning documents that fit your life situation.

The latter category appears only if you asked for document suggestions in the program's introduction (see "Figuring Out Which Estate Planning Documents You Need," in Part 2).

If you've already created a document, you'll also see the category "Documents You've Created," which provides an easy way to find your documents.

② List of Document Names

This list shows all document names in the currently selected category.

- Document names in *black* type (and preceded by a page icon) represent templates for documents you can create.
- Document names in *blue* type represent actual documents you've created; these names are listed directly below the template names and contain an identifier (such as the name of the person who created the document). For example, Patricia Jenkins' name in blue below the document name "Will" (the template for creating a will) represents the will made by Patricia Jenkins.

③ Document Status Line

If you select the name of a previously created document (in blue type), its creation date appears in this status line directly below the list of document names, along with the document's status—either "in progress" or "completed."

④ Create/Open Document Button

Click this button after you've selected the template or document you want to work on. The name of the button changes depending on whether the document name you've selected represents a template or an actual document:

- If you've selected a template name, the button is **Create Document**.
- If you've selected the name of an already created document, the button is **Open Document**.

⑤ Description of Selected Document or Category

When you select a category (from the drop-down category list) or a document name (from the list of document names), this text describes the category or document you've selected. If you've selected a document name, this description includes a link to a sample document of the same type, so you can see what a finished version looks like.

Learning About Your Document Options

To find out what documents you can make with Quicken WillMaker Plus:

1. Go to the Document List (if you aren't already there) by clicking **Document List** on the navigation bar.

2. Choose a category of documents from the drop-down category list. (If you haven't yet created a document, you'll see "Make a Selection" here.)

3. Read the description of the category on the right-hand side of the screen.

4. Click a document name and read its description at right.

5. Repeat the above steps as often as needed.

Once you know what your options are, you can select a document to work on.

BEHIND THE SCENES

Many documents, one portfolio file. Documents you've created are listed under "Documents You've Created." You might think that these documents are each stored in their own, separate file. In fact, Quicken WillMaker Plus saves all the documents you create in one portfolio file, which also contains the contact information you enter in your Contact List. The file is named "Portfolio of [*Your Name*].pfl" using the name you entered during the program's introduction.

This "one file" approach allows Quicken WillMaker Plus documents to share contact information and saves you time. (You don't need to reenter names and addresses when you refer to the same people in multiple documents.) Plus, you can change contact information easily in one place—the Contact List (described in Part 6)—and let the program extend the changes to all relevant documents.

To find out more about portfolio files and how to use them to manage your documents, see Part 5.

Starting Your Document

The first step in creating a new document in Quicken WillMaker Plus is selecting the document interview. You can create a completely new document or make a different version of a document you've already created.

Starting a Completely New Document

To start a completely new document:

1. Go to the Document List (if you aren't already there) by clicking **Document List** on the navigation bar.
2. Choose a category of documents from the drop-down category list.
3. Select the name (in black type) of the document you want to create. (Remember, names in black type represent document templates, while names in blue type represent documents already created.)
4. Click **Create Document**.

The first screen of your document interview appears. If it's a checklist, see "Using Checklists for Interview Management," below, for tips about using the checklist to navigate an interview and monitor your progress. Otherwise, simply proceed through the interview screens in order and supply the requested information.

BEHIND THE SCENES

Know when your document is actually created. Clicking **Create Document** starts the interview process, but the program doesn't actually create your document until you enter some information on an interview screen and save it by moving on to the next screen. If you merely select a document and read an introductory interview screen, you haven't created that document.

Starting a New Document Based on an Existing Document

SKIP AHEAD

If you haven't created a document. You can skip this section if you haven't yet created any documents.

Sometimes, you may need a new document that's very similar to one you've already created. For example, you may want to create a pet care agreement for your dog before you leave on vacation using the agreement you created last year as a template. Quicken WillMaker Plus lets you easily duplicate and edit existing documents to create new ones—except in the cases of certain estate planning documents (see below).

Note that you don't need to duplicate a document just to make changes to it—simply revise the document itself as described in Part 4.

To start a new document based on an existing document:

1. Go to the Document List (if you aren't already there) by clicking **Document List** on the navigation bar.

2. From the drop-down category list, select "Documents You've Created."

3. Select the name (in blue type) of the document you want to duplicate and edit. (Remember, names in black type represent document templates, while names in blue type represent documents already created.)

4. Choose **Edit > Duplicate Document**. (If this command is unavailable, see the cautionary note below.) A new listing for the duplicated document (with "duplicate (1)" in its name) appears just below the document name you selected in Step 3.

5. Select the new duplicate document, if it isn't already selected.

6. Click **Open Document**.

The first screen of the document interview appears. All the interview screens for this document contain the same answers as the document you duplicated.

> **CAUTION**
>
> **Some estate planning documents should not be duplicated.** Having more than one of certain documents—will, living trust, health care directive, final arrangements document or durable power of attorney for finances—*for the same person* can create legal problems. For this reason, Quicken WillMaker Plus doesn't let you use the **Duplicate Document** command for these documents. You can, however, very easily create an identical will for your spouse or partner. (See "Creating an Identical Will for a Spouse or Partner," below.)

As you click through the interview screens, carefully review each question and change your answers, when necessary, to suit the new document. For example, if you're creating a temporary guardianship authorization for your son based on the one for your daughter, you will change some of the data on the "Information About Your Child" screen, such as the child's name and date of birth.

CAUTION

Know whose documents you're licensed to create. The end user licensing agreement for Quicken WillMaker Plus prohibits you from preparing wills or other documents for people outside your immediate family or for commercial purposes. If you are interested in licensing Quicken WillMaker Plus for commercial purposes, call Nolo at 510-549-1976, or go to www.nolo.com/bizdiv/professional.cfm.

Creating an Identical Will for a Spouse or Partner

SKIP AHEAD

If you haven't created a will and aren't married or partnered. You can skip this section if you haven't yet created a will and aren't married or in a domestic partnership.

Some married couples or couples in a long-term domestic partnership may want to create identical wills, where all the provisions in the will— such as beneficiaries, alternate beneficiaries and children's guardians— are the same, except that the spouses' or partners' names are reversed. For example, if you make a will and name your spouse or partner as your executor, the identical will for your spouse or partner will name you as your spouse's or partner's executor.

Married couples or partners are not required to create identical wills. But for those who want to do so, Quicken WillMaker Plus offers a feature specifically for this purpose.

TIP

Work on the will interview together. Because the first spouse or partner to write a will is in effect creating the will for both of you, we suggest that the two of you complete the will interview together, discussing and agreeing to all decisions and choices.

When you have completed the will for one spouse or partner, here's how to duplicate it for the other:

1. Go to the "Congratulations" screen for the will of the first spouse or partner. (See "Getting to the 'Congratulations' Screen" in Part 4.)

2. Click **Duplicate for Spouse**.

3. The Document List appears after you read an advisory dialog box and click **OK**. The duplicated will appears on the list with the status description "in progress."

4. Double click the duplicated will (or select it and click the **Open Document** button).

5. The checklist for the duplicated will appears after you read an advisory dialog box and click **OK**. Note that none of the parts on this checklist are checked, even though this will contains the information carried over from the first will; these parts will be checked when you have reviewed the information.

6. For each part in the checklist, click through all interview screens to make sure the second spouse or partner agrees with the choices the first one has made. You can change the information in this will, but keep in mind that these changes will not be reflected in the will of the first will-writing spouse or partner.

7. When you've reviewed all screens, you can preview and print the completed will as described in Part 4.

Proceeding Through a Document Interview

Once you start the interview for the document you selected, all you have to do is click through the screens in the interview and supply the information needed to correctly generate your document.

This section of the manual shows you how to navigate through an interview using the various data entry formats you may encounter along the way. Each document in Quicken WillMaker Plus has its own set of interview screens, but they all use the same basic process and formats.

Read each interview question carefully and consult the program's help resources (the onscreen Guide, the Legal Manual and this Users' Manual) to help you decide on your answers. (For more information about help resources and how to access them, see "Getting Oriented" in Part 2, or read Part 7, "Getting Help.")

Moving Forward

To move to the next screen in an interview, use any of the following methods:

- Click **Next**.
- Choose **Navigate > Next**.
- Press ALT+RIGHT ARROW.
- Use the TAB key to move the keyboard focus to the **Next** button, then press the ENTER key or the SPACEBAR. (The keyboard focus is on a button when a dotted outline surrounds the button.)

If the information requested on the current screen is optional, you can go on to the next screen without supplying the information. However, if the information is required, the program won't let you move to the next screen without answering.

If you're not sure how to answer, we suggest you quit the program and return to the interview later; when you return, the interview will pick up where you left off. Or, you can give a placeholder answer and move on—but if you do so, you may need to come back and change several answers later, because later parts of the interview may be determined by your answer.

Moving Backward

To go back to the previous screen in an interview, use any of the
following methods:

- Click **Back**.
- Choose **Navigate > Back**.
- Press ALT+LEFT ARROW.
- Use the TAB key to move the keyboard focus to the **Back** button,
  then press the ENTER key or the SPACEBAR. (The keyboard focus
  is on a button when a dotted outline surrounds the button.)

> **CAUTION**
>
> **Don't lose data when you backtrack.** Quicken WillMaker Plus doesn't
> record what you've entered on the current screen until you move to the next
> screen. If you enter or change an answer and then try to go back to the previous
> screen, the program warns you that your answer or change won't be saved. To save
> your answer before backtracking, first click **Next** to move one screen forward; then
> back up to previous screens.

If you are working on a document that has a checklist, you have
an additional method for going backward: Use the checklist to reopen
sections of the interview you've already completed. To find out more
about checklists, see "Using Checklists for Interview Management,"
below.

Revising Answers You've Entered

Because Quicken WillMaker Plus sometimes chooses interview questions
based on your answers to earlier questions, revising one answer may
affect everything that comes after it. So, after you go back to revise
a recent answer (using any of the methods described in "Moving
Backward," above), you'll need to continue going forward, one screen
at a time, making any necessary corrections. If the document has a
checklist, use the checklist to reopen the section of the interview that
contains the answer you want to change; then click forward through that

entire section, making changes as needed. (See "Using Checklists for Interview Management," below.)

Using Checklists for Interview Management

SKIP AHEAD

Not all documents use checklists. You can skip this section *unless* you are creating one of the following estate planning documents: will, living trust, final arrangements document, health care directive, durable power of attorney for finances or information for caregivers and survivors form. Only these documents use checklists in their interviews; all others have shorter interviews, so the checklist format isn't necessary.

When you start an estate planning document in Quicken WillMaker Plus (except the revocation of health care directive and the revocation of power of attorney), the first screen is the interview checklist. This checklist provides an overview of the parts of the interview, so you know which topic is covered in each part.

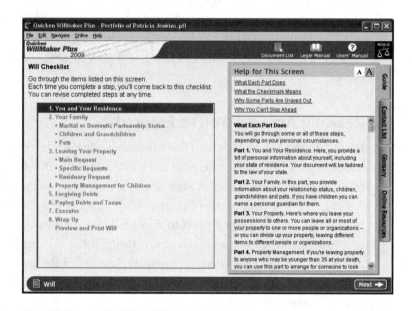

The checklist helps to keep track of which parts of an interview you've completed and simplifies the process of going back to change an answer. Rather than stepping through the whole interview, you can go directly to the part you want to change.

Understanding Checkmarks and Dimmed List Items

The checkmarks on a checklist show which parts of the interview you have completed. Dimmed items are unavailable for you to work on.

List items are dimmed:

- to prevent you from working on interview parts out of order, or
- to prevent you from working on interview parts that aren't relevant to your situation.

Quicken WillMaker Plus determines which parts of the interview don't apply to you based on the answers you've given to previous questions. For example, in the trust interview, if you say in "3. Property to Be Held in Trust" that you want all your trust property to go to one person, then "5. Residuary Beneficiaries" is dimmed because it's not relevant to your situation.

Working on Document Parts

In most documents that have checklists, you must go through the interview parts in order. However, you can return to previously completed parts (parts with checkmarks) in any order.

The one exception to the above rule is the information for caregivers and survivors form. After completing the introductory part of this document, you can work on the remaining parts in any order you wish.

To work on a document part listed in the checklist:

1. Select the name of the document part in the checklist.
2. Click **Next** (or use any other method of forward movement described in "Moving Forward," above).

The first screen in the selected part of the interview appears. If you have selected **Preview and Print,** you will go directly to the "Congratulations" screen. There you can preview, print or export your document. (For more information about performing these tasks, see Part 4.)

Answering Interview Questions

A Quicken WillMaker Plus interview may ask you to supply information in any or all of the following ways:

- typing into text-entry boxes
- using icons to select names and dates
- adding items to list boxes
- choosing radio-button options
- choosing check-box options
- selecting from pick lists, or
- selecting from drop-down lists.

This section explains how to use each of these formats. For instructions on how to answer specific interview questions, consult the Guide on the right side of each interview screen.

As you proceed through the interview, keep in mind that the program doesn't save the information you enter on a given screen until you move forward to the next one.

BEHIND THE SCENES

Some questions are answered automatically. On some interview screens, you may find answers already filled in with information, such as the address or phone number for a person or organization. Quicken WillMaker Plus finds this information, which you entered previously, in your Contact List and automatically inserts it for you. If you revise automatically inserted information on the interview screen, it will also be revised in the Contact List and in all documents that use this information.

Typing Into Text-Entry Boxes

On some screens, you type information—such as a name, address, fraction, date or description of an item of property—in a text-entry box. (If you can't type into the box and you see an **Add to List** button on the same screen, the box is actually a list box; see "Adding Items to List Boxes," below.)

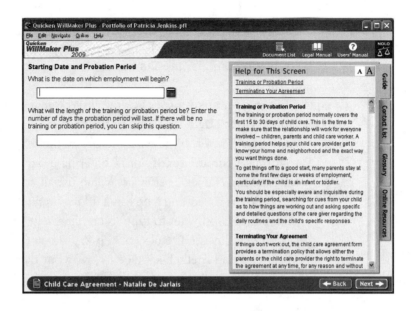

Most text-entry boxes hold a single answer to an interview question. However, you will also encounter text-entry boxes in which you can enter multiple names or other items on separate lines.

Both types of text-entry box require the same basic steps:

1. If the text-entry box doesn't have a blinking cursor in it, click in the box or press the Tab key as needed to put the cursor in the box.

2. Type in your answer (or click the **Insert Name From Contact List** or **Select a Date** icon next to the box, if applicable). When appropriate, refer to the example below the box to see how to format your answer. If you're entering a name, see "Tips for Entering Names," below, for some useful advice.

3. If the box is a text-entry box that allows multiple items to be entered and you want to type in another item, press Enter to start a new line and return to Step 2.

4. Proofread and spell check (see below) your data before proceeding to the next screen.

TIP

Double-check formatting—especially of phone numbers and zip codes. While Quicken WillMaker Plus checks some data for correct formatting, telephone numbers and zip codes aren't checked (to allow for international contact data, phone extensions and so on). Be sure to review the format of your answer before moving to the next screen.

CAUTION

Watch out for automatic Enter-key navigation. On most interview screens, pressing the Enter key triggers the default navigation button, which is usually the **Next** button. If you are in the habit of pressing Enter after you type in an answer, you may find yourself jumping to the next screen unintentionally. Remember, the only time you need to press Enter while typing in data is if you want to start a new line in a text box that allows multiple items. (Pressing Enter at other times will probably send you to the next screen.)

Using Icons to Select a Name or Date

To save you from retyping information, the program includes some shortcuts for entering names and dates.

Pasting in Contact List Names

When the answer to an interview question is a name that is already in your Contact List, you can avoid retyping it by pasting it in from your Contact List. The **Contact List** icon, which looks like a notepad page with two people on it, appears next to text-entry boxes where a name is requested.

To paste a Contact List name into a text-entry box:
1. Click the **Contact List** icon next to the text-entry box in which you want to paste the name.
2. Select the name you want to paste by clicking it.

If you are pasting multiple names from your Contact List into a text-entry box that allows multiple entries, you can either select and paste the names individually or use the **Select Multiple Names** feature.

To find out more about the Contact List, including how to edit contact information, see Part 6.

Selecting Dates

When the answer to an interview question is a date, you can use the **Select a Date** calendar icon, which appears next to text-entry boxes where dates are requested.

To insert a date into a text-entry box:
1. Click the **Select a Date** icon next to the text-entry box in which you want to enter a date. This opens a calendar below the date-entry box, with today's date already selected.
2. What happens next depends on what date you want to insert:

- If you want to insert today's date, click on the day on the calendar.
- If you want to insert a different date:
  1. To change the year of the selected date, click the year, then use the arrows that appear to the right of the year.
  2. To change the month of the selected date, use the arrows to the left and right of today's month and year.
  3. To change the day of the selected month and year, click on the day you want to use.

Checking Your Spelling

You can make sure that the spelling of your answers to interview questions is correct using Quicken WillMaker Plus's built-in spell checker. Here's how:

1. Type in your answer, as described in "Typing Into Text-Entry Boxes," above.
2. If your cursor is not flashing in the text box you want to spell check, click inside that text box.
3. Choose **Edit > Check Spelling**. If there's a word the spell checker doesn't recognize, you'll see the **Check Spelling** dialog box.
4. Use the buttons in the **Check Spelling** dialog box to either:
   - *change* the spelling of the selected word
   - *ignore* the selected word
   - *add* the selected word to your user dictionary, so that spell checker will allow this word on this screen and recognize it any time you use it while creating Quicken WillMaker Plus documents.
5. When each word in the text box has "passed" spell check, the **Check Spelling** dialog box closes automatically.
6. If there's more than one text box on the current interview screen, repeat Steps 2 through 5.
7. When each text box has "passed" spell check, click **Next** to move to the next interview screen.

Tips for Entering Names

Because a name used in one part document interview may appear again in that document (or in others), Quicken WillMaker Plus keeps track of all the names you enter and stores them in your Contact List.

Using this list, the program checks your answers for logical inconsistencies and alerts you if a name entered in one place can't be used there based on answers you've given earlier.

To enable Quicken WillMaker Plus to perform its error checking correctly, and keep your Contact List as accurate as possible, follow these tips when entering names:

- Use full names, first name first.
- Be consistent: Use the same exact name for a person or organization throughout the document interview. If you use a full name in one answer and a nickname in another, the program will assume they are different and add both to the Contact List.
- Carefully check the spelling of all names before you leave the screen. The program assumes different spellings are different people and adds both names to the Contact List.
- If the program fills in a name automatically after you've typed in a few characters (guessing that it is a name from your Contact List), check that it truly is the name you want to enter. If it isn't, continue typing the correct name. (To turn off the "automatic completion" feature, choose **Edit > Preferences**.)
- Enter only one name per line. To begin a new line for an additional name, follow the onscreen instructions.
- Whenever possible, use the Contact List to paste in names that you've entered previously, as described in "Pasting in Contact List Names," above.

If you discover you entered a name incorrectly and want to change it, choose **Edit > Manage Contact List** to correct the name in the Contact List; the program will make the correction in all documents where the name occurs. To find out more about working with the Contact List, see Part 6.

Adding Items to List Boxes

On some interview screens, you'll need to enter items in a list box and provide additional information about each listed item. For example, the will interview asks you to list each of your children and provide each child's gender and date of birth.

When you encounter an empty list box, the keyboard focus is on the button for adding list items, making this button the default choice.

Each screen with a list box contains detailed instructions on how to use its particular list, but all use the same basic steps.

To add an item to a list box:

1. Click **Add to List**. (In some cases, the name of this button may be customized to reflect items contained in the list, for example, **Add a Child**.)

2. Answer whatever questions appear about the item you're adding.

3. Click **Next** or **OK** to return to the screen with the list box.

Once you've added all your items to the list, you can use the **Change** and **Remove** buttons as needed to change or remove selected items.

Choosing a Radio-Button Option

Some interview questions require you to choose one answer from several options using a list with radio buttons. When you click one radio button to select its option, any previous selection is erased. The selected option is the one with the black dot in the center of the button.

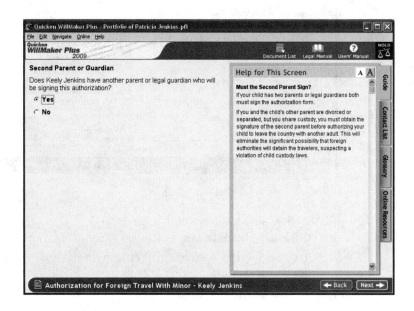

To choose a radio-button option:

- Click the radio button next to the option or use the ARROW keys on your keyboard to select it.

If an option is already selected when the screen appears, make sure it's the answer you want to give. If it isn't, choose a different option before you move on to the next screen.

Choosing Check-Box Options

If a question requires you to choose one or more options from a list, the program displays a list with check boxes. You can select as many options from the list as you need.

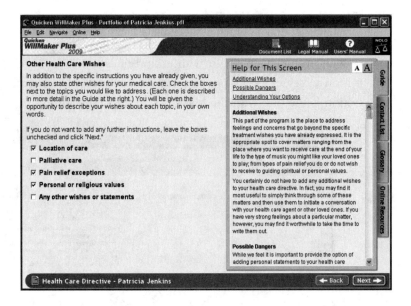

To choose a check-box option:

- Click the check box next to the option to mark it with a ✔ (or use the TAB key to select the option, then press the SPACEBAR to mark the box with a ✔).

To remove a ✔ from a check box:

Click the check box to clear it (or use the TAB key to select the option, then press the SPACEBAR to clear the ✔ from the check box).

When you've made sure that only the options you want are checked, you can move on to the next screen.

Selecting From a Pick List

Some interview screens with long lists of selection options—such as a list of all the states in the U.S.—require you to choose one answer from a pick list.

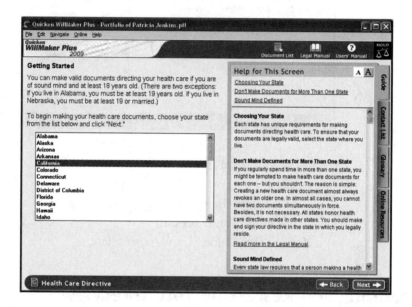

To choose an option from a pick list:

1. Use the scroll bar or Arrow keys to see the entire list, if necessary (or type a letter to move the selection bar to the first list item that begins with that letter).
2. Click the option you want to select (or use the Arrow keys to select it).

Selecting From a Drop-Down List

Some interview questions require you to choose one answer from a drop-down list.

To choose an option from a drop-down list:

1. Click the arrow to the right of the list space to display a list box below the space. Use the scroll bar or ARROW keys to see the entire list, if needed.

2. Click the option you want to select.

Stopping and Restarting Your Interview

You can stop an interview in progress at any time, either by quitting the program or by navigating to another part of the program—for example, clicking the **Document List** icon to return to the Document List.

When you select the name of a document that was not completed in the Document List, the status line below the list shows the document's creation date and the description "in progress." When you open the document, you'll return to the screen where you left off.

> **CAUTION**
>
> **Keep document-switching to a minimum.** While the program lets you work on multiple interviews at the same time, doing so can be confusing. We suggest you work on one interview at a time.

Saving Your Data

Because Quicken WillMaker Plus automatically saves the information you provide on an interview screen when you move on to the next one (unless you've turned off the **Automatically save changes** feature in the program preferences), you generally don't need to worry about saving data. The program saves all of your documents and contact information in your portfolio. (Portfolios are explained in Part 5.)

If you have turned off the **Automatically save changes** feature in the program preferences, you'll need to save data manually at frequent intervals. The program asks if you want to save changes whenever you quit.

To save data manually:

- Choose **File > Save**.

To change your preference for the **Automatically save changes** feature:

1. Choose **Edit > Preferences** to open the **Preferences** dialog box.
2. Click the check box next to **Automatically save changes** to turn this feature on if it's off (or off if it's on). A check mark (✔) indicates the option is on.

We strongly recommend you leave this feature on.

For more information on saving and backing up your data, see Part 5.

Completing Your Interview

When you've completed all the interview screens for a document, the program has all the information it needs to assemble and print your document. The next step takes you to the "Congratulations" screen, which lets you view, print, revise and export your document. This screen appears automatically when you complete the interview—unless the interview for your document uses a checklist, in which case you need to select **Preview and Print** from the checklist, then click the **Next** button.

To learn more about working with your completed document, see Part 4.

Reviewing, Changing and Printing Your Documents

A fter you've completed your document interview, Quicken WillMaker Plus uses your answers to create a finished document. The "Congratulations" screen, which appears at the end of each interview, lets you look at the document and make any necessary changes before you print it out.

This part of the Users' Manual explains how to get to the "Congratulations" screen and use its options to review, change and print your document. It also discusses how to export your document to a text file.

 SKIP AHEAD

This part of the manual doesn't cover how to print contact information or help topics. To find out about printing your Contact List, see "Printing Your Contact List" in Part 6. To learn about printing topics from the onscreen Guide or online manuals, see Part 7.

Getting to the "Congratulations" Screen

How you reach the "Congratulations" screen depends on whether or not your document uses a checklist:

- *If your document does use a checklist*, you can reach the "Congratulations" screen from the checklist after you've completed all required parts of the document. Double click **Preview and Print** at the bottom of the checklist (or select **Preview and Print** and click **Next**). The following documents use checklists: will, living trust, final arrangements document, health care directive, durable power of attorney for finances and information for caregivers and survivors form.
- *If your document doesn't use a checklist*, the "Congratulations" screen automatically appears when you complete the final screen of the document interview and click **Next**. After that, the "Congratulations" screen appears every time you open the document from the Document List.

The "Congratulations" screen provides options for previewing and printing your document, changing your answers and returning to the Document List.

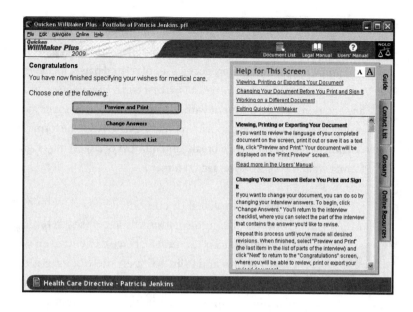

TIP

Special option for will writers. For wills, the "Congratulations" screen also provides a **Duplicate for Spouse** button, which you can use to create an identical copy of the will for your spouse or partner. (For more information about this process, see "Creating an Identical Will for a Spouse or Partner" in Part 3.)

Reviewing Your Document in Print Preview

We recommend that you use Print Preview to carefully review your finished document. If you want to change any of your answers, you can do so before you print your document.

> **CAUTION**
>
> **Signing instructions not included in Print Preview.** In addition to your document, each interview produces a set of related pages, including instructions on how to sign your document and make it legal. These signing instructions, and any additional pages, print out with the document (if you specify so in the **Print** dialog box) but they don't appear in Print Preview. Also, the format of the printed document (line breaks, page breaks and number of pages) may slightly differ in format from the version you see on screen.

To review your completed document:

1. Go to the "Congratulations" screen (see "Getting to the 'Congratulations' Screen," above), if you aren't already there.

2. Click **Preview and Print** to open the document preview.

3. If the document is a will, living trust, durable power of attorney for finances or health care directive, you'll see a dialog box asking which specific documents in the document set you would like to display. If you don't want to display all of them, uncheck the ones you don't want before clicking **OK** (but be sure to include all of them when you print out the version you intend to sign and make legal).

4. In the document preview, use the scroll bar or press the Up and Down Arrow keys to move through the document and read it carefully, making sure the information is correct. (If you're curious about the hash marks ("////") that appear at the end of some pages, see the "Behind the Scenes" note, below.)

5. If you're not ready to print or export the document, click **Close Preview** on the left side of the document to return to the "Congratulations" screen.

BEHIND THE SCENES

Those "////" marks on your document are there for a reason. Quicken WillMaker Plus uses "////"—also known as "hash marks"—in its printed documents as both a precaution and a legal necessity. They prevent someone from inserting additional language into blank spaces in the document after you have signed it. If you print an exported document (see "Exporting Your Document to a Text File"), make sure that any hash marks in the version you print match those in the version displayed in Print Preview.

Revising Your Document

As you are reading your document, you may find information that you want to change. If so, you need to return to the document interview and provide new answers. How you do this depends on whether the document uses a checklist or not. (To find out how to change the *appearance* of your document—fonts, page margins and so on—see "Changing How Your Document Looks," below.)

Revising a Document That Uses a Checklist

If the document you want to revise is an estate planning document that uses a checklist, use the checklist to go directly to the part of the document interview containing the information you need to change. (To find out more about checklists, see "Using Checklists for Interview Management" in Part 3.)

To return to the appropriate part of your document interview and make changes:

1. Go to the "Congratulations" screen by clicking **Close Preview** or **Back** in Print Preview. (If you're not in Print Preview, see "Getting to the Congratulations Screen," above.)

2. Click **Change Answers** to get to the checklist for your document.

3. Double click the name of the interview part you need to revise (or select it and click **Next**).

4. Click through the screens in that part of the interview and review the information you previously entered, making changes as needed. When you've made it through all the screens, you'll return to the checklist.

5. If needed, repeat steps 3 and 4 for any other interview parts you need to revise.

6. Double click **Preview and Print** on the checklist (or select it and click **Next**) to return to the "Congratulations" screen.

After you've made your changes, review your document once again in Print Preview before you print it.

Revising a Document That Doesn't Use a Checklist

If the document you want to change doesn't use a checklist, you need to return to the first interview screen for the document, then step through the interview screen by screen to make all the changes you want to make.

To reopen your document interview and make changes:

1 Go to the "Congratulations" screen by clicking **Close Preview** or **Back** in Print Preview. (If you're not in Print Preview, see "Getting to the 'Congratulations' Screen," above.)

2. Click **Change Answers** to go to the first interview screen for your document.

3. Click through the screens in the interview and review the information you entered previously, making changes as needed. When you've made it through all the screens, you'll return to the "Congratulations" screen.

After you've made your changes, review your document once again in Print Preview before you print it.

Changing How Your Document Looks

Most of the time, you won't need to change the default formatting for your documents. However, if you do need to make formatting changes—changes to fonts, margins, spacing and so on—you can do so.

There are two places in Quicken WillMaker Plus where you can reformat documents:

- The **Print Options** dialog box lets you change fonts and adjust page margins, line spacing and footer format.
- The **Print** dialog box lets you add a watermark ("Draft" or "Duplicate") to the document you are printing.

Both of these dialog boxes also let you specify basic printer setup options, including some that affect the look of your document: page orientation (portrait or landscape) and image quality.

To find out more about accessing these dialog boxes to make formatting adjustments, see below.

TIP

Restoring default format settings. If you decide to experiment with formatting adjustments, keep in mind that you can restore the default print-option settings at any time by choosing **File > Print Options,** then clicking **Use defaults.**

Adjusting Fonts, Footers, Margins and Spacing

To make adjustments to fonts, footers, margins and line spacing:

1. Choose **File > Print Options** (or click **Print Options** if you're in Print Preview). The **Print Options** dialog box opens.
2. Modify the option settings in the dialog box to make the changes you want. For more information about changing specific settings, see their descriptions below.
3. Click **OK**.

When you return to the displayed document, your changes will be reflected.

```
 Print Options                                              [X]

  ┌─Page Margins:──────────────┐  ┌─Line Spacing:────────────┐
  │                            │  │  ○ Tight spacing         │
  │  Top   [0.75"]  Bottom [0.45"] │                          │
  │                            │  │  ◉ Standard spacing      │
  │  Left  [1.25"]  Right  [1.25"] │                          │
  │                            │  │  ○ Loose spacing         │
  │  ☑ Footers in smaller type │  └──────────────────────────┘
  │  ☑ Footers in bold type    │

    ( Font... )  ( Setup... )  ( Use defaults )   ( Cancel )  ( OK )
```

The **Print Options** dialog box includes the following elements:

Page Margins

These margins are measured in inches. To fit more text on each page, decrease the margin size by typing in smaller margin measurements.

Line Spacing

These options let you control how tightly spaced the text will be on the printed document. To fit more text on a page, select **Tight spacing**.

Footers in smaller type

When this option is checked, the type size of the footers at the bottom of each printed page will be smaller than that of the document text.

Footers in bold type

When this option is checked, the footers at the bottom of each printed page will appear in bold type.

Font...

Click this button to change the font, or its size, in a Windows **Font** dialog box.

Setup...

Click this button to change the printer, paper or network properties in a Windows **Print Setup** dialog box. (You can also specify printer and paper properties in the dialog box that appears when you choose **File > Print**.)

Use defaults

Click this button to restore all options specified in the **Print Options** dialog box to their default values.

Adding a Watermark to Identify a Draft or Duplicate Copy

If the copy you're printing is a draft or duplicate, we recommend adding a watermark to identify it as such, so it won't be confused with a final, signable document.

To add a watermark to your document, follow the steps in "Printing Your Document," below. When the **Print** dialog box appears, select **Draft** or **Duplicate** in the **Watermark** box (in the lower left corner) found on the bottom left-hand corner before clicking **OK**.

> **CAUTION**
>
> **Don't sign draft and duplicate copies.** To avoid confusion, sign only the final version of your document, making sure it does not have a draft or duplicate watermark.

Printing Your Document

To print your completed document:

1. Go to the "Congratulations" screen (see "Getting to the 'Congratulations' Screen," above), if you aren't already there.
2. Click **Preview and Print** to open the document preview.
3. If the document is a will, living trust, durable power of attorney for finances or health care directive, you'll see a dialog box asking which specific documents in the document set you would like to display. If you don't want to print all of them, uncheck the ones you don't want before clicking **OK** (but be sure to include all of them when you print out the version you intend to sign and make legal).
4. Click **Print** (or choose **File > Print**) to open the **Print** dialog box.
5. Adjust the printing options available in the dialog box if necessary. If you are adding a watermark, see "Adding a Watermark to Identify a Draft or Duplicate Copy," above. If you are specifying page ranges and including signing instructions in your printout, see the cautionary note below.
6. Click **OK**.

> **CAUTION**
>
> **Page range counts may include instructions.** When you print your document, signing instructions are included unless you click **No** under **Print signing instructions** (found in the bottom right-hand corner of the **Print** dialog box). When included, these instructions print before the document.
>
> If you enter page numbers in the **From:** and **To:** boxes of the **Print range** section of the **Print** dialog box without turning off the option to print signing instructions, keep in mind that Quicken WillMaker Plus counts from the first page actually printed, which is the first instruction page (some documents have more than one instruction page). Be sure to factor these extra pages in when you are specifying the range of pages you want to print.

If you're curious about slight differences between the printed version and the version you saw in Print Preview—or if you'd like to learn more about the hash marks ("////") that print at the end of some pages—see "Reviewing Your Document in Print Preview," near the beginning of Part 4.

Exporting Your Document to a Text File

It's easy to export a document to a text file. You may need to do this if:

- you are experiencing problems printing your document from Quicken WillMaker Plus, or
- you need to email a copy of your document to someone who doesn't own a copy of Quicken WillMaker Plus.

However, we strongly advise against exporting your document to another program for the purpose of editing document language. Editing your exported document can create significant problems, as noted below. Don't forget that Quicken WillMaker Plus offers a substantial range of formatting options (see "Changing How Your Document Looks," above) for fine-tuning your document's appearance.

> **CAUTION**
>
> **Don't edit the language of your exported document.** Making changes to the language of a Quicken WillMaker Plus document can create confusion, contradictions and legal problems that you may not be aware of. If you have questions about the language in a document, or if you would like to change its language, take the document to an experienced estate planning attorney and get advice on how to accomplish your goals.

The one type of edit that may be necessary is adjusting the hash marks ("////"), headers and footers to ensure the version you print matches the version displayed in Print Preview.

To export your document:

1. Go to the "Congratulations" screen (see "Getting to the 'Congratulations' Screen," at the beginning of Part 4), if you aren't already there.
2. Click **Preview and Print** to open the document preview.
3. If the document is a will, living trust, durable power of attorney for finances or health care directive, you'll see a

dialog box asking which specific documents in the document set you would like to display. If you don't want to export all of the documents, uncheck the ones you don't want before clicking **OK** (but be sure to include all of them when you export a version you intend to sign and make legal).

4. Click the **Export** icon (or choose **File > Export Document**). After you see a warning message and click **Continue**, you'll see the **Export Document** dialog box.

5. Type a unique name for the file in the **File name** box. (If you don't use a unique name, any other file you have previously created with the same name will be erased.)

6. Select a file type—either Rich Text Format (.rtf) or plain text (.txt)—from the **Save as type** drop-down menu. If your word processor can read Rich Text Format, select this option, which preserves more formatting.

7. Click **Save**.

8. You'll then see a dialog box asking whether you'd like to view the exported file. Click **Yes** to open the file in your default word processor. If you click **No**, you'll need to use My Computer or Windows Explorer to locate your exported file so you can open it.

To view or print the exported document, you'll have to open it with a word processing or text editing program—preferably Microsoft Word or Word Viewer (see below). Be sure to read the instructions in the exported file about how to place the proper headers and footers to correctly format your document—then delete these instructions before printing out your document.

TIP

Open your exported .rtf file in Microsoft Word or Word Viewer. If you export your document in .rtf (Rich Text Format) and open it in a program other than Microsoft Word or Word Viewer, your documents may have problems (such as missing formatting, incorrect page numbering or missing signature lines) that you'll need to correct manually. If you don't have Word, you can download Word Viewer for free from Microsoft.com's Download Center.

Managing Your Documents in Portfolios

I n Quicken WillMaker Plus, a "portfolio" is the file where your documents and Contact List are saved. Portfolios have the extension ".pfl."

If you simply want to create a few documents for yourself with Quicken WillMaker Plus, you may not ever need to know about portfolios. The Document List (see Part 3) offers plenty of basic document-management capabilities: You can see what documents you've created, and you can open them to revise or print. Plus, the program automatically saves your documents and makes back-up copies on your computer.

However, if you need to perform more complex document-management tasks, such as moving your documents to other locations or protecting them with passwords, you need to learn a bit about portfolios.

This part of the Users' Manual introduces portfolios and describes how to create and save portfolios, password-protect them and back them up.

Understanding Portfolios

A Quicken WillMaker Plus portfolio stores all of the documents a person creates in one file, along with that person's Contact List information.

This "one file" approach offers important advantages:

- You can easily share contact information (and changes in that information) among documents.
- It helps prevent confusion that might arise from keeping your documents in multiple places.

Portfolios can be a bit confusing if you're used to programs that save each document in a separate file. Remember: With Quicken WillMaker Plus, you can create many documents, but they're all stored in one portfolio.

Creating a Portfolio

Quicken WillMaker Plus uses the name you enter in the introduction to create a portfolio file for you.

If you decide to create additional portfolios, you can return to the "Enter Your Name" screen with the simple menu command described below. We recommend that each person in your family who uses Quicken WillMaker Plus creates a separate portfolio file, to avoid confusion about whose documents are in what file. (To find out how to share contact information among users, see Part 6.)

To create a portfolio:

1. Go to the "Enter Your Name" screen, if you're not already there, by choosing **File > New Portfolio**.

2. Type your name (or, if the portfolio is for someone else, have that person type his or her name) in the text entry box.

3. Click **Next** or press ENTER.

4. When you next see the **Save File** dialog box (either now or later, depending on your saving preferences), check that the default file name and save location are what you want, then click **Save**. For more information about saving portfolios, see "Saving Your Portfolio," below.

Unless you specify otherwise, the program names the portfolio "Portfolio of [*name you entered*].pfl" and saves it to your **My Documents** (Windows 2000 and XP) or **Documents** (Windows Vista) folder. It also creates an identical back-up portfolio to use if a problem occurs with the original file. (To find out more about back-up portfolios, see "Opening a Back-Up Portfolio," below.)

Opening a Portfolio

If there are multiple portfolios on your computer, it's important to pay attention to which one you have open at any given time—and to know how to switch among them.

Each time you start Quicken WillMaker Plus, the program automatically opens the portfolio that was open the last time you quit the program. You can't have more than one portfolio open at a time; so if you open another portfolio, the program automatically closes the one that was open.

How you open a portfolio depends on whether you've used it recently or not.

Opening a Recently Used Portfolio

To open a portfolio you used recently:

1. Choose **File > Recent Files** to see a submenu of recently used portfolios.
2. Click the name of the portfolio you want to use.

The program opens the portfolio you selected.

Opening a Previously Created Portfolio

Sometimes, you need to open a portfolio that was created some time ago—perhaps in an earlier version of the program—and hasn't been recently used.

To open a previously created portfolio:

1. Choose **File > Open Portfolio** to bring up the standard **Open** dialog box used for opening files in Windows.

2. Locate the file you want to open. In most cases, it will be in your **My Documents** (Windows 2000 and XP) or **Documents** (Windows Vista) folder. If you can't find it, use the Windows Search feature (**Start > Search**) to search for all files on your computer with a ".pfl" file extension.

3. Click **Open**.

After you open a file created with a pre-2009 version of the program for the first time, you'll see a message about file conversion (confirming that you converted an older file into the current format).

> ⓘ **CAUTION**
>
> **Some documents from older versions of the program can't be converted.** If you've opened a portfolio created with a pre-2009 version of Quicken WillMaker Plus, it's possible that some of your old documents won't appear in the Document List. This happens only if we've made such substantial revisions to a document that we can no longer support earlier versions—or if the document template in question is no longer available in the program. In addition, you may be required to review some document interviews completed in your pre-2009 version of WillMaker before you can print them out in the 2009 edition. To find out details about differences in program versions, consult the **What's New** file installed with the program. (See "Checking Out the Program Folder" under "Installing Quicken WillMaker Plus" in Part 2.)

Saving Your Portfolio

If the **Automatically save changes** feature is turned on in the program preferences, the program automatically saves data to the currently open portfolio as you move from one interview screen to the next. If this feature is turned off, you'll need to save data manually.

To find out how to save data manually and how to change your program preferences, see "Saving Your Data" in Part 3.

Protecting Your Portfolio With a Password

If your computer has multiple users, you may want to ensure the privacy of your Quicken WillMaker Plus documents by assigning your portfolio a password. Once you've done so, no one can unlock your portfolio without knowing the password.

This section of the manual describes how to lock and unlock a portfolio, as well as how to change a portfolio's password.

Locking a Portfolio

To lock the currently open portfolio:

1. Choose **File > Lock Portfolio** to open the **New Password** dialog box.

2. Enter the password you want to use (the program asks you to do this twice to make sure you typed it correctly), along with a hint to help you remember the password. *Note that your password is case sensitive*, so you'll need to remember exactly how you entered it.

3. Click **OK** for this dialog box and the subsequent one, which tells you your portfolio has been locked.

The next time you try to open the portfolio, the program will display a **Portfolio Locked** dialog box. You'll need to enter the password and click **OK** to open the file.

> **TIP**
>
> **Take care when choosing your hint.** Once your portfolio is locked, you can't open it without first entering the correct password. While the program does let you unlock a portfolio or change its password (see below), you can't do so unless the portfolio is already open. So, be careful when you choose your password and make your hint as useful as possible. For example, instead of just saying "name of favorite horse" for your hint, say "name of favorite horse (no caps or abbreviations)," so you'll remember you spelled it "mistered" instead of, say, "MrEd."

Unlocking a Portfolio

To unlock the currently open portfolio:

- Choose **File > Unlock Portfolio**.

A dialog box informs you that your portfolio has been unlocked.

Changing a Portfolio's Password

To change the password assigned to the currently open portfolio:

1. Choose **File > Change Portfolio Password** to open the **New Password** dialog box.
2. Enter the new password you want to use, along with a hint to help you remember the password.
3. Click **OK** for this dialog box and the next one that displays, which tells you your portfolio has been locked.

Opening a Back-Up Portfolio

Whenever Quicken WillMaker Plus creates a portfolio, it also creates an identical back-up copy of it. Each time the program saves data to your portfolio, it also saves the same data to your back-up portfolio. This back-up can come in handy if a problem ever occurs with your original file.

Unless you specify otherwise, Quicken WillMaker Plus stores back-up portfolios in the **Nolo Documents Back-Up** subfolder of your **My**

Documents (Windows 2000 and XP) or **Documents** (Windows Vista) folder.

To protect you from accidentally overwriting your back-up portfolios, Quicken WillMaker Plus doesn't let you open portfolios stored in the **Nolo Documents Back-Up** folder. If you encounter a problem with a portfolio and need to open its back-up portfolio, you must first copy the back-up portfolio out of the back-up folder and into another location.

To open a back-up portfolio:

1. In Windows, locate the **Nolo Documents Back-Up** folder. If it isn't in your **My Documents** (Windows 2000 and XP) or **Documents** (Windows Vista) folder, use the Windows Search feature to find it.

2. Open the **Nolo Documents Back-Up** folder and locate the back-up portfolio you want to open.

3. Copy the back-up portfolio and paste it into a different folder or onto the desktop, using your favorite Windows method for copying and pasting files. Remember the name and location of this copied portfolio.

4. In Quicken WillMaker Plus, choose **File > Open Portfolio**.

5. Locate and open the copied portfolio, as described in "Opening a Previously Created Portfolio," above.

Managing Your Contact Information

When you enter information about people and organizations in document interviews, Quicken WillMaker Plus automatically adds it to your Contact List. This saves you from having to enter it again in other documents. The Contact List is stored in your portfolio with the documents you create.

While the program creates and maintains your Contact List in the background, you can also work directly with your Contact List. For example, changing a name in the Contact List changes that name in all the documents that contain it. You can also access your Contact List for other contact-management purposes, such as printing information about your contacts or importing contact information from another portfolio.

This part of the Users' Manual discusses how to:

- access your Contact List
- add names to your Contact List
- revise contact information you've already entered
- delete names from your Contact List
- locate names in your documents
- import contacts from another portfolio, and
- print your Contact List.

Accessing Your Contact List

Quicken WillMaker Plus provides two ways for you to access your Contact List:

- The onscreen Guide lets you view or edit Contact List entries during an interview.
- The **Manage Contact List** dialog box provides a wider range of Contact List management options.

For tasks other than editing previously entered contact information during an interview, use the second option.

Accessing Contact List Entries From the Guide

If you are in the middle of an interview, the onscreen Guide offers a handy way for you to view or edit the information in your Contact List.

To access the Contact List entries from the Guide:

- Click the **Contact List** tab on the right-hand edge of the Guide.

A list of the names in your Contact List appears in the Guide. Click any name to view or edit its associated contact information (address, phone number and so on).

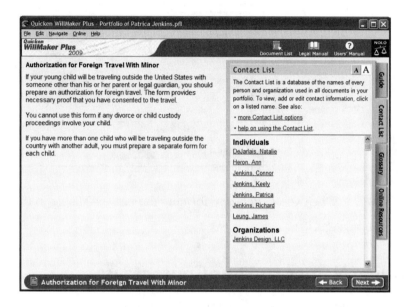

Accessing Contact List Management Options

To access a full range of options for managing your Contact List:

- Choose **Edit > Manage Contact List**.

The **Manage Contact List** dialog box appears, with buttons for adding, deleting, revising, importing and printing contact information and for locating documents that contain specific names. (For more information on these tasks, see below.)

When you're done performing the tasks available in this dialog box, click **Done**.

Adding Names to Your Contact List

Whenever you type a name into a text box during a document interview and go to the next interview screen, Quicken WillMaker Plus checks to make sure the name isn't already in your Contact List, then adds it. If you like, you can also enter names directly into the Contact List.

To add the name of a person or organization directly into your Contact List:

1. Choose **Edit > Manage Contact List** to display the **Manage Contact List** dialog box, if it's not already displayed.
2. Click **Add** to display the **Name Information** dialog box.
3. Type the name in the **Name** text-entry box.
4. Click the appropriate radio button to identify whether you have named a male, a female or an organization.
5. Type in any additional information in the appropriate areas of the **Additional Information** box.
6. Click **OK** to return to the **Manage Contact List** dialog box.

Revising Contact Information

To revise the information for a particular name in your contact list, you first need to access the **Name Information** dialog box for that contact name. You can access this dialog box in either of two ways; which method you use depends on how you have accessed your Contact List (see "Accessing Your Contact List," above):

- If you clicked the **Contact List** tab in the Guide, click the contact's name from the list showing in the Guide.
- If you are using the **Manage Contact List** dialog box, select the contact's name, then click **Edit**.

Once the **Name Information** box is showing, make any changes you want to make, then click the **OK** button.

Deleting Names From Your Contact List

If a name is not used in any of the Quicken WillMaker Plus documents
in your portfolio, you can delete it from the Contact List as follows:

1. Choose **Edit > Manage Contact List** to display the **Manage
   Contact List** dialog box, if it's not already displayed.
2. Select the name you want to delete.
3. Click **Delete**.

appears. (See "Locating Names in Your Documents," just below.) You can then revise the documents to remove the name. When the name is no longer used in any documents, you'll be able to delete the name from the Contact List. (For information about revising documents, see "Revising Your Document" in Part 4.)

Locating Names in Your Documents

To find out which of the documents in your portfolio contain a particular name:

1. Choose **Edit > Manage Contact List** to display the **Manage Contact List** dialog box, if it's not already displayed.
2. Select the name you want to locate.
3. Click **Locate Name** to display the **Documents Containing This Name** dialog box.
4. When you have noted which documents contain the name in question (you may want to write down the document names), click **OK**.

Importing Contacts From Other Contact Lists

If your family members have created separate portfolios (see "Creating a Portfolio" in Part 5), you can share contact information for contacts you have in common. You do this by importing Contact List data from one portfolio into another.

To import Contact List information from another portfolio into the one currently open:

1. Choose **Edit > Manage Contact List** to display the **Manage Contact List** dialog box, if it's not already displayed.

2. Click **Import** to open the **Select the file you want to import names from:** dialog box.

3. Locate and select the Quicken WillMaker Plus portfolio from which you want to import Contact List information. (If you're having trouble finding it, use the Windows Search feature (**Start > Search**) to search for all files on your computer with a ".pfl" file extension.)

4. Click **Open**.

5. Read the dialog box that tells you how many names you've imported, then click **OK**.

When you import names, only those names *not* already in your portfolio are added.

Printing Your Contact List

To print the information in your Contact List:

1. Choose **Edit > Manage Contact List** to display the **Manage Contact List** dialog box, if it's not already displayed.

2. Click **Print** to open the **Print** dialog box.

3. Adjust the printing options available in the dialog box if necessary, then click **OK**.

Your contact information is printed with people listed first, then organizations. Names are in alphabetical order by first name of person or first word of organization name—unless you checked the **Sort Contact List by last name** box in the **Manage Contact List** dialog box. If you checked this box, the list is printed in alphabetical order by last name of person or last word of organization name.

Getting Help

A ny time you have a question about how to do something with Quicken WillMaker Plus, help is close at hand. The key to answering your question as quickly as possible is knowing which help resource to consult.

The table below shows which help resource to use for the type of help you need. It also refers you to specific sections of Part 7 that will help you use these resources.

Using the Onscreen Guide

The Guide that you see on the right-hand side of each interview screen in Quicken WillMaker Plus helps you answer the specific questions on that screen. The text includes both legal and practical information related to the current screen, plus links to related topics in the electronic manuals and on the Internet. In addition, the tabs along the right edge of the Guide provide quick access to your Contact List information, a glossary of legal terms and a page with links to online resources.

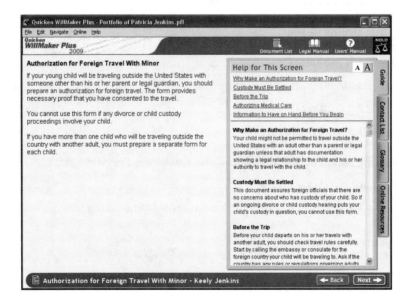

What You Need	Help Resource to Consult	Section(s) of Part 7 to Read
Help understanding how to complete the current interview question or screen	The onscreen Guide (right-hand side of screen)	"Using the Onscreen Guide"
In-depth legal information to help you decide how to answer an interview question	The Legal Manual (printed or electronic version)	"Using the Electronic Manuals"
Definitions of legal terms	The Glossary in the onscreen Guide or Nolo's online glossary	"Looking Up Definitions of Legal Terms" and "Accessing Online Resources"
Help locating a lawyer	Nolo's online Lawyer Directory	"Accessing Online Resources"
Practical advice about how to use the program	This Users' Manual (printed or electronic version)	"Using the Electronic Manuals," plus other applicable sections of this manual (consult the Index or the Table of Contents)
Help fixing a problem you're having with the program	This Users' Manual (printed or electronic version)	"Dealing With Problems"
Additional assistance for a problem you haven't been able to solve using the manual	Nolo Technical Support	"Contacting Nolo Technical Support and Customer Service"

You don't need to do anything to access the Guide; it automatically appears on each interview screen. As you move to a new screen, the Guide text changes to provide specific help for that screen.

This section provides some tips for using the Guide and describes how to:

- change the Guide's font size
- copy text from the Guide, and
- print help topics from the Guide.

Tips for Finding Information in the Guide

Sometimes, the "Help for This Screen" displayed for a particular page is extensive. To help you quickly find what you're looking for, here are some tips:

- Click the topic names at the top of the Guide, directly under "Help for This Screen," to go directly to those topics instead of having to scroll through the text.
- For more in-depth information on a topic than is shown in the guide, click "Read more" links when they appear. These links open a relevant part of one of the electronic manuals in a separate window. (For more information about these manuals, see "Using the Electronic Manuals," below.)
- Web links, which are underlined and preceded by a "globe" icon , open a separate browser window in which you can view a related website. When you've looked at the website, you can return to Quicken WillMaker Plus by closing or minimizing your browser, using your Windows taskbar, or pressing ALT+TAB.
- If you need access to online resources or help with terminology, click the **Online Resources** or **Glossary** tab. (See "Accessing Online Resources" and "Looking Up Definitions of Legal Terms," below.)

Changing the Guide's Font Size

The two **A** icons in the title bar at the top of each Guide page let you change the font size of the text in the Guide:

| Help for This Screen | A A |

- To show the text in a smaller font size, click the icon with the smaller **A**.
- To return the text to the larger font size, click the icon with the larger **A**.

The change of font size will take effect immediately.

Copying Text From the Guide

To copy text from the Guide and paste it into an email or word processing document:

1. Select the text you want to copy.
2. Copy it to your clipboard by pressing CTRL+C.
3. Click where you want to insert the text, then paste it there by pressing CTRL+V.

Printing Help Topics From the Guide

To print the Guide text for the screen you're currently viewing:

1. Choose **File > Print Guide Topic** to open the standard **Print** dialog box.
2. Make any changes you want to the print options, then click **OK**.

Using the Electronic Manuals

Quicken WillMaker Plus's help system includes electronic versions of the program's two manuals:

- this Users' Manual, which provides practical advice to help you use the program, and

- the Legal Manual, which contains in-depth legal information written in plain English to help you answer the program's interview questions knowledgeably.

This section describes how to:

- access the electronic manuals
- navigate a manual's contents
- print a topic from a manual
- print a chapter or entire manual, and
- view a PDF version of the Users' Manual.

Accessing the Electronic Manuals

You can access an electronic manual in any of the following three ways:

- from the **Help** menu (choose **Help > Quicken WillMaker Users' Manual** or **Help > Quicken WillMaker Legal Manual**)
- by clicking the manual's icon on the navigation bar above the Guide, or
- by clicking a "Read more" link in the Guide text.

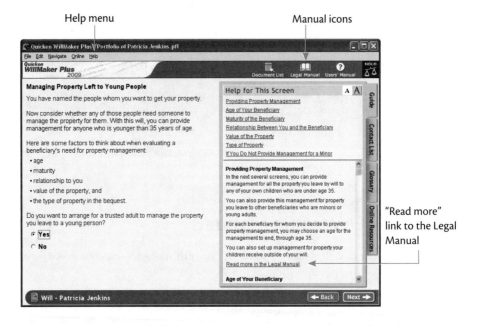

Navigating a Manual's Contents

When you open one of the manuals as described above, it appears in its own window on top of the main Quicken WillMaker Plus program window. If you click the **Show** button on the button bar at the top of the window, the window expands to include a navigation pane along the left side, offering you additional navigation options. The expanded manual window includes three main areas (described in detail below):

- the topic pane
- the button bar, and
- the navigation pane.

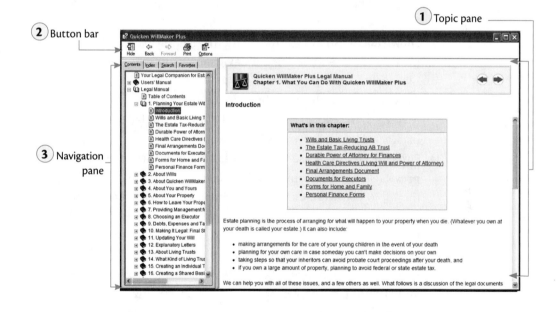

1 Topic Pane

The topic pane displays the text of the manual. The area at the top tells you which manual, chapter and topic you're viewing.

At the top (upper right corner) and bottom of each topic are arrows that link to:

- the *previous* topic in the current chapter (or the last topic in the previous chapter, if you're at the beginning of a chapter), and

- the *next* topic in the current chapter (or the first topic in the next chapter, if you're at the end of a chapter).

Many topics include underlined links to related topics and websites. You can click on them to go to related manual sections or websites; the latter open in a separate browser window.

② Button Bar

The button bar at the top of the manual window contains the following buttons:

- **Show/Hide.** Displays (or hides) the navigation pane, which provides access to additional navigational options. (See "Navigation Pane," below.)
- **Back.** Takes you through the manual topics you've already reviewed, in reverse order. (This button is similar to the backward arrow in your Web browser.)
- **Forward.** If you've used the **Back** button to return to a previously viewed topic, you can use this button to move to the topic you were viewing when you clicked the **Back** button. (This button is similar to the forward arrow in your Web browser.)
- **Print.** Opens a dialog box that gives you the option of printing sections of the manual. (See "Printing a Topic From a Manual" and "Printing a Chapter or Entire Manual," below.)
- **Options.** Opens a menu list that contains items for all the buttons listed above (for easy keyboard access to these options), plus a few other options. The **Internet Options** command opens Internet Explorer's **Internet Options** dialog box. The **Search Highlight On/Off** command turns highlighting for search terms on or off.

③ Navigation Pane

The navigation pane doesn't appear when you first open the manual window; you need to click **Show** (in the button bar) to see it. The navigation pane has four tabs:

- **Contents.** Displays the manual's table of contents. You can use the **+/–** icons next to the manual and chapter titles to show or hide the chapter names and topics. If you have opted to locate the currently displayed topic, the topic name is highlighted in the table of contents. To display a topic listed in the table of contents in the topic pane, double click the topic name.

- **Index.** Displays the manual's index. To display a topic listed in the index in the topic pane, double click the topic name in the index (or select it and click the **Display** button at the bottom of the pane).

- **Search.** Displays a search tool that provides a full-text search of every page in both manuals. Type the words you want to search for in the text-entry box, then click the **List Topics** button. The search tool lists all topics that contain the words you searched for. Topic names are prefaced to identify whether the information is in the Legal Manual ("LEGAL"), the Users' Manual ("USER"), a sample document ("SAMPLE") or a help topic accessible from a dialog box ("HELP"). To display a topic in the topic pane, double click its name (or select its name and click the **Display** button near the top of the pane).

- **Favorites.** Displays a list (initially blank) of your favorite topics. You can (when the topic is showing in the topic pane) remove and display topics by using the buttons below the Favorites list.

To hide the navigation pane, click the **Hide** button on the button bar.

Printing a Topic From a Manual

To print the text of the manual topic you're currently viewing:

1. Click **Print** on the window's button bar. What happens next depends on whether the navigation pane is hidden

or showing; if it's hidden, the **Print** dialog box appears immediately, so you can skip the next step.

2. If the navigation pane is showing, you'll see the **Print Topics** dialog box; select the option **Print the selected topic** and click **OK** to open the **Print** dialog box.

3. In the **Print** dialog box, make any changes you want to the print options, then click **Print**.

Printing a Chapter or Entire Manual

To print a chapter of the Users' Manual or Legal Manual after you have opened its electronic version:

1. Display the **Contents** tab in the window's navigation pane. (See "Navigating a Manual's Contents," above.)

2. Select the name of the manual or chapter you want to print by clicking it. (If only the manual's names are showing and you want to print a chapter, click the + icon next to the manual's name to display the chapter titles.)

3. Click **Print** on the window's button bar to open the **Print Topics** dialog box.

4. Select the option **Print the selected heading and all subtopics**.

5. Click **OK** to open the **Print** dialog box.

6. Make any changes you want to the print options, then click **Print**.

The method described above prints the manual's pages as they appear in the electronic version. If you are printing part of the Users' Manual and would prefer for the pages to appear as they do in the printed version, you can open the PDF version as described below and print from that version.

Viewing a PDF Version of the Users' Manual

The electronic version of the Users' Manual that you can access from the program is designed to work well on screen but lacks the illustrations and some of the formatting found in the printed version. So, we've also included a PDF version with the same formatting as the printed manual.

You can view it if you have Adobe Acrobat Reader version 5.0 or greater installed on your computer. (You can download Adobe Reader for free from www.adobe.com.)

To view the PDF version of the Users' Manual in Adobe Reader:

- From the Windows taskbar, choose **Start > Programs** (or **All Programs**) **> Quicken WillMaker Plus 2009 > Users' Manual**.

Looking Up Definitions of Legal Terms

When you're answering interview questions, you may encounter a legal or estate planning term you're not familiar with. To find out what the term means, you can look up its definition in the program's glossary or consult Nolo's online glossary (see "Accessing Online Resources," below).

To look up the definition of a term in the program's glossary:

1. Click the **Glossary** tab on the right-hand edge of the Guide to open the glossary. At the top of the glossary, you'll see all the letters of the alphabet. Directly below are the glossary terms in alphabetical order.

2. At the top of the glossary, click the letter that begins the word you want to learn about. You'll then see a list of all glossary terms that begin with that letter.

3. Find the term you're interested in, scrolling if necessary to see more of the list, and click it to see its definition.

Many of the terms used in the definitions are underlined, indicating that those terms are also defined in the glossary. To see the definition of an underlined term, click on it.

Accessing Online Resources

Nolo provides many online resources that complement the help features available within Quicken WillMaker Plus. These resources include a directory of lawyers in specific geographical areas, a glossary defining hundreds of legal terms and much more.

You can access Nolo's online resources in either of the following two ways:

- by clicking the **Online Resources** tab on the right-hand edge of the Guide and then clicking an underlined link to the specific resource you want, or
- by choosing **Online > Nolo on the Web**.

In either case, a Web page opens in a separate browser window.

Dealing With Problems

If you encounter a technical difficulty while running the program, this manual is the first resource you should consult. Which section you should read depends on the type of problem you're experiencing:

- If you're having trouble installing Quicken WillMaker Plus because the setup program doesn't launch, see "Jump-Starting the Setup Program," below.
- If you're having trouble printing from the program, see "Correcting Printing Problems," below.
- If you're having trouble with the program's Web Update feature (discussed in "Updating Your Version of the Program," in Part 2), see "Handling Web Update Problems," below.
- If you're encountering an error message, consult the table in Appendix C. This table explains the meaning of each error message and describes what to do if you encounter it.

If none of the above situations apply and you can't find a section of this manual that helps with your problem, look in the **Troubleshooting** file in your **Quicken WillMaker Plus 2009** program folder (see "Checking Out the Program Folder" in Part 2); you may find advice relevant to your problem.

If none of the above suggestions help, contact Nolo Technical Support. (See "Contacting Nolo Technical Support and Customer Service," below.)

Jump-Starting the Setup Program

When you insert the Quicken WillMaker Plus Installation CD into your CD-ROM drive, setup should launch automatically. If it doesn't, here's what to do:

1. Choose **Start > Run...** (Windows 2000 or XP) or **Start > All Programs > Accessories > Run...** (Windows Vista).
2. Type **D:\AUTORUN** (you may have to substitute the letter of your CD-ROM drive for "D").
3. Click **OK**.

Correcting Printing Problems

If you're having a printing problem in Quicken WillMaker Plus, try the following remedies:

- If you are having trouble getting your document to print, go to the **Print Setup** dialog box (**File > Print Setup**) and make sure the settings for your printer are correct, then click **OK** and try to print again.
- If you are not satisfied with the formatting of a printed document, go to the **Print Options** dialog box (**File > Print Options**) to make adjustments. For example, if you're getting a page with very little text and lots of hash marks ("////"), try making the bottom margin larger (changing it from 0.45 inch to 0.6 inch will usually correct the problem). (For information about why hash marks are legally necessary, see "Reviewing Your Document in Print Preview" in Part 4.)

If neither of the above suggestions help, you can export your document and print it using your word processor (see "Exporting Your Document to a Text File" in Part 4)—and please contact Nolo Technical Support to report the problem, so we can investigate the problem and fix it, if necessary. (See "Contacting Nolo Technical Support and Customer Service," below.)

Handling Web Update Problems

If you encounter problems with the program's Web Update feature (see "Updating Your Version of the Program" in Part 2), check the table below. If any of the situations listed there apply to you, try the suggested remedy for your problem.

CAUTION

Web Update isn't designed to work with proxy servers and other corporate VPN configurations. If you are trying to update the program behind a corporate proxy server and getting various error messages, you won't be able to use Web Update. Web Update is designed for the home user with a basic firewall. Unfortunately, we can't support proxy servers and other corporate VPN (Virtual Private Network) security configurations.

If none of the above suggestions help, and you can't find relevant advice in the **Troubleshooting** file (see "Checking Out the Program Folder" under "Installing Quicken WillMaker Plus" in Part 2), contact Nolo Technical Support (see below).

When contacting Nolo Technical Support about a Web Update problem, include the following details in addition to those normally required for other types of problems:

- the type of Internet connection you have (modem dial-up, DSL, or other), and
- the name of your Internet service provider.

If you are:	Try this remedy for your problem:
A Windows 2000 or XP user getting an error message because you don't have the administrator privileges required for installing program files ...	Switch to a user with administrator privileges or have your system's security settings changed. If necessary, contact your network administrator or read Windows documentation on changing security settings.
A Windows Vista user encountering a "User Access Control" dialog box when the update finishes ...	Click **Continue** in the dialog box or enter an administrator password as prompted.
Using a firewall or security application (see below for the case of Windows XP Service Pack 2) and receiving warnings ...	Add "f1.nolo.com" to the "trusted site" list. If you still can't complete the update after making this addition, you may need to turn off your firewall program while retrieving the update, then turn it back on.
A Windows XP Service Pack 2 user getting a Windows Security Alert asking whether you want to keep blocking or to unblock your Quicken WillMaker's Internet connection ...	Select **Unblock**. Once you have unblocked Quicken WillMaker Plus, you should be able to download future Web Updates.

Contacting Nolo Technical Support and Customer Service

If you're encountering a problem that isn't addressed in this section of the manual or Appendix C, you may find an answer on Nolo's website. Nolo's Technical Support department posts FAQs with answers to common user questions and problems.

To find the FAQ page for this program, go to Nolo's Technical Support page at www.nolo.com/support/software_faq.cfm.

If you can't find a solution on the FAQ page, contact Nolo Technical Support directly.

Email address: support@nolo.com
Phone number: 510-549-4660
Phone hours: 9:00 a.m. to 5:00 p.m. Pacific time, Monday through Friday

When you call, try to be in front of the computer with which you are having the problem. Also, whether you are emailing or calling, be sure to have the information noted below on hand.

Information to Have on Hand

When you contact Nolo Technical Support about a problem, please include the following information in your email (or have it ready before you call):

- the version of Quicken WillMaker Plus you're running (which should be 8.0 or higher)
- the point in the program where the problem occurred
- whether you can duplicate the problem
- the brand and model of computer you are using
- the brand and model of printer (if you are having trouble printing)
- the name of your Internet service provider and the type of Internet connection you have (if you are having a problem that involves connecting to the Internet)

- which version of which operating system your computer is running (for example, Windows 2000 version 5.00.2195 or XP Home Service Pack 2), and
- the amount of RAM on your computer.

If you're not sure which model of computer you have, how much RAM it has or which version of the operating system it's running, see below.

Finding Information About Your Computer System

How you find information about your computer system depends on which operating system it's running.

Windows Vista:

- Choose **Start > Computer > System Properties**.

Windows operating systems other than Vista:

1. Right click the **My Computer** icon on your desktop.
2. Select **Properties**.
3. Choose the tab that contains the information you need.

Menu Options

T his appendix lists the commands available in each of the program's menus and describes what they do. To access any menu option:

1. Click the menu in Quicken WillMaker Plus's menu bar.
2. Select the command.

If you prefer not using your mouse, just type the first letter in the menu name while pressing the ALT key, then type the letter underlined in the option name.

File Menu

New Portfolio

Use this command to create a new Quicken WillMaker Plus portfolio.

Open Portfolio...

Use this command to open portfolios made with Quicken WillMaker Plus 2009.

Save

Use this command to manually save your currently open portfolio. You do not need to use this command if **Automatically save changes** is on.

Save As...

Use this command to rename your portfolio and/or save it to another location on your computer.

Lock/Unlock Portfolio

Use this command to lock your portfolio and give it a password. If your portfolio is locked, no one can open it without first entering the password. If you want to unlock a portfolio you've locked, you'll first need to enter the password you assigned to it.

Change Portfolio Password

Use this command to change your password. This command is available only if you have previously locked your portfolio.

Print Options...

Use this command to change the formatting for your documents, including page margins, line spacing, font type and font size. We recommend keeping the default settings.

Print Setup...

Use this command to open the standard **Print Setup** dialog box for the currently chosen printer.

Print Guide Topic...

Use this command to print the Guide topic displayed in the current interview screen. If you don't see this command, click the **Guide** tab and then try opening the **File** menu.

Print Contact List...

Use this command to print the Contact List for the currently open portfolio. If you don't see this command, click the **Contact List** tab and then try opening the **File** menu.

Export Document...

Use this command to save your displayed document as a text file that you can view, edit or print with a word processor.

Recent Files

Use this command to open a recently used portfolio file (.pfl). This submenu lists up to five files.

Exit

Use this command to quit the Quicken WillMaker Plus program.

Edit Menu

Undo

Use this command to undo the last typing or editing action you performed, provided you haven't left the screen on which the changes were made.

Cut

Use this command to remove selected text and add it to the Clipboard.

Copy

Use this command to copy selected text to the Clipboard, without removing it.

Paste

Use this command to insert text that you have previously cut or copied at the blinking cursor, or to replace selected text with text that you have previously cut or copied.

Delete

Use this command to delete selected text without adding it to the Clipboard. The selected text will not be saved.

Select All

Use this command to select all the text in the currently active text field.

Check Spelling

Use this command to check the spelling of text you typed in answering an interview question. Make sure your mouse cursor is inside the text box where you typed your answer before choosing **Edit > Check Spelling**.

Duplicate Document

Use this command to create a new document by duplicating one you've already created. To use this command, you must select the document you want to duplicate in the Document List.

Delete Document

Use this command to delete a document you've already created. To use this command, you must select the document you want to delete in the Document List.

Duplicate Will for Spouse/Domestic Partner

Use this command to make an identical will for your spouse or registered partner. For details on how couples can use this command to create identical wills, see "Creating an Identical Will for a Spouse or Partner" in Part 3.

Manage Contact List...

Use this command to add, modify or delete names in the Contact List, and to enter additional information about names previously entered.

Preferences...

Use this command to customize your version of Quicken WillMaker Plus. You can use the **Preferences** command to specify the following:

- whether your data will be saved automatically or manually
- whether you want the program to fill in names automatically as you type them, based on entries in your Contact List
- whether you want the program to fill in related fields automatically after you enter a name
- whether you want the program to check for Web Updates automatically when you start it up
- the font size of the Guide text, and
- the folder where your backup portfolios are stored.

Navigate Menu

Back

Use this command to go back to the previous screen.

Next

Use this command to move ahead to the next screen.

Go to Document List

Use this command to switch to a different Quicken WillMaker Plus document interview. This command takes you to the Document List, from which you can start a new document or work on one you've already created.

Go to Introduction

Use this command to view the series of introductory screens you saw the first time you used the program.

Go to Interview

Use this command to start the interview of a document you've selected in the Document List, or to return to the interview if you're previewing the document in Print Preview.

Preview Document

Use this command to preview your completed document. You can use this command only after you have completed the document interview.

Online Menu

Web Update

Use this command to update your copy of Quicken WillMaker Plus by downloading the latest updated files from the Web. Before you use this command, you must have a live Internet connection.

Online Registration

Use this command to register your copy of Quicken WillMaker Plus. You'll need a Web browser and an Internet connection to use this command.

Nolo on the Web

Use this command to access Nolo's website at www.nolo.com. You'll need a Web browser and an Internet connection to use this command.

Help Menu

Quicken WillMaker Users' Manual
Use this command to display an electronic version of this manual.

Quicken WillMaker Legal Manual
Use this command to display an electronic version of the Legal Manual.

Product Support
Use this command if you need help with the program.

Suggestion Box
Use this command to see a Web page where you can give us feedback and suggestions about this program.

Keyboard Shortcuts
Use this command to see how to operate the program using a keyboard rather than a mouse.

About Quicken WillMaker Plus 2009
Use this command to see information about which version of the program you're running, plus detailed information about all the program files you've installed.

Keyboard Shortcuts

This section lists keyboard shortcuts for performing the following types of actions:
- choosing options and exiting the program
- opening and saving portfolios
- displaying help resources
- navigating within and among screens, and
- navigating in a text-entry box.

To see this information when you're running the program, choose **Help > Keyboard Shortcuts**.

Choosing Options and Exiting the Program

Press ...	To ...
ENTER	Trigger the default button (as indicated by a thicker outline) or the selected button (if there is no default)—unless you are in a text-entry box that allows multiple entries, in which case pressing ENTER will start a new line of text.
ESC	Trigger the **Cancel, Close** or **No** button in a pop-up dialog box.
ALT+F4	Exit the program.

Opening and Saving Portfolios

Press ...	To ...
CTRL+O	Open an existing portfolio.
CTRL+S	Save the current portfolio when the **Automatically save changes** function is turned off.

Displaying Help Resources

Press ...	To ...
F1	Open the electronic version of the Users' Manual in a separate window.
CTRL+SHIFT+G	View the **Guide** tab at the right of an interview screen ("Help for This Screen").
CTRL+SHIFT+C	View the **Contact List** tab at the right of an interview screen.
CTRL+SHIFT+L	View the **Glossary** tab at the right of an interview screen.
CTRL+SHIFT+O	View the **Online Resources** tab at the right of an interview screen.

Navigating Within and Among Screens

Press ...	To ...
TAB	Move to the next part of the screen (such as a text box, list, button or group of option buttons).
SHIFT+TAB	Move to the previous part of the screen (such as a text box, list, button or group of option buttons).
DOWN ARROW	Highlight the next option button (in a group when one option button is selected), or the next item (in a selected list).
UP ARROW	Highlight the previous option button (in a group when one option button is selected), or the previous item (in a selected list).
ALT+RIGHT ARROW	Go to the next interview screen.
ALT+LEFT ARROW	Go back to the previous interview screen.

Navigating in a Text-Entry Box

Press ...	To ...
ENTER	Start a new line, if the box allows entry of multiple items.
LEFT ARROW	Move one character to left.
RIGHT ARROW	Move one character to right.
UP ARROW	Move one line up.
DOWN ARROW	Move one line down.
HOME	Move to the beginning of the line.
END	Move to the end of the line.
CTRL+HOME	Move to the beginning of the text-entry box.
CTRL+END	Move to the end of the entered text.
CTRL+LEFT ARROW	Move one word to left.
CTRL+RIGHT ARROW	Move one word to right.
CTRL+Z	Undo the most recent text editing action you have taken on the current screen, if the change has not yet been saved.
CTRL+X	Cut the selected text to the Clipboard.
CTRL+C	Copy the selected text to the Clipboard.
CTRL+V	Paste the contents of the Clipboard.
DELETE	Delete the selected text.
CTRL+A	Select all text in the current text-entry box.
CTRL+SHIFT+S	Check spelling of text in current text-entry box.

Error Messages

The table below describes what each error message means and what you should do if you encounter it. If the table entry for your error message suggests that you contact Nolo Technical Support, see "Contacting Nolo Technical Support and Customer Service" in Part 7 for contact information.

Error	What It Means	What You Should Do
[CD-ROM drive] is not accessible. The device is not ready	The CD you inserted is not being read.	Reinsert the CD. Wait ten seconds and double click the CD-ROM drive icon. If that doesn't solve the problem, contact Nolo Technical Support.
[Name you're trying to edit information about]'s [name or gender] can't be changed. It's probably being used in a critical place in some document—for example, a frozen trust.	Editing this information could affect the legality of another document you've made.	Think about whether this change really needs to be made. If so, check other documents to see whether they require the same revision. If they do, you can make the revisions by creating new versions of the documents in question. Please read the appropriate sections of the Legal Manual before you start creating new document versions in this manner.
A check on your interview answers revealed that some of your data is out of date or missing. Please review your answers by clicking "Change Answers" and reviewing the entire interview.	The program has determined that some of your data is out of date or missing.	Review all interview screens and make the necessary entries and revisions. If this problem continues, contact Nolo Technical Support.
An error exists in this Help file. Contact your application vendor for an updated Help file.	There's a problem opening the topic you selected in the program's Help system.	First, close the windows for any open Help files (including those from other programs), keeping Quicken WillMaker Plus open. Then, repeat what you did that caused the error message. If the problem persists, contact Nolo Technical Support.
An error occurred: couldn't find the requested path name.	Quicken WillMaker Plus couldn't find the path for a file it is trying to open.	Contact Nolo Technical Support.
An error occurred while assembling the document.	The resource files of the program might be damaged.	Reinstall the program and try again. If that doesn't work, contact Nolo Technical Support.

Error	What It Means	What You Should Do
Internal error: attempt to overwrite existing file.	Quicken WillMaker Plus is attempting to overwrite an existing file without permission.	Try to remember the steps you performed before the error appeared, then contact Nolo Technical Support.
Please select a part or option.	You clicked **Next** (or pressed ENTER) before you made a checklist selection.	Make a selection before clicking **Next** (or pressing ENTER).
Quicken WillMaker Plus cannot open that file (because it is read-only).	Quicken WillMaker Plus was not allowed to open a file, either because it is in use or because it is read-only.	Make sure the file is located on your computer's hard drive in the My Documents folder, and check that neither the file nor the disk is locked.
Quicken WillMaker Plus was not shut down properly the last time it was run. Please run Web Update to make sure your copy of the program is up-to-date. If this problem continues, contact Nolo Technical Support.	Either (1) a bug in Quicken WillMaker Plus caused the program to crash the last time you used it, or (2) you turned off your computer while Quicken WillMaker Plus was still running.	Run Web Update. If the problem was Quicken WillMaker Plus, an update to fix the problem may be available. Also, make sure that you exit Quicken WillMaker Plus before shutting down your computer. If this problem continues, contact Nolo Technical Support.
Sorry, a needed resource cannot be found.	The resource files of the program might be damaged.	Reinstall the program and try again. If that doesn't work, contact Nolo Technical Support.
Sorry, an internal data-module error occurred.	Something serious is wrong with the internal data structures.	Contact Nolo Technical Support.
Sorry, an internal error occurred.	Something serious is wrong with the program because of a disk error, a memory error or a bug.	Quit, restart the program, and attempt to repeat what you did. The problem may clear up on its own. If not, try reinstalling Quicken WillMaker Plus. If that doesn't work, contact Nolo Technical Support.

Error	What It Means	What You Should Do
Sorry, but this version of Quicken WillMaker Plus requires Internet Explorer version 6.0 or greater. Please install Internet Explorer 6.0 or later on your machine. Quicken WillMaker Plus will now exit.	Your system does not meet the minimum requirements to run Quicken WillMaker Plus.	If you don't run Internet Explorer, install it. If you run an old version, upgrade. You can download Internet Explorer free from Microsoft.com's Download Center.
Sorry, Quicken WillMaker Plus can open only one portfolio at a time.	You attempted to open more than one Quicken WillMaker Plus portfolio.	Open only one portfolio at a time.
Sorry, this file cannot be read by Quicken WillMaker Plus.	You are trying to open a file that Quicken WillMaker Plus doesn't recognize.	If you are sure the file you are attempting to use is a Quicken WillMaker Plus portfolio file (that is, it has the extension ".pfl"), try a back-up copy (see "Opening a Back-Up Portfolio" in Part 5). If that doesn't work, contact Nolo Technical Support.
Sorry, this file has been corrupted and cannot be read.	Your portfolio file has been seriously corrupted and cannot be read.	Use the backup portfolio with the same name.
Your document is not yet complete. Please complete the interview before printing your document.	The program has determined that it does not have all the information it needs to print your document.	Review all interview screens and enter any missing information. If you still can't print, contact Nolo Technical Support.

Index

A

abstract of trust. *See* certification of trust

AB trusts
death of beneficiary, 312
death of spouse or partner, 312, 324–325
final beneficiaries, 265–268
"formula" clause, 256
original trustees, 246–248
overview, 7–8, 149–151, 244–246
paperwork for surviving spouse, 331
property management for young people, 268–273
property to put in trust, 251–263
sample trust, 274–287
specific beneficiaries, 263–265
splitting the trust, 330–331
successor trustee, 248–251
surviving spouse's duties and rights, 325, 331–332
when to use, 161–164
See also disclaimer AB trusts; living trusts
advance health care directives. *See* health care directives
affidavit of assumption of duties, 327
age limits
for making a health care directive, 389

for making a will, 18
UTMA property management, 96
airplanes, transferring to a trust, 302
"aka" (also known as), entering in WillMaker, 46
Alabama
health care agent restrictions, 401
pregnancy and health care directives, 426
witnessing and notarizing of health care directives, 433
Alaska
health care agent restrictions, 401
pregnancy and health care directives, 426
shared trusts and community property, 218
witnessing and notarizing of health care directives, 433
alternate attorney-in-fact
choosing, 350–351
defined, 336
different powers for, 366
gifts to, 359
alternate beneficiaries of a trust
AB trusts, 264
individual trusts, 187
shared basic trusts, 223–224
alternate beneficiaries of a will
married/partnered couples with children, 75–78

married/partnered couples without children, 78–79

residuary beneficiaries, 90–92

single parents, 81–82

single people, 83–84

for specific bequests, 87–89

beneficiary transactions, by attorney-in-fact, 355

bill of sale form, 14

birth certificates, requesting, 11

blood transfusions, 413

boats, transferring to a trust, 302

body donations. *See* organ donations

bond for executors or property managers, 31–32, 107

brokerage accounts

transferring to a trust, 302–303

See also securities

burial decisions

final arrangements, 454–455

health care agent and, 409–410

business interests

transactions by attorney-in-fact, 353–354

transferring to a trust, 303–305

bypass trust. *See* AB trust

C

California

attorney-in-fact acceptance statement, 370

durable power of attorney rules, 370

health care agent restrictions, 401

pregnancy and health care directives, 426

property taxes and transfers, 301

self-proving laws, 127

shared trusts and community property, 218

witnessing and notarizing of health care directives, 433–434

cancel membership or subscription form, 14

cardiopulmonary resuscitation, 413, 416

caretakers, bequests to, 88

cash, 180, 216, 260

caskets and urns, 460–462

certification of trust, 294–296, 297–299

charitable trusts, 152

child care agreement and instructions, 12

children

death of and new will, 133

entering information about in WillMaker, 52–53

lawsuits by, 154

overlooked, 154

See also minor children

children's property management

AB trusts and, 268–273

examples of, 103–104

individual trusts and, 188–192

overview, 94–95

pot trust, 98, 100

property managers, 101–103

shared basic trusts and, 224–229

See also child's subtrust; Uniform Transfers to Minors Act

child's subtrust, 97, 99–100

AB trust and, 272–273

administration of, 329

individual trust and, 191–192

shared living trust and, 228–229

civil unions. *See* same-sex couples

closely held corporations. *See* corporations

coguardians for children's property, 31

Colorado

health care agent restrictions, 401

pregnancy and health care directives, 426

transferring real estate to a trust, 300

witnessing and notarizing of health care directives, 434

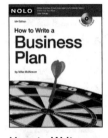

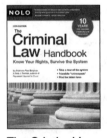

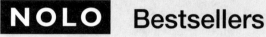

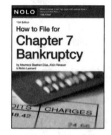

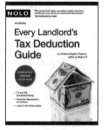

Get the Latest in the Law

 Nolo's Legal Updater
We'll send you an email whenever a new edition of your book is published!
Sign up at **www.nolo.com/legalupdater**.

 Updates at Nolo.com
Check **www.nolo.com/update** to find recent changes in the law that
affect the current edition of your book.

 Nolo Customer Service
To make sure that this edition of the book is the most recent one, call us at
800-728-3555 and ask one of our friendly customer service representatives
(7:00 am to 6:00 pm PST, weekdays only). Or find out at **www.nolo.com**.

 Complete the Registration & Comment Card ...
... and we'll do the work for you! Just indicate your preferences below:

Registration & Comment Card

NAME   DATE

ADDRESS

CITY   STATE   ZIP

PHONE   EMAIL

COMMENTS

WAS THIS BOOK EASY TO USE?   (VERY EASY)   5   4   3   2   1   (VERY DIFFICULT)

☐ Yes, you can quote me in future Nolo promotional materials. *Please include phone number above.*

☐ Yes, send me **Nolo's Legal Updater** via email when a new edition of this book is available.

Yes, I want to sign up for the following email newsletters:

    ☐ **NoloBriefs** (monthly)
    ☐ **Nolo's Special Offer** (monthly)
    ☐ **Nolo's BizBriefs** (monthly)
    ☐ **Every Landlord's Quarterly** (four times a year)

☐ Yes, you can give my contact info to carefully selected
partners whose products may be of interest to me.

QWMB5

NOLO

Send to: **Nolo** 950 Parker Street Berkeley, CA 94710-9867, Fax: (800) 645-0895, or include all of
the above information in an email to regcard@nolo.com with the subject line "QWMB5."

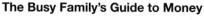